W9-AOH-724

Social Problems in America

Social Problems in America

Costs and Casualties in an Acquisitive Society

Second Edition

Harry C. Bredemeier
and Jackson Toby

John Wiley & Sons, Inc.
New York · London · Sydney · Toronto

Library of Congress Cataloging in Publication Data

Bredemeier, Harry Charles.
   Social problems in America.

   Includes bibliographical references.
   1. U.S.—Social conditions. 2. Social problems.
I. Toby, Jackson, joint author. II. Title.
HN57.B65 1972   309.1'73   72-1137

ISBN 0-471-10005-6
ISBN 0-471-1006-4 (pbk.)

Printed in the United States of America.

10 9 8 7 6 5 4 3 2 1

Preface

In our teaching of "social problems," we have been impressed with the seeming lack of continuity between one topic and the next in many textbooks. A "social problems" course often provides a Cook's tour of personal and social pathologies rather than a systematic analysis of the significance of the symptoms held up to view. We wondered whether sociological theory could impart a coherent framework to the social problems field. We concluded that this was possible if sociologists were willing to chop conventional topics up and recombine them in new ways.

This we have done in the present book. The result is somewhat disconcerting—even to us, the authors. When we look at the table of contents, we see no familiar "Alcoholism" or "Family Disorganization" staring back. As a colleague, who saw the galley proofs, pointed out, he would not have known that ours is a social problems textbook were it not for the title. Truth to tell, however, most of the familiar problems *are* in the book. Look at the index if you are skeptical. We hope that the theoretical advantages of our framework will justify the far-reaching revisions we have made in the usual organization of social problems courses.

A second difficulty with many social problems textbooks is that they often seem dull to the student. Partly this is because of the telephone-directory organization just mentioned: the subject seems to change very rapidly. Partly it is because very few sociologists can write six hundred pages of scintillating exposition. Recognizing *our* literary shortcomings and yet wishing to present the material in as interesting a manner as possible, we decided to use illustrative readings. Do not be deceived, however. This is not just a collection of articles.

v

We systematically defined for ourselves the characteristics of an illustration called for by our conceptual scheme and then scoured the literature to find an article that would meet our demands. Despite the small proportion of text which we have written ourselves, we consider ourselves authors rather than editors.

Now that we have differentiated our product positively, we must also concede its limitations. We do not present statistics on the extent or seriousness of the social problems we discuss. By way of justification, we might point out that statistical data quickly become outdated. Second, we do not, except by implication, proffer solutions. We feel that "solutions" can be most fruitfully considered after an understanding of the nature and sources of problems has been developed. We hope that these omissions will be taken care of by the instructor in his own way through lectures and supplementary readings. Third, and finally, the over-all impression of American society conveyed by our book may be negative. In our effort to show the genesis of social problems in America, we emphasize those aspects of American society which (we believe) produce problems, and, necessarily, we ignore aspects of American society which (we believe) are achievements of human spirit. Specifically, we suggest that a competitive struggle for material possessions and social status produces a high rate of human casualties and certain inefficiencies in social organization. Nevertheless, we do not mean to imply that materialistic concerns are wholly destructive. The high standard of living which materialistic concerns help to bring about is more than gadgetry. It means longer life expectancy, less disease, less physical suffering and discomfort. A high standard of living means greater potential opportunity for widespread participation in the intellectual and artistic triumphs of society. Materialistic concerns also constitute a favorable climate for the development of science, technology, and rationality. Furthermore, it may be that a fairly high level of material welfare is a prerequisite for personal liberty and community self-government.

We believe that sociology should describe the functioning of social arrangements as accurately as possible, and the factors making for weakness and strife are just as important scientifically as those making for cohesiveness and strength. It so happens that the division of labor within sociology allocates to the social problems field a lugubrious enterprise: auditing casualties and costs. We, the authors, are not dismayed by our survey. Analysis of the forces generating casualties is a necessary step in reducing them. We hopefully anticipate a more favorable balance sheet in the twenty-first century.

It would be indecent to end this preface without acknowledging the many ways in which we have been aided by Mrs. Belle Sicurella and Mrs. Harriet Zucker.

Harry C. Bredemeier
Jackson Toby

January 1972

Contents

Social Problems in America

chapter 1
Introduction:
human needs and social problems

Benjamin Franklin's advice to leaders of the American Revolution, "We must hang together or we shall certainly hang separately," could well serve as the slogan of the human race. Human beings cannot survive at all in isolation from one another, and they have abilities that enable them to profit handsomely from joint action. Both aspects of man—his extreme dependence and his augmented capacities when united with others—are based on a combination of biological and sociocultural characteristics.

CONSPICUOUS CHARACTERISTICS OF HUMAN BEINGS

1. *Plasticity.* In an ant society the ant with the role of laying eggs is biologically forced to lay eggs. She can no more escape her egg-laying destiny than a fish can decide to walk instead of swim. With man it is different. No human being is biologically compelled to be a devoted mother or a conscientious worker or a brave soldier. This freedom from highly specific biological determination of behavior is what is meant by man's plasticity. Relatively few of his actions are genetically built in. The range of possible responses to a stimulus on the part of a human being is very great. He can, for example, respond to a pain in his side by suspecting witchcraft and employing a sorcerer to charm it away, by thinking of appendicitis and summoning a surgeon, or by believing that it is "psychosomatic" and visiting his psychiatrist. In other words, human beings react to stimuli in terms of what they have learned. Moreover, they can learn from others' experiences as well as their own.

2. *Symbol Making and Symbol Using Capacity.*   Basic to the human ability to learn is the capacity to make and use symbols.[1] Lower animals perceive what they perceive directly—that is, without the intervention of symbols. Man, on the other hand, is not the prisoner of his immediate experience. He can relate the tree he saw yesterday to the tree he sees today and to the idea of a tree. If man_1 could tell man_2 about a tree he had seen only if man_2 saw the same tree at the same time, communication would be a meager affair. Luckily, ideas that refer to classes of objects are able to convey meanings even though experience is not identical. That is why symbols are so useful. They vastly expand the range of communication that is possible and the range of stimuli that can elicit human response.

3. *Dependence.*   Even on a purely physical level, man is extraordinarily dependent on his fellows. Human infants are helpless at birth, and for several years thereafter they cannot survive without nurturance. In adulthood, the dependence is no less pronounced, although, being less spectacular, it usually passes unnoticed until something happens to disrupt orderly coordination, such as a nationwide transportation strike. Then people begin to realize how dependent they are on the coordination of their action with the actions of others whom they may neither know nor care to know. One of the critical problems of human society stems from the fact that coordination is both essential and problematical. That is, in view of the relative freedom of man from biological determination, it cannot be taken for granted that the necessary coordination will be forthcoming as it is in an ant or a termite society. (One writer has suggested that we can understand much about human behavior if we think of human beings as creatures with anthropoid equipment who are trying to live like termites.)

Both in childhood and adulthood, peoples' dependence on one another—their interdependence—takes the form of four kinds of problems that each faces with respect to the others. Everyone needs (partly as a result of his biological nature and partly as a result of his personality structure) to *obtain* some things *from* others (money or food, for example); to *dispose* of some things *to* others (labor services, for example); to *retain* some things *from* others (secrets or personal property, for example); and to *contain* some things *in* others—that is, keep the things away from themselves (noise or disease, for example). Those "others" have the same kinds of needs, and the problematic issue of social life is the manner in which those needs of people can be coordinated. What Smith needs to obtain from Jones must be something Jones can be induced to dispose of. What Smith needs to dispose of to Jones must be something Jones can be

---

[1] A symbol is any observable entity—a sound, a gesture, a written mark—that arbitrarily stands for something else.

induced to accept. What Smith needs to keep out must be something Jones is willing to hold on to. What Smith needs to retain must be something Jones can be induced to keep out or leave alone.

What is meant by saying that human beings are creatures with anthropoid equipment who are trying to live like termites is that the members of a termite society face exactly the same problems, but the problems are solved by the *genetic* program that governs each termite's behavior. Man is dependent on shared symbolic programs for the synchronization and dovetailing of one another's obtaining, disposing, containing, and retaining needs. And this seems to be a more precarious mechanism because shared symbolic programs require that men cooperate in the assignment of meanings to the symbols they use. The meaning of a symbol is, by definition, arbitrary. Unlike the relationship between clouds and rain, the relationship between a symbol and the thing it stands for does not exist in nature. (For example, there is no biological reason why a feeling of hostility should result in the expression, "Go to hell!") Meaning is put there by the consensus of human beings. Without such consensus, communication is impossible. The necessity of maintaining a common symbol system is thus a basic form of mutual dependence. At the same time, however, perfect consensus on the meanings of symbols never exists. Since the meanings are arbitrary, individuals within a community may attach symbolic meanings to objects and events that other members of the community have not attached to them.[2] Thus, man is dependent on shared symbolic programs, which are always imperfect and which, therefore, prevent the human problems of interdependence that they are designed to solve from having other than imperfect solutions.

Man's dependence on symbols goes further. Smith is, for the most part, dependent on symbols not only for ways of inducing Jones to accept what Smith wants to dispose of (and so on), but also *for the determination of what he wants to dispose of in the first place.* To be sure, the Smiths of the human world are genetically programmed to need oxygen, certain vitamins, protection from cold, and so on. But, except in extreme cases of maladaption, the things men are *culturally* programmed to want and need are more relevant for our efforts to understand them. These include such things as expressions of approval, caviar, fur coats, Picasso paintings, and so on. Moreover, man is entirely dependent on cultural programs for the *ways* in which he must induce his fellows to coordinate their needs with his.

Symbols are to human beings what instincts are to other animals. Symbols are the glasses through which man looks at the world; an adult human being can scarcely perceive anything without the intervention of symbols. As an illustra-

---

[2]When individuals attach symbolic meanings to objects or events that are incomprehensible to other members of the community, such individuals are labeled psychotic.

tion of this principle, consider what happens when you are hungry. You do not simply crave food (anything at all that is nutritious). You crave beefsteak rather than horsemeat; and even starvation might not induce you to eat grubs, worms, mice, or another human being. These things are edible; human beings eat them in other parts of the world. But Americans are symbolically conditioned to regard certain nutritious objects as "food," and other equally nutritious objects as revolting. So, provided that the symbols are clear—provided that you know what the menu consists of—you are either gastronomically interested or you are nauseated. Similarly, symbols determine who is sexually attractive to Americans and on what occasions; it is never the sex drive alone that does so. There is no biological reason why college students are more likely to grow amorous in a parked car by moonlight than at 10:30 during a sociology lecture.

In short, symbols organize man's perceptions; they abstract aspects of reality for him to pay attention to. They tell him what to see or hear and how to respond to what he sees and hears. Determination by symbols is thus the distinctive character of human responses: It leads simultaneously to man's greatest triumphs and his most grievous errors. No animal but man could discover atomic energy because none but he can invent the symbol "atom." On the other hand, no animal but man has incinerated members of his own species because none but he can invent the symbols "National Destiny" and "inferior races." On the one hand, symbolic development frees man to think and to love as lower animals cannot possibly do. On the other hand, it makes possible a special kind of slavery, enslavement to one's misperceptions of reality. The hallucinations and delusions of a psychotic person are dramatic examples of symbolic enslavement, but all human beings distort reality to some extent.

4. *Self-evaluation.*   Related to man's dependence on symbols is his self-consciousness. Unlike the horse or the cat, the human being is inescapably self-conscious; he perceives himself as an object.[3] He can be proud or ashamed of himself. He can treat himself as a tool to serve some "higher purpose," or he can elevate himself into a cause that everything else should serve. He often comes to love himself so much that he cannot conceive of the world without himself in it, but at the same time he is intellectually aware that all human beings die. The

[3]"Perceiving the self as an object" should not be confused with "perceiving the self *objectively.*" The human capacity for objectifying makes self-evaluations not only possible but inescapable. However, these self-evaluations are not necessarily objective. On the contrary, psychology has documented what political theory has long asserted, that no man can be trusted to be a fair judge in his own case. We often take a generous view of our own failings and an exaggerated view of our own virtues—although it is equally possible to err in the opposite direction by imputing all virtue and nobility to others and all sin and evil to ourselves. To be objective about oneself is extremely difficult.

incompatibility between his intellectual awareness and his self-love may drive him to attempt to perserve his self from the threat of extinction by identifying it with some more permanent object: science, the United States, God, the human race, the Master Race.

Self-consciousness implies another dimension of man's dependence on his fellows: dependence on the attitudes of others. He is influenced in his self-evaluation by the evaluations that he learns that others make of him. Human beings need more than food, shelter, and clothing; they crave praise, affection, esteem, and other symbolic rewards. Human beings develop an image of themselves that is a complex mixture of their perceptions of others' images of them and their reactions to those perceptions. When people communicate to you that they perceive you as bad, ugly, stupid, or awkward, you are psychologically wounded. You may respond to the wound by enduring it, by coming to perceive yourself as bad, ugly, stupid, or awkward; or you may respond to it by hotly asserting the opposite. But however you respond, you are influenced by the attitudes of others.

This process of evaluation by others leads to defensive manuevering in order to minimize the pain of an unfavorable self-evaluation. Such maneuvering is of central concern here because the assumption of this book is that the individual's satisfactions or frustrations influence his relations with other people. He is constantly engaged in the process of evaluating himself in terms of the symbolic standards that he knows other people use in evaluating him. Just as human beings respond to pains in the side according to their interpretation of the *meaning* of a pain in the side, so they respond to themselves in terms of social cultural standards of evaluation that they have learned. They must adjust in one way or another to the self-images developed thereby. Under certain conditions these adjustments involve behavior that constitutes "social problems" and under other conditions these adjustments involve behavior considered socially desirable. What these conditions are will be discussed in a later section of the book. At this point more attention will be given to the standards by which people are evaluated by themselves and by others; and a little later we shall return to the issue of how people induce one another to help them meet those standards.

Four kinds of standards that nearly all human beings acquire can be distinguished. The first two, standards of adequacy and standards of authority, are symbolic yardsticks that assess the individual's conformity to impersonal rules. The other two, standards of gratification and standards of security, prescribe the kinds of satisfactions the individual learns to need, crave, demand, or expect.

THE STANDARDS OF SELF-EVALUATION

1. *Standards of Adequacy.*   Every group or society has tasks for its members to perform—growing crops, hunting buffalo, building bridges, studying chemistry,

and so on. The recognition of different degrees of skill or competence at those tasks is also found universally; and the ideas of how competent one should be are what we mean by "standards of adequacy." Whatever the human individual is doing, shooting a bow and arrow or ordering wines to go with a dinner, his behavior is measured (by himself and others) according to some cultural standard of competent performance. Measuring up to the standard gives the individual a feeling of achievement and self-satisfaction; falling below it produces a painful sense of failure, of self-devaluation, of shame.

2. *Standards of Authority.* Not only are there, in all human societies, standards of *how* people should do various things; there are also cultural judgements of *what* things people should do and be. In American society it is generally considered better to be a banker than to be a ditch-digger; or to be a college graduate than not to be one. But there are also certain things that *some* people are supposed to do, but not other people. Regardless of competence, for example, some activities are culturally regarded as the prerogative of men, or adults, or whites (or, in black groups or nations, of blacks), and so on. It is not only such attributes as sex, age, or skin color on which differential rights are pegged; rights are differentially attached to statuses that may be achieved. Policemen have certain rights denied to others, who have *duties* toward the police (who also have duties toward them). Generals have authoritative rights different from those of privates; teachers have authority in the classroom that children do not have; and so on.

"Authority" may be regarded as a *stock* of "rights," comparable to the way in which "wealth" is a stock of purchasing power. How rights and authority are distributed in a society— that is, who has which rights to do various things—is a significant determinant of peoples' self-evaluations. Standards of authority are ideas about how rights and duties should be allocated.

3. *Standards of Gratification.* So far the standards discussed have been impersonal yardsticks, which people use to help them answer the question, "Am I deserving?" Consider now the standards people use to answer a different, though related, question: "What is it that I deserve?" The first of the latter sort of standards, standards of gratification, are the cultural norms that define fulfillment: what it is that gives life "point," makes it worth living. In the United States, for example, boys may learn that driving an automobile at high speeds is "fun"; girls may learn that spending the summer months hitchhiking through Europe is exciting. If the individual fails to secure enough of the experiences that his society defines as intrinsically worthwhile, he feels he is missing out on something; he is dissatisfied.

4. *Standards of Security.* In addition to the symbolic definitions of fulfillment, the individual learns what constitute (in his society) desirable emotional bonds

with other people, and these become part of his expectations. In American society, where romantic love is prominent, solidarities between adult males and adult females are emphasized. The ideal is one of great intensity and intimacy between a man and a woman. In other cultures other solidarities are emphasized: among siblings; between the generations of a family line; among adolescents of the same sex. But in all societies the individual learns to want to be accepted by other people. He learns his culture's conception of the feeling of "belonging." To the extent that he does not experience it, he feels rootless, lonely, and insecure.

THE MODES OF TRANSACTION

Those four standards—of adequacy, authority, security, and gratification— are also closely related to what we shall call the "modes of transaction" by which the members of a society relate to one another. Transaction modes are the "ways" in which Smith tries to induce Jones to give him what his standards tell him he needs; to get Jones to accept what Smith wants to dispose of; and so on.

The basic point is that, when one member of a human society says to another, "Give me X," or "Please accept Y from me," or "Please keep Z away from me," or "Please don't take W away from me," the other can always reply, "Why should I do what you are asking?" Termites cannot do this, which is what makes human coordination so much more problematical.

In fact, not only *can* human beings say, "Why should I?," they *must* say it. They "must" say it because *only the existence of shared cultural answers to that question can induce them to comply with one another's requests.* To the degree that people are well socialized into their societies, they do not *consciously* ask, "Why should I?" every time someone makes a request; they know the answers so well that the question does not arise. But their behavior implicitly supplies answers to that question.

There are five answers to the "Why should I?" question. We shall list them swiftly, and then consider in further detail each one and its relations to the standards of self-evaluation discussed above. The answers are: (1) Because you do not have a choice in the matter; I shall coerce you into compliance. (2) Because if you do, I shall make it worth your while by doing something *you* want *me* to do. (3) Because it is your duty, and if you do, you will have self-respect and the respect of others, whereas if you don't you will have a bad conscience and the authorities (God; the State; etc.) will punish you. (4) Because doing so is an efficient means for achieving a goal you desire. (5) Because you care about my welfare—you love me—and this will increase my welfare.

The first of those answers—the coercive answer—we shall not deal with in this book, except as a *problem*. For it is the answer given when *shared cultural symbols have broken down*. It is the answer given when men live in Hobbes' state of "war of all against all," in which life is "solitary, mean, nasty, brutish, and short." We shall come back to it in Part II of this book when we examine such breakdowns. The other four answers are manifestations of four different cultural modes of coordinating the transactions among interdependent members of a human society. These four transaction modes governing the interrelations of people to one another are related to the standards by which people assess themselves. It might appear at first glance that a person's effort to meet a given *standard* could be carried out in any of the four kinds of *modes* we have distinguished (not counting the coercive mode), so that we should have 16 different kinds of institutionalized action (four standards times four modes). However, the relationship between modes and standards is not of that nature. Rather, each mode is associated with a certain standard, as we shall see by considering them one by one.

"Making It Worth While" and Adequacy Standards

We said above that cultural standards of adequacy are "ideas of how competent one should be." In some situations one person is interested in another primarily in terms of his competence at doing something the first person wants done. In other words, the only thing about Smith that is of interest to Jones in some situations is how effective Smith is at satisfying one or more of Jones' needs. If Smith says to Jones, "Please give me X," and Jones replies, "Why should I?," the only satisfactory answer Smith can give is, "Because I have the ability—the competence—to make it worth your while." Jones then examines Smith with only one question in mind, "Does he?" When the relationship between Smith and Jones is of this nature, we speak of a "utilitarian" type of transaction. Elsewhere, we refer to this as a "bargaining" mode of transaction; and in the previous edition of this book we called it the "negotiated exchange" principle. These latter terms connote a process of offers and counter offers or haggling; and while utilitarian norms often do involve such a process, it is not their essence. Their essence is mutual usefulness; under this mode, one person is interested in the other only so far as the other is useful to him at the moment. *If* actions are coordinated, they are coordinated through a series of judgments that causes it to be at least temporarily worth one's while to comply with the other's request because the other has the instrumental competence to *make* it worth one's while. When the mode relating people to one another is the utilitarian mode, people evaluate one another and themselves by standards of adequacy.

"Duty" and Standards of Authority

In some situations, the relevant issue about another person is *not* how adequate he is at, say, directing traffic, but whether he has the *right* to direct it. We do not ordinarily consider whether it is efficient or effective or worthwhile or pleasant to stop when a traffic policeman holds up his hand and says, "Stop." We stop because it is our duty to do (in that situation) what he tells us to do; and it is his right to tell us. He has the authority, and while we may hope he *got* it by proving his competence, the only relevant fact at the moment is that he *has* it. Here we are in the realm of "legality" and "bureaucracy," whereas in the case of "instrumentalism," we were in the realm of "the market." They are different worlds. In each of them, the multiplicity of interdependent human actions usually get coordinated; but the procedures, vicissitudes, and dangers of non-coordination are different. Each generates its own species of "social problems." In the legal-bureaucratic mode of interpersonal relations, evaluative standards are standards of authority.

"Cooperation" and Standards of Gratification

On a football team, if the quarterback tells the right guard to take out the opposing tackle, the effective answer to the guard's question, "Why should I?" is, "Because you want our team to win, and the most effective thing you can do to realize that goal on this next play is to do what I tell you." It is true that at the moment of play, the quarterback has the *authority* to call the signal; but it has been tacitly agreed that at a given signal the guard acts in a certain way *because* that seems to be most efficient in the cooperative enterprise. To take another example, when a physician tells a patient to take a certain medicine and the patient says, "Why should I?", the answer that is ordinarily taken for granted is, "Because it will make you better"—that is, because *in the nature of things*, compliance will help to achieve the *patient's* goal; and it is assumed that the physician shares that goal. It is not, as in the utilitarian case, that the *physician* will make it worth the patient's while to comply (by paying him, for example); it is that the *world* is built in such a way that compliance will be efficient.

"Adequacy," to be sure, is involved here also; the physician is presumed to be an expert on physiology and drugs. But the important consideration is that the physician-and-the-patient and the quarterback-and-the-guard share the same goal as the standard of gratification rather than separate goals as in the utilitarian case. As we shall see, American standards of gratification do not usually put people in cooperative relationships; they more often put them in competitive relations; and this is a source of certain problems.

Standards of gratification tell people what are gratifying ends in themselves, and whether these are shared or private. They state the major premise to which cooperation must add the minor premise of an argument that compliance will yield gratification.

"Love" and Standards of Security

There are situations in which one person does something for another because he values the welfare of the other as an end in itself. In such cases, if A asks B to do something and B says, "Why should I?," the sufficient answer for A to give is, "Because it will make me happy." The standards of security we spoke of above tell people with whom they expect to carry out transactions in this mode. They define norms and boundaries of friendship, solidarity, loyalty, care, and love. They are standards of "security" in the sense that to be in such a relationship is to feel secure about the chances of getting one's needs met.

In sum, standards of adequacy are associated with utilitarian modes of interpersonal relations; standards of authority are associated with legal-bureaucratic modes; standards of gratification determine whether relations will be cooperative or competitive; and standards of security tell people with whom (or whether) they may count on other peoples' care, solidarity, and concern.

CONCLUSION

Human beings need one another. One aspect of this dependence is the individual's adoption of group standards of adequacy, authority, gratification, and security. This means that he needs to feel that he can do competently the tasks his fellows think he ought to do; that what he is or does is the right thing to be or do; that he is getting a sense of fulfillment out of life; and that he "belongs," that there are others who care about him and about whom he cares, whose lives are closely interwoven with his. These feelings are necessary if the individual is not to be a conscious or unconscious rebel against the arrangements of his society. Moreover, they are interdependent. The individual cannot enjoy pleasures if he is anxious about his competence at his job, if he feels inferior because of a low I.Q. or a brown skin, or if he feels that no one cares whether he lives or dies. When these feelings of satisfaction are not available through socially acceptable experiences, one may seek to obtain them through socially unacceptable experiences. Thus, individual frustrations are transformed into social problems.

THE PLAN OF THIS BOOK: In part I, we shall examine in turn the particular *American* version of each of those four standards and transaction modes. Part II, the core of the book, is the "social problems" part. It is divided into nine sections, some of which contain only one chapter. We shall explain the logic of the organization of this part of the book in the introduction to part II.

PART I

American Standards and Transaction Modes

The aspects of the human condition discussed in Chapter 1 are *general* aspects of human beings everywhere at all times. This book is about *American* social problems, so we must describe the American versions of these conditions, versions that provide the script by which Americans act out their lives. The next four chapters are addressed to this task.

The theme of Chapter 2 ("Materialism in a Secular Society") is that American standards of gratification and goal-seeking tend to be secular and material-istic, implicitly contributing an explanation for the fact that cooperation has not been a dominant American value. We cite the role of science in shaking men's allegiance to transcendental goals and in contributing to the secularization of religion and the American preoccupation with goods.

Chapter 3 ("Utilitarianism in a Market Society") describes the emphasis in American society on utilitarian norms of the marketplace and on the conception of adequacy as successful "making out" in negotiations with others. The Ameri-can legal tradition insists that people should freely bargain for themselves and that one is worth what he can earn on the market. We illustrate some of the pressures on people to act in terms of these doctrines.

Chapter 4 ("Self-Orientation in a Competitive Society") suggests that Ameri-can culture has emphasized self-oriented *competition* with others more than a solidary *relationship* with them. It examines the American faith in competition and the ubiquity of competition in several different areas of life.

Chapter 5 ("Acquiescence to Authority in an Organizational Society") considers American attitudes toward duty and authority, both particularly American ambivalences toward bureaucracy, liberty, freedom, dissent, and law-abidingness and more universal dilemmas of social organization.

Jan Lukas/Rapho Guillumette

chapter 2
Materialism in a secular society

Human beings are dependent on cultural definitions to survive—and also for a *reason* to survive. Only man among living creatures is capable of asking, "Why exist?" Only man can find life "pointless," "not worth living." This happens when the cultural definitions of his society lose their power to interpret the world for him. It happens also when a society as a whole begins to question its cultural definitions. Urban industrial society is susceptible to this second type of pointlessness because of its devotion to rationality and, more specifically, to science. To say that a man's thinking is unscientific or irrational is almost as insulting as to call him a coward. But, as scientists are the first to admit, a man's willingness to be objective about the subject of his study, although a prerequisite for objectivity, is incompatible with unquestioning faith in God, in country, in family. Joseph Wood Krutch, in a passage from his book, *The Modern Temper,*[1] shows how the critical examination of life has taken some of the meaning out of it.

It is not by thought that men live. Life begins in organisms so simple that one may reasonably doubt even their ability to feel, much less think, and animals cling to or fight for it with a determination which we might be inclined to call superhuman if we did not know that a will to live so thoughtless and so unconditional is the attribute of beings rather below than above the human level.

[1]From *The Modern Temper* by Joseph Wood Krutch, copyright, 1929, by Harcourt Brace Jovanovich, Inc.; renewed, 1957, by Joseph Wood Krutch. Reprinted by permission of the publishers.

All efforts to find a rational justification of life, to declare it worth the living for this reason or that, are, in themselves, a confession of weakness, since life at its strongest never feels the need of any such justification and since the most optimistic philosopher is less optimistic than that man or animal who, his belief that life is good being too immediate to require the interposition of thought, is no philosopher at all.

In view of this fact it is not surprising that the subtlest intellectual contortions of modern metaphysics should fail to establish the existence of satisfactory aims for life when, as a matter of fact, any effort to do so fails as soon as it begins and can only arise as the result of a weakening of that self-justifying vitality which is the source of all life and of all optimism. As soon as thought begins to seek the "ends" or "aims" to which life is subservient it has already confessed its inability to achieve that animal acceptance of life for life's sake which is responsible for the most determined efforts to live and, in one sense, we may say that even the firmest medieval belief in a perfectly concrete salvation after death marks already the beginning of the completest despair, since that belief could not arise before thought had rendered primitive vitality no longer all-sufficient.

The decadent civilizations of the past were not saved by their philosophers but by the influx of simpler peoples who had centuries yet to live before their minds should be ripe for despair. Neither Socrates nor Plato could teach his compatriots any wisdom from which they could draw the strength to compete with the crude energy of their Roman neighbors, and even their thought inevitably declined soon after it had exhausted their vital energy. Nor could these Romans, who flourished longer for the very reason, perhaps, that they had slower and less subtle intellects, live forever; they too were compelled to give way in their time to barbarians innocent alike both of philosophy and of any possible need to call upon it.

The subhuman will to live which is all-sufficient for the animal may be replaced by faith, faith may be replaced by philosophy, and philosophy may attenuate itself until it becomes, like modern metaphysics, a mere game; but each of these developments marks a stage in a progressive enfeeblement of that will to live for the gradual weakening of which it is the function of each to compensate. Vitality calls upon faith for aid, faith turns gradually to philosophy for support, and then philosophy, losing all confidence in its own conclusions, begins to babble of "beneficent fictions" instead of talking about Truth; but each is less confident than what went before and each is, by consequence, less easy to live by. Taken together, they represent the successive and increasingly desperate expedients by means of which man, the ambitious animal, endeavors to postpone the inevitable realization that living is merely a physiological process with only a physiological meaning and that it is most satisfactorily conducted by creatures who never feel the need to attempt to give it any other. But they are at best no more than expedients, and when the last has been exhausted there remains nothing except the possibility that the human species will be revitalized by some race or some class which is capable of beginning all over again.

Can it be that Krutch is right, that science has pulled the rug from under us by destroying the beliefs men live by? Or is his pessimism unjustified? After all, the current revival of interest in religion would seem to belie the notion that faith is dead. Let us see how Will Herberg analyzes America's return to religion.[2]

What do Americans believe? Most emphatically, they "believe in God"; 97 per cent according to one survey, 96 per cent according to another, 95 per cent according to a third. About 75 per cent of them, as we have seen, regard themselves as members of churches, and a sizable proportion attend divine services with some frequency and regularity. They believe in prayer: about 90 per cent say they pray on various occasions. They believe in life after death, even in heaven and hell. They think well of the church and of ministers. They hold the Bible to be an inspired book, the "word of God." By a large majority, they think children should be given religious instruction and raised as church members. By a large majority, too, they hold religion to be of very great importance. In all of these respects their attitudes are as religious as those of any people today, or, for that matter, as those of any Western people in recent history.

Yet these indications are after all relatively superficial; they tell us what Americans say (and no doubt believe) about themselves and their religious views; they do not tell us what in actuality these religious views are. Nowhere are surface appearances more deceptive, nowhere is it more necessary to try to penetrate beyond mere assertions of belief than in such ultimate matters as religion.

We do penetrate a little *deeper*, it would seem, when we take note of certain curious discrepancies the surveys reveal in the responses people make to questions about their religion. Thus, according to one trustworthy source, 73 per cent said they believed in an afterlife, with God as judge, but "only 5 per cent [had] any fear, not to say expectation, of going [to hell]." Indeed, about 80 per cent, according to another source, admitted that what they were "most serious about" was not the life after death in which they said they believed, but in trying to live as comfortably in this life as possible. And in their opinion they were not doing so badly even from the point of view of the divine judgment: 91 per cent felt that they could honestly say that they were trying to lead a good

---

[2] From *Protestant, Catholic, Jew,* by Will Herberg. Copyright © 1955 by Will Herberg. Reprinted by permission of Doubleday and Company, Inc.

life, and 78 per cent felt no hesitation in saying that they more than half measured up to their own standards of goodness, over 50 per cent asserting that they were in fact following the rule of loving one's neighbor as oneself "all the way"! This amazingly high valuation that most Americans appear to place on their own virtue would seem to offer a better insight into the basic religion of the American people than any figure as to their formal beliefs can provide, however important in themselves these figures may be.

But perhaps the most significant discrepancy in the assertions Americans make about their religious views is to be found in another area. When asked, "Would you say your religious beliefs have any effect on your ideas of politics and business?", a majority of the same Americans who had testified that they regarded religion as something "very important" answered that their religious beliefs had no real effect on their ideas or conduct in these decisive areas of everyday life; specifically, 54 per cent said no, 39 per cent said yes, 7 per cent refused to reply or didn't know. This disconcerting confession of the irrelevance of religion to business and politics was attributed by those who appraised the results of the survey as pointing to a calamitous divorce between the "private" and the "public" realms in the religious thinking of Americans. There is certainly a great deal of truth in this opinion, and we shall have occasion to explore it in a different context, but in the present connection it would seem that another aspect of the matter is more immediately pertinent. *Some* ideas and standards undeniably govern the conduct of Americans in their affairs of business and politics; if they are not ideas and standards associated with the teachings of religion, what are they? It will not do to say that people just act "selfishly" without reference to moral standards of any kind. All people act "selfishly," of course; but it is no less true of all people, Americans included, that their "selfishness" is controlled, mitigated, or, at worst, justified by some sort of moral commitment, by some sort of belief in a system of values beyond immediate self-interest. The fact that more than half the people openly admit that their religious beliefs have no effect on their ideas of politics and business would seem to indicate very strongly that, over and above conventional religion, there is to be found among Americans some sort of faith or belief or set of convictions, not generally designated as religion but definitely operative as such in their lives in the sense of providing them with some fundamental context of normativity and meaning. What this unacknowledged "religion" of the American people is, and how it manages to coexist with their formal religious affirmations and affiliations, it is now our task to investigate.

"Every functioning society," Robin M. Williams, Jr. points out, "has to an important degree a *common* religion. The possession of a common set of ideas, rituals, and symbols can supply an overarching sense of unity even in a society riddled with conflicts." What is this "common religion" of American society, the "common set of ideas, rituals, and symbols" that give it its "overarching sense of unity"? Williams provides us with a further clue when he suggests that "men are always likely to be intolerant of opposition to their central ultimate values." What are these "central ultimate values" about which Americans are "intolerant"? No one who knows anything about the religious situation in this country would be likely to suggest that the things Americans are "intolerant" about are the beliefs, standards, or teachings of the religions they "officially" acknowledge as theirs. Americans are proud of their tolerance in matters of religion: one is expected to "believe in God," but otherwise religion is not supposed to be a ground of "discrimination." This is, no doubt, admirable, but is it not "at least in part, a sign that the crucial values of the system are no longer couched in a religious framework."?

What, then, is the "framework" in which they *are* couched? What, to return to our original question, is the "common religion" of the American people, as it may be inferred not only from their words but also from their behavior?

It seems to me that a realistic appraisal of the values, ideas, and behavior of the American people leads to the conclusion that Americans, by and large, do have their "common religion" and that that "religion" is the system familiarly known as the American Way of Life. It is the American Way of Life that supplies American society with an "overarching sense of unity" amid conflict. It is the American Way of Life about which Americans are admittedly and unashamedly "intolerant." It is the American Way of Life that provides the framework in terms of which the crucial values of American existence are couched. By every realistic criterion the American Way of Life in the operative faith of the American people. . . .

The American Way of Life is, of course, conceived as the corporate "way" of the American people, but it has its implications for the American as an individual as well. It is something really operative in his actual life. When in the *Ladies' Home Journal* poll, Americans were asked "to look within [themselves] and state honestly whether [they] thought [they] really obeyed the law of love under certain special conditions," 90 per cent said yes and 5 per cent no when the one to be "loved" was a person belonging to a different religion; 80 per cent said yes and 12 per cent no when it was the case of a member of a different race; 78 per cent said yes and 10 per cent no when it concerned a business competitor—but only 27 per cent said yes and 57 per cent no in the case of "a member of a political party that you think is dangerous," while 25 per cent said yes and 63 per cent said no when it concerned an enemy of the nation. These figures are most illuminating, first because of the incredible self-assurance they reveal with which the average American believes he fulfills the "impossible" law of love, but also because of the light they cast on the differential impact of the violation of this law on the American conscience. For it is obvious that the figures reflect not so much the actual behavior of the American people—no people on earth ever loved their neighbors as themselves as much as the American people say they do—as how seriously Americans take transgressions against the law of love in various cases. Americans feel they *ought* to love their fellow men despite differences of race or creed or business interest; that is what the American Way of Life emphatically prescribes. But the American Way of Life almost explicitly sanctions hating a member of a "dangerous" political party (the Communist party is obviously meant here) or an enemy of one's country, and therefore an overwhelming majority avow their hate. In both situations, while the Jewish-Christian law of love is formally acknowledged, the truly operative factor is the value system embodied in the American Way of Life. Where the American Way of Life approves of love of one's fellow man, most Americans confidently assert that they practice such love; where the American Way of Life disapproves, the great mass of Americans do not hesitate to confess that they do not practice it, and apparently feel very little guilt for their failure. No better pragmatic test as to what the operative religion of the American people actually is could be desired.

It is not suggested here that the ideals Americans feel to be indicated in the American Way of Life are scrupulously observed in the practice of Americans; they are in fact constantly violated, often grossly. But violated or not, they are felt to be normative and relevant to "business and politics" in a way that the formal tenets of "official" religion are not. That is what makes the American Way of Life the "common religion" of American society in the sense here intended.

. . . The "common faith" of American society is not merely a civic religion to celebrate the values and convictions of the American people as a corporate entity. It has inner, personal aspects as well; or rather, side by side and in intimate relation with the civic religion of the American Way of Life, there has developed, primarily through a devitalization of the historic faiths, an inner, personal religion that promises salvation to the disoriented, tormented souls of a society in crisis.

The inner, personal religion is based on the American's *faith in faith*. We have seen that a primary religious affirmation of the American is his belief in religion. The American believes that religion is something very important for the community; he also believes that "faith," or what we may call religiosity, is a kind of "miracle drug" that can cure all the ailments of the spirit. It is not faith in *anything* that is so powerful, just faith, the "magic of believing." "It was back in those days," a prominent American churchman writes, recalling his early years. "that I formed a habit that I have never broken. I began saying in the morning two words, 'I believe.' Those two words *with nothing added* . . . give me a running start for my day, and for every day" (emphasis not in original).

The cult of faith takes two forms, which we might designate as introvert and extrovert. In its introvert form faith is trusted to bring mental health and "peace of mind," to dissipate anxiety and guilt, and to translate the soul to the blessed land of "normality" and "self-acceptance." In earlier times this cult of faith was quite literally a cult of "faith healing," best expressed in what H. Richard Niebuhr has described as the "man-centered, this-worldly, lift-yourselves-by -your-own-bootstraps doctrine of New Thought and Christian Science." Latterly it has come to vest itself in the fashionable vocabulary of psychoanalysis and is offering a synthesis of religion and psychiatry. But at bottom it is the same cult of faith in faith, the same promise that through "those two words, 'I believe,' with nothing added," all our troubles will be dissipated and inner peace and harmony restored.

The cult of faith has also its extrovert form, and that is known as "positive thinking." "Positive thinking," thinking that is "affirmative" and avoids the corrosions of "negativity" and "skepticism," thinking that "has faith," is recommended as a powerful force in the world of struggle and achievement. Here again it is not so much faith in anything, certainly not the theocentric faith of the historic religions, that is supposed to confer this power—but just faith, the psychological attitude of having faith, so to speak. And here too the cult is largely the product of the inner disintegration and enfeeblement of the historic religions; the familiar words are retained, but the old meaning is voided. "Have faith," "don't lose faith," and the like, were once injunctions to preserve one's unwavering trust in the God from Whom comes both the power to live and the "peace that passeth understanding." Gradually these phrases have come to be an appeal to maintain a "positive" attitude to life and not to lose confidence in oneself and one's activities. "To believe in yourself and in everything you do"; such, at bottom, is the meaning of the contemporary cult of faith, whether it is proclaimed by devout men from distinguished pulpits or offered as the "secret of success" by self-styled psychologists who claim to have discovered the "hidden powers" of man. What is important is faith, faith in faith. Even where the classical symbols and formulas are still retained, that is very often what is meant and what is understood.

Herberg seems to be saying that American society retains the outward forms of religiosity but has emptied it of biblical content. Or, to put it another way, our faith in faith reflects a widespread recognition that we need something to believe in. If we lack faith in Divine purpose, we will worship at lesser shrines. We may make a religion out of self-gratification (hedonism). We may make a religion out of our nationality or social class (groupism). We may also make a religion of *things*, of the tangible entities which seem more real to a population impressed with the triumphs of atomic physics and antibiotics. The worship of things (materialism) is not, however, undertaken with a clear conscience. Americans are far more interested in the symbolic rather than the physical aspect of cars and houses and clothes. Americans are materialistic by default—because they try to use "things" to express their search for the meaning of existence. Aldous Huxley, in the following excerpt from his book, *Jesting Pilate*.[3] captures this paradoxical quality of American materialism.

Turning over the pages of the Chicago telephone directory, I came upon a full-page advertisement of a firm of undertakers, or "morticians," as they are now more elegantly styled in America. The type was large and bold; my face was fatally caught. I interrupted my search to read, in twenty lines of lyrical prose, an appreciation of the incomparable Service which Kalbsfleisch and Company were rendering to Society. Their shop, I learned, was a mortuary chapel in the Gothic style; their caskets (the grosser English would call them coffins) were elegant, silk-lined and cheap; their motor-hearses were funereally sumptuous; their manners towards the bereaved were grave, yet cheering, yet purposefully uplifting; and they were fortunate in being able to "lay the Loved Ones to rest in———graveyard, the cemetery Unusual." Service was their motto and always would be. Service wholehearted and unflagging. And to prove that they meant it, personally and individually, they had reproduced two photographs, one of Mr. Kalbsfleisch, the Governing Director of the Firm, and the other of charming Mrs. Kalbsfleisch, Licensed Embalmer.

I remained for some time in meditative contemplation of Mrs. Kalbsfleisch's smile; I re-read more than once her husband's poetical and uplifting prose. The page on which I now gazed was something more, I reflected, than a mere page of advertising in a telephone book. It was a page out of contemporary American history. Something is happening on the Western shore of the Atlantic, something that has already made America unlike any other country in the world, something that threatens to separate it still further from the older civilizations, unless (which God forbid) the older civilizations should themselves fall victims to the same distorting process. To any one who reads and inwardly digests Mr. Kalbsfleisch's advertisement in the Chicago telephone book, the nature of this strange historical process becomes clear. The page is a symptom and a revealing symbol [of changes in established values] . . . .

There are two ways in which the existing standards of value may be altered. In the first case, the very existence of values may be denied. In the second, values are admitted, but the mode in which they are assigned changed: things which in the past had been regarded as possessing great value are disparaged or,

---

[3]From *Jesting Pilate*, by Aldous Huxley, pp. 305-314. 1926, 1954 by Aldous Huxley. Reprinted by permission of Harper & Brothers, New York.

more often, things which were previously of small value come to be regarded as precious.

In Europe such attempts as have been made to alter the existing standard of values have generally taken the form of denials of the existence of values. Our belief that things possess value is due to an immediate sense or intuition; we feel, and feeling we know, that things have value. If men have doubted the real existence of values, that is because they have not trusted their own immediate and intuitive conviction. They have required an intellectual, a logical and "scientific" proof of their existence. Now such a proof is not easily found at the best of times. But when you start your argumentation from the premises laid down by scientific materialism, it simply cannot be discovered. Indeed any argument starting from these premises must infallibly end in a denial of the real existence of values. Fortunately human beings are capable of enormous inconsistencies, and the eighteenth-and nineteenth-century men of science, whose conception of the universe was such that values could not be regarded by them as possessing any sort of real existence, were in practice the most ardent upholders of the established standards of values.

Still the materialist conception of the universe could not fail to exert an influence. The generation of Arnold and of Tennyson sat uncomfortably on the horns of what seemed an unescapable dilemma. Either the materialist hypothesis was true; in which case there was no such thing as value. Or else it was false; in which case values really existed, but science could not. But science manifestly *did* exist. The electric telegraph and the steam engine were there to prove it. The fact that you could go into any post office and communicate almost instantaneously with the antipodes was felt to be a confirmation of the materialistic hypothesis then current among men of science. It worked, therefore it was true, and therefore our intimate sense of the existence of values was a mere illusion. Tennyson and Arnold did not want it to be an illusion; they were distressed, they were inwardly divided. Their intellects denied what their feelings asserted; and the Truth (or rather what was at that time apparently the Truth) was at war with their hopes, their intuitive convictions, their desires. The European intellectuals of a later generation accepted the conclusions logically derivable from the scientific-materialist hypothesis and resigned themselves—almost with glee— to living in a devaluated world. Some of them are still with us, and the theories which they propounded, as corollaries to the main value-denying theory from which they started, are still influential. Claiming to speak as the apostles of scientific truth, they stripped art of its significance, they reinterpreted human life in terms, not of its highest spiritual aspects, but of its lowest. (I am using the terms "highest" and "lowest," which they, of course, would repudiate as nonsensical.) A less sophisticated generation had regarded the Sistine frescoes as being somehow superior to a prettily patterned rug, *Macbeth,* as more important than *The Rape of the Lock.* Illusion! According to the apostles of scientific truth, one was really just as good as the other. Indeed, the *Rape* and the patterned rug were actually superior to *Macbeth* and the Michelangelo frescoes, as being more finished and perfect works of art: they aroused, it was explained, intenser "esthetic emotions." Art thus satisfactorily disposed of, religion was next "explained" in terms of sex. The moral conscience was abolished (another illusion) and "amuse yourself" proclaimed as the sole categorical imperative. The theories of Freud were received in intellectual circles with acclaim; to explain every higher activity of the human mind in terms of incest and coprophily came to be regarded not only as truly scientific, but also as somehow virile and courageous. Freudism became the *realpolitik* of psychology and philosophy. Those who denied values felt themselves to be rather heroic; instinctively they were appealing to the standards which they were trying, intellectually, to destroy...

But the influence of these *ci-devant* "scientific" deniers of value has not been wide. In most human beings the intuitive sense of values is too strong to be seriously affected by intellectual arguments, however specious. They are revolted by the denial of values; they insist on interpreting the world in terms of high and low. Unfortunately, however, they are apt to make mistakes and to call things by the wrong names, labelling "high" what should rightly be low, and "low" what ought to be high....

The morticians, and with them all the Business Men of America, are as whole-heartedly enthusiastic about Service as was ever St. Francis or his divine Master. But the activities which they designate by the word "Service" happen to be slightly different from those which the Founder of Christianity called by the same name....

...It is on the same ground that they perform necessary jobs well that American Business Men claim to be doing Service, and Service of the highest value. They overlook the significant historical fact that all the valuable things in life, all the things that make for civilization and progress, are precisely the unnecessary ones. All scientific research, all art, all religion are (by comparison with making coffins or breakfast foods) unnecessary. But if we had stuck to the merely necessary, we should still be apes.... By exalting the merely necessary to an equality with the unnecessary, the American Business Man has falsified the standard of values. The service rendered by a mortician or a realtor has come to be regarded as the equivalent of the service rendered by an artist or a man of science. Babbitt can now honestly believe that he and his kind are doing as much for humanity as the Pasteurs and the Isaac Newtons. Kalbsfleisch among his silk-lined caskets knows himself to be as good as Beethoven. Successful stockbrokers, certain that Business is Religion, can come home after a day of speculation on the Exchange, feeling as virtuously happy as Buddha must have felt when he had renounced the world and received his great illumination.

Note that Aldous Huxley's argument involves two points: (a) a misinterpretation of science tends to undermine faith generally, and (b) the everyday business of life tends to be regarded as the main point of life. Although he does not explicitly denounce the American preoccupation with "things," Huxley implies that materialistic standards of evaluation have crept into sectors of American life where they should not be. As an example of this phenomenon, consider that the "leading" minister of a community is the minister with the largest and wealthiest congregation, not the minister whose life comes closest to Christian ideals.

Americans seem insatiable for material evidences that life is worth living and that they are getting the most out of life. Whether they are the "driven executives and professionals" or the anxious security-seeking "millions who man the assembly lines . . . [and] file the letters," it is their material standard of living that seems to preoccupy them.[4] Indeed, technological progress comes to be identified in the minds of many as essential to the democratic process itself.

If our interpretation is correct, the materialism of American society is a substitute for the moral certainty that used to be provided by traditional religion. In a sense, economic pursuits are part of a spiritual quest. But the material preoccupations that give life meaning have incidental effects. Thus, tensions over financial problems may worsen the quality of family life. A recent book by a distinguished British sociologist attempts to demonstrate the deleterious consequences of this seepage of material values into human relations by contrasting the British and American handling of blood transfusions. What follows is an excerpt from a review of this book.[5]

No American can read *The Gift Relationship: From Human Blood to Social Policy,* by Richard M. Titmuss (Pantheon, $6.95) without shame. We are generally aware that American health services are in bad shape. They are enormously expensive, both absolutely and as a share of Gross National Product; they are inequitably distributed, both geographically and socially; they are not terribly effective in improving health; they are very badly coordinated—if indeed they can be said to be coordinated at all; they are difficult of access and comprehension.

---

[4] Jules Henry, *Culture Against Man,* New York: Vintage, 1963.

[5] From Nathan Glazer, "Blood," *The Public Interest,* No. 24 (Summer 1971), pp. 86-89. Copyright © National Affairs, Inc., 1971. Reprinted by permission.

All this we more or less knew, and it is a heavy charge to set against the several advantages of the American system—that fairly good but costly health services by well-trained people are available in most places for most people and that our chaos offers the advantage—still one not to be lightly thrown away—of providing a multiplicity of patterns and models of health and of foreclosing none completely.

Professor Titmuss's study of the systems for the collection and use of blood and blood products in health services in the United Kingdom and the United States suggests forcefully that the charges against the American health system are far graver than those I have suggested, and its several advantages are, on examination, no advantages at all. He has had the ingenious idea of examining a very specific area of medical practice and treatment, and he asks how it is handled in England and the United States.

In England, blood and blood products are completely removed from the marketplace. Blood is not sold by donors, nor do they get any advantage of any kind from giving blood. They do not by giving blood provide blood for family and friends, or pay off the blood used by themselves and their families, or accumulate credits for themselves or for specific institutions. Nor can blood be sold. The blood that is needed is provided by the National Blood Transfusion Service. Because there is no market in blood, even private patients—those who do not take advantage of the National Health Service but become patients in private hospitals—get blood free. There is heavy and increasing use of blood in England, as in this country, for surgery, for accidents, in obstetrical practice, for the preparation of blood products used in testing and treatment. The system of voluntary donors, who give often and regularly, provides all that is needed. Donors are a cross-section of the healthy population. The amount of blood wasted (blood is wasted when it is not used within 21 days, though products made from blood can last for a much longer time) is infinitesimal—one per cent or so. The number of infections arising from blood taken from sick donors, or donors infected with serum hepatitis or other diseases that are carried through the blood, is very small, of the order of magnitude of one per cent or so.

Let us contrast this with the American situation. Professor Titmuss estimates that in the United States only 7 per cent of blood is given completely voluntarily by donors. A good part—it is hard to estimate the proportion owing to poor statistics but perhaps a third—is bought and sold on an open market. The rest is given under varying degrees of compulsion, ranging from the mildest—the pressure to give blood for family and friends—to the quite specific obligation to repay blood used, or the building up of blood insurance under various programs. While 40 per cent of blood is collected by the Red Cross, 20 to 30 per cent by 6,000 hospital blood banks, 15 to 20 per cent by community blood banks, and all these do not pay donors, the fact is that no blood is free. Hospitals charge for its use. The cost is so high that hemophiliacs, or those suffering from serious accidents or special surgery, can be bankrupted by the bills. (Some part presumably is covered by insurance, other parts by Medicare and Medicaid—even so, many individuals will find themselves saddled with enormous yet quite real debts for blood.)

This is the beginning of the contrast. Despite the enormous charges for blood, blood is in permanent short supply in this country. Not enough donors come forward, whether paid, tied, or completely voluntary. Between 1956 and 1966-67, American blood collections rose 17 per cent. In England and Wales, the increase in collections for this period was 77 per cent. If one takes into account the fact that American population rose much faster than English, American blood collections per capita did not rise at all, or may have declined. The estimates for waste in American blood collections—primarily through out-dating —run as high as 30 per cent, as against one per cent in England and Wales.

The permanent blood shortage has led pharmaceutical companies into the practice of plasmapheresis—in which great quantities of blood can be taken, at frequent intervals, from donors, and the red cells removed and reinjected. This permits donors to be bled more often, and for greater quantities. It may have as yet undefined dangers to the health of donors.

At the same time, the blood here is of much poorer quality. Because so much is collected from those selling blood to make money, a substantial proportion of donors are Skid Row types, drug addicts, and others among whom the risk of hepatitis is extremely high. The carrier of hepatitis need not know he has it, but whether he knows it or not, there is an incentive for the paid donor whose need for money is urgent to conceal it. A good part of American blood supplies comes from prisoners, who are given various incentives to contribute, and among these, too, the risk of hepatitis is high. Thus the risk of hepatitis from blood transfusion, and the risk of death, is much higher in the United States than in England.

Because of the perpetual shortage, the United States uses, for the casualties of Vietnam, blood bought in the Far East (the system in Japan also depends in large measure on paid donors, with equivalent risks). Thus, the United States is engaged in the purchase of blood on the international market.

Professor Titmuss points out that in this country it is the poor who sell blood, the rich who buy it—the middle classes manage through insurance schemes, but are still subject to the risks inevitable in the paid donor approach. Whereas England provides blood free to private patients and exports excess eyes for transplants (contributed free to the National Health Service) without charge, the United States is already dependent in some measures on overseas supplies;

and to the movement of blood from the poor to the rich internally, we may soon add a movement of blood from poor countries to rich countries internationally.

The American commitment to a free market in blood operates at many levels. The individual may sell his blood. He may sell to a commercial blood bank. The blood bank sells it to pharmaceutical companies, profit-making hospitals, and non-profit hospitals. All these sell blood to patients. If hospitals borrow blood, they must repay it. If one area is short of blood, it must import from another, and then repay in blood. This leads to practices of hospital hoarding of blood, which leads to waste, as some have too much and must dispose of it. It leads to a great deal of shipment of blood from one area to another. Because shipment of blood is more efficient when blood is combined into large pools, the risk of hepatitis increases—one bad donation may infect the whole. In England blood is not pooled to the same extent, owing to these risks. With all this buying and selling, there is an enormous addition to the Gross National Product—at the cost of delayed operations, insufficient supplies, the spreading of infection and the danger of death.

Titmuss concludes with this overwhelming indictment:

> From our study of the private market in blood in the United States we have concluded that the commercialization of blood and donor relationships represses the experience of altruism, erodes the sense of community, lowers scientific standards, limits both personal and professional freedoms, sanctions the making of profits in hospitals and clinical laboratories, legalizes the hostility between doctor and patient, subjects critical areas of medicine to the laws of the marketplace, places immense social costs on those least able to bear them—the poor, the sick, and the inept—increases the danger of unethical behavior in various sectors of medical science and practice, and results in situations in which proportionately more and more blood is supplied by the poor, the unskilled, the unemployed, Negroes and other low-income groups and categories of exploited human populations of high blood yielders. Redistribution in terms of blood and blood products from the poor to the rich appears to be one of the dominant effects of the American blood banking systems.

Moreover, on four testable non-ethical criteria the commercialized blood market is bad. In terms of economic efficiency it is highly wasteful of blood; shortages, chronic and acute, characterize the demand and supply position and make illusory the concept of equilibrium. It is administratively inefficient and results in more bureaucratization and much greater administrative, accounting and computer overheads. . . . In terms of quality, commercial markets are much more likely to distribute contaminated blood; the risks for the patient of disease and death are substantially greater. Freedom from disability is inseparable from altruism.

CONCLUSION

Civilized man has lost the élan that comes from a commitment to some important purpose. Since it is impossible for human beings to live without *some* conception of a point to life, Westerners seem often to be engaged in a desperate effort to fill the void left by the disappearance of earlier and "naive" faiths. Turning specifically to America, Will Herberg believes that the resurgence of traditional religion, although it may be motivated by a search for identity and meaning, results in an empty formalism. The outward forms of American religiosity surround a core set of values distinctly more hedonistic than idealistic. Whether or not Americans are godless, they do not dare to be churchless.

What is left for many Americans is an escape from the dread fear of "pointlessness" into a mad round of materialistic preoccupations and distractions. They try to persuade themselves and others that they *are* doing something important; but the things that seem "important" are, Huxley suggests, material things that can show up in the Gross National Product. Even the vital activity of blood transfusions becomes in the United States, according to Titmuss, a materialistic activity—with considerable material disadvantages, as well as possible moral ones.

chapter 3
Utilitarianism in a market society

American society has gone very far in institutionalizing a market mentality. That is to say, an American usually asks himself when contemplating an arrangement with other persons, "What's in it for me?" And, on the other hand, he expects others to agree to the arrangement only if he can make it "worth their while." It would be a mistake to infer from this that Americans are more selfish than members of other societies. The point is rather that one of the governing principles of American society is that of negotiated exchange. The individual is expected to secure what he needs and wants from others by contracting a mutually advantageous arrangement. Thus, your claim to an income rests on the wages you can induce an employer to give you; the quality of housing you obtain depends on the bargain you make with landlords or mortgage companies; your chance for favorable legislation depends on the pressure you can exert on your representatives.

No principle, of course, is institutionalized with thoroughgoing consistency; thus there are exceptions to the principle of utilitarianism. Americans do not expect small children to make it worth their parents' while to feed them.[1] Certain categories of persons—children, the mentally ill, the very old—are not expected to negotiate on their own behalf. Actually, the boundary separating those capable of negotiating on their own behalf and those needing the protection of society has been redrawn again and again in American history. Thus, legislation regulating the working conditions of women and children was once

[1] On the other hand, the claim of an American child for food, clothing, and shelter does depend on the bargain his parents are able to drive with other persons in the economy.

held to be unconstitutional. Note the reasoning in the Supreme Court decision of Adkins v. Children's Hospital (1923)[2] in which the importance of the negotiated exchange principle is clearly stated.

The case arose from an Act of Congress in 1918, which created a public agency in the District of Columbia with powers to regulate the wages and working conditions of women and children. This was an effort to substitute a *legal* principle for the *negotiated-exchange* principle for determining how much someone should get. The act said, in effect, that a public agency should decide what was "decent" or "proper," at least in the case of women and children, rather than let bargaining power settle the matter.

Congressmen may have been motivated at the time by a feeling of solidarity and care of disadvantaged persons; they may even have felt that citizens could cooperate more effectively in a national "team" effort if their basic needs were more adequately met. Those are two others of the four transaction modes discussed in Chapter 1. We do not know about such motivations; our aim at the moment is to show how ingrained in the American fabric at the time was the "utilitarian" or "negotiated exchange" mode.

The Board created by Congress found that a hotel and a certain young woman 21 years of age had negotiated a contract under which the young woman worked as an elevator operator for $35 a month and two meals a day. She was satisfied, saying that she could not successfully bargain for higher wages and was willing, therefore, to accept this negotiation. The hotel was satisfied also. But the Board ruled that the hotel ought not to drive such a hard bargain.

Here is what the Supreme Court said.

The feature of this statute which, perhaps more than any other, puts upon it the stamp of invalidity is that it exacts from the employer an arbitrary payment for a purpose and upon a basis having no causal connection with his business, or the contract or the work the employee engages to do. The declared basis, as already pointed out, is not the value of the service rendered, but the extraneous circumstance that the employee needs to get a prescribed sum of money to insure her subsistence, health and morals. The ethical right of every worker, man or woman, to a living wage may be conceded. One of the declared and important purposes of trade organizations is to secure it. And with that principle and with every legitimate effort to realize it in fact, no one can quarrel; but the fallacy of the proposed method of attaining it is that it assumes that every employer is bound at all events to furnish it. The moral requirement implicit in every contract of employment, *viz*, that the amount to be paid and the service to be rendered shall bear to each other some relation of just equivalence, is completely ignored. The necessities of the employee are alone considered and these arise

[2]*Adkins v. Children's Hospital*, 261 U.S. 525 (1923).

outside of the employment, are the same when there is no employment, and as great in one occupation as in another. Certainly the employer by paying a fair equivalent for the service rendered, though not sufficient to support the employee, has neither caused nor contributed to her poverty. On the contrary, to the extent of what he pays he has relieved it. In principle, there can be no difference between the case of selling labor and the case of selling goods. If one goes to the butcher, the baker or grocer to buy food, he is morally entitled to obtain the worth of his money but he is not entitled to more. If what he gets is worth what he pays he is not justified in demanding more simply because he needs more; and the shopkeeper, having dealt fairly and honestly in that transaction, is not concerned in any peculiar sense with the question of his customer's necessities. Should a statute undertake to vest in a commission power to determine the quantity of food necessary for individual support and require the shopkeeper, if he sell to the individual at all, to furnish that quantity at not more than a fixed maximum, it would undoubtedly fall before the constitutional test. The fallacy of any argument in support of the validity of such a statute would be quickly exposed. The argument in support of that now being considered is equally fallacious, though the weakness of it may not be so plain. A statute requiring an employer to pay in money, to pay at prescribed and regular intervals, to pay the value of the services rendered, even to pay with fair relation to the extent of the benefit obtained from the service, would be understandable. But a statute which prescribes payment without regard to any of these things and solely with relation to circumstances apart from the contract of employment, the business affected by it and the work done under it, is so clearly the product of a naked, arbitrary exercise of power that it cannot be allowed to stand under the Constitution of the United States. . . .

The liberty that the Supreme Court was protecting in this decision was, in short, the liberty to receive whatever one could succeed in bargaining for. Since this decision, the principle of negotiated exchange has been tempered considerably; and the Supreme Court, since 1937, has validated legislation regulating wages, hours, and working conditions, not only for women and children, but for men as well.

Another departure from the negotiated-exchange principle is this: American society provides some services to its members without regard to what they contribute in exchange. Thus, all children are entitled to elementary education, and all members of the community are entitled to police and fire protection. Finally, in application, the exchange principle is softened: Americans insist on certain ethics in negotiations. They frown on lying and other kinds of deliberate deception. They are shocked when a surgeon performs unnecessary operations even though his patients agree to them. Nevertheless, despite the exceptions, the principle is clear: ideally, Americans feel entitled only to what they are able to get through free negotiations in the marketplace.

Economists have stated the principle with relentless logic. They call it the exchange theory of value. According to this theory, the remuneration received by a factor of production (including human beings) should be equal to the value added by the last unit of that factor. Here is the way Harvard professor Thomas Nixon Carver put it in a book entitled *Essays in Social Justice*.[3]

If there should be too many of one kind of laborers at one particular spot, so that no more could be produced with one more of that kind, and no less with one less of that kind, the physical product of a man of that kind at that spot is exactly nothing, and therefore his value is exactly nothing. But if the number of a particular kind of laborers is so small and the other factors are so abundant that one more laborer of this particular kind would add greatly to the product of the combination, then it is not inaccurate to say that his physical product is very high. That being the case, his value is very high. This, therefore, is the principle which determines how much a man is worth, and consequently, according to our criterion of justice, how much he ought to have as a reward for his work. To pay him more than that would take something from other producers. If the total addition which a certain individual can make to the total product of the community is one dollar a day, or, which means the same thing, if the total reduction in the production of the community when he ceases to work is one dollar a day, and if he is actually consuming two dollars a day, then there would be one dollar a day more for some one else if he should emigrate or die. The extra dollar which he receives, at the expense of some one else, is either given him for love or benevolence, according as the others look upon him. It is not given him for the sake of justice.

How much is a man worth? As much as someone is willing to pay him for his muscle power, brainpower, or his goods or capital—whatever he is offering. Sometimes it may be his good looks, as in the case of movie stars whom people pay to watch. If the goods or services (or looks) one has to offer to others are not worth much to those others, then one is worth little.

This principle—modified somewhat by minimum wage legislation, public housing, and similar legal principles—tends to dominate American transactions. Nor is the principle of negotiated exchange confined to cases of wages or prices. Consider the following observation of Willard Waller, made over 30 years ago.[4]

During the winter term the preponderance of men assures to every coed a relatively high bargaining power. Every summer witnesses a surprising re-

---

[3]Reprinted by permission of the publishers, Harvard University Press, Cambridge, Massachusetts, from Thomas Nixon Carver, *Essays in Social Justice*, 1915, pp. 177, 184, 200-201.

[4]Willard Waller, "The Rating and Dating Complex," *American Sociological Review*, Vol. 2 (October 1937), p. 736.

versal of this situation. Hundreds of women school teachers flock to this school for the summer term, and men are very scarce; smooth, unmarried boys of college age are particularly scarce. The school teachers are older than the boys; they have usually lost some of their earlier attractiveness; they have been living for some months or years within the school-teacher role. They are man-hungry, and they have a little money. As a result, there is a great proliferation of highly commercialized relations. The women lend their cars to their men friends, but continue to pay for repairs and gasoline; they take the boys out to dinner, treat them to drinks, and buy expensive presents for them. And many who do not go so far are available for sex relations on terms which demand no more than a transitory sort of commitment from the man.

Again, observe the operation of the principle in the case of relations between congressmen and their constitutents. True, students of democratic government have long debated whether legislators should primarily represent their constituents or should, through study of the issues arrive at their own independent judgment of what is best for the country. The fact is, however, that the American device for protecting the country against despotism—making lawmakers responsive to the electorate—means that legislators receive and hold their positions only so long as they make it "worth their constituents' while" to vote for them. It also means that legislators who wish to be retained in office must please those persons to whom they owe their positions—not others, and not posterity, because posterity cannot vote yet.

In other words, the principle that you are entitled to what you can make it worth someone's while to give you applies here also, as Alistair Cooke shows in the following comparison of the American Congress and the British Parliament.[5]

. . . Englishmen usually leave Washington with the complaint that Congress is not, and seems to have no intention of becoming, the House of Commons. I spend some part of every year begging British and French journalists to start their study of American government not in Washington but in the places the men in Washington come from; so they may understand why a man from the goat country of Texas, west central Texas, keeps up such a lively interest in mohair and army uniforms, and why a man from California sometimes seems to have nothing on his mind but water, unless it is the oil that flows under it.

By such little expeditions it is possible for a foreigner to learn at the start one of the great differences between a Congressman and a member of Parliament. . . .

[5]From an address delivered by Alistair Cooke, "Ethics in Congress and Parliament," at the Twentieth Annual Herald Tribune Forum. Reprinted by permission of Alistair Cooke and the New York Herald Tribune.

When a man goes to Westminster, he does not go as a one-man delegation from an industry or a crop. . . . Very often he may have only a rough idea of what his constituents do for a living. For there is no locality rule in the British system, which is not an oversight but a provision meant to leave the member of Parliament comparatively free to give his best to the affairs that concern the nation as a whole. This is quite different from watching the Congress bring up a bill and expecting your man to amend it in your interest.

A small glimpse of the pressures imposed on a Congressman by this principle of "responsiveness to his constituents" is provided by Stephen K. Bailey and Howard D. Samuel in their book, *Congress at Work*. We quote below a brief section of that study.[6]

> "Let's be realistic," a member [of Congress] might say. "I owe my election in part to an organization. Sad as it may seem, the support of those who make the electoral machinery spin is not always conditional upon my voting record. In fact, most of what in political parlance is called 'the mob' don't care how I vote. They want to know what I have done for *them*—and done for them lately: aid in getting a government contract, assistance in straightening out an immigration case, help in getting a judgeship for a loyal party member. If I want to be returned next election, this is a part of the hidden cost of campaigning, and the necessary price for having a Congress at all. Do I have to compromise my ethics occasionally? Of course I do."

Perhaps the essential significance of negotiated exchange as a principle of American life is the pressure it exerts to define other persons strictly in terms of their utility to oneself. Another human being is either irrelevant or can be "used" in some way. William H. Whyte, Jr. shows this effect in the following account of his job-training experience with the Vick Company.[7]

> Shortly before we were to set out from New York, the president, Mr. H. S. Richardson, took us up to the Cloud Club atop the Chrysler Building. The symbolism did not escape us. As we looked from this executive eyrie down on the skyscraper spires below, Golconda stretched out before us. One day, we gathered, some of us would be coming back up again—and not as temporary guests either. Some would not. The race would be to the swiftest.
>
> Over coffee Mr. Richardson drove home to us the kind of philosophy that would get us back up. He posed a hypothetical problem. Suppose, he said, that you are a manufacturer and for years a small firm has been making paper cartons

---

[6]From *Congress at Work* by Stephen K. Bailey and Howard D. Samuel, pp. 4-5.

[7]William H. Whyte, Jr., *The Organization Man*, New York: Doubleday-Anchor, 1965. Copyright © 1956 by William H. Whyte, Jr. Reprinted by permission of Simon & Schuster, Inc.

for your product. He has specialized so much to service you, as a matter of fact, that that's all he does make. He is utterly dependent on your business. For years the relationship has continued to be eminently satisfactory to both parties. But then one day another man walks in and says he will make the boxes for you cheaper. What do you do?

He bade each one of us in turn to answer.

But *how much* cheaper? we asked. How much time could we give the old supplier to match the new bid? Mr. Richardson became impatient. There was only one decision. Either you were a businessman or you were not a business-man. The new man, obviously, should get the contract. Mr. Richardson, who had strong views on the necessity of holding to the old American virtues, advised us emphatically against letting sentimentality obscure fundamentals. Business was survival of the fittest, he indicated, and we would soon learn the fact.

He was as good as his word. The Vick curriculum was just that—survival of the fittest. In the newer type of programs, companies will indeed fire incom-petents, but a man joins with the idea that the company intends to keep him, and this is the company's wish also. The Vick School, however, was frankly based on the principle of elimination. It wouldn't make any difference how wonderful all of us might turn out to be; of the thirty-eight who sat there in the Cloud Club, the rules of the game dictated that only six or seven of us would be asked to stay with Vick. The rest would graduate to make way for the next batch of students.

Another difference between Vick's approach and that now more charac-teristic became very evident as soon as we arrived in the field. While the work, as the company said, was educational, it was in no sense make-work. Within a few days of our session at the Cloud Club, we were dispatched to the hinterland—in my case, the hill country of eastern Kentucky. Each of us was given a panel delivery truck, a full supply of signs, a ladder, a stock of samples, and an order pad. After several days under the eye of a senior salesman, we were each assigned a string of counties and left to shift for ourselves.

The merchandising was nothing if not applied. To take a typical day of any one of us, we would rise at 6:00 or 6:30 in some bleak boarding house or run-down hotel and after a greasy breakfast set off to squeeze in some advertis-ing practice before the first call. This consisted of bostitching a quota of large fiber signs on barns and clamping smaller metal ones to telephone poles and trees by hog rings. By eight, we would have arrived at a general store for our exercise in merchandising. Our assignment was to persuade the dealer to take a year's supply all at once, or, preferably, more than a year's supply, so that he would have no money or shelf space left for other brands. After the sale, or no-sale, we would turn to market research and note down the amount sold him by "chisel-ing" competitors (i.e., competitors; there was no acknowledgment on our report blanks of any other kind).

Next, we did some sampling work: "Tilt your head back, Mr. Jones," we would suddenly say to the dealer. For a brief second he would obey and we would quickly shoot a whopping dropperful of Vatronol up his nose. His eyes smarting from the sting, the dealer would smile with simple pleasure. Turning to the loungers by the stove, he would tell them to let the drummer fella give them some of that stuff. After the messy job was done, we plastered the place with cardboard signs, and left. Then, some more signposting in barnyards, and ten or twelve miles of mud road to the next call. So, on through the day, the routine was repeated until at length, long after dark, we would get back to our lodgings in time for dinner—and two hours' work on our report forms.

The acquisition of a proper frame of mind toward all this was a slow process. The faded yellow second sheets of our daily report book tell the story. At first, utter demoralization. Day after day, the number of calls would be a skimpy eight or nine, and the number of sales sometimes zero. But it was never our fault. In the large space left for explanations, we would affect a cheerful humor—the gay adventurer in the provinces—but this pathetic bravado could not mask a recurrent note of despair.[8]

To all these bids for sympathy, the home office was adamantine. The weekly letter written to each trainee would start with some perfunctory remarks that it was too bad about the clutch breaking down, the cut knee, and so on. But this spurious sympathy did not conceal a strong preoccupation with results, and lest we miss the point we were told of comrades who would no longer be with us. We too are sorry about those absent dealers, the office would say. Perhaps if you got up earlier in the morning?

As the office sensed quite correctly from my daily reports, I was growing sorry for myself. I used to read timetables at night, and often in the evening I would somehow find myself by the C & O tracks when the George Washington swept by, its steamy windows a reminder of civilization left behind. I was also sorry for many of the storekeepers, most of whom existed on a precarious credit relationship with wholesalers, and as a consequence I sold them very little of anything.

The company sent its head training supervisor to see if anything could be salvaged. After several days with me, this old veteran of the road told me he knew what was the matter. It wasn't so much my routine, wretched as this was.

---

[8]I quote some entries from my own daily report forms: "They use 'dry' creek beds for roads in this country. 'Dry!' Ha! Ha! ... Sorry about making only four calls today, but I had to go over to Ervine to pick up a drop shipment of ¾ tins and my clutch broke down. ... Everybody's on WPA in this country. Met only one dealer who sold more than a couple dozen VR a year. Ah, well, it's all in the game! ... Bostitched my left thumb to a barn this morning and couldn't pick up my first call until after lunch. ... The local brick plant here is shut down and nobody's buying anything. ... Five, count 'em, *five* absent dealers in a row. ... Sorry about the $20.85 but the clutch broke down again. ..."

It was my state of mind. "Fella," he told me, "you will never sell anybody anything until you learn one simple thing. The man on the other side of the counter is the *enemy*."

It was a gladiators' school we were in. Selling may be no less competitive now, but in the Vick program, strife was honored far more openly than today's climate would permit. Combat was the ideal—combat with the dealer, combat with the "chiseling competitors," and combat with each other. There was some talk about "the team," but it was highly abstract. Our success depended entirely on beating our fellow students, and while we got along when we met for occasional sales meetings the camaraderie was quite extracurricular.

Slowly, as our sales-to-calls ratios crept up, we gained in rapacity. Somewhere along the line, by accident or skill, each of us finally manipulated a person into doing what we wanted him to do. Innocence was lost, and by the end of six months, with the pack down to about twenty-three men, we were fairly ravening for the home stretch back to the Cloud Club. At this point, the company took us off general store and grocery work and turned us loose in the rich drugstore territory.

The advice of the old salesman now became invaluable. While he had a distaste for any kind of dealer, with druggists he was implacably combative. He was one of the most decent and kindly men I have ever met, but when he gave us pep talks about this enemy ahead of us, he spoke with great intensity. Some druggists were good enough fellows, he told us (i.e., successful ones who bought big deals), but the tough ones were a mean, servile crew; they would insult you, keep you waiting while they pretended to fill prescriptions, lie to you about their inventory, whine at anything less than a 300 per cent markup, and switch their customers to chiseling competitors.

The old salesman would bring us together in batches for several days of demonstration. It was a tremendous experience for us, for though he seemed outwardly a phlegmatic man, we knew him for the artist he was. Outside the store he was jumpy and sometimes perspired, but once inside, he was composed to the point of apparent boredom. He rarely smiled, almost never opened with a joke. His demeanor seemed to say, I am a busy man and you are damned lucky I have stopped by your miserable store. Sometimes, if the druggist was unusually insolent, he would blow cigar smoke at his face. "Can't sell it if you don't have it," he would say contemptuously, and then, rather pleased with himself, glance back at us, loitering in the wings, to see if we had marked that.

Only old pros like himself could get away with that, he told us in the post-mortem sessions, but there were lots of little tricks we could pick up. As we gathered around him, like Fagin's brood, he would demonstrate how to watch for the victim's shoulders to relax before throwing the clincher; how to pick up the one-size jar of a competitive line that had an especially thick glass bottom and chuckle knowingly; how to feign suppressed worry that maybe the deal was too big for "the smaller druggist like yourself" to take; how to disarm the nervous druggist by fumbling and dropping a pencil. No mercy, he would tell us; give the devils no mercy.

We couldn't either. As the acid test of our gall the company now challenged us to see how many drugstores we could desecrate with "flange" signs. By all the standards of the trade this signposting should have been an impossible task. Almost every "chiseling competitor" would give the druggist at least five dollars to let him put up a sign; we could not offer the druggist a nickel. Our signs, furthermore, were not the usual cardboard kind the druggist could throw away after we had left. They were of metal, they were hideous, and they were to be screwed to the druggists' cherished oak cabinets.

The trick was in the timing. When we were in peak form the procedure went like this: Just after the druggist had signed the order, his shoulders would subside, and this would signal a fleeting period of mutual bonhomie. "New fella, aren't you?" the druggist was likely to say, relaxing. This was his mistake. As soon as we judged the good will to be at full flood, we would ask him if he had a ladder. (There was a ladder out in the car, but the fuss of fetching it would have broken the mood.) The druggist's chain of thought would not at that moment connect the request with what was to follow, and he would good-naturedly dispatch someone to bring out a ladder. After another moment of chatter, we would make way for the waiting customer who would engage the druggist's attention. Then, forthrightly, we would slap the ladder up against a spot we had previously reconnoitered. "Just going to get this sign up for you," we would say, as if doing him the greatest favor in the world. He would nod absent-mindedly. Then up the ladder we would go; a few quick turns of the awl, place the bracket in position, and then, the automatic screw driver. Bang! Bang! Down went the sign. (If the druggist had been unusually mean, we could break the thread of the screw for good measure.) Then down with the ladder, shift it over to the second spot, and up again.

About this time the druggist would start looking up a little unhappily, but the good will, while ebbing, was still enough to inhibit him from action. *He* felt sorry for us. Imagine that young man thinking those signs are good looking! Just as he would be about to mumble something about one sign being enough, we would hold up the second one. It had a picture on it of a woman squirting nose drops up her nostrils. We would leer fatuously at it. "Just going to lay this blonde on the top of the cabinet for you, Mr. Jones," we would say, winking. We were giants in those days.

The principle of negotiated exchange is an institutionalized procedure for the allocation of goods and services in American society. It helps to solve the basic distributive problem. However, it also has implications for the personality of the individual—quite apart from what it allocates to him in the way of material benefits. It is a basis of self-assessment. Thus, the individual's feelings of adequacy, worthiness, security, *and* gratification stem in part from his success in applying the principle of negotiated exchange.

Consider the following suggestions (offered to college seniors by the Placement Office) for making a good impression on corporate recruiters. They seem to deny the uniqueness of the applicant in the course of packaging an attractive product.

Introduction—The employment interview is one of the most important events in your working career. In the period of 20 to 30 minutes, you are expected to present and sell your product—YOURSELF.

The primary ingredient in any successful interview is enthusiasm and self-confidence. There are some general rules that will help you in being successful.

I. PREPARATION—As in any sales job it is very important that you know your product and the purchaser.

    YOUR PRODUCT—In order to sell yourself, you must determine:

    (1) What type of work you want to do? Why you want to do it?
    (2) What qualifies you for this type of work? Is it your experience? education? personality? abilities? aptitudes? or interest?
    (3) Where are you willing to work? Are you limiting yourself to a certain industry, geographic location, salary range, etc. A helpful exercise, after you have determined the type of work you wish to do is to list in one column all the qualifications the job requires and in another column how you can show that you have them.

For example:	Television Control Technician
Technical and Personal Requirements	*How Can I Show I Have Them*
Good knowledge of electronic and electrical circuits	My school record. My work experience.
Ability to analyze situations	Suggestion award I received for solving the unexplained short circuits.
Must make decisions on the spot.	Ability demonstrated by specific examples.

Another aid in analyzing yourself is to have answers for the following questions, which are frequently asked: (As reported by 92 companies surveyed by Northwestern University)

(1) What are your future vocational plans?
(2) How do you spend your spare time? What are your hobbies?
(3) In what type of position are you most interested?
(4) What jobs have you held? How were they obtained and why did you leave?
(5) Why did you choose your particular field of work?

(6) Why did you—or didn't you attend college?

(7) What qualifications do you have that make you feel that you will be successful in your field?

(8) Do you prefer any specific geographic location? Why?

(9) What personal characteristics are necessary for success in your chosen field?

(10) Do you prefer working with others or by yourself?

(11) What have you learned from some jobs you have held?

(12) Do you like routine work?

(13) Do you like regular hours?

(14) What is your major weakness?

(15) Do you demand attention?

(16) Do you have an analytical mind?

(17) Are you willing to go where the company sends you?

(18) What type of books do you read?

(19) What jobs have you enjoyed the most? The least? Why?

(20) What are your special abilities?

(21) Do you like to travel?

(22) How about overtime work?

(23) What kind of salary do you expect?

You cannot rehearse your role in an upcoming interview because you don't know what cues will be given to you. The important part is to know yourself and the company.

It is your job to sell yourself and not under- or over-sell. You should be enthusiastic and perceptive. You must seek out what is wanted and then present it.

There are a few things that may happen that you should be aware of.

1. Surprise, direct questions—Some interviewers may open with questions like:

   (a) What can I do for you?

   (b) Tell me about yourself.

   (c) Why are you interested in this company?

This is your opportunity to present your strengths right off the bat. Point out why the company should hire you.

2. Keep following the interviewer's lead. Don't answer in just yeses and nos. On the other hand, don't talk too much.

3. Be prepared to answer a few personal questions.

4. Sit up in your chair and look alert and interested at all times. Don't look tense, but don't relax so much that you look slouchy.

5. Look your interviewer directly in the eye—and keep doing it from time to time during your conversation. Don't be overly serious; a frequent smile will help.

6. A few interviewers like to do most of the talking and judge you by your reactions—the interest, comprehension and intelligence you show. Others speak very little. Their attitude is that it is your job to sell yourself. That is where you will have to call on your knowledge of yourself and your interest in the work his company does.

7. In selling yourself try to appear factual and sincere, not bloated with conceit.

8. Most interviewers will follow a rather simple question and answer formula. If such is the case your ability to answer quickly and intelligently is of great importance. If your answers are confused and contradictory your cause is lost. The greatest preventive against contradictory answers is plain unembroidered truth.

9. Ask some definite questions about the company. This demonstrates interest as well as giving you information.

10. If you get the impression that the interview is not going well and that you have already been rejected, don't let your discouragement show. You have nothing to lose by continuing the appearance of confidence, and you may gain much. The last few minutes often change things.

REMEMBER YOUR SUCCESS WILL DEPEND ON:

(1) YOUR APPEARANCE (dress conservatively)

(2) YOUR KNOWLEDGE OF YOURSELF

(3) YOUR KNOWLEDGE OF THE COMPANY

(4) YOUR ENTHUSIASM AND SELF-CONFIDENCE

CONCLUSION

The way in which the measurement of "worth" by exchange value has traditionally been linked in America with the values of freedom and efficiency is revealed in the decision of the United States Supreme Court in the *Adkins* case and in the writings of Thomas Nixon Carver. Freedom means, according to this reasoning, the right to pay as little as you must for what you need; the right to get as much as you can for what you offer; and the correlative duty to accept what you can get. Moreover, adds Carver, this is both efficient and just. Utilitarianism, indeed, is so basic to American culture that it permeates many institutions besides the strictly "economic." It is to be observed in sexual relations and in politics, where votes and political support are exchanged for legislation and political favors. Given the widespread institutionalization of this principle, people inevitably come to judge themselves in terms of their marketability. The paradoxical result is that a principle justified by Justice Sutherland and Thomas Nixon Carver in terms of individualism ends up as a major threat to individuality.

United Artists

chapter 4
Self-orientation
in a competitive society

Alfred P. Doolittle sings in "My Fair Lady,"

> The Lord above made man to help his neighbor
> No matter where—on land or sea or foam.
> But, with a little bit of luck,
> When he comes around, you won't be home.

The song is supposedly English, but the sentiment is characteristically American. Its folklore expressions are legion: "Trust in God—but keep your powder dry"; "God helps him who helps himself"; "Do unto others as they would do unto you—only do it first"; "The hell with you, Jack; I got mine." These are the pungently irreverent summaries of a basic American principle: You sink or swim on your own. Bonds of solidarity, team-cooperative enterprises, and senses of duty are observable in American life, but they are exceptions to a more pervasive self-orientation.

Self-orientation is the other side of the coin of freedom of choice: if I am free to choose what to do with my life, then so are you—but your freedom means that I cannot expect help from you, and you can't expect it from me. People do get helped out of "charity" but the word on American lips has a condescending sound. As theologian Reinhold Niebuhr remarked, it is easier to give charity than to do justice.

Success and failure in America are considered to result from individual achievement, but achievement is obligatory. The individual has a moral responsibility to be personally "successful." How successful? More successful than others. America is a competitive society, and one's success is measured by how many others he has outdistanced and by how far.

In a competitive society, the range of roles open to the individual is wide, but, by the same token, he cannot claim a role merely by virtue of being born. He must *earn* the right to a role. He must demonstrate qualities or perform actions that are then evaluated by society and compared with the qualities and performances of all the other people who wish to occupy that role. In short, a competitive system is a little like a jungle. Only the fittest obtain the highest rewards of the system.[1] You live in a world filled with rivals and potential rivals, with persons who want your job, your reputation in the community, your girl friend. Lewis Carroll might have been describing a competitive system when he had the Red Queen say in *Through the Looking Glass*, "Now, here, you see, it takes all the running you can do, to keep in the same place. If you want to get somewhere else, you must run at least twice as fast as that!" In a competitive society, every aspect of life tends to be defined as a contest, and one's sense of adequacy, of worthiness, of security, and even of pleasure hinges on whether one is a winner or a loser. This has at least two consequences. For one, contests are usually set up so that there are many losers and few winners; this means that the majority, in addition to not getting the rewards that contests allocate, are publicly humiliated. Second, the winners are never sure how long they can continue to be winners. They know that their margin of superiority is small; rivals are close behind. Thus fear of failure haunts the successful.

Societies do not *have* to be competitive; societies differ in the emphasis their culture places on competition. One distinguished student of American society, Robin Williams, has suggested the difference between competitive and noncompetitive values, and the way in which Americans emphasize the former, in the following passage.[2]

The tension level of any social grouping is in part a function of the relative emphasis in that group's culture upon *participation in common values* as over against individual or group *acquisition of scarce "goods."*

In every social system people act in orientation to certain values which can be shared by everyone, and which are not scarce in the sense that one individual's sharing will reduce others' enjoyment of the value. The most ready and conspicuous examples are religious salvation, and group (e.g., national) prestige. All adherents to a religious faith can participate in its values—all, for example,

[1] In the history of social thought, the analogy between a competitive system and a jungle has often been made. See, for example, Richard Hofstadter, *Social Darwinism in America* (Boston: Beacon Press, 1955).

[2] Robin M. Williams, Jr., *The Reduction of Inter-Group Tensions* (New York: Social Science Research Council, 1947), pp. 55-56.

can have salvation—without any member's "success" detracting from that of any other member. Similarly, in this respect, all Americans are presumed to share in any increase or decrease in the prestige of the nation considered as a collectivity. National prestige as such is "participated in" rather than "divided up." On the other hand, in every social system people also act in orientation to scarce, divisible, and divisive values. This is, of course, true even of those who share a common culture in such other respects as language, religion, family mores, political ideology, and so on. The main classes of scarce, divisible values are: wealth, power, and prestige within a given group or culture. In any given state of the economy, the more economic goods held or consumed by one individual, the less there are for others. Power consists of control over others; hence it is inherently scarce and distributive. Prestige status is meaningful only in terms of relative ranking within a system: for one individual or group to be "high" requires that others be ranked "lower."

Thus every society has to work out some equilibrium of relative emphasis upon these two broad classes of action orientation. It seems to be generally agreed among serious students of American society that our culture places a rather extraordinary stress upon competition for distributive values. The "competitive" motif is not merely a matter of such competition being permitted; rather, the striving for "success" is positively enjoined to such an extent that in many areas and classes it approaches the status of a culturally obligatory pattern. At the same time, American society—at least in comparison with many older, more stable, more homogeneous societies—appears historically to have a relatively low development of the shared, nondivisible values. These two aspects seem clearly interrelated. Thus insofar as emphasis upon religious, otherworldly values has declined, this must in itself reinforce tendencies for "worldly" competition, other things being at all equal.

The competition which is significant for the analysis of group hostility is not just any kind of competition but that which revolves around basic security in subsistence and status. In this connection the importance of status-mobility in the United States is difficult to overstress. Rising and falling on the status-prestige scale is nominally free, and in actuality has been very widespread, i.e., the dominant institutional pattern has been that of achieved rather than ascribed status. In fact, "intensive competition" and "emphasis upon achieved status" are merely two formulations of the same situation. As Charles Horton Cooley pointed out, there are only two polar systems for ranking individuals in the social order: either inherited status or some form of competition.

Americans do not, for the most part, get satisfaction from national prestige (a team-cooperative relationship) or from carrying out traditional duties. They get it from achieving competitively.

In a sense developed by S. M. Lipset in the next selection, the emphasis on competitive achievement has always been somewhat at odds with another American value, that of equality. Here is how Lipset views the tensions between equality and achievement.[3]

On the one hand, our society is shown to be suffering from elaborate corruption in business practices, and in labor and law enforcement practices; from a growing concentration of business power; from the influences of mass media operated by entertainment tycoons seeking to satisfy the lowest common denominator in popular taste; and from a wasteful expenditure of resources in products designed only for conspicuous consumption and enhancement of social status.

On the other hand, ours is shown to be an affluent, highly democratic society in which the distribution of income, status symbols and opportunities for social mobility is becoming more even-handed all the time; in which tolerance for differences in culture, religion and race is growing; and in which there is an increasing demand for the best in art, literature and music. This outburst of self-criticism and self-analysis has been brought on, I believe, by anxiety over traits and trends which we Americans find hard to reconcile, but which form around two basic American values which are not entirely compatible and never have been. These are Equality and Achievement.

When I say that we value Equality, I mean that we believe all persons must be given respect simply because they are human beings; we believe that the differences between high- and low-status people reflect accidental, and perhaps temporary, variations in position—differences which should not be stressed in social relationships. The emphasis on equality has pervaded much of American culture. It was reflected in the introduction of universal suffrage in America long before it came in other nations; in the fairly consistent and extensive support for a unitary school system at all levels so that all might have a common background; and in the pervasive antagonism to any domination by an elite in the fields of culture, politics or economics. Foreign visitors throughout the nineteenth and twentieth centuries have constantly remarked in their writings on the aggressive equalitarianism of the American people.

Most foreign observers have also been impressed by the value we have put on Achievement—by our belief that everyone, regardless of his background, should try to "succeed." Until the emergence of the Communist states, there had been no other society which compared with America in the emphasis placed on "getting ahead." The strength of the value of Achievement is closely related, of

[3] Lipset, S. Martin, "Equal or Better in America," *Columbia University Forum*, Spring, 1961 (Vol. 4), pp. 17-21. Reprinted from Columbia FORUM, Spring, 1961, Vol. IV, No. 2. Copyright 1961 by The Trustees of Columbia University in the City of New York.

course, to the importance of the value of Equality. The ideal of equality helped to institutionalize the idea that success should be the goal of all, no matter the accidents of birth, class or race. In societies where social status has been more obviously related to inherited qualities, there is necessarily less emphasis on achievement.

Historically, the relation between the forceful American themes of equality and achievement has been close and complex. Tocqueville, for example, noted that equalitarianism maximizes competition among the members of a society, and that the abolition of hereditary privilege opens "the door to universal competition." A detailed analysis of the descriptions of American society written by foreign visitors in the late nineteenth century shows that these commentators generally agreed that "social and economic democracy in America far from mitigating competition for social status, intensified it." Some European socialists, in particular, were surprised to find American workers so deeply involved in conspicuous consumption—that is, imitating the middle-class style of life—and reported that the very feeling of equality itself presses workers in America to "make a show," since in America a worker could hope to demonstrate his achievements to others.

But if equalitarianism has encouraged competition for status, for advancement, it has also made individuals extremely uncertain about their social position; that is, it makes them uncertain just how much they *have* achieved, and leaves them insecure about their prospects to maintain or pass on their achieved higher status to their children. In fact, many of the foreign visitos who have been so impressed with the equalitarianism of social relations in America, have also suggested that it is precisely because of the emphasis on equality and opportunity that Americans have been more status-conscious than those who live in the more aristocratic societies of Europe. Many have reported that it has been easier for the *nouveaux riches* to gain acceptance in English high society than in American. English observers, from Harriet Martineau and Frances Trollope in the 1830's to James Bryce in the 1870's and Denis Brogan in recent years, have described the way in which the very absence of a legitimate aristocratic tradition, in which social rankings are unquestioned, forces Americans to emphasize status. In a more class-conscious society, everyone is aware of class distinctions and can therefore ignore them on many occasions: they will remain what they are. But in a social system in which such distinctions conflict with the basic belief that all are socially equal, those with a claim to higher status must assert that claim in a variety of ways or lose their right to it.

In all societies committed to equalitarianism, the "successful"—those who have achieved status—will seek to undermine the aims of the equalitarian society in order to retain and pass on their privileged position. This inherent challenge to the abolition of class limits has been checked in part in America by the recurrent victories of the forces of equality in the political order. Much of American

political history, as Tocqueville pointed out over 130 years ago, can be interpreted as a struggle between proponents of democratic equality and would-be
aristocracies of birth and wealth. In terms of political parties, the linkage of the
Democrats to the working-class and lower-status ethnic groups makes them the
dominant party—according to the polls, a large majority think of themselves as
Democrats and the election registration rolls also indicate a large Democratic
advantage. This creates major difficulties for the Republicans, who are identified
in the public mind as the party of wealth and big business. In America, to be
identified with the common man is a considerable advantage. In recent decades,
whenever a majority of voters choose on the basis of *domestic* issues, as they
seem to do in state and Congressional elections, they choose the equalitarian
Democrats. The Republicans are well aware of their disadvantage in this and seek
in their campaign tactics to place the emphasis on other issues, particularly
foreign policy matters, or on the personal qualities of candidates.

The ideal of a traditional elite governing our own country is clearly anath-
ema to our equalitarian ethos. This seems to be the opposite of the British
situation, in which political observers suggest that the situation which Bagehot
described still exists to some extent, that a large segment of the lower strata
believe it proper that members of leading families, who are accustomed to ruling,
should in fact rule. Thus the Anglo-Canadian political sociologist, Robert Mac-
Kenzie, has suggested that the Tories, unlike the Republicans, are actually
advantaged by the fact that they are identified with traditional wealth and
authority.

The stress on equality and achievement has also meant that in comparison
with, say Britain, America is what one might call a particularly "ends-oriented,"
rather than "means-oriented," society. In a country which places an extreme
emphasis on the importance of success, people are led to feel that the game must
be won, no matter what methods are employed to win it. The worst thing that
can happen, they feel, is to lose, to be perceived to be a failure. In contrast, the
ethos of the more rigidly stratified or aristocratic societies stresses the value of
playing the game well, and implies that one must conform to the behavior
appropriate to one's station. Such societies usually contain special sets of goals
for each stratum within them. And consequently a worker who is the son of a
worker is less likely to feel himself a personal failure than would a man with a
comparable background in America—the American's values insist on the progressive achievement of higher status for all. This does not mean that people in more
rigidly stratified societies such as Britain do not resent having low status, but
rather that each man is less likely to feel the need to do something extraordinary
about it himself. Deprived people in such countries have rather tended to try to
improve their situation collectively through class political movements.

Sociological students of crime have suggested that the much greater prevalence of organized vice and racketeering in America, as compared with that in

England and other well-to-do countries of northern Europe, reflects the greater pressure on those with deprived social backgrounds to find individual ways of succeeding when the more legitimate fields are closed to them. Columbia sociologist Daniel Bell has pointed out that the rackets have attracted members of minority ethnic groups who are denied other opportunities. He suggests that the rackets must be seen as one of the principal "ladders of social mobility in American life."

Public opinion studies of situations in which officials have been clearly involved in corrupt activities but still retain widespread electoral support indicate that many Americans will knowingly tolerate such practices if they are accompanied by accomplishments, by getting things done. This is not a new phenomenon; many nineteenth-century foreign travellers were disturbed by the ready public acceptance of those who succeeded regardless of the means they had employed to get ahead. Thus Charles Dickens reports as typical of opinion in the mid-nineteenth-century America which he visited the following comments about a man who had succeeded by dubious methods, but was held in high repute:

"He is a public nuisance, is he not?"

"Yes, sir."

"A convicted liar?"

"Yes, sir."

"He has been kicked, cuffed, and caned?"

"Yes, sir."

"And he is utterly dishonourable, debased, and profligate?"

"Yes, sir."

"In the name of wonder, then, what is his merit?"

"Well, sir, he is a smart man."

Much of the unique character of the American labor movement may be interpreted in the same way. For workers, as for other Americans, the emphasis on ends, on pecuniary success, combined with the absence of the kind of class consciousness characteristic of less equalitarian societies, has helped to foster acceptance, if not approval, of various devices to permit union officials to "get ahead." In no other country do heads of unions earn as much in relation to the earnings of their members as in the United States. The incomes of major American labor leaders astonish Europeans, who think of such officers as the leaders of a lower class who should reflect the status of their class. The same emphasis on success has meant an acceptance of the right of union officials to be private businessmen, even to be employers. The job of a union leader is regarded by many workers as a means of getting ahead, not as a way of life. There is no reason, therefore, why a union leader should not get as much as he can for himself and his family, as long as he does not injure his members' interests.

The ends-orientation of Americans, as contrasted with the greater stress on means in societies which retain elements of aristocratic norms, is reflected also in the tactics and strategy of the American labor movement as a body. In contrast to most European unions, American unions have had little interest in radical political ideologies or programs which are concerned with changes in the overall social system or the class order. But while ideologically conservative and often narrowly self-interested in their objectives, the American labor movement has in some ways been more violent and militant in its tactics than have the seemingly more Marxist-oriented unions in other industrial nations. American unionists have not been loath in the past to use physical violence, up to and including the dynamiting of buildings, in the struggle for their ends—higher wages and better working conditions. They have employed mobsters in labor disputes (as have employers), and even today they are freer with the use of the strike weapon than any other set of non-Communist Western unionists. American labor has been brutally aggressive, much like American industry.

While I have argued that pressures which come from the interplay of the ideals of Equality and Achievement account for the prevalence of certain forms of deviant or nonconformist behavior, it is also possible that these same basic values contribute to the American over-sensitivity to the judgment of others, to our tendency to conformism and "other-directedness."

It is strange how frequently commentators on the American scene have remarked upon this quality of the national character. Most of the English travellers in America from 1785 to 1835 mentioned "the acute sensitiveness to opinion that the average American revealed." But though most of the nine-teenth-century travellers disliked the "other-directed" behavior which they reported, many pointed out that there is an intimate relationship between such behavior and the basic American values—values which the more liberal among them approved. They suggested that it is the very emphasis on equality, the dislike of pretensions to permanent status, that makes Americans so sensitive to the opinions of others. Summarizing the remarks of various British writers on America, an American, John Graham Brooks, wrote some fifty years ago:

> One deeper reason why the English are blunt and abrupt about their rights . . . is because class lines are more sharply drawn there. Within these limits one is likely to develop the habit of demanding his due. He insists on his prerogatives all the more because they are narrowly defined . . . In a democracy everyone at least hopes to get on and up. This ascent depends not upon the favor of a class, but upon the good-will of the whole . . . To make one's self conspicuous and disagreeable is to arouse enmities that block one's way.

But America's is not the first social system to call forth comments suggesting that conformism may stem from a conflict between stratification and equalitarian values. In Plato's *Republic* we find a description of the consequences of equalitarian democratic life that reads as if it came from one of the travellers' reports on America. Plato writes that in such societies fathers fear their sons, schoolteachers flatter their pupils, the old seek to imitate and win the good opinion of the young, and equality prevails in the relations of men and women. And according to Plato, the main result of all these things is to make the souls of the citizens extremely sensitive.

Above all, equalitarianism seems to promote consideration for the rights and feelings of others. This is seen in extreme form in the efforts in schools to avoid hurting the feelings of the less bright or popular students by various practices designed to avoid public invidious distinction. At the same time, it intensifies the strength of the achievement value, which demands that all strive by every means possible to secure or maintain a status above the average. While one may point to the kindliness and idealism of Americans as desired consequences of the central unifying values of the society, one may look on corruption and conformism as unanticipated but inherent consequences of these values. America presses students, ethnic groups, businessmen, union leaders, politicians, and scholars to "innovate"—to get ahead. And then we wonder why there is cheating on exams, rackets among low-status ethnic groups, embezzlement in white-collar jobs, dictatorships in unions, and graft among politicians. Though we deplore the fact that there seems to be too much conformism in the way people behave and speak, we should not forget what many of the nineteenth-century foreign travellers to America knew, that an open and necessarily ambiguous class structure made status-striving, the desire to get ahead, tantamount to conformity. It seems to me that the growing strength of the same values of Achievement and Equality in the Soviet Union have had similar consequences. In Russia, for example, cheating on examinations and bribery of university admissions officers are now something of a scandal, and the upper strata can give Americans lessons in status-seeking, conformist behavior and in conscpicuous consumption.

All this is not to say that corruption and conformism are necessary consequences of equalitarian democracy. There is in fact much evidence that America is in other ways becoming a more moral and less conformist society. Our concern with Equality is reflected in the field of race relations; as Gunnar Myrdal pointed out twenty years ago, the most important single argument of the Negroes is the fact that their second-class citizenship violates a basic postulate of the American Creed. The successful efforts to spread and equalize educational opportunities are clearly linked to the belief in equal opportunity.

Through much of American history, those advocating public education argued that such measures were essential to making equality a reality. And by the mid-Nineteen-Fifties, American education crossed two historic benchmarks:

a majority of all high school students now actually graduate, and a majority of such graduates go on to institutions of higher learning. The equalization of educational opportunities has meant that an ever-increasing proportion of the population is now exposed to, in Eric Larrabee's words, that "modest range of cultural experience that the arts represent." Book sales have increased remarkably; the annual expenditure has almost doubled since 1950. Popular magazines have become better. According to C. J. McNaspy, the Metropolitan Museum of Art in New York had almost four million visitors in 1959, twice the figure at the Louvre, and three times the number to visit the Metropolitan twenty years earlier. *The Times Literary Supplement* is rightly impressed by the presence of over one thousand community symphony orchestras in the United States; there were less than 100 in 1920.

America is not a simple country to understand. Jennie Lee, Aneurin Bevan's wife, and a British Left Socialist leader in her own right, once wrote of her despair that after five trips to this country she felt it was impossible to "get any coherent picture of America . . . And the more Americans explained America to me, the more blurred the picture became." What is confusing is the fact that the institutions and practices of this country fluctuate between the two related values, which are also polarities, Equality and Achievement. Tocqueville could see the latter value as causing Americans to shun public affairs as "a troublesome impediment, which diverts them from their occupation and business," yet he could also call attention to the amazing propensity of Americans to form voluntary associations of all kinds to achieve socially desirable ends. The seeming contradiction between the emphasis on success, and the felt acceptance even by the very successful of the value of Equality can be seen in some measure in American patterns of philanthropic giving. Foreign travellers in the nineteenth century noted this trait to give away wealth, long before there were income and inheritance taxes.

It is easy to discuss American culture from an integrated positive or negative point of view . . . to stress the extent to which it has become a corrupt, irresponsible mass society characterized by a high degree of conformity; or conversely, to emphasize the extent to which it has expanded the possibilities for all to partake in the "higher life," by increasing access to the preconditions for individual freedom and self-expression—greater education, more leisure from petty routine tasks, and greater economic security. To recognize that many of the social supports of what we like and dislike are often rooted in identical institutions and values is difficult. But such recognition does not mean we must passively accept the bad because of its ties to the good. Rather it implies the need for a constant struggle to preserve and extend these positive institutions, for only through the efforts to maintain and extend Equality have the corrupting effects of the necessary emphasis on Achievement been prevented from dominating the society.

Although Lipset points to certain ways in which equality and achievement are opposites, there is a sense in which they only seem to be opposites—at least as they have evolved in American society. The American version of equality is essentially equality of *opportunity* rather than equality of *rewards*. Even the other-directedness that Lipset links to the equality value often takes a form influenced by the pervasiveness of competition. William H. Whyte, Jr., makes this clear in the short excerpt that follows.[4]

The figures of speech younger executives use to describe the situation they now find themselves in are illuminating. The kind of words they use are "treadmill," "merry-go-round," "rat race"—words that convey an absence of tangible goals but plenty of activity to get there. The absence of fixed goals, as we remarked before, may make them seem less ambitious, less competitive than their forebears, but in the more seemingly co-operative climate of today lies a prod just as effective. They are competing; all but the fools know this—but for what, and against whom? They don't know, and there is the trap. To keep even, they must push ahead, and though they might like to do it only slightly, who is to say what slightly is. Their contemporaries are in precisely the same doubt, and thus they all end up competing against one another as rapaciously as if their hearts were set on the presidency itself.

This co-operative competition can be observed rather clearly in the post-graduate business schools. At one school an up-and-coming plant manager told me that he was puzzled at the apparent lack of ambition in the others. Since they represented a good chunk of the cream of their age group in U.S. corporation life, he couldn't understand why so few of them had no specific goal in mind. (He wanted to be president of his corporation's major subsidiary.) "But the funny thing is," he told me, "that they work just as hard as I do. Frankly, I'm knocking myself out to get top grades because that will mean a lot to the people back in New York. The only thing the others here are working for is just to get an okay grade. But the grades here depend on how everybody else does, so how can you tell what a good grade is? They can't take any chances so they do just as much night work, give up just as many week ends as I do."

Back at the office the job of steering the right middle course requires more and more skill. The increasingly "democratic" atmosphere of management has opened up opportunities for the executive, but it has also made more difficult the task of sizing up the relative rankings around the place and judging the timing of one's pushes. The overt differences in status and office amenities are much less than before, but the smaller the differences the more crucial they can

---

[4]William H. Whyte, Jr., *The Organization Man*, New York: Doubleday Anchor Books, 1965, pp. 176-178. Copyright © 1956 by William H. Whyte, Jr. Reprinted by permission of Simon & Schuster, Inc.

become to the individual. It is easy to joke about whether or not one has a thermoflask on his desk or whether the floor is rubber tiled or carpeted, but the joking is a bit nervous and a number of breakdowns have been triggered by what would seem a piddling matter to the observer. Where does one stand in this shifting society in which standing depends so largely on what other people think? Even a thermoflask is important if it can serve as a guidepost—another visible fix of where one is and where others are.

"You get into a certain position," one forty-year-old executive explains, "and you start getting scared that somebody else might want the job you have. You can't tell who he might be, so you take on the protective coloring so you won't look as if you are ambitious and have the others move in on you." The best defense against being surpassed, executives well know, is to surpass somebody else, but since every other executive knows this also and knows that the others know it too, no one can ever feel really secure. Check vacation records, and you will find that the higher up the man is, the more likely is the vacation to be broken up into a week here and a week there and, furthermore, to be rescheduled and postponed to suit the company rather than the family. "I like to take my vacation in two or three stretches instead of three or four weeks," One executive confesses. "I don't do it for my health. If you go away for three weeks, when you come back you find that they have rearranged your entire job. Someone has to carry on while you are gone and they are in your files, and when you get back the people will ask you questions about your job on account of what others did while you were away. I don't blame them, mind you; I would do exactly the same thing." (In *Blandings' Way*, Eric Hodgins has sketched a commuter's reverie that has occurred to many a management man. Today, the executive thinks miserably to himself, is the day they *find me out*.)

Even those who are not particularly driven to achieve, says Whyte, are driven to compete, and consequently may be just as insecure as the genuinely achievement-oriented person. In another analysis of the competitive pressures, C. Wright Mills suggested that among lower-level white-collar workers, occupational competition can produce less traumatic (but still uncomfortable) results. The struggle for status goes on in the neighborhood and on vacation as well as in the world of work. The white-collar worker may not himself know whether he has won or lost, and those who came into contact with him in some specific segment of his existence may be even less sure.[5]

The sharp split of residence from work place, characteristic of urban life since the Industrial Revolution, is most clearly manifested in the big city suburb,

[5]From *White Collar* by C. Wright Mills, pp. 254-258. Copyright 1951 by Oxford University Press, Inc., New York. Reprinted by permission of the publishers.

where work associates are formally segregated from neighbors. This means that the subordinate may compete in two status worlds, that of work place in the big city and that of residence in the suburb.

At the work place, it is difficult, even in large enterprises, to inflate real occupational status, although great status tensions are likely to be lodged there. But actual job position is not so well known to those whom one meets away from work. It may be that to the extent that status aspirations and claims are frustrated at work, there is a more intense striving to realize them off the job. If the status struggle within the job hierarchy is lost, the status struggle outside the job area shifts its ground: one hides his exact job, claims prestige from his title or firm, or makes up job, title, or firm. Among anonymous metropolitan throngs, one can make claims about one's job, as well as about other bases of prestige, which minimize or override actual occupational status.

The place of residence, which is a signal of income and style of life, limits this inflation of status; for neighbors, like job associates, will not readily cash in higher claims. Among them, the first, often the only, impression one makes may permit a brief success in status claiming, sometimes as a sort of mutual deal.

"Under modern conditions," Thorstein Veblen wrote, "the struggle for existence has, in a very appreciable degree, been transformed into a struggle to keep up appearance." Personal worth and integrity may count for something but "one's reputation for excellence in this direction does not penetrate far enough into the very wide environment to which a person is exposed in modern society to satisfy even a very modest craving for respectability. To sustain one's dignity—and to sustain one's self-respect—under the eyes of people who are not socially one's immediate neighbors, it is necessary to display the token of economic worth, which practically coincides . . . with economic success." . . .

"One does not 'make much of a showing' in the eyes of the large majority of the people whom one meets with," Veblen continued, "except by unremitting demonstration of ability to pay. That is practically the only means which the average of us have of impressing our respectability on the many to whom we are personally unknown, but whose transient good opinion we would so gladly enjoy. So it comes about that the appearance of success is very much to be desired, and is even in many cases preferred to the substance . . . the modern industrial organization of society has practically narrowed the scope of emulation to this one line; and at the same time it has made the means of sustenance and comfort so much easier to obtain as very materially to widen the margin of human exertion that can be devoted to purposes of emulation."

Of an eighteenth-century nobility, Dickens could say that "dress was the one unfailing talisman and charm used for keeping all things in their places," but in a mass society without a stable system of status, with quick, cheap imitations, dress is often no talisman. The clerk who sees beautifully gowned women in the movies and on the streets may wear imitations if she works hard and, skipping the spiced ham sandwich, has only cokes for lunch. Her imitations are easily found out, but that is not to say they do not please her. . . .

The prestige enjoyed by individual white-collar workers is not continuously fixed by large forces, for their prestige is not continuously the same. Many are involved in status cycles, which, as Tom Harrison has observed, often occur in a sort of rhythmic pattern. These cycles allow people in a lower class and status level to act like persons on higher levels and temporarily to get away with it.

During weekdays the white-collar employee receives a given volume of deference from a given set of people, work associates, friends, family members, and from the transient glimpses of strangers on transport lines and street. But over the week end, or perhaps a week end once a month, one can by plan raise oneself to higher status: clothing changes, the restaurant or type of food eaten changes, the best theater seats are had. One cannot well change one's residence over the week end, but in the big city one can get away from it, and in the small town one can travel to the near-by city. Expressed claims of status may be raised, and more importantly those among whom one claims status may vary— even if these others are other strangers in different locales. And every white-collar girl knows the value of a strict segregation of regular boy friends, who might drop around the apartment any night of the week, from the special date for whom she always dresses and with whom she always goes out.

There may also be a more dramatic yearly status cycle, involving the vacation as its high point. Urban masses look forward to vacations not "just for the change," and not only for a "rest from work"—the meaning behind such phrases is often a lift in successful status claims. For on vacation, one can *buy* the feeling, even if only for a short time, of higher status. The expensive resort, where one is not known, the swank hotel, even if for three days and nights, the cruise first class—for a week. Much vacation apparatus is geared to these status cycles; the staffs as well as clientele play-act the whole set-up as if mutually consenting to be part of the successful illusion. For such experiences once a year, sacrifices are often made in long stretches of gray weekdays. The bright two weeks feed the dream life of the dull pull.

It should not be thought that competition is merely an economic phenome-non. It pervades many aspects of American life. Thus, the competitive struggle for dates on a college campus can be just as rugged as the competitive struggle for customers in the garment district. Waller's classic analysis of the "rating and dating"[6] analysis points up an inherent difficulty of a competitive system: there is every likelihood that victory in the struggle has nothing to do with the needs of the competitors. As a classroom demonstration of this generalization, Jackson

[6] Willard Waller, "The Rating and Dating Complex," *American Sociological Review*, Vol. 2 (October, 1937), pp. 727-737.

Toby sometimes asks his students about their criteria for selecting dates. They say they seek girls who are pretty, well-poised, good conversationalists, have good sense of humor, and so forth. And what about girls who do not meet these standards? "Oh, they are the dogs, and we steer clear of them." But what happens to "dogs"? Don't they want dates too? "Perhaps," a student will suggest, "the unpopular boys date the unpopular girls, thus taking care of everybody." Unfortunately, if Waller's data are correct, this does not happen. *Common* standards of attractiveness exist; the same girls are liked (or disliked) by most of the boys. Even an unpopular boy does not want to date an unpopular girl.

Competition for dates and, ultimately, for spouses is a symmetrical process; that is to say, girls and boys *mutually* choose one another. Mutuality of choice is characteristic of much role allocation in the United States, although sometimes one of the choosers is a collectivity rather than an individual. For example, on American campuses freshmen compete among one another for fraternity bids and fraternities compete among themselves for pledges. The following analysis is an attempt to explain the operation of the fraternity system in terms of prestige competition very similar to that involved in dating behavior.[7]

The key that unlocks most of the mysteries of the fraternity system is that on every campus some fraternities are good, others are better, and one, perhaps, is the best. These terms refer, of course, not to their moral character but to their prestige. Whereas membership in a high ranking fraternity is a notable achievement, it is hardly worth joining a low ranking one at all. Freshmen realize quite soon that one fraternity is not just as good as another, although amnesia sets in by the sophomore year—after the pledging and the initiations are over. Those who have settled for a less desirable fraternity seem convinced that theirs is the best little old fraternity in the world. They are boosters. They will tell you about the "swell bunch of guys" at their House and the wonderful times they have.

It's not all talk. If their fraternity does not have the recognition on the campus that is clearly its due, the members try to build it up, to put it across. That means winning intra-mural contests, electing the brothers to Student Council, participating in extra-curricular activities—especially Varsity sports, and, last, and probably least, keeping up the scholastic average of the House. No fraternity is reconciled to a humble position in the campus firmament. Since those occupying a place in the sun show no inclination to move out of it, a fraternity man works as hard as he can to keep his fraternity in the same relative position it was a year ago. Occasionally changes take place in the prestige hierarchy. One fraternity is ruined by scandal; another manages to attract

---

[7]Jackson Toby, "Competition for Prestige: the Engine That Drives the Fraternity System," unpublished lecture.

personalities who improve its relative position. But, more often, the years come and go; the best fraternity is still the best; and the fraternity of last resort is still, to speak frankly, the last resort.

There are at least two factors in this stability. One is real estate. Some fraternity houses are more attractive than others: they are more expensive, better furnished, or more conveniently located. Second, and more important, the pledging system handicaps the fraternities of *lesser* prestige. Promising freshmen are snapped up by the best fraternity because it can generally exercise first choice. The less the prestige of the fraternity, the lower the standards it can afford to maintain in recruiting pledges. After all, there is a limit to the choosiness of a rushing committee. Men must be found to carry the financial burden of the House. But the less glamorous the pledge of today, the less glamorous the brother of tomorrow. Thus, the pledging system operates as a kind of flywheel, perpetuating the competitive advantages and disadvantages of each fraternity.

Of course, freshmen are shopping around for the right fraternity just as diligently as rushing committees are searching for pledges who will add luster to their House. So it is not enough for the brothers to be favorably impressed by a freshman. *He* has to be convinced that he can do no better. He weighs the relative desirability of pledging himself to some other fraternity. It is not uncommon for a half a dozen fraternities to solicit the membership of a particularly attractive freshman. This fortunate fellow usually accepts the bid of the highest ranking fraternity among them, if he knows which is which—but not always. He may have a close friend who has not been invited to pledge to that fraternity. As a result, he may pledge himself to a fraternity of lesser prestige or to none at all. Were it not for such instances, where the logic of pledging is modified by the human beings who apply it, the fraternities constituting the college Inter-Fraternity Council might be as rigidly ordered as Indian castes.

The human element is involved in pledging in yet another way. Someone must decide who will and who will not be an asset to the fraternity. This entails not only correct assessment of the freshman while he is a freshman but a prediction of what he will be like as a senior. Each fraternity has a rushing committee saddled with this task. Smokers are specially arranged during rushing season to help the committee get personal impressions. However, it is no secret to the freshman that he is being looked over. The tension which this knowledge contributes to the situation does not make the committee's work any easier. Nevertheless, rushing committees have definite ideas about candidates. They do not abandon the attempt to evaluate freshmen because of the obvious difficulty of the problem. Nor should it be thought that their criteria are so vague that any freshman desirous of joining a fraternity will be invited to pledge to one fraternity if not to another. Many a freshman attends the smokers of half a dozen fraternities and does not receive a bid from any of them. This is because the notion of the type of fellow who is an asset varies little from fraternity to fraternity. A boy who is sufficiently poised, outgoing, and well-rounded to look promising to one rushing committee will very likely attract attention elsewhere. On the other hand, the freshman who is obviously ill-at-ease despite the forced cordiality of the brothers, who drinks the beer he is offered as though it were his first glass, who is frightened because he has no idea what is expected of him, and who reacts to a conversational gambit like a stag brought to bay, such a freshman is not likely to strike *any* fraternity as a good prospect.

Occasionally, a boy whom no rushing committee considered worth bothering with as a freshman becomes a Big Man On Campus by his junior or senior year. This is, however, unusual. It is not that the appraisals of the rushing committees are necessarily good—although the committees certainly *try* to recruit potential B.M.O.C.'s. It is simply that fraternities wield great power; hence they are usually able to prevent a barbarian, however remarkable, from becoming, say, president of the Student Council. To put it another way, the chances for becoming a B.M.O.C. are so much greater if one is a member of a prominent fraternity that its rushing committee could probably choose freshmen for membership at random and make a disproportionately large number of them into campus leaders by the time they are seniors. Hence, it is not often apparent that the rushing committees overlooked good fraternity material. The boys missed by the rushing committees do not have equality of opportunity for campus social and political success. Furthermore, it is always possible to recruit the Varsity athlete, who slipped through unnoticed as a freshman or sophomore, after he makes the team and establishes his reputation. This is the common explanation when a prominent barbarian joins a fraternity in his junior year.

Mistakes in the other direction are more visible. Boys who struck the rushing committee as nuggets at the smoker may, on closer examination, turn out to be clinkers. Every fraternity has a few members that the majority would like to see drafted or graduated in a hurry. Of course, pledging is only apprenticeship, not membership. It is *possible* to rectify the error of inviting an albatross to pledge before fastening it around the neck of the fraternity by an initiation. But rectification at this stage is not easy. Although the vote of a single brother is technically enough to blackball a pledge, fraternity members are reluctant to dash the expectations of someone they have gotten to know. Sentiment against him must be quite strong, and even then a few friends may be able to persuade the majority to let him in. A supporter of an unpopular pledge in one fraternity threatened to blackball all the other pledges that year if his friend were not admitted to membership. His friend got in. In other words, a fraternity is usually stuck with the pledges it started with. Hence, every rushing committee has nightmares about the current batch of pledges.

The rushing committee has a twofold problem. One is to select freshmen who are personally congenial to the brothers. The other is to maintain—and, if possible, augment—the relative standing of the fraternity by pledging freshmen who will be a credit to it. There are occasions when these two objectives are incompatible. For instance, a wealthy freshman may be personally unappealing, but he may be invited to pledge because the fraternity cannot afford to let another fraternity get him. Or, a boy with many social graces may be relegated to the shadow-world of the barbarians because the fraternity dares not pledge a Catholic, a Jew, or a Negro. Thus, actions which appear snobbish on the surface often turn out to be motivated by an excess of competitive zeal. They are hastily disposed of and conveniently forgotten.

What worries rushing chairmen most is that a hectic scramble to choose and be chosen is not conducive to accurate evaluation. Fraternities which select pledges on the run may repent their selections at leisure. Consequently, many fraternities start lining up pledges long before the rushing period officially opens. Far from waiting for candidates to make a beaten path to the fraternity door, some fraternities do not even wait for the freshmen to arrive on the campus. They launch an aggressive campaign as soon as the Admissions Committee of the college makes known the names of the high school students entering college in the fall. Besides providing more time for study of the freshman class, an early start may enable the rushing committee of one's own fraternity to indoctrinate promising freshmen *first.*

An early start depends on the resources of the fraternity for contacting and assessing incoming freshmen when they are still in high school. Will the brothers take time out of their summer vacations to visit remote corners of the state? Can the alumni be counted on to snoop in the fraternity's behalf? Sometimes the brothers and the alumni show diligence on its behalf above and beyond the call of loyalty. For example, confidential information from the office of the Dean of Students or the Admissions Office may find its way mysteriously to a rushing committee. Many fraternities make a preliminary investigation of a prospective pledge before he occupies his dormitory room. What was his high school record? Athletics? Politics? Cheer leading? Scholarship? Debating? Does he come from a respectable family? Would his parents fit in if asked to be chaperons at a fraternity function? Did they go to college? Is his father an alumnus of the fraternity—or of some other good fraternity? Is his family able to give him a substantial allowance? Will he have a car at college? The simplest way to get answers to these questions is personal recommendations. Perhaps one of the brothers comes from the same town as the freshman and knew him in high school. Such testimony can be decisive because it is presumed that the brother is fully aware of fraternity standards and would call attention to any deficiency in the candidate's qualifications. But a recommendation from an alumnus, especially an active one, also carries weight. Sometimes a freshman will arrive on the campus shortly after letters introducing him have been received by the fraternity.

It would be wrong to conclude that, except for relative prestige, one fraternity is exactly like another. Each has its distinctive rituals; each is unique in the particular personalities it has combined within it. Moreover, there are variations in interests from one House to another. One has a reputation for mountaineering; another harbors the campus poker sharks. But every fraternity, regardless of size, religious affiliation, or financial resources, is competing with other fraternities for campus glory. Success in this competition is not promoted by too scrupulous a regard for youngsters unable to get into the fraternity of their choice—or to any fraternity at all. Of course, some students do not join fraternities even though the fraternities would be glad to have them. All barbarians are not disappointed Greeks. Some boys believe fraternities to be undemocratic or immoral. Some are forbidden to join by their parents. Some avoid membership because of the time, the expense, or the possible obstacles to study which membership entails. But there are others who feel themselves rejected by the fraternities. They suffer in silence, yearning for the convivial life which appears to go on behind the pillared facades.

The irony of the fraternity system is that fraternities do not practice brotherhood toward the loneliest students on the campus. Freshmen sever their social roots in coming to live at college. They are homesick until the gap created in their lives by reduced contact with family and hometown chums is filled by college friends. Those who become members of fraternities fill the gap quickly, almost automatically. Those who do not join fraternities have to make new friends slowly, one by one. And, paradoxically, it is precisely those who find the readjustment from home to college most difficult that the fraternities are least likely to want. They are boys who are sometimes rebuffed but, more often, just ignored, for they are too shy to make advances. On the other hand, freshmen sufficiently endowed with social skills to make their way without the help of ready-made friendships are much more likely to be recruited by the fraternities. Whereupon they get the benefit of additional opportunities to ease the transition from home to college.

CONCLUSION

That American society relies upon competition to allocate roles in the economic area of life needs no particular documentation. This chapter has illustrated the *pervasiveness* of competition as a governing principle in noneconomic activities. Toby and Waller show how the principle operates in dating and fraternity life, and both emphasize an important implication of the principle—that "others" are threats to one's success because one's chances of being chosen depend on how one is invidiously compared with others. Toby, moreover, calls attention to one rather little-noticed consequence of competition: The tendency for competition to perpetuate a ranking system when competitors are mutually choosing and being chosen.

Whyte describes the operation of competition among junior executives in the modern corporation and calls attention to the diffuse anxiety generated by the awareness that productivity is measured in competitive terms, that adequacy depends on how much others are doing and getting. On lower white-collar levels, Mills shows how the struggle for symbols of competitive success extends into the leisure time activities of white-collar workers.

chapter 5
Acquiescence to authority
in an organizational society

Chapter 1 emphasized that a conspicuous characteristic of human beings is dependence on one another. The anthropologist Ralph Linton put this characteristic and some of its attendant difficulties epigrammatically. "We are, in fact," he said, "anthropoid apes trying to live like termites, and, as any philosophical observer can attest, not doing too well at it."[1] What Linton was pointing to is another of the characteristics emphasized in Chapter 1: the *mechanism* human beings use to bring about the coordination required by the interdependence is a *cultural* mechanism. It is not the sure biological mechanism of specialization that termites enjoy, but the more precarious one of symbolic definitions.

Part of these symbolic definitions are standards in terms of which people evaluate one another. In order for those symbolic standards to successfully direct and channel people's behavior, so that individuals can both understand and rely on one another, at least some of the standards must be viewed as absolute. Thus, in the course of socialization, standards become internalized as constitutive parts of personalities; and one of the standards that people internalize is the *standard that they should not question certain standards.*

Sigmund Freud has described this characteristic of human life in terms of cultural restrictions on the opportunities for individual gratification. This sacrifice of freedom is legitimated by the individual's feeling that the restrictions are fair—and they seem fair when they apply to everyone and are approved by a large segment of the population instead of by a small minority. In short, Freud believed that the personality accepts cultural controls, albeit grudgingly.[2]

[1]Ralph Linton, *The Tree of Culture*, New York: Alfred A. Knopf, 1955, p. 11.

[2]Sigmund Freud, *Civilization and Its Discontents*, New York: W.W. Norton & Co., 1961, pp. 42-43.

The liberty of the individual is no gift of civilization. It was greatest before there was any civilization, though then, it is true, it had for the most part no value, since the individual was scarcely in a position to defend it. The development of civilization imposes restrictions on it, and justice demands that no one shall escape those restrictions. What makes itself felt in a human community as a desire for freedom may be their revolt against some existing injustice, and so may prove favourable to a further development of civilization; it may remain compatible with civilization. But it may also spring from the remains of their original personality, which is still untamed by civilization and may thus become the basis in them of hostility to civilization.

Freud emphasized the *psychological* processes by which people become law-abiding. There are also social processes important in generating and maintaining incentives to obey the law. The sociologist and political scientist, Robert M. MacIver, has described these as follows.[3]

The sense of the social order as controlling the behavior of human beings, since it is not fully instinct-governed as with the ants and bees, requires the establishment of social sanctions to secure it against the strains and pulls of contrary impulses. In the very simplest societies, where the community is a group of nearly autonomous, nearly self-sufficient families and where the conduct of each is within the perspective of all, there may be no need for any further sanctions than those that depend on the immediate reaction of the folk against the violator of custom, of the "customary law." But the further we move from the simplicity of this situation the more do we find the confirmation of authority by institutional devices of increasing formality.

The routinized respect for age or ancestry or skill or prowess confers authority on individuals so that they are presumed to speak for or to represent the folk, to embody its spirit or its virtue. This personal authority may have little or no paraphernalia of office. But when the person becomes the instituted chief, especially when the line of chieftainship is established by heredity or otherwise, authority gains a new dimension. Now the person in authority is set further apart from his fellow men. He undergoes the equivalent of sanctification. He cannot be approached as a person among other persons, differing perhaps in degree. Now as the embodiment of authority he differs in kind. Some peoples carry the process further than do others. But the tendency exists everywhere. Authority is thus safeguarded, stabilized, removed in a measure from the competition for power. . . .

All institutions, whether dignified by ceremony or not, tend to implant in men a sense of the authority that maintains them. Since the state is the guardian

[3]Reprinted with permission of The Macmillan Company from *The Web of Government* by Robert M. MacIver. Copyright © 1947, 1968 by Robert M. MacIver. pp. 42-47; 61; 74-79; and 83-84.

and maintainer, at least in a formal sense, of all social institutions the might of its authority is omnipresent. Whatever men do, whatever they strive for, predicates under normal conditions the existing frame of institutions. Our dependence on institutions becomes identified with our dependence on authority, and the value we attach to institutions is reflected in our respect for authority.

In the more sophisticated society we may distinguish between respect for the personal qualities of the ruling group and respect for the large body of institutions they preside over. We may, at times, have little regard for "politicians" and much regard fo;the system, including the form of government. But for the less sophisticated, and especially in the simpler societies, no such distinction is easily drawn. And even the most abstract philosopher is apt to confound the two.

It is true that groups of different backgrounds and different indoctrinations will have different standards of lawabidingness. It is true that the kind of government will affect in some measure both the degree and the spirit in which men obey the laws. But . . . in every society, save during the throes of revolution, there is a firmament of order. The acceptance of its terms is an expression of the sentiments that bind men everywhere in social union. They obey the law not merely because they recognize the legitimacy of its source, nor mainly because they are convinced of the rationality of its contents. They obey not merely because they consider it their obligation to the state. And they certainly do not obey solely because they fear the sanctions attached to the law, the "fear of the consequences" on which Thomas Hobbes laid such stress. Neither the fear of punishment nor the fear of the larger consequences of law-breaking to society can explain the common observance of the law.

All the motivations we have here mentioned are involved but they do not operate in their simplicity, as single and sufficient determinants of men's behavior . . .

The vast majority of men have the habit of law-abidingness . . .

Men obey because they are social beings—or, if you prefer it, because they are socialized beings, trained and indoctrinated in the ways of their society. All the motivations that are evoked and active in their social circle conspire to make them, on the whole, law-abiding. We cannot then answer the question why men obey the law by adducing merely *political* considerations. Law-abidingness is the pragmatic condition of and response to the whole firmament of social order . . .

The question whether it is the duty of the citizen always to obey the law has generally arisen where the individual or the group has been confronted with two conflicting claims on loyalty, where Antigone has to choose between the command of her king and the sacred custom of the kin, where Orestes has to choose between the respect due his mother and the obligation to avenge his father, where the persecuted religious sect has to choose between the law of the temporal power and the ordinance of God, where the pacifist has to choose between the order to take up arms and the dictate of his conscience or his faith.

By authority we mean the established *right*, within any social order, to determine policies, to pronounce judgments on relevant issues, and to settle controversies, or, more broadly, to act as leader or guide to other men. When we speak of *an* authority we mean a person or body of persons possessed of this right. The accent is primarily on right, not power. Power alone has no legitimacy, no mandate, no office. Even the most ruthless tyrant gets nowhere unless he can clothe himself with authority. . . .

Authority exists in every sphere for every group according to its kind. There is authority in religion, in education, in business, in science, in the arts. There is authority within every organization, or it could carry on no function whatever. There is authority inside the groups that fight against authority. There is authority among the boys who skirmish with the boys in the next street, and there is authority in an anarchist assembly. There is no order without authority. This authority is vested in persons, whether as accepted superiors or as the agents of organized groups. We speak broadly of a man as being an authority if his word carries weight with others. Thus a man may be an authority on the nature of God, on astro-physics, on cuneiform inscriptions, on the language of the Bantus, on the playing of bridge, and so on endlessly. But in the stricter sense an authority is a man or a body of men vested with the right to make decisions and to maintain the order that prevails within any system or area of social organization. In this sense an authority does not act in his private capacity, but always by virtue of a right conferred upon him for this purpose by society.

In the passages quoted, MacIver alludes to the phenomenon of individuals being unable or unwilling to obey their society's laws because they are impelled by contradictory moral principles. We shall return to this phenomenon later in this chapter. It is made especially significant in American society by the American ethos of "individualism." But before turning to the dilemmas and ambiguities created by the tensions between "individualism" and the need to abide by authoritative decisions, we must stress the necessity of group coordination. As economists are fond of pointing out, the productivity of contemporary society is due to the division of labor—in short, to cooperation in the performance of specialized tasks.[4] The dominance of homo sapiens on the planet is a result of individual *specialization*—provided that the specializations are somehow coordinated so as to produce a collective result.

The more specialized a society is, the more complex it is and, potentially, the more productive it is. But the more complex it is, the more imperative and the more difficult it is to achieve the requisite degree of coordination. One solution to the coordination problem has been the evolution of "bureaucratic"

[4]John Kenneth Galbraith, *The New Industrial State*, Boston: Houghton-Mifflin, 1967, pp. 60-63.

forms of organization, where the subordination of individual discretion to bureaucratic rules and bureaucratic authority is carried very far. It is carried so far that "bureaucratic" is more an epithet in the minds of most Americans than a neutrally descriptive word. Still, bureaucracy seems to be an essential device in modern societies, as Peter Blau makes clear in the following selection.[5]

Our high standard of living is usually attributed to the spectacular technological developments that have occurred since the Industrial Revolution, but this explanation ignores two related facts. First, the living conditions of most people during the early stages of industrialization, after they had moved from the land into the cities with their sweatshops, were probably much worse than they had been before. Dickens depicts these terrible conditions in certain novels, and Marx describes them in his biting critique of the capitalistic economy. Second, major improvements in the standard of living did not take place until administrative procedures as well as the material technology had been revolutionized. Modern machines could not be utilized without the complex administrative machinery needed for running factories employing thousands of workers. It was not so much the invention of new machines as the introduction of mass-production methods that enabled Henry Ford to increase wages and yet produce a car so cheaply that it ceased to be a luxury. When Ford later refused to make further administrative innovations, in the manner of his competitors, the position of his company suffered, but after his grandson instituted such changes the company manifested new competitive strength. Rationalization in administration is a prerequisite for the full exploitation of technological knowledge in mass production, and thus for a high standard of living.[6]

Let us examine some of the administrative principles on which the productive efficiency of the modern factory depends. If every worker manufactured a complete car, each would have to be a graduate of an engineering college, and even then he could not do a very good job, since it would be impossible for him to be at once an expert mechanical engineer, electrical engineer, and industrial designer. Besides, there would not be enough people with engineering degrees in the country to fill all the positions. Specialization permits the employment of many less-trained workers, which lowers production costs. Moreover, whereas the jack-of-all-trades is necessarily master of none, each employee can become a highly skilled expert in his particular field of specialization.

[5]Reprinted by permission from Peter Blau, *Bureaucracy in Modern Society*, New York: Random House Studies in Sociology, 1956, pp. 16-19, 28-32.

[6]To be sure, activities of trade unions have greatly contributed to the raising of our standard of living by forcing employers to distribute a larger proportion of their income to workers. Without administrative efficiency in the production and distribution of goods, however, there would be less income to distribute, and fewer goods could be bought with a given amount of income. Moreover, the strength of unions also depends on an efficient administrative machinery.

What has been taken apart must be put together again. A high degree of specialization creates a need for a complex system of coordination. No such need exists in the small shop, where the work is less specialized, all workers have direct contact with one another, and the boss can supervise the performance of all of them. The president of a large company cannot possibly discharge his managerial responsibility for coordination through direct consultation with each one of several thousand workers. Managerial responsibility, therefore, is exercised through a hierarchy of authority, which furnishes lines of communication between top management and every employee for obtaining information on operations and transmitting operating directives. (Sometimes, these lines of communication become blocked, and this is a major source of inefficiency in administration.)

Effective coordination requires disciplined performance, which cannot be achieved by supervision alone but must pervade the work process itself. This is the function of rules and regulations that govern operations whether they specify the dimensions of nuts and bolts or the criteria to be used in promoting subordinates. Even in the ideal case where every employee is a highly intelligent and skilled expert, there is a need for disciplined adherence to regulations. Say one worker had discovered that he could produce bolts of superior quality by making them one-eighth of an inch larger, and another worker had found that he could increase efficiency by making nuts one-eighth of an inch smaller. Although each one made the most rational decision in terms of his own operations, the nuts and bolts would of course be useless because they would not match. How one's own work fits together with that of others is usually far less obvious than in this illustration. For the operations of hundreds of employees to be coordinated, each individual must conform to prescribed standards even in situations where a different course of action appears to him to be most rational. This is a requirement of all teamwork, although, in genuine teamwork the rules are not imposed from above but are based on common agreement.

Efficiency also suffers when emotions or personal considerations influence administrative decisions. If the owner of a small grocery expands his business and opens a second store, he may put his son in charge even though another employee is better qualified for the job. He acts on the basis of his personal attachment rather than in the interest of business efficiency. Similarly, an official in a large company might not promote the best-qualified worker to foreman if one of the candidates were his brother. Indeed, his personal feelings could prevent him from recognizing that the qualifications of his brother were inferior. Since the subtle effects of strong emotions cannot easily be suppressed, the best way to check their interference with efficiency is to exclude from the administrative hierarchy those interpersonal relationships that are characterized by emotional attachments. While relatives sometimes work for the same company, typically they are not put in charge of one another. Impersonal relationships assure the detachment necessary if efficiency alone is to govern administrative decisions. However, relationships between employees who have frequent social contacts do not remain purely impersonal, as we shall see.

These four factors—specialization, a hierarchy of authority, a system of rules, and impersonality—are the basic characteristics of bureaucratic organization. Factories are bureaucratically organized, as are government agencies, and if this were not the case they could not operate efficiently on a large scale.

By "bureaucracies," most people mean giant corporations or government agencies. But the essence of bureaucracy—rules and the authorities who enforce them—are ubiquitous in social life. Ubiquitous also is a steady, almost incessant, drumbeat of messages about the importance of conforming to the rules. A vivid example of rules and educational pressures to obey them (or to pay the price of not doing so) is provided in an experience of one of the authors of this book. Jackson Toby (who specializes in criminology) once devised an experiment in which he tried to do three things. One was to contribute to the education of his undergraduate students at Rugers University by involving them in a special seminar with adolescent delinquents. The second was to contribute to the rehabilitation of the delinquents by getting them to associate with the Rutgers students in the seminar, the subjects of which were the sources and nature of delinquency. The third was to understand the processes of interaction that developed in the seminar. For the last reason, all discussions were taped.

Here is an excerpt from one of the meetings. It shows, in an incidental but dramatic way, the operation of bureaucratic rules in a school system, the costs of nonconformity, and above all, the relentless pressure on individuals to recognize the strategic necessity to conformity.

Tom: Sometimes you can't really control yourself. When I was in school, the teachers, they give me a lot of trouble. I tried to avoid it, but sometimes I just couldn't. One day I was in school, and I didn't feel good. I had a fight at home with my father.... [a pause] They was real funny in our school. During the change of periods, if you go to the bathroom, they don't want you combing your hair because they say you take too long to get back to your classes. So I was in there, combin' my hair. So the teacher walked in and said, "Hey, boy, put that comb away." So I said, "All right, I'll put it away." So I put it away. Then he says to me, "Button your shirt up." I said, "All right," and was going back to my class, buttoning my shirt up. Then he pushed me against the wall and said, "I told you to button your shirt up." I says, "I am." He pushed me again, and I hit him because he was pushing me. He took me down to the office, and I told the principal that he was pushing me. The principal says, "I don't want to hear anything from you because you're an instigator in school." And he threw me out of school. So it's all according to how you feel. Like that teacher, he didn't have no right pushing me, right?

Dr. Toby: I appreciate your telling this story, Tom. It gives us an opportunity to consider another situation involving self-control. Let's ask Tom questions about this story so that we really get to understand what happened, why it happened, and whether Tom was behaving childishly or not. Maybe this was just a rough situation. But let's see if we can come to understand it as well as possible. Yes?

Rutgers Student: Can I ask some questions?

Dr. Toby: Sure.

Rutgers Student: Do you think that getting this one good shot at the teacher, even if he was wrong, was worth getting kicked out of school?

Tom: No, it wasn't worth getting kicked out of school, but I was just aggravated when he pushed me, so I hit him. But after I got thrown out of school, I did think twice. But it was too late. Most of the time I went to school, I had trouble with the teachers.

Rutgers Student: Was it just an impulse or did you think about it and say, "Oh, the hell with this!" and just punch him?

Tom: I don't know. When he pushed me, I just got up and hit him. That's all.

Rutgers Student: Instantly? You didn't think?

Tom: No, I didn't think.

Rutgers Student: It was just impulse then.

Tom: Yes.

Dr. Toby: I haven't been in high school for a long time. Is walking around with one's shirt unbuttoned a crime in high school? I don't get it.

Jim: It's not a serious crime, but the teachers make a big issue of it.

Dr. Toby: Do they?

Jim: Yeah.

Rutgers Student: What are the rules at school? Do you have to have your shirt buttoned clear up to the top?

Tom: No, you have to have this one buttoned right here. [indicating the next button to the top] And you can't have your collar up.

Rutgers Student: So you know about the rules.

Tom: Yeah. And there's another thing too. Me, I never wear a belt. They make you wear a belt in school. They won't let you go in there without a belt. I don't see that. As long as you come to school clean and dress right, they can't make you wear a belt. Right?

Dr. Toby: Well, I don't know whether they can or they can't.

Tom: Well, I don't see that. As long as you come to school and you're clean, it's all right. I don't see they have a right to make you wear a belt.

Dr. Toby: Well, now, you're talking about whether they *should* have such a rule or not. You're saying they shouldn't have such a rule. But they do have it. I don't make the rules and you don't make the rules. Once the rules are there, then you can do one thing or the other: You can obey the rules, or you can get kicked out. And you have to decide what you want to do. Right?

Tom: Right.

[Tom then refers to "other kids" in his school who also break rules, and, he alleges, they don't receive the treatment he receives. Toby picks this up in the following way.]

Dr. Toby: We don't have them here. We're not talking about them, we're talking about you.

Tom: I thought I was pretty good in school.

Dr. Toby: Oh, you thought you were pretty good. Why were you in the principal's office so often?

Tom: I don't know.

Dr. Toby: Well, tell us some of the reasons.

Tom: When I was in the classroom, I never did nothing. And when I did want to do something, like get in a discussion with all the kids, I'd raise my hand, and the teacher would say, "I don't want to hear you. Go back to sleep." [laughter from class]

Dr. Toby: Why was that?

Tom: Because every day I went in there, I never did nothing. I never did my homework, never carried books home with me.

Dr. Toby: You weren't playing according to the rules of the game. Why not?

Tom: Because I didn't want to go to school.

Dr. Toby: Oh! Well, if you didn't want to go to school, then I apologize for all the things I was thinking. You didn't behave childishly. You did exactly right. You wanted to get kicked out, and you were.

Tom: No, I didn't want to get kicked out, but I didn't want to go to school. I just had to go to school because my mother told me to go. And I didn't want to go out and work, so I figured I would stay in school.

Dr. Toby: I'm not sure I quite get that. Either you wanted to be in school or you didn't want to be in school.

Tom: Well, see, I didn't want to go to school, but I knew if I was out of school, I'd have to go to work. And I didn't want to go to work.

Rutgers Student: Which did you think was worse?

Tom: Going to work.

Dr. Toby: So you wanted to be in school?

Tom: Yes.

Dr. Toby: You wanted to be in school, but you didn't want to obey any of the rules.

Tom: Yes.

Dr. Toby: That's like the old expression "You want your cake and you want to eat it too." You can't have both. If you wanted to be in school, then you had to obey the rules, or get kicked out.

Tom: I don't know. To me, I thought the teachers was lazy, because we'd go into class and the teacher would put one thing down for all her classes that would come in. It would be on the board, and all the kids had to do it. Some of the kids used to take seven books home a night. And I knew if I had taken one of them books home, I never would have got out. I would have been home doing my homework all night. And I figure that you only go to school from 9 to 3; that's it. I don't want to hear about homework because I want to go out when I get home. [laughter]

Dr. Toby: I see. You thought only the teachers should do homework, not the students?

Tom: They're getting paid for it.

Dr. Toby: I see. So you didn't want to do any homework.

Tom: No.

Dr. Toby: That was one of the things you didn't want to do. What other things didn't you want to do? [Silence] Gene?

Gene: Well, he could've tried another school.

Dr. Toby: But all schools would have asked him to do homework. No?

Gene: What about Vocational School?

Dr. Toby: Is there no homework in Vocational School?

Gene: Not the type of homework you do in a regular school.

Dr. Toby: Do you know? Have you been in Vo-Tech?

Gene: No, but I have a few friends there.

Dr. Toby: Did you think about transferring to another school? Gene suggested that.

Tom: Yeah, but if I went to another school, I'd be a freshman. And I heard that if you're a freshman, they make you do all kinds of stuff. I wouldn't have did it. I would start fighting with them, and I would get suspended from that school, too.

Dr. Toby: I see. You didn't think you could obey the rules in the other school.

Tom: No.

Dr. Toby: Some rules were by the teachers and some by the students. You didn't want to take any guff from the students either.

Tom: No.

Dr. Toby: What other rules didn't you want to obey? You didn't want to do homework; you didn't want to dress the way the teachers wanted you to dress; you wanted to spend a lot of time combing your hair—

Tom: No, I figure you have the breaks [the time between classes]—I always made it to class, I never was late to the class; but there's a lot of girls around. And you can't leave your hair messed up all the time. [laughter]

Dr. Toby: Let me say that this problem that Tom has told us about is everybody's problem. That is to say, the natural thing to do in all these situations is what you damn please. If you get angry, the natural thing is to hit somebody; and if you see something you like, the natural thing to do is to take it.

Tom: You couldn't say that, can you? [in a shocked tone]

Dr. Toby: Sure, it's the natural thing to do, but grown-up human beings don't do the natural thing. They control themselves when they feel like hitting someone who gets them angry. And they resist the impulse to steal when they see something they like that isn't theirs. Learning to be grown-up is learning to do the *unnatural* thing.

"Learning to be grownup is learning to do the *unnatural* thing!" What Toby meant is what we have been emphasizing in this chapter. Human beings must have rules; but there is no biological "naturalness" about their conforming to them.

The matter of law abidingness is further complicated in American society by the cultural emphasis placed on "individualism" and "individual self-assertion," which often makes rules appear even more "unnatural." The hostility toward rules in American culture accounts for the special warmth Americans feel toward Henry David Thoreau. Thoreau's defense of *non*-law abidingness in his famous essay, "On Civil Disobedience," follows.[7]

All men recognize the right of revolution; that is, the right to refuse allegiance to, and to resist, the government, when its tyranny or its inefficiency are great and unendurable. But almost all say that such is not the case now. But such was the case, they think, in the Revolution of '75. If one were to tell me that this was a bad government because it taxed certain foreign commodities

[7]Reprinted by permission from Henry David Thoreau, *The Writings of Thoreau*, New York: Random House, 1937, pp. 638-640, 644-649, 659.

brought to its ports, it is most probable that I should not make an ado about it, for I can do without them. All machines have their friction; and possibly this does enough good to counterbalance the evil. At any rate, it is a great evil to make a stir about it. But when the friction comes to have its machine, and oppression and robbery are organized, I say, let us not have such a machine any longer. In other words, when a sixth of the population of a nation which has undertaken to be the refuge of liberty are slaves, and a whole country is unjustly overrun and conquered by a foreign army, and subjected to military law, I think that it is not too soon for honest men to rebel and revolutionize. What makes this duty the more urgent is the fact that the country so overrun is not our own, but ours is the invading army.

... Unjust laws exist: shall we be content to obey them, or shall we endeavor to amend them, and obey them until we have succeeded, or shall we transgress them at once? Men generally, under such a government as this, think that they ought to wait until they have persuaded the majority to alter them. They think that, if they should resist, the remedy would be worse than the evil. But it is the fault of the government itself that the remedy *is* worse than the evil. *It* makes it worse. Why is it not more apt to anticipate and provide for reform? Why does it not cherish its wise minority? Why does it cry and resist before it is hurt? Why does it not encourage its citizens to be on the alert to point out its faults, and *do* better than it would have them? Why does it always crucify Christ, and excommunicate Copernicus and Luther, and pronounce Washington and Franklin rebels?

One would think, that a deliberate and practical denial of its authority was the only offense never contemplated by government; else, why has it not assigned its definite, its suitable and proportionate penalty? If a man who has no property refuses but once to earn nine shillings for the state, he is put in prison for a period unlimited by any law that I know, and determined only by the discretion of those who placed him there; but if he should steal ninety times nine shillings from the state, he is soon permitted to go at large again.

If the injustice is part of the necessary friction of the machine of government, let it go, let it go: perchance it will wear smooth,—certainly the machine will wear out. If the injustice has a spring, or a pulley, or a rope, or a crank, exclusively for itself, then perhaps you may consider whether the remedy will not be worse than the evil; but if it is of such a nature that it requires you to be the agent of injustice to another, then, I say, break the law. Let your life be a counter friction to stop the machine. What I have to do is to see, at any rate, that I do not lend myself to the wrong which I condemn. ...

A minority is powerless while it conforms to the majority; it is not even a minority then; but it is irresistible when it clogs by its whole weight. If the alternative is to keep all just men in prison, or give up war and slavery, the State will not hesitate which to choose. If a thousand men were not to pay their tax-bills this year, that would not be a violent and bloody measure, as it would be to pay them, and enable the State to commit violence and shed innocent blood. This is, in fact, the definition of a peaceable revolution, if any such is possible. If the tax-gatherer, or any other public officer, asks me, as one has done, "But what shall I do?" my answer is, "If you really wish to do anything, resign your office." When the subject has refused allegiance, and the officer has resigned his office, then the revolution is accomplished. But even suppose blood should flow. Is there not a sort of blood shed when the conscience is wounded? Through this wound a man's real manhood and immortality flow out, and he bleeds to an everlasting death. I see this blood flowing now. . . .

The authority of government, even such as I am willing to submit to—for I will cheerfully obey those who know and can do better than I, and in many things even those who neither know nor can do so well—is still an impure one: to be strictly just, it must have the sanction and consent of the governed. It can have no pure right over my person and property but what I concede to it. The progress from an absolute to a limited monarchy, from a limited monarchy to a democracy, is a progress toward a true respect for the individual. Even the Chinese philosopher was wise enough to regard the individual as the basis of the empire. Is a democracy, such as we know it, the last improvement possible in government? Is it not possible to take a step further towards recognizing and organizing the rights of man? There will never be a really free and enlightened State until the State comes to recognize the individual as a higher and independent power, from which all its own power and authority are derived, and treats him accordingly. I please myself with imagining a State at last which can afford to be just to all men, and to treat the individual with respect as a neighbor; which even would not think it inconsistent with its own repose if a few were to live aloof from it, not meddling with it, nor embraced by it, who fulfilled all the duties of neighbors and fellow men. A State which bore this kind of fruit, and suffered it to drop off as fast as it ripened, would prepare the way for a still more perfect and glorious State, which also I have imagined, but not yet anywhere seen.

On the one hand, then, the Amercan value system insists fiercely on the supremacy of the individual and the primacy of the individual conscience. An enduring legacy of our Hebraic-Greco ancestry, it is expressed in its most radical form in the Protestant Reformation. On the other hand, *no* human society can endure in which most people do not conform to most of their status obligations most of the time, whether they individualistically feel like it or not. American society, then, also contains the moral commandment, "Thou shalt do thy duty." Moreover, the duty one must do cannot be left to the discretion of each individual; it is a duty imposed by an authority.

The originator of the Protestant Reformation, Martin Luther, puts this emphatically, indeed, vehemently. Speaking of the "free will" of man, Luther said that it must be understood to "allow man 'free will' not in respect of those who are above him, but in respect only of those beings who are below him. . . . God-ward man has no 'free will,' but is a captive, slave, and servant either to the will of God or to the will of Satan."[8]

With respect to the secular world, Luther was even more passionate on the subject.

> Even if those in authority are evil or without faith, nevertheless the authority and its power is good and from God. . . . Therefore, where there is power and where it flourishes, there it is and there it remains because God has ordained it. . . . God would prefer to suffer the government to exist no matter how evil, rather than to allow the rabble to riot, no matter how justified they are in doing so. . . . A prince should remain a prince no matter how tyrannical he should be. He beheads necessarily only a few since he must have subjects in order to be a ruler. . . . Let everyone who can, smite, slay, and stab, secretly or openly, remembering that nothing can be more poisonous, hurtful, or devilish than a rebel. It is just as when one must kill a mad dog; if you do not strike him, he will strike you, and a whole land with you.[9]

Luther's purplish prose and literal appeals to religion are, of course, out of style in modern secular society. Moreover, his one-sided rejection of Thoreau's one-sided espousal of individualism is too extreme for contemporary Americans. Still, the ambivalence remains; and many thoughtful Americans have struggled to formulate a rationale that would balance the claims of individualism against the claims and necessity of law-abidingness.

Two such rationales will serve to give the flavor of the struggle. One is that of MacIver, whom we quoted above on the necessity of laws. In that excerpt, MacIver was dealing with, among other things, the question, "Why *do* men obey the law?" But there is another question that thoughtful men must ask themselves—"Why ought men to obey the law?" MacIver briefly reviews certain answers, and indicates his own, in the short excerpt that follows.[10]

In his book *The Sanctity of Law* **J. W. Burgess pointed out that men have rested the obligation to obey on two main grounds. One is the legitimacy of the source from which law proceeds, in other words the right ascribed to the**

---

[8]Quoted by Erich Fromm, *Escape from Freedom* (New York: Holt, Rinehart, and Winston, 1941), p. 76. Reprinted by permission.

[9]*Ibid.*, p. 82.

[10]MacIver, *op. cit.*, pp. 74-75.

law-making authority, whether divine appointment, constitutional right, or some contractual agreement between ruler and subject. The other is the rationality of content, in other words the intrinsic merit of the law itself, its contribution to the system of values we uphold or cherish. The two grounds are often conjoined, and often no distinction is drawn between them. But the answer so far given remains inadequate. There is very often considerable division of opinion about the merit of particular laws, and they are nevertheless accepted and obeyed. On the other hand, even if the legitimacy of the source is acknowledged, that does not preclude the recognition of other authorities or other obligations, with the demands of which the law of the state may be in conflict. The issue of the primacy of one authority over another has constantly arisen. Should Antigone obey the command of her king or the contradictory command of her religion and of her kinship bond? Should we obey conscience against law or law against conscience? And so forth. Some, like Plato and Thomas Hobbes and Hegel, have made the law of the state paramount over all others. Many have placed "the law of God" above the law of man. Some, like Protagoras, Friedrich Nietzsche, George Sorel, have denied that there is any inherent legitimacy in government— at least unless it is the particular kind of government they advocate. They have claimed that governments rule in the interest of a group or class and that obedience is more a matter of expediency than of obligation. Others, like Harold Laski in his *Grammar of Politics*, have held that the citizen is obligated to obey a particular law only if that law satisfies his own sense of justice. Others—and with this view the present writer is in sympathy—hold that obedience is obligatory except when in the considered judgment of the citizen disobedience promotes the greater welfare of the society as a whole in which he lives. It is clear, however, that on a question such as this there is no hope of consensus. The answers given will differ not only with the kind of government under contemplation but also with the value-system of the respondent.[11]

For MacIver, the thoughtful 20th century American, *obedience is obligatory*, save under one circumstance: "When in the considered judgment of the citizen, disobedience promotes the general welfare of the society as a whole in which he lives." Notice in the first place that there is still implicit in this the moral principle that it is the duty of the individual to promote the general welfare of the *society as a whole*. Disobedience that promotes only the welfare of the disobedient person himself, or some subgroup of which he is a member, is not being condoned. In the second place, even this formula, so typically American, can generate severe problems, as we shall see in later chapters. A second interesting rationale for bringing the two contradictory sentiments into balance was offered by Woodrow Wilson.[12]

[11]*Ibid.*, pp. 74-75.

[12]Reprinted by permission from Woodrow Wilson, *The New Freedom* (New York: Doubleday and Co., 1913 and 1931), pp. 277-288.

What is liberty?

I have long had an image in my mind of what constitutes liberty. Suppose that I were building a great piece of powerful machinery, and suppose that I should so awkwardly and unskillfully assemble the parts of it that every time one part tried to move it would be interfered with by the others, and the whole thing would buckle up and be checked. Liberty for the several parts would consist in the best possible assembling and adjustment of them all, would it not? If you want the great piston of the engine to run with absolute freedom, give it absolutely perfect alignment and adjustment with the other parts of the machine, so that it is free, not because it is let alone or isolated, but because it has been associated most skillfully and carefully with the other parts of the great structure.

What is liberty? You say of the locomotive that it runs free. What do you mean? You mean that its parts are so assembled and adjusted that friction is reduced to a minimum, and that it has perfect adjustment. We say of a boat skimming the water with light foot, "How free she runs," when we mean, how perfectly she is adjusted to the force of the wind, how perfectly she obeys the great breath of the heavens that fills her sails. Throw her head up into the wind and see how she will halt and stagger, how every sheet will shiver and her whole frame be shaken, how instantly she is "in irons," in the expressive phrase of the sea. She is free only when you have let her fall off again and have recovered once more her nice adjustment to the forces she must obey and cannot defy.

Wilson uses the American symbol of "freedom" to justify *laws*—and by implication, to justify the duty to obey laws (unless, as MacIver would say, not obeying the laws would *more effectively* "adjust" individuals to the needs of the "machine"). The issue of how to resolve the conflict between the American sentiment that individual freedom of judgment is good and the American sentiment that conformity to law is good is once again a public issue. Protests against American military intervention in Vietnam and against the continuing subordination of black Americans are leading some Americans to replay the Thoreau solution. We shall discuss those actions in Chapters 13, 15, and 16. But the same events are leading others to reaffirm the American value of law abidingness. We bring this chapter to an end with two such reaffirmations. One was made by the philosopher, Sidney Hook, in response to an invitation to address certain questions by the New York *Times*. Two of the questions were "What justifies an act of civil disobedience? What are, or should be, the limits of civil disobedience?" A third question asked whether civil disobedience was justified in the particular case of the Vietnam war. Hook's reply is as follows.[13]

[13] Reprinted by permission from Sidney Hook, "A Right Way to Remedy a Wrong, a Wrong Way to Secure a Right," New York *Times Magazine*, November 26, 1967, pp. 124-126. © 1967/65/68/58 by the New York Times Company. Reprinted by permission.

The right of dissent is integral to a free society; otherwise it lapses into tyranny. But there must be limits to dissent when it takes the form of action; otherwise the result is anarchy.

Actions are civilly disobedient when they openly defy on grounds of conscience laws that have been sustained by the supreme legal authorities. To a democrat, resort to civil disobedience is never politically legitimate where methods of due process are available to remedy evils. If these remedies are unavailing and the issue appears of transcendent importance, a democrat may on moral or religious grounds resort to civil disobedience in the hope that he will open the minds of his fellow citizens to second thoughts. In that case he must willingly accept his punishment. Otherwise he has abandoned his faith in democracy, and in effect acts as if he were at war against the democratic community. In that event the community has the duty to protect itself against him, and to constrain him if he resorts to warlike actions instead of argument.

The limits of civil disobedience in a democracy begin when it becomes uncivil, when resistance to law, passive or active, takes the form of violence or has consequences leading to social chaos. This is the aim of those critics of American Vietnam policy who urge "resistance" rather than "dissent." They often rationalize their resistance by denying that we live in a democratic society. Having failed to influence national policy by rational means within the law, they seek to coerce the community by obstructive techniques outside the law. They scoff at majority rule which is a necessary but not a sufficient condition of our Bill of Rights democracy.

A free society can recognize and respect the scruples of a conscientious objector to war who civilly disobeys the law and accepts his punishment. But if he forcibly tries to prevent others from fulfilling their duty to their country he is neither a genuine pacifist nor a democrat.

Some who have already gone beyond dissent to "resistance" have shown by their actions that they no longer believe in the democratic process. Wherever they have the power to do so, they deny to those who disagree with them the right to be heard, they disrupt meetings, threaten bodily harm to speakers, trespass and take over public places, and act more like Storm Troopers or the Communist squads that used to break up Socialist meetings.

The law is not always wrong and the voice of conscience is not always right—especially when consciences conflict. If the dictate of a man's conscience cannot withstand rational analysis and criticism by those who disagree with him, this is presumptive evidence of the unwisdom of acting on it.

I do not believe that civil disobedience with respect to American Vietnam policy, if one is opposed to it, is justified. The issues are not black and white, but large and complex, about which intelligent men of goodwill and character may differ. There are no easy solutions. All-out escalation or scuttle-and-run are not the only alternatives to present policy. . . .

The practice of "resistance" is self-defeating and therefore politically unintelligent. Public revulsion at its excesses will strengthen the hawks and build up popular support for them. It will also harden the resolution of present policymakers.

Resort to resistance creates a precedent which will have a pernicious effect on the quality of future public debate. The appeal to the streets and violent mass action will take the place of the appeal to evidence, good sense and common interest, on which a healthy democracy depends.

By inspiring a backlash of reaction, resistance will make dissent more difficult, and tempt those who are sickened by civil disorder to support extreme measures of repression. Democracy in the long run is not viable unless its citizens recognize that there is a right way to remedy a wrong and a wrong way to secure a right.

The second concluding statement of the American value of law-abidingness is that of Erwin Griswold, former Dean of the Harvard Law School and now (1970) Solicitor General of the United States.[14]

We must draw two fundamental distinctions when we speak of dissent; the first involves primarily legal and moral variables and divides permissible from unpermissible dissent; the second presupposes that the dissent is tolerable but involves the social and political considerations of whether, or when or how the protest *should* be made. The latter is not a question of right, but of judgment and morals, even of taste, and a proper sense of restraint and responsibility, qualities which are or should be inherent in the very concept of civil liberties.

We must begin any analysis of these questions with the undoubted fact that we live in a society, an imperfect and struggling one no doubt, but one where Government and order are not only a necessity but are the preference of an overwhelming majority of the citizenry. The rules that society has developed to organize and order itself are found in a body of law which has not been imposed from outside, but has been slowly built up from experience expressed through the consent of the governed, and now pervades all aspects of human activity. Inevitably there are occasions when individuals or groups will chafe under a particular legal bond, or will bridle in opposition to a particular governmental policy, and the question presents itself, what can be done?

Vocal objection, of course—even slanderous or inane—is permissible. But the fact that one is a dissenter with a right to express his opposition entitles him to no special license. Thus, in expressing views that are themselves wholly immune to official strictures he gains no roving commission to ignore the rules and

---

[14]Reprinted by permission from Erwin Griswold, "Dissent—1968 Style," The George Abel Dreyfus Lecture on Civil Liberties, given at the Tulane University School of Law, New Orleans, Louisiana, April 16, 1968.

underlying assumption of society that relate in a neutral way to activity rather than to the maintenance or expression of ideas. Thus, I submit that one cannot rightly engage in conduct which is otherwise unlawful merely because he intends that either that conduct or the idea he wishes to express in the course of the conduct is intended to manifest his dissent from some governmental policy. I cannot distinguish in principle the legal quality of the determination to halt a troop train to protest the Vietnam war or to block workmen from entering a segregated job site to protest employment discrimination, from the determination to fire shots into a civil rights leader's home to protest integration. The right to disagree—and to manifest disagreement—which the constitution allows to the individuals in those situations—does not authorize them to carry on their campaign of education and persuasion at the expense of someone else's liberty, or in violation of some laws whose independent validity is unquestionable.

This distinction runs deep in our history, but has too frequently been ignored in this decade. But the line is a clear one, and we should reestablish it in the thinking and understanding of our people. While I share Professor Harry Kalven's assessment that the "generosity and empathy with which [public streets and parks] are made available [as a "public forum"] is an index of freedom,[15] I regard as unassailable the limitation that the mere fact that a person wishes to make a public point does not sanction any method he chooses to use to make it. Yet there seems to be currently a considerable tendency to ignore if not to reject this limitation. Certainly many of the modern forms of dissent, including those I have just mentioned, proceed on the basis of the contrary proposition. Only last Term the Supreme Court was asked to sustain the right of demonstrators active in a cause that most of us here and the Court itself no doubt regarded as laudable, to lodge their demand for an end to segregation on the grounds of a city jail where, it seemed, biased treatment was being accorded prisoners. The argument was made that a demonstration at that site was "particularly appropriate", irrespective of the consequences. Speaking for the Court, Justice Black rejected this rationale, explaining that[16]

> Such an argument has as its major unarticulated premise the assumption that people who want to propagandize protests or views have a constitutional right to do so whenever and however and wherever they please.

That notion the Court expressly "vigorously and forthrightly rejected."

Another form of protest that can never, in my view, be excused or tolerated, is that which assumes the posture of a violent and forcible assault on public order, whatever the motivation. The interests at stake in such a situation must transcend the validity of the particular cause and the permissibility of adhering

---

[15]Kalven, *The Concept of the Public Forum: Cox v. Louisiana*, 1965 Supreme Court Review 12.

[16]*Adderley v. Florida*, 385 U.S. 39, 47-48.

to it. Violent opposition to law—any law—or forcible disregard of another's freedom to disagree falls beyond the pale of legitimate dissent or even of civil disobedience, properly understood; it is nothing short of rebellion.

The utter indefensibility of violent opposition to law is that it proceeds on the foolhardy and immoral principle that might makes right. Centuries ago Rousseau rejected this approach as a viable political alternative:[17]

> For, if force creates right, the effect changes with the cause: every force that is greater than the first succeeds to its right. As soon as it is possible to disobey with impunity, disobedience is legitimate; and, the strongest being always in the right, the only thing that matters is to act so as to become the strongest. But what kind of right is that which perishes when force fails?

To permit factions the resort to force when they feel—however correctly—that a particular law or policy is wrong would be to renounce our own experience and that of the Founders. In support of this view, I offer two sentences written by Justice Frankfurter: "Law alone saves a society from being rent by internecine strife or ruled by mere brute power however disguised."[18] And, "Violent resistance to law cannot be made a legal reason for its suspension without loosening the fabric of our society."[19]

What is at stake is not mere order but also the lessons of history. True freedom and substantial justice come not from violent altercations or incendiary dissent. "No mob has ever protected any liberty, even its own."[20] While the First Amendment embodies a distrust of the collective conscience of the majority in areas of fundamental liberty, it no more intended to leave the limits of freedom to the judgment of coercive dissenters. "Civil government cannot let any group ride rough-shod over others simply because their 'consciences' tell them to do so."[21]

These reflections have dealt with the question when law and government may tolerate dissent, or dissent manifested in certain ways, and I have suggested that it is illicit to violate otherwise valid laws either as a symbol of protest or in the course of protest, and secondly that I regard it as indefensible to attempt to promote a viewpoint either by flagrant violence or by organized coercion. Now I will turn finally to the second distinction to which I referred earlier in this lecture. That is, assuming a legal or moral right to protest, what considerations of prudence and responsibility should infuse the determination to exercise these rights.

First, you will note that I imply that a line may be drawn between legal and

[17]*The Social Contract*, Bk. I, Ch. 3.

[18]*United States* v. *United Mine Workers*, 330 U.S. 258, 308.

[19]*Cooper* v. *Aaron*, 358 U.S. 1, 22.

[20]*Terminiello* v. *Chicago*, 337 U.S. 1, 32 (Jackson, J., dissenting).

[21]*Douglas* v. *City of Jeanette*, 319 U.S. 157, 179 (opinion of Jackson, J.).

moral rights to dissent. I am not now referring to what I accept as the genuine possibility that one may exercise his constitutional right to dissent in a way that, because of recklessness or unfairness, makes his conduct ethically improper. I mention this distinction, however, because I believe awareness and evaluation of it should always be taken into account in considering an exercise of the right to dissent. But for the present, I mean to concentrate on the converse of this distinction, that there may be a moral right to dissent without a corresponding legal privilege to do so. It is in this context that "civil disobedience" must be viewed.

Earlier, I observed that our system contemplates that there may be a moral right to "civil disobedience" (properly understood) that exists notwithstanding a "legal" duty to obey. I also referred to the source of this moral right: the ultimate sanctity of a man's own conscience, as the intellectual and volitional composite that governs his conception of his relation to Eternal Truth. I wish now to emphasize the considerations which, in my view, condition the existence and exercise of this moral right, because I believe the current rhetoric—which sometimes seems to consecrate "civil disobedience" as the noblest response in the pantheon of virtues—has obscured the nature and consequence of this activity. To define my term—I mean by "civil disobedience" the deliberate violation of a rule ordained by constituted government because of a conscientious conviction that the law is so unjust that it cannot morally be observed by the individual.

The most important point to be stressed is that this decision is one that should be made only after the most painful and introspective reflection, and only when the firm conclusion is reached that obedience offends the most fundamental personal values. It is self-evident that routine or random non-compliance with the law for transient or superficial reasons would negate the first principles of civilized behavior. Unless society can safely assume that *almost* without exception individuals will accept the will of the majority even when to do so is grudging and distasteful, the foundation of secure liberty will rather rapidly erode. John Locke, who in his profound *Letter Concerning Toleration* analyzed and defended the right of obedience to conscience over civil law in case of severe conflict, thereafter cautioned in his essay *Concerning Civil Government:*[22]

> May [the sovereign] be resisted, as often as any one shall find himself aggrieved, and but imagine he has not right done him? This will unhinge and overturn all polities, and instead of government and order, leave nothing but anarchy and confusion.

Last year, in delivering this lecture, Arthur Goodhard observed, "Thus, it has

[22]Ch. XVIII, para 203.

been correctly said that obedience to the law is a major part of patriotism."[23] He meant this not as a castigation of dissent or as an outburst of flag-waving chauvinism, but rather as a formulation of a central political truth: That if human society is to enjoy freedom, it cannot tolerate license. Henry David Thoreau is generally regarded as the most notable American exponent of civil disobedience, and all of us share admiration for his determination. But we must not ignore the vital aspect of Thoreau's nonconformity—his passionate attempt to dissociate himself from society. He was, as Harry Kalven has put it, "a man who does not see himself as belonging very intensely to the community in which he was raised,"[24] and who sought constantly but futilely to reject the society to which he had not voluntarily adhered.

Thoreau's poignant attitude was charming enough in mid-nineteenth century America. But it was, essentially, an effort to withdraw from the realities of life and it was, I suggest, myopic even then, for it was painfully inconsistent with the fact that man is a part of society by nature, by geography, and by citizenship. Unlike a member of a purely artificial group, like a bar association or country club, a citizen cannot resign from the "social compact" because he protests policies of the regime. Now in the last third of the Twentieth Century, we must be even more cognizant that there is nothing noble or salutary about fore-doomed attempts to abdicate membership in society. Complex problems demand rational attention that can come only from personal focus on solutions and never from stubbornly turning one's back on harsh and unpleasant realities.

This is precisely what non-conformity as a way of life is. It is the essential irrationality of the "hippie movement"—a mass endeavor to drop out of life. It is a protest of sorts, of course, but one that can bear no fruit, because it takes issue with what is not only inevitable, but more importantly, indispensable—social regulation of individual behavior.

Stretched to its logical extreme, this also is civil disobedience, and for this reason I urge that before any man embarks upon a unilateral nullification of any law he must appreciate that his judgment has not merely a personal significance but also portends grave consequences for his fellows.

In determining whether and when to exercise the moral right to disobey the dictates of the law, it must also be recognized that society not only does not but cannot recognize this determination as entitled to legal privilege. It is part of the Gandhian tradition of civil disobedience that the sincerity of the individual's conscience presupposes that the law will punish this assertion of personal principle. In the very formation of our country, in the Federalist Papers,

---

[23]*Recognition of the Binding Nature of Law*, 41 Tul. L. Rev. 769, 773 (1967).

[24]"On Thoreau" in *Civil Disobedience* 25, 28 (Center for the Study of Democratic Institutions 1966).

Hamilton explained the reason why government cannot compromise its authority by offering a dispensation for individual conscience:[25]

> Government implies the power of making laws. It is essential to the idea of a law, that it be attended with a sanction; or, in other words, a penalty or punishment for disobedience. If there be no penalty annexed to disobedience, the resolutions or commands which pretend to be laws will, in fact, amount to nothing more than advice or recommendation.

Thus, it is of the essence of law that it is equally applied to all, that it binds all alike, irrespective of personal motive. For this reason, one who contemplates civil disobedience out of moral conviction should not be surprised and must not be bitter if a criminal conviction ensues. And he must accept the fact that organized society cannot endure on any other basis. His hope is that he may aid in getting the law changed. But if he does not succeed in that, he cannot complain if the law is applied to him.

CONCLUSION

To paraphrase a remark of Freud (contained in the first reading in this chapter), the individual would have more liberty without authoritative rules and their enforcement, but his liberty would be of little value. It would be the freedom to be coerced by the unrestrained liberty of anyone who is more powerful. The more complex a society becomes, the greater are the difficulties of coordinating individual actions into a cohesive whole. Bureaucratic forms of coordination can solve the problem, but they breed problems of their own. One of the problems is generated by the tension between the emphasis on conformity to rules ("the law") and the value Americans put on individualism of the Thoreau type. How can society maximize opportunities for dissent from the rules while minimizing coercive violations of others' liberties?

[25]The Federalist, Number 15

PART II
Social
Problems

"Social problems" are actions by persons that some other people think ought not to be engaged in. Sometimes the persons engaging in the "problem" behavior agree that their actions ought not to be engaged in. Both observers and starving persons are likely to agree that people ought not to starve. Similarly, many narcotics addicts, as well as their observers, agree that heroin ought not to be taken. Almost everyone agrees that depressions or "runaway" inflation, wars, disease, riots, and murder are "problems" that ought to be "solved." In other cases, the acting individuals do *not* agree that their behavior is a problem. For them, the problem is that others think there is a problem. Hippies do not feel that hippies are problems; squares are the problem. Mormons did not feel that their polygynous practices were a social problem; the arrogant interference by non-Mormons with Mormon beliefs was the problem.

Is there any way to avoid this relativity of "social problems"? Is there a valid way of saying that something is "really" a social problem, whatever people think about it subjectively? We doubt it. Human action constitutes social problems to the degree that a major segment of society (1) does not like it and (2) believes it can be ameliorated.

Let us assume that enough consensus exists in American society on which kinds of actions are problems in this sense and ignore the questions of whether some behavior is a problem or how serious a problem it is. Let us focus rather on the question, how can we understand the behavior people engage in that a major segment of the society *calls* problems? This focus is on behavior and on its social definition. Human beings act, as we pointed out in Chapter 1, so as to obtain some things from others, dispose of some things to others, to retain some things from others, and to contain some things in others. They do so by utilizing certain transaction modes in interaction with other people. There are, then, three elements in an action: the "want" or "need" of the actor; the type of transaction he uses to satisfy that want; and the relationship he has with others in his situation.

Each of those three elements may be viewed by observers (and/or by the actor himself) as one that ought to prevail or as one that ought not to prevail. (1) The want pursued by the actor may be regarded as culturally *prescribed* or *proscribed*. (2) The type of transaction he uses may be regarded as culturally prescribed or proscribed. (3) It may be felt that the actor should *remain in the relationship* with a given transacting partner, or there may be no obligation on him to maintain it. Putting these possibilities together, we obtain the classification of social problems shown in Table 1.

Table 1
TYPOLOGY OF SOCIAL PROBLEMS

	Pursuing Prescribed Wants		*Pursuing Proscribed Wants*	
	Using Prescribed Types of Transaction	Using Proscribed Types of Transaction	Using Prescribed Types of Transaction	Using Proscribed Types of Transaction
Maintaining a Given Relationship	Pathologies of Conformity	Success by Hook or Crook	Ritualism	Explosion
	B	C	D	E
Not Maintaining It	Search for Greener Pastures	Disaffiliation	Search for New Meanings	Search for Oblivion
	F	G	H	I

Part II of this book is divided into nine sections. Sections B through I have the titles shown in the cells of Table 1. (Section A will be discussed shortly.) Each type of social problem will be considered in the nine sections, but a brief explanation of Table 1 will give the reader a preliminary overview.

Section B deals with social problems that are pathologies of conformity. The point is that human beings are capable of maintaining that certain wants should be pursued by certain types of transaction in certain relationships—and then objecting strongly to the fact that many people do this. Thus, some behavior defined as a social problem is the result of *conformity* to materialism, bargaining, legal or bureaucratic duties, or individualistic self-orientation.

Section C describes a social problem that results from striving for approved wants in the context of the approved relationship but using types of transactions *not* supposed to be used. We call such problems "success by hook or crook" problems.

Section D deals with problems of a ritualistic kind of behavior—that is, people go through the motions of using the types of transaction they are supposed to use and remaining in the approved relationship, but in fact reject the wants the culture of their society says they should strive to satisfy.

In Section E we deal with problem behaviors that result from remaining in an approved relationship while trying to satisfy disapproved wants by disapproved means. The prototype is explosive vengefulness toward a spouse, in which one drops both the original purpose of the relationship and the approved type of transaction and expresses hostility.

Sections F-I deal with cases in which the relationship itself is ruptured. Section F considers the use of approved transactions in the pursuit of approved goals, but at the cost of searching for new partners. Such behavior is not always regarded as a problem, but sometimes it is. We call it the "search for greener pastures." In other cases (Section G), the rupture of the relationship is accompanied by the use of disapproved types of transactions. We call such actions "disaffiliation"; they include both extruding some people—forcing them out of a relationship—and seceding from membership in a social system. Section H deals with the problem generated when people break off approved relations, and, although using approved types of transactions, search for new meanings in life by rejecting the culturally approved goals prescribing what people *should* strive for. Finally, Section I is entitled "Search for Oblivion." These are problems generated when people drop out of all aspects of the society and culture—at the extreme, through suicide.

In addition to describing these eight types of social problems, Part III is concerned with another type (in Section A). This section, entitled "Human Suffering," is based on the assumption that standards of gratification, security, authority, and adequacy reviewed in Chapter 1 themselves create a kind of social problem, namely, the psychic pain experienced by people when they fail to measure up to standards they have internalized. Those experiencing the pain (and others who observe empathically their suffering) may regard such pain as costly and preventable—and therefore as a social problem.

Section A
HUMAN SUFFERING

chapter 6
The failure to meet standards

The culture of American society tells what the good things of life are, what to be ashamed of, what a man or a woman should be like, and so on. But societies do not necessarily make it easy for members to measure up to cultural standards; and when members cannot, a uniquely human kind of suffering results. Much of what American society regards as its social problems reflects this suffering. Poverty, for example, is a problem mainly because those of us who are not poor understand (or think we understand) how uncomfortable it is to be without sufficient financial resources in a society where most of the good things of life are not free. Poverty might still be regarded as a problem even if it were widely believed that the poor are as happy as the affluent; poverty might even be considered a more insidious problem because those afflicted with it do not realize that they ought to be resentful of their many disadvantages. But a large proportion of "social problems" evoke widespread concern because of a humanitarian desire to reduce suffering. In the rest of this chapter we shall illustrate the failure to measure up to the four cultural standards described in Chapter 1. In most cases the people who fail to measure up experience psychic pain; in some cases the observer watching their failure feels sympathetic and perhaps uncomfortable.

FAILING TO MEET STANDARDS OF GRATIFICATION

Standards of gratification tell people what the good things of life are—what a desirable level of living is, or what sort of people are attractive or ugly. In all societies, some people do not measure up to such standards. For example, migrant farm laborers in the United States live in the kind of poverty widely regarded as un-American.[1]

The valleys of California and Arizona and the suburbs of the Middle West are filled with the cabin slums of Mexican-Americans, Negroes, and poor whites trying to settle down. After a few years a migrant who cannot escape the stream is broken by it. The poverty, anxiety, homelessness, and isolation wear away his spirit. It is this apathy that is often called acceptance and makes people say, "They like things that way."

"We're always goin' someplace," said a sandy-haired Oklahoma migrant, "but we never git noplace." In a tired, flat voice, an old woman in a Michigan field put it only a little differently: "I been ever' place, and I got no place."

A migrant minister in a Belle Glade camp asked a woman in his camp church if she was going on the season again. "I don't know. Ever' year I go up broke, and I come back broke. I don't know why I go even."

Migrant workers are Americans cut off from the material goods the American culture tells them they should enjoy. They cannot bargain successfully (they have nothing much worth anyone's while); they have no legal or bureaucratic rights to a good living; they are not loved; they are not members of a cooperative team, other members of which might help them. And they lack coercive power.

Other Americans in a similar position are many of the "retired" aged.[2]

Edmund MacIntosh was depending on the theory that hard-boiled eggs and opened cans of Spam need no refrigeration. And he was sick.

He had also depended on the theory that if you work hard, live frugally, and mind your own business, you'll get by without help. And now he was seventy-four years old and needed help.

Mr. MacIntosh depended on hard-boiled eggs because his hotel room has no refrigerator and he can't afford to eat out. He is trying to live on his $50-a-month Social Security check. Room rent is $38.50 a month, which provides a room with clean linen every two weeks and clean towels every day. The remainder goes for food and chewing tobacco. Every week friends on the same floor buy him two dozen eggs, seven small cans of V-8 juice, two cans of Spam, a carton of dry cereal (because the box says, "Minimum daily requirement of vitamins") and his tobacco. He boils his eggs at once and eats them morning and

[1]From Truman Moore, "Slaves for Rent," *Atlantic Monthly*, May, 1965, p. 122. Copyright © 1965 by Truman Moore. Reprinted by permission.

[2]From Ben Bagdikian, *In the Midst of Plenty*, Boston: Beacon Press, 1964, pp. 103-111. Copyright © by Ben Bagdikian. Reprinted by permission of Beacon Press.

evening. He stretches a can of Spam for three days or so. It has cost him violent nausea to discover that hard-boiled eggs and opened Spam need refrigeration in warm weather.

He was trying to eat on $11.50 a month, or 38 cents a day. The Department of Agriculture thinks that the cleverest shopper for the minimum needs of an old man has to have a dollar a day. . . .

About a year ago, after almost ten years as the old man who always came around cutting lawns, automation hit Edmund MacIntosh. He was made obsolete by power lawn mowers.

They was using more and more of them. I couldn't afford one and when I used the people's mower it took only half the time as with a hand mower and by and by my people realized that, hell, they might as well do it themselves. I don't blame them. With a power mower it's no work at all. But I just wasn't getting enough work to stay alive. That's when I went to the Social Security people. I knew I had Social Security coming to me when I reached sixty-five but I was getting along cutting grass so I went to the Social Security people and asked them if I'd lose anything by not taking it right then. They told me no, it would just pile up, so I let it. But when those power mowers came in and I wasn't making enough to eat, I went to the Social Security people. I didn't mind doing that. Now, welfare, that's charity and that's something else. But Social Security, that's yours, you work for that yourself.

So last year I went to the Social Security. They was awfully nice and I picked up my back pay and started my $50 a month. I try living on the $50 but it just doesn't work. Some months it's all right, some months it's not. I hate to use all my money in the bank from my Social Security savings because it's all I've got. But now I need help.

Mr. MacIntosh was lucky. Only because he was over 72 did his uncollected Social Security pension accumulate. He was also lucky he could steadily withdraw money from this nest egg to augment his monthly payments.

He spit some tobacco from his reclining position. He didn't quite make it to the green plastic wastebasket on the floor.

Well, they've told me about welfare and I didn't much like the idea of that. But I've done about everything I can to cut out my outgo. I moved to a cheaper hotel here and now they're going to tear this one down. I sold my TV for $15.50 and I miss it now. Maybe I'll have to go to welfare. But I don't know where to go and I'm not able to go out any more. If I try walking my head swims and I'm afraid if I got outside I'll fall down and the cops will think I'm a wino. . .

The last time I left this city was seven years ago. Last time I left this block was two weeks ago. I took a cab to Third and Main for a haircut that cost me 50 cents. Cab costs 85 cents. I get my hair cut at the barber school. But they don't seem to have no taxi school for a cheap ride.

Sometimes in the evening, Edmund MacIntosh will walk to the elevator on his floor and ride down to the "lobby" of his hotel, a corridor of depression where ashen old men sit in torn plush sofas beside a row of orange steel barrels marked "Scrap."

Most of the time he lies on his bed, listening to a cracked plastic radio, mostly to news and discussion programs.

I like the radio, though I miss my TV. I don't have the money to buy a newspaper. The janitor here's a nice fellow and he brings me an old one now and then. On the radio I like to hear political talks. Best thing I like is the President's press conference. I'm a Democrat in politics. My Daddy was and my granddaddy was. We believed all Republicans go to hell when they die and I didn't want to go to hell. I voted last year for Governor Brown and Mayor Yorty. I voted for Kennedy. I've voted all my life ever since I was old enough. Fact is, I was accused once of voting before I was old enough. I was nineteen years old, pretty near old enough.

He fears the day when even his walking to the elevator will stop and the time when he will not have kind friends. As it is, a couple on the floor look in on him every day. The janitor brings him old papers. Another man does his shopping every week. But the hotel will be torn down and Edmund MacIntosh will be moved among strangers.

What I need most is a doctor. But I don't know no doctor I can call. I need something for my eyes. Four years ago I went to the hospital and they scraped them and I could read a newspaper without glasses. Now if I shut my right eye I can't see that doorknob over there. My hearing's going, too.

I asked him what things he missed most, now that he is alone in his hotel room. He pulled with his arms against the steel rod of his headboard and let himself look out the window at the bare earth hill and the gray concrete that made his view of the world.

Things I miss? You haven't got enough paper.

He was silent for awhile. He was good-natured and matter-of-fact.

My eyes are getting dimmer. I keep having these dizzy spells. I keep getting sick to my stomach. There's not a thing on my stomach right now. I guess what I want more than anything else is a doctor. Some good medicine.

He paused some more.

I'd like to go to church. I went a year ago but I don't know if I'll be able to go again. I can't right now and it's a little hard for me to tell when I will again. *If* I will again. Straight up, that is. I need a suit of clothes. I'd love to go to a picture show. They may sound like asking for everything in sight, but I miss things like that.

He chewed some more and spit again. He missed again.

All right. A man ain't going to have everything all his life. Sure, I'd like to be able to walk around without getting dizzy. And go to church. And go to a picture show. But maybe if I just had some good company I guess that would be all right, too. I ain't had a letter in twelve months. And that was from the bank about my account.

There are other ways of feeling poor besides not having money. A person who falls below the standards of acceptable physical attractiveness in terms of height, body build, profile, or skin condition tends to gravitate to the periphery of social life—to a mental slum. Erving Goffman called the failure to have culturally prescribed or preferred attributes, "stigma."[3]

The stigmatized individual tends to hold the same beliefs about identity that we do; this is a pivotal fact. His deepest feelings about what he is may be his sense of being a "normal person," a human being like anyone else, a person, therefore, who deserves a fair chance and a fair break . . . Yet he may perceive, usually quite correctly, that whatever others profess, they do not really "accept" him and are not ready to make contact with him on "equal grounds." Further, the standards he has incorporated from the wider society equip him to be intimately alive to what others see as his failing, inevitably causing him, if only for moments, to agree that he does indeed fall short of what he really ought to be. Shame becomes a central possibility, arising from the individual's perception of one of his own attributes as being a defiling thing to possess, and one he can readily see himself as not possessing.

The immediate presence of normals is likely to reinforce this split between self-demands and self, but in fact self-hate and self-derogation can also occur when only he and a mirror are about:

When I got up at last . . . and had learned to walk again, one day I took a hand glass and went to a long mirror to look at myself, and I went alone. I didn't want anyone . . . to know how I felt when I saw myself for the first time. But there was no noise, no outcry; I didn't scream with rage when I saw myself. I just felt numb. That person in the mirror *couldn't* be me. I felt inside like a healthy, ordinary, lucky person—oh, not like the one in the mirror! Yet when I turned my face to the mirror there were my own eyes looking back, hot with shame . . . when I did not cry or make any sound, it

---

[3]Erving Goffman, STIGMA: Notes on the Management of Spoiled Identity, © 1963, Prentice-Hall, Inc.

became impossible that I should speak of it to anyone, and the confusion and the panic of my discovery were locked inside me then and there, to be faced alone, for a very long time to come.

Over and over I forgot what I had seen in the mirror. It could not penetrate into the interior of my mind and become an integral part of me. I felt as if it had nothing to do with me; it was only a disguise. But it was not the kind of disguise which is put on voluntarily by the person who wears it, and which is intended to confuse other people as to one's identity. My disguise had been put on me without my consent or knowledge like the ones in fairy tales, and it was I myself who was confused by it, as to my own identity. I looked in the mirror, and was horror-struck because I did not recognize myself. In the place where I was standing, with that persistent romantic elation in me, as if I were a favored fortunate person to whom everything was possible, I saw a stranger, a little, pitiable, hideous figure, and a face that became, as I stared at it, painful and blushing with shame. It was only a disguise, but it was on me, for life. It was there, it was there, it was real. Every one of those encounters was like a blow on the head. They left me dazed and dumb and senseless everytime, until slowly and stubbornly my robust persistent illusion of well-being and of personal beauty spread all through me again, and I forgot the irrelevant reality and was all unprepared and vulnerable again.

Another writer provides a more detailed picture of the consequences suffered by those who are grossly unattractive by American standards.[4]

Mary Benchley, a 34-year-old housewife and the mother of a one-year-old girl, is a fourth-generation Protestant American of Dutch and Scotch descent. She lives with her husband, 17 years her senior, to whom she has been married six years. Mr. Benchley is a mechanic who makes $130 a month working for a small firm. This is a second marriage for both of them.

Mrs. Benchley had come to the plastic surgery clinic to request correction for a marked deformity of the lip. A plain-looking woman, dressed poorly and without particular care, she was shy, but frank and responsive. She had been born with a harelip and cleft palate. Although the harelip had been operated on when she was one year old, her upper lip was noticeably short and retracted, and she was unable to bring her lips together. The nose was also deformed because of the extreme width and flatness of the right nostril. The teeth were poorly aligned and a front one was missing. In view of the fact that the patient had never had any formal speech training, she spoke remarkably well.

Mrs. Benchley stated that neither she nor her mother had realized that

[4]From Frances Cooke Macgregor et al., *Facial Deformities and Plastic Surgery*, 1953, pp. 30-36. Courtesy of Frances Cooke Macgregor and Charles C. Thomas, Publisher, Springfield, Illinois.

further correction in her appearance could be made. Just recently, however, she had learned about the clinic from a neighbor who was interested in her plight. She had immediately come in search of help because she wanted to "look better" for the sake of her child: "She will want me to look more presentable when she grows up."

Mrs. Benchley was born in a small upstate town and was the youngest of four children. There were two boys and two girls. She described her father, a laborer, as "a man I never considered to be my father because of what he did to me." He was a poor provider and an alcoholic. He frequently lost his temper and became violent; once he threw a lamp at his wife and hit her in the stomach. At this time, she was pregnant with Mary and later attributed the child's deformity to this incident. Since the father seldom worked and could therefore not pay the rent, the family was forced to move from one town to another because of repeated evictions. The patient's mother was a hard-working, protective, and kindly woman who took the needs of her children seriously. Though she never blamed her husband for the deformity of the child, there were occasions later on when she told Mary that she had tried to interrupt the pregnancy and expressed guilt feelings about it.

When Mary was five and began to play with other children, she became aware that she was different from them. They taunted her because of her impaired speech and the way she looked. When she told her mother about the teasing, the mother tried to explain to her that she had been "born this way" and that it was not her fault. In grammar school, the children laughed and made fun of her, calling her "split lip" and "crooked talking." Often she was driven to tears and asked herself, "Why did this have to happen to me?" She hated school and played hooky a great deal because she was so ashamed. "I was afraid to recite because of the children's laughing." She had only one friend, a little girl who "invited me to her parties and knew how I felt in school. She used to stand up for me and fight back if the others teased me. She could understand my speech the most. She died when I was 12 and I was heartbroken." Most of the time Mary remained alone or played games with her closest sibling, a brother two years older than herself. When the other siblings were invited to parties from which she was excluded, the mother took her on picnics and tried to comfort her as much as possible. Both the mother and a Christian Science practitioner who took an interest in the child tried to help her speak correctly.

When Mary was 10 years old, her father made sexual advances toward her: "He told me I had to do things like this as no man would ever want me anyway." When this occurred a second time, the child became worried and told her mother. The mother promptly made her husband leave the home, and from then on, was forced to support the children herself.

Although Mary was of average intelligence, her school performance was poor. Because the family had moved so often, she had attended eight different grammar schools. Each change involved new and trying situations with other children. "They made fun of me because of the way I talked and the way I looked and said I wasn't normal." When she was 14 and in the eighth grade, it became necessary for her to go to work.

In applying for jobs, Mary found her appearance to be a considerable handicap. A job in a nursery school was refused her on the grounds that children would take exception to her looks. She was denied a minimal office job because "They wanted someone prettier." The only work she was able to obtain was as a domestic. When she was 15, she decided that she had to face her situation and "make the most of it." She worked harder on her speech and spent her free hours reading in the library to educate herself. She was never included in the activities other adolescents cherished but would go to the movies alone or sometimes with a boy she knew. One day when he made sexual advances to her, she submitted to him, though she regarded her behavior as wrong. "Nevertheless," she said, "I did it because he was the first boy who was nice to me, and since I probably would never have anyone, I decided I might as well." . . .

Mrs. Benchley claimed that her whole life had been greatly influenced by her appearance and by her speech defect. While she found it exceedingly embarrassing and difficult to make people fully understand her when she talked (she carried a slip of paper with her name written on it), she felt that her appearance had been the greater handicap in obtaining jobs and making friends. She stated that not only had people ridiculed her and stared at her, but she had been the victim of pity, questions, jokes, and nicknames. All her life she felt rejected by others because of her deformity, and this caused her to feel depressed, inferior, and anxious. Even so, she persisted in her attempts to cope with her situation. While her second marriage and, particularly, the birth of her child gave her a greater sense of security, and while the friendly neighbor and inclusion in the women's coffee club made her feel more accepted, she was still extremely shy and fearful of strangers or of being in public places.

In some ways Mary Benchley was lucky. She was able to make her appearance acceptable by plastic surgery. After that, the barriers to social participation were down. Sometimes the rejected individual can do very little about the characteristics that reduce his acceptability. The physically handicapped come to mind at once: the blind, the deaf, and the crippled. Perhaps the worst situation of all is that in which the individual hopes he can do something to correct his deficiency but finds he cannot. The pathos of stuttering, for example, comes from the stutterer's desperate effort to speak fluently.

Failing to Meet Standards of Security

The foregoing excerpts are examples of failing to meet standards of gratification. A second standard mentioned in Chapter 1 is that of security; the cultural conception of "belonging." In all societies the individual learns to want to be accepted by other people. But each society answers the question, "Which other people?" and "What kind of acceptance?" in different ways. The following excerpt from a novel about a twelve-year-old Southern girl (Frankie) illustrates the frequent identity crisis at adolescence.[5] In American society the insecurity of adolescents is taken for granted. Still, the psychic pain that accompanies the search for meaningful relationships is real—and helps to explain drug use, delinquency, and assorted forms of adolescent rebellion.

There was in the neighborhood a clubhouse, and Frankie was not a member. The members of the club were girls who were thirteen and fourteen and even fifteen years old. They had parties with boys on Saturday night. Frankie knew all of the club members, and until this summer she had been like a younger member of their crowd, but now they had this club and she was not a member. They had said she was too young and mean. On Saturday night she could hear the terrible music and see from far away their light. Sometimes she went around to the alley behind the clubhouse and stood near a honeysuckle fence. She stood in the alley and watched and listened. They were very long, those parties.

"Maybe they will change their mind and invite you," John Henry said.

"The son-of-a-bitches."

Frankie sniffed and wiped her nose in the crook of her arm. She sat down on the edge of the bed, her shoulders slumped and her elbows resting on her knees. "I think they have been spreading it all over town that I smell bad," she said. "When I had those boils and that black bitter smelling ointment, old Helen Fletcher asked what was that funny smell I had. Oh, I could shoot everyone of them with a pistol."

She heard John Henry walking up to the bed, and then she felt his hand patting her neck with tiny little pats. "I don't think you smell so bad," he said. "You smell sweet."

"The son-of-a-bitches," she said again. "And there was something else. They were talking nasty lies about married people. When I think of Aunt Pet and Uncle Ustace. And my own father! The nasty lies! I don't know what kind of a fool they take me for."

"I can smell you the minute you walk in the house without even looking to see if it is you. Like a hundred flowers."

"I don't care," she said. "I just don't care."

"Like a thousand flowers," said John Henry, and still he was patting his sticky hand on the back of her bent neck.

[5]The selections from Carson McCullers, *The Member of the Wedding*, 1946, pp. 14-15, 39-41, 50-52, 176, are reprinted by permission of and arrangement with Houghton Mifflin Company, Boston, Massachusetts, the authorized publishers.

Frankie sat up, licked the tears from around her mouth, and wiped off her face with her shirttail. She sat still, her nose widened, smelling herself. Then she went to her suitcase and took out a bottle of Sweet Serenade. She rubbed some on the top of her head and poured some more down inside the neck of her shirt.

"Want some on you?"

John Henry was squatting beside the open suitcase and he gave a little shiver when she poured the perfume over him. He wanted to meddle in her traveling suitcase and look carefully at everything she owned. But Frankie only wanted him to get a general impression, and not count and know just what she had and what she did not have. So she strapped the suitcase and pushed it back against the wall.

"Boy!" she said. "I bet I use more perfume than anybody in this town."

... "And you know what Janice remarked?" asked Frankie. "When Papa mentioned about how much I've grown, she said she didn't think I looked so terribly big. She said she got the major portion of her growth before she was thirteen. She did, Berenice!"

"O.K.! All right."

"She said she thought I was a lovely size and would probably not grow any taller. She said all fashion models and movie stars—"

"She did not," said Berenice. "I heard her. She only remarked that you probably had already got your growth. But she didn't go on and on like that. To hear you tell it, anybody would think she took her text on the subject."

"She said—"

"This is a serious fault with you, Frankie. Somebody just makes a loose remark and then you cozen it in your mind until nobody would recognize it. Your Aunt Pet happened to mention to Clorina that you had sweet manners and Clorina passed it on to you. For what it was worth. The next thing I know you are going all around and bragging how Mrs. West thought you had the finest manners in town and ought to go to Hollywood, and I don't know what all you didn't say. You keep building on to any little compliment you hear about yourself. Or, if it is a bad thing, you do the same. You cozen and change things too much in your own mind. And that is a serious fault."

"Quit preaching at me," Frankie said.

"I ain't preaching. It is the solemn truth."

"I admit it a little," said Frankie finally. She closed her eyes and the kitchen was very quiet. She could feel the beating of her heart, and when she spoke her voice was a whisper. "What I need to know is this. Do you think I made a good impression?"

"Impression? Impression?"

"Yes," said Frankie, her eyes still closed.

"Well, how would I know?" said Berenice.

"I mean how did I act? What did I do?"

"Why, you didn't do anything."

"Nothing?" asked Frankie.

"No. You just watched the pair of them like they was ghosts. Then, when they talked about the wedding, them ears of yours stiffened out the size of cabbage leaves—"

Frankie raised her hand to her left ear. "They didn't," she said bitterly. Then after a while she added. "Some day you going to look down and find that big fat tongue of yours pulled out by the roots and laying there before you on the table. Then how do you think you will feel?"

. . . .

. . . For a long time now her brother and the bride had been at Winter Hill. They had left the town a hundred miles behind them, and now were in a city far away. They were them and in Winter Hill, together, while she was her and in the same old town by herself. The long hundred miles did not make her sadder and make her feel more far away than the knowing that they were them and both together and she was only her and parted from them, by herself. And as she sickened with this feeling a thought and explanation suddenly came to her, so that she knew and almost said aloud: *They are the we of me.* Yesterday, and all the twelve years of her life, she had only been Frankie. She was an *I* person who had to walk around and do things by herself. All other people had a *we* to claim, all others except her. When Berenice said *we*, she meant Honey and Big Mama, her lodge, or her church. The *we* of her father was the store. All members of clubs have a *we* to belong to and talk about. The soldiers in the army can say *we*, and even the criminals on chain-gangs. But the old Frankie had had no *we* to claim, unless it would be the terrible summer *we* of her and John Henry and Berenice—and that was the last *we* in the world she wanted. Now all this was suddenly over with and changed. There was her brother and the bride, and it was as though when first she saw them something she had known inside of her: *They are the we of me.* And that was why it made her feel so queer, for them to be away in Winter Hill while she was left all by herself; the hull of the old Frankie left there in the town alone.

"Why are you all bent over like that?" John Henry called.

"I think I have a kind of pain," said Frankie. "I must have ate something."

John Henry was still standing on the banisters, holding to the post.

"Listen," she said finally. "Suppose you come on over and eat supper and spend the night with me."

"I can't," he answered.

"Why?"

John Henry walked across the banisters, holding out his arms for balance, so that he was like a little blackbird against the yellow window light. He did not answer until he safely reached the other post.

"Just because."

"Because why?"

He did not say anything, and so she added: "I thought maybe me and you could put up my Indian tepee and sleep out in the back yard. And have a good time."

Still John Henry did not speak.

"We're blood first cousins. I entertain you all the time. I've given you so many presents."

Quietly, lightly, John Henry walked back across the banisters and then stood looking out at her with his arm around the post again.

"Sure enough," she called. "Why can't you come?"

At last he said. "Because, Frankie, I don't want to."

"Fool jackass!" she screamed. "I only asked you because I thought you looked so ugly and so lonesome."

Lightly John Henry jumped down from the banisters. And his voice as he called back to her was a clear child's voice.

"Why, I'm not a bit lonesome."

Frankie rubbed the wet palms of her hands along the sides of her shorts and said in her mind: Now turn around and take yourself on home. But in spite of this order, she was somehow unable to turn around and go.

. . . .

. . . The wedding was like a dream outside her power, or like a show unmanaged by her in which she was supposed to have no part. The living room was crowded with Winter Hill company, and the bride and her brother stood before the mantelpiece at the end of the room. And seeing them again together was more like singing feeling than a picture that her dizzied eyes could truly see. She watched them with her heart, but all the time she was only thinking: I have not told them and they don't know. And knowing this was heavy as a swallowed stone. And afterward, during the kissing of the bride, refreshments served in the dining room, the stir and party bustle—she hovered close to the two of them, but words would not come. They are not going to take me, she was thinking, and this was the one thought she could not bear.

When Mr. Williams brought their bags, she hastened after with her own suitcase. The rest was like some nightmare show in which a wild girl in the audience breaks onto the stage to take upon herself an unplanned part that was never written or meant to be. You are the we of me, her heart was saying, but could only say aloud: "Take me!" And they pleaded and begged with her, but she was already in the car. At the last she clung to the steering wheel until her father and somebody else had hauled and dragged her from the car, and even then she could only cry in the dust of the empty road: "Take me! Take me!" But there was only the wedding company to hear, for the bride and her brother had driven away.

Clearly, Frankie could not solve her problems by accompanying her brother and her sister-in-law on their honeymoon. But how else could she be a full-fledged human being? She felt big and clumsy; she thought she had an unpleasant body odor; she knew that the older girls did not want her in their club; there were some "nasty lies" about older people that she did not understand. Eventually, the reader smiles, Frankie's troubles will disappear; in two or three years they will be only a painful memory. But new insecurities are possible. Consider, for example, the anxieties that some women develop because they think that they are no longer "single" but an unplucked blossom on the family tree. In the following scene from William Inge's play, *Picnic*,[6] desperate effort is expended to deal with this insecurity. Rosemary, a school teacher, does not want to be an "old maid," and she regards Howard as her last chance at matrimony.

Howard: Honey, you're not yourself tonight.

Rosemary: Yes, I am. I'm more myself than I ever was. Take me with you, Howard. If you don't I don't know what I'll do with myself. I mean it.

Howard: Now look, Honey, you better go upstairs and get some sleep. You gotta start school in the morning. We'll talk this over Saturday.

Rosemary: Maybe you won't be back Saturday. Maybe you won't be back ever again.

Howard: Rosemary, you know better than that.

Rosemary: Then what's the next thing in store for me? To be nice to the next man, then the next—till there's no one left to care whether I'm nice to him or not. Till I'm ready for the grave and don't have anyone to take me there.

Howard (in an attempt to be consoling):   Now Rosemary!

Rosemary: You can't let that happen to me, Howard. I won't let you.

Howard: I don't understand. When we first started going together, you were the best sport I ever saw, always good for a laugh.

Rosemary (in a hollow voice):   I can't laugh any more.

Howard: We'll talk it over Saturday.

Rosemary: We'll talk it over *now*.

Howard (squirming):   Well—Honey—I . . .

Rosemary: You said you were gonna marry me, Howard. You said when I got back from my vacation, you'd be waitin' with the preacher.

Howard: Honey, I've had an awful busy summer and . . .

Rosemary: Where's the preacher, Howard? Where is he?

Howard (walking away from her):   Honey, I'm forty-two years old. A person forms certain ways of livin', then one day it's too late to change.

Rosemary (grabbing his arm and holding him):   Come back here, Howard. I'm

[6]From *Picnic*, by William Inge, pp. 76-79. Copyright 1953 by William Inge. Reprinted by permission of Random House, Inc., New York.

no spring chicken either. Maybe I'm a little older than you think *I* am. I've formed my ways too. But they can be changed. They *gotta* be changed. It's no good livin' like this, in rented rooms, meetin' a bunch of old maids for supper every night, then comin' back home alone.

Howard: *I* know how it is, Rosemary. My life's no bed of roses either.

Rosemary: Then why don't you do something about it?

Howard: I figure—there's some bad things about every life.

Rosemary: There's too much bad about mine. Each year, I keep tellin' myself, is the last. Something'll happen. Then nothing ever does—except I get a little crazier all the time.

Howard (hopelessly):   Well . . .

Rosemary: A *well*'s a hole in the ground, Howard. Be careful you don't fall in.

Howard: I wasn't tryin' to be funny.

Rosemary: . . . and all this time you just been leadin' me on.

Howard (defensive):   Rosemary, that's not *so!* I've not been leading you *on.*

Rosemary: I'd like to know what else you call it.

Howard: Well—can't we talk about it Saturday? I'm dead tired and I got a busy week ahead, and . . .

Rosemary (she grips' him by the arm and looks straight into his eyes):   You gotta marry me, Howard.

Howard (tortured):   Well—Honey, I can't marry you, *now.*

Rosemary: You can be over here in the morning.

Howard: Sometimes you're unreasonable.

Rosemary: You gotta marry me.

Howard: What'll you do about your job?

Rosemary: Alvah Jackson can take my place till they get someone new from the agency.

Howard: I'll have to pay Fred Jenkins to take care of the store for a few days.

Rosemary: Then get him.

Howard: Well . . .

Rosemary: I'll be waitin' for you in the morning, Howard.

Howard (after a few moments' troubled thought):   No.

Rosemary (a muffled cry):   Howard!

Howard: I'm not gonna marry anyone that says, "You gotta marry me, Howard." I'm not gonna. *(He is silent. Rosemary weeps pathetic tears. Slowly Howard reconsiders.)* If a woman wants me to marry her—she can at least say "please."

Rosemary (beaten and humble):   "Please" marry me, Howard.

Howard: Well—you got to give me time to think it over.

Rosemary (desperate):   Oh, God! Please marry me, Howard. Please . . . *(She sinks to her knees.)* Please . . . please . . .

Howard (embarrassed by her suffering humility):   Rosemary . . . I . . . I gotta have some time to think it over. You go to bed now and get some rest. I'll drive over in the morning and maybe we can talk it over before you go to school. I . . .

Rosemary: You're not just tryin' to get out of it, Howard?

Howard: I'll be over in the morning, Honey.

Rosemary: Honest?

Howard: Yah. I gotta go to the courthouse anyway. We'll talk it over then.

Rosemary: Oh, God, please marry me, Howard. Please.

Howard (trying to get away):   Go to bed, Honey. I'll see you in the morning.

Rosemary: Please, Howard!

Howard: I'll see you in the morning. Good night, Rosemary. *(Starting off.)*

Rosemary (in a meek voice):   Please!

Howard: Good night, Rosemary.

Frankie and Rosemary suffered from the absence of that security which comes from personal care and belonging. But American norms emphasize a different source of security than membership in a solidary group. They emphasize, especially for men, the security that comes from having the ability to make it *worth other people's while* to meet one's needs. Security, in this sense, is a skill that is in demand by others.

Not having such a skill generates the pain of failing to meet *appreciative* standards, as in the case of the migrant Brents and the aged Ed MacIntosh. But that pain is not only the pain of being broke. Being poor is also the pain of failing to conform to the American *sine qua non* of security—having something someone else is willing to pay you for with respect as well as with money. The American poor are worthless in the straightforward sense that what they have to offer is worth little or nothing to others. And to feel worthless is painful indeed.

The anthropologist Elliot Liebow studied street-corner men in Washington, D.C. who felt that pain. Liebow's report reflects the insecurity of life on the street corner where Tally, Liebow's major informant, hung out.[7]

Lethargy, disinterest and general apathy on the job, so often reported by employers, has its street-corner counterpart. The men do not ordinarily talk about their jobs or ask one another about them. Although most of the men know who is or is not working at any given time, they may or may not know what particular job an individual man has. There is no overt interest in job specifics as they relate to this or that person, in large part perhaps because the specifics are not especially relevant. To know that a man is working is to know approximately how much he makes and to know as much as one needs or wants

[7]From Elliot Liebow, *Tally's Corner*, Boston: Little, Brown & Co., 1968, pp. 56-59, 61-63. Reprinted by permission. Copyright © 1967 by Little, Brown and Company (Inc.).

to know about how he makes it. After all, how much difference does it make to know whether a man is pushing a mop and pulling trash in an apartment house, a restaurant, or an office building, or delivering groceries, drugs, or liquor, or, if he's a laborer, whether he's pushing a wheelbarrow, mixing mortar, or digging a hole. So much does one job look like every other that there is little to choose between them. In large part, the job market consists of a narrow range of nondescript chores calling for nondistinctive undifferentiated, unskilled labor. "A job is a job."

A crucial factor in the streetcorner man's lack of job commitment is the overall value he places on the job. *For his part, the streetcorner man puts no lower value on the job than does the larger society around him.* He knows the social value of the job by the amount of money the employer is willing to pay him for doing it. In a real sense, every pay day, he counts in dollars and cents the value placed on the job by society at large. He is no more (and frequently less) ready to quit and look for another job than his employer is ready to fire him and look for another man. Neither the streetcorner man who performs these jobs nor the society which requires him to perform them assesses the job as one "worth doing and worth doing well." Both employee and employer are contemptuous of the job. The employee shows his contempt by his reluctance to accept it or keep it, the employer by paying less than is required to support a family. Nor does the low-wage job offer prestige, respect, interesting work, opportunity for learning or advancement, or any other compensation. With few exceptions, jobs filled by the streetcorner men are at the bottom of the employment ladder in every respect, from wage level to prestige. Typically, they are hard, dirty, uninteresting and underpaid. The rest of society (whatever its ideal values regarding the dignity of labor) holds the job of the dishwasher or janitor or unskilled laborer in low esteem if not outright contempt. So does the streetcorner man. He cannot do otherwise. He cannot draw from a job those social values which other people do not put into it. . . .

Tally and I were in the Carry-out. It was summer, Tally's peak earning season as a cement finisher, a semiskilled job a cut or so above that of the unskilled laborer. His take-home pay during these weeks was well over a hundred dollars—"a lot of bread." But for Tally, who no longer had a family to support, bread was not enough.

> "You know that boy came in last night? That Black Moozlem? That's what I ought to be doing. I ought to be in his place."
>
> "What do you mean?"
>
> "Dressed nice, going to [night] school, got a good job."
>
> "He's no better off than you, Tally. You make more than he does."
>
> "It's not the money. [Pause] It's position, I guess. He's got position. When he finish school he gonna be a supervisor. People respect him. . . . Thinking

about people with position and education gives me a feeling right here [pressing his fingers into the pit of his stomach]."

"You're educated, too. You have a skill, a trade. You're a cement finisher. You can make a building, pour a sidewalk."

"That's different. Look, can anybody do what you're doing? Can anybody just come up and do your job? Well, in one week I can teach you cement finishing. You won't be as good as me 'cause you won't have the experience but you'll be a cement finisher. That's what I mean. Anybody can do what I'm doing and that's what gives me this feeling. [Long pause] Suppose I like this girl. I go over to her house and I meet her father. He starts talking about what he done today. He talks about operating on somebody and sewing them up and about surgery. I know he's a doctor 'cause of the way he talks. Then she starts talking about what she did. Maybe she's a boss or a supervisor. Maybe she's a lawyer and her father says to me, 'And what do you do, Mr. Jackson?' [Pause] You remember at the courthouse, Lonny's trial? You and the lawyer was talking in the hall? You remember? I just stood there listening. I didn't say a word. You know why? 'Cause I didn't even know what you was talking about. That's happened to me a lot."

"Hell, you're nothing special. That happens to everybody. Nobody knows everything. One man is a doctor, so he talks about surgery. Another man is a teacher, so he talks about books. But doctors and teachers don't know anything about concrete. You're a cement finisher and that's your specialty."

"Maybe so, but when was the last time you saw anybody standing around talking about concrete?"

Failing to Meet Standards of Adequacy

It is painful not to have the good things (including good bodies) one's culture praises, and it is painful to lack the solidarities and general approval one's culture implies one should have. A related kind of pain comes from failing to meet cultural standards of adequacy. Inept fishermen in a fishing village feel such pain as did, no doubt, cave men clumsy at ax-wielding. The likelihood of such pain is increased when competence is defined not in terms of a standard of adequacy at fishing or ax-wielding or automobile assembly, but in terms of being better than others *in general*. When it is not being good at one's job that entitles one to a sense of competence but rather being good *at competing for good jobs*, frustration is more likely. Thus, the American occupational system—because it generates a hierarchy of occupational prestige—increases the tendency to feel inadequate. Americans are competitively ranked not only in terms of the jobs they hold but in other ways such as "intelligence." How smart are we supposed to be? As close to the smartest as possible. With respect to those who are dumb, we do not say, "They happen to have certain qualities but not others." We do not even say, "There but for the grace of God go I." We are more likely to say, "Ugh!" But if those of normal intelligence respond in this way, so also do those who do not measure up to cultural standards of intellectual competence; such standards are part of *their* culture also. The problem is worst for those intellectually aware that they are not intellectually competent *enough*. The "mentally retarded," then, have the double burden of their comparative incompetence and the *additional* pain of stigmatization, as is shown in the following passage from Edgerton's book, *The Cloak of Competence.* [8]

We, in our everyday affairs, regularly and easily accuse others and ourselves of stupidity. We joke about real or fancied incompetence, we estimate the IQ's of our friends and foes, we make invidious comparisons of all kinds about the intelligence of many persons with whom we come into contact. Usually we mean little by these remarks and usually neither we nor the victims of our speculations or accusations suffer very much as a result.

For the ex-patient of an institution for the mentally retarded, however, matters are very different. The ex-patient *must* take his intelligence very seriously, for he has been accused and found guilty of being so stupid that he was considered incompetent to manage his own life. As a consequence, he has been confined in an institution for the mentally incompetent. This research has shown, and our common sense would agree, that such an accusation of stupidity has a shattering impact. The stigma of having been adjudged a mental retardate is one which the ex-patients in this study reject as totally unacceptable. Hence, their lives are directed toward the fundamental purpose of denying that they are in fact mentally incompetent. These former patients must at all times attend to the practical problems of seeming to others to be competent and of convincing themselves that this is so. The label of mental retardation not only serves as a humiliating, frustrating, and discrediting stigma in the conduct of one's life in the community, but it also serves to lower one's self-esteem to such a nadir of worthlessness that the life of a person so labeled is scarcely worth living. Thus the "moron" who is released from Pacific State Hospital must "deny," must "pass" with himself. He cannot, and he does not, accept the official "fact" that he is, or ever was, mentally retarded.

To understand the processes of passing and denial in the period following the ex-patients' release from the institution, we must first review prior events in the life experiences of these persons. In an earlier study, the pre-hospital and

[8]From Robert Edgerton, *The Cloak of Competence*, Berkeley: University of California Press, 1967, pp. 144-150, 153-165. Reprinted by permission of The Regents of the University of California.

hospital careers of the same patients who formed the cohort for this research were examined. It was rarely possible to reconstruct the pre-hospital biographies of these patients in adequate detail, yet it was possible to determine that their pre-hospital experiences were typically highly mortifying. These experiences commonly involved both direct and indirect communication by normal persons to the retarded person to the effect that his or her intelligence was deficient. Parents, peers, teachers, neighbors, and even strangers presented a consistent refrain of rejection and humiliation. Notwithstanding this concerted onslaught, the retardate resisted the accusation that he was mentally retarded, and he usually found allies in the form of parents or peers who would aid him in denying that his intellect was subnormal.

However, entry into Pacific State Hospital presents the retarded person with a new dilemma. Although he is by now thoroughly familiar with mortification and has probably developed means of self-defense against suggestions of mental deficit, he is surely not prepared for the experiences that the hospital will inflict upon him. The cumulative impact of the initial period of hospitalization (at the time of the research) was greatly mortifying, leaving the patient without privacy, without clear identity, without autonomy of action, without relatives, friends, or family, in a regimented and impersonal institution where everything combines to inform him that he is, in fact, mentally inadequate. A typical patient reaction is seen in the following words of a teen-age boy who was newly admitted to the institution: "Why do I got to be here with these people? I'd rather be dead than in here."

At this point, when the hospital's impact has taken full effect, the patient's self-esteem has probably reached its low point. However, at this critical point, circumstances arise to provide the patient with an opportunity to aggrandize himself and reconstruct his damaged self-esteem. This opportunity results from (1) the presence in the hospital of large numbers of manifestly severely retarded persons with whom comparisons of intellectual ability may profitably be made— the newly admitted mildly retarded person is clearly superior to most of the more severely retarded patients in the hospital, thus it is not surprising that he concludes that he does not really belong in a hospital that contains such patients; (2) friendly, accepting peer-group relationships that, in comparison with pre-hospital relationships, sustain a positive conception of self—these relationships often provide the patient with the first instances of acceptance by peers that he has ever experienced; (3) contacts with well-meaning employees who encourage favorable self-esteem—many of these employees not only provide acceptance and affection but also do much to provide authoritative assurance that the patient truly is not retarded.

The patients in the research cohort, then, had an opportunity to rebuild and even to aggrandize their self-esteem while in the hospital. Nonetheless, they felt acutely uncomfortable about being in the hospital and hoped for release. There is no necessary contradiction implied. The patients were able to aggrandize their self-esteem by being in the hospital, but a vital feature of their own aggrandizement was their contention that they did not belong there in the first place. In addition, the patients seldom appreciated either hospital confinement or its regulations. As a result, freedom from institutional confinement was a primary goal for every patient in the cohort.[9]

Release, when it came, was always received as an expression of justice, long overdue. Again and again, the words "I never belonged there in the first place" were recorded. As one ex-patient put it: "I was never mental like the others that couldn't remember nothing or do nothing." Members of the cohort commonly saw their release as confirmation of the error of the original diagnosis of mental retardation that had sent them there, and as affirmation of their right as "normal" persons to live their own lives, "without anybody telling me what to do." Release from the hospital was indeed the beginning of their right to live "like anybody else," but it was emphatically not the end of their problems, nor of their need for passing and denial. They now had to face the multiple challenges of living independently in the "outside" world. Each former patient knew that failure to meet these challenges would not only be ruinous to self-esteem—it might also lead to a forcible return to the hospital. Consequently, the outside world was entered cautiously and fearfully.

One of the first needs of the ex-patients was concealment of their institutional history, a "past" which, if revealed, could be gravely discrediting. This concealment was regularly attempted through a stereotyped "tale" which explained and excused their confinement in the hospital by revealing the "real" reason they were there. Such excuses were collected from all of the forty-eight ex-patients. The excuses fell into nine categories. The excuses, with the number of persons who gave them, are as follows: "nerves" (2), mental illness (2), alcoholism (3), epilepsy (4), sex delinquency (5), criminal offenses (5), physical illness—usually a need for surgery—(7), need for education (8), and the enmity of, or abandonment by, parent or relative (12). The first four categories of excuses admit of some degree of mental or physical abnormality; the last five excuses admit nothing more than errors of conduct, and sometimes admit nothing at all. Examples of a typical excuse within each category:

"Nerves": "I don't miss that institution. I should have been put out of there years ago; they shouldn't have kept me in there like they did. That's what I think. They kept me too long. I only went there 'cause I was nervous, but they kept me so long I got worse. They ruined my life. Those people in that

_____
[9] A few patients were not eager to be discharged from hospital supervision after they were living in a community on "work leave" status, but all patients in the cohort wanted to leave the confines of the hospital itself.

institution was much worse than me. I'm just as good as anyone in there or anybody I've seen on the outside."

Mental illness: "That place was horrible. Everybody there was crazy. You know, there was one girl that actually ate a table—took bites right out of a table. Another girl stood on her head and drank milk. I was a little crazy myself, that's why I went there, I guess. But I got over it OK."

Alcoholism: "I used to be a pretty heavy drinker. Now I kind of control myself a little bit. That's why I went to that institution. The drinking mostly brought it on. When I stopped drinking I got out OK."

Epilepsy: "Well, the hospital was good in some ways—I made friends with the girls, but I really didn't belong with those other patients. (Why?) Well, they're mental, you know. Low mental."

Sex delinquency: "When I was younger I used to make mistakes with boys. I was put in that hospital so's I could learn to behave myself with boys. I done OK. You learn when you get older. But I sure didn't belong in there with all those dopey people."

Criminal behavior: "Yeah, I was in there because of the robberies I was doing when I was a kid. Cops caught me, so I was sent up to that place. I was never supposed to be there with those mental patients. I was there because of those robberies, you know."

Physical illness: "That hospital was OK. If it wasn't for that place I wouldn't be alive today. I went in when I was only fifteen and I had three surgical operations. I was only there on the surgery ward because of my kidneys. I didn't have nothing to do with them handicapped patients."

Need for education: "Well, that place didn't do me no good. I was sent there to go to school because I missed lots of school when I was little. But I didn't get much schooling in there. Might just as well not of been there. I never belonged in a place with all those low-grade patients. I was just there for my schooling."

Enmity of, or abandonment by, a parent or relative: "I got plenty of kick coming. I spent five years in that hole just because my stepfather always hated me. As soon as my mother died he got together with some doctor and framed me into that place. I never should of been in no place like that full of those mentally handicapped patients. Those people need to be there because they can't take care of themselves. Hell, look at me. I can take care of myself OK. It was a real frame-up to put me in that place."

Entering the world outside the hospital, or as the ex-patients put it, "life on the outs," means facing an often bewildering array of demands for competence. The reaction to this initial contact with the outside world is typically a kind of "release shock." All patients experienced this shock. Some reacted by exaggerated attempts to remain inconspicuous: "I didn't say nothing to nobody. I would just listen and stay out of the way. After work I'd come straight home and stay in my room. Sometimes I'd be shakin' all over by the time I got home." Others sought a personal guide to direct their actions in the earliest days: "I was all confused, sort of puzzled up. I don't know what I'd done if Mrs. — hadn't of shown me the ropes. I just didn't know how to do nothing. Mrs. — had to show me how to shop and go places and everything. Oh boy, I was real scared in those days." All remarked that this period of release shock was extremely difficult for them. A man who married another cohort member remembers it this way: "I did twelve years in that hospital, so I know what rough times is like, but it was even tougher outside. A man's got to worry about working every day and stuff. Ain't nobody going to feed you on the outside. It wasn't no cherries for us, I'll tell you." . . .

FINDING A MATE

For many reasons, it is imperative that the ex-patient find a mate—if possible, a marriage partner. Ideally this mate should be a normal person. A woman discussed the matter this way: "Every girl wants to marry an outside guy. I know I did. I tried everything to find one. I bought nice clothes and tried to talk right, and I went to nice places. And I didn't go around with no hospital guys either. When I finally married an outside guy I knew my troubles were over." A man sees it as follows: "A guy usually wants to get married, but mostly he can't meet no outside girls. He can only get hospital girls or whores or something. I'm still single because I ain't found no outside girl yet." Another woman states the matter as succinctly as is possible; when asked if she knew another ex-patient in the cohort she said: "Oh yeah, she's doing real good. She's really made good. She married an outside guy."

Many of the ex-patients are satisfied to be married to anyone, even another ex-patient. A man said, "Before I was married I never used to have the same kind of life as other people. I was left out of so many things. Now that I got my wife (an ex-patient) I feel like I'm OK. I feel like I'm just as good as anybody." Another woman made her feelings plain when she answered the question "Are you happy?" by saying incredulously, "Well, I'm married, ain't I?"

Marriage for the ex-retardate is a highly meaningful status to achieve. Not only does it partake of most of the meanings it possesses for normal persons, it also serves dramatically to emphasize their newly won status as free and full members of the outside world. As patients in the hospital they had been denied the right to marry, or to bear children. By the time of the research, all but fourteen of the forty-eight cohort members had married. But bearing children continued to be a problem.

Forty-four of the forty-eight ex-patients had undergone "eugenic" sterilization before their release from the hospital. Indeed, during the period of their institutionalization, sterilization was generally viewed by the administration as a prerequisite to release. The form letter sent to parents or guardians to request permission for the operation stated, *inter alia*, that sterilization would "permit parole, leave of absence, and visits with less fear of undesirable complications." Consequently, unless there was a profoundly negative reaction on the part of a relative or guardian, surgical sterilization of both males and females was routinely performed.[10]

A few ex-patients, almost without exception the single men, approved of sterilization on the grounds that it gave them greater freedom to enjoy sexual relations without fear of pregnancy. As one male put it, "It ain't so bad. This way I can play around with the girls and I don't have to worry about getting into no trouble." However, most of the ex-patients held strongly negative feelings about sterilization. They objected to it because it suggested to them their mortifying, degrading, and punishing past; sterilization for them had become an ineradicable mark of their institutional past. As such, it served as a permanent source of self-doubt about their mental status. One woman gave expression to this doubt in the following typical fashion: "I still don't know why they did that surgery to me. The sterilization wasn't for punishment, was it? Was it because there was something wrong with my mind?" Another woman gave these words to her torment: "I love kids. Sometimes now when I baby-sit, I hold the baby up to myself and I cry and I think to myself, 'Why was I ever sterilized?' "

But more important to the present discussion is the extent to which sterilization impedes the course of "passing." As the following characteristic remarks should indicate, it sometimes does so to a marked degree:

(A woman) "Naturally, when a girl comes out of the hospital and meets a guy and gets married—well, if she is sterilized, then the guy wonders why she can't have no children. She's either got to tell the guy the truth or lie to him and say, 'Well, I had an accident,' or something."

(A woman) "Two or three times I could've got married but I didn't dare tell the man I was sterilized. How could I tell a man a thing like that?"

(Another woman) "I was all engaged to marry a man that I really loved. He loved me, too, but one day we were sitting and talking with his mother and father and they were saying how happy they would be when we were married and had children. I couldn't do it, because his parents wanted us to have children. When I heard this, I said, 'No, I don't never want to get married.' I almost told her (the mother) why but I just couldn't bear to tell her."

Another sterilized woman lies to all her friends, telling them that she has a seventeen-year-old daughter. She says, "I feel like being in that hospital wrecked my life. They made it so I can't have kids."

[10]Not only is eugenic sterilization no longer performed at Pacific State Hospital as a routine prerequisite to release, but currently employed medical and psychological criteria for performing such surgery are so demanding that very few patients are now being sterilized.

Women regularly explain the prominent abdominal sterilization scar to their husbands or lovers as the result of an appendectomy. "When I first had, you know, sex with a guy after getting out (of the hospital), I could just feel him looking at my scar and wondering what it was. I was gonna cover it up, but then I thought that would look bad, so I told him it was my appendix scar. He believed me OK." This is a nice irony, since sterilization surgery at the hospital was usually described to the patient as an appendectomy rather than what it actually was.

Men, too, can suffer this same dilemma. One man was inordinately proud that he had courted and married a normal girl. He had revealed nothing of his past to her, least of all his sterilization. But after several childless years of marriage, he was feeling immense guilt and anxiety about his infertility. "It almost worried me to death. I was scared she would find out about me and divorce me." Then, without his knowledge, his wife went to a doctor and discovered that *she* could not have children. He was tremendously relieved and has still not told his wife anything about his own sterility.

It is evident, then, that sterilization can complicate the problems of passing by standing as a permanent and visible mark of a secret and humiliating institutional past.

Those born less competent mentally than their society's standards call for suffer in ways the reading has described. But almost everyone is less competent that his society's standards call for. For some, it may happen suddenly, as when technological change makes irrelevant an occupational competence on which one prided oneself. For others, it happens slowly, as the process of aging inexorably erodes competences. Fast or slow, occupational inadequacy is painful, as the reader learns in the following excerpt from a novel, *The Square Trap.*[11] In the novel a middle-aged Mexican-American (Vidal) resolves to end dependence on unemployment compensation by resuming an old trade, sandal making.

Vidal began to walk toward Spring and Second Streets, and as he walked he felt some of the old purpose in his step, the rush of excitement which had always made his heart pound before the first morning of a new job, which might be the job that would mean his security and good fortune. Everything was happening as it should and he walked rapidly, humming to himself, feeling alive and vital, full of plans.

... On Spring Street he ... finally chose to enter a store whose windows advertised second-hand machinery, tools, and cut-rate leather findings. The raw smell of hides and leather stirred memories long dormant, and with excited gestures Vidal touched the spools of waxed thread, the supple and stiff leathers,

---

[11]From Irving Shulman, *The Square Trap*, Boston: Little, Brown, & Co., 1953, pp. 224-228. Copyright 1953, by Irving Shulman. Reprinted by permission.

cans of wax and polish, and the hand tools of his trade, much better and finer than those he had used as a boy. But he recognized the tools, knew what they were for, and this knowledge made him feel like striking himself proudly on the chest. A trade was never forgotten. A trade was an everlasting gift. A trade was a heritage.

Deliberately, with great care, he put aside leathers for soles and uppers, choosing them for strength, texture, and finish, and picked over inner linings, thongs, waxed threads, heels, buckles, needles, cutting and shaping knives, augers, tacks, and several patterns.

. . . [When he had selected the items he could afford, Vidal thanked the clerk and said], "Please put them in a strong bag for me."

"You don't want them wrapped?"

Vidal shook his head and laughed. "A strong bag. I want to look at what I've bought."

. . . In the street Vidal hefted the bag, enjoyed its weight, and wondered what Rosa would say when she saw him spread the patterns, leather, and tools on the kitchen table. And as he conjured and saw the tableau, his excitement and optimism began to leave him. His wife might think he was a fool but she would never say so. What Pepe thought didn't matter. Helen and Tomas would not approve of his plan, would think it was stupid and impractical. Furthermore, they would say to him: He, who preached constantly about saving money, had gone off and foolishly squandered almost ten dollars. After this had been thoroughly yelled out, they would begin to insult the old country and the old days and tell him there was no room in the United States for skilled handicrafts, at least not for people of their class.

They couldn't be right. They didn't dare to be right. But maybe they were right and as Vidal considered this unhappy possibility he realized that he needed some fortification for his courage, and in a drugstore he bought a bottle of wine, uncorked the bottle in a doorway, raised the lip to his mouth and took a long drink. Then another drink. Then a third one, but not quite as long. Still the doubts persisted. In ten minutes Vidal had finished the bottle and although he felt lighter on his feet he had not been able to recapture the first enthusiasm which had warmed far more and far better than the wine.

. . . He muttered aloud to himself and noticed his lips and tongue seemed to be thick and expression was difficult. Tonight he wanted to explain very carefully and thoroughly to his family his reasons for buying the articles in the paper bag. Another bottle of wine—just half a pint—was what he needed and he still had enough money in his pocket to buy one.

With considerable gravity Vidal greeted his family, placed the bag on the kitchen table, and sat down heavily.

"We were worried," his wife said to him. "Shall I put away your hat?"

"If you want to," Vidal replied. "I'm not going out any more tonight. . . .

It's very warm in here, Rosa. Very warm."

His wife hurried to open the back door and the kitchen window.

"Help your mother, Pepe," Vidal barked at his son.

Pepe stood up as if getting to his feet were a nuisance. "Sure, Pop."

Vidal restrained himself; this wasn't the time for quarrels or shouting. . . . "Do you want to know what I've done?" he asked his wife and daughter. "Would you like to see what I have in the bag? Would you Pepe?"

"We would," Helen replied and calmed her mother's anxiety by a quick look and wave of the hand.

Helen, Pepe, and their mother crowded around the table and watched Vidal remove his shoemaking supplies, tools, and patterns from the bag. And as Vidal arranged them on the table, Rosa started as she saw the leather and shoemaker's twine, but Helen again restrained her mother with a touch on the arm. Pepe pursed his lips and shook his head; this was a new pitch for his father.

"You know what these are?" Vidal pointed to the spread-out articles on the table.

His wife nodded and turned away as she replied, "To make shoes."

"Sandals," Vidal corrected her as he stood up, swayed, and sat down quickly. Although it was difficult to be impressive sitting down, it was safer. "These are the tools and materials of my craft. You remember, Rosa?" he asked her, "how well I made sandals?"

His wife looked anxiously at her daughter as the glimmerings of Vidal's purpose penetrated her bewilderment. "You have gotten a job with a shoemaker?" she asked hopefully.

Vidal smiled drunkenly. "Better than a job," he said to her, "I am going into business for myself. I am going to become a maker of sandals."

"Father!" Helen stared at him with amused anger.

"Geez, Pop, you're kiddin'," Pepe said to him.

. . . As they watched in silence Vidal removed his coat, loosened his tie, and rolled the sleeves of his shirt. Individually and as a group, they feared the tragedy which was about to take place, yet none could stop its performance . . . [They watched him] blink his eyes as he opened one of the patterns, smoothed it on the table, and stagger as he held the pattern in place with both hands. Breathing heavily he stared at the designs, oriented them, and looked for a moment at his family. They were no encouragement to him as he chose a piece of hard leather for the soles, and almost like a magician who is about to pull a rabbit from his hat showed it to Pepe before he placed it underneath the pattern. With great and deliberate care he began to choose a knife, but an uncertain movement of his hand swept all the tools from the table to the floor.

"Vidal—" his wife kneeled to help him recover the tools—"show us tomorrow. It would be a better time."

"This very night!" Vidal shouted and flung the tools on the table. "That was an accident. Every shoemaker needs more than a table to work on. And I'll show you," he said with emphatic challenge, "that I can still make sandals."

He ruined one section of leather.

Then Vidal tore the pattern. Stubbornly, and with anger, he cut into the leather and traced the rough outline of a sole, but nothing seemed to come right to him. The tools were strange, as if he had never used them before, and he was unable to cut the sharp and precise sections required for a pair of sandals. His wife, sons, and daughter watched silently, knowing they could not stop him and alarmed by the thought of what might happen if they attempted an interruption of this labor by which their father attempted to prove to them that he was still master of his household. And they watched him as they might have a sorry and grotesque comedy single, in which the performer is incompetent, unskilled, and ill versed in his part, but determined, despite the catcalls and jeers of the audience, to play his role through to the last gesture and point of punctuation.

Slowly Vidal raised his hands and turned them. There were his fingers: thickened, scarred, and stiff with age and the punishment of unyielding manual labor; these were the fingers and hands of a sandalmaker. And he had forgotten much. But his hands: the blunt nails; the crooked middle and index fingers of his left hand, broken by a falling crate and set by a friend so they had not healed properly; the crisscross ridges of scars caused by brambles and thorns and gravel; the thickened calloused rings of flesh on his palms. His hands; ugly and crippled, unable to measure up to the demands he made of them.

"I can't do it," he admitted to his family.

Something had to be said, but no one knew what to say.

"I can't do it," Vidal repeated, "I've wasted the money," he looked at the laden table. "Everything," he swept the leather, pattern, and tools to the floor. "Everything."

"It's all right," his wife whispered. "It's all right, Vidal."

"I can't go on," Vidal turned his hands slowly. "I can't—I can't make sandals. My hands are dead."

The painful feeling of being inadequate intellectually or occupationally is easily understood. The feeling of sexual inadequacy, though common and very painful, is more likely to be mistaken for some other problem. A psychiatrist reports in a popular magazine on a case of a woman who feared she was "frigid."[12]

Mary came to me first with the kind of report I hear so often. She just felt "awful." She was tired all the time but she couldn't sleep at night. She stayed up

[12]From Anonymous, "The Doctor Talks about Frigidity," © McCall's 1957. Reprinted by permission.

later and later, but when she finally did smoke the last cigarette and read the last magazine and put out the light she still wasn't sleepy. The slightest rustle, the sound of a car in the street might wake her again.

Mary didn't feel like eating and she did look thin. She had lost fifteen pounds in her five years of marriage. She was worried about her temper. She loved her child, yet often she knew that she treated her as if she were nothing but badness and trouble. Then tossed in as if an afterthought, she added the statement: "I don't have any interest in sex *at all*."

Though it came last, I was sure that Mary's worry about no longer getting pleasure, fulfillment, release and greater closeness to her husband through the sexual relationship was enough to trigger all her other complaints.

It was some time before Mary admitted that her husband too seemed uninterested in sex. She was sure he was disappointed in their marriage and would be having an affair with someone else if he could afford the time and money.

Finally, after she had given me approximately fifty more reasons why their marriage didn't work, she came back to the point. She asked, "How often *should* you have sexual relations?"

I told her that I didn't know how often she *or* her husband should have sexual relations. "But suppose you tell me how often you do?" Mary told me that they rarely ever did. In fact, she said, she had just about given up trying because Roger was so obviously uninterested. Mary was convinced that he didn't love her at all.

I was reasonably certain that this wasn't true, but I told Mary it was important to try to find out how their life had deteriorated to the bad state which she described. . . .

It was not until after their daughter Wendy was born that the lonely nights began to tell on Mary and the extra strain of responsibility and the extra hours that went with it began to have their effect on Roger. Probably because she had more time to think, Mary noticed a difference. Roger seemed preoccupied and indifferent. More and more Mary would find Roger asleep when she came to bed. Sometimes Mary would try to wake him.

One night after giving the baby her eleven-o'clock feeding she felt especially affectionate to Roger and succeeded in arousing him. But he could not make love to her. After this experience she felt that Roger was no longer interested in her. She attributed the episode to her own inadequacy as a sexual partner. For Roger it was equally devastating. He began to avoid Mary for fear of a repetition of this humiliating experience.

Mary redoubled her efforts to interest Roger in order to prove to herself that she, at least, was still normally interested in sex. Of course the results were unsatisfying for her, because she was too preoccupied to enjoy herself or consider her partner. She found she was *feeling* less and less. The less she felt, the more anxious she became and the less important the sexual experience became to her as an expression of love. With the real inability to experience sexual pleasure came a new and overpowering fear—frigidity. This was what brought her to my office. . . .

The first thing I did for both of these two young people was to assure them that they were normal in every way. Roger, like Mary, was well educated in the textbooks and believed that a really virile man should be able to make love to his wife on demand, patiently stimulating her interest to match his own. Mary, for her part, believed that she should always be excited at the thought of sexual relations and should always reach a climax.

As a matter of fact, many marriages start off this way. A young woman in love and recently married may be stimulated merely by the thought of her husband when she feels a very deep need for him. The progress of her sexual excitement is not impeded by thoughts of work, children, responsibilities, worry about bills or anything else. Neither is her husband's.

But there comes a point in marriage, as there did in Mary's, where strain or worry or fatigue affects one or the other or both the partners. Something alters the sexual drive. In Roger's case it was too much work and uncertainty about his ability to be an adequate father so soon.

This should have been no problem, except that Mary was living up to unreal standards of sexual behavior. Judging her husband's performance by those standards, she concluded that his lack of interest was induced by her inadequacy. He concluded that his tiredness and lowered sexual vitality were evidence of his failure as a man. Because he couldn't bear that failure he tried to avoid making love to his wife.

Mary and Roger felt sexually inadequate because they judged themselves in terms of *romantic* standards of erotic performance. The books they had read and the movies they had seen had not provided them with a *realistic* basis for married love. Nothing was wrong with their perceptions; the trouble lay in the definitions of sexual adequacy provided by American culture.

Failing to Meet Standards of Conformity to Legitimate Authority

Cultural standards say to people, "This is the good life; and if you don't enjoy it, too bad for you." They also say, "This is how to be secure, and if you can't do it, too bad," and "This is how competent you should be, and this is what you should be competent at; and if you're not, you aren't worth much."

But cultures say as well, "These are your rights and duties—because that's the way this system *is*; and if you claim rights we deny you, or violate duties we assign you, then you'll be punished." Americans, in other words, are expected to *conform* to the obligations of their statuses and often to authorities who have the responsibility to make them live up to status obligations. Sometimes these status obligations seem arbitrary in terms of the intrinsic requirements of the role.[13]

The tall young Negro was very well dressed. He was wearing a white shirt, regimental tie, three-button suit, and polished shoes. He spoke in an educated voice to the Negro woman interviewer at the state employment office. He seemed an ideal type for some professional or semi-professional job except for one thing—he had the damnedest "Afro" haircut I'd ever seen: his hair grew out high and straight from his head in all directions.

Yet to me he looked both natural and of a piece—the haircut suited him admirably—but not to the interviewer, for I heard her tell him he should cut his hair if he wanted to get a good job. He refused and the next day, when he was back again to talk to the personnel officer of a large utility company, his hair was still "Afro" style. He didn't get the job, of course.

I took him outside the office and we sat in my car, talking about what had happened.

"What do you people want from me?" he asked bitterly. "You tell me I should be proud of my descent, so I let my hair grow instead of getting it processed. I spend a lot of money on this haircut. It costs me six dollars to get it fixed like this, and I have to put hair spray on it every day to keep it neat. I try to keep neat and clean. This morning I took a shower, used a deodorant, put on a clean white shirt, had my mother press my pants, and came down to look for a job. But all they want me to do is cut my hair. Mister, I'm the only one in my whole family who graduated from high school. I even have a year of junior college. But I'm not going to cut my hair. I'm going to wear it 'Afro' even if I don't get a job."

"What will you do?"

"Hustle. I'll get a couple of girls working for me and a few other hustles going. I'll make out. Screw the job if I can't look the way I want."

When I talked with the employment service interviewer about why she hadn't argued with the personnel man when he said he wouldn't hire the kid because of his haircut, she got angry. "He should cut his hair. He should look like everybody else, like the employer wants him to look. It's not my job to argue with employers."

The nonrational requirement that an employee wear a certain kind of suit or a certain style of haircut is easing. Variety in personal grooming inconceivable 20 years ago is acceptable today. With this increase in freedom comes increased

[13]From Paul Jacobs, *Prelude to Riot*, New York: Random House, 1966, pp. 97-98. Reprinted by permission.

demand for release from remaining traditional status requirements, one of the strongest of which is sex-role requirements. Sexual traditions not only require the relegation of women to disadvantaged occupational and social roles—an injustice that the Women's Liberation Movement calls to public attention, it insists also that men and women direct their sexual interest toward the opposite sex. Recently homosexuals have begun to protest the psychological and social pounding they take for a nonconforming sexual preference. The following are excerpts from the public announcement by a well-known middle-aged writer of his sexual preferences, his life history, and his resentment of the pressures to conform.[14]

Have my heterosexual friends, people I thought were my heterosexual friends, been going through an elaborate charade all these years? I would like to think they agree with George Weinberg, a therapist and author of a book on therapy called "The Action Approach," who says, "I would never consider a person healthy unless he had overcome his prejudice against homosexuality." But even Mr. Weinberg assumes that there is a prejudice, apparently built-in, a natural part of the human psyche. And so my heterosexual friends had it, maybe still have it? The late Otto Kahn, I think it was, said, "A kike is a Jewish gentleman who has just left the room." Is a fag a homosexual gentleman who has just stepped out? Me?

I can never be sure, of course, will never be sure. I know it shouldn't bother me. That's what everybody says, but it does bother me. It bothers me every time I enter a room in which there is anyone else. Friend or foe? Is there a difference?

When I was a child in Marshalltown, Iowa, I hated Christmas almost as much as I do now, but I loved Halloween. I never wanted to take off the mask; I wanted to wear it everywhere, night and day, always. And I suppose I still do. I have often used liquor, which is another kind of mask, and, more recently, pot.

Then, too, I suppose if my friends have been playing games with me, they might with justice say that I have been playing games with them. It took me almost 50 years to come out of the closet, to stop pretending to be something I was not, most of the time fooling nobody.

But I guess it is never easy to open the closet door. When she talked to the Daughters of Bilitis, a Lesbian organization, late last summer, Kate Millett, author of "Sexual Politics," said: "I'm very glad to be here. It's been kind of a long trip. . . . I've wanted to be here, I suppose, in a surreptitious way for a long time, and I was always too chicken. . . . Anyway, I'm out of the closet. Here I am."

Not surprisingly, Miss Millett is now being attacked more because of what

[14]Merle Miller, "What It Means to Be a Homosexual," New York *Times Magazine*, January 17, 1971, pp. 10-11, 48-49, 57. Reprinted by permission.

she said to the Daughters of Bilitis than because of what she said in her book. James Owles, president of Gay Activists' Alliance, a militant, nonviolent organization concerned with civil rights for homosexuals, says: "We don't give a damn whether people like us or not. We want the rights we're entitled to."

I'm afraid I want both. I dislike being despised, unless I have done something despicable, realizing that the simple fact of being homosexual is all by itself despicable to many people. . . .

In the nineteen-fifties, McCarthy found that attacking homosexuals paid off almost as well as attacking the Communists, and he claimed they were often the same. Indeed, the District of Columbia police set up a special detail of the vice squad "to investigate links between homosexuality and Communism."

The American Civil Liberties Union recently has been commendably active in homosexual cases, but in the early fifties, when homosexuals and people accused of homosexuality were being fired from all kinds of Government posts, as they still are, the A.C.L.U. was notably silent. And the most silent of all was a closet queen who was a member of the board of directors, myself. . . .

They say that the Depression and the World War were the two central experiences of my generation, and that may be. I certainly had more than enough of both, but I was never really hungry for food. It was love I craved, approval, forgiveness for being what I could not help being. And I have spent a good part of my life looking for those things, always, as a few psychologists have pointed out, in the places I was least likely to find them. . . .

I was 4 years old when I started school. My mother had told them I was 5; I was somewhat precocious, and she may just have wanted to get me out of the house. But butch haircut or not, some boys in the third grade took one look at me and said, "Hey, look at the sissy," and they started laughing. It seems to me now that I heard that word at least once five days a week for the next 13 years, until I skipped town and went to the university. Sissy and all the other words—pansy, fairy, nance, fruit, fruitcake, and less printable epithets. I did not encounter the word faggot until I got to Manhattan. I'll tell you this, though. It's not true, that saying about sticks and stones; it's words that break your bones.

I admit I must have been a splendid target, undersized always, the girlish voice, the steel-rimmed glasses, always bent, no doubt limp of wrist, and I habitually carried a music roll. I studied both piano and violin all through school, and that all by itself was enough to condemn one to permanent sissydom.

I ate carloads of Wheaties, hoping I'd turn into another Jack Armstrong, but I still could neither throw nor catch a baseball. I couldn't even see the thing; I'd worn glasses as thick as plate-glass windows since I was 3 ("You inherited your father's eyes, among other weaknesses.") I sold enough Liberty magazines to buy all the body-building equipment Charles Atlas had to offer, but it did no good. I remained an 89-pound weakling year after year after year. And when the voices of all the other boys in my class had changed into a very low baritone, I was still an uncertain soprano, and remained that until I got to the University of Iowa in Iowa City and, among other disguises, lowered my voice at least two octaves so that I could get a job as a radio announcer on the university station. . . .

Growing up in Marshalltown, I was allowed to take out as many books as I wanted from the local library, and I always wanted as many as I could carry, 8 or 10 at a time. I read about sensitive boys, odd boys, boys who were lonely and misunderstood, boys who really didn't care all that much for baseball, boys who were teased by their classmates, books about all of these, but for years nobody in any of the books I read was ever tortured by the strange fantasies that tore at me every time, for instance, my mother insisted I go to the "Y" to learn how to swim. They swam nude at the Y, and I never went. Lead me not into temptation. In gym—it was required in high school—I always tried to get in and out of the locker room before anybody else arrived.

And in none of the books I read did anybody feel a compulsion, and compulsion it surely was, to spend so many hours, almost as many as I spent at the library, in or near the Minneapolis & St. Louis railroad station where odd, frightening things were written on the walls of the men's room. And where in those days, there were always boys in their teens and early 20's who were on their way to and from somewhere in freight cars. Boys who were hungry and jobless and who for a very small amount of money, and sometimes none at all, were available for sex; almost always they were. They needed the money, and they needed someone to recognize them, to actually see them.

That was the way it happened the first time. The boy was from Chicago, and his name was Carl. He was 17, and I was 12 and the aggressor. I remember every detail of it; I suppose one always does. Carl hadn't eaten, said he hadn't eaten for two days. His father was a plumber, unemployed, and his mother was, he said rather vaguely, "away, hopefully forever." I remember once I said, "But why don't you go home anyway?" And he said, "Where would that be?"

Years later a boy I met on West 42d Street said it best, about the boys in my childhood and the boys on all the streets of all the cities where they wait. He was the next-to-youngest child in a very poor family of nine, and once he ran away from home for two days and two nights, and when he got back, nobody knew that he had been gone. Then, at 19, he discovered The Street, and he said, "All of a sudden here were all these men, and they were looking at me."

The boys who stopped by at the M. and St. L. in Marshalltown all had stories, and they were all anxious to tell them. They were all lonely and afraid. None of them ever made fun of me. I was never beaten up. They recognized, I guess, that we were fellow aliens with no place to register. . . .

There were often black boys on the freight trains, and we talked and had sex. Their stories were always sadder than anybody else's. I never had any hangups about the color of somebody's skin. If you were an outcast, that was good enough for me. I once belonged to 22 organizations devoted to improving the lot of the world's outcasts. The only group of outcasts I never spoke up for publicly, never donated money to or signed an ad or petition for were the homosexuals. I always used my radio announcer's voice when I said "No." . . .

I have been back to Marshalltown only briefly in all the years since my escape, but a few years ago, I did return to a reunion of my high school class. I made the principal speech at the banquet, and at the end there was enough applause to satisfy my ego temporarily, and various of my classmates, all of whom looked depressingly middle-aged, said various pleasant things, after which there was a dance.

I have written about that before, but what I have not written about, since I was still not ready to come out of the closet, is that a little while after the dance began, a man whose face had been only vaguely familiar and whose name I would not have remembered if he had not earlier reminded me came up, an idiot grin on his face, his wrists limp, his voice falsetto, and said, "How about letting me have this dance, sweetie?" He said it loud enough for all to hear.

I said, "I'm terribly sorry, but my dance card is all filled up." By no means the wittiest of remarks, but under the circumstances it was the best I could manage.

Later, several people apologized for what he had said, but I wondered (who would not?) how many of them had been tempted to say the same thing. Or would say something of the kind after I had gone. Fag, faggot, sissy, queer. A fag is a homosexual gentleman who has just left the room. . . .

George Weinberg says, "The 'homosexual problem,' as I have described it here, is the problem of condemning *variety* in human existence. If one cannot enjoy the fact of this variety, at the very least one must learn to become indifferent to it, since obviously it is here to stay."

The fear of it simply will not go away, though. A man who was once a friend, maybe my best friend, the survivor of five marriages, the father of nine, not too long ago told me that his eldest son was coming to my house on Saturday: "Now please try not to make a pass at him."

He laughed. I guess he meant it as a joke; I didn't ask.

And a man I've known, been acquainted with, let's say, for 25 years, called from the city on a Friday afternoon before getting on the train to come up to my place for the weekend. He said, "I've always leveled with you, Merle, and I'm going to now. I've changed my mind about bringing — [his 16-year-old son]. I'm sure you understand."

I said that, no, I didn't understand. Perhaps he could explain it to me.

He said, "— is only an impressionable kid, and while I've known you and know you wouldn't, but suppose you had some friends in, and. . . .?"

CONCLUSION

The process of socialization into American culture (or into any culture) inflicts pain on those who are being socialized, in many cases great pain. One reason for this pain is that successful socialization into a culture requires internalization as a part of oneself of the standards of judgment of that culture. A second reason is that those standards of judgment are usually sufficiently high that many people cannot measure up to them.

Standards of living, standards of beauty, standards of intimacy and belonging, standards of competence and adequacy, standards of sexual prowess and pleasure, standards of propriety, and standards of manliness set requirements. But there are no guarantees of the genes, the socialization, the experiences, or the luck that will enable one to meet those standards. For those who fall short, their pain is a problem, as it is for those who are luckier but remain empathic.

Section B

PATHOLOGIES OF CONFORMITY

Often, labor unions are able to exert pressure on employers, not by striking, but by "going by the book," that is, by following to the letter the rules laid down by management. This may seem paradoxical—that by punctilious conformity, operations may be impaired. Reflection resolves the paradox. "Going by the book" is comparable to the situation discussed in the introduction to Part I, which pointed out that scientific principles never operate in pure form. So with rules. It is difficult to design rules that cover all exigencies of complex situations. Moreover, any concrete problem like running a railroad is governed by rules that mutually limit one another. The rules that men devise need to be flexibly interpreted and applied differently in the light of circumstances and other rules. Rigid conformity to every detail governing tests of safety of railroad equipment, for example, can effectively tie up railroads.

On a broader scale, a paradox of human existence is that *conformity* to the norms and transaction modes of American life reviewed in Part II can lead to consequences that nearly everyone deplores, even those who finally support the norms. This makes for perplexing dilemmas. People are told to behave in certain ways—they are told that their success and self-respect hinge on behaving in those ways; and yet doing so too much results in cries of outrage. It brings to mind the child, admonished by his parents to be truthful, who reports to the arriving guest that his parents wished they had never issued the invitation.

The four chapters of this section, Chapters 7 through 10, scrutinize the social problems generated in America by people's zealous conformity to the principles of materialism, commercialism, self-oriented competition, and authority.

chapter 7
Pathologies of conformity to materialism

As the introduction to Part II pointed out, social problems do not always stem from the violation of social standards. Many problems develop because of the intrinsic nature of social standards. In this chapter and the next three, we shall look at pathologies resulting from conformity to central values of American society.

Conformity to one value, materialism, leads people to a preoccupation with cars, houses, color TV sets, and so on. A leading American economist, John Kenneth Galbraith, has pointed out some disadvantages of this preoccupation.[1]

The legacy of wants, which are themselves inspired, are the bills which descend like the winter snow on those who are buying on the installment plan. By millions of hearths throughout the land it is known that when these harbingers arrive the repossession man cannot be far behind. Can the bill collector be the central figure in the good society?

In 1955 the median income of the American family before taxes was $3960. Of all families within the income range from $3000 to $4000, 48 percent had installment payments to meet. For nearly a third of these the payments commanded more than a fifth of the family income before taxes.

Galbraith asks, "Can the bill collector be the central figure in society?" Probably not, but he looms devastatingly large in the lives of many Americans. Galbraith describes the use of consumer debt in aggregative, macroscopic terms,

---

[1] John Kenneth Galbraith, *The Affluent Society*, New York: Houghton Mifflin, 1958, p. 202.

as befits an economist. A sociologist might wish to look at one of the "millions of hearths throughout the land" on which the bills "descend like the winter snow," such as the hearth of Marion Rairigh.[2]

I'll never forget the day we stopped kidding ourselves and realized what a terrible fix we had got into by trying to keep up with all of our neighbors.

It had started when we looked around and told ourselves that if other people could keep up all those payments, we could do it too. When we couldn't make it, we got desperate and tried to borrow money. Then we sold our new home, figuring that ought to pull us out. Next we tried to turn some things back for the amounts we still owed on them, but even that didn't work. Then came that day when I reached the airline shops to go to work as usual, and my supervisor called me aside.

"Marion, what's this all about?" he asked. "A Palo Alto firm has attached your pay."

His tone was kindly enough, but I can remember only one other time in my life that I ever came so close to real panic—the day during the war when our bomber was so badly shot up we thought she'd crash.

I knew the company fired employees who didn't pay their bills. Our nice new suburban home was already gone, our new car, our fancy food freezer and our TV set were gone, we still owed more than we could possibly pay, and now it seemed that my job was gone. . . .

It was in February, 1953, when we all piled into our old 1941 car for the trip out of the snow to California—Bernice and I and our three children. Our oldest, Mary Florence, was only seven then; Aleta Fern was five, and Daniel Floyd was three. The car was bulging and the kids were yipping, but we didn't mind. We were sure things were going our way at last. I was going to be making nearly seventy-five dollars a week, and to me that seemed a fortune.

We were practically broke when we got to Palo Alto and moved into a motel. It was cheap, as motels go—twenty dollars a week for two little rooms. Even so, it didn't take us long to persuade ourselves that it would be only good business to buy a new house.

I would come back in the evenings to our crowded, hot little motel unit, and Bernice would be looking pretty tired and harassed, handling three children in that cluttered little space.

"Look, honey, I don't see why we don't go ahead and buy a house," I said. "You know my mother told us she would give us five hundred dollars any time we were ready to get a home of our own, and that would cover the whole down

[2]From Marion F. Rairigh, "We Couldn't Pay Our Bills," as told to Elmont Waite. First published in the *Saturday Evening Post*. Copyright 1958 by The Curtis Publishing Company. Reprinted by permission of Brandt & Brandt, New York, agents for Marion F. Rairigh.

payment, the way they're selling these places in California. Monthly payments couldn't be more than this dump, we know that."

We hadn't found any bargains in rentals either—not with three small children. So we looked around at new homes for sale and found a three-bedroom, ranch-style house in a new subdivision in Sunnyvale. It cost $11,500, but the down payment was only $500, plus $250 in closing costs. After a month on my new job, I figured I could scrape up the $250. Payments would be only seventy-two dollars a month, including taxes and insurance.

I remember the day we paid our little deposit to hold the place, standing in the middle of that bare living room, with the kids scooting around, laughing and giggling. We were feeling a little frightened and a little proud of ourselves, and tremendously excited. This was a palace!

We passed two more danger signs right there, without even opening our eyes. In the first place, I was a brand-new employee with the airline and if there were any cutback at all I'd be out of work. This problem of job security never entered my mind. Fortunately, I never was laid off, but the big risk was certainly there.

In the second place, neither Bernice nor I had any idea what a new house costs after you've bought it.

One extra cost we hadn't anticipated didn't really hurt; it was more of an annoyance than a problem. Taxes and insurance promptly rose, so that our seventy-two-dollar monthly payment became seventy-eight dollars.

"But what are we going to use for furniture?" Bernice asked. That did hurt us.

We bought the house in March, 1953, and didn't get possession until May first, so we had a little time to save a few dollars. But we didn't save enough to pay cash for furniture—even secondhand furniture. We did buy a used stove for cash, and we made a $100 down payment on a lot of new furniture. We got only what we thought we had to have, but the total bill was nearly $1000, so we owed $900—agreeing to pay it at $40.49 a month. No matter what kind of a rose-colored pencil you use to add that to a seventy-eight-dollar house payment, the total still comes out $118.49 every month.

Another cost we hadn't figured at all was landscaping. The subdivision homes had no lawns. We had thought we'd wait a while for ours, but one day I heard a couple of our neighbors talking. They didn't see me.

"I don't see why some people around here don't get their lawns in," one of them said. "The dust is terrible. How long do we have to put up with this?"

I walked quietly away and went down to price some grass seed. I figured maybe forty dollars, but, including a few garden tools, the bill came to nearly $100, and I had to borrow the $100. So there was fourteen dollars a month to be paid on that loan, raising our monthly total to $132.

Early that summer, too, the heat coming through our uninsulated roof made the house almost unbearable in the afternoons. So a salesman didn't have much trouble persuading me that insulating the ceilings would be a fine investment. Of course, he was right. It would make the house worth more—and think how much cooler it would be! Well, that job cost $200 and the payments were twelve dollars a month. That made our monthly debt payments total $144, but I don't believe I ever bothered to add them up.

That's another danger sign I'd like to point out. When you buy things on credit, always keep track of how much you are committed to pay every month. Hardly anyone seems to know how much money he owes nowadays or even how much he must pay every month and how long it will take to get out of debt. You don't need elaborate bookkeeping. You can add the figures on a scrap from a grocery sack, jotting the answers on a calendar—but do it! It may well keep you from getting in too deep, the way we did.

I'm certain I never realized how much I already owed when the water-softener salesman came to our door one day.

"Could you use some extra money?" he asked.

By the time he explained that we'd have to buy a water-softener to save money on water and soap, we were hooked. Bernice was saying, "Well, our clothes did wash easier back in Colorado where we had soft water." So I wound up owing $300 more and our monthly payments rose by $14. I know now that it made our monthly installments total $158.

About that time it began to dawn on me how far our home was from my job. The old '41 car was giving out. I tried riding busses for a while; then arranged to get rides with another fellow. Finally, Bernice got a windfall—a $600 settlement as a result of an auto accident she had been in, back in Colorado. We used the check to buy a 1947 car—a pretty good one—for cash. With what little money was left, we bought a few more things for the house, including curtains. Somehow we were managing to make both ends meet, although there was no safety margin left.

Then came what we first thought was a wonderful break—although I think now it pushed us closer to the brink. I came home one hot August evening and Bernice was wearing her I've-got-a-secret look. "Guess what?" she demanded. "I've got a job too!" She was doing a little dance step around the kitchen, she was so proud of herself. I wasn't too happy abou the idea, but we did need the money. The job, on the night shift in a cannery, paid fifty-five dollars a week plus frequent overtime.

I think real disaster began right then. First we bought a good used TV set for $200—at $15 per month. Our children had been everywhere except at home, because all the neighbors had television, so it was easy to talk ourselves into that one, and to ignore the fact it made our monthly installments go up to $173.

Next thing we knew, we had signed up for a bargain food-freezer deal—$500, including all kinds of food, and payments of only forty dollars a month. If I had stopped to add, I'd have known it boosted our monthly payments to a total of $213.

The last straw was something I've never been able to explain. I walked in one day to look at new automobiles in a showroom—nothing but casual curiosity.

"That old car of yours is exactly what we need for a customer of ours!" the salesman exclaimed. "I'll tell you what we'll do—"

It was, he said, a "fantastic" deal on a demonstrator. So I came out driving a new model, saddled with a new $100-a-month payment. That made our installments total $313 every month, practically my whole salary, so all our regular expenses had to come out of Bernice's earnings.

By pinching pennies, we were just able to keep our heads above water. Looking back on those days, I know neither of us was happy, in spite of all our fancy new possessions. We were trapped. We had to keep plugging away to keep up with all those bills, and we worried continually.

The crash came, finally, just as Christmas, 1953, was drawing near. I got up early one morning to get my own breakfast as usual, and there was Bernice, already putting on the coffee.

"Hey, honey, you shouldn't be up at this hour, with that night job of yours," I said.

Never one to beat around the bush, she blurted it right out, "I don't have a job. I got laid off."

I'm not a very big man, and it felt as though a huge prize fighter had just belted me in the solar plexus. I was getting the half-and-half out of the refrigerator and I must have jumped, because a slurp of cream splattered on the floor.

"Oh, no!" I said. "What are we going to do now?"

Bernice looked as though she were going to cry. I put my arm around her and told her we'd get along, and she'd probably be able to get another job.

Well, she couldn't. There were no other jobs. For the second time we had sailed blindly past that big danger sign I mentioned—job security. Lots of families I know seem to rely on the wife's earnings as we did, without ever stopping to think that they may vanish any minute. Even if the husband's job is secure, the wife may be fired, or get sick, or have a baby, and then what?

We did the only thing we could do. We skipped the December car payment. Then Bernice got sick and doctor's fees were added to our pile of unpaid bills, so we missed our December house payment.

In January, 1954, we missed a second car payment. We knew we simply had to make the January house payment, but Bernice telephoned me at work one day.

"I just got back from the doctor's office," she said. "Mary Florence fell and hurt herself in the neighbor's yard; she hit a sprinkler head in the lawn, and the X ray showed her collarbone is broken."

That knocked out our house payment for the second month.

There was nothing I could do but get out of that car deal somehow. I gave the car back to the dealer, but did that cancel what we owed on it? No, sir! We still owed $600. It's legal, and not uncommon. Models had changed and the car had depreciated faster than I had been paying for it, even at $100 a month.

So we still owed $600, and had no car at all. Other creditors were beginning to hound us, and it got so we hated to see the mailman coming. I had already tried to borrow enough money to clear up all our bills and then pay at a smaller rate on the one loan, but I couldn't. I did get one small loan that month, however, that covered a few of our debts and let us buy an old 1941 car for $100 cash, but we were still broke, still deeply in debt, and the loan payment itself added $21.68 a month to our obligations.

Bernice tried place after place, but couldn't find a job anywhere.

"We might as well admit it," she said, as we sat glumly in the living room one night. "I don't stand a chance of getting another job, since the cannery season is over. I haven't any special training."

We decided, then and there, that we'd have to sell the house. We even looked forward to getting rid of it, hoping we might get a little peace of mind.

But selling our house didn't clear our bills. We were three months behind in the house payments by then, and the sale price left us only $200, after paying the house loan and the water-softener and insulation bills.

We moved to a $46.50 rental unit in the Lindenville public-housing project in South San Francisco, taking nothing but our old car and our furniture—and more bills than we could possibly pay.

The firm we owed for the food freezer had taken it back, but there again I was stuck. They sold it to someone else, cheap, and I still owed for the difference, plus a second lot of food I hadn't paid for. This was the bill that brought the attachment of my pay check, in June, 1954, and by that time it amounted to more than $500—as much as the original price of the freezer.

The personal economic crisis of the Rairighs is a problem resulting from conformity to materialistic values. Another problem occurs when a materialistic passion for production distorts a society's understanding of what is going on. The economist and political scientist, Adolph A. Berle, Jr., calls attention to some of those distortions in the following analysis of the American infatuation with the Gross National Product. He wrote of the GNP of 1968, but what he says is true of the much greater GNP of today.[3]

[3]From Adolph A. Berle, "What GNP Doesn't Tell Us," *Saturday Review*, August 31, 1968, pp. 10-12. Copyright 1968 Saturday Review, Inc. Reprinted by permission.

It is nice to know that at current estimate the Gross National Product of the United States in 1968 will be above 850 billions of dollars. It would be still nicer to know if the United States will be better or worse off as a result. If better, in what respects? If worse, could not some of this production and effort be steered into providing more useful "goods and services"?

Unfortunately, whether the work was sham or useful, the goods noxious, evanescent, or of permanent value will have no place in the record. Individuals, corporations, or government want, buy, and pay for stuff and work—so it is "product." The labor of the Boston Symphony Orchestra is "product" along with that of the band in a honky-tonk. The compensated services of a quack fortune teller are "product" just as much as the work of developing Salk vaccine. Restyling automobiles or ice chests by adding tail fins or pink handles adds to "product" just as much as money paid for slum clearance or medical care. They are all "goods" or "services"—the only test is whether someone wanted them badly enough to pay the shot. . . .

Any audit of social result, any system of social indicators, requires solving two sets of problems. First, with all this Gross National Product reflecting payment to satisfy wants, did America get what it paid for? In getting it, did it not also bring into being a flock of unrecorded but offsetting frustrations it did not want? Essentially, this is economic critique. Second—and far more difficult— can a set of values be put forward, roughly expressing the essentials most Americans would agree their society ought to be, and be doing, against which the actual record of what it was and did can be checked? This second critique, as economists rightly contend, is basically philosophical.

As for the economic critique, let us take the existing economic record at face. Work was done, things were created, and both were paid for. The total price paid this year will be around $850 billion. But, unrecorded, not included, and rarely mentioned are some companion results. Undisposed-of junk piles, garbage, waste, air and water pollution come into being. God help us, we can see that all over the country. Unremedied decay of parts of the vast property we call "the United States" is evident in and around most American cities. No one paid for this rot and waste—they are not "product." Factually, these and other undesirable results are clear deductions from or offset items to the alleged "Gross National Product" we like so well.

The total of these may be called "disproduct." It will be a hard figure to calculate in dollar figures. Recorded as "product" is the amount Americans spent for television sets, stations, and broadcasts. Unrecorded is their companion disproductive effect in the form of violence, vandalism, and crime. Proudly reported as "product" are sums spent for medical care, public health, and disease prevention; unheralded is the counter-item, the "disproduct" of loss and misery as remediable malnutrition and preventable disease ravage poverty areas. Besides our annual calculation of "gross" national product, it is time we had some idea of Gross National Disproduct. Deducting it, we could know what the true, instead of the illusory, annual "net national product" might be. (Economists use "Net National Product" to mean Gross National Product less consumption of capital—but it is not a true picture.)

There is a difference, it will be noted, between "disproduct" and "cost." Everything made or manufactured, every service rendered by human beings, involves using up materials, if only the food and living necessities of labor. These are "costs." They need not enter into this calculation. Conventional statistics already set up a figure for "capital consumption," and we deduct this from "Gross National Product." That is not what we have in mind here. We are trying to discover whether creation of "Gross National Product" does not also involve frustration of wants as well as their satisfaction. Pollution of air and water are obvious illustrations but there are "disproducts" more difficult to discern, let alone measure.

Scientists are increasing our knowledge of these right along. For example, cigarettes (to which I am addicted) satisfy a widespread want. They also, we are learning, engender a great deal of cancer. Now it is true that at some later time the service rendered in attempting to care for cancer (generated by cigarettes manufactured five years ago) will show up as "product"; so the work of attempted cure or caretaking will later appear as a positive product item. But that item will not be known until later. What we do know without benefit of figures is that against this year's output of tobacco products whose cash value is recorded we have also brought more cancer into being—an unrecorded "disproduct." We know at the end of any year how many more automobiles have been manufactured. We also know that each new car on the road means added injury and accident overall. Carry this process through our whole product list, and the aggregate of "disproduct" items set against the aggregate of production will tell us an immense amount about our progress toward (or retrogression from) social welfare.

Once we learn to calculate disproduct along with product and discover a true "net," as well as a "gross," we shall have our first great "social" indicator. We shall know what the country accomplished.

It could be surprising and disillusioning. It might disclose that while satisfying human wants as indicated by the "gross" figure, in the process we had also violated, blocked, or frustrated many of these same wants and, worse, had done a great deal we did not want to do. Carrying the calculation further, we would probably find (among other things) that while satisfying immediate wants from today's productivity, we had been generating future wants (not to say needs) to repair the damage, waste, and degeneration set up by current production.

Some of today's "gross" product carries with it a mortgage—it sets up brutal defensive requirements that must be met by tomorrow's work and things. Some forms of productivity may prove to generate more decay, damage, or waste annually than their total amount, while neglect of some production may annually place a usurious claim on future years. Failure to maintain cities at acceptable standards is a case in point: it sets up huge but unrecorded claims on the manpower and product of coming decades. It is entirely possible to score annual increases of Gross National Product as we presently figure it—and yet, after reckoning "disproduct," be little better off at the end of any year than at its beginning.

Problems on an even larger scale than the costs to *American* society of preoccupation with GNP are created for the entire planet by the American pursuit of material production. With about 6 percent of the world's population, the United States consumes about 40 percent of the total planetary output of raw materials, not counting food.[4] Consider what this means for the future of the rest of the world. At the rate of population growth now prevailing, there will be close to 7 billion people on the earth by the year 2000.[5] (There are now about 3½ billion.) Even if, by means no one can be certain about now, the planetary population by 2000 could be limited to "only" 5 billion, the planetary level of consumption of resources would have to be 25 times greater than the American level of 1970, if the rest of the planet is to have in 2000 the living levels enjoyed by Americans in 1970.[6]

But "before any area can reach the per capita energy and mineral consumption rate of the United States, it must first build up its industry to that level. Were the whole world to have done this ... the presently estimated world supplies of the ores of ·most industrial metals, produceable by present technology would have been exhausted well before such a level of industrialization could have been reached."[7] Put another way, every American in 1970 required, on the average, that over 20 tons of raw material be dug from the earth every year and processed to give him the level of life he then knew. If all five billion inhabitants of the planet in 2000 are to have that life, 100 billion tons a year would have to be dug, which is impossible. Moreover, the better-grade ores are being used up first, and to process poorer and poorer grades requires the use of greater and greater quantities of energy. "The conclusion to be drawn is not that 5 billion persons living at present United States standards would require 25 times as much energy as the United States does today. Rather than 25, the factor for some metals could be in the hundreds. And even at 25 times the present U.S. consumption of coal, oil, and gas, the human race would burn up the earth's

[4] *Population Bulletin*, Vol. 26, No. 2, June 1970, p. 3.

[5] Undated Population Reference Bureau press release, early 1970.

[6] *Pop. Bull.*, op. cit., p. 4.

[7] M. King Hubbard, *Energy Resources: A Report to the Committee on Natural Resources of the National Academy of Sciences, National Research Council*, 1962. Quoted in *Ibid.*

estimated resources of fossil fuels not in a matter of centuries, but in a few decades."[8]

Materialistic preoccupations threaten the biophysical environment. They also may damage the human personalities that hope to live in that environment. Consider the college students who are enrolled for the wrong reasons.[9]

I recall talking to a young pre-med major just last spring. He had failed both his zoology and his chemistry. After I glanced at his grades, I asked him why he wanted to become a doctor. His unusually frank and disarming answer was simply, "to make money."

"Why do you want to make this much money?" was my next question.

"My father believes that money is the only reason why a boy should go to college."

"Is there another possible reason that a young man might like to become a doctor?" I asked.

"None that I can think of!" was his clincher.

I give myself credit for keeping my temper and not shouting, "I'd hate to call you in an emergency." But then I was sure as it is humanly possible to be that he would never become even a college graduate, much less an M.D.

Then there was the coed who could not pass a chemistry course. Yet she was in pre-nursing because her mother is a frustrated nurse. She probably would have done well in business college or perhaps even in an elementary teaching curriculum, so long as she did not have to use chemistry.

Because we have a large and rigorous engineering program at W.S.U., I see more pre-engineering students than perhaps any other group. As the young man sits across from me, my invariable first question is simply, "Why do you want to be an engineer?"

A tremendous segment of this group of students will answer just as simply, "Because my father told me that engineers make a lot of money."

I can still remember how amazed and disgusted at parental pressures I became when I first began to counsel students at a state university larger than W.S.U. I was attempting to interpret a profile to a high school senior who planned to enroll at the university the following September. Although his scores in mathematics and science were very low, the tests showed high interest in music. He intended, however, to become an engineer.

I asked a few pointed questions calculated to probe the motives behind intention. Finally, he blurted out, "My dad teaches engineering on this campus, and he wants me to become an engineer."

[8]*Ibid.*, p. 7.

[9]From Lewis M. Magill, "A Word to Overanxious Parents: Get off Johnny's Back," *Saturday Review*, Feb. 15, 1964, p. 66. Copyright 1964 Saturday Review, Inc. Reprinted by permission.

I excused myself for a moment, found a telephone outside my office, and called his high school band director to discover whether the interest tests reflected an aptitude for music. The director assured me that the boy could do excellent work in music school. But when I returned and suggested that perhaps he should consider majoring in music, he seemed so thoroughly brain washed that he became almost inarticulate.

Finally, when he left my office, I added as a parting question, "Do you really want to be an engineer?"

He gulped out a muffled, "No."

Within an hour I received a telephone call from an indignant *mother*, who asked me what right I had to interfere in family matters. She screamed into the phone for fifteen or twenty minutes and then fairly shrieked, "Well, if it's any satisfaction to you, he's going to major in music."

Enduring her shouting was, I felt, a small price to pay for the salvation of a human soul.

Any counselor on a college campus can multiply my examples by infinity. And yet for some reason many parents cannot rid themselves of the notion that they can totally direct their children's lives and selfishly seek vicarious satisfaction in launching their children into careers that presumably will bring prestige to the family or that will salve an old frustration.

One more point must be made. Most of the parents about whom I have written are not uneducated or illiterate. In fact, professional people are the worst with whom we have to deal. I make no claim to be a sociologist, but I believe sincerely that the more prestigious the occupation, the more unreasonable parents tend to be. Certainly, M.D.s are the most stubborn group we encounter in knowing what is *right* for their children. Whether they are subconsciously impressed by the great prestige now attached to being a doctor or whether they are far too used to having their slightest orders carried out and their prescriptions followed to the letter, I have reluctantly come to the conclusion that it is a wise doctor who knows his own child.

And those in my profession—college professors—are in some ways almost as bad. Perhaps we get intoxicated by our captive audience, or perhaps we just have faith in the delusion that it is impossible for us to have "dim" children (to use that wonderful British expression). Without attempting to delineate a hierarchy, I would list engineers, dentists, lawyers, officers in the armed forces, and pharmacists as following close behind. The working man, on the other hand, is generally so happy that his children have a chance to go to college that he keeps his hands off, although I can cite some obvious exceptions.

I can think of no better way of emphasizing the points I have been trying to make than to quote in full (with some modifications to protect the innocent) a letter I received several years ago.

To whom it may concern:

To get to the point, I do not want to be reinstated! Today my mother is mailing the application for re-enrollment and the application for reinstatement. It is none of my doing, because I do not want to return to W.S.U. I would rather attend . . . (here he names a trade school). There has been a great deal of trouble in our home because of this.

I do not want my parents to know about this letter, so please do not acknowledge this, or return an answer. Just simply do not reinstate me! Please do what I am asking, as it is very important to me.

If this letter is disregarded, I will not meet the requirements of reinstatement if I am reinstated. Whether I am qualified to be reinstated or not, I do not know. But, I do know that I do not want to be reinstated!

I hope I have made myself clear to you.

If you think that you must return an answer to this letter, please mail your answer to . . . (an address other than the one on the application).

I hope you will please do as I ask. I do not want my parents to know about this letter to you. It is very important to all concerned.

Please, please do as I ask you.

Thank you.

We obliged the young man.

CONCLUSION

In Chapter 2 it was suggested that Americans are materialistic by default, that we try to use "things" to express our search for the meaning of existence. In an age of anxiety, we hope that science can save us. In an age that has lost its faith, we turn to tangible reality—to stall showers, air-conditioned cars, frozen foods, television, jet airplanes—and try to forget that the basic questions remain unanswered. When satisfactions are not forthcoming, when the individual finds himself failing to live up to the adequacy, authority, gratification, or security standards of American society, one possible response is to emphasize "things" even more relentlessly.

The identification of the meaning of life with materialism was what Emerson had in mind when he wrote:

> 'Tis the day of the chattel,
> Web to weave, and corn to grind;
> Things are in the saddle,
> And ride mankind.

From the consumer's point of view, materialism means the vision that one more gadget, one more convenience, one recent model of something, will be the thing to make life pleasant and worthwhile. From the producer's point of view, it means the devotion of more and more resources to whipping up the demand for more things, newer things, different things.

Quite apart from the human potentialities that go undeveloped as a result of exclusive preoccupation with things, critical issues are ignored by a public that is too preoccupied with meeting installment payments to notice what might be happening to civil liberties or the United Nations.

Ken Heyman

chapter 8
Pathologies of
the market mentality

The principle of negotiated exchange means that, once having found someone in a position to meet your needs, you must persuade him to do so by making it "worth his while." What do you have that *he* wants? How much of it are you prepared to give him? Bargaining is most fully institutionalized in the economic system, and its operation in this sphere of American life is usually considered desirable. Even in the marketplace, however, negotiated exchange can be carried too far. When it becomes sufficiently relentless, social problems ensue, especially when one of the bargainers is weaker or more ignorant than the other. Consumers, for example, are ordinarily in a poor position to evaluate the claims of competing advertisers—or even to avoid products containing harmful ingredients. The Pure Food and Drug Administration and the Federal Trade Commission are Federal agencies which operate to counteract an adage of the market place, *caveat emptor* (let the buyer beware). There are also state and municipal agencies which protect the consumer in various ways. The bargaining principle, strictly construed, commands that you give him as little as possible and try to get as much as possible. This principle is not usually *strictly* construed; it is often tempered by other considerations, such as the *needs* of the person with whom you are bargaining, or some other principle of "fairness." For example, during World War II, sellers of gasoline, meat, and other scarce goods were expected *not* to sell their supplies to the highest bidder, but rather to ration them in accordance with *equally* distributed ration books. For peacetime examples: If you are a shoe salesman, you are expected to exert some effort to make sure that the shoes you exchange for your customer's money really fit him. Women are not expected to sell their sexual services to the highest bidder. Physicians are,

150

at least by some interpretations of the Hippocratic Oath, not supposed to refuse to treat patients because the patients cannot pay enough. And so on.

When, however, the principle of negotiated exchange is widely and deeply institutionalized and when individuals feel themselves threatened by their inability to obtain what they need, those tempering values may be discarded. Whatever it is you have to sell, sell it to the highest bidder—and make him bid as high as possible.

Since you are entitled only to what you can make it worth someone's while to give you, you *owe* people only what they make it worth your while to give them. You are conforming, not deviating, when you are reluctant to give them more. Such conformity, however, may generate social problems. For example, if the kind of housing you can make it worth a landlord's while to give you is slum housing, giving you more than slum housing is charity, not an obligation. A slum landlord is obliged to give his tenants only what they make it profitable for him to give them.[1]

A man I shall call Dan Marner, a typical metropolitan slum landlord, once had a friend. He was a real friend, not just another useful contact in the local Bureau of Buildings or land-record office, and before he and Dan broke up over a roofing contract he gave him a Christmas present. It was a game of Monopoly.

Dan never used it. He studied the rules carefully and then shelved it. For several years it has lain in a ledger case beside his scarred desk, gathering office dust. "It was those 'Community Chest' cards you got to pick," said the estranged friend later. "Dan Marner couldn't bring himself to give anything to charity even in a game."

Dan himself explains that the game sounds foolish. To him it probably does: In Monopoly, the winning player usually must acquire the most expensive properties on the board—"Park Avenue" and "the Boardwalk." Dan knows that real estate doesn't work that way. In the twenty years he has been working the shabby side of his city's map, he hasn't had to pay the "Community Chest" or "Go to Jail" once, and he has been a consistent winner. On paper, indeed, he is a millionaire, the title owner of 327 deeds. Each month he grosses $6,000 from rents and auxiliary sources. His expenses are comparatively small—his three sons act as office and field assistants, slum tax assessments are low, and Dan never repairs houses voluntarily.

At sixty-two, Dan is a dour, bespectacled man, wise in the ways of the drab districts that dot every metropolis on the eastern seaboard—districts built before the Civil War, paved with Victorian cobblestones, and peppered today with

[1]From "The Life and Times of a Slum Landlord" by William Manchester, as it appeared in *The Reporter*, November 15, 1956, pp. 24-26. Copright 1956 by The Reporter Magazine Co. reprinted by permission of the Harold Matson Company, Inc.

pawnshops, cut-rate drugstores, and warped doors bearing the crudely chalked names of tenants. The increase of traffic in the interiors of cities long ago sent the original householders to suburbs on the perimeter. Into the vacuum they left, men like Dan moved—first as managers, later as landlords.

Dan's headquarters is in a dingy office building on the edge of the slum. There his tenants—some colored, some white—bring their weekly money and humbly wait in line while his sons stamp their rent books, which are small and black and resemble bankbooks. Some tenants send money orders, but none mail cash. Long ago they learned that since there is no record of a cash mailing, they have no recourse if Dan tells them their envelopes have been lost in the mails. Like many professional slum landlords, he has a reputation for sharp practice. The office building, which he shares with several competitors, is known in the trade as "the Den of the Forty Thieves."

Dan's reputation doesn't affect his business, and so it doesn't bother him. Within obvious limits, he is candid, and he will open his records to the outsider who guarantees him anonymity. They reveal that his typical house was built about forty-five years ago, is on the outskirts of the downtown area in his city, is overcrowded, lacks plumbing, has no central heating, and frequently lacks heating equipment altogether. Dan rents it for $28 a month. It costs the occupant $9 more for utilities, which means that the typical tenant, who makes less than $2,000 a year, spends a quarter of it on housing characterized by defective wiring, blind rooms, an outside toilet, a leaking roof, and massive rat infestation.

Unless he is goaded by the law, Dan pockets the two per cent depreciation allowed him under the Federal tax laws and mends nothing. Suggestions that he should do otherwise baffle him. To Dan, his career is not merely defensible; it is admirable.

"What I did," he says, peering over his steel-rimmed glasses at the files of paying tenants, "any of them could do." ·

That is a difficult argument to answer, because it is literally true. Like most of the other Forty Thieves, Dan is a product of the slum. His rise is a kind of twisted Horatio Alger story. Tubercular as a youth, he left school in the seventh grade, married early, and was earning $18 a week in a canning factory when the depression threw him on relief. In 1934, after two years on the dole, he rented a vacant house, agreeing to clean it for the first two weeks' rent. He swiped a rusty bedspring from a junk yard, set it up on four soapboxes, and advertised a room for rent. Saving his coins and assembling other makeshift beds, he converted the vacant building into a profitable flophouse.

The owner of the house, an elderly woman who had inherited money and moved to a suburb, admired Dan's ingenuity. She owned five occupied buildings in the same block. Times were hard, the occupants were in arrears, and she appointed Dan her rent collector. He was so persistent at extorting money from his neighbors that one, in exasperation, slugged him. The story made the papers. The public may have disapproved of Dan's methods but other absentee property owners decided he was just the man they needed. He became the busy manager of several estates, charging, under standard practice, a five per cent commission on the rents he collected.

Actually he charged much more, if those who knew him then are to be believed. According to them, Dan, knowing that absentee landlords rarely visit their properties, extracted money from them for repairs he never made. At the same time, it is contended, he jacked up rents on his own authority and kept the difference. Dan admits none of this. But it is a matter of record that in two years he had saved enough to buy his first house, a two-story shack offered by the city in a tax sale.

The following year he bought his second house in a low-income white neighborhood. Dan moved a Negro family in and took advantage of the neighbors' panic to buy four more homes in the same block at bargain prices. He had to mortgage everything he had to do it, but today the street is a respectable colored district, a faithful producer of weekly money orders. He has acted as a "blockbuster" on several occasions since, serving as an incidental agent of desegregation.

Dan goes into debt frequently. Every cent he makes goes into new property. In courthouse circles he has a reputation for not being able to answer a judgment without selling a house. If a house becomes burdensome, he usually finds it profitable to have the mortgage foreclosed. He will keep it until he has cleared his investment and then cut off payments to the building-and-loan association. Occasionally the auctioneer will fail to meet his expectations, and he will be obliged to pay the association a small deficiency decree, but as a rule he finds foreclosure cheaper than a broker's commission.

All other things being equal, Dan prefers colored tenants to white. Negroes, confined to the slum by social pressures, are of all types. White families can live elsewhere, however, and those he gets are inclined to be irresponsible. There is one exception to this: The handicapped of all races are sound risks. Late in the 1930's, for example, Dan took in a veteran of the Argonne, a chronic victim of combat shock. The man, unmarried, received $125 a month from the Veterans Administration. He regularly turned his check over to Dan, who saw to it he was supplied with coffee and beans from the corner grocery until his death, which Dan deeply regretted.

Exploiting the handicapped may seem beneath a millionaire, but Dan doesn't look at it that way. "Life is dog eat dog," he says, shrugging and spreading his hands. "It's survival of the fittest." His fortune has been built from stacks of small change, and no device is too petty for him. If a Department of Highways inspector insists he repair one of his sidewalks—a twenty-five-dollar job—Dan dutifully takes out a Bureau of Buildings permit, indicating that he intends to do the work. The permit costs one dollar and gives him thirty days' grace. By then the inspector is looking over another neighborhood. When he returns next year and finds the walk worse, Dan will explain that he has been unable to find a contractor. He will take out another permit as evidence of his good faith. He is prepared to go on from permit to permit, always promising and never performing, to avoid paying that $25.

On the other hand, he knows all his rights. Since Dan's days as a rent collector, the city has established a small-claims court, and he is one of its steadiest customers. In theory, the court is for taxpayers who cannot afford to press extensive suits. Actually, two-thirds of its docket entries are rent cases, with the city acting as agent for complaining landlords. If a tenant falls into arrears, Dan drops into the court, fills out a slip, and pays a one-dollar fee. A policeman then serves a summons on the tenant. Most occupants of slum homes are terrified of authority. Frequently the lax tenant will borrow the cash that day and rush to Dan, who will also recover the one-dollar summons charge from him.

Dan's big property gains were made during the war. On the eve of Pearl Harbor, he was worth about $100,000. He held title to thirty-four houses, acquired at public tax sales, from out-of-town heirs unfamiliar with local values, or from hard-pressed owners needing quick cash. Each month, his records show, he was grossing between $850 and $900 in rentals, and he was branching out. He had become a professional bondsman, pledging his property as collateral. His eldest son hung around police stations soliciting business. Dan always made certain his bonds were secured by chattel mortgages, and he always demanded the maximum legal interest—ten per cent in Federal court, five in local courts. Each year he met a score of bonds and took in upward of two thousand dollars in bail fees. He had plenty of free capital—too much, indeed, to suit him. "I was uneasy," he says. "I figured someone would find out and make an excuse to sue me for something."

Unfortunately, investment opportunities were limited. The specter of competition was rearing its head: Other landlords were bidding against Dan at auctions, and the market was tight. He wanted to pioneer a new field by buying a block of Victorian mansions on the slum fringe and converting them into apartments, but the zoning statute prohibited it. Then, at the appropriate time, the Japs attacked. War industry boomed, and the city was invaded by Southerners who wanted to work but had no place to live. Dan took a plunge. He bought the block, went to the zoning-appeals board, and explained he would house the war workers if the board would overlook the law. It worked: His peculiar contribution to the war effort was accepted.

"I didn't get the Army-Navy 'E'," he recalls, "but I got a precedent, and in 1946 I got rid of all those hillbillies by moving one Negro family in."

Dan's one serious challenge has come from the local Health Department.

Late in the war the department set up a housing bureau, and under its leadership a team of inspectors invaded the slum, looking for infractions of the law. In one fourteen-block area, with 791 properties, they found 13,589 health, building, fire and electrical violations. Notices were issued ordering repairs, and the team moved on, checking off kerosene space heaters, outdoor hoppers, exposed wiring, and sagging walls. A week later they struck the first of Dan's blocks.

The campaign was a real threat to him. Structural repairs are expensive— mending his houses properly would have taken more money than he had, or so he now says. He began by protesting that his property rights were being invaded, but the inspectors had strong public support. Protest failing, Dan quietly told each of his tenants he could buy the house he was renting with no down payment. The terms were farcical; Dan retained the deeds, and he was permitted to cancel the contract if one weekly payment was one day late. Most occupants fell for the "buy-instead-of-rent" gimmick, however, until Dan started forwarding Health Department notices to them. Ownership, he piously explained, implies responsibility.

The department argued that Dan was still the landlord, and a legal battle opened to determine where ownership really lay. Meanwhile, Dan had opened a contracting sideline. He outfitted a man in neat white coveralls, with the word INSPECTOR embroidered over the left breast pocket, and sent him out to trail bona fide Health Department inspectors. After the Health Department men had gone, Dan's "inspector" would call and ask the bewildered tenant if he might look at the house. Usually he was admitted without question.

Inside, he would explain that this or that had to be done. When the frightened occupant, thinking of himself as the house's owner, asked where repairmen might be found the "inspector" said he had friends who did work at cut-rate prices. The prices were, of course, inflated, for Dan extracted a referral fee from the plumbers and roofers he sent out. Under this ingenious arrangement, the repairs were not only made; Dan made a profit on them. According to one report, Dan's "inspector" dismantled a furnace on the coldest day of 1949, left, and returned the following day with an installment-sale furnace contract. The shivering householder signed.

The courts decided that Dan, as deed holder, was legally responsible. Since then he has been erecting cardboard partitions and installing inferior wiring— doing the work, in short, but in the worst possible fashion. The Health Department keeps after him, and he has paid a few ten-dollar fines for failure to comply with its notices. But he is still the winner. Ten years after its ambitious opening, the department's campaign is hopelessly bogged down in detail. By fighting it every step of the way, Dan is defeating it.

Outside the Health Department and a few civic organizations interested in slum clearance, there is little local interest in Dan. The business community is almost wholly indifferent. Some of its members, one suspects, secretly admire him. They think of him as a shrewd trader, a self-made man, an individualist who is defying bureaucracy and managing to get away with it.

Dan is all those, and more. He is a symbol of the spreading rot in metropolitan areas, and his story has as many implications for economists as for moralists. Since 1935, when Dan bought his first house, the assessed value of his properties has dropped twenty-seven per cent, meaning his municipality gets nearly $8,000 less in taxes from them each year. The city is spending forty-five per cent of its income in the slums and getting six per cent of its taxes there.

The forty-five per cent is spent in many ways. The neighborhood Dan converted to apartments during the war now leads the city in juvenile delinquency, with twenty cases per thousand population annually. Patrolmen are necessary in every block: after midnight they meet under street lamps and pivot, back to back, like sentries. About one-third of the city's inhabitants live in the slums, but they account for eighty-three per cent of its syphilis and seventy-one per cent of its tuberculosis—one of Dan's blocks has five active TB cases today. The cost of slums in petty thefts, bastardy cases, and social parasites is incalculable, but census figures show that eighty-one per cent of the welfare cases are concentrated there.

Dan's admirers may not know it, but they all contribute to his loot through the relief rolls. A home-owner with an assessment of $9,500 pays three weeks' rent each year in taxes. Through their unfortunate tenants, Dan and his colleagues get a big slice of this.

Such implications have no interest whatever for Dan. His outlook is expressed in a few catch phrases: dog eat dog, tooth and claw, survival of the fittest. He came up the hard way, and he argues anyone else can do it, though if pressed he will modestly admit that stamina, brains, and what he calls "realism" are necessary for success.

Confronted with hard bargainers like Dan Marner, the poor get inadequate housing because they have little to offer in exchange for better housing. Their bargaining position is also weak because they lack information about the comparative quality and value of products they buy. Consequently, they pay more for lower quality than do more knowledgeable American consumers.[2]

The numerous accounts of [consumer] exploitation fall under several general headings. Some reveal the high-pressure sales techniques to which these families are subjected. Others relate to the misrepresentation of the price of goods. And still others refer to the substitution of inferior goods for those ordered. Included here are accounts of the sale of reconditioned goods as new.

[2]Reprinted with permission of The MacMillan Company from *The Poor Pay More* by David Caplovitz © 1967 by The Free Press, a Division of The Macmillan Company. pp. 141-154.

The repetitiveness of the incidents is quite striking. Some families were victimized by unethical television repairmen, a few by the same company. Another group were victims of the pots-and-pans salesmen; encyclopedia salesmen show up in several of the accounts, as do the peddlers selling sink attachments.

As we shall see, the incidents touch upon a number of themes. These include the role of the mass media in setting off the chain of events with alluring ads; the anonymity of many of the credit transactions to the point where the consumer is not sure who the merchant is; the bewilderment of the consumer in the face of powerful forces brought into play by the merchant; and the hopelessness, frustration, and resignation of many in the face of exploitation.

BAIT ADVERTISING AND THE SWITCH SALE

A sizable number of the families had been victimized by "bait" advertising. Responding to advertisements for sewing machines, phonographs, washing machines, and other items offered at unusually low prices, they succumbed to the salesmen's "switch-sale" technique by buying a much more expensive model.

The technique is illustrated by the story of a 26-year-old Negro housewife:

> *I saw a TV ad for a $29 sewing machine,* so I wrote to the company and they sent down a salesman who demonstrated it for me. It shook the whole house, but I wanted to buy it anyway. But he kept saying it would disturb all the neighbors by being so noisy, and *went out to the hall and brought in another model costing $185. . . .*

> I actually had to pay $220. He promised if I paid within a certain amount of time I would get $35 back. *But since my husband was out of work, we couldn't pay within the time period,* so I didn't get the refund. . . . *I was taken in by the high-pressure sales talk.*

A middle-aged Puerto Rican husband was victimized by a variant of this racket. Instead of responding to an ad, he received a call from a salesman saying that his wife had won a sewing machine:

> He brought the machine to the house. It was worth $25, and we ended up buying another one for $186. A friend of mine bought a similar machine, maybe better than mine, for $90. *They tricked me into buying the machine for $186 on credit.*

In these cases, the reactions are much the same, the feeling of being tricked by a high-pressure salesman. In each instance, a purchase was made at a price higher than the anticipated one.

The "switch sale" is by no means limited to sewing machines. A 28-year-old Negro housewife told the following story about a phonograph sale:

I saw an advertisement in the paper *for a $49 Hi-Fi set.* The ad said: "Phone for free demonstration," so I did. The salesman came a few days later, bringing a set that was different from the one I saw advertised. I told him it wasn't the set I saw in the paper, but he said it was, so we hassled for a while. He kept high-pressuring me, saying he had one in the car he knew I would like. So finally, I told him to bring it up. He did, and played it for me.

I asked him to leave it so my husband could hear it, but he said "no." Then I asked him to come back later when my husband would be home and he said "no" again. Well, I decided to gamble and signed the papers. [Later they mailed a coupon book. The set came to $175.]

He asked me for a down-payment, so I gave him my old radio and got $10 off. *And right after that, my husband came in. He didn't want the set, but the salesman told him we couldn't return it.* Later my husband examined the set. The salesman had said it contained four woofers and two tweeters, but my husband found out they didn't exist. We called the store, but they said we couldn't change it, so we had to pay the full amount.

Once the set stopped working. We phoned the store and got free repairs. *But the second time the set broke down, we called the store and were told that the company no longer dealt in Hi-Fi sets, only in sewing machines.*

One law of the commercial jungle facing the low-income consumer is vividly dramatized in this irreversibility of the credit transaction. Tacit in all dealings with ethical merchants is the right to exchange merchandise if the customer is not satisfied. Not so in the low-income market. Once the signature is obtained on the contract, the sale is consummated. It should be noted that the husband returned in time to register his displeasure to the salesman. But the concept of the satisfied customer is foreign to such hit-and-run transactions. Even when the couple discovered that the phonograph did not measure up to the salesman's claims, they were still unable to exchange it. As we shall see, this is not an isolated occurrence. Other families also discovered that the principle of exchange does not apply to them. The "run-around" this couple received when seeking service is also fairly typical. The explanation given seems quite thin, and yet it was apparently enough to free the store from the complaining customer. The incident also illustrates the way "easy credit" breaks through traditional constraints upon consumption. However reluctant at first, this housewife was still able to indulge her impulse to buy without consulting her husband.

Bait advertising was reported by a 37-year-old Negro mother living on welfare. She had seen a newspaper ad, placed by a 125th Street furniture store, announcing the reupholstering of couches with good material for $49.95:

I phoned them and they sent out a salesman. I told him I saw the ad and wanted my couch covered for $49.95. I asked him to show me the material.

He pulled out some patterns and looked at them and said, "These aren't so hot. I really want to give customers something they'll be satisfied with." Then he flipped to the higher-priced patterns—*but I didn't know they were higher-priced then.* I picked out a pattern and asked him how much. He told me $149. *But I only had $49 in cash and wanted to pay only in cash, so I told him that this was too high. He praised the material so much, talking about its quality and durability, that I finally told him that if I could get an account I'd take it. He gave me a contract. I just took a quick look and signed it.* They sent for the couch and returned it two weeks later. The work on the seams of the pillows was awful. . . . Six months later, the wire in the spring popped out the side and the other side had a pointed end on it.

By now the elements of the process are familiar: the "bait ad," the high-pressure salesman, the purchase of a much more expensive item, and, as often happens, dissatisfaction with the merchandise. Of particular interest in this case is the fact that the woman had every intention of paying cash when she responded to the ad but was converted into a credit buyer in spite of her intent.

A 45-year-old white housewife reported the "switch sale" in connection with encyclopedias:

About four years ago I saw an encyclopedia advertised on TV. I called for a salesman and he showed me a set, but it wasn't worth the money. He then talked me into buying a more expensive set.

Like other victims of bait advertising, this woman encountered further difficulties. Although promised an annual yearbook for $3.00, she never received it or recovered her money.

The idea of the unusual bargain takes other forms besides bait advertising. Sometimes the consumer is "hooked" by the promise of free merchandise. A 30-year-old Puerto Rican husband told us that he had once received a phone call from someone who promised him a present:

The man brought a wastepaper basket as the present and he also had with him a vacuum cleaner which he demonstrated. *He talked me into buying the vacuum cleaner even though I thought the price was too high.* I felt "high-pressured."

Another variant of the "something for nothing" appeal is based on the principle of the "pyramid club." Consumers are promised a refund if they help the salesman find a certain number of customers. One instance, reported by an 18-year-old Negro housewife, involved the added inducement of an outright monetary gift:

My mother sent the vacuum cleaner salesman here. He said that he would give me $5 just to talk to me. Then he said that if I got him nine more sales I could have the vacuum cleaner free. I wasn't able to find any customers and I can't work the vacuum cleaner with all its attachments. I don't want it and I've stopped making the payments on it.

Here we see an example of the great disparity between the more traditional logic of these consumers and the law of installment buying. Whether or not the consumer wants the merchandise has no bearing on the merchant's right to payment once the contract is signed.

The "contest" theme is a popular one in the exploitation of consumers. A 32-year-old Negro housewife told us that she entered a contest by filling out a coupon in a Third Avenue store:

Later I was told I won first prize—$30 off on a set of silverware. A man came four different times with different silverware—some used, some with pieces missing. He told us to keep the set for the time being, and that he would return with the set we wanted. Before we ever received the set we ordered, they sent a final notice to pay or my husband's salary would be garnisheed. My husband told his boss who told him to take the silver back to the place and leave it. My husband did take it back, but the man refused to give him a receipt.

Another Negro housewife told of a puzzle contest tied in with the purchase of encyclopedias:

In different comic books my husband found puzzle-contest ads. The prizes were for $10,000, $5,000, and $1,000, plus a lot of other prizes. Over a period of about two years, while he was solving different puzzles, he was required to buy a book a month for $1.98 each. My husband bought twenty of these books. After he got the whole set, he wrote to find out about his position in the puzzle contest. In return he received more puzzles to solve. This went on for some time. Then the firm stopped sending puzzles. And they never did answer any of his letters asking about the contest.

It is apparent that these schemes are able to work because of the naivete of the consumers. This reader of comic books undoubtedly worked on the additional puzzles in good faith.

Some salesmen misrepresent themselves as officials of the Housing Authority. As we noted earlier, some families found themselves buying sink panels from men they thought were Housing-Authority employees. The 18-year-old housewife victimized by the vacuum-cleaner salesman was also a victim of this practice:

Soon after we moved in, a man came saying he was part of the housing management. He installed the cabinets under the kitchen and bathroom sink. Then he told me they cost $19. I thought he meant *both* cost $19, but I found out that they were $19 each. They're not worth it. But I didn't do anything about it.

Another woman, a 37-year-old Puerto Rican, signed a contract for a set of encyclopedias thinking that she was filling out Housing-Authority forms:

When I first moved, a man who said he was the manager asked me to sign some papers. *It turned out I signed for encyclopedias thinking I was signing some housing authority forms* as a new tenant. I went to the Legal Aid Society to complain. The case is still in court. My husband was threatened with a garnishee by the encyclopedia company. *[She said the company went out of business. The account has been taken over by KIP, Inc., and they are the firm suing the family for $96.]*

This incident points up more than the practices of unscrupulous salesmen. It also shows the complex web of business institutions involved in credit transactions which the traditional consumer finds so difficult to understand.

The poor get exploited by hard bargainers because despite their poverty they hunger for the material benefits of an affluent society and because their ignorance makes them gullible. Not only the poor are vulnerable to commercial exploitation. Nearly everyone lowers his defenses against commercial exploitation after the death of a loved one; and American funeral expenses reflect this vulnerability.[3]

In 1960, Americans spent, according to the only available government estimate, $1.6 billion on funerals, setting thereby a new national and world record. The $1.6 billion is, as we shall see, only a portion of what was actually spent on what the death industry calls "the care and memorialization of the dead." Even this partial figure, if averaged out among the number of deaths, would amount to the astonishing sum of $942 for the funeral of every man, woman, child, and stillborn babe who died in the United States in 1960. This is a record unmatched in any previous age or civilization.

The $1.6 billion figure that is given for our national burial bill is furnished by the U.S. Department of Commerce census of business under the heading "personal expenditure for death expense." Since it includes personal expenditures only, it does not include burial expenditures by cities and counties and by private and public institutions for the burial of indigents, welfare recipients, and persons confined in public institutions, nor does it include burial expenditures by the armed forces for military personnel. How much do these public expendi-

---

[3]From Jessica Mitford, "The Undertakers' Racket," *Atlantic*, June 1963, pp. 56-62. Reprinted by permission of Robert Lantz-Cadida Donadio Literary Agency, Inc. Copyright © 1963 by Jessica Mitford.

tures amount to annually? Nobody knows, for there is no centrally maintained source of information. The burial of indigents, for example, is a matter of city or county concern. There is a wildly disparate variation in costs and procedures. Some counties contract with funeral directors for casket, service, and burial for as little as $70; some pay as much as $300 for casket and service alone.

Another substantial item of funeral expense which is not included in the Department of Commerce figure is the cost of shipping the dead by train or plane. These charges must be considerable; one in ten of all the dead is shipped elsewhere for burial. Train fare for a corpse is double the cost of a single first-class ticket for a live passenger. The standard rate for air shipment of human remains is two and one half times the rate for other air freight; the average transcontinental fare for a dead body is $255.78.

Funeral flowers are not included in the Department of Commerce figures. These account for a good bit more than half of the dollar volume of all sales by retail florists in the United States.

Last, the Department of Commerce statistics leave out of account entirely the very considerable amounts spent each year by Americans who in increasing numbers buy graves and mausoleum crypts for future occupancy. This mushrooming business, running into hundreds of millions of dollars annually, is known in cemetery parlance as "pre-need" selling.

It would be a conservative guess that these extras, if added to the Commerce Department's base figure of $1.6 billion, would bring the nation's burial bill to well over $2 billion. A little over three fourths of all funerals are what the industry calls "regular adult funerals." The remainder are limited-service funerals for infants and limited-fee funerals for indigents and servicemen, handled by contract with government agencies. The Department of Commerce figure averages out to $1160 for each regular adult funeral. The more realistic figure of $2 billion yields a nationwide average of $1450 for the disposition of the mortal remains of an adult American.

Funeral people, confronted with the charge that they are responsible for the staggering cost of dying, loudly protest their innocence; how can it be their fault, if fault it be, they say. It is up to the individual family to decide how much to spend on a funeral, and if more is spent by Americans on death than is spent for conservation of natural resources, for fire or police protection; if funeral expenditures exceed personal expenditures for higher education, that's only because funeral buyers are exercising their inalienable right to spend their money as they choose.

"How much should a funeral cost?" says Wilbur Krieger, managing director of the National Selected Morticians. "That's like asking how much should I pay for a house or how much for a car. You can buy at all prices." Most funeral advertising stresses the same thought: "The decision of how much to spend for a funeral always rests with the family."

Very occasionally, somebody within the industry will spill the beans. Such a one was W. W. Chambers, self-styled "slab-happy" mortician of Washington, D.C., who has built up a million-dollar mortuary empire. "It's the most highly specialized racket in the world," he declared, testifying before a congressional committee in 1947. "It has no standard prices; whatever can be charged and gotten away with is the guiding rule. My competitors don't like my habit of advertising prices in black and white, because they'd rather keep the right to charge six different prices for the same funeral to six different people, according to what they can pay. Why, some of these bums charge a family $90 to bury a poor little baby in a casket that costs only $4.50." Scoffing at the suggestion that an undertaker is a "professional man," Chambers said any good plumber could learn how to embalm in sixty days. He added that he could embalm a human body for forty cents and an elephant for $1.50.

Foreigners are astonished to learn that almost all Americans are embalmed and publicly displayed after death. The practice is unheard of outside the United States and Canada. As Alfred Fellows, an English jurist, wrote in *The Law of Burial*, "A public exhibition of an embalmed body, as that of Lenin in Moscow, would presumably be dealt with as a revolting spectacle and therefore a public nuisance."

I asked a London undertaker if he had ever conducted an open-casket funeral, in which the mourners file by to look at the embalmed corpse. He answered that such a thing would be considered so absolutely weird, so contrary to good taste and proper behavior, so shocking to the sensibilities of all concerned that he thinks it could never become a practice in England. The overwhelming majority of English of all classes, he said, settle for a simple wooden coffin and a small gathering (six or seven is average) of the immediate family at the funeral service. Cremation is sharply on the increase there, and in 90 percent of cases the ashes do not wind up in an elaborate urn housed in a niche in some columbarium, but are scattered over the countryside or in a garden. . . .

The seller of funerals has, one gathers, a preconceived, stereotyped view of his customers. To him, the bereaved person who enters his establishment is a bundle of guilt feelings, a snob, and a status seeker. The undertaker feels that by steering his customer to the top-priced casket, he is giving him his first dose of grief therapy, for, according to a trade magazine, "the focus of the buyer's interest must be the casket, vault, clothing, funeral cars, etc.—the only tangible evidence of how much has been invested in the funeral—the only real status symbol associated with a funeral service."

Whether or not one agrees with this rather unflattering appraisal of the average person who has suffered a death in the family, it is nevertheless true that the funeral transaction is generally influenced by a combination of circumstances which bear upon the buyer as in no other type of business dealing: the disorientation caused by bereavement, the lack of standards by which to judge the value of the commodity offered by the seller, the need to make an on-the-spot decision, general ignorance of the law as it affects disposal of the dead, and the ready availability of insurance money to finance the transaction. These are worth analyzing because they predetermine to a large extent the outcome of the transaction.

The buyer's frame of mind will vary, obviously, according to the circumstances which led him to the funeral establishment. The great majority of funeral buyers, as they are led through their paces at the mortuary—whether shaken and grief-stricken or merely looking forward with pleasurable anticipation to the reading of the will—are assailed by many a nagging question: What is the right thing to do? I am arranging this funeral, but surely this is no time to indulge my own preferences in taste and style. What will her family and friends expect? How can I avoid criticism for inadvertently doing the wrong thing? And, above all, it should be a nice, decent funeral—but what *is* a nice, decent funeral?

Which leads us to the second unusual aspect of the funeral transaction: the buyer's almost total ignorance of what to expect when he enters the undertaker's parlor. What to look for, what to avoid, how much to spend. The funeral industry estimates that the average individual has to arrange for a funeral only once in fifteen years. The cost of the funeral is the third largest expenditure, after a house and a car, in the life of an ordinary American family. Yet even in the case of an old relative whose death may have been fully expected and even welcomed, it is most unlikely that the buyer will have discussed the funeral with anybody in advance.

Because of the nature of funerals, the buyer is in a quite different position from one who is, for example, in the market for a car. Visualize the approach. The man of prudence and common sense who is about to buy a car consults a consumer's research bulletin or seeks the advice of his friends; he knows in advance the dangers of rushing into a deal blindly. In the funeral home, the man of prudence is completely at sea without a recognizable landmark or bearing to guide him. It would be an unusual person who would examine the various offerings and then inquire around about the relative advantages of the Monaco casket by Merit and the Valley Forge by Boyertown. In the matter of cost, a like difference is manifest. The funeral buyer is generally not in the mood to compare prices here, examine and appraise quality there.

The third factor which confronts the buyer is the need to make an on-the-spot decision. Impulse buying, which should ordinarily be avoided, is here a built-in necessity. The convenient equivocations of commerce—"I'll look around a little, and let you know," "Maybe, I'll call you in a couple of weeks if I decide to take it"—simply do not apply in this situation.

Popular ignorance about the law as it relates to the disposal of the dead is a factor that sometimes affects the funeral transaction. People are often astonished to learn that in no state is embalming required by law except in certain special circumstances, such as when the body is to be shipped by common carrier.

The funeral men foster these misconceptions, sometimes by coolly misstating the law to the funeral buyer and sometimes by inferentially investing with the authority of law certain trade practices which they find convenient or profitable to follow. This free and easy attitude toward the law is even to be found in those institutes of higher learning, the colleges of mortuary science, where the fledgling undertaker receives his training. For example, it is the law in most states that when a decedent bequeaths his body for use in medical research, his survivors are bound to carry out his directions. Nonetheless, an embalming textbook disposes of the whole distasteful subject in a few misleading words: "Q: Will the provisions in the will of a decedent that his body be given to a medical college for dissection be upheld over his widow? A: No . . . No-one owns or controls his own body to the extent that he may dispose of the same in a manner which would bring humiliation and grief to the immediate members of his family."

I had been told so often that funeral men tend to invent the law as they go along (for there is a fat financial reward at stake) that I decided to investigate this situation at firsthand. Armed with a copy of the California code, I telephoned a leading undertaker in my community with a concocted story: my aged aunt, living in my home, was seriously ill—not expected to live more than a few days. Her daughter was coming here directly; but I felt I ought to have some suggestions, some arrangements to propose in the event that—Sympathetic monosyllables from my interlocutor. The family would want something very simply, I went on, just cremation. Of course, we can arrange all that, I was assured. And since we want only cremation, and there will be no service, we should prefer not to buy a coffin. The undertaker's voice at the other end of the phone was now alert, although smooth. He told me, calmly and authoritatively, that it would be "illegal" for him to enter into such an arrangement. "You mean it would be against the law?" I asked. Yes, indeed. I took a deep breath and pressed on: "In that case, perhaps we could take the body straight to the crematorium in our station wagon?" A shocked silence, followed by an explosive outburst: "Madam, the average lady has neither the facilities nor the inclination to be hauling dead bodies around!" (Which was actually a good point, I thought.)

I tried two more funeral establishments and was told substantially the same thing: cremation of an uncoffined body is prohibited under California law. This was said, in all three cases, with such a ring of conviction that I began to doubt the evidence before my eyes in the state code. I reread the sections on cremation, on health requirements; finally I read the whole thing from cover to cover. Finding no reference to an uncoffined body, I checked with an officer of the Board of Health, who told me there is no law in California requiring that a coffin be used when a body is cremated.

It is, however, true that most privately owned crematoria have their own privately established rule that they will not cremate without a coffin. After all, why not? Many are in the casket-selling business themselves, and those that are not depend for their livelihood on the goodwill of undertakers who are.

Cemetery salesmen are also prone to confuse fact with fiction to their own advantage in discussing the law. Cemeteries derive a substantial income from the sale of vaults. The vault, a cement enclosure for the casket, is not only a money-maker; it facilitates upkeep of the cemetery by preventing the eventual subsidence of the grave as the casket disintegrates. In response to my inquiry, a cemetery salesman (identified on his card as a "memorial counsellor") called at my house to sell me what he was pleased to call a "pre-need memorial estate"— in other words, a grave. After he had quoted the prices of the various graves, the salesman explained that a minimum of $120 must be added for a vault, which, he said, is "required by law." Why is it required by law? To prevent the ground from caving in. But suppose I should be buried in one of those eternal caskets made of solid bronze? Those things are not as solid as they look; you'd be surprised how soon they fall apart. Are you *sure* it is required by law? I've been in this business fifteen years, I should know. Then would you be willing to sign this; (I had been writing on a sheet of paper, "California State Law requires a vault for ground burial.") The memorial counsellor swept up his colored photographs of memorial estates, backed out the door, and fled down the street.

The fifth unusual factor present in the funeral transaction is the availability to the buyer of relatively large sums of cash. The family accustomed to buying every major item on time—car, television set, furniture—and to spending to the limit of the weekly paycheck suddenly finds itself in possession of insurance funds and death-benefit payments, often from a number of sources. It is usually unnecessary for the undertaker to resort to crude means to ascertain the extent of insurance coverage. A few simple and perfectly natural questions put to the family while he is completing the vital-statistics forms will serve to elicit all he needs to know. For example, "Occupation of the deceased?" "Shall we bill the insurance company directly?"

The undertaker knows, better than a schoolboy knows the standings of the major league baseball teams, the death-benefit payments of every trade union in the community, the social security and workmen's compensation scale of death benefits, the veterans' and servicement's death benefits.

At the lowest end of the scale is the old-age pensioner, most of whose savings have long since been spent. He is among the poorest of the poor. Nevertheless, most state and county welfare agencies permit him to have up to $1000 in cash; in some states he may own a modest home as well, without jeopardizing his pension. The undertaker knows that under the law of virtually every state the funeral bill is entitled to preference in payment as the first charge against the estate. (Efforts in some states to pass legislation limiting the amount of the priority for burial costs to, say, $500 have been frustrated by the funeral lobby.) There is every likelihood that the poor old chap will be sent out in high style unless his widow is a very knowledgeable customer.

In short, the marketing principle applies to bereaved persons as well as to customers for other services. We see in this case the pathology involved in the market mentality more generally. The utilitarian use of human beings for the sake of enhancing one's bargaining power takes other forms, forms less directly commercial and more clearly pathological.[5] The involvement of "The Mob" in legitimate businesses is a case in point.

In the spring of 1964, Jerry Catena and his brother Gene wangled a contract from a manufacturer to wholesale an offbreed brand of detergent in the New Jersey area. Forthwith they began to push their "Brand X," as we'll call it here, through one of their front outfits, the Best Sales Co. of Newark. Best Sales has salesmen aplenty, of a sort—some 600 members of the gang that Jerry was running for Vito Genovese, plus others, such as representatives of the Amalgamated Meat Cutters and Butcher Workmen, and the Teamsters. Both had organized workers in food chain stores in New Jersey.

To move the Best Sales detergent, Catena eventually pulled all the stops of Cosa Nostra power.

First, butchers' union agents began pointedly dropping word in food marts that the Best Sales product was a good thing. "Good people in that company," store managers were told, "particular friends of ours." Most of them got the message—and laid in a supply of the detergent, dutifully priced at 70¢ per box.

Early in 1964, the Catenas began thinking big, drawing a bead on the huge A & P chain. If the A & P could be "persuaded" to sell the product, or maybe even to push it over the big-name brands, the Catena boys would surely end up as soap czars.

There was no objection by A & P to testing the Catena detergent—indeed, it seemed for a few days that the Best Sales product was being favorably considered.

In April, however, A & P consumer tests disclosed that Catena's product didn't measure up to other brands—no sale. Within a few days, to add insult to injury, word reached Gene Catena that his detergent had been rejected *because A & P had learned that the Catenas were selling it.*

Gene, in a fury, promised to "knock A & P's brains out." And he tried.

On a May night in 1964, a fire bomb was tossed into an A & P store in

[5]From Sandy Smith, "The Mob," *Life* 63:10, September 8, 1967, pp. 103-104. Reprinted by permission. © 1967 Time Inc.

Yonkers, N.Y. The store burned to the ground.

A month later, another Molotov cocktail touched off a fire that destroyed an A & P store in Peekskill, N.Y. In August, an A & P store on First Avenue in Manhattan was gutted, and in December, an A & P store in the Bronx.

Even then, though thoroughly frightened, executives of the chain did not connect the incendiary fires with their rejection of the detergent. The Catenas tried again to spell it out, in a more pointed way.

On the night of January 23, 1965, Manager James B. Walsh closed a Brooklyn A & P store and got into his auto to go home. A few blocks from the store, one of his tires seemed flat, and he got out to fix it. A car pulled up and four men got out. They killed Walsh with three pistol shots.

About two weeks later, on the evening of February 5, store manager John P. Mossner drove home to Elmont, N.Y. from his A & P supermarket in the Bronx. As he got out of his car in his driveway, a lone gunman stepped out of the shadows and shot him dead.

Two months after Mossner's murder, one more A & P store burned in the Bronx. The blaze had been started with a fire bomb.

Meanwhile, the butchers' union had begun negotiations on a new labor contract with A & P. The company's contract offers were rejected. The union made counterproposals which A & P considered outrageous. The butchers threatened to strike, and the Teamsters let it be known they would not cross the picket lines.

The A & P officials were growing frantic in the face of the apparently motiveless murders and fire-bombings and the deadlocked union negotiations. In desperation they appealed to the federal government for assistance of some kind.

It took about a month for government informants to link the terrorism with the Catena detergent sales company. But proving that connection by producing the informants in a courtroom was out of the question. Accordingly, U.S. District Attorney Robert Morgenthau brought Jerry Catena himself before a federal grand jury. On his way into the jury room the puzzled gangster asked a government official why he had been called.

"We want to know about your marketing procedures," the official said.

"Marketing of what?" asked Catena.

"Detergent."

Ah, *detergent!* As of that moment, the A & P's terror ended. Catena appeared briefly before the grand jury and hurried from the grand jury and hurried from the courthouse. At their very next negotiating session, the strike-threatening butchers signed the A & P contract they had rejected weeks before.

A few days later, a federal investigator ran into one Gerardo Catena in lower Manhattan and asked pointedly how things were going in the detergent business. Catena's muttered answer was close to pleading.

"I'm sorry," he said. "I'm getting out of detergent."

And that was all. To try to muscle a mob-backed product onto A & P shelves, Catena or thugs in his employ had burned out five supermarkets and had murdered two innocent store managers in cold blood. And yet, because the government could not jeopardize its own informants by bringing them into court, Catena suffered only the minor inconvenience of a grand jury appearance and the failure of his detergent scheme. Gene Catena died a month ago, of natural causes. Jerry Catena, the hoodlum boss, and his bomb throwers and murderers continue to walk around free.

CONCLUSION

Many people look at the social problems consisting of merchants who exploit the poor, funeral directors who take advantage of the bereaved, mobsters who use force to sell their wares, and landlords like Dan Marner, and attribute the causes to the bad character of the "villains." "Evil people cause such problems," many people think.

A sociological diagnosis places the emphasis differently. A *social structure* organized so that the individual is dependent on making it worth other peoples' while to supply his needs tempts many persons to conform relentlessly to the bargaining principle. We do not mean that everyone who participates in the marketplace is ruthless; for many people, other American standards temper their commercial tendencies. Still others are lucky enough or talented enough so that the market for their services is brisk without any special effort on their part. For many, however, the market commandment, "Thou shalt prosper only by successful bargaining," leads to behavior we consider social problems.

Ken Heyman

chapter 9
Pathologies of conformity
to self-oriented competition

Competition, Americans believe, is the flywheel of progress. Doubtless, under certain conditions, it is. Under other conditions, however, the self-oriented drive to surpass or eliminate competitors imposes high social costs. As an illustration, consider the ruthless techniques employed by segments of the American railroad industry in fighting competition from trucking companies. What follows are parts of the official record in the United States District Court for the Eastern District of Pennsylvania.[1]

   ... the use of long-haul trucks for interstate hauling of freight had increased so enormously by May of 1949 that it was a matter of immediate and vital self-interest to the railroads to do something about the erosion of what had been up to this time almost an exclusive monopoly of long-haul freight transportation. At first blush, to the ordinary person it would appear that the primary concern of the railroads might have been directed to improving service and to attempt to meet by more flexibility and speedy delivery the growing competition of the truckers. The evidence in this case has disclosed there were certain areas wherein the trucks could not compete. It was testified that the trucks would not compete with the railroads in taking the coal out of the mountains of West Virginia since one diesel engine could take a great number of cars on the downgrade of the West Virginia mines to the Norfolk breakwater. That the railroads would continue to enjoy this type of business was completely self-

[1]From Noerr Motor Freight, Inc. et al. v. Eastern Railroad Presidents' Conference et al., 113 *Fed. Supp.* 737.

172

evident. On the other hand, the greater flexibility of the truck and the speedier delivery of goods were elements in the competitive market which the railroads might themselves have attempted to meet by the use of trucks or otherwise. The door-to-door feature of truck delivery was also important. However, the record in this case is barren of any attempt on the part of the railroads to adjust their thinking and their actions to meet this definite threat to a segment of business theretofore enjoyed by them. They engaged in what has been termed throughout the trial of this case as a "concert of action" to "improve their position" in the long-haul freight competitive market. And here is how they did it.

In May of 1949 the evidence discloses that the top executives of the Pennsylvania Railroad, before attending the May 19th, 1949, meeting of the [Eastern Railroads Presidents] Conference, were considering a campaign for Federal and State taxes against users of highways, waterways, etc. The recommendation which came out of this consideration was that they should explore the possibility of organizing private motorists and other groups to be held out to the public as completely nonrailroad inspired for the sole purpose of restricting the truckers by making their operations so expensive that they could not operate at a profit. The obvious corollary is that the railroads would be the beneficiaries of these restrictions. On May 19th, 1949, at a meeting of the Conference, there was appointed a Competitive Transportation Committee with Subcommittees designated Legal, Research, and Public Relations. David I. Mackie, then vice-president of the Delaware & Lackawanna Railroad, was made Chairman of the Legal Committee. Raymond J. Littlefield, tax agent and later general agent of the Pennsylvania Railroad, was made Chairman of the Research Committee. Thomas J. Deegan, Jr., then executive vice-president of the Chesapeake & Ohio Railroad, later staff vice-president of the Allegheny Corporation, operators of the New York Central Lines, was made Chairman of the very important Public Relations Subcommittee. While these three subcommittees maintained an effective liaison, the most active and most potent of the committees was the Committee on Public Relations. Deegan and his subcommittee determined on a plan of operation. The single objective of the campaign was harassment of the long-haul truckers. One of the objectives was the enactment of legislation, not under the sponsorship of the railroads but by others acting on their behalf, by what was called in inoffensive and pleasing language, "The third-party technique."

The campaign was to begin in New York, New Jersey and Ohio, and other states were to be brought in later as the program developed, consistent with the degree of success of the program. It was also determined that the campaign should be handled through an independent public relations firm. . . .

A presentation was made by the defendant-Byoir firm prior to the execution of the contract on August 15, 1949. . . . After the contract was awarded a memorandum of agreement was executed providing for payment to Byoir of

$75,000 a year, plus reimbursement of each and every expense of any sort involved in the campaign. Byoir immediately organized a staff to put the program into effect and execution. . . .

While the ultimate objective is shrewdly set forth as legislation affecting the truckers, the intermediate goals are also set forth, all designed and aimed at injury to the truckers. These objectives, including the crystalization of motorist resentment arising from commercial heavy truck operations over the roads, were designed to arouse the public generally of the need to obtain new methods of financing public highways and by methods which would not appear to emanate from railroad sources.

MAGAZINE ACTIVITIES

One of the most unusual of Byoir's employees, the head of the Magazine Department, was Patricia Lochridge Hartwell. Mrs. Hartwell, whose professional name while she was with Byoir was Patricia Lochridge, joined the Byoir organization in November of 1949 and was assigned to the ERPC account. She thereupon set out to develop magazine articles which would portray the railroads' point of view and would be unfavorable to the trucking interest. Her method of operation was to interest an editor of a magazine in a story and if the editor thought it had sufficient merit he might assign one of his staff writers or editors to do the piece. In that event Mrs. Hartwell would furnish the writer with the data which Byoir had compiled, which data of course was always slanted against the truckers. She also made use of free-lance writers. She would interest them in a particular story and pay them while they researched the proposed story at Byoir's or at other places, which amounts in many instances ran into several hundreds of dollars. Since the ultimate aim was to hurt the truckers, any such payments were reimbursed by the railroads, and should the free-lance writer be able to sell the article to a magazine the entire fee went to the writer. In other words, Byoir paid the writer during the preparation of the article and the magazine paid him for writing it. In the extremely limited number of instances that a writer contemplated an article which would be favorable to the railroads' point of view with respect to the truckers, Byoir extended every facility it possessed for use of the writer and at no cost to the writer.

The worth of such a project in the attainment of the ERPC goal cannot be minimized. In addition to the ordinary extensive circulation which the magazines themselves possessed, it was possible, at railroad expense, to circulate reprints of the articles widely to civic organizations, state, city and government officials, as well as to legislators and other individuals who were concerned with public opinion. While it is true that her efforts in every case did not meet with complete success, she was successful in having enough magazine articles released to make an important contribution to the railroads' antitruck campaign. Without attempting to individuate the details of each article, it will be sufficient to recount some of the articles published and Byoir's connection with them.

The first article, "The Giants Wreck Highways" with a subtitle "Heavy Trucks Are Making Their Runs On Your Tax Dollars," appeared in the April, 1950 issue of *Everybody's Digest*. It was based almost completely upon Byoir's research and development. In the same month Byoir claimed credit for having furnished minor research and comment for an article by Senator Joseph C. O'Mahoney entitled, "What Bad Roads Are Costing Us," which appeared in the April, 1950 issue of the *American Magazine*. . . .

An article which represented an extremely important item in the railroads' campaign against the truckers was that which appeared in the April, 1952 issue of the *Country Gentleman*. This article by Emilie Hall, described as "You Can Have Better Roads" was referred to by the magazine as a "new chapter in the farm roads story." The writer was discovered by Horace Lyon, a Byoir employee assigned to the ERPC account, and Mrs. Hartwell did most of the research and editing for the article, with Jim Miller and Dick Strouse of Byoir helping in some last minute rewrites. Quoting Mrs. Hartwell's appraisal of the publication of this article: "This was a difficult job to put across, entailing two complete rewrites of the article to satisfy both a pixie author and a difficult editor. This was accomplished without too much pain and the underlying philosophy of the ERPC account came through in the final draft." After various complications Lyon and Lochridge were able to get the article endorsed in a box which appeared on the first page of the article by the president of the all-important Association of American State Highway Officials. This article received widespread distribution at the hands of Byoir but more importantly a motion picture based on this article was made for distribution to farm groups throughout the country. The story of how this motion picture came into existence, the purpose behind the picture, and the ultimate success of the endeavor is significantly interesting.

For some seventeen years one Fred O. Bailey had served as reporter and farm editor of the United Press Association. During the years 1945, 1946 and 1947 he had served as Legislative Counsel of the National Grange. Subsequent to 1947 he served a number of national magazines in the farm field as a reporter and columnist. According to the testimony of David I. Mackie, one of those magazines served was the *Country Gentleman*. During the year 1951 Bailey had discussed the formation of a Farm Roads Foundation but nothing came of it during that year. However, the general idea of such a Foundation was to cooperate with and assist farm organizations and farm groups in planning for an adequate balanced roads program to serve their needs. The first and only function of the Farm Roads Foundation up until May of 1953, the date of Mr. Bailey's deposition in this case, was the distribution of a film, "Highways and

Byways, U.S.A.," based upon the story in the *Country Gentleman* magazine, "You Can Have Better Roads." The evidence in this case discloses beyond peradventure of doubt that the moving force in the making of this film was the Western Association of Railroads. Bailey was approached by representatives of that association and offered an outright grant of a picture for distribution. It was not until this offer had been made that the Farm Roads Foundation was incorporated and came into being. The evidence is also crystal clear that Byoir, in conjunction with representatives of the Western Railroads Association, had been working on a script for this picture. In fact, Byoir edited the script. Dudley Pictures of Hollywood were commissioned by the association of railroads to make the picture and the cost of making the picture was divided between the Eastern, Western and Southern railroads on a basis of 18% to the Southern railroads and 41% each to the Eastern and Western railroads. The assessment to the Eastern railroads was $62,500. Based on the above percentages of assessment it would appear, therefore, that the cost of the film to the three railroad associations exceeded $150,000. This film, the cost of the public distribution of which (and it was most extensive) has always been borne through a grant by the railroads, was exhibited at the trial of this case and the film and a transcript thereof have been filed of record. The film is professional and skillfully done. It demonstrates clearly the needs of the farmers for auxiliary roads and suggests united, combined, intelligent community efforts to obtain the necessary funds to bring about this very desirable result. The lasting impression, however, created by the picture is contained in a very few sentences of the dialogue and as the picture concludes; the lasting impact of the film is that big trucks do not pay their fair share of highway construction and maintenance. While extremely expensive it constituted a very important piece of propaganda carrying a terrific impact upon its viewers. Mr. Bailey, whose cooperation had been sought in the editing of the script, was completely unaware of the very important role played by Byoir. He had no idea of the cost of the film nor of the cost of distribution which was borne by the railroads. Two distribution companies were employed to distribute the film through their regular agencies to farm groups and other interested parties. It was distributed free of charge for showing in regular moving picture houses. 186 colored prints were made in 16 millimeter size and 10 black and white 16 millimeter size copies were made for showing on TV. The testimony indicates that considerable use was made of the film on TV. Four 35 millimeter copies were made for showing in regular motion picture theaters. To a viewer of the picture it would appear that the sponsors were the *Country Gentleman* and the Farm Roads Foundation. No suggestion either in the title, dialogue or screen credits indicated the connection of the railroads with this film. Viewed as it was by millions, the effect was most certainly to build up prejudice in the public mind against the trucking industry. . . .

ROAD TEST ONE—MARYLAND

In 1949 the Governors Conference requested the Council of State Governments to study and report upon the matter of reasonable and uniform standards of motor-vehicle maximum-size-and-weight limitations. At the call of Governor Lausche of Ohio and cosponsored by highway officials from 14 midwestern and eastern states, a conference was held at Columbus, Ohio, on December 5 and 6, 1949, to consider the size and weight problem as a matter of interregional concern. Early in the deliberations of the conference, it became apparent that an objective determination of the effects of *axle loads* of various magnitudes would afford the only possibility of eventual agreement of the entire membership on the important question of axle-load limitations.

The conference formed itself into the Interregional Council on Highway Transportation and appointed a Committee on Test Roads. This special committee met in Baltimore, Maryland, on January 9 and 10, 1950, to inspect a test-road location proposed by representatives of the Maryland State Roads Commission. After visiting the site of the proposed test road, the committee decided that the project identified as Road Test One—Maryland was feasible and recommended that tests be conducted at the joint expense of the participating state highway departments and with Highway Research Board direction of the project. The highway departments of the following states: Connecticut, Delaware, Illinois, Kentucky, Maryland, Michigan, New Jersey, Ohio, Pennsylvania, Virginia, Wisconsin and the District of Columbia, executed contracts with the National Academy of Sciences, of which the Highway Research Board was a component part, agreeing to participate financially in the cooperative venture. The project was administered and supervised by the said Highway Research Board through a small Project Executive Committee and an Advisory Committee. The Advisory Committee included one representative from each participating state, the Bureau of Public Roads, the Automobile Manufacturers Association, the Petroleum Industry, the American Trucking Association, and the Department of the Army. The Bureau of the Public Roads provided personnel and instruments for measurements of surface roughness, slab strains and deflections caused by the test loads, soil surveys, and other necessary instrumentation and testing services, and also provided the services of the project engineer and three assistants.

The principal object of the test was to determine the relative effects on a particular concrete pavement of four different *axle loadings* on two vehicle types. The loads employed were 18,000 and 22,400 pounds per single axle, and 32,000 and 44,800 pounds per tandem axle. The tests were conducted on a 1.1-mile section of Portland cement-concrete pavement constructed in 1941 on U.S. 301 approximately 9 miles south of La Plata, Maryland. The pavement consisted of two 12 ft. lanes, each having a 9-7-9 in. cross-section and reinforced with wire mesh. The road at the beginning of the test was in fairly good condition and insofar as the records of the Maryland Road Commission could determine the entire length of the test site was constructed on good granular subbase material.

There were four separate test sections. The first, which was the west lane of the southern half mile of the pavement under test, was subject to 18,000 lbs. single axle load; the second, which was the east lane of the southern half mile, was subject to 22,400 lbs. single axle load; the third, which was the west lane of the northern 0.6 mile, was subject to 32,000 lbs. tandem axle load; and the fourth, which was the east lane of the northern 0.6 mile, was subject to 44,800 lbs. tandem axle load.

The test truck operations began on June 12, 1950, for Sections 1 and 2, single axle loads, and the tandem heavier trucks on the eastern end began operation on June 23, 1950. Operations of all test trucks were continuous, on a 24-hour day, seven-day week basis, except when necessary to interrupt operations for vehicle and pavement maintenance and service, meals and rest stops for drivers, and special tests, such as strain and deflections. In addition, operations were suspended for 24 hours for three holidays during 1950: July 4, Labor Day and Thanksgiving Day. The drivers worked three 8-hour shifts and were allowed a 10-minute rest period each hour and 30 minutes for a meal in the middle of the shift. The 18,000 lb. axle load totaled 111,889 miles; the 22,400 lb. axle load totaled 111,792 miles; the 32,000 lb. tandem axle load totaled 106,668 miles; and the 44,800 lb. tandem axle load totaled 59,256 miles due to cessation of operations during the month of November occasioned by excessive damage to that part of the test highway.

This was to be, and was, insofar as the Highway Research Board was concerned, a completely objective test. Mr. Herbert S. Fairbanks, Deputy Commissioner of the Bureau of Public Roads and Chairman of the Highway Research Board, estimated in his testimony in this case that the stress placed on the road during the pendency of this test would approximate 40 years of normal usage of the same road. Contrary to the general understanding of the content of the subsoil of the road, it became very evident as the test progressed that certain portions of the road, particularly that over which the heavier trucks ran, had a subgrade which consisted in great part of fine grain soil. When water permeated the fine grain soil the deflection caused by the weight of the trucks would push the water and solid matter from the subbase of the road and eventually this would create a hole or pocket under the road. The weight of the truck would then crack the concrete immediately over the hole or pocket. The water which would lodge in these pockets or holes would be "pumped" up through the expansion joints of the road. While test procedures might have allowed normal maintenance of the roads, such as filling in and reinforcing these cavities under the road, deliberately and in the interest of scientific knowledge minimal maintenance was indulged in throughout the entire period of the test. Naturally this resulted in much faster deterioration than would be the case had normal maintenance been carried out.

It will be recognized that the impetus for this test came from Governor Lausche of Ohio. His Director of the Ohio Department of Highways, T. J. Kauer, Chairman of the Interregional Council on Highway Transportation, as such, had extremely close contacts with all features of the test. It will also be recalled that Harold Cohen, Chief of Public Relations of the Ohio Department of Highways, was a very close associate of Stull, Byoir's representative in Ohio. The purpose of this test was a scientific determination of what a road of this character could carry safely. The distortion of this aim and purpose, and the peculiar conduct of Messrs. Kauer, Cohen and Clinton Johnson, Director of Publicity for the Maryland Roads Commissions, makes an interesting chapter in the Byoir-railroad antitruck campaign. It was the purpose of Byoir to obtain as early as possible any information from this test which would support their theory that the *gross weight* of the truck (whereas the test was an examination of the effects of *axle-load weights*) was alone responsible for breaking up roads. With this in mind close liaison was kept with Kauer, Cohen and Johnson. The records of the Byoir organization show that Johnson during the course of this test was a frequent visitor at the Byoir offices in New York and that the expenses of his visits were borne by Byoir and reimbursed by the railroads. There also appear in the evidence many vouchers which indicate that the railroads reimbursed Byoir for entertainment of Johnson and his wife. Ultimately he became an employee of the ERPC, receiving $1,000 per month plus expenses from December of 1952 through September of 1953. A further inference may be drawn from the fact that in an undated memorandum (P-121) from Hardy, Byoir's New Jersey and Pennsylvania agent, to Mr. Deegan, Hardy noted that in checking over the agenda of an ERPC meeting it occurred to him that Deegan might not want to discuss Johnson at the open meeting. He further mentioned that he talked to Littlefield about this and that he was interested in Deegan's idea. Hardy's explanation that the reason they might not want to discuss Johnson at the open meeting was because it was a mere matter of slight detail does not satisfy the Court. (R.745) While out-and-out bribery of Mr. Johnson has not been proven by a preponderance of evidence, the Court is satisfied that the plaintiffs have proved that Mr. Johnson, because of the above-mentioned factors, was not an objective public employee, but rather was working for the interests of the railroads in order to further his own personal goal of obtaining a lucrative position with the ERPC.

There is no doubt and the record abundantly proves that Byoir actually did get information about the test as it progressed. It was the purpose of Mr. Fairbanks and his associates that no conclusion be published until the full committee had time for a mature consideration of all of the factors involved in the test. From time to time, however, Byoir put out releases which indicated that big trucks, in the sense of gross weights rather than axle loads, were the primary factor in destroying the roads and highways of this country. Byoir even released pictures terming the Maryland Road Test as a "Crackathon"; pictures which showed the pumping action when heavy trucks ran over joints where the subsoil was of fine grain sand rather than the granular subsurface which withstood the test of all of the weights with remarkable durability. If a "Crackathon" is a highly technical and scientifically controlled attempt to crowd into a period of several months the effect of roughly four decades of road use in order to determine what factors ultimately result in the break up of roads, Byoir used the proper appellation in describing the Maryland Road Test. But this Court finds that Byoir meant, and the reading public so interpreted it as meaning, that a "Crackathon" was the result which invariably followed from the use of heavy trucks on concrete roads. In a word—big trucks are the sole procuring cause of road destruction, rather than the true nature of the test which was to crack the road under controlled conditions.

Mrs. Hartwell likewise entered into this picture. She spent about a week at the site of the test, taking notes and watching the progress of the test, and did her best to get releases which would favor the railroads. She also sent a woman free-lance writer to the scene with instructions to represent herself as an editor of *Colliers*, which she was not. As such purported editor she was well received by all at the site including representatives of the American Trucking Association and she was accorded every courtesy possible. Her report to Mrs. Hartwell is a masterpiece of the venomous approach which any one connected with Byoir took toward the heavy trucks.

One particular feature of the test and Byoir's approach to it deserves special mention. A running motion picture of the test at selected times was made for the Bureau of Public Roads. At the conclusion of the test and with the approval of Mr. Fairbanks, this motion picture was edited and narrated by a competent Washington, D.C. news commentator. The original so-called "long version" of the motion picture was shown at the trial of the case and the Court was impressed with the completely objective approach to the problem and the fair comments of the narrator. Viewing the motion picture at the end of one day's session, the Court felt that the picture clearly demonstrated that the most important cause of cracking of concrete highways was the presence of a fine grain silty or clay soil subgrade. One important statement was made in the long version of the film:

> The test shows conclusively that a concrete pavement, of the strength and dimensions of the test road, will support indefinitely, without structural failure, single-axle loads as great as 22,400 pounds—*if* there is a subgrade, of adequate thickness, of non-plastic, granular soil. The equivalent of such support must be supplied by the design of roads *in the future.*

Among others, this important statement was carefully removed from the later shortened version of the film.

When people or organizations (such as a group of railroad companies) compete in a no-holds-barred fashion, not only are their competitors damaged, but the public is also misled. This may be dangerous in a democracy. Indeed, the public is often the victim of a small group's determination to protect its *own* interests—in what many consider typically American fashion. The "small group" may be a political entity such as a municipality, which acts in a rational self-interested way to keep *its* taxes down or keep *its* property values high, in disregard of the costs it thereby imposes on others. Consider the phenomenon of one community benefiting by polluting the water of all communities downstream from it.[2]

Last September [1960] the United States government filed a suit against St. Joseph, Missouri, the first time the Federal government has ever brought suit against a city. The suit was filed in desperation, after three years of unsuccessful attempts to persuade the city to stop polluting the Missouri River.

St. Joseph, which publicizes itself as the "Home of the Pony Express," also has some old-fashioned notions about sanitation. The city and its industries have been pouring raw sewage into the Missouri River for more than a century.

On occasion the waters south of it have become so thick that some of the hardier entrepreneurs in the area have taken to their boats and worked up a good business peddling the grease they skimmed from the surface. A Public Health Service engineer who inspected the sewage flow into the river testified that it is not safe to come in contact with the water.

The Missouri River is a boundary between Kansas and Missouri. Twenty-four miles south of St. Joseph, the city of Atchison, Kansas, takes its water supply from the polluted river. Atchison goes to extraordinary lengths to purify the water, but with limited success. An Atchison resident testified during a Public Health Serice hearing: "We have grown accustomed to it, but at times . . . the chlorine content was such as to cause a serious odor and also some sickness among people in Atchison." His wife's parents had moved to town to enjoy the amenities of urban life, he said, but they were hauling their drinking water in from the farm.

CRACKING DOWN

The U.S. Public Health Service brought health officials of Kansas and Missouri together for a conference with spokesmen for St. Joseph and eighteen of its industries in June, 1957, but little was accomplished until the Federal govern-

[2]From William L. Rivers, "The Politics of Pollution," *The Reporter*, March 30, 1961, pp. 34-35. Copyright 1961 by The Reporter Magazine Co. Reprinted by permission.

ment pushed the Water Pollution Board of Missouri into cracking down. In 1958, St. Joseph held a bond-issue referendum for a sewage-treatment plant. The voters rejected it. A year later, the Public Health Service held a five-day public hearing that resulted in a notice to the city and the eighteen industries to stop polluting the river; they were given a schedule that was designed to get sewage-treatment facilities into operation by June, 1963.

The industries that had been polluting the water gave in at that point. When city officials rejected as inadequate their offer to contribute $1,350,000 toward construction of a plant that would serve the entire area, industry leaders got together and decided to build their own facilities. St. Joseph conducted a $9,500,000 bond-issue referendum last May. The voters rejected it again, this time more decisively, prompting a newspaper to applaud them for "pioneer independence and be damned if they aim to stand still while some bureaucrats in Washington tell them what to do." The "bureaucrats" then brought the suit against St. Joseph for failing to keep to the schedule of sewage-plant planning and construction.

The case of U.S. v City of St. Joseph, which is still pending, is a small symbol of the breakdown in efforts to control wastes that endanger the health and welfare of millions. Although this is the only suit that has ever been filed under the Federal Water Pollution Control Act, the problem is so general and persuasion has accomplished so little that others are sure to follow.

St. Joseph is not the only city that has been accused of turning a river into a sewer. In fact, St. Joseph itself is the victim of the dirty habits of cities and industries farther north. The Missouri River begins in Montana and winds through the Dakotas into Iowa, reaching its first urban complex at Sioux City. There, according to Public Health Service engineers, "Floating excrement and other sewage solids were obvious, and gas bubbles from sludge deposits rose to the surface." The point where the Floyd River meets the Missouri "appeared almost clogged with untreated packing plant wastes. Where the water was not red with bloody wastes, it was gray with decomposing organic wastes. Offensive odor filled the atmosphere." At Omaha, 135 miles down the river, some of the grease passes through the plant intake, coating the walls of the concrete basins used in treating the water. Omaha's complaints, however, must be balanced against its own sewage-disposal practices: fish taken from the river below Omaha sometimes taste like kerosene, and crows ride on the patches of solid grease that flow from its packing houses.

The Missouri has been described as a thousand-mile sewer, but it is no more polluted than many another U.S. waterway. Thirty thousand municipal and industrial sewers empty directly into waters that are used to supply municipal water-treatment plants. In earlier days, even sanitary engineers repeated the rhyme that justified dumping filth into water: "Dilution is the Solution to Pollution." There is reason to doubt that this ever was true, but it is certainly not true today. The purifying properties of water are being used up so rapidly by increasing quantities of new oxygen-demanding wastes that many streams and rivers barely flow. Fifty million pounds of solid sewage go into water every day.

In a Public Health Service hearing, a Louisiana farmer testified that ninety-five of his 140 cattle died from drinking the water in the creek that ran beside his ninety-acre farm. When the creek overflowed, the trees along the banks began to die, and more than sixty acres could no longer be used for pasture or for growing crops. A trapper added: "Everything has been killed in that creek, and the fur-bearing animals have done quit traveling it. There's nothing for them; not even a frog."

Cleaning the nation's water is a political challenge that arouses implacable resistance. St. Joseph was taken to court only after many conferences, warnings, and a hearing. Throughout the hearing, a transcript of which ran to 426 pages, the city's attorney spoke of the "alleged" pollution despite clear evidence that untreated sewage from eighty thousand people was being dumped into the river every day.

Much of the foot dragging by municipalities can be explained by an axiom of local politics: building a water-treatment plant to clean up the water used by voting citizens is almost always easy to accomplish; however, a sewage plant that will treat a community's wastes benefits only the neighboring communities downstream. A Public Health Service official says that he detects a slow change in this selfish attitude, in part because of the growing popularity of water sports, which need clean water, in part because "almost all cities are downstream from at least one other city."

In contrast, the resistance of industry to enforcement actions is growing, even though many manufacturing plants cannot use polluted waters. By 1980, industry will need nearly twice as much water as agriculture and all municipalities combined. And the nation's industries are by far the worst polluters, dumping twice as much waste as the municipalities.

Spokesmen for industry do not deny that industrial pollution is a critical problem, but they claim that their research program will lead to improvement. Leonard Pasek, an executive of Kimberly-Clark Corporation, told a Senate committee that the National Council for Stream Improvement, which is financed primarily by pulp and paper companies, has a research budget of several million dollars a year. In many cases, competitive pricing makes the cost of building sewage-treatment plants prohibitive. An executive of a plant that produces soda ash said during a Public Health Service conference that forcing his company to install treatment facilities would drive production costs so high that his plant would close down because it would be unable to compete with the other nine soda-ash producers.

People or organizations imbued with the competitive spirit may not be nasty or even indifferent to the harm they do. Frequently, self-oriented competitors are aware of the social problem they are creating and would rather not create it. But they feel helpless to stop competing unilaterally. They cannot afford to assume costs that are not a similar burden on all their competitors. For example, consider the problem of air pollution.[3]

In contrast to the widespread recognition of the losses caused by the impairment of the human factor, the social costs of air and water pollution have attracted much less attention. This is probably due to the fact that the causal relation between productive activities and air and water pollution is more complex and less easily seen than the relatively clear connection that exists between private production and, say, industrial accidents. Moreover, whereas the impairment of human health by industrial accidents and occupational diseases tends to affect a relatively well-organized group of persons all of whom have a strong interest in the prevention of the risks and dangers to which they are exposed in their daily work, the harmful consequences of the pollution of the atmosphere and the contamination of water by various kinds of industrial waste products are usually felt by a highly heterogeneous, unorganized group of persons. Their reaction is, therefore, less articulate than that of injured workers in the case of industrial accidents and occupational diseases. Nevertheless, there can be no doubt that the social costs of air and water pollution are considerable. In the United States these costs may well reach several billion dollars annually. The present . . . [discussion] is devoted to a study of the social costs of air pollution . . .

. . . While the domestic use of coal continues to be a contributing cause of atmospheric pollution, it is primarily the emanations of smoke and gas from industrial establishments, railroads and large heating plants which, at present, cause most of the prevailing air pollution. Indeed, the large-scale replacement of man and horse power by such energy resources as bituminous coal and oil has made air pollution a common and characteristic phenomenon around many industrial centers. Nor can it be assumed that the replacement of coal and oil by atomic energy may one day eliminate the pollution of the atmosphere. On the contrary, recent experiments with radioactive disposal systems seem to indicate that radioactive waste materials—solids, liquids, and gases—may get into the air and represent not only short-lived but long-lived risks for neighboring cities and countries. In fact, if not properly controlled, the problem of air pollution in the atomic age may well become world-wide.

The manner in which present industrial production tends to give rise to air

[3]From Karl William Kapp, *The Social Costs of Private Enterprise*, Cambridge, Mass. Harvard University Press, 1950, pp. 67-74, 76-78. Reprinted by permission.

pollution need not occupy us to any great extent. Suffice it to point out that the formation of smoke and other gaseous emanations is almost invariably a sign of improper and incomplete combustion of fuels; in other words, the existence of smoke is always indicative of technical inefficiencies in the use of energy resources. Such inefficiencies fail to be eliminated whenever the private returns (or savings) obtainable from their elimination are not high enough to cover the private costs involved. The fact that the resulting pollution of the atmosphere may cause substantial losses to other people will not and cannot normally be considered in the cost-return calculations of private enterprise. . . .

The most obvious of the ill effects of smoke are those evidenced in the progressive destruction and premature deterioration of building materials, metals, paint coatings, merchandise, etc. Thus the various sulphur compounds contained in smoke have a destructive effect on stone and metals, corroding or disintegrating "practically all kinds of building materials (slate and granite possibly excepted); marble tends first to turn green and then black, limestone deteriorates very rapidly, turning to gypsum owing to its great affinity for sulphur. The absorption of sulphur causes the stone to expand, thus rendering it soluble and powdery so that particles are constantly washed or blown away." Materials such as stone, mortar, concrete, etc., are "soiled by soot and the necessary cleaning by wire brush and detergent chemicals, a sandblast or other drastic methods, is not only costly, but injures the stone itself." Metals, if exposed to smoke-polluted air, suffer not only from soot and tar but also from the presence of obnoxious gases and acid vapors. While "the destruction of iron is most noticeable, for it is the metal in most common use and it is more readily corroded than the majority of metals," there is hardly any metal which is not susceptible to the corrosive action of smoke. In fact, "the sulphuretted hydrogen in smoke blackens, disfigures or tarnishes nearly all metals. Copper and bronze rapidly darken . . . aluminum is affected by vapors and acids, many metals become pitted from electrochemical action and even gold and gilded articles become dull."

Protective paint coatings applied to metallic surfaces and other materials are subject to contamination by atmospheric carbon and dust which tends to reduce their protective efficiency and makes necessary frequent washing. . . .

Furthermore, smoke-polluted air affects the interior of buildings and interior decorations. Air-conditioning and ventilating equipment in particular are subject to corrosion and have been seen to fail within a period of three months owing to smoke-polluted air. Similarly, factory smoke is responsible for the deterioration of the quality and value of all kinds of merchandise, causing substantial losses to wholesale and retail businesses. In addition, air pollution causes social losses as a result of the necessity of more frequent household cleaning and washing.

The social costs of atmospheric pollution go far beyond the losses resulting from the more rapid deterioration of building materials, metals, and paint coatings. Several students of the problem of air pollution have pointed to the injurious effects which the loss of daylight and of ultraviolet light may have upon human health. The most important damages to persons seem to be caused by the inhalation of smoke-polluted air. The poisonous compounds and soot particles contained in smoke-polluted air may serve "as carriers of the obnoxious products of human fatigue which irritate the sensitive membranes of the eyes, nose, throat, lungs, and gastro-intestinal tract, increase the susceptibility to gastro-intestinal, pulmonary and nasopharyngeal disorders, diminish the potential reserve, working capacity, and well-being of the individual, increase fatigue, irritability and malcontent, and may tend to hasten premature decay."

Other less direct effects of air pollution on human health are revealed by the following brief analysis of the influence which factory smoke may have upon weather and general meteorological conditions. To be exact, air pollution and weather conditions influence each other. The presence of smoke in the atmosphere tends to increase the relative humidity and affects adversely the character of daylight; and similarly, high temperatures, low winds and high relative humidity add to the intensity of air pollution in any given locality. In particular, it was found that "smoke lessens the duration and intensity of sunshine; reduces the intensity of daylight, the limit of visibility and the diurnal winter temperature; increases humidity, mists, the frequency and duration of fogs and possibly alters the electrical potential." Moreover, "fogs may become mixed with smoke to such an extent that their color is changed from white to brown, or even black, and prevent sunlight from penetrating to the level of the street. Heat rays as well as light rays are thus stopped so that evaporation of the fog is retarded." . . .

Investigations of the smoke nuisance and its effects on light in the United States established the fact that "city fogs are more persistent than country fogs, principally because of their increased density due to the smoke that accumulates in them." This, in turn, leads to less intense sunshine as well as to "fewer hours of sunshine in the cities than in the surrounding country."

A special study of the loss of light due to smoke on Manhattan Island emphasizes that "in some cases the average hourly or daily percentage loss was greater than 50. The average percentage loss for the whole year was 16.6 for clear days, 34.6 for cloudy days, and 21.5 for all days. The percentage loss on cloudy days was, therefore, about twice as great as on clear days."

In the light of these findings it is not difficult to understand why a smoke-filled atmosphere may have far-reaching effects upon human health and all animal and plant life. The loss of sunshine and the exclusion of ultraviolet radiation reduces physical vitality and makes the human body more susceptible to colds and other bacterial infections. Moreover, humidity intensified by smoke increases the solid poisonous contents of the air, aggravates various pathological conditions of the body, reduces the sensibility of some organs and depletes the vital potential. Fogs likewise "increase the prevalence of diseases and augment the death rate." Still other disadvantages accrue from the fact that artificial light made necessary by the loss of sunshine has injurious effects on human health inasmuch as colorless daylight is superior for visual efficiency and optical health.

It must be noted, however, that the gradual absorption by the human system of the poisonous products of imperfect combustion does not necessarily "give rise to any definitely recognizable actue disorder or specific disabilities. But the process of slow poisoning may insidiously eat away like a mild cancer at vital tissues and thus in time deplete our potential reserve . . ."

Numerous investigations by private and public agencies have yielded a wealth of evidence and quantitative estimates of the social losses caused by air pollution in different industrial localities. Careful studies have been made with a view to measuring the amount of carbon, ash, tar, iron oxide and sulphur dioxide in the air which in the form of dust settles in and around industrial communities. For example, it has been found that 1,800 tons of dust settle per square mile per year in the center of the city of Baltimore, while three miles from the center only 800 tons of settled dust were recorded, and ten miles out in the country the settled dust was 340 tons per square mile per year.

Several monetary estimates of the social costs of air pollution have been made; the earliest and most detailed of these estimates are those of the Mellon Institute of Industrial Research of the University of Pittsburgh in 1913. According to the Smoke Investigation of the Mellon Institute, the smoke nuisance costs the people of Pittsburgh approximately $9,944,740 per annum. This figure applies to conditions prevailing in 1913. More recent estimates place the losses caused by smoke in Pittsburgh at $9.36 per person per year. Later investigations in Pittsburgh convinced the Institute "that we were safe in estimating the cost to each man, woman and child in the city at about $15 each year." Studies made in other places, among them New York, Chicago, Cincinnati, Salt Lake City, Boston and Baltimore have revealed losses amounting to "from $10 to $30 per capita." Estimates for Cleveland range as high as $80 for each family. The total costs of the smoke nuisance in New York City are placed at about $100,000,000 per year. For the country as a whole "the annual bill for smoke . . . lies in the neighborhood of $500,000,000, of which $140,000,000 is said to represent the cost of spoiled merchandise and of building cleaning." H. W. Wilson of the U.S. Geological Survey likewise placed the loss which the country as a whole suffers as a result of smoke at over $500,000,000 "in damage done to merchandise, defacement on buildings, tarnishing of metals, injury to human life and to plant life, the greatly increased labor and the cost of housekeeping and the losses of the manufacturers due to imperfect combustion of coal." Air pollution has become a problem because business firms do not wish to incur the expense of installing smoke traps on their chimneys unless their competitors are forced to assume the same obligation.[4]

This pathology of competition might be removed by requiring all competitors to accept the same costs, thus giving none an advantage over the others. Some costs of competition are not so easily avoided. The strain on individuals may produce a variety of human casualities. One social scientist found that countries with high achievement motivation tended to have high death rates because of repression and inhibition (ulcers and high blood pressure) and that nations whose populations sought personal power tended to have high death rates from aggressiveness and acting out (murder, suicide, and alcoholism).[5]

In another way, individuals become casualties of the competitive pressure of American society. We spoke earlier of air pollution as a cost of competition, but air pollution is not simply unpleasant or economically costly; it is dangerous to human health. So is the private pollution of one's personal air through smoking. Insofar as smoking helps people to adjust to the pressures of competition, such diseases as lung cancer and emphysema may be indirect costs of competitive stress. In addition to physical costs of competitive striving, there are sometimes costs to human dignity and to such values as trust and acceptance. We spoke earlier of the use of people as instrumental things; the point here is similar. Distrust and suspicion can be generated by self-oriented competitiveness, which in turn can generate offensive and defensive spying and prying.[6]

Surveillance of the teammates on the job in private industry has shot up at such a rate in recent years that the phenomenon might seem to have pathological overtones. At thousands of plants no one is to be trusted in any sense in which we've traditionally known the word. No one's motives and integrity are to be taken for granted.

One justification offered for stepping up the surveillance is pilferage; but there has always been pilferage, and in today's economy there is much more to pilfer. Then there is the alleged constant hazard of theft of secret processes being developed. During and after World War II such guarding of secret military processes became commonplace, but now the same rules of guarding are being applied to new zipper designs, to a formula for new shades of lipstick, and to mock-ups of a built-in light for milady's leg shaver. . . .

---

[4]The latest type of air pollution—radioactive fallout resulting from the testing of atomic weapons—can be attributed to international military competition rather than to conventional economic competition.

[5] Stanley A. Rudin, "The Personal Price of National Glory," *Trans-Action*, September-October, 1965, pp. 4-7.

[6]From Vance Packard, *The Naked Society* (Pocket Books, 1964), pp. 63-64. Copyright © 1964 by Vance Packard. (New York: David McKay Company, Inc.) Reprinted by permission of the publisher.

One head of an investigative "consulting" organization specializing in managers explained: "Let's suppose, for instance, you think a guy is having a bad time on his job. It might pay to leave a bug in there for a week just to see how he is treating people and how he is getting along. You don't try to hurt the guy or fire the guy. You want to know what areas you have to fortify in his performance."

More commonly, however, surveillance is done by fulltime operatives. They can cause cameras—either hidden or unobtrusive—to pan and tilt, by remote control, over the work areas and can see who is doing what in the recreation or coffee area.

Is electronic snooping a social problem? It *is* to the extent that large numbers of people resent the invasion of their privacy. Competitive zeal makes for electronic snooping; it may also underlie human abrasiveness of other kinds. Sibling rivalry probably exists in all societies to some degree, but it is surely sharper in a society whose members are accustomed to compete for nearly everything. One anthropologist has pointed out that the residents of American homes for the aged compete with one another in terms of the numbers of visitors they receive.[7] Competition "thrusts the achievement drive into the face of Death himself." That the competition for love within the family is heightened too is to be expected. Perhaps this is another cost of life in a competitive and materialistic society.

CONCLUSION

If we do not have alternatives to choose among, we are less free. But in order for us to have alternative sources of transportation, of communities in which to live, of goods and services of all kinds, there must be many suppliers of those things. From the point of view of those many suppliers, *our* alternatives are *their* competitors.

From our perspective, competition among them is desirable. It gives us alternatives, and it keeps them vying to please us. But, as is true so often in human affairs, every benefit has a cost. The cost of competition includes the insecurity it generates and the toll in health it exacts. On occasion, a high price is paid by the total society just because people are doing what they are supposed to do in a competitive system, namely, watch out for themselves. We then get such unpleasant results as pollution. And we sometimes find competitors shifting from efforts to please us to efforts to injure one another.

[7]Jules Henry, *Culture Against Man*, New York: Vintage Books, 1963, pp. 448-450.

chapter 10
Pathologies of conformity
to authority

Chapter 5 discussed the necessity for people to learn a sense of duty—a habit of conformity to rules and to duly constituted authority that enforces rules—so that orderly social life is possible. This chapter discusses social problems created by the individualistic strain in American values that prizes such *non*conformists as Henry David Thoreau, also noted in Chapter 5. That valuation of nonconformity often springs from the American insistence on the importance of getting a job done well. The test of an action is, for many Americans, whether it works. As Chapters 10, 11, and 12 will show, conformity does not always work. For example, conformity is costly when the rules are irrational or the authority to be obeyed is incompetent. Which is better, to do one's duty, which may mean disaster for everyone; or to do what seems efficient, which may mean undermining the bases of authority? William H. Whyte, Jr. alludes to this dilemma as the split between the Protestant Ethic of individualism and the Social Ethic that endorses acquiescence (duty-fulfillment).[1]

If you wanted to put in fiction form the split between the Protestant Ethic and the Social Ethic of organization life, you might, if you wanted to be extreme about it, come up with a plot situation something like this.

A middle-management executive is in a spot of trouble. He finds that the small branch plant he's helping to run is very likely to blow up. There is a way to save it: if he presses a certain button the explosion will be averted. Unfortu-

[1]From William H. Whyte, Jr., *The Organization Man*, New York: Doubleday Anchor, 1965, pp. 269-275, 276-291. Reprinted by permission.

nately, however, just as he's about to press a button his boss heaves into view. The boss is a scoundrel and a fool, and at this moment he's so scared he is almost incoherent. Don't press the button, he says.

The middle-management man is no rebel and he knows that the boss, stupid as he is, represents The Organization. Still, he would like to save everyone's life. Thus his dilemma: if he presses the button he will not be acting like a good organization man and the plant will be saved. If he doesn't press it he will be a good organization man and they will all be blown to smithereens.

A damn silly dilemma, you might say. Almost exactly this basic problem, however, is the core of the biggest-selling novel of the postwar period, Herman Wouk's *The Caine Mutiny*, and rarely has a novel so touched a contemporary nerve. Much of its success, of course, was due to the fact it is a rattling good tale, and even if the author had ended it differently it would still probably have been a success. But it is the moral overtones that have made it compelling. Here, raised to the nth degree, is the problem of the individual versus authority, and the problem is put so that no reader can duck it. There is no "Lady or the Tiger" ending. We must, with the author, make a choice, and a choice that is presented as an ultimately moral one.

The boldness of it makes *The Caine Mutiny* something of a landmark in the shift of American values. Popular fiction in general ... has been going in the same direction for a long time, and *The Caine Mutiny* is merely evolutionary in this respect. But it is franker; unlike most popular fare, it does not sugar-coat the precept to adjustment by trapping it up with the words of individualism. It is explicit. Author Wouk puts his protagonist in a dilemma and, through rigorous plotting, eliminates any easy middle course. The protagonist must do what he thinks is right or do what the system thinks is right.

The man caught in the dilemma is one the reader can identify himself with. He is Lieutenant Maryk, the executive officer of the mine sweeper *Caine*. Maryk is no scoffer, but a stolid, hard-working man who just wants to do his job well. He likes the system and all his inclinations lead him to seek a career in the Regular Navy.

Ordinarily he would lead an uneventful, productive life. The ship of which he is executive officer, however, is commanded by a psychopath named Queeg. At first Maryk stubbornly resists the warnings about Queeg voiced by Lieutenant Keefer, an ex-writer. But slowly the truth dawns on him, and in a series of preliminary incidents the author leaves no doubt in Maryk's—or the reader's—mind that Queeg is in fact a bully, a neurotic, a coward, and what is to be most important of all, an incompetent.

In many similar instances subordinates have found ways to protect themselves without overtly questioning the system—they can make requests for mass transfer and thereby discipline the superior, control him by mass blackmail, and the like. Wouk, however, proceeds to build a climax in which such reconciliations are impossible. He places the *Caine* in the midst of a typhoon.

Terrified, Queeg turns the ship south, so that it no longer heads into the wind. Maryk pleads with him to keep it headed into the wind as their only chance for survival. Queeg, now virtually jabbering with fear, refuses to turn the ship around into the wind. The ship is on the verge of foundering.

What shall Maryk do? If he does nothing he is certain that they are all lost. If he takes advantage of Article 184 in Navy Regulations and relieves Queeg temporarily of command for medical reasons, he is in for great trouble later.

Maryk makes his decision. With as much dignity as possible he relieves Queeg of command and turns the ship into the wind. The ship still yaws and plunges, but it stays afloat. As if to punctuate Maryk's feat, the *Caine* passes the upturned bottom of a destroyer that hadn't made it.

Eventually there is a court-martial for Maryk and his fellow officers. The defense lawyer, Barney Greenwald, makes what appears to be highly justified points about Queeg and, through skillful cross-examination, reveals him to the court as a neurotic coward. The court acquits Maryk. Queeg's career is finished.

Then the author pulls the switch. At a party afterward, lawyer Greenwald tells Maryk and the junior officers that *they*, not Queeg, were the true villains of the piece. Greenwald argues that Queeg was a regular officer, and that without regular officers there would be no going system for reserves to join later.

Whyte was interested in the public reaction to this implied thesis of Wouk's that it was the authority of the Navy that ought to have been preserved at all costs. He even has the lawyer, Greenwald, throw a glass of champagne in the face of Keefer, the intellectual fellow-officer who had urged Maryk on to his mutiny.

It could be argued that the public's acquiescence was only apparent and if people had bothered to think about the moral they would have protested it. To get some idea of what would happen if people had to think about its implications, I tried a modest experiment. In co-operation with the authorities of a small preparatory school, I initiated an essay contest for the students. The subject would be *The Caine Mutiny*. Prize winners would be chosen for the literary excellence of their essays and not for their point of view, but it was the moral issue of *The Caine Mutiny* that was their subject. Here are the ground rules we announced:

The essay, which should be between 500 and 1,000 words in length, should consider the following problems:
  I. What is the central moral issue of **The Caine Mutiny**?
  II. How does the author, Herman Wouk, speaking through characters in the book, regard the resolution of the moral issue?

III. How do the resolution of the moral issue and the author's judgment of that resolution accord with life as you know it?

At length the essays were finished, and when we sat down to read them we were pleased to find how well they had grasped the essential issue. In a sense, it was a highly nondirective test; not surprisingly, they had gone to some effort previously to cadge some hints from the teachers, and it was obvious they tried hard to cadge hints from Wouk. How they felt about the mutineers depended considerably on how they thought he felt; and, understandably, they were somewhat confused as to what side they were meant to disapprove. On the whole, however, they did grasp the essential issue at stake. Each interpreted its relevance to his life somewhat differently, but most of them saw the problem as that of individual independence versus the system.

With one exception they favored the system. Collusion may have fortified them in this, but their phrasing, and their puzzlement over Wouk's position, left little doubt that their feeling was genuine. Several disagreed with Wouk, but the grounds on which they disagreed with him were that he was too easy on the mutineers. Here is a sampling of final paragraphs:

> In everything we do there are certain rules and regulations we have to abide by, and, like Willie Keith, the only way we will learn is through experience. We have to abide by the rules of our particular society to gain any end whatsoever.

> I cannot agree with the author in that I believe that one should obey orders to matter what the circumstances.

> It seems that life in general is like a baseball game; everywhere there are rules and laws set up by many people for the ultimate benefit of all. Yet there are people who think as the young rookie that their actions should be directed by what they feel is right, not by what everyone else has determined. True, there may be partly extenuating circumstances; but unless the reason is more than subjective, the one who breaks society's laws will be punished by fine, jail, or even death.

> This is another example of why a subordinate should not have the power to question authority.

> Morally, however, the very act that Maryk committed is against the law.

> The underlying causes of the *Caine* mutiny have their parallel in everyday life. . . . The teacher who allows personal dislike to enter into his grading; the politician who blames his mistakes on others; both of these are examples of fraudulency. . . . Greenwald, Maryk's lawyer, confused Queeg and twisted his words so that Queeg was made to look stupid.

Men have always been subjected to the whims of those in command; and so it will be in the future. This plan must exist or anarchy will be the result.

Writing in the 1950's, William Whyte saw a social problem. The tension between individual self-assertion and self-expression, on the one hand, and the need for conformity to status obligations and authority, on the other, had swung too far toward acquiescence. In the 1960's, the civil rights struggle, student militancy, and other sources of turmoil seemed to deny Whyte's thesis that Americans are acquiescent slaves of society. What is the true state of American individualism? What would Americans actually *do* if authorities told them to behave in ways they believed wrong? This is the question that Stanley Milgram, a psychologist at Yale, asked himself and an account of his experimental effort to find the answer is reproduced here.[2]

In its most general form the problem may be defined thus: if X tells Y to hurt Z, under what conditions will Y carry out the command of X and under what conditions will he refuse. In the more limited form possible in laboratory research, the question becomes: if an experimenter tells a subject to hurt another person, under what conditions will the subject go along with this instruction, and under what conditions will he refuse to obey. The laboratory problem is not so much a dilution of the general statement as one concrete expression of the many particular forms this question may assume. . . .

SUBJECT POPULATION

The subjects used in all experimental conditions were male adults, residing in the greater New Haven and Bridgeport areas, aged 20 to 50 years, and engaged in a wide variety of occupations. Each experimental condition described in this report employed 40 fresh subjects and was carefully balanced for age and occupational types. The occupational composition for each experiment was: workers, skilled and unskilled: 40 per cent; white collar, sales, business: 40 per cent; professionals: 20 per cent. The occupations were intersected with three age categories (subjects in 20s, 30s, and 40s, assigned to each condition in the proportions of 20, 40, and 40 per cent respectively).

THE GENERAL LABORATORY PROCEDURE

The focus of the study concerns the amount of electric shock a subject is willing to administer to another person when ordered by an experimenter to give the

---

[2]From Stanley Milgram, "Some Conditions of Obedience and Disobedience to Authority," *Human Relations*, Vol. 18, February 1965, pp. 57-61, 65-67, 72-73, 74-75. Reprinted by permission.

"victim" increasingly more severe punishment. The act of administering shock is set in the context of a learning experiment, ostensibly designed to study the effect of punishment on memory. Aside from the experimenter, one naive subject and one accomplice perform in each session. On arrival each subject is paid $4.50. After a general talk by the experimenter, telling how little scientists know about the effect of punishment on memory, subjects are informed that one member of the pair will serve as teacher and one as learner. A rigged drawing is held so that the naive subject is always the teacher, and the accomplice becomes the learner. The learner is taken to an adjacent room and strapped into an "electric chair."

The naive subject is told that it is his task to teach the learner a list of paired associates, to test him on the list, and to administer punishment whenever the learner errs in the test. Punishment takes the form of electric shock, delivered to the learner by means of a shock generator controlled by the naive subject. The teacher is instructed to increase the intensity of electric shock one step on the generator on each error. The learner, according to plan, provides many wrong answers, so that before long the naive subject must give him the strongest shock on the generator. Increases in shock level are met by increasingly insistent demands from the learner that the experiment be stopped because of the growing discomfort to him. However, in clear terms the experimenter orders the teacher to continue with the procedure in disregard of the learner's protests. *Thus, the naive subject must resolve a conflict between two mutually incompatible demands from the social field. He may continue to follow the orders of the experimenter and shock the learner with increasing severity, or he may refuse to follow the orders of the experimenter and heed the learner's pleas. The experimenter's authority operates not in a free field, but against ever-mounting countervailing pressures from the person being punished.*

A few technical points need to be considered before the findings of the study are described. For the purpose of delivering shock, a simulated shock generator is used, with 30 clearly marked voltage levels that range from 15 to 450 volts (and each activated by one of 30 individual lever switches set in a horizontal line). The naive subject is given a sample shock of 45 volts to convince him of the authenticity of the instrument. The generator bears verbal designations that range from "Slight Shock" to "Danger: Severe Shock."

The responses of the victim are standardized on tape, and each protest is coordinated to a particular voltage level on the shock generator. Starting with 75 volts the learner begins to grunt and moan. At 150 volts he demands to be let out of the experiment. At 180 volts he cries out that he can no longer stand the pain. At 300 volts he refuses to provide any more answers to the memory test, insisting that he is no longer a participant in the experiment and must be freed. In response to this last tactic, the experimenter instructs the naive subject to treat the absence of an answer as equivalent to a wrong answer, and to follow the usual shock procedure. The experimenter reinforces his demand with the statement: "You have no other choice, you must go on!" (This imperative is used whenever the naive subject tries to break off the experiment.) If the subject refuses to give the next higher level of shock, the experiment is considered at an end. A quantitative value is assigned to the subject's performance based on the maximum intensity shock he administered before breaking off. Thus any subject's score may range from zero (for a subject unwilling to administer the first shock level) to 30 (for a subject who proceeds to the highest voltage level on the board). For any particular subject and for any particular experimental condition the degree to which participants have followed the experimenter's orders may be specified with a numerical value, corresponding to the metric on the shock generator.

This laboratory situation gives us a framework in which to study the subject's reactions to the principal conflict of the experiment. Again, this conflict is between the experimenter's demands that he continue to administer the electric shock, and the learner's demands, which become increasingly more insistent, that the experiment be stopped. The crux of the study is to vary systematically the factors believed to alter the degree of obedience to the experimental commands, to learn under what conditions submission to authority is most probable, and under what conditions defiance is brought to the fore. . . .

At first no vocal feedback was used from the victim. It was thought that the verbal and voltage designations on the control panel would create sufficient pressure to curtail the subject's obedience. However, this was not the case. In the absence of protests from the learner, virtually all subjects, once commanded, went blithely to the end of the board, seemingly indifferent to the verbal designations "Extreme Shock" and "Danger: Severe Shock." This deprived us of an adequate basis for scaling obedient tendencies. A force had to be introduced that would strengthen the subject's resistance to the experimenter's commands, and reveal individual differences in terms of a distribution of break-off points.

This force took the form of protests from the victim. Initially, mild protests were used, but proved inadequate. Subsequently, more vehement protests were inserted into the experimental procedure. To our consternation, even the strongest protests from the victim did not prevent all subjects from administering the harshest punishment ordered by the experimenter; but the protests did lower the mean maximum shock somewhat and created some spread in the subject's performance; therefore, the victim's cries were standardized on tape and incorporated into the regular experimental procedure.

The situation did more than highlight the technical difficulties of finding a workable experimental procedure: it indicated that subjects would obey authority to a greater extent than we had supposed. It also pointed to the importance of feedback from the victim in controlling the subject's behavior.

One further aspect of the pilot study was that subjects frequently averted their eyes from the person they were shocking, often turning their heads in an awkward and conspicuous manner. One subject explained: "I didn't want to see the consequences of what I had done." Observers wrote:

> . . . subjects showed a reluctance to look at the victim, whom they could see through the glass in front of them. When this fact was brought to their attention they indicated that it caused them discomfort to see the victim in agony. We note, however, that although the subject refuses to look at the victim, he continues to administer shocks. . . .

There are reasons to feel that, on arrival, the subject is oriented primarily to the experimenter rather than to the victim. He has come to the laboratory to fit into the structure that the experimenter—not the victim—would provide. He has come less to understand his behavior than to *reveal* that behavior to a competent scientist, and he is willing to display himself as the scientist's purposes require. Most subjects seem quite concerned about the appearance they are making before the experimenter, and one could argue that this preoccupation in a relatively new and strange setting makes the subject somewhat insensitive to the triadic nature of the social situation. In other words, the subject is so concerned about the show he is putting on for the experimenter that influences from other parts of the social field do not receive as much weight as they ordinarily would. This overdetermined orientation to the experimenter would account for the relative insensitivity of the subject to the victim, and would also lead us to believe that alterations in the relationship between subject and experimenter would have important consequences for obedience.

In a series of experiments we varied the physical closeness and degree of surveillance of the experimenter. In one condition the experimenter sat just a few feet away from the subject. In a second condition, after giving initial instructions, the experimenter left the laboratory and gave his orders by telephone; in still a third condition the experimenter was never seen, providing instructions by means of a tape recording activated when the subjects entered the laboratory.

Obedience dropped sharply as the experimenter was physically removed from the laboratory. The number of obedient subjects in the first condition (Experimenter Present) was almost three times as great as in the second, where the experimenter gave his orders by telephone. Twenty-six subjects were fully obedient in the first condition, and only 9 in the second (Chi square obedient *vs.* defiant in the two conditions, 1 d.f. = 14.7; $p < .001$). Subjects seemed able to take a far stronger stand against the experimenter when they did not have to encounter him face to face, and the experimenter's power over the subject was severely curtailed.

Moreover, when the experimenter was absent, subjects displayed an interesting form of behavior that had not occurred under his surveillance. Though continuing with the experiment, several subjects administered lower shocks than were required and never informed the experimenter of their deviation from the correct procedure. (Unknown to the subjects, shock levels were automatically recorded by an Esterline-Angus event recorder wired directly into the shock generator; the instrument provided us with an objective record of the subjects' performance.) Indeed, in telephone conversations some subjects specifically assured the experimenter that they were raising the shock level according to instruction, whereas in fact they were repeatedly using the lowest shock on the board. This from of behavior is particularly interesting: although these subjects acted in a way that clearly undermined the avowed purposes of the experiment, they found it easier to handle the conflict in this manner than to precipitate an open break with authority.

Other conditions were completed in which the experimenter was absent during the first segment of the experiment, but reappeared at the point that the subject definitely refused to give higher shocks when commanded by telephone. Although he had exhausted his power via telephone, the experimenter could frequently force further obedience when he reappeared in the laboratory.

Experiments in this series show that the physical *presence* of an authority is an important force contributing to the subject's obedience or defiance. Taken together with the first experimental series on the proximity of the victim, it would appear that something akin to fields of force, diminishing in effectiveness with increasing psychological distance from their source, have a controlling effect on the subject's performance. As the victim is brought closer, the subject finds it harder to administer shocks to him. When the victim's position is held constant relative to the subject, and the authority is made more remote, the subject finds it easier to break off the experiment. This effect is substantial in both cases, but manipulation of the experimenter's position yielded the more powerful results. Obedience to destructive commands is highly dependent on the proximal relations between authority and subject.

TENSIONS

The description of final scores does not fully convey the character of the subjects' performance, and it would be useful to interrupt our reporting of quantitative relationships to remark on the subjects' general reaction to the situation.

One might suppose that a subject would simply break off or continue as his conscience and temperament dictated. Yet this is very far from what happened. There were powerful reactions of tension and emotional strain in a substantial proportion of the participants. Persons were observed to sweat, tremble, stutter, bite their lips, and groan as they found themselves increasingly implicated in the experimental conflict. Some sense of the subjects' mood can be gotten from a transcript of their remarks at break-off point. Here are the remarks of two defiant subjects:

Is he banging? . . . Is he hurt out there? Well, I don't want to be responsible for anything that happens to him. No, I can't go on with it. I don't know whether he's all right or not. I mean he may have a heart condition or something; I wouldn't feel right doing it. He's banging for help. He's evidently in trouble or he wouldn't bang . . . I don't see any sense to this—to knocking him out or something. I just can't see it.

(Subject refuses to administer shocks)   *[Subject 0108]*

The man is banging. He wants to get out . . . I'm sorry. If the man wants to get out I'd just as soon stop . . . I don't want to administer any more [extremely excited] . . . I will gladly refund the check, but I will not harm this man . . . I'm sorry, I will not give him any more if he obviously wants to get out. There is no money in the world that will make me hurt another individual. *[Subject 010X]*

And here is a transcript from an obedient subject. He began the experiment calmly, but became increasingly tense as the experiment proceeded. After administering the 150-volt shock, he began to address the experimenter in agitated tones:

150 volts delivered. You want me to keep going?

165 volts delivered. That guy is hollering in there. There's a lot of them here. He's liable to have heart condition. You want me to go?

180 volts delivered. He can't stand it! I'm not going to kill that man in there! You hear him hollering? He's hollering. He can't stand it. What if something happens to him? . . . I'm not going to get that man sick in there. He's hollering in there. You know what I mean? I mean I refuse to take responsibility. He's getting hurt in there. He's in there hollering. Too many left here. Geez, if he gets them wrong. There's too many of them left. I mean who is going to take responsibility if anything happens to that gentleman? *[The experimenter accepts responsibility.]* All right.

195 volts delivered. You see he's hollering. Hear that. Gee, I don't know. *[The experimenter says: "The experiment requires that you go on."]*—I know it does, sir, but I mean—hugh—he don't know what he's in for. He's up to 195 volts.

210 volts delivered

225 volts delivered

240 volts delivered. Aw, no. You mean I've got to keep going up with the scale? No sir. I'm not going to kill that man! I'm not going to give him 450 volts! *[The experimenter says: "The experiment requires that you go on."]*—I know it does, but that man is hollering in there, sir . . .

Despite his numerous, agitated objections, which were constant accompaniments to his actions, the subject unfailingly obeyed the experimenter, proceeding to the highest shock level on the generator. He displayed a curious dissociation between word and action. Although at the verbal level he had resolved not to go on, his actions were fully in accord with the experimenter's commands. This subject did not want to shock the victim, and he found it an extremely disagreeable task, but he was unable to invent a response that would free him from E's authority. Many subjects cannot find the specific verbal formula that would enable them to reject the role assigned to them by the experimenter. Perhaps our culture does not provide adequate models for disobedience. . . .

LEVELS OF OBEDIENCE AND DEFIANCE

One general finding that merits attention is the high level of obedience manifested in the experimental situation. Subjects often expressed deep disapproval of shocking a man in the face of his objections, and others denounced it as senseless and stupid. Yet many subjects complied even while they protested. The proportion of obedient subjects greatly exceeded the expectations of the experimenter and his colleagues. At the outset, we had conjectured that subjects would not, in general, go above the level of "Strong Shock." In practice, many subjects were willing to administer the most extreme shocks available when commanded by the experimenter. For some subjects the experiment provides an occasion for aggressive release. And for others it demonstrates the extent to which obedient dispositions are deeply ingrained, and are engaged irrespective of their consequences for others. Yet this is not the whole story. Somehow, the subject becomes implicated in a situation from which he cannot disengage himself.

The departure of the experimental results from intelligent expectation, to some extent, has been formalized. The procedure was to describe the experimental situation in concrete detail to a group of competent persons, and to ask them to predict the performance of 100 hypothetical subjects. For purposes of indicating the distribution of break-off points judges were provided with a diagram of the shock generator, and recorded their predictions before being informed of the actual results. Judges typically underestimated the amount of obedience demonstrated by subjects. . . .

Forty psychiatrists at a leading medical school . . . predicted that most subjects would not go beyond the tenth shock level (150 volts; at this point the victim makes his first explicit demand to be freed). They further predicted that by the twentieth shock level (300 volts; the victim refuses to answer) 3.73 per cent of the subjects would still be obedient, and that only a little over one-tenth of one per cent of the subjects would administer the highest shock on the board. But . . . the obtained behavior was very different. Sixty-two per cent of the subjects obeyed the experimenter's commands fully. Between expectation and occurrence there is a whopping discrepancy.

Why did the psychiatrists underestimate the level of obedience? Possibly, because their predictions were based on an inadequate conception of the determinants of human action, a conception that focuses on motives *in vacuo*. This orientation may be entirely adequate for the repair of bruised impulses as revealed on the psychiatrist's couch, but as soon as our interest turns to action in larger settings, attention must be paid to the situations in which motives are expressed. A situation exerts an important press on the individual. It exercises constraints and may provide push. In certain circumstances it is not so much the kind of person a man is, as the kind of situation in which he is placed, that determines his actions.

Many people, not knowing much about the experiment, claim that subjects who go to the end of the board are sadistic. Nothing could be more foolish as an overall characterization of these persons. It is like saying that a person thrown into a swift-flowing stream is necessarily a fast swimmer, or that he has great stamina because he moves so rapidly relative to the bank. The context of action must always be considered. The individual, upon entering the laboratory, becomes integrated into a situation that carries its own momentum. The subject's problem then is how to become disengaged from a situation which is moving in an altogether ugly direction. . . .

Almost a thousand adults were individually studied in the obedience research, and there were many specific conclusions regarding the variables that control obedience and disobedience to authority. Some of these have been discussed briefly in the preceding sections, and more detailed reports will be released subsequently.

There are now some other generalizations I should like to make, which do not derive in any strictly logical fashion from the experiments as carried out, but which, I feel, ought to be made. They are formulations of an intuitive sort that have been forced on me by observation of many subjects responding to the pressures of authority. The assertions represent a painful alteration in my own thinking; and since they were acquired only under the repeated impact of direct observation, I have no illusion that they will be generally accepted by persons who have not had the same experience.

With numbing regularity good people were seen to knuckle under the demands of authority and perform actions that were callous and severe. Men who are in everyday life responsible and decent were seduced by the trappings of authority, by the control of their perceptions, and by the uncritical acceptance of the experimenter's definition of the situation, into performing harsh acts.

What is the limit of such obedience? At many points we attempted to establish a boundary. Cries from the victim were inserted; not good enough. The victim claimed heart trouble; subjects still shocked him on command. The victim pleaded that he be let free, and his answers no longer registered on the signal box; subjects continued to shock him. At the outset we had not conceived that such drastic procedures would be needed to generate disobedience, and each step was added only as the ineffectiveness of the earlier techniques became clear. The final effort to establish a limit was the Touch-Proximity condition. But the very first subject in this condition subdued the victim on command, and proceeded to the highest shock level. A quarter of the subjects in this condition performed similarly.

The results, as seen and felt in the laboratory, are to this author disturbing. They raise the possibility that human nature, or—more specifically—the kind of character produced in American democratic society, cannot be counted on to insulate its citizens from brutality and inhumane treatment at the direction of malevolent authority. A substantial proportion of people do what they are told to do, irrespective of the content of the act and without limitations of conscience, so long as they perceive that the command comes from a legitimate authority. If in this study an anonymous experimenter could successfully command adults to subdue a fifty-year-old man, and force on him painful electric shocks against his protests, one can only wonder what government, with its vastly greater authority and prestige, can command of its subjects. There is, of course, the extremely important question of whether malevolent political institutions could or would arise in American society. The present research contributes nothing to this issue.

In an article titled "The Dangers of Obedience," Harold J. Laski wrote:

> . . . civilization means, above all, an unwillingness to inflict unnecessary pain. Within the ambit of that definition, those of us who heedlessly accept the commands of authority cannot yet claim to be civilized men.

> . . . Our business, if we desire to live a life, not utterly devoid of meaning and significance, is to accept nothing which contradicts our basic experience merely because it comes to us from tradition or convention or authority. It may well be that we shall be wrong; but our self-expression is thwarted at the root unless the certainties we are asked to accept coincide with the certainties we experience. That is why the condition of freedom in any state is always a widespread and consistent skepticism of the canons upon which power insists.

Professor Milgram concludes his research report with the suggestions that Americans will do almost anything if the demand comes from seemingly legitimate authority. The atrocities that American soldiers committed against unarmed Vietnamese civilians at My Lai illustrate his point. "Perhaps," he found himself concluding, "our culture does not provide adequate models for disobedience." The authors of this book do not think that the problem is providing "models for disobedience." (Other chapters of this book show that there are many such models in American society—they constitute other social problems!) The problem, rather, is teaching members of a society to make more sophisticated distinctions between situations in which a rule or an authority should be obeyed and those in which the rule should be violated or the authority figure defied. It is silly (and socially destructive) to neglect all status obligations and defy all authorities. Which acts of defiance are worth the cost?

One might expect that one place in society where authority is challenged appropriately is the university. Part of the tradition of academic men is that the free exchange of ideas is their lifeblood. "Academic freedom" to speak one's mind and to dissent from mere authority when authority seems wrong is cherished by America's academic (and other) intellectuals. Yet under some conditions even academics become too acquiescent. Sociologists Paul Lazarsfeld and Wagner Thielens studied the effect on American college and university faculties of the national hysteria about Communism sparked by Senator Joseph McCarthy during the early 1950's.[3]

As one attempts to get a composite picture of the limitations these teachers felt in approaching their classes, five themes stand out. First, some teachers omitted certain topics which they believed, on professional grounds, ought to be discussed. Other respondents slanted their presentation away from their professional convictions, or balanced an intellectually preferred but controversial position with discussion of a more popular opposing viewpoint. All three ended up by giving students an altered version of what in their best judgment was the truth. Other teachers, while they did not modify presentations as directly, nevertheless detached themselves from personal responsibility for the views they discussed. Finally, some respondents took rather elaborate precautions to avoid getting into difficulty over controversial issues.

THE OMISSION OF CONTROVERSIAL MATTERS

It is hardly surprising that specific omissions occurred in connection with the classroom study of Communism, Soviet Russia, and Red China. During the difficult years the suspicion of subversion could be based on sins far less grievous in an accuser's eye than open and impartial discussion of these topics in the classroom. One historian gave a reading assignment on the constitution of the

[3]From Paul F. Lazarsfeld and Wagner Thielens, *The Academic Mind*, New York: The Free Press, 1958, pp. 197-200, 203-204. Reprinted by permission of The Macmillan Company. The demagogic late Senator Joseph McCarthy of Wisconsin was a different breed of cat from the still active and nonacquiescent Senator Eugene McCarthy of Minnesota. It is also necessary, coincidentally, to remind the reader that the reference in the Lazarsfeld-Thielens piece to an "ex-Wallacite" is to the left-wing Presidential candidate of the Progressive Party in 1948, former Vice-President Henry A. Wallace, *not* to the conservative Presidential candidate of the American Independent Party in 1968, the Governor of Alabama, George Wallace!

Soviet Union, only to find that "the mere fact that I said they had a constitution made the students think that I was a Commie." Another professor, assigning works by Karl Marx to his students, sent them to the public library of a neighboring city when he found that the college library did not have sufficient copies; he later learned that the names of all those asking for the books were written down. It was in such a climate that the omissions occurred. A West Coast geographer, aware that as an ex-Wallaceite he was already open to criticism, reported his decision that a lecture on the geography of the U.S.S.R. might be too risky. Other respondents said they no longer assigned "The Communist Manifesto" or bulletins sent out by the Soviet Embassy. Less frequently, the omission was on a larger scale: there were a few college administrations which completely dropped certain courses on these topics.

The reader will notice that the examples used in this chapter often deal with Communism. It is not our task to say how matters involving Russia and Communism should be presented in the classroom. Different schools and different departments will disagree over the proper handling of these topics. But the problem, it seems clear, is the contemporary instance of a much older dilemma: how should institutions of higher learning deal with matters on which the larger community has, perhaps only temporarily, taken an uncompromising stand? We are attempting here simply to point out the constraints adopted by some teachers and schools when they faced this problem.

While it was mentioned most frequently, Communism was not the only specific topic teachers withheld from students. Novels of protest from the 1930's were also sometimes found too dangerous for classroom use; a West Coast sociologist, accustomed to assigning James. T. Farrell and *What Makes Sammy Run*, had to be "more careful now." More than one Southern professor, under orders from the school president or by his own reluctant decision, completely avoided the subject of race in class. Social security was still a bad word in some quarters. Religious matters were sometimes considered too hot to handle; Darwinism was discussed in only the most guarded terms at a small New England school with a predominance of Catholic students, and at a major West Coast university plans to conduct a seminar on religion were dropped because the topic was "too controversial."

Teachers avoided not only particular subjects, but also discussion of considerably broader areas, such as "political and economic problems," "any criticism of the status quo," and "explorations of the merits of dissent." Sometimes the topic itself was not the cause of the omission. One respondent did not assign a textbook he considered ideal because the author had been involved in a controversial investigation. An objection from a powerful source to one chapter of a book, or in unusual cases even a single word, was sometimes enough to cause it to be discarded.

It should be added that a few professors, rather than baldly concede that they omitted certain topics and areas in their classrooms, preferred to rationalize the procedure. One said he refused to deal at all with such issues unless conclusive scientific evidence could be brought to bear on them. Another postponed discussion of a controversial issue until, as he put it, "the thing was cleared up." And a third respondent said, "I'm less willing to discuss controversial issues; I don't eliminate them, but if there's a choice between a controversial or a noncontroversial issue, I take the noncontroversial." Whatever the merits of these different approaches, they share in common a reluctance to air many unresolved but important issues.

SLANTING THE PRESENTATION

Rather than shun a subject completely—and sometimes total avoidance is impossible—teachers often chose to slant their presentation of it. This is particularly true, again, of respondents who had to deal with Communism and Soviet Russia in their courses. In typical instances, an economist became critical of Russian economic forms, a political scientist underplayed his approval of certain administrative devices developed by the Russians, a historian concealed his support of the recognition of Red China and stressed the opposing view instead. Replacing textbooks may have the same effect; an economist at a private New England school reported a "trend toward conformity . . . Five years ago they picked John Maynard on Russia, now they pick Rostow."

In a few cases, interestingly enough, teachers slanted their approach to a controversial subject in the direction, not of the popular, but of the unpopular viewpoint. A Midwestern teacher, for example, suspected that in an effort to compensate for his students' prejudices against the Soviet Union, he may have neglected to point out the defects of the Russian system sufficiently. When a subject is highly controversial, an impartial presentation may indeed be difficult.

"BALANCING" THE PRESENTATION

The wish to forestall attack, which prompted some teachers to omit or slant material, led others to "balance" remarks they expected to be received unfavorably with statements of more conventional opinion. A respondent, already quoted in an earlier chapter, made it a practice to follow any criticism of the United States with one of Russia. And if a favorable reference to Communism was made, it was often carefully surrounded with distinctions and disclaimers. One teacher said:

> In discussing communism, I sometimes say that communism (small "c") is probably the most ideal form of economic organization yet devised, yet I carefully differentiate communism with a little "c" from Russian Com-

munism. I point out that communism would work only in a society of angels, because it fails to take into consideration the imperfections—laziness, etc.—inherent in human nature.

This comment permits us to return to an earlier point. Let us forget for a moment that it deals with communism, with all its present connotations. Suppose that the teacher had simply been describing a vision of a good society. *Any* such vision, whatever it might be, would conflict with the beliefs of some sector of the community. The offended group might feel strongly that their beliefs should not be challenged. How should a teacher communicate to his students such a vision, or indeed any view at sharp variance with prevailing opinions? Is he entitled to describe it as graphically as he can, so his students will understand it clearly? The teacher just quoted had come to the theoretical conclusion that a true communist society would have a high economic efficiency. He would certainly reduce the impact of his point by hastily making a balancing observation that imperfect human beings could never establish a true communist society. An abstract idea of this sort often requires a forceful and vigorous presentation to be understood by students. This would be more difficult to accomplish if the teacher were also anxious to make sure that no one thought he was talking about Russian Communism. The teacher's timing of his remarks would be dictated, not by his judgment of how best to put across his points, but by prudence. He probably would not dare, for example, to postpone discussion of the inherent flaws of communism to the next lecture so students could consider its advantages at leisure. . . .

Among the teachers who most clearly sensed new constraints on their classroom work were several who had experienced an extensive change in their environment. Teachers who had recently moved from a Northern school to a Southern school where race topics were not discussed, or from a non-denominational school to a denominational one, were often sharply conscious of the more restrictive character of their new colleges. Also, a few teachers who had been away on leave from their campuses for a year or two said they had immediately noticed a different atmosphere on their return.

But those who simply suspected that a change had occurred, without being able to pin it down exactly, were likely to be troubled; they sensed that they might have in some way retreated, but they were not quite sure. A typical comment came from an introspectively-inclined Southern economist:

I feel a rather tenuous connection between a changing intellectual environment and my own teaching practices. It's not so much an avoidance of controversial issues, as a feeling of hesitancy or uncertainty in pursuing a discussion of these issues in the classroom. I don't have any idea how that feeling has affected my teaching. I am aware of it as a subjective thing.

Such a comment suggests that if a pressure is sufficiently subtle and continuous, a teacher may respond to it without realizing he has changed his behavior. In such a situation, too, the impulse to exercise caution may seem almost a reflex, unpremeditated and somewhat disconcerting. Witness the remark of a California teacher: "I recently made some pretty obvious comments about Governor Knight's tax program without mentioning any names; I wondered why I just hadn't come out with it." Clearly a less self-perceptive teacher might easily overlook this kind of change. All in all, it appears likely that for every teacher who was actually conscious of shifting his classroom stand, there were more who had unwittingly either drifted along with the times completely, or partially reoriented their positions.

SOME CONSEQUENCES

When constraints occur in the classroom, certain consequences are inevitable. A student cannot react to an idea unless he hears it stated; if a teacher chooses to avoid discussion of controversial issues of the day, some students will remain unaware that they exist. A slanted classroom presentation denies to the student the privilege of hearing the other side. Furthermore, as many teachers pointed out, a vicious circle of increasing constraint can develop; a teacher who surrenders today his right to discuss what he considers peripheral may find tomorrow that he cannot discuss the central. In any case, whenever teachers do not speak out, but go along uncomplainingly with the dominant forces of the day, colleges and universities as strongholds of reform and progress are weakened.

Other consequences, if less sweeping, may nevertheless substantially alter established academic custom. It has long been the practice of many teachers to try out their new ideas, their new formulations and interpretations, upon their students; innumerable textbooks and journal articles contain tributes to the students who have tested them in preliminary versions. And yet if the ideas in such works are somehow unconventional by today's standards, many teachers are no longer willing to risk them on students. As one teacher put it, "How far may I speculate and come out with outrageous opinions, which may turn out in the future to be conventional ones?" If today's conjectural extravagance can become tomorrow's truth, to inhibit it is costly.

In short, educational achievement is no guarantee that the critical line between acquiescence and rebellion will be properly drawn—although it helps. By way of analogy, recall that the Orson Welles dramatization of an invasion from Mars frightened thousands of radio listeners during the 1930's; some tried to flee in their automobiles.[4] The poorly educated were disproportionately represented among the panic-stricken because they lacked the sophistication to evaluate the seeming evidence of their ears. In the 1970's, levels of formal

[4]Hadley Cantril, *The Psychology of Social Movements*, New York: Wiley, 1941.

education are rising and sophistication is growing. Fewer people would be stampeded by such a broadcast today. For the same reason, more high school students are questioning arbitrary rules of personal grooming ("dress codes") and improper orders from persons in authority are more likely to be disobeyed, even by soldiers. Still, My Lai happened quite recently, and there will doubtless be other scandals of acquiescence. But we should not expect final solutions of perennial problems. In every situation the line between acquiescence and rebellion must be drawn afresh.

CONCLUSION

Conforming to authority is like taking substances into the body for the sake of maintaining one's health. Sometimes the substances are, like castor oil, unpleasant in the short run, but under certain conditions vital. Sometimes the substances are, like heroin, soothing in the short run—yet ultimately ruinous. Sometimes they are, like juicy steaks, pleasant in the short run and beneficial. Sometimes they are, like lye, painful in the short run and ruinous as well.

The moral commandment, "Conform to authority!" (the possible message of *The Caine Mutiny*) is like the moral commandment, "Take substances into your body!" Both are asinine unless conditions for doing so are specified. It is the same with the moral commandment, "Don't conform to authority!" Unless conditions are specified, it, too, is asinine.

Conformity to authority is often essential if everyone is to achieve his own ends. This may even be true if the authority is incompetent. In a traffic jam, for example, what is often needed is *someone* to decide who should move first; and even the motorist who moves last may be better off than he would be if he and all the others had refused to budge. Whether the traffic officer who makes the decision might have made it more wisely is often unimportant.

One trouble is that conformity may become addictive. Then pathologies of conformity arise as "social problems." They may be pathologies of nonthinking robotism, which is objectionable because it is a sellout of human potentials; or the pathologies of more blatant self-destruction or destruction of others. The opposite trouble is that *non*conformity may become addictive. It leads to megalomaniacal self-indulgence rather than robotism—as well as to self- and other-destruction, as later chapters will show.

Human beings find it difficult to avoid swinging from one extreme to another with respect to "authority." In the 1950's and early 1960's, there was a wave of alarm about the social problem of "the conformists," "the silent generation," "the organization man," the crew-cutted "men in grey flannel suits." In the late 1960's and early 1970's there was a wave of alarm about the "nonconformists," the "rebellious generation," the "anarchic hippies," the long-haired "boys and girls in too-tight jeans."

Perhaps human beings must accept the tension of living with the realization that authority is necessary *and* that addiction to it is menacing. Although this tension is too much for some people to endure, many of us can learn to live with it and to weigh at each choice point whether we are being robots or megalomaniacs. *Both* questions need *always* to be asked.

The authors of this book believe that that is one of the tensions that keep us human. *Perhaps* it is too bad that we are neither unthinking turnips nor omniscient gods; but the fact is that we play in a different ball game. We had better accept it; it is the only game we have.

To be specific about the illustrations presented in this chapter, our own opinions are these.

1. Certainly Maryk should have relieved Queeg of command, in view of all the evidence he had.
2. Certainly Maryk's action should have been evaluated afterward, to see whether he had been megalomaniacal rather than prudent.
3. Certainly the gravity of mutiny should have been underscored, and the compulsive denigrators-of-authority-for-the-sake-of-denigrating-authority, like Keefer, should have been put down.
4. Certainly we should bend every effort to give Americans the abilities to act like Maryks and not like most of Milgram's subjects.

Section C
SUCCESS
BY HOOK
OR CROOK

One thing that can go wrong in social life is that some people learn to long for what their culture defines as desirable, but the types of transactions by which they are supposed to pursue such goals do not work. If their conformity to the cultural prescription of the desirable is strong enough and if they are determined enough, they pursue success "by hook or crook." They use whatever type of transaction with others that promises to work. If the approved one works for them, they use it and are regarded as conformists. If a different type of transaction works better for them in their particular situation (or in view of their personality structures or background or physical attributes), they deviate; their actions become "social problems."

Different sorts of social problems are created by different combinations of prescribed transactions and those actually used. Thus, when utilitarian bargaining (the negotiated exchange principle) is prescribed, the problem of favoritism or nepotism arises when people relate to one another in terms of loyalty or solidarity. The problem of "red tape" or "legalistic interference" arises if they seek to relate to one another bureaucratically. The problem of "collusion" arises if the transaction used is cooperation.

If legal (bureaucratic) modes are prescribed, the social problem of "bribery" is generated when people relate by bargaining for mutual advantage; that of favoritism or nepotism is again generated if they call loyalty into play; that of "conspiracy" or "collusion" if they try to use cooperation.

When cooperation is prescribed (such as when members of a football team are supposed to cooperate in pursuing victory for the team), the use of individualistic bargaining is usually regarded as "selling out"; the use of legal-bureaucratic procedures is regarded as "legalistic bickering"; and loyalty to other than team members is regarded as "betrayal" if the loyalty is to a member of the opposing team and as "favoritism" if a team members gets to carry the ball because he is the coach's nephew rather than because he is the best ball carrier.

Finally, in those cases in which loyalty is prescribed, the social problem of "prostitution" is generated by people who resort to bargaining; that of "formalistic nit-picking" by people who define the relationship legalistically; and that of "exploiting" loved ones if team-cooperative transactions are attempted, as in the case in which a father drafts his children into the family business rather than considering their best interests.

Some of those problems are regarded as more serious than others. We shall not attempt to illustrate all of them in this book—not even all the more serious ones. In this section we shall focus our attention rather on a type of social problem that results from the determined pursuit of a prescribed goal by proscribed transaction types, but a type not mentioned in the foregoing typology, namely, the use of coercion. Coercion, in stable and orderly societies, is the one type of transaction proscribed for everyone except for representatives of the state, which has (in stable societies) a monopoly on the legitimate use of force.[1] Still, coercion is often an effective albeit illegitimate means; and if the prescribed means are not effective, a certain proportion of determined goal-seekers will inevitably use it.

In the present section of the book, three kinds of problems generated in this way will be considered. Chapter 11 deals with "forthright thievery." Chapter 12 deals with more subtle ways of "making out"; and Chapter 13 deals with the special kind of coercion called "resistance." We shall discuss the differences among the three types in the separate chapters.

---

[1]Still another type of social problem is created when representatives of the state who are *supposed to* use force under certain conditions do not in fact do so. When policemen accept bribes or "look the other way" for friends or relatives, we speak of "corruption."

chapter 11
Grabbing what you want

If you don't have goods or services that other people want—professional skills, good looks, money, charm, or whatever commands attention in the market place—you cannot bargain effectively for what you want. The other types of interpersonal transactions might still enable you to obtain what you want and need. You might have a legal *right* to what you want, or you might persuade a colleague to give it to you as a contribution to a joint effort, or a friend or relative might love you enough to give it to you. Suppose that none of these alternative transaction types are available. Then you must either do without what you want, or use coercion. If you can't afford to do without it, the resort to coercion is a tempting possibility. One form of coercion, stealing, is not necessarily *easy*; the skills involved in professional theft may be impressive.[1]

We know something about the intricate "M.O.'s" of unrespectable thieves from the police who apprehend them. We know much less about thieves with respectable positions in society. Among those whose respectability may provide a better-than-average opportunity to steal (and get away with it) are those on whom society relies to control theft, namely, the police. Since policemen are as likely as anyone else to be confronted with the dilemma of either giving up a monetary goal or resorting to theft, sometimes cops become robbers. The following autobiographical account was given to a journalist by an ex-policeman during a sentence in Colorado State Prison for his part in a Denver police scandal.[2]

[1] John Bowers, "Big City Thieves," *Harpers*, February, 1967, pp. 50-53.
[2] From Ralph Lee Smith, "Cops as Robbers," *The Nation*, February 1, 1965, pp. 102-107. Reprinted by permission.

My partner and I noticed that the door of a small uptown shop was open. We radioed the dispatcher that we were entering. That's standard procedure. If you are going to enter a premises in the line of duty you call the dispatcher to tell him. He usually sends out a covering car with a sergeant or lieutenant in it to give you help or protection if you need it. Well, we radioed the dispatcher, then we pulled up the car and went in with our guns drawn. A thing like that is a real kind of case—you never know if some shots are going to start coming at you from some dark corner. But nobody was there.

"We put up our guns and my partner walked to the safe and started fiddling carefully with the dial. The door popped right open. 'I thought so,' he said. 'They left it on day lock. When they do that, all you have to do is turn it to one right number and she opens.' He reached inside and pulled out a wad of money. Then he looked at me with complete earnestness. 'You know, John,' he said, 'they don't lose a thing. They will claim it on their insurance—in fact, they'll claim more than they lost, and they'll get it without question. Now don't tell me that you can't use a little of this.' We ended up splitting it, and we gave some to the sergeant who came down to cover the case. He needed some too. It was the first money I took. I wasn't 'hooked' yet—that is, I wasn't a regular thief or burglar. But I had taken my first stolen money.

"Soon after that my partner and I surprised a couple of guys hauling some merchandise out of a warehouse. We caught them in a dark alley, drew our guns, and told them to get their hands up. They quickly identified themselves—they were policemen. My partner and I put up our guns. I suddenly realized that I probably didn't care very much any more. I was closer to being hooked."

He stopped for a moment, and took out a cigarette. It remained unlit in his hand as he went on.

"It's funny," he said, "but I think the thing that hooked me was the thing that happened a few nights later. It was a small thing, nothing compared to the kinds of jobs we were in after that. But you know, we were talking about the revelations I had. This was my next revelation, and it brought me in contact with the business community of the town.

"One night my partner and I were cruising down a dark alley late at night. A light snow was falling, and it had been falling since about 8 P.M. There were no tire tracks or footprints in the alley. Suddenly I noticed that the back door of a warehouse seemed to be open about a foot. There was a timber jammed up against it. It looked as if the door had drifted open a short way until it had been stopped by the timber.

" 'Stop the car,' I said to my partner. He stopped the car, we put the spotlight on the door, and I walked over. There was no sign that the door had been forced. Still, I liked to do things thoroughly. 'Call the dispatcher and tell him I'm entering,' I said. Then I went in and turned on the light.

"It was a small warehouse belonging to a manufacturer of fur coats. There were coats on racks and piles of skins around. Things were in order and I saw no sign of burglary.

"In a few minutes the lieutenant pulled up in a second car, and he had the owner of the place with him. The owner came in and walked halfway down the center aisle. Suddenly he gasped.

" 'My God!' he said. 'They're gone!'

" 'What's gone?' I asked.

" 'Over against the wall there,' he said excitedly. 'I had piles of skins on pallets. They're gone!'

" 'Pallets and all?'

"He didn't bat an eyelash. 'Pallets and all!' he said.

" 'How many skins were there?'

" 'A couple of hundred of them.'

" 'What were they worth?'

" 'Between $6 and $7.50 each.'

"This meant a loss of $1,200 to $1,500. I was skeptical. 'Look,' I said. 'I don't think anybody took anything here. There's no sign that the door was forced. It's been snowing since about 8 P.M. and there were no footprints or car tracks of any kind anywhere in the alley before my partner and I pulled in here.'

"He turned on me furiously. 'Are you doubting my word?' he shouted. Then he looked at me and his tone changed. 'By the way,' he said with a smile, 'do you fellows know your wives' sizes? We're grateful to you for the protection you give us. I'd like to give you each a coat for what you've done here.'

"I don't know if you can understand it. But somehow that was the end. 'Yes,' I said, 'I know my wife's size and I'll take one.'

" 'What about your patrol partner?' the man asked.

" 'He'll take one too,' I said.

" 'And how about the lieutenant outside?'

" 'I *know* he'll take one,' I said—and I was right.

"After we had all gotten our coats the lieutenant said to me, 'Fill out a loss report.' I filled it out, describing the loss just the way the man told me, and the man signed it.

"The next day the loss report went through the detective bureau and a detective called me in. 'Do you think that stuff was really stolen?' he asked me. 'I don't know,' I told him. 'All I know is, if you want a nice new fur coat for your wife you can go over there and get one.' The detective promptly went over and got himself a coat. The loss report went in to the insurance company and the insurance company paid off with no muss or fuss."

Lawyers call this type of justification "self-serving." The dishonest policeman, like the dishonest citizen, needs to rationalize his departure from honesty norms; one way to do this is to claim that everyone is crooked, that "nobody else cares, and why the hell should I?" Of course, this feeling is not restricted to the police. It is encouraged by a materialistic society in which self-orientation and an attitude of "What's in it for me?" are expressions of competition and negotiated exchange.

The exploitative use of others for one's own gain is well illustrated in the "con game." Although physical coercion is rarely used in confidence games, the victim is *psychologically* manipulated to the point of coercion.[3]

The modern wire store is operated by one regular insideman who poses as a Western Union official, a variable staff of shills, and a staff of several outsidemen or ropers. These ropers travel the country over looking for victims who have money and can be played for the wire. Some ropers depend largely on luck to enable them to find a mark and do very well by this haphazard method; others are more systematic, resorting to advertisements for "business opportunities" inserted in metropolitan newspapers, and carefully interviewing and sifting out the resulting clientele; the most enterprising have agents who locate prospective marks, investigate their financial standing, and compile a list from which the roper can select the fattest and juiciest. There is one restriction which, though it was formerly ignored especially in New York, is now rigidly observed: the mark must not be a resident of the city where he is to be trimmed.

Wherever the roper finds his mark, he knows that each one is an indivdual problem and that the play must be varied somewhat for each victim. Consequently, in an account of the wire it has seemed best to simplify it in order to present the general principles of the game without confusing the reader by the infinite possible variations in the play.

In order to visualize the wire in operation, let us assume that a roper whom we shall christen Louis Sanborn has been told that one John Bates, owner of a small department store in Providence, is a prospect for the wire. So Mr. Sanborn visits Mr. Bates, represents himself as the agent for a large corporation which is buying up small stores, and gets his victim's confidence. Mr. Bates is pleased to find a buyer for the business because it has not been too profitable. The two spend several days going over the matter. Sanborn blows hot and cold, then finally decides to buy and makes Bates a very generous tentative offer, subject to the final approval of his superiors. Mr. Bates snaps it up. So Mr. Sanborn takes an option on the business and invites Bates down to New York to consummate the deal.

They arrive in New York around noon and take up quarters at the Fairdale. Mr. Sanborn phones his "main office" and reports that their attorneys are occupied with another deal and will not be available until the following day.

[3]From David Maurer, *The Big Con*, Indianapolis, Indiana: The Bobbs-Merrill Company, Inc., Pocket Book edition, 1940, pp. 32-52. Copyright © 1940, 1968, reprinted by permission of the publishers, The Bobbs-Merrill Co., Inc.

Then he excuses himself and makes a private call from a phone booth to his insideman, whom we shall call Charley Maxwell.

"I have a businessman from Providence," he says. "What time can we play for him?"

Maxwell consults his appointment book. "How about half past two this afternoon?" he asks.

"Fine," says Sanborn. "We'll be there."

When he returns to the room he finds his victim ready for lunch. They go down to the dining room. There, during luncheon, Sanborn plants the first seeds for the play to come. He casually mentions the fact that his cousin is manager of the central office of the Western Union here in New York.

"On my way up I tried to locate a friend in New London," he explains. "Charley wanted to see him about some kind of deal, but he was out of town."

Luncheon progresses. They talk of the pending sale of Mr. Bates' business. When it is time to depart, Sanborn picks up the check and again brings up his cousin. "We aren't in any hurry," he says, "and Charley's office is just around the corner from here. Would you mind walking around that way with me? I think you'll like Charley."

And Mr. Bates does like cousin Charley, for he has a dignified and attractive personality which puts Bates immediately at his ease. He is one of the best insidemen in New York. When they arrive, he is very busy directing the activities of a staff of telegraphers. In the midst of this wholesome hum and clatter the introduction is made.

"Where are you staying, Louis?" asks Charley.

"Over at the Fairdale," says Louis. "Mr. Bates is here on business with me and he is over there too."

"Why, you're just around the corner," observes Charley. "What about our man in New London? Have you talked to him?"

"Not yet," says Louis. "He was out of town."

Cousin Charley rolls up his sleeves another notch and adjusts his green eyeshade. "I want to talk to you about him later, but I can't entertain you here. The inspectors will be around any minute now and it wouldn't look good to have a couple of strangers loafing in the office. I think you understand the situation. Now you two go on down to the hotel and as soon as inspection is over I'll join you there in the lobby. It won't take long. Good-by."

Little does Mr. Bates suspect that the Western Union office he has just been in is entirely fake, that the energetic whir of teletypes was for his benefit only, that as soon as he left, it ceased entirely, the Western Union sign came down, and that cousin Charley put on his coat and dropped his manner of dignified, conscientious executive. The outward appearances have been so convincing, the stage set with such precision, that it does not occur to him to question its authenticity.

Half an hour later, in street clothes, Charley meets Mr. Bates and Mr. Sanborn in the hotel lobby. "It's all over," he remarks, "and they're gone. Now, Louis, how about Brown? You said that you'd find him and bring him along."

Louis explains that he learned that Brown is out of town for two weeks. He ventures to suggest tentatively that perhaps his friend here, Mr. Bates, could be persuaded to fill in on the deal. Cousin Charley looks somewhat shocked at this suggestion and gives Mr. Bates an appraising look.

"How long have you known this gentleman, Louis?" he asks.

"Not very long," answers Louis, "but long enough to know that he is a responsible man, with his own business in Providence. He is O.K. I feel sure that you can depend on him."

Mr. Bates' very natural discomfort in this situation is quickly allayed by cousin Charley, who turns upon him full force the benign rays of his personality and suggests that they talk the matter over confidentially. Mr. Bates begins to feel that he likes Mr. Maxwell even better than he does Mr. Sanborn. Charley Maxwell already "has his con."

They go up to Sanborn's suite and relax. Mr. Maxwell rises to the occasion and "tells the tale" with such dignified sincerity that even the cynical Mr. Sanborn is touched by his fine acting. He explains to Mr. Bates that he has worked for a heartless corporation for years; that he has had advancement, but never what he had been promised and assured; that the company has neglected him when it should have promoted him, and that he has decided to resign.

We must not assume that Mr. Bates is a fool. He has been about a bit himself, he manages his own business and he flatters himself that he knows a good deal about people. If he ever saw character, there it is in Charley Maxwell. He is not so much touched by the facts which Maxwell has outlined, but by the manner in which they are presented. Instead of a dissatisfied, disgruntled employee, he begins to see before him a man with the makings of a fine executive who has been neglected and wronged.

"And," Mr. Maxwell adds, "I have decided that when I resign, I will not be poor. I know how to swing a deal by which I can make a very good profit without hurting my company in the least. But I must have the assistance of an honest and dependable man, one who is able to put up some funds in return for a share of the profits. Louis' friend, Mr. Brown, was the man I had in mind. Now he cannot be located. I must act quickly, for I may not have the opportunity a second time. Are you interested?"

Mr. Bates is chary. Is Maxwell trying to make a touch? What is this deal? Is it legitimate? How much would he have to invest? And, though he does not say so, the really serious question: *How much is the profit involved?* He stalls for more information.

Mr. Maxwell drops the question of financing and tells him about the deal. He explains that through his central office pass the race results for all the bookmakers in the city, that the horse-poolrooms are growing fat on the profits from gambling on races, that rich men with inside information can win through the bookmakers, but that the poor fellow with only a form-sheet to guide him always loses more than he makes. He says that he has worked out a system whereby he can beat the bookmakers at their own game by delaying the results long enough to phone them to his assistants who are to be stationed next door to the poolroom and who will bet on the races after they are run. Then the results will be released, and of course their bets will pay a very neat profit. And no one will suffer but the rich and dishonest bookmakers.

Once the mark has gone this far, he seldom backs out. If he does, further pressure may be put on him or he may be dropped altogether. But we will assume that Maxwell's smooth voice and sincere manner have had their effect. Bates likes the proposition and sees in it a high profit with no risk. It is a sure thing.

"Now," says Mr. Maxwell, aside to Mr. Bates, "Louis doesn't understand much about this business and I will count on you to take the responsibility of seeing that everything goes all right. You and he go on down to this address on 48th Street and look the place over. Then go into the drugstore next door and wait for a call from me at three sharp. I'll give you the name of the winner and hold up the results just long enough for you to go next door and place your bet. I can't hold them for more than three or four minutes. That way we can see whether or not our system will work, and of course you and Louis can keep anything you win for yourselves. If it works out, we will want to try something bigger."

Mr. Bates and Louis follow the instructions they have received. They visit the poolroom and find there all the paraphernalia that go with a booking establishment. Races are chalked on the blackboard. The ticker is thrumming merrily. Prosperous gentlemen are winning and losing large bets nonchalantly. The caller calls the races with great zest. Bets of $10,000 to $20,000 are laid casually. Very large amounts of cash are changing hands like nickels in a crap game. Everywhere there is cash. The patrons peel off large bets from fat bank rolls or from bulging wallets. The cashier counts out $40,000 winnings without batting an eye. Louis and Mr. Bates are much impressed. A little of the fever of that atmosphere has worked its way into Mr. Bates' blood.

Three o'clock approaches. They return to the drugstore. Maxwell gives them, shall we say, Seabiscuit as winner. They hasten back and plunge into the thick and throbbing atmosphere. Both Mr. Bates and Louis put a ten-dollar bill on Seabiscuit to win. Mr. Bates feels a queer sensation of mingled guilt and triumph. It is a wonderful feeling to bet on a sure thing, even for ten dollars. They have hardly placed their bets when the caller says the magic words, "They're off!"

Then he calls the race. Seabiscuit wins, at 4-1. Our pair of innocents collect fifty dollars each. The larceny in Mr. Bates' veins begins to percolate. He can already see a fortune stretching out ahead of him. Why, there is no limit—except the resources of the bookmaker—to what one could make out of this thing. And there are thousands of bookmakers.

They look about them while they await the next race. The same air of dignified, restrained feverishness prevails. No one seems to notice them. Mr. Bates looks the crowd over. It is not large, but it is sporty. Brokers with pasty faces. Sportsmen, tanned and casual. A financier with a Vandyke and highly tailored clothes. The thick blue haze wherein mingle the thin silver streams from a dozen fine cigars. They are betting, joking, absorbed in themselves.

Mr. Bates is a little taken aback at the nonchalant way in which these men handle money. He likes it, and would like to feel that he is a part of it. But he knows that he isn't. He turns to his friend Sanborn. The next race is coming up. They retire to the 'phone for more information. Then they bet fifty dollars each on War Admiral to win at 4-1. He does.

This nets them $250 apiece. "I think I'll shoot the works on the next race," says Mr. Bates. Sanborn counsels caution. After all, this thing is just starting. This is only an experiment to see if their plan will work. Charley knows what he is about, and perhaps they had better do as he says and place only small bets. But Mr. Bates is hooked. He returns to the telephone, awaits a horse, and comes back with the firm intention of placing the $250 on his nose. Louis cautiously refrains from betting this time.

Mr. Bates hurries to the window to place his bet. He has the $250 in his pocket, ready to be laid. But there are several men just ahead of him. They are laying down very big bets. He cannot help noticing the fat, sleek piles of fives, tens, twenties, fifties and hundreds in the cashier's drawer. He sees the piles of bills on the shelf behind the cashier. He sees the deft hands swiftly paying out and taking in thousands of dollars. He grows impatient. Time is short. The race will be called any moment now. He pushes the line along, but it doesn't seem to move fast enough. He shifts his weight from one foot to the other and peers ahead. Only one man, now. Laying a fifteen thousand dollar bet. Will he never get that money counted down? The man moves casually away, biting the end off a heavy cigar. Mr. Bates removes the wadded bills from his pocket. Challedon. Charley said Challedon to win.

"They're off!" shouts the caller.

Mr. Bates stands there, futilely fingering his money. Betting is closed. Challedon. . . . Where is Challedon? He lags to the rear. He is under wraps. The caller reads off the ticker with such animation that he might as well have been an eyewitness. Will Challedon never make his move? Here it is. They enter the stretch with Challedon moving up. He is booted home a winner. And 6-1. Mr. Bates does a little sketchy mental arithmetic and wonders why he wasn't just one ahead in the line at the window.

He doesn't know it, but he has been given the "shut-out" or the "prat-out," a clever method of stepping up the larceny in the veins of a mark when the manager feels that he is not entering into the play enthusiastically enough. It may be repeated several times so that the mark is fully impressed with what he has missed. The shills who surround the mark at the window usually play for more than the mark is being played for; if the mark is being played for $25,000, the air is full of $50,000 bets; thus the mark always feels like a piker instead of a plunger. Furthermore, ambitious marks must not be allowed to get too much of the store's cash into their pockets.

Mr. Bates returns to Louis. "Tough luck," says Louis.

A suave-looking gentleman approaches them. He is quiet, polite, but authoritative. And just a little condescending. Mr. Bates doesn't know just why, but he feels embarrassed.

"Are you the gentlemen who have been placing these small bets?" he asks, waving a pair of slips.

"We just made a fifty-dollar bet, if you call that small," says Louis.

The manager looks at them with patronizing good nature. "Well, I'll have to ask you not to place any more small bets here," he says. "We have other poolrooms for working men. Small bets make too much bookkeeping for us." He smiles and gently starts them toward the door. Mr. Bates feels patronized. He doesn't like it.

"How much does a man have to bet here?" asks Louis.

"A thousand dollars is usually the lower limit," answers the manager, smiling. "Beyond that, you can go as high as you like. Come back, gentlemen, some other time."

As they pass the doorman, they see Maxwell coming down the street. "Did it work?" asks cousin Charley. "If it did, we can all make a fortune."

"We won a couple of hundred dollars apiece on two bets," volunteers Louis. "But we never got any further. They called us pikers because we didn't bet high enough."

"Never mind that, my boy," answers Charley. "When the time comes we will arrange to bet high enough to suit them. Let's go over to the hotel. I want to discuss this thing further with you in private."

Up in the suite at the Fairdale Mr. Bates hears what he wants to hear.

"This particular poolroom," says cousin Charley, "is the one that I have marked to work on. I know that they have very extensive financial backing. Their volume of business must be tremendous."

Mr. Bates, with a mind full of greenbacks, reflects that it certainly must be.

"They can lose a million and never miss it," continues Charley. "My plan is to take eight or nine hundred thousand in four or five days, then quit. What do you gentlemen say?"

Mr. Bates and Louis agree that it would indeed be a desirable course of action.

"But we have to have cash to finance it," says Charley. "That is why I was so concerned about Brown. He could dig up the cash we need. Let's see, I believe you were thinking that you might raise some for us?"

"How much would you need?" asks Mr. Bates, fearful of appearing too anxious.

"Do you think you would be willing to finance it?" asks Charley. "After all, you know, I haven't much except my salary and Louis here is just getting a start. How much can you raise?"

Mr. Bates studies. He figures on an envelope. His mind is a whirl of mortgages, real estate, government bonds. It may take a couple of weeks to sell his business. Bonds would be the quickest. Government bonds.

"I think I could pick up twenty-five thousand within the next couple of days. Or maybe sooner," he adds, mindful of the potential Mr. Brown. "Is your friend definitely out?"

Mr. Maxwell is very cool and practical. "I hate to let Brown down," he muses. "But I think this arrangement will be fine. How much did you say you could raise? Twenty-five thousand? How is this money? In cash?"

"No, no," says Mr. Bates, "in bonds. Government bonds. I'll have to have my banker sell them and forward me a draft for the proceeds."

"That would be fine," says Charley.

"Now," says Mr. Bates, "how do you intend to split the profits? I would want to pay you whatever is right, but if I put up the money, I ought to get a good share of the profits. Otherwise it wouldn't pay me to get into it."

Mr. Bates suddenly feels important. All he needs is the information. He has the cash. That is the important thing. These men can be paid off at his own price if he finances it now, quickly, before someone else is cut in.

"I have thought that over," says cousin Charley. "Since the plan is mine, I think I ought to have at least fifty per cent. And we should cut Louis in for about twenty per cent for his cooperation. That would leave you thirty per cent which would make you a very good return on your investment."

Mr. Bates doesn't like that arrangement. He wants to cut those men out of all he can. Of course they must have something, but why let Louis in on it at all? And Maxwell. Why, he would go to prison if this thing ever became known. He schemes and argues. As they dicker, Maxwell humors him by working out a compromise whereby he and Bates will split ninety per cent of the profit, and Louis will get the remaining ten. Mr. Bates still feels that they have been too generous with Louis. He moves immediately to phone his banker in Providence. But Maxwell interposes.

"This deal must be kept absolutely secret," he argues. "If you phone in for money in a hurry, your banker may become suspicious. You know how bankers are. He may feel that you are making a mistake to dump a block of bonds like that on the market right now. It will be a little more expensive, but much safer if you catch a train out of here this afternoon and talk to your banker personally tomorrow. Explain that you are buying some real estate here in the city and want to pay down that much cash."

"But," interposes Bates, turning to Louis, "what about that appointment with your lawyers?"

"Don't worry about that," says Louis. "I'll take care of everything for you. Just send me a telegram as soon as you know when you'll be back and I'll fix things up at the office."

"That's right," says Charley. "And you'd better add a note in that telegram which will let me know how much money you are bringing. But we don't want anyone to suspect you are bringing it. So let a thousand dollars equal, say, one 'bushel.' Then you can say, 'Bringing twenty-five bushels' and I'll know you are prepared to go right ahead with the deal."

This stage of the game is known as "the send." It is a strange fact that, once a good insideman "tightens up" a mark, he can be sent anywhere for his money and will usually return despite all obstacles. For example, during the week of July 3, 1939, the metropolitan papers carried stories on the case of Mr. Leonard B. Reel, a public accountant of Beach Haven, New Jersey, who, with his wife, was put on the send from Mexico City. The couple flew to Philadelphia and brought back $74,000 which they lost on the rag to the Velvet Kid. They reported that they made the trip with some difficulty, having been forced down en route by storms four different times. If the con men think that they can get away with using the mails, they may not use "the send."

Mr. Bates agrees that it will be best to make the trip. There must be no slips. For a moment he fears what might happen if this scheme came to light. Then he remembers that he is only financing it. He feels better. Also, the $250 in his wallet will more than cover his expenses on the trip home. Mr. Bates watches his pennies. But on the other hand, is it safe to leave the deal open here? Suppose Brown—or someone else—turned up with the ready cash?

"You have decided definitely that I am to finance it?" he asks.

"Yes, indeed," says Charley. "Here is my hand on it. We'll shake hands all the way around. That swears us all to keep this deal absolutely secret."

They all shake hands, though having Louis cut in on the deal still sticks in Bates' crop. After all ten per cent isn't much, and Louis still holds the key to the sale of his store. Well, he'll get that ten per cent back and more when Louis' company takes up that option.

Three days later he is back in New York with a draft for $25,000. He is at a high pitch of excitement. This business turns over a profit quicker than anything he has ever seen. And he gets a strange sense of elation—the same feeling, magnified a thousand times, that he felt when he had that first ten dollars on Seabiscuit and watched him romp home. He has a sure thing.

Maxwell takes him to a bank which has been fixed. Mr. John Bates endorses the check, and now has $25,000 in cash. It burns holes in his pockets.

"This afternoon I think we can work," says Charley. "I'll find out what the best odds are, you stay near the 'phone booth, and I'll tell you what to bet just before each race. I'll get any last-minute change in odds as they come through over the wire, and we'll take all that into consideration. We'll work the same as we did the other day. Now hold on tight to that money." Then he goes back to directing the destinies of a minor province in the great empire of the Western Union.

The next few hours are critical ones for the con men. Between now and post-time the mark is most likely to have a "brain-blow" and lose his head. Marks have been known to go to the police with the whole story right at this point, and a "wrong" copper might lay a trap for the con men and get the mark to co-operate. Or the mark might worry about so large a gamble and look up some friend or acquaintance to consult about the matter; of course any of these might tip the whole thing off. Occasionally the victim insists on seeking the advice of his wife, in which case wiser con mobs encourage such a move, for they have learned that such a consultation usually works in their favor. Some marks simply get cold feet at the last moment and go on about their business, or return home.

So a "tailer" is put on Mr. Bates during all the time that he is not with either of the con men. The tailer, a man of ample experience in such matters, can tell immediately by the mark's actions how he is getting along. If he consults the police, the tailer reports back immediately and the con men may simply not see him any more, or they may phone him and tell him that the Western Union has become suspicious and that the deal must be postponed. However, if he has consulted a "right" copper or detective, the con men know that they are safe, for they can pay their way as soon as the score comes off. They go right ahead and play for him knowing that the police will not "knock" him or tip him off to what is happening. If it seems necessary, the insideman himself or his fixer will go down and have a chat with the officer in order to be sure there will be no slips. Meanwhile, Mr. Bates, if he has had any traffic with police, feels better in the knowledge that the officers of the law are not suspicious of the men with whom he is dealing or of the deal (if he lets that out) which he is contemplating.

Meanwhile, Louis stalls the victim along with the pending sale of his store, which, during the play, fades into the background. Some marks become so feverish that, during the period of the tie-up, they apparently forget all about the original reason for their coming to the city where the big store is located, or resent the roper's attempts to continue negotiations for the business while this big deal is in the air.

Post-time finds Mr. Bates and Louis haunting the phone booth, awaiting the call which will come sometime during the afternoon. Bates hugs his $25,000. Louis handles his quarry skillfully, knowing just how to arouse his anticipations and how far to go in quieting the doubts which may be troubling his mind.

At last the phone jangles. Mr. Bates rushes into the booth. It is Maxwell.

"Hello," he says, "is that you Louis?"

"No, this is John Bates."

"Well, I've got the winner. Hurry right on over and place the money on Flying Lill. Call Louis to the phone, will you?"

Louis talks briefly to Charley. "O.K.," he says. "I understand. Place it all on Flying Lill. Good-by, Charley."

They hurry over to the poolroom and plunge into the atmosphere of synthetic excitement. There on the odds-board is Flying Lill, 5-1. Mr. Bates feels a momentary sinking in the pit of his stomach. His mouth is dry and his hands tremble. Louis takes the bills from his hands and pushes them through the cashier's window. "Flying Lill to win," he says. "Twenty-five thousand."

The cashier gives him his slip and begins to count the money. "They're off!" calls the announcer, and the next two minutes are hectic ones. It is Unerring by a length. Flying Lill second. Lady Maryland third.

Mr. Bates is stunned. *Unerring won.*

"Wait a minute," says Louis, "there must be something wrong. It isn't official yet." He looks with mingled sympathy and anxiety into Mr. Bates' ashen face.

But it is official. The announcement cuts through the smoke and clatter like a great somber gong. It is official.

"We've lost," says Louis, and they go out into the street.

It may occur to Mr. Bates that he has been betrayed. His mind is probably such a chaos that he cannot think at all. He may break into sobs immediately, and wildly tear his hair. But we will assume that he is a gentleman and that he restrains his emotions and reserves his judgments until he learns what has happened. Louis has already solicitously begun the "cooling-out" process which will pave the way for Maxwell's smooth patter.

They meet Charley, who can only partly conceal his jubilation, a short distance from the Western Union office. He is talking in terms of winning $125,000. Mr. Bates tells him that Louis bet the horse to win, but that it placed and they lost. Charley turns on Louis in a fury. "Don't you know what the word *place* means?" he roars. Louis tries to justify his mistake on the basis of their misunderstanding of the word *place*. But Maxwell will have none of it. He rakes that young man over the coals until he hangs his head in red-faced shame and humiliation. Mr. Bates is very likely to come to Louis' defense, on the grounds that he, too, misunderstood. Then Mr. Maxwell turns on him and gives him also a piece of his mind. But finally he cools off.

"Well," he says, "we'll never make that mistake again." Then he takes Mr. Bates in hand in such a way that the "cooling-out" process is perfect and Mr. Bates lives only until he can raise enough money to give the plan a second trial. When Charley Maxwell cools a mark out, he stays cooled out. And if he has decided that the mark is good for another play—as about fifty per cent of them are—he will "feel him out" to see whether or not he can raise more cash; some marks have been beaten four or five times on the same racket. If he knows he has been swindled, or if he cannot raise any more money, he is "blown off" and disposed of as quietly as possible. Let us assume that Mr. Bates, being the perfect mark, is good for another play. Mr. Maxwell retains his confidence to such an uncanny extent that he will do almost anything he is told to do. So he is "put on the send" again for $20,000, which he borrows, using real estate as collateral.

The second play takes up just where the first left off. The only delay is caused by obtaining Mr. Bates' money. Louis knows how to handle the deal regarding Mr. Bates' business and assures him that everything is going along fine, but that his corporation is going to investigate the department store further before they sign the final papers. Usually, if the mark is good for a second play, he is by this time so wrapped up in the wire that he has practically dropped the legitimate deal. Some con mobs will send a tailor along home with the mark to see if he consults the police before returning. The tailer may pose as an agent for the corporation which is interested in the mark's business.

The big store, the boost, and all the necessary stage-settings are again called into play. When the time comes to make the big bet, the sting is put in a little differently. Over the phone Mr. Maxwell gives the mark Johnny J. at 6-1 to win. Mr. Bates and Louis bet the $20,000, making sure that there is no misunderstanding this time regarding that tricky word *place*. The betting is heavy all around them, though Mr. Bates does not realize that those bank rolls have seen much service as props. The $50,000 in cold cash laid down by the better just ahead of him is real money; it makes an impression.

"They're off!" says the caller. The room quiets. The smoke drifts in swirls. The gamblers listen with polite eagerness. It is Johnny J. by a neck.

Mr. Bates feels a great exhilaration; his fingers and toes tingle; a warm wave of relief sweeps over him. His horse has won $140,000. Now to take his share and build it up into a fortune.

"Let's cash it right away," urges Louis, "before something happens to it."

Mr. Bates waves the ticket before the impassive cashier, who is imperturbably stacking big bills; Mr. Bates has never seen so much loose cash. It is everywhere. The cashier looks at him with polite indifference.

"Cash this, cash this, please," says Mr. Bates, pushing the ticket under the grating.

"Just a minute, sir," says the cashier. "I'm sorry, but those results are not yet official. Wait a minute."

"Flash!" says the caller. "Flash! A mistake in colors. It was Silverette by a neck, Johnny J. second, Technician is third. This is official."

Mr. Bates vaguely hears a man beside him say to his friend, "I'm very glad that horse disqualified. I had $7,000 on Silverette."

"I'm not," says his friend. "That damned Johnny J. cost me just twenty thousand. . . ."

Mr. Bates is dazed. He remonstrates with the manager. He cries and curses his luck. He suspects that he has been swindled but doesn't know how. The manager is polite, firm and impersonal. The heavy play goes right on for the next race. Louis, crying and complaining as if it were his $20,000 which went glimmering, leads him out into the street. The outside air only intensifies the terrible feeling of loss and despair in Mr. Bates' heart. To him money is a sacred thing. This is terrible.

Outside on the street they meet Charley. He looks tired and worried. He is nervous and distraught. He listens absently to the tale of woe. "Yes, that is terrible," he agrees. "But right now I am in terrible trouble myself. The Western Union detectives have been investigating the delay in race results and I'll be lucky if I only lose my job. If they pin anything on me, I'll go to prison. Maybe all three of us."

Mr. Bates hasn't thought of this angle since Charley first explained the deal to him. Fear now adds its agony to despair. They talk over the possibilities of arrest. Maxwell advises that Bates and Louis leave town as quickly and quietly as possible. They return to the hotel. Louis obligingly gets the time for the next train to Providence. It leaves at 10:00 P.M. Mr. Bates, worried, nervous, broken, agrees to take it. Charley promises that, if this thing blows over, he himself will raise enough money to play the game again and will give Mr. Bates all his money back, and some profit to boot. Then he leaves, so that he may not be picked up. Louis draws Mr. Bates aside.

"How much money do you have?" he asks.

Mr. Bates looks in his wallet. "Less than fifty dollars," he answers. "And I have to pay my hotel bill."

"Well," offers Louis, "I have nearly a hundred and fifty. You have had a bad break and I hate to see you stranded. You have been a fine sport to take it the way you do. Here, let me lend you seventy-five to get home on. You can pay it back any time. And remember," he adds, "our auditors will be at your place next week. Then I'll have everything in good shape at this end and we'll close the deal."

Mr. Bates takes the money which is pressed on him. He is surprised. Louis is a pretty nice fellow after all. He is ashamed of the way he has felt about him recently. Still in a daze, he shakes the proffered hand and Louis departs. "I'll be back about nine-thirty," he says, "to see that you get to the train safely. Wait for me in the lobby."

From now on, it is up to a local tailer to keep close tab on Mr. Bates to see what he may do, reporting any tendency he may show to consult the police. Mr. Maxwell may have him paged to the telephone and continue the cooling process by phone. The tailer watches closely; if, after this conversation, Mr. Bates consults the house detective or a detective he has stationed in the lobby, the tailer reports immediately to Maxwell, who puts the machinery of the fix into operation. Or, Louis may deliberately delay his arrival at the hotel to see his victim off. As the time for departure approaches and Louis fails to appear, Mr. Bates may get nervous and make a phone call to the police, or consult a detective already stationed in the hotel. The tailer can predict the mark's reactions with a good deal of accuracy, for he has had ample opportunity to study at first hand the psychology of the trimmed mark.

Just before ten, at the tailer's signal, Louis appears with a good excuse for lateness, bundles Mr. Bates carefully into a cab, hurries him to the station, buys his ticket for Providence, and puts him on the train. He waits solicitously until the train pulls out.

As soon as the mark is safely on his way, Mr. Maxwell meets his roper, the manager and the boost at the hangout. He is a meticulous bookkeeper. He gives each one a plain envelope containing his share of the score, and drops a word about an appointment for eleven-thirty on Wednesday. And so the big store goes on.

The big-city thieves and the predatory cops differ from the con man in that they do not deal directly with the victims of their coercion. Different from all of them is the holdup man who not only deals directly with his victim, but utilizes naked force. Here is an account of that road to success by a professional armed robber, written during the enforced leisure of a prison sentence.[4]

The holdup was a relatively rare form of crime forty or fifty years ago, though well publicized even then. Nowadays it is the most common form of serious crime. It would be interesting to know the reasons for this sudden rise in popularity. No doubt the ever-increasing complexity of our way of life has had something to do with it. Psychologists declare that excessive discipline is likely to result in impulses of cruelty and destruction, and it seems probable that the innumerable social pressures to which the individual is subjected in our society

[4]Everett DeBaun, "The Heist: The Theory and Practice of Armed Robbery," *Harper's Magazine*, February 1950, pp. 69-77.

give rise to aggressive feelings ultimately requiring outlets—certainly our preoccupation with bloodthirsty comics, movies, radio programs, and mystery and detective fiction is not accidental. And certainly the stickup is an aggressive action of classic directness and simplicity.

Such an explanation may account in part for the innumerable holdups of drug stores and filling stations, the frequent heists pulled with glass pistols, cap pistols, water pistols, air guns; the haberdasheries and cigar stores stuck up as Jesse James might have stuck up banks; the sadistic little jobs whose main purpose seems to be maltreatment of the victims: the Lovers Lane holdups, the cab-drivers robbed of fares and tips. Such holdups undoubtedly have a large emotional, or neurotic, component. Obviously, the motivation is not a rational weighing of risks against possible gain, for banks might be robbed almost as cheaply—not that bank robbery is lightly punished, but that we punish robbery of any type more severely than several varieties of murder (in some states by death), a lesson in applied Christianity as pointed, in its way, as our custom of requisitioning lives though not money in time of war, or the size of the vote polled by Norman Thomas.

There are more tangible reasons for the emergence of the holdup as a *professional* technique, though here too emotional and social factors of course are present. Technological change occurs in the underworld, as elsewhere. During the past few generations several ancient and dishonorable professions have given way to others better suited to the times. In comparison with the burgeoning of the holdup, the decline of the box-busting racket is a case in point. Forty or fifty years ago, the safe-cracker was considered the prince of thieves. Though the best of the modern boxmen can open modern safes as efficiently as the petermen of half a century ago could open those of that day, the profession is fast on the down-grade. Cash simply is not kept in safes as it was. For the most part, business is carried on by check, and checks are worthless as loot. Similarly, securities are now seldom readily negotiable, stamps are giving way to postage meters, jewelry is a drug on the market—"slum," as it is familiarly called, brings but from 15 to 20 per cent of the replacement value at fence, while silver is hardly worth carrying off, and watches can be disposed of for no more than a portion of the value of the metal in the cases. Furthermore, that infallible source of cash in large amounts, the bank, is no longer vulnerable to the safe-cracker, thanks chiefly to the time lock, a device which may be set to jam the bolt mechanism for a period during which a vault may not be opened even by some one possessing the combination. Consequently, the Max Shinburnes, Leonidas Leslies, Chauncy Johnsons, Adam Worths, Bob Scotts, and Jimmy Hopes who during the last quarter of the past century burglarized banks of sums said to total close to a hundred million dollars—a number of the individual "scores" were for more than a million—have gone the way of the horse and buggy. Their present-day counterparts are top-grade holdup-men—"heist-men" in the underworld argot. . . .

A seventeenth-century cookbook advises those who would prepare jugged hare first to catch their hare. To pull a heist, first find your "mark." A mark may be any considerable sum of money or the equivalent in readily convertible swag. Professional heist-men judge marks in terms of the probable cash return relative to the risks involved.

Marks are either dug up or tipped off. When a heist-man says that he has dug one up, he means that he has found it himself. He may have sought it out, tailing ladies who appear in public festooned like Christmas trees with jewels, or armored cars making deliveries of payrolls, for instance. Or he may just have stumbled upon it, like one who was introduced by a casual resort acquaintance into a private poker game in which some $12,000 was in play, or another who noticed that the proprietor of a saloon where he occasionally stopped for a beer made a practice of cashing pay-checks for employees of a nearby refinery. Marks that have been tipped off are those that have been pointed out by others. One who tips off marks is called a fingerman or tipster; he may or may not be of the underworld. Sometimes pickpockets, gamblers, and other footloose grifters tip marks off to heist-men as a side-line. The standard remuneration for this service is 10 per cent of the gross score. A surprisingly large number of marks are tipped off by legit, or ostensibly honest, people, and no few are put up (whence, incidentally, the colloquial expression "put-up job") or prearranged: a truck driver would like a share of the value of the load of cigarettes or whiskey he will be carrying; a jeweler wants to beat his insurance company; a bank manager wishes to cover his embezzlements. As the police are well aware of this, many heist-men fight shy of such tips, for the legit citizen, having odd notions of honor by the thief's standards, is likely to break down under close questioning, and promises of immunity for himself, and finger his partners as thoroughly as he formerly fingered the mark.

Other things being equal, the cash mark is always preferable. There is nothing like a bank for cold cash in large amounts, and until recently the "jug" was beyond argument the best type of mark by professional criteria. It is true that for many years banks of any size have had what looks to be formidable protection, but in robbery as in warfare of other types the aggressor has a heavy advantage. Armed guards, vaults with walls of steel and concrete several feet in thickness, and elaborate alarm systems did not prevent heist-mobs from knocking over an average of about two banks a day during the early thirties. In 1934, however, Congress passed an act making bank robbery a federal offense and bringing it under the jurisdiction of the FBI, a police organization having almost unlimited funds and unique facilities, the most important of these being a corps of stool-pigeons probably as extensive as any outside Russia. Simultaneously, the flat twenty-five-year sentence for bank robbery became mandatory, and the government established a special prison for "jug-heists" (the species populates Alcatraz almost 100 per cent), operated on principles that would turn the stomach of a Turk. These additional risks require that others be at a minimum if a bank is to be marked nowadays, and the same is true of the mails. . . .

Given a mark, the next step is mobbing up, or getting together the men who will work the job. A working unit of underworld professionals of any type is called a mob. There are "single-o" heist-men, such as the one known in the papers as Slick Willie, who has robbed large and well-protected banks single-handed, but the vast majority of the brotherhood work in mobs. A heist-mob may comprise from two to six or eight members—the type of mark is usually the determining factor. Thus, the "same" mob—*i.e.*, several of a group of stick-up men who sometimes work together—may be five-handed for a jug-heist and three-handed for a payroll job. There are excellent reasons why the mob is generally of the minimum size compatible with efficient operation. One is selfish: "The smaller the mob, the bigger the cut." The other is protective: each additional member adds to the risk of a fall, paradoxical as this may seem. The answer is that the professional runs little danger of falling either *en flagrante* or, despite the highly imaginative information ladled out for popular consumption along this line, as a result of acute detective work. Almost always he is caught because of information given to police.

Eddie suddenly squares his debts and springs with a new car, for instance, or begins shooting high craps and buying drinks for the house, or buys a fur coat for Marge, who cannot resist throwing the needles to that catty Doris, who puts two and two together and confides the result to Nettie, whose husband Louie peddles dope or does a bit of pimping or wants to get City Hall's okay to book numbers or horses in his cigar store. In every city, police permit numerous Louies to operate in consideration for periodical cash donations, plus just such favors as the one Louie is now in a position to confer. If Eddie cannot stand up under the beatings he will now undergo as a matter of police routine, or if Marge knows who his partners are and can be talked or frightened into trading the information for a lighter sentence for him, the whole mob may fall.

Popular notions notwithstanding, the basic units of a heist-mob are not a "mastermind" and some servile morons who carry out his orders. As a matter of fact, among "heavy" thieves no one gives orders for the good reason that no one takes them—the heavy is as independent a character as walks the earth. Within the mob, equality reigns. All share equally in risk and gain. All have equal authority. This is not to imply that the members of a mob simply behave as they please on the job. There a rather rigid discipline prevails, but all have had a voice in the plan being carried out and authority has been delegated willingly.

The true essentials of a heist-mob are a wheel-man and a rod-man. The former is a skilled driver, often a specialist who takes no other part (this is preferred practice). Yet if the mob is short-handed or somewhat slipshod in operation he may work the inside with the others. The rod-man's title is self-explanatory. A rod is a gun. Since most holdups involve the close control of a number of people during the course of the actual robbery, most mobs have two or more gun-wielding members. In special cases, a mob may use a man on the outside in addition to the man on the wheel. For example, the getaway route for a job located in the business section of a city may begin with a run down a narrow alley or a one-way street, in which case a tail, a car or truck which cuts in behind the getaway car and blocks the way long enough for the former to get a sufficient jump, may be used. But the great majority of heist-mobs work with a single man on the wheel and either two or three on the inside.

A mob forms rather casually. Eddie, let us say, has a promising mark. He decides that it can "go" three-handed. Thinking over the experienced men of his acquaintance who are out for action he fixes on Big Pete. His choice is based upon several considerations. Pete has a rep as a good man, which means that he is known to be trustworthy, dependable, and resourceful. When he makes a meet, or engagement, he keeps it. He has plenty of belly, or courage. He has shown that he is a sticker who will not panic and leave the others to shift for themselves in the event of trouble, and he has repeatedly stood up, or kept his mouth shut, under police questioning—American police question prisoners; only foreigners torture them. Furthermore, he will not burn, or cheat, his partners; he does not flash, or make a show of his money; and he has an air of calm authority which is valuable on the job: he can control a whole roomful of people without frightening them so that someone may do something foolish.

Eddie and Pete talk the job over—"cut it up," they say. If a tip is involved, Eddie lets Pete know that there will be a tipster's end (10 per cent) to come off the top, or before any deductions have been made, but without telling him who the tipster is, just as he will not tell the latter who will work the job, for by his code anyone who deals with him is entitled to full protection, and he considers them bound by the same standard. Other details are discussed. Yes, between them, the two can handle the inside without trouble. Probably they could handle the whole thing, but to be on the safe side they had better have a man on the wheel.

Since the mark is Eddie's, he is boss in this respect. He "owns" the job; it is therefore his right to select those who are to participate. Anyone who does not wish to work with any of the others may pull out, or withdraw. If one who pulls out should thereupon get his own mob together and take the job, Eddie would feel morally justified in shooting him, though if another mob working independently happened to beat Eddie to the job he would not consider himself wronged. If something happened to prevent him from taking part in the touch and Pete filled in another man and took it, Eddie would be entitled to half an end, or share, even though he was in prison when the job came off.

In this case, there is no trouble in filling the mob. Both Eddie and Pete are friendly with Bangs, so called from his habit of causing his car to backfire during chases to the end of instilling a proper caution in amateur pursuers, who seldom require much encouragement to imagine they are being shot at. One of them looks him up and inquires casually if he wants "a little action on the wheel." Bangs asks questions: what kind of action? what's in it? who is working? If the answers, which are given in general terms, are to his liking, he says, "Okay, I'm in," and the mob is complete. Only then is he given specific details.

The detailed planning and preparation which constitutes the next stage is the most important part of the heist. If this layout is done well, the mark is in the bag. The robbery itself becomes a simple transaction lasting but a few moments—sometimes less than thirty seconds.

Professionals agree that casing is far and away the most important part of laying out a heist. This word, which like many others of underworld origin is coming into popular use, is from the argot of faro, once as popular a betting game as craps is today. It originally referred to a record of the cards played as kept on an abacus-like contraption called a "case." As used in the underworld, the word means gathering information from observation.

Even when the tip includes detailed information, a good mob cases its marks with care. Tipsters often err. One mob, whose tipster worked in the place to be taken, was furnished with a layout-chart so complete that they did not bother casing the inside, to their subsequent sorrow, for the tipster had neglected to indicate that the partitions setting off the office they were to rob did not extend to the ceiling, and police were waiting for them when they came out.

Several matters are cased with particular care. The size of the score is checked in advance whenever possible—tipsters are likely to be very optimistic about the size of a prospective touch. If the mark is a bank, checking may involve little more than a glance at the quarterly statement, available at the local library or Chamber of Commerce, and the size of payrolls may be estimated satisfactorily from the number of employees, but most other kinds of mark are difficult to case accurately for size. A knowledge of the floor plan, arrangement of furniture, placement of doors and windows, and so forth, is essential to a fast, smooth piece of work.

On the theory that it helps to know where trouble is likely to come from, some heist-men like to get an advance look at the people on the inside as well. Impressionable young squirts who attend the movies too often and an occasional old towser who has had his job for thirty years—"heroes," the heist-man calls them sardonically—may, if not closely watched, rise in defense of the insurance company's stockholders, especially if women or big bosses are present. It is always well to know how many women must be dealt with, since they are an occupational hazard of the first order which I will describe later on. Armed guards are of course cased with care, though unless ensconced in a protective cage or turret they represent a threat more apparent than real, since they cannot go about with cocked pistols. A well-executed job takes so little time that alarm systems call for little or no attention, unless the mark is a bank. Bank heists usually take several minutes.

Sometimes ingenuity is required to case a job without attracting attention. Unless there is heavy pedestrian traffic, outside casing is usually done from a car or the window of a nearby building. Various ruses are resorted to in casing the inside, the commonest being the pose of having business to transact. This can be excellent vocational training—at least, it proved to be in the case of Keister (Suitcase) John, an old-timer who came by his moniker in honor of a battered salesman's case full of janitor supplies which he used as a prop, religiously charging off the full original cost of the outfit, some forty dollars, against the nut, or expense, of every job he worked. A time came when jokes about his "ten grand" suitcase circulating in the hangouts came to the ears of police, and John went to stir. There he came to the conclusion that he was becoming too old and too well-known to continue in his wicked ways, so upon release he set up in the building maintenance business, in which he prospered.

Generally speaking, casing is the job of the inside-men. The wheel-man has work of his own. The procurement of the getaway car is one of his responsibilities. There are many car-thieves who will deliver to specifications of year and make for moderate fee, but heist-men seldom patronize them for reasons of security. The simple job of stealing a car may be considerably complicated by the wheel-man's personal predilections. Most of them have strong convictions concerning various makes of car for this particular kind of service. Certain makes, widely known as "dogs on the get-out," which is to say that they accelerate slowly from a standing start, automatically are ruled out. In general, a small, fast car of common make is preferred for work in city traffic, but a heavy one where the get-away entails a long run over country roads. Having procured a suitable car, the wheel-man provides it with license plates which are not hot and plants it, or places it somewhere out of harm's way, until it is needed.

The wheel-man's other major responsibility is the layout of the get, or getaway route, a simple matter if the job is in a city and the mob intends to piece up there but complicated if a run to another locality is in prospect, as is usually the case if the mark is located in a small community. In the latter event, he must cruise back roads and country lanes until he has pieced together a route which by-passes towns, main highways, and, so far as is possible, roads followed by telephone lines. He runs this route until thoroughly familiar with it, and may even chart it in detail:

> L over bridge
> 40 for S-bend mi. 4
> R fork Bull sign mi. 6½
> weaves over 55 gravel. . . .

Such a chart is called a "running get." The back-country getaway—the idea of a specific route, which was once a close professional secret—is said to have been tipped off to the FBI by Brown Derby Bentz, a bank robber until recently in Alcatraz and there for this reason shunned by many of his professional brethren. Whether or not the rap is a right one for Bentz, the principle of the get is now so well known that a movie glorifying the G-men has been based upon it.

There will be other details requiring attention. Perhaps the job is located in a town whose approaches may quickly be blocked off. If so, the mob may want to hide out in town until the heat has somewhat subsided, in which case a suitable plant, or hideout, will be required. There will have to be bags for the money—the paper shopping bags used by housewives are as good as any. And there is the matter of guns.

Mobs composed of men who often work together may have a small armory of weapons belonging to the mob as a whole, but as a general thing each man furnishes his own weapon, usually a pistol. Revolvers are preferred to automatics, for many of the Colt .45's circulating in the underworld came originally from army or other federal sources, and if one is used on a job the G-heat may assume it has been stolen and enter the case on that basis. Moreover, if the magazine clip of an automatic is kept loaded for a protracted time its spring may become "tired" and the gun may jam when used. The sub-machine guns so common in the movies are rarely used in real-life holdups. They are cumbersome, difficult to acquire, and at once bring the crime under federal jurisdiction. Sprayers, which are automatic pistols of a foreign make provided with a detachable stock and custom-made magazines holding fifty or more bullets, are sometimes used on jobs where there are a large number of people to be controlled, but sawed-off shotguns are cheaper, far easier to obtain, less lethal (except at pointblank range), and more effective in terms of shock effect upon the victims.

The job is ready to go when it has been cased and the other details have been attended to. The mob will have met several times to cut up, or talk things over, and to lay the job out, or make a detailed plan of action. The preparations in their entirety will have taken anywhere from a few hours to several weeks, depending upon the mark and the class, or quality, of the mob—the better the mob, the more thorough the layout.

As has been intimated, there is not much to the holdup itself if the layout has been well done. Each man knows just what to do on the job, when to do it, and what to expect of the others. Unforeseeable complications aside, the actual robbery is largely a matter of going through the motions on schedule. The term "schedule" is used advisedly, for the time element is important—so important that the time taken to "get in, get it, and get out" is a good measure of professional competence. It is not unusual for a class mob to carry out a run-of-the-mill holdup in half a minute. . . .

In working a heist, the mob usually goes out from a meet, or appointment held a short time before the job is to go. Here the layout is gone over again, clothes are changed—if the mark is in a factory district the mob may work in coveralls, if in a business district in business suits; the idea is to remain as inconspicuous as possible—and other last-minute details are attended to. The members of the mob leave singly and go to the mark by separate routes in order to avoid the possibility of being seen together by coppers to whom they may be known. Possibly they do not rod up, or arm themselves, until they reach the job, just in case one of them might be stopped and searched. The wheel-man brings the guns in the car.

The mob meet the car a block or so from the mark and rod themselves up. They walk to the job; the wheel-man pulls ahead and parks near the entrance in such a way that he can swing out from the curb in a hurry. If possible, the inside-men work covered, or masked. This usually can be managed without difficulty unless the place must be entered directly from the street, and even then if scarves fastened with pins so that they may quickly be twitched up over the mouth and chin are used—the lower part of the face is the most easily identifiable.

Covered or bald, the mob enters as casually as any other visitors. Melodramatics are for the movies. One man does the talking: "All right, folks, stay where you're at! Keep quiet! Keep your hands where I can see them! Nobody but the insurance company is gonna get hurt, so take it easy." Generally this fellow stands near the door where he can keep the whole room under observation as well as intercept anyone who may come in while the robbery is in progress. He is an authoritative figure, the center of attention. Most witnesses hardly notice the other inside-men, who go about their job of collecting the score as quickly and with as little fuss as possible.

So far as may be, the mob are calm and polite on the job. "Cowboying," or the wild brandishing of pistols and shouting of orders in all directions is frowned upon; fear has made more heroes than courage ever has. People will not be gratuitously abused. The professional does not become so tensed up by fear and excitement that he strikes out blindly upon insignificant provocation. As one puts it: "When you're out on a heist you're out to get the dough and keep out of trouble. Halloween's the night for scaring people." However, courtesy on the job does not include softness or indecision. A holdup may easily become a shambles if the people under the gun think they detect nervousness or hesitation on the part of the man behind it.

The boys are particularly careful if women are present. Nobody can tell how women will react—at least, such is the considered opinion of the heist-men with whom I have cut up this situation. Looks tell nothing. One who has all the earmarks of a lady pipefitter may just roll her eyes and swoon, while the little mouse who looks so scared a man itches to pat her on the head and say something soothing is really cooly examining the mob for warts or moles or counting the hairs on their knuckles as a means of future identification. Guns or no guns, some women will give out large pieces of their minds, and the less of this commodity they have to spare the more generous they appear with it. There are old ladies—one heist mob had a harrowing experience at the hands of a motherly soul who got into the middle of a loan-office heist before she realized what was going on. Then she was horrified and spoke severely to the mob. They should be ashamed, for she could tell that they were good boys at heart who had got off on the wrong foot. Since this was precisely what the boys secretly thought of themselves, they were moved; they ordered one of the clerks to destroy the record of the old lady's loan at once. This intended kindness only shocked her more, and she began to pray for them. The boys sweated copiously and might even have left if the manager, who had the combination to the safe, had not been due at that moment. . . .

Sometimes screamers can be a real hazard on the job, as when the mob must be inside for several minutes, but on the ordinary job they are more bothersome than dangerous and the mob ignores them. In some circumstances, as when there is a safe which must be opened, it may take the mob several minutes to get the score, but usually it is merely a matter of picking it up and carrying it out. The man on the door remains a few seconds to give the others time to get to the car, for despite his warning someone will probably throw up a window and begin yelling as soon as he leaves. As he comes out, the car already is inching ahead.

It is off the instant his foot touches the running board. Unless a policeman is where he cannot avoid responding to the cries coming from the window—policemen on a beat are seldom eager to career along in chase of someone who may shoot back; they are not paid or very well trained for that kind of work and are likely to shoot their revolvers on double action, to the peril of spectators in upstairs windows—or unless some civilian in search of excitement gives chase, reckless driving is not indulged in. The car whisks around the first corner, takes several others in quick succession, then straightens out for a run of two or three blocks down a street having little traffic.

If no chase car shows up behind, the getaway car heads for wherever the front car—one legitimately owned by one of the mob—is parked. Meanwhile, the inside-men may accompany him, or, if they want to play it safe all the way, go into the receptacle provided: where there is no pedestrian traffic outside, the mob may not take time on the job to put the loot into bags but carry it out in a wastepaper basket or any other handy container. One of the mob takes the score and pistols in the front car to the place prearranged for the meet. The other inside-men may accompany him, or, if they want to play it safe all the way, go separately. The wheel-man continues in the getaway car to another part of the city, where, having wiped down the interior to remove fingerprints, he ditches it.

By the time he arrives at the meet, the money probably already has been pieced up into as many piles as there are members of the mob. "There she is," one of the others says. "Latch onto one."

Armed robbery is the blue collar form of outright thievery, whereas the con game is almost an entertainment version, a drama. There is also a more genteel form that goes by the name of embezzlement. In the short excerpt that follows from a classic study of embezzlers, notice the steps by which a man gets trapped into feeling the necessity to "borrow" other people's money.[5]

... At the time of his commitment this man was forty-two and had been the president of his bank. He was sentenced for violating the law in connection with operations calculated to keep his bank open during the depression. ... He became the cashier of a country bank in another state and advanced rapidly [but] he was called back to Wisconsin to manage a bank which needed to be extricated from financial difficulties. He says, howeer, that he did not know how serious the difficulties were. ... He succeeded in putting the bank on a better-paying basis temporarily, but the depression again placed it in jeopardy. To keep the bank open he falsified the statements, hoping that time would dispel its difficulties. Matters went from bad to worse, however, until it was necessary to close the bank. ...

Why did this man who had been brought up in a good home, who had made money and was highly respected, and who had been trained in banking methods, finally engage in legal embezzlement, while his brother, also a bank manager, brought his institution through the same severe crisis successfully? ... Two or three aspects of this man's history may furnish a clue. 1. As the oldest child in the family he had been thrown upon his own resources early and had gradually learned to trust his own judgment. His youngest brother frequently pleaded with him during the difficulties to cut down on his scale of living, resign from an impossible situation, and allow the bank to be closed. *His pride doubtless prevented his accepting this advice, for to do so would have been to admit poor judgment in accepting the presidency of the bank without a more thorough investigation, but also the failure of his efforts to solve its difficulties, and loss of prestige in the community.* ... His previous success had engendered a pride in his ability to handle difficult situations which his resignation would have hurt. Like many a banker, he took chances during the depression and finally lost. He seems to have made no personal profit from any of the illegalities. He had no intention of cheating anyone, but only a strong desire to save the bank and with it not only his own investment but that of his stockholders and depositors.

[5]From *Other People's Money*, 1953, by Donald R. Cressey, pp. 45-47. Reprinted by permission of Donald R. Cressey and the publishers, The Free Press, Glencoe, Illinois. Cressey quotes in this excerpt from John L. Gillin, *The Wisconsin Prisoner* (Madison: The University of Wisconsin Press, 1946), pp. 186-188, by permission of the publisher.

One essential difference between this man and his brother, who is cited as a "control" case, lies in the fact that the latter had no occasion to define his banking problems as non-shareable [with other people who might have helped him].

The history of the brother differs at some points. He was an extrovert, whereas the prisoner was an introvert. His reputation in the community was based on sound business practices and modest social activities which intrenched him in the esteem of the inhabitants; the prisoner moved about and had to rebuild his reputation anew in each town he lived in. *The brother sought help in his banking deals both from his board of directors and from other bankers; the prisoner had learned to play a lone hand and did so in the management of the Wisconsin bank.* The brother had been careful never to be involved in the disputes of the community, with whose social and business life he was intimately familiar. The prisoner had been thrust into a bitter feud between social and business groups of the community and had become the punching bag of both factions. The brother's bank was examined regularly by the State Banking Commission; the prisoner was encouraged to adopt shady methods by a "hands off" policy of the examiners, who hoped he might succeed in pulling the bank through. The brother was governed to some extent in his personal life by the standards of his depositors, and his wife always lived simply, particularly during the depression. The prisoner, on the other hand, though he kept within his income, always lived on a higher scale than his country depositors. He invited criticism by keeping polo ponies, building a pretentious home, and sending his wife to Europe many times.

CONCLUSION

Confronted with the principle that others will give him what he wants only if it is worth their while to do so; confronted with the fact that it is apparently *not* worth their while; and resolved not to accept defeat, the individual has only one avenue left: to *take* what he needs and give *nothing* in return. He can take it by elaborately manipulating the other person's own readiness to get something for nothing (the con game); or he can take it more directly (the heist). And "it" need not be money. The con game may be played with the coin of symbols of affection as well as with dollars. The principle is: When others have what would make your life meaningful, when they will not share it with you, and when you refuse to do without it, you seize it. This is the principle that results in such social problems as rape, theft, fraud, school cheating, adulteration of food, misleading advertising, and the political con game of demogoguery.

Burk Uzzle/Magnum

chapter 12
More subtle making out

The variations on the thievery theme reported in Chapter 11 are obvious ways of coercing people's minds, bodies, or possessions. More subtle ways exist to induce people to give one what one wants against their will—and this more subtle assault on their wills is a type of coercion, too. The person trusted by other people to act in the latters' interests is in a position to exploit them simply by violating his trust. The criminologist who coined the phrase "white-collar crime" describes seven different ways in which businessmen sometimes behave in this fashion.[1]

Executives and directors of a corporation are trustees, in the eyes of the law, and have the duty of managing the affairs of the corporation in the interest of the corporation as a unit. At the same time, these executives have personal interest and other interests, which may conflict with their duties as executives of the corporation. While every person in a position of responsibility confronts this situation, many corporate executives make strenuous efforts to secure positions in which they may have an opportunity to violate the trust for which they are legally responsible.

A total of 64 accusations of violation of trust and misapplication of corporate funds has been made against executives of 41 of the seventy large corporations. These include violations of trust in the interest of a particular executive, of a small group of executives, of a particular group of security holders, of investment banks, and of other corporations with which these executives are

[1]From Edwin H. Sutherland, *White Collar Crime*, New York: Dryden Press, 1949, pp. 153-158. Copyright 1949 by Holt, Rinehart & Winston, Inc. Reprinted by permission of Holt, Rinehart & Winston, Inc.

connected. In some of these cases, the crime is committed against the corporation rather than by the corporation, but it is difficult to differentiate the two types of offenders in most of the cases.

These violations of trust are of several types. One of the most clear-cut, as well as least frequent, violations of trust is ordinary embezzlement of corporate funds by executives of a corporation. The chief executive of one corporation, after he had been displaced, was found to be short in his account with the corporation by more than three million dollars. He was permitted to make a settlement without an official court action.

A second way in which executives of corporations have violated trust is by organizing personal companies to render services to their corporations. In doing this they act both as buyers and sellers of the services and make bargains which are advantageous to their personal companies. Some of these personal companies may be limited to specific services, such as foreign sales or lighterage service, and these probably cause no serious loss to the corporation; other personal companies may be placed in the corporate structure so that they can drain off a large share of the corporate profits. The stockholders of one corporation sued the executives in connection with such a personal company for $50,000,000 which was claimed to have been misapplied.

The third way in which executives violate trust is by using their knowledge to make private purchases of stocks or of commodities and selling these to the corporation at a large profit. The executive of a corporation has inside knowledge that his corporation must purchase more land for the plant, he makes a private purchase of the best available land and sells it at a considerable profit to the corporation.

A fourth way in which executives violate trust is by using their official positions for personal advantage rather than for corporate advantage. A stockholder of a corporation offered to sell a large block of stock to the corporation; several of the directors of the corporation influenced the Board to vote against the purchase of this stock; then they organized a syndicate and purchased this stock privately.

The fifth type of behavior which may involve violations of trust is the appropriation of enormous salaries and bonuses by the executives of a corporation. Accusations have been made on this count against the executives of 25 of the seventy corporations. These huge awards are described in the charges as illegal appropriations by officers who are in a position to manage the corporation in their own interest and as cognate with embezzlement. On the other hand, the defense is made by the executives that the number of persons qualified for executive positions in large corporations is small, that large awards are necessary in order to secure good executives, that these huge payments are incentives to greater efficiency, and that they are therefore economical in the long run. John C. Baker, however, in a statistical analysis found a slight tendency for corporations which paid high salaries to have smaller earnings, and greater fluctuations in earnings than in those which paid low salaries.

Stockholders are seldom able to determine from the corporate reports the salaries paid to their executives. In some of the earlier cases not even the directors knew the salaries of the executives. One of the large corporations recently was fined for making false reports to the Securities and Exchange Commission in the effort to conceal a special fund for executive bonuses. Also, in some cases an executive received a large salary from a parent corporation and additional large salaries from each of several subsidiaries. Many executives of corporations have protested vigorously against publicity regarding salaries and bonuses.

These huge salaries and bonuses are frequently paid in years when the corporations have a net loss as well as in years when they have a net gain. The chief executive of one of the seventy corporations received a salary and bonus of approximately $1,000,000 a year, plus additional payments to cover his income tax, although this corporation had paid no dividends on common stocks for many years. The principal executives of another corporation received bonuses over a twenty-year period, which exceeded the dividends on common stocks for that period.

Many stockholders have sued the executives of corporations for misapplication of corporate funds in the payment of these bonuses to themselves, generally with little success. In one of these cases a judge was convicted of taking a bribe. In other cases it has been revealed that the executives have paid the complainants large sums from corporate funds to drop the suits. In one suit, however, the executives were ordered to reimburse the corporation by approximately $6,500,000 for funds illegally appropriated to themselves as bonuses, with a part of the period of illegal appropriation exempted by the statute of limitations.

The sixth type of violation of trust is the profit of one group of security holders, including the executives of a large corporation, at the expense of other security holders. Several decisions have been made on this point against the seventy corporations. In two cases the courts enjoined corporations from paying dividends on common stocks until the accrued dividends on preferred stocks had been paid. In another case the court enjoined a corporation from issuing new bonds which took precedence over previous mortgages. The stockholders of another corporation voted in favor of a plan of reorganization, on information supplied to them by the executives of the corporation. They discovered later that the reorganization was very favorable to certain securities which were held principally by the executives of the corporation. Charges have been made that unsecured bank creditors are frequently given precedence in reorganization proceedings; A. J. Sabath, chairman of the Congressional Committee on Reorganizations, stated regarding one reorganization that it was marked by "collusion, fraud, and conspiracy." In some cases corporations in financial difficulties were managed for a period of years by agents of investment banks, who controlled the corporation through special management shares. In at least one case of this kind, the agents of the investment bank looted the corporation.

The final method of violation of trust is through the looting of a subsidiary by a parent corporation, when the subsidiary is controlled but not wholly owned by the parent corporation. A simple example of this is the purchase of the assets of the subsidiary by the parent company at a price far below the amount that could have been secured from other purchasers. In this case, the parent company was, in substance, both buyer and seller, but the minority stockholders of the subsidiary secured a decision which forced a higher payment. In another case in which a subsidiary was about to be separated by court action from the parent company, the subsidiary paid to the parent company approximately $50,000,000 for rights which were of no value. A settlement was made in this case, with the approval of the court.

Some of these businessmen were unscrupulous; they would steal whether they were executives or taxi-drivers. Most of them, however, simply believed in self-reliance. They did not feel they were stealing from the stockholders—any more than customers who cheat the Bell Telephone Company worry about the widows and orphans who own shares of American Telegraph and Telephone. In short, many Americans do not consider it *wrong* to put personal interests ahead of loyalty to a corporate employer or of honesty with the tax collector. For the same reason, many Americans vote for candidates who will protect their interests as veterans, farmers, businessmen, or old people rather than for candidates who, they think, will promote the general welfare of the nation. Clearly, this creates difficulties. The American economy, characterized as it is by giant corporations, cannot function efficiently unless employees make the best judgment they can on behalf of their companies. Similarly, the American political system, characterized as it is by swarms of regulatory agencies, cannot function efficiently unless officials and voters place societal goals ahead of personal advantage.

Under special circumstances, the self-reliance principle tends to generate social problems in quite a different way. Consider an individual who has failed to earn enough money to realize his goals in terms of esteem, adequacy, security, or gratification. He interprets the self-reliance principle to mean that he must not let other people know about his failure. For one thing, he cannot let them know how lacking in self-reliance he is. For another, he does not feel he has any right to expect anybody to help him. This is the sort of situation in which the idea occurs to him of "borrowing" other people's money, if it happens to be temporarily accessible to him. By violating his trust—temporarily, he believes—he can still regard himself as self-reliant.

Business executives driven by ambition for the good things of life to exploit others illustrate "success by hook or crook." At the other end of the status system, other exploitative maneuvers may be observed, different in detail but identical in motivation. Seth Levine calls one such set of practices, "the unemployment-insurance game."[2]

It is a few minutes before eight on a bleak winter morning in the New York shoe factory of which I am part-owner and general manager. The place is abnormally quiet, except for the occasional clank of massive steel elevator doors opening and shutting. Men shuffle to the dressing-rooms to change their clothes, exchange perfunctory greetings with fellow workers, and move on to their machines. At eight o'clock when the power switches are thrown, the production line will start up with a roar.

Suddenly a phone rings in the shoe-lasting room. The foreman takes the call from Joe Minati's wife. "He's got a hundred and one fever," she says, "and won't be in today."

Joe is a roughing machine operator who works midway on the production line. His job is to buff the shoes' bottom surfaces, to which soles are then cemented. He alone handles this job on the eight hundred pairs the factory produces daily. Feeding shoes to Joe on the production line are twenty-five lasters and a dozen other workers. They can keep going without him, but by quitting time the racks will pile up from Joe's machine to the lasters' benches. If he is out for more than a day, the lasters will have to be laid off. On the other side of Joe's station, the operators are already hit by the jog jam. Unfinished work may keep them busy for an hour or two. But with nothing funneling through Joe's machine, they will be through at ten o'clock.

A fellow employee cannot be shifted over to Joe's skilled job, for an inexperienced man or one who is out of practice can ruin too many shoes. However, the plant superintendent must somehow keep our highly seasonal product moving to the retail stores on time. So he implores the workers down the line to co-operate and hang around until the union office opens and a replacement can be found.

Shortly after ten o'clock a substitute rougher—Henry Smith—appears bearing a union pass. But he is not ready to start work until two hurdles are crossed—first, the matter of pay. As a piece worker, Joe was getting 2.5 cents a pair which amounts to about $2.50 an hour. Henry wants to be paid on a time basis—a reasonable request, since a new man is bound to be slow until he "works into" the particular machine, product, and factory conditions. But the figure he names—$3 an hour—seems a slight case of extortion. The going rate in the

---

[2]From Seth Levine, "The Unemployment-Insurance Game," *Harper's Magazine*, Vol. 223, No. 1335, August 1961, pp. 49-52. Copyright © 1961 by Harper's Magazine, Inc. Reprinted by permission.

industry is $2.50. Since the superintendent is in a box he agrees to pay $3 and hopes that Henry will not be on the job long.

The second hurdle is more vexatious. Henry is collecting unemployment insurance and wants the factory to pay him "off the record," that is, in cash. If the superintendent insists on putting him on the payroll, he won't work. To Henry it is a simple matter of arithmetic. As a skilled worker, his normal weekly wage is a hundred dollars or more. He is now collecting $50 a week in unemployment insurance. For each day that he works he loses a quarter of his weekly benefits—$12.50. A six-hour stint at our roughing machine will give him a wage of $18, but his net will be only about $14 after deductions for federal and state income taxes, Social Security and disability taxes, and the cost of carfare, lunch, and coffee breaks. Subtracting the $12.50 lost from his unemployment benefit, he figures he will make only $1.50 by working for a day.

What is the plant superintendent to do? If he threatens to report the matter to the unemployment-insurance office, Henry will know this is an empty bluff. Few employers will take the trouble to lodge a complaint which may well involve a hearing and a wasted day away from the factory. Ninety times out of a hundred, the "help-out's" terms are accepted.

To collect unemployment-insurance benefits while working is illegal, a plain case of fraud; but very few workers see it this way. For example, many who are hired as permanent factory employees expect to work the first week or two "off the record." Thus they continue to collect benefits until they decide if they like the job and qualify for it. Similarly, many workers who retire collect both Social Security payments and company or union-management pensions, as well as unemployment-insurance benefits for the full period allowed under law.

When production is low in seasonal industries, workers who are employed for only a few hours a day commonly expect either to be paid off the record or at some future time when full production resumes. Thus they can continue to collect their unemployment benefits during the slack season.

A really shocking loophole was provided in 1958 by a New York state law which was a statutory restatement of earlier administrative practice. This permits workers to collect unemployment benefits while on paid vacation if—for the week preceding or following it—they are "less than substantially fully employed." ("Fully employed" is defined as four days or more of work in a given week.) Thus a worker who is laid off for two days, either before or after his vacation, is eligible for tax-free unemployment benefits for the two-week vacation period, amounting possibly to $100.

News of this windfall ran through our factory like wildfire early in June last year. We were scheduled to close for vacation during the first two weeks in July. Except for a handful of newcomers, nearly all our workers were entitled to two weeks' paid vacation. Yet there was scarcely one who did not spend the month of June devising ways to be laid off for a few days before or after vacation. As they figured it out, there seemed to be no point in working the week before or after vacation for a mere $100, when, if they were laid off, they could get three weeks of unemployment benefits amounting to $135. (At that time the maximum benefit in New York was $45 per week. It has since been raised to $50.) Figuring in the taxes and costs of going to work, they made a profit of $50 with a third week of vacation thrown in.

"Hook or crook" adjustments to the strains of American society impose costs, not only to those who are manipulated, but also to the manipulators. There is often a warping of character. Thus, students who cheat differ from Sutherland's business executives and Levine's workers collecting unemployment insurance benefits only in the context and the detailed methods of their problematic behavior. John Harp and Philip Taietz show some of the social factors that influence cheating in the article that follows.[3]

Without norms of academic integrity, the stability and continuity of the academic system could not be maintained. Educators view any violation of the norms of academic integrity both as an ethical problem and as a negation of one of the objectives of education, i.e., the development of independent critical thinking. Students themselves regard cheating as morally wrong. Yet cheating is a common phenomenon on American college campuses as a number of studies have shown. In 1952 a study conducted in eleven colleges found that nearly two-fifths of the students polled admitted cheating. A recently completed nationwide study reports that 49 per cent of the students cheat. Another study reveals the following incidence of cheating reported by seniors: 26 per cent at Columbia, 30 per cent at Cornell, 52 per cent at Fordham, and 54 per cent at Notre Dame.

Colleges vary in the formal and informal means they use to communicate the norms of academic integrity and the associated sanctions. It is quite possible that the norms may be vague and variously interpreted in regard to specific items of behavior. Furthermore, the norms of academic integrity do not have the same salience for all subgroups in the academic system. For example, studies have shown that the incidence of reported cheating is higher among fraternity members than among independents.

CHEATING AS A FORM OF DEVIANCY

A recent nationwide study reported on student definitions of cheating. Both faculty and students considered "copying on a term paper or other assignment"

---

[3]From John Harp and Philip Taietz, "Deviancy and Opportunity Structure: A Study of Cheating Among College Students." A revision of an article by John Harp and Philip Taietz entitled, "Academic Integrity and Social Structure: A Study of Cheating Among College Students," *Social Problems*, 13, No. 4, Spring 1966. Reprinted by permission.

as a form of cheating. It is evident that both parties regard cheating as a contravention of legitimate rules governing academic integrity. One should point out, however, that the concept legitimacy as used in the sociological literature implies a moral validity. It is worthy of mention therefore that data from two previous studies involving a number of universities show that a majority of students regard cheating as "morally wrong" or believe that "students are morally obliged not to cheat." The latter results leave little chance for disparity between the legal and moral aspects of legitimacy. The legal aspects of legitimacy are therefore given a strong moral reinforcement. . . .

The present analysis will emphasize the more immediate social environment, namely, the social situations that give rise to patterns of behavior representing a contravention of norms governing academic integrity. Are students socialized to a covert norm of cheating as they progress through college and are there certain structures which facilitate this socialization process and provide solutions for students with particular adaptive problems? These are the principal questions which will serve to guide our analysis.

Various measures of cheating were developed for a stratified random sample of male students enrolled in the three largest colleges of an Ivy League university. Two forms of cheating essentially agreed upon by faculty and students as comprising a class of acts which violate norms of academic integrity were selected. They were "cheating on tests and final exams" and "cheating on term papers and reports." Contrary to the results of a recent study, the two measures were not found to be intercorrelated. Nor were similar patterns of relationships found with external variables. A low amount of variation for the cheating on exams variable may partially explain our low correlations. Continuing the search for additional measures of deviancy which cover a greater range of behaviors led us to explore the relationships between cheating, cutting classes, and tardiness in submitting class assignments. They were not related nor was a scale of deviant acts of the order cited obtainable from the present data.[4]

Cheating on term papers was chosen as the indicator for intensive analysis since (1) a much higher incidence was reported than was true for the other

[4]A recent study of scholastic dishonesty in two large southern universities utilized an index comprised of the following six items:

1. Seeking information about a final exam from students who had already taken it.
2. Copying from another student's paper during a quiz.
3. Collusion in a take-home assignment.
4. Lying about an absence.
5. Bringing written information into an examination and using it.
6. Purchasing a final exam from a bootlegger.

It was further reported that the items scaled and acceptable coefficients of reproducibility and scalability were obtained. See Charles M. Bonjean and Reece McGee, "Scholastic Dishonesty Among Undergraduates in Differing Systems of Social Control," *Sociology of Education*, 38 (Winter, 1965), p. 130.

variables—50 per cent of all students reported cheating on term papers—and (2) it represents a type of behavior which requires some semblance of organization.

STRUCTURAL SOURCES OF DEVIANCY

Beginning with the largest organizational unit within the university, namely the various colleges, one observes that they may reflect differences in curriculum such as emphasizing vocational objectives, as well as differences in individual characteristics resulting from variations in admissions procedures. Both of these influences are operative for the three colleges included in the sample. They consist of Arts and Sciences, Agriculture and Engineering respectively. The latter two are considerably more vocational than Arts and Sciences, and differ significantly with respect to their students' verbal SAT scores.

Following the freshman year a significant difference in the incidence of cheating on term papers is found for the three colleges. Forty-two and fifty per cent of the students in Agriculture and Engineering reported cheating compared with twenty-six per cent for Arts and Sciences. For all colleges the incidence of cheating is highest during the junior and senior years. Past studies have also reported a larger amount of cheating for students in the more vocationally oriented colleges than for those whose curricula do not share this emphasis. . . .

[A] higher incidence of cheating is reported by fraternity members in all three colleges when compared with non-fraternity members. There is however a significant difference between colleges in the incidence of cheating by fraternity members with the highest incidence reported by the more vocational colleges. Both college affiliation and fraternity membership appear to be exercising an influence on student conduct.

OPPORTUNITY STRUCTURES AND DEVIANCY

A more adequate explanation for the higher incidence of cheating on term papers for fraternity members would view the organizations as opportunity structures both in the sense of providing the physical facilities necessary for the behavior and the requisite normative support. Parsons notes this duality of opportunity by referring to "a concrete resource aspect on the one hand, a normatively controlled 'mechanism' or standard aspect on the other."[5] The availability of illegitimate means is controlled, as Cloward points out, by various criteria and in the same manner as conventional means.[6] One must be concerned with both differentials in access and differentials in fulfillment. Cloward comments on this as follows:

[5]Talcott Parsons, "Some Considerations on the Theory of Social Change," *Rural Sociology*, 26 (September, 1961), p. 230.
[6]Richard A. Cloward, "Illegitimate Means, Anomie, and Deviant Behavior," *American Sociological Review*, 24 (April, 1959), p. 173.

Some occupations afford abundant opportunities to engage in illegitimate activity; others offer virtually none. The businessman, for example, not only has at his disposal the means to do so, but, as some studies have shown, is under persistent pressure to employ illegitimate means, if only to maintain a competitive advantage in the market place.

The competitive nature of higher education in the United States may offer a parallel to the business world in this respect.

Although the presence of an opportunity may serve as a necessary antecedent for the adaptive behavior described as cheating on term papers, it is not sufficient to explain why all members of these social groups do not cheat. Having identified certain environmental influences we must also explain why they are not completely successful and to do so requires that we juxtapose the parts played by individual and group influences on deviant behavior. Proceeding in this way should also enable us to more closely identify the functions performed by the opportunity structure in question. Access to legitimate means was described by Robert R. Merton as a function of one's position in the social structure. It is our contention that a more relevant source of variation with respect to accessibility of legitimate means rests with the individual's ability or capacity to comply with them. The question arises therefore: Is there any evidence to indicate that structures of this kind facilitate the adaptive response of cheating for students who lack the ability to follow the more legitimate course?

First we observe that the adequacy of role capacity or ability as measured by verbal SAT scores and cumulative averages is negatively associated with the adaptive response indexed by cheating on term papers. However, ... in the College of Engineering, students whose ability and performance are relatively low and who belong to fraternities comprise a significantly higher proportion of deviants than those members who placed higher on ability and performance. Stated another way, our evidence suggests the fraternity system viewed as an opportunity structure may provide illegitimate adaptive solutions for students who score low on ability and performance.

The anything-for-success ethic to which some business executives, some workers, and some students are driven is found elsewhere, too. One of the disturbing places in which it is found is politics. What is disturbing is not so much that some politicians are crooked (if some business executives, why not some politicians?) as that the ethic is pervasive among *voters*. And, as an anonymous legislator reveals in the following article, the ends for which voters will manipulate candidates are often picayune.[7]

---

[7]From A Kentucky Legislator, "How an Election was Bought and Sold," *Harper's Magazine*, Vol. 221, No. 1325, October 1960. Copyright © 1960, by Minneapolis Star and Tribune Co., Inc. Reprinted by permission.

Last year I was elected to the Kentucky legislature after paying off many of the citizens of my district with the money and whiskey they demanded in return for their votes. Many of the men who sit with me as legislators were elected in the same way.

This is nothing new in Kentucky but I think it is time that some politician, somewhere, tell the straight—and embarrassing—story of how a candidate may be compelled to pay for votes in this country if he is to be elected. It may be that the political customs of my Kentucky county are very much more decadent and corrupt than those of the nation at large, but after talking frankly with other politicians, I strongly doubt it. I believe that the appalling practices I am about to describe could be uncovered—with local modifications and many refinements, to be sure—in all of the states and in most of their precincts.[8]

The district which elected me—and in which I have spent most of my life—lies in the Kentucky coal fields. Some of the country's largest coal producers conduct large-scale mining operations here. In addition, a number of small "truck mines" have plants within the district. Practically the entire population depends in some way on the coal industry.

The area was originally settled at the beginning of the nineteenth century by frontiersmen from North Carolina and Virginia. Most of them were of Scotch, Irish, English, and German extraction. Their descendants lived as hunters and farmers until the coming of large-scale mining developments just before the first world war. Then the coal corporations imported large numbers of immigrants from south and southeastern Europe and a small horde of Alabama and Mississippi Negroes. Other workers flocked into the region from different parts of the United States. In the ten years between 1910 and 1920 the population increased immensely.

The coal companies built "camps" or company-owned towns to house this large new labor force. Company ownership ended, in most instances, about a decade ago and the towns are now "free." The county contains a number of towns, and the rural areas between them are dotted with houses and farms. Its precincts have long been a battleground between the local Democratic and Republican party organizations with the Democrats enjoying a decisive edge for the last several years.

A desire to "do something about" the state's dismal public roads and schools led me into the race for the state legislature in 1959 as a Democrat. The extent to which bribery of the voters can figure importantly in an election became clear to me only during the five hectic days before November 3.

---

[8]But there is considerable evidence that they happen most in areas—whether Republican or Democratic—of low income and education, such as city slums and depressed rural communities. *The Editors [of Harper's Magazine]*

HELP FROM THE CLANS

In my state, as in most Southern states, a long list of state officials run for office simultaneously with the governor and lieutenant-governor, and so do all the one hundred state representatives and half the state senators. Each of these many candidates usually has an assortment of relatives, friends, and followers who hope to get a political job or other benefit from his election. Campaigns are usually long and bitterly contested. The candidates become more and more desperate and inventive. The only question asked about an election maneuver is, "Will it work?"; few people wonder, "Is it right?"

On Thursday morning—the fifth day before the election—I passed the courthouse and saw intense little clusters of people waving their arms and shaking their heads. Spokesmen for individual candidates, or for their "straight tickets," were appealing for votes and loudly denouncing the opposition.

Soon after I arrived at my campaign headquarters the telephone rang and the voice of a woman in a nearby precinct assured me she would like to work for me "on election day." She pointed out that there were five voters in her household that she could "handle," besides the fact that she had many friends whom she could influence. She thought she should have $10 for her work plus $10 for gasoline with which to "haul them to the polls." She named several successful candidates whom she had helped in previous elections and who, she averred, had only praise for her. She needed a little money right now because her husband was out of work.

The fiction of buying votes by pretending to hire precinct workers has now become routine. The candidate or his political supporters either shell out the sum required or risk losing the household in question to the enemy. In a single precinct a candidate will sometimes find himself with a half-dozen "hired workers"—generally women or disabled and unemployed men. This blackmail is sometimes brought by the same person against several candidates so that money is extorted from two or three on the same slate. The "work" consists of "lining up" members of the family and other relatives, and handing out a few cards near the polling places or in the precinct.

And now such calls, some similar, some with variations, came thick and fast and from all parts of the district. One woman said she preferred to be for me but that my opponent had just left her home. He had offered her $10 to work for him and she was going to accept it unless I brought her the same sum that very day. Another had been promised $20 to work for the straight Democratic ticket but her two daughters had got "out of line" and were threatening to vote against me and my running mate for the other legislative chamber unless they received $10 each to work for us. Still a third had received a $20 bill and some political cards from my opponent and she had agreed to work for him. However, if I would give her the same sum she would "throw his cards away" and work for me because after all, though she was a registered Republican, she was a Democrat at heart.

At last came a short respite from these demands for cash but my ordeal had just begun. From then until the polls were closed, I was subjected to unremitting pleas for money and barely disguised threats of retaliation in the voting booths unless it were promptly forthcoming.

As I turned from the telephone three smiling ladies from a local PTA entered the room. They were the finance committee of their chapter and were engaged in a fund-raising drive. The money was to be spent for library books and other needed equipment and they were sure each of the candidates would be delighted to donate to such a good cause. Then, too, the names of all contributors would be read to the assembled members that night while special pains would be taken to mention those who had "refused to help the school." These busybodies had no sooner departed in triumph with my check when the bland face of a Protestant lay preacher appeared at my door. He declared his whole-hearted support for me and piously declared I was the "best man for the office." He had talked to his flock, of whom there were more than seventy adult members, and they were "just about all" for me. Then he came to the point. His church had undertaken to enlarge its building and, with God's help, he was soliciting funds for that purpose. He and his entire congregation (and the Almighty, too) would be extremely grateful for any assistance I could render them in this righteous cause. While my nerveless fingers signed the check he predicted a fine majority for me in his precinct.

Next came a man whose house had burned some three weeks before, destroying all his household effects. He was destitute and was "doing all he could" for me. If I could help him with a little donation he and all his close relatives would be at the polls "at the break of day" to vote for me and the straight ticket.

Meanwhile my wife had arrived and was receiving callers. In Kentucky citizens can vote at eighteen and a high-school girl had come to demand a bit of election cash. She had become interested in politics in her civics class and was "just dying" to work for me, and for the small sum of ten bucks! When my wife sweetly explained that I had already spent all my money, she inquired where my opponent might be found and left.

THE PRICE OF FIDELITY

At last I managed to escape the gougers to attend a finance committee meeting scheduled for that afternoon. Present were the Democratic managers of the county campaign, some of the candidates, several local Democratic office-holders, and a number of influential and seasoned politicians. The purpose of the meeting was to determine how best to parcel out the "war chest" to the several precincts.

A considerable sum had been cleared at a fund-raising dinner at which a prominent and distinguished party member had appeared as the principal speaker. The greater part, however, had been contributed by those whose personal interests were at stake in the election: the candidates and their supporters; job seekers; politicians looking ahead to future local elections; coal operators anxious to obtain fuel orders for state buildings and institutions; and contractors and others who did business with the state and had found it beneficial to be on "the inside of the track."

The money collected had been sorted and stacked on a table in the center of the room. A considerable portion was in $10 and $20 bills which had been made ready for the "workers," "haulers," and "leaders." Most of it, though, was in crisp new $1 bills, and the total heaped together amounted to nearly a good round English peck.

The treasurer, who had been responsible for the safekeeping of the money, read a list of contributors and of itemized disbursements he had made for telephone calls, printing, and rent for the county campaign headquarters. The balance was carefully counted and was the "net available for the organization." A sigh swept round the room when it became clear that the money available was wholly inadequate for the demands sure to be made upon it.

An old politician cleared his throat and started the discussion:

"Now, men, let's start with the colored. We all know what it takes to get the nigger vote and if we don't fork it over the Republicans will get every damn one of them. They've got at least ten leaders who have to have a $20 bill apiece, and each voter has to have two dollars. Then they ought to have about three gallons of liquor for the ones that want a drink. If we come across like I say, and handle everything just right we'll get 'em all and that's at least two hundred straight-ticket votes. I say $650 for the niggers to start off with."

The wisdom of this pronouncement was recognized and after discussion two gentlemen were agreed upon as the ones to take the "sweetening" to the Negro communities for distribution on the eve of the election. The infidelity of the "nigger voters" was duly discussed and certain safeguards were agreed upon to make sure they would vote as they had been paid to do. For instance, it was believed that in some precincts an election officer could arrange to vote for them under a pretense of showing the voters how to work the machines.

Someone recalled that in the days before voting machines the best solution to this problem was the "chain ballot"—a scheme by which the voter dropped a folded blank piece of paper into the ballot box in lieu of the ballot, concealed the unmarked ballot, and brought it to the precinct captain waiting outside the polls. The voter was paid for the blank ballot and the precinct captain would mark it as desired and deliver it to a second voter. The latter would enter the polling place, receive his own ballot from the officials, enter the booth, hide the unmarked ballot on his person, and emerge to deposit the marked ballot in the box before the eyes of the election officers. This process could be repeated all day long.

However, though the chain ballot was no longer possible, if the precinct election officials would co-operate the situation could still be handled and one's money's worth received.

This discussion largely took care of two precincts and consideration was then given to a third. Two "good men" were agreed upon "to haul out the voters" and sums were allocated to pay them and a number of workers. Then a tricky problem was presented. The precinct chairman reported "Old Lady Blank is bad out of line. She's got forty-seven votes in her family—children, grandchildren, and their wives and husbands—that she can absolutely handle. I promised her fifty to work for our side and she laughed at me. She said that unless she gets $150 she's goin' to vote every one of 'em under the Log Cabin!"

These tidings plunged the group into gloom. The extra $100 would strain the funds but all agreed that Old Lady Blank was "mean as hell" and would carry her threat into execution unless her demands were promptly met. A bundle of 150 crisp new dollar bills was sadly set aside for her benefit.

In another precinct the head of a large clan had to be mollified. The vote might be close in his precinct and if he tried hard he could probably bring in a total of seventeen votes. So it was decided that one of the chairman should visit him on the following day and assure him that if and when a Democratic administration got into office, one of his sons would be slipped onto the public assistance rolls "as soon as possible." This son was reported to be "pretty sick and not able to work." In addition, he was to be handed a $20 bill "to get out his vote with." This sum appeared ample in view of the fact that he and all his following lived within easy walking distance of the polling place.

By this means the county was gone over precinct by precinct. The money allotted each was placed in a suitably marked envelope and dispatched by a trusted courier to the designated precinct chairman or other workers. When the last precinct had been dealt with, the stacks of cash had vanished and it was discovered that $600 were still needed. To fill this gap one of the gentlemen took it upon himself to visit a quarry operator and assure him the local bigwigs would help him to get some profitable road-gravel contracts "after the first of the year if he would chip in and help out."

The next three days were spent in frantic campaigning. I made last-minute appearances before teachers' groups to pledge support for their projected legislative program. I was compelled to scurry about from one local union hall to another to squelch a rumor planted by my opponent among members of the United Mine Workers that I was anti-union and had expressed sentiments not wholly critical of the Taft-Hartley Act. I also found time to donate to a couple of charities I had never heard of, and to buy raffle tickets of doubtful legality from a half-dozen or more patriotic and fraternal organizations. Time also had to be found to visit the general managers of the coal companies and to state that I was sane, sound, sensible, and conservative and to implore them to "line up their office workers" for me. And through it all I was beset—singly and in murderous packs—by bushwhackers who demanded money: (a) to compensate them for past labors in my behalf and for the electioneering they proposed to do on election day, (b) to hire persons to carry voters to the polls (apparently few people any longer walk there or drive their own cars), or (c) to appease those who were offended because they did not receive a share of the "campaign pot."

Of course, the Grand Old Party was far from quiet during this critical interval. A few days before the election one of their party leaders spoke to a crowd in the county circuit courtroom. His listeners showed small interest in his speech until he got down to business and declared that the National Committee was going to be able to send some money down to Kentucky "to help put over the ticket." At this splendid passage the crowd cheered up and applauded fervently.

About 7:00 P.M. on election eve a messenger came flying all wild with haste and fear to inform me that "the Republicans have got in amongst the niggers with money and liquor and are trying to tear things all to hell!" He and I sped to the trouble spot and found a large group of Negroes assembled in the local grade-school building listening while a Republican orator talked to them about Abraham Lincoln, Chief Justice Warren, and the "great school-integration decision of the Supreme Court." Many of his listeners had been comforted with 100-proof cordials. However, we were consoled when, a few minutes later, one of the Negro leaders spied our parked car and came out to talk to us. He assured us the Negroes were only being courteous to the Republican "white folks" and intended only to get a little whisky and money from them and then vote the Democratic ticket. "That Abraham Lincoln stuff is all right," he said, "but we ain't forgot about Franklin D. either." He also took advantage of the occasion to request an extra $20 with which to keep some waverers in line.

No one knows how widespread is corruption of the political process. Nor, for that matter, does anyone know how widespread are the manipulative activities of business executives, "unemployed" persons, or students. In another area of life—the major American industry of gambling—the tendency to cheat other people is more clearly the rule rather than the exception, perhaps because it is essentially an attempt to get something for nothing.[9]

[9]From Mario Puzo, "Why Sally Rags is a Winning Gambler," *New York Times Magazine*, February 25, 1968, pp. 28 ff. © 1967/65/68/58 by the New York Times Company. Reprinted by permission.

In the lexicon of the gambler, a middle is a sure thing. In that long-ago summer baseball season, our middle had its start when a New York newspaper listed Washington as the 7-8 favorite in an out-of-town game. This meant that those betting with bookies would have to put up $8 to make $5 if they bet the favorite Washington, or $5 to make $7 if they bet the underdog. (This is the system that assures the bookie of *his* middle, or "percentage": if the favorite wins, he loses $5 and makes $5, breaking even; if the underdog wins, he loses $7 and makes $8.) But as it happened, the New York newspaper had goofed; the real betting odds, set by the nationwide Syndicate, had Washington as the 7-8 underdog.

Most bookmakers, of course, couldn't have cared less what the newspaper said. But in that same summer, a very prosperous and very tough butcher, dreaming his own dreams of glory, had turned bookie and was servicing a small town in New Jersey. The butcher-bookmaker had no protection or underworld contacts and no access to the official "line." Also, he must have been pretty dumb. He was using this faulty "line" in the newspaper; and by going along with Washington as the favorite, he was giving bettors a chance to grab a middle. And it was in the nature of things for Ragusin to nose out this butcher-bookmaker—it was his destiny.

So we traveled out to New Jersey; and there, where Washington was the favorite, we bet on the underdog team and against Washington, putting up $5 to make $7. Then we hurried back to New York to Ragusin's bookmaker, who had Washington as the underdog, and put our money on Washington, again laying $5 to make $7.

No matter which team won, we won. If Washington won, we would lose our $5 in New Jersey but win $7 in New York; if New York won, the figures would be reversed. Thus, we had to gain $2 on the exchange. Of course, we bet more than fives and sevens.

This was the perfect middle, and I must admit I never enjoyed gambling more. During that week, Ragusin caught several newspaper mistakes, and we practically commuted to New Jersey. By the end of the week, of course, the bookmaker was back in his butcher shop, and we were out of business, but we had made a huge sum for $60-a-week clerks. It was typical of Ragusin's generosity when things went well with him that he picked up all the travel and eating tabs during the operation. . . .

[The author of the article reports also on how another gambler, Sally Rags, had achieved a "middle" on bets at the race track.]

I asked him about the unshaven man at the trotters. Sally laughed when I said I'd seen him buying all those $50 tickets. He said he didn't mind my seeing him because harness racing is so notoriously crooked that it didn't matter. The authorities had had to do away with the twin doubles because the fixing of four races in a single night by greedy gamblers had created an indiscreet and dangerous situation.

He admitted that the unshaven man had given him information about a fixed race. "I had to give the guy half the profits, and I had to promise not to bet more than $500. The horse paid 4 to 1, so I cashed $2,000 worth of tickets, but I only made a clear profit of $750." He insisted, however, that such tips did not always work out; there were sometimes accidents, mishaps, even a deliberate misleading to mask a big and more private coup.

"What happens when he gives you a loser?" I wanted to know.

Sally Rags shrugged. "He never does that unless he's given you a couple or three winners before, so you're always ahead. And what I lose comes out of his cut on the next horse he gives me."

I asked what would happen if the unshaven man gave him two losers in a row. Sally said, "He can't give me two loser in a row."

"He never gives anybody two losers in a row?" I asked.

Sally Rags shrugged. "I don't know what he does with other people. He knows he can't give me two losers in a row."

"Is that the way it is?" I asked. I was really surprised.

He laughed. It was a genuinely nice laugh at my innocence. "That's the way it is," he said.

I was surprised because I knew him as a man not physically strong, not mentally vicious, not cruel. I knew him as an extremely agreeable companion who loved sporting events and worshipped some of the great athletes. He rooted as enthusiastically as any college boy. And I had reason to know he was generous.

There is a hint in Sally Rags' confidence that a tipster would "never" give him two losers in a row of some *not*-so-subtle transaction modes that also lurk in the background of another form of manipulation: the loan-shark business. Ruthless advantage is taken of people who feel themselves to be desperately in need of money.[10]

. . . .There are, all investigators agree, four operating levels. On the top level is the family boss. Just under him are his trusted principal lieutenants. The lieutenants have their own subordinates to whom they funnel money for investment, and these third-echelon underlings, besides lending out much of it themselves, split up the rest of the money and pass it down to the fourth and lowest level, the working bookie and street-corner hoodlum. Sergeant Salerno gave a graphic description of the way it all works. He said:

"A big racket boss could have a Christmas party in his home, to which he

[10]From Fred J. Cook, "Just Call 'the Doctor' for a Loan," *New York Times Magazine*, January 28, 1968, pp. 55-57, 65-67. © 1967/65/68/58 by the New York Times Company. Reprinted by permission of Barthold Fles, Literary Agent.

invites 10 trusted lieutenants. He doesn't have to write their names down. He knows their names. They are friends of his. . . . He can take one million dollars, which is not an inconceivable amount of cash, and distribute that, $100,000 per man to these 10 men. All he has to tell them is, 'I want 1 per cent a week. I don't care what *you* get for it. But *I* want 1 per cent a week.'

"He does not have to record their names. He does not have to record the amount. They are easy enough to remember. And if you stop to think that, 365 days later, at the next year's Christmas party, the only problem this gang leader has is where he is going to find five more men to hand out half a million dollars that he earned in the last year on the same terms. . . . "

This usurious interest (the gang chieftain's 1 per cent a week becomes 52 per cent a year) is known in the trade as vigorish—or "the vig." (There is a theory that the term derives from the word "vicarage" and refers to the contributions given the vicar by his parishioners.) Naturally, the rate goes up as the money is filtered through the various echelons, and each takes its cut. On the second level, where the principal lieutenants dwell, the vigorish may amount to 1.5 or 2 per cent a week, and on the lowest operating level, where most ordinary loans are made, it will be 5 per cent a week—260 per cent a year. And the underworld, ruthless and insatiable, has a whole arsenal of neat devices by which even this horrendous figure can be hiked.

The Doctor is one of those top-level lieutenants who would be invited to the big chief's Christmas party. Only in his case, he would probably not be given a piddling $100,000 to put to work, but something more like a million. "He is a big, big money mover," says one detective. "They trust him. He has hundreds of thousands of dollars working at any one time."

Rarely, if ever, does the Doctor participate in the direct lending of his hoard of cash. He works through his subalterns, parceling out his share of the underworld treasury among as many as 30 underlings on the third echelon of the pyramid; they make the actual loans and collections and, in turn, put some of the money to work through street-corner bookies and hoods. Under such circumstances, life for the Doctor becomes one unvarying round of seemingly innocent social contacts.

Since he is a late-night man-about-town, the Doctor hardly ever rises much before noon. He may then have a late brunch with his bride, daughter of a Mafia chieftain, and then he will get into his Cadillac and begin his rounds. His first stop is almost invariably at the home of his former, divorced wife with whom he apparently maintains amicable relations. Detectives theorize that the former wife's home is probably a contact point at which he picks up messages or cash that may have been left for him. After a short stay here, the Doctor drives on to a small business office that he maintains as an ostensibly legitimate front. Detectives have been unable to discern any real business being conducted here, and they deduce that the office serves as another contact point.

After the office stop, the Doctor's routine may vary slightly, depending upon the day of the week. Monday is especially busy in the loan-shark racket. It is the day when new loans are being laid out, when collections are made, when the misdeeds of defaulters must be weighed and penalties assessed. The Doctor regularly visits his favorite Italian social club, where he sits around chatting with old cronies; but it is noticeable that, on this one day of the week, his stay is always more protracted and his talk longer and more earnest.

After the business at the club has been transacted, it's off to the plushier bistros of Manhattan, where the Doctor circulates, much like the lord of the manor, with maître d's bowing and scraping and bartenders bobbing their heads in welcome and subservience. They all know they had better. Many are so deeply in hock to the Doctor themselves that they will probably never again be able to call themselves free men, and in some instances the pit has been dug so deep that the Doctor is in fact the secret owner of the business. A favorite rendezvous in the past, a plush restaurant just off Park Avenue in the midtown section, was forced to close eventually because his silent partnership became too loud and the State Liquor Authority revoked the liquor license.

"You can watch all this activity, and it's most frustrating," says a detective who has camped on the Doctor's trail. "He goes into a place, has a drink, chats with the bartender who is a 'steerer' of his [sending along loan customers]. Perhaps he picks up a message or some cash that has been left. How can you tell? It's all very casual, very hard to detect. Perhaps he wanders off to the men's room, and, just by chance, one of his lieutenants follows, and a word is dropped or money changes hands. There is little you can do about it."

Inevitably, with a business as intricate as the Doctor's it becomes necessary, as it is not in a more streamlined operation, to keep some detailed records. It is fairly simple for the family boss who has parceled out $1-million in chunks of $100,000 to each of 10 principal lieutenants to keep his accounts in his head; but when you split up hundreds of thousands of dollars into hundreds of chunks, the transactions become too complicated. Even an agile brain cannot retain the details without the help of a written record. Authorities have been successful in obtaining one such account sheet of the Doctor's. It contains a long column of figures that look as if they were taken from a bank's daily ledger. Scanning the column at random, one notices amounts ranging from $13,000 to $43,000, each representing a loan. Some of the loans are identified only by nickname or initial; others have names spelled out beside them—including names of subsidiary Mafia figures to whom the Doctor apparently had funneled some of his money.

"We're sure this sheet represents loan-sharking business," the prosecutor who has it says, "but when we questioned the Doctor about it, his alibi was that this was just an ancient record, representing transactions from years and years ago when he was in the bookmaking business."

Even when authorities get an undubitably current record, it is extremely difficult to make much sense, still less a legal case, out of the mysterious chicken scratches. One investigative unit recently came into possession of a red-covered, loose-leaf pocket notebook containing the record of transactions of a bookie-shark on the lowest level of the Doctor's ring. The flyleaf carries an unexplained notation: $15,000.

"This apparently was the money entrusted to him to lend out," a detective says.

The $15,000 item is followed by these other unexplained entries: $7,300, $3,900, $700. Out at the side of the page, the last sum is broken down into three other amounts: $250, $350, $100—apparently representing three smaller loans that made up the $700.

Who got the money? There is no way of telling.

"The guy who had this book carried it in his head," the detective says. "He knows who got the $7,300, who got the $3,900; he doesn't have to put down names."

Some of the inside pages of the notebook do contain more information. In transactions involving week-by-week payments over periods of several months, the shark had to keep a careful record. But even here the entries tell little. There are designations like "Brother," "Billy," "Fred." Just who they are is anybody's guess. One of these accountings shows that $500 was lent to be paid back at a rate of $50 a week for 12 weeks—a mere $600 for $500. Regular payments were made, except for one week. However, the borrower paid $100 the next week, was never delinquent again and the account was marked closed at the end of the 12 weeks.

Not all borrowers were so lucky. One account in this book deals with a loan that started out at $11,600. The borrower—whose name appeared beside the figures—made regular payments at the start, but then the burden obviously became too heavy. His payments lapsed for weeks. Penalties were assessed. These and the accumulations of vigorish boosted the indebtedness, despite what had been paid, to $16,898. There the account ends—permanently. The man who borrowed but could not pay was found murdered in a city alleyway, and investigators trying to solve the case are operating on the theory that he paid with his life for having had the bad judgment to cost the syndicate money.

Such gory episodes point up a fact of life: the borrower is always at the mercy of the shark, and the shark, backed by all the awesome, terroristic power of the Mafia, is utterly ruthless. Coupled with his ruthlessness is a devilish cunning that is always devising new ways of getting people in his power—and then driving them right through a wall.

Take the case of the prosperous bar owner who tried to do his daily good deed, found himself caught in the middle and was almost devoured by a shark. The bar owner had a good, free-spending customer whom he had known for quite some time. One day the customer confided that he was in a financial bind and needed to borrow some fancy cash. So the bar owner, trying to do a favor for a patron, passed him on to his favorite loan shark. The customer and the shark made their deal, and for a time everybody was happy. But then the customer, evidently unable to pay, skipped the city—and the sharp ivories of the loan shark closed on the bar owner who was informed *he* was responsible for and had to make good the loan.

"If you introduce someone to a loan shark," says one investigator, "you make yourself responsible for the payments. If the friend you've recommended takes off for Florida or Samoa, leaving the debt unpaid, they come to *you* to collect. It is just like co-signing a note in legitimate business. This is one way many bartenders and bar owners find themselves suddenly in deep, deep trouble."

The trouble gets just as deep as the loan shark in his generosity chooses to make it, for the shark makes up the rules of the game as he goes along, and the other player, the borrower, hasn't a thing in the world to say about it. If a borrower defaults for a couple of weeks or a month, the shark can assess any penalty that comes into his usurious mind—and the borrower has to pay or flee the country or risk being dumped in some dank gutter.

Frank Rogers, in his testimony before the Commission of Investigation, cited a case that began with a $6,000 loan to a businessman. The borrower made three payments, then missed two. For this heinous offense, the loan shark decided that the $6,000 would now be converted into $12,000, with the accompanying double vigorish. When the hapless borrower could not begin to pay this suddenly doubled load, the shark upped the principal to $17,000, then $25,000. "Just by simple mandate from the loan shark," Rogers testified, "you are in an irreversible situation. He says, 'This is the loan,' and that is it."

Once a victim has been driven completely through the wall by such devices, the shark sometimes grins his suddenly friendly smile and says, "O.K., I'm now your partner. I own half your business."

This doesn't mean he's really forgiving anything, he's simply stopped piling it on. But he still expects his vigorish on the old loan—and half his new "partner's" profits besides. The situation then rapidly deteriorates to the point of utter hopelessness, which is what the shark wants. Then he may say magnanimously, "Look, we will swap even. We will forget the loan, you forget the business. It is now all mine." The entire process, Rogers said, sometimes takes less than six months.

Although the loan shark's tactics are not subtle, his "cover" (lending money to persons in need) is a more subtle way of making out than forthright thievery. Even thievery is often defined as a necessary "hustle."[11]

---

[11]See, e.g., Malcolm X, with Alex Haley, *The Autobiography of Malcolm X*, New York: Grove Press, 1964, pp. 84-91.

Or, as Al Capone put it, "Everybody has his racket, but there are legit rackets and illegit rackets." Under certain conditions of need or desire, when prescribed means do not work, people are tempted to make out by hook or crook. Our last selection for this chapter makes clear the processes of such temptation. Bensman's and Gerver's account of criminal behavior in an airplane factory has the advantage of showing how an entire social system (in this case the factory) may have the social problem behavior woven into the texture of its operating principles.[12]

The tap is a tool, an extremely hard steel screw, whose threads are slotted to allow for the disposal of the waste metal which it cuts away. It is sufficiently hard so that when it is inserted into a nut it can cut new threads over the original threads of the nut.

In wing assembly work bolts or screws must be inserted in recessed nuts which are anchored to the wing in earlier processes of assembly. The bolt or screw must pass through a wing plate before reaching the nut. In the nature of the mass production process alignments between nuts and plate-openings become distorted. Original allowable tolerances become magnified in later stages of assembly as the number of alignments which must be coordinated with each other increase with the increasing complexity of the assemblage. When the nut is not aligned with the hole, the tap can be used to cut, at a new angle, new threads in the nut for the purpose of bringing the nut and bolt into a new but not true alignment. If the tap is not used and the bolt is forced, the wing plate itself may be bent. Such new alignments, however, deviate from the specifications of the blueprint which is based upon true alignments at every stage of the assembly process. On the basis of engineering standards true alignments are necessary at every stage in order to achieve maximum strength and a proper equilibrium of strains and stresses.

The use of the tap is the most serious crime of workmanship conceivable in the plant. A worker can be summarily fired for merely possessing a tap. Nevertheless, at least one-half of the work force in a position to use a tap owns at least one. Every well-equipped senior mechanic owns four or five of different sizes and every mechanic has access to and, if need be, uses them. In fact, the mass use of the tap represents a widespread violation of this most serious rule of workmanship.

The tap is defined as a criminal instrument, primarily because it destroys the effectiveness of stop nuts. Aviation nuts are specifically designed, so that, once

[12]From Joseph Bensman and Israel Gerver, "Crime and Punishment in The Factory," *American Sociological Review*, Vol. 28, August 1963, pp. 590-595. Copyright © by the American Sociological Association. Reprinted by permission.

tightened, a screw or bolt cannot back out of the nut under the impact of vibration in flight. Once a nut is tapped, however, it loses its holding power and at any time, after sufficient vibration, the screw or bolt can fall out and weaken the part it holds to the wing and the wing itself.

In addition, the use of a tap is an illegal method of concealing a structural defect. If the holes, for example, were properly drilled and the nuts were properly installed, the use of the tap would be unnecessary, since specifications calling for alignment would be fulfilled. Whenever a tap is used, there are indications of deviations from standards. Furthermore, such deviations make subsequent maintenance of the airplane difficult since maintenance mechanics have no records of such illegal deviations from specifications. Taps can be used in certain cases by special mechanics when such usage is authorized by engineers and when proper paper work supports such use. But such authorization usually requires one to three days for approval.

The tap, then, is an illegal tool, the use or possession of which carries extreme sanctions in private organizational law, but which is simultaneously widely possessed and used despite its illegal status. The problem of such a pattern for the meaning of private organizational law is to account for the wide acceptance of a crime as a means of fulfilling work requirements within a private organization, the aircraft plant.

THE SOCIALIZATION OF THE WORKER

To most workers entering an aircraft plant the tap is an unknown instrument. Dies which thread bolts, i.e., the process opposite to tapping, are relatively well known and are standard equipment of the plumbing trade. The new worker does not come into this contact with the tap until he finds it impossible to align the holes in two skins. In desperation and somewhat guiltily as if he had made a mistake, he turns to his partner (a more experienced worker) and states his problem. The experienced worker will try every legitimate technique of lining up the holes, but if these do not succeed, he resorts to the tap. He taps the new thread himself, not permitting the novice to use the tap. While tapping it he gives the novice a lecture on the dangers of getting caught and of breaking a tap in the hole, thereby leaving telltale evidence of its use.

For several weeks the older worker will not permit his inexperienced partner to use a tap when its use is required. He leaves his own work in order to do the required tapping and finishes the job before returning to his own work. If the novice demonstrates sufficient ability and care in other aspects of his work he will be allowed to tap the hole under the supervision of a veteran worker. When the veteran partner is absent, and the now initiated worker can use the tap at his own discretion he feels a sense of pride. In order to enjoy his new found facility, he frequently uses the tap when it is not necessary. He may be careless in properly aligning perfectly good components and then compensate for his own carelessness by using the tap.

He may forego the easier illegal methods (which are also viewed as less serious crimes) of greasing and waxing bolts or enlarging the misaligned holes and indulge himself in the more pleasurable, challenging and dangerous use of the tap. Sooner or later he inevitably runs into difficulties which he is technically unprepared to cope with. When his partner and mentor is not available, he is forced to call upon the assistant foreman. If the situation requires it, the foreman will recommend the tap. If he has doubts about the worker's abilities, he may even tap the hole himself. In doing this, he risks censure of the union, because as a foreman he is not permitted to handle tools.

At the time the research was conducted, there were four levels of foremen. These were: assistant foreman (one star); foreman (two stars); assistant general foreman (three stars), and general foreman (four stars). The stars are on the foremen's badges and are the insignia of rank. The assistant foreman is the immediate supervisor of a work crew. The four star is the shop supervisor. The two and three star foremen have authority over increasingly larger sections of the assembly line. In the following discussion the foreman refers to the one star, assistant foreman, unless otherwise noted.

While the foreman taps the hole, he also lectures on the proper and technically workmanlike ways of using the tap: "The tap is turned only at quarter turns . . . never force the tap . . . it has to go in easy or it's likely to snap . . . if it snaps, your ass is in a sling and I won't be able to get you out of it."

The foreman warns the worker to make sure "not to get caught, to see that the coast is clear, to keep the tap well hidden when not in use, and to watch out for inspectors while using it." He always ends by cautioning the worker, "It's your own ass if you're caught."

When the worker feels that he is experienced and can use the tap with complete confidence, he usually buys his own, frequently displaying it to other workers and magnanimously lending it to those in need of it. He feels himself fully arrived when a two star foreman or, even higher, an assistant general foreman borrows his tap or asks him to perform the tapping. The worker has now established his identity and is known as an individual by the higher ups.

Once the right to use the tap is thus established, the indiscriminate use of it is frowned upon. A worker who uses a tap too often is considered to be a careless "botcher." A worker who can get his work done without frequently using a tap is a "mechanic," but one who doesn't use the tap when it is necessary does not get his own work done on time. Proper use of the tap requires judgment and etiquette. The tap addict is likely to become the object of jokes and to get a bad work reputation among workers, foremen and inspectors.

AGENCIES OF LAW ENFORCEMENT

The enforcement of the plant rules of workmanship devolves upon three groups: foremen, plant quality control and Air Force quality control. The ultimate and supreme authority resides in the latter group. The Air Force not only sets the blue print specifications, but also and more importantly, can reject a finished airplane as not meeting specifications.

Furthermore, the Air Force inspectors reinspect installations which have been previously "bought" by plant quality control. If these installations do not meet Air Force standards they are "crabbed," i.e., rejected. When this happens, the plant inspectors who bought the installations are subject to "being written up," i.e., disciplinary action for unintentional negligence which may lead to suspensions, demotions or in extreme cases loss of jobs. The Air Force inspector has the absolute right to demand that any man be fired for violating work rules.

There were only two Air Force inspectors to a shop at the time of these observations, so that it was almost impossible for Air Force inspectors to police an entire shop of over 2,000 men. As an Air Force inspector walks up the line, it is standard procedure for workers to nudge others workers to inform them of the approach of the "Gestapo." When tapping is essential and when it is known that Air Force inspectors are too near, guards of workers are posted to convey advance notice of this approach to any one who is actively tapping. This is especially true when there are plant drives against the use of the tap.

In all instances, when the Air Force inspector is in the vicinity, workers who have a reputation for open or promiscuous use of the tap are instructed by the assistant foreman to "disappear." Such types can return to work when the "coast is clear."

Despite the Air Force inspectors' high authority and the severity of their standards, they are not sufficiently numerous to be considered the major policing agency for detecting and apprehending violators of the rules of workmanship. Plant quality control is the actual law enforcement agency in terms of the daily operations of surveillance. There are approximately 150 plant inspectors to a 2,000 man shop. They work along the assembly line along with the workers. In some cases a panel of inspectors is assigned to inspect the work done by a number of crews who are supervised by a two star foreman. In this system a call book which guarantees the equal rotation of inspections is kept. When a worker has completed a job and requests an inspection, he enters his wing number and the requested inspection in the call book. The inspector, after completing an inspection, marks the job as completed and takes the next open inspection as indicated in the call book.

A result of either type of inspection setup is the free and intimate intermingling of inspectors, and workers. In off moments, inspectors and workers gather together to "shoot the breeze and kill time." Inspectors, unlike workers, may have long waiting periods before their next assignment. During such periods out of boredom and monotony they tend to fraternize with workers. This causes conflict between the role of "good egg" and the role of policeman. A cause of leniency on the part of inspectors is intrinsic to the relationship between mechanics and themselves in circumstances not involving the tap. There is a sufficient amount of mechanical work which is not easily and immediately accessible to inspectors. This is particularly true if the inspector does not want to spend several hours on a fairly simple inspection. In order for the inspector to complete his work and make sure that the work he "buys" will be acceptable to later inspectors, he must rely on the workmanship of the mechanic. In brief he must have faith not only in the mechanic's workmanship but also in his willingness not to "louse him up." If the inspector gets the reputation of being a "bastard," the mechanic is under no obligation to do a good job and thus protect the inspector. Since the penalties for the use of the tap are so severe, no inspector feels comfortable about reporting a violation. A number of subterfuges are resorted to in an effort to diminish the potential conflict.

There is a general understanding that workers are not supposed to use a tap in the presence of plant inspectors. At various times this understanding is made explicit. The inspector frequently tells the workers of his crew: "Now fellas, there's a big drive now on taps. The Air Force just issued a special memo. For God's sakes, don't use a tap when I'm around. If somebody sees it while I'm in the area, it'll be my ass. Look around first. Make sure I'm gone."

At other times the verbalization comes from the worker. If a worker has to use a tap and the inspector is present, he will usually wait until the inspector leaves. If the inspector shows no signs of leaving, the worker will tell him to "Get the hell outa here. I got work to do and can't do it while you're around."

If the worker knows the inspector he may take out the tap, permitting the inspector to see it. The wise inspector responds to the gesture by leaving. Of course, a worker has already "sized up" the inspector and knows whether or not he can rely upon him to respond as desired.

When there is an Air Force-inspired drive against the tap, the inspectors will make the rounds and "lay the law down": "I want no more tapping around here. The next guy caught gets turned in. I can't cover you guys any more. I'm not kidding you bastards. If you can't do a decent job, don't do it at all. If that s.o.b. foreman of yours insists on you doing it, tell him to do it himself. He can't make you do it. If you're caught, its your ass not his. When the chips are down, he's got to cover himself and he'll leave you holding the bag!"

For about three or four days thereafter, taps disappear from public view. The work slows down, and ultimately the inspectors forget to be zealous. A state of normal haphazard equilibrium is restored.

Other types of social relations and situations between workers and inspectors help maintain this state of equilibrium. An inspector will often see a tap in the top of a worker's tool box. He will pick it up and drop it into the bottom of the box where it cannot be seen easily. Perhaps he will tell the worker that he is a "damned fool for being so careless." The inspector thus hopes to establish his dependability for the worker, and creates a supply of good will credit, which the worker must repay in the form of protecting the inspector.

Another typical worker-inspector situation occurs when a mechanic is caught in the act of tapping, and the inspector does not look away. The inspector severely reprimands the mechanic, "throws the fear of God into him," holds him in suspense as to whether he will turn him in, and then lets him go with a warning. This, generally, only happens to new workers. Occasionally when a worker has a new inspector and no previously established trust relationship, the same situation may arise. In both cases they are in integral part of the socialization of the worker to the plant or, rather, to a specific phase of its operation.

THE ROLE OF THE FOREMAN

Another type of ceremonial escape from law enforcement through pseudo-law enforcement involves the foreman. In rare cases an inspector will catch a worker using the tap, reprimand him and turn him over to his foreman. The foreman then is forced to go through the procedure of reprimanding the errant worker. The foreman becomes serious and indignant, primarily because the worker let himself get caught. He gives the worker a genuine tongue lashing, and he reminds him once again that he, as foreman, has to go to bat so save the worker's neck. He stresses that it is only because of *his* intervention that the worker will not lose his job. He states, "Next time be careful. I won't stick my neck out for you again. For God's sakes don't use a tap, *unless it's absolutely necessary.*"

The worker is obliged to accept the reprimand and to assume the countenence of true penitent, even to the extent of promising that it won't happen again. He will say, "Awright, awright. So I got caught this time. Next time I won't get caught." Both the foreman and worker play these roles even though the worker tapped the hole at the specific request of the foreman. The most blatant violation of the mores in such a situation is when the worker grins and treats the whole thing as a comic interlude. When this happens, the foreman becomes truly enraged, "That's the trouble with you. You don't take your job seriously. You don't give a dam about nothing. How long do I have to put up with your not giving a dam!"

The public ritual therefore conceals an entirely different dimension of social functions involved in the use of the tap. It is inconceivable that the tap could be used without the active or passive collusion of the foreman. As noted, the foreman instructs the worker in its use, indicates when he wants it used, assists the worker in evading the plant rules, and when the worker is caught, goes through the ritual of punishment. These role contradictions are instrinsic to the position of the foreman. His major responsibility is to keep production going. At the same time he is a representative of supervision, and is supposed to encourage respect for company law. He is not primarily responsible for quality since this is the province of plant quality control, i.e., inspection. He resolves the various conflicts in terms of the strongest and most persistent forms of pressures and rewards.

The work requirements of a particular foreman and his crew are determined by the Production Analysis Section, another staff organization. Workers call it Time Study although this is only one part of its function. Production Analysis determines, on the basis of time studies, the amount of men to be assigned to a specific crew, the locations of crews on the line, and the cutting-off points for work controlled by a particular foreman. Having done this, they determine the work load required of a foreman and keep production charts on completed work. These charts are the report cards of the foreman. At a moment's glance, top supervision can single out foremen who are not pulling their weight. In aviation assembly, since the work cycle for a particular team is relatively long (four to eight hours) and since a foreman has relatively few teams (usually three) all doing the same job, any slow-down which delays one team damages the foreman's production record in the immediate perceivable terms of the report card. Moreover, delay caused by the inability of one crew to complete its task prevents other crews from working on that wing. The foremen of these crews will complain to the two or three star foremen that they are being held up and that their production records will suffer because of another foreman's incompetence.

As a result of these considerations, the pressures "to get work out" are paramount for the foreman. There is a relatively high turnover among foremen, even at the two star level. In the last analysis, production records are the major consideration in supervisory mobility. All other considerations—e.g., sociability, work knowledge, personality, etc.—are assumed to be measured by the production chart.

In this context the foreman, vis à vis the ticklish question of the tap, is compelled to violate some of the most important laws of the company and the Air Force. Crucial instances occur at times when the Air Force institutes stringent anti-tap enforcement measures. When key holes do not line up it may be necessary, as an alternative to using the tap, to disassemble previous installations. The disassembling and reassembling may take a full eight hours before the previously reached work stage is again reached. The production chart for that eight-hour period will indicate that no work has been done. In such a situation the worker may refuse to tap a hole since he risks endangering his job. The foreman also may be reluctant to request directly that the worker tap a hole. To get the work done he therefore employs a whole rhetoric of veiled requests such

as "Hell, that's easy ... you know what to do ... you've done it before."
"Maybe you can clean out the threads," or "Well, see what you can do."

If the worker is adamant, the foreman will practically beg him to do the
right thing. He will remind him of past favors, he will complain about his chart
rating and of how "top brass doesn't give a dam about anything but what's on
the chart." He usually ends his plea with: "Once you get this done, you can take
it easy. You know I don't work you guys too hard most of the time."

If the veiled requests and pitiful pleadings don't produce results, the foreman
may take the ultimate step of tapping the hole himself. He compounds the
felony, because he not only violates the rules of workmanship but also violates
union rules which specifically state that no foreman can use a tool. To add insult
to injury, the foreman furthermore has to borrow the tap in the midst of an
anti-tap drive when taps are scarce.

From the viewpoint of production the use of the tap is imperative to the
functioning of the production organization, even though it is one of the most
serious work crimes. This is recognized even at official levels, although only in
indirect ways.

Taps, being made of hard steel, have the disadvantage of being brittle. If not
handled carefully, they may break within the nut. This not only makes further
work impossible, but makes for easier detection of the crime. To cope with such
a problem, the tool crib is well equipped with a supply of tap extractors. Any
worker can draw an appropriately sized tap extractor from the tool crib. All
these are official company property. He can do this even amidst the most severe
anti-tap drives without fear or the danger of punishment.

CONCLUSION

The creative ingenuity of mankind is responsible not only for the marvels of
science, engineering, and the arts but also for embezzlement, "beating the
system," cheating, corruption, crooked gambling, pseudolegitimate financial
lending, hustlers of never-ending variety, and clever—but dangerous—social arrangements for breaking social rules. Creativity is something intrinsic to human
beings. How it emerges is influenced by the pressures of the social structure and
the opportunities it presents—or denies—to people.

SUPPORT DRAFT REFUSERS
RESIST! RESIST! RESIST!
RECORD
RESISTERS

chapter 13
Resistance

Pursuing goals by any means that promise success—cases of success by hook or crook—can be classified into two groups: cases in which individuals seek purely personal (usually material) gain and other cases, equally generative of social problems, in which individuals seek collective goals or even the furtherance of an abstract moral principle. The indifferences of such deeply committed persons to the legitimacy of the means they use is legendary. The nineteenth-century social philosopher and activist, Georges Sorel, put the matter well.[1]

> During the Terror [of the French Revolution], the men who spilt the most blood were precisely those who had the greatest desire to let their equals enjoy the golden age they had dreamt of, and who had the most sympathy with human wretchedness: optimists, idealists, and sensitive men, the greater the desire they had for universal happiness, the more inexorable they showed themselves.

Georg Simmel, a German sociologist, described this phenomenon in more general terms.[2] When individuals consider that they are "mere representatives of supra-individual claims" and are "fighting not for themselves but only for a cause," he wrote, they

[1]Georges Sorel, *Reflections on Violence*, tr. T. E. Hulme, New York: Peter Smith, 1941, p. 195.
[2]From Georg Simmel, *Conflict*, tr. Kurt H. Wolff, New York: The Free Press, 1955, p. 39. Reprinted by permission.

... can give the conflict a radicalism and a mercilessness which find their analogy in the general behavior of certain very selfless and very idealistically inclined persons. Because they have no consideration for themselves, they have none for others either; they are convinced that they are entitled to make anybody a victim of the idea for which they sacrifice themselves. Such a conflict which is fought out with the strength of the whole person while the victory benefits the cause alone, has a noble character.

The kind of social problem we are calling "resistance" results from self-righteous idealism, not from cynicism. Consider the following account of a student disruption at the University of Chicago in 1969; it would not have been undertaken had the students not believed—sincerely—that they were fighting for a noble cause.[3]

Student rebels chanting "fascist pig" forced the suspension today of a session of the special disciplinary committee convened by the University of Chicago to deal with the 10-day occupation of the school's administration building.

Nearly 50 demonstrators screamed and swore in the second such disruption of a disciplinary committee session in two days.

One student, Sally Yagol, 20 years old, of Evanston, Ill., ran to the committee table in the law school building and pounded on it until Dallin H. Oaks, the committee chairman, recessed the meeting.

The 50 demonstrators were seated in back rows of the room when the open hearing began this morning. As soon as Mr. Oaks began to speak, a male demonstrator shouted: "We're having our own hearing! It's going to deal with political suppression at this university! Anyone with short hair who is over 30 will not be allowed!"

The demonstrators then began a chant, "sixty-one, sixty-one" referring to the number of student suspensions announced last week for some of the persons involved in the take-over of the administration building.

"Please be quiet," Mr. Oaks said. "This is a public hearing. If you're not quiet, it soon will become a private hearing."

A demonstrator shouted, "Listen to him. That's Dallin Oaks, chief of the pigs."

"I appeal to your fairness," Mr. Oaks said.

"Fairness! Fairness! Fascist pig! Fascist pig!," the demonstrator screamed.

When Mr. Oaks, the committee members and the dean of students, Charles O'Connell, left the buildings, shouting demonstrators attempted to pursue them, but were restrained by student bailiffs and the university police.

[3]From the New York *Times*, February 9, 1969. Reprinted by permission.

The demonstrators broke free, raced around the building, but failed to find Mr. Oaks and the committee. However, they cornered the assistant dean of students, James Vice, in the lobby and berated him.

One girl demonstrator ran her fingers through the assistant dean's hair and murmured, "I just love vice."

As the demonstrators filed from the building they sang "God Bless America," completing the song with a shout, "God Damn America!"

The sit-in was started Jan. 30 to protest the university's decision against renewing the contract of Mrs. Marlene Dixon, a sociology professor.

In the previous year (1968) students at Columbia University were prepared to bring the University to a halt because they felt it wrong to construct a gymnasium that did not also serve the Harlem community and because of their principle that a university ought not to lend itself to secret military research.[4] From the students' point of view, the social problem was the callousness of Columbia to the needs and interests of the black ghetto neighboring the University and the "betrayal" of academic values through participation in military research. The students might have said that the administration's behavior in both respects was an example of "pathologies of conformity to materialism" and to "bargaining." They might even have argued that it was the *administration's* determination to achieve its own goals at almost any cost that is an example of "success by hook or crook." The administration was behaving *legally*, but the disruptive students were saying, in effect, that legality was irrelevant; the University was acting *immorally*. When men believe that legally permitted behavior is morally wrong and when they feel that the regular machinery for getting their views felt is not effective, they resist. This self-righteousness poses problems for a society that tax the minds and skills of those responsible for the society's integration. Former Supreme Court Justice Abe Fortas tried to stake out a reasoned position on the problem.[5]

The term "civil disobedience" has been used to describe a person's refusal to obey a law which he believes to be immoral or unconstitutional. John Milton's famous defiance of England's law requiring licensing of books by official censors is in this category. He openly announced that he would not comply with it. He assailed the censorship law as an intolerable restriction of freedom, contrary to the basic rights of Englishmen.

But the phrase "civil disobedience" has been grossly misapplied in recent

[4]The Cox Commission, *Crisis at Columbia: Report of the Fact-finding Commission Appointed to Investigate the Disturbances at Columbia University in April and May, 1968*, New York: Vintage, 1968.

[5]Justice Abe Fortas, "The Limits of Civil Disobedience," The New York *Times Magazine*, May 12, 1968, pp. 29 ff.

years. Civil disobedience, even in its broadest sense, does not apply to efforts to overthrow the government or to seize control of areas or parts of it by force, or by the use of violence to compel the government to grant a measure of autonomy to part of its population. These are programs of revolution. Revolutionists are entitled, of course, to the full benefit of constitutional protections for the advocacy of their programs. They are even protected in the many types of *action* to bring about a fundamental change, such as the organization of associations and the solicitation of members and support at the polls. But they are not protected in the use of violence. Programs of this sort, if they are pursued, call for law enforcement by police action.

But there is a form of civil disobedience other than the refusal to obey a law because of disapproval of that particular law. This is the violation of laws in order to publicize a protest and to bring pressure on the public or the government to accomplish purposes which have nothing to do with the law that is breached. The great exponent of this type of civil disobedience was Gandhi.

The first type, as in Milton's case—the direct refusal to obey the specific law that is the subject of protest—may sometimes be a means, even an essential means, of testing the constitutionality of the law. For example, a young man may be advised by counsel that he must refuse to report for induction in order to challenge the constitutionality of the Selective Service Act. This is very different from the kind of civil disobedience which is not engaged in for the purpose of testing the legality of an order within our system of government and laws, but which is practiced as a technique of warfare in a social and political conflict over other issues. Frequently, of course, civil disobedience is prompted by both motives—by both a desire to make propaganda and to challenge the law. This is true, for example, in many instances of refusal to submit to induction.

Here let me be clear about a fundamental proposition. The motive of civil disobedience, whatever its type, does not confer immunity for law violation. Especially if the civil disobedience involves violence or a breach of public order prohibited by statute or ordinance, it is the state's duty to arrest the dissident. If he is properly arrested, charged and convicted, he should be punished in accordance with the provisions of law, unless the law is invalid in general or as applied.

He may be motivated by the highest moral principles. He may be passionately inspired. He may, indeed, be right in the eyes of history or morality or philosophy. These are not controlling. It is the state's duty to arrest and punish those who violate the laws designed to protect private safety and public order.

In both the Negro and the youth rebellions, the critical question is one of method, of procedure. The definition of objectives and the selection of those which will triumph are of fundamental importance to the quality of our society, of our own lives and those of our descendants. But the survival of our society as a free, open, democratic community will be determined not so much by the specific points achieved by the Negroes and the youth generation as by the procedures—the rules of conduct, the methods, the practices—which survive the confrontations. Procedure is the bone structure of a democratic society, and the quality of procedural standards which meet general acceptance—the quality of what is tolerable and permissible and acceptable conduct—determines the durability of the society and the survival possibilities of freedom within the society. . . .

It would be foolish to expect that these dissident groups—Negroes and youth—would confine themselves to the polite procedures that other segments of our society would wish. We can hardly claim that their deserving demands would be satisfied if they did not vigorously assert them. But we can, I think, insist that the methods which they adopt be within the limits which an organized, democratic society can endure.

An organized society cannot and will not endure personal and property damage, whatever the reason or occasion.

An organized society will not endure invasion of private premises or public offices, or interference with the work or activities of others if adequate facilities for protest and demonstration are otherwise available.

A democratic society must tolerate criticism, protest, demand for change, and organizations and demonstrations within the generally defined limits of the law to marshal support for dissent and change. It should and must make certain that facilities and protection where necessary are provided for these activities.

Protesters and change-seekers must adopt methods within the limits of the law. Despite the inability of anyone always to be certain of the line between the permissible and the forbidden, as a practical matter the lines are reasonably clear.

Any mass demonstration is dangerous, although it may be the most effective constitutional tool of dissent. But it must be kept within the limits of its permissible purpose. The functions of mass demonstrations, in the city or on the campus, are to communicate a point of view; to arouse enthusiasm and group cohesiveness among participants; to attract others to join; and to impress upon the public and the authorities the point advocated by the protesters, the urgency of their demand and the power behind it. These functions do not include terror, riot or pillage.

In my judgment, civil disobedience—the deliberate violation of law—is never justified in our nation when the law being violated is not itself the target of the protest. So long as our Governments obey the mandate of the Constitution and assure facilities and protection for the powerful expression of individual and mass dissent, the violation of law merely as a technique of demonstration constitutes an act of rebellion, not merely of dissent.

Civil disobedience is violation of law. Any violation of law must be punished, whatever its purpose, as the theory of civil disobedience recognizes. But violations directed not against laws or practices that are the subject of dissent, but to unrelated laws which are disobeyed merely to dramatize dissent, may be morally as well as politically unacceptable. . . .

Animating all of this in our society is the principle of tolerance. The state must tolerate the individual's dissent, appropriately expressed. The individual must tolerate the majority's verdict when and as it is settled in accordance with the laws and the procedures that have been established. Dissent and dissenters have no monopoly on freedom. They must tolerate opposition. They must accept dissent from their dissent. And they must give it the respect and the latitude which they claim for themselves. Neither youth nor virtue can justify the disregard of this principle, in the classroom, in the public hall or on the streets. Protest does not justify hooliganism.

Fortas says that "The functions of mass demonstrations . . . are to communicate a point of view . . . and to impress upon the public and the authorities . . . the urgency of [demonstrators'] demands . . ." He then adds, "These functions do not include terror, riot or pillage." But there is the rub. Terror, riot, or pillage may be regarded by the resistors—and may sometimes be in fact—the best available means to impress on the public and the authorities the resistors' sense of urgency.

Much depends on the "impressionability" of the public and the authorities. When a group wants to get a message across to authorities, the effectiveness of the methods it uses depends as much on the receptiveness of the authorities as it does on the dissenting group. If the message is, "See how deeply we care about this," and if the authorities regard anything less than violence as not caring enough to matter, then violence is invited—if the resistors do indeed care that deeply.

An American principle emphasized in Chapter 3 is that you are entitled to what you can make it worth someone's while to give you. And the value placed on nonconformity makes Americans suspicious of the idea that people should obey authorities just because they are authorities. Therefore, when Americans are faced with authorities who seem to them "wrong," it is an easy step to the conviction, "We can make them listen to us only by making it worth their while." If "they" do not need anything "we" have—that is, if we have nothing with which to make it worth their while—what shall we do? Assuming that we do not give up, we can always resort to one thing "we" *always* have that "they" want—namely, our *non*violence, *non*terror, or *non*pillage.[6]

The economist and gamesmanship strategist, Thomas Schelling, put the matter succinctly in a slightly different context.

---

[6]Black student leaders at a University of Wisconsin rally said, "We feel that the only power we have is the power to disrupt." New York *Times*, February 9, 1969.

The ordinary healthy high-school graduate, of slightly below average intelligence, has to work fairly hard to produce more than $3,000 or $4,000 of value per year; but he could destroy a hundred times that much if he set his mind to it, according to the writer's hasty calculations. Given an institutional arrangement in which he could generously abstain from destruction in return for a mere fraction of the value that he might have destroyed, the boy clearly has a calling as an extortionist rather than as a mechanic or clerk.[7]

In short, when Americans are convinced of the rightness of their goals, when they reject a duty to obey, and when they believe that others will not cooperate with them, they bargain. If they have no positive counters with which to bargain, they may use negative ones. They succeed by hook or crook: by either violent or nonviolent resistance.

Resistance may sometimes be symbolic rather than a resort to naked force. Even when it is symbolic, though, and especially when the symbolic gesture is eloquent, it often raises comparable concern as an act of violence. Symbols are powerful determinants of human behavior, as Chapter 1 emphasized. Symbolic gestures of resistance, therefore, are perceived by many as a social problem. The symbolic gesture of burning draft cards is considered by a University of Minnesota professor of law, who regrets governmental efforts to deal with such "problems" by seeking to punish the resisters. Professor Martin's discussion reflects the difficulty of deciding which is "the social problem": the symbolic resistance or its suppression.[8]

Toward the end of June, a remarkable demonstration took place in Washington, across the street from the Supreme Court building. Twelve women, standing in a circle and holding hands, burned a dozen draft cards furnished them for that purpose by male anti-war protesters. Burning one's own draft card is no longer a phenomenon. This variation on the familiar ceremony is explained by the participants' desire to condemn not only the war and the draft but to protest as well (and perhaps circumvent) a recent Supreme Court decision, *United States v. O'Brien*. In that case, the Court upheld against constitutional challenge the puerile dare to dissenters issued by Congress in 1965: "Burn a draft card and you face up to five years in jail and a fine of $10,000."

The Columbia University uprising catalyzed a flood of commentary on the permissible limits of civil disobedience. Although much of it has come from lawyers (including such prominent men as Supreme Court Justice Abe Fortas, Solicitor General Erwin Griswold, and ABA President Earl Morris), judgments

[7]Thomas Schelling, *The Strategy of Conflict*, New York: Oxford University Press, 1963, p. 141.

[8]From Peter W. Martin, "The Draft Card Burners," *The Nation*, July 22, 1968, pp. 42-45. Reprinted by permission.

about the propriety of civil disobedience—conduct that is by definition illegal—necessarily derive from moral rather than legal principles. Before an act of protest raises moral issues, however, it must be clear that it is in truth civil disobedience and not the perfectly lawful exercise of the right of free speech guaranteed by the First Amendment. The definition of this boundary of civil disobedience is a legal problem and was the task addressed by the Supreme Court in the O'Brien case.

The boundary is not so easy to discern as many statements of the issue would suggest. The typical, too-simple approach is epitomized by this comment of a judge, made while sentencing a convicted draft card burner:

> You have the right of dissent. You have the right to disagree with those in authority.... But you have no right to violate the law simply because you disagree with it. If you have that right, then so does every other citizen. Instead of a free society, we have anarchy.

The dichotomy here drawn between dissent and violating the law is deceptively sharp. Concealed is the fundamental conflict which exists between the individual's right to all effective means of expression and society's interest in prohibiting harmful conduct, a conflict that demands some mutual accommodation. . . . The guarantee of the right of free speech extends not only to traditional forms of expression, written and oral but also, to some extent, to conduct which symbolically expresses a point of view. It is this range of First Amendment protection that makes it no easy matter to distinguish civil disobedience from constitutionally shielded dissent.

On March 31, 1966, David O'Brien, then 19 years old, burned his Selective Service registration certificate, standing on the steps of the South Boston Courthouse before a sizable crowd that included members of the press. He was subsequently convicted of violating the criminal provisions of the Universal Military Training and Service Act of 1948, amended by Congress in 1965 to provide a $10,000 fine or five-year prison term for anyone who "knowingly destroys" or "knowingly mutilates" his registration certificate or classification notice (the "draft cards" of common parlance). O'Brien appealed, arguing that the First Amendment barred Congress from punishing his conduct. After mixed success in the U.S. Court of Appeals, his case reached the Supreme Court. Rarely has the Court had a better opportunity to clarify the relationship between free speech and civil disobedience.

The purpose of O'Brien's act was to communicate. He told the jury that he burned his draft card publicly "so that other people would re-evaluate their positions with Selective Service, with the armed forces, and re-evaluate their place in the culture of today, to hopefully consider my position." On the other hand, the statue in question merely prohibited conduct which arguably interfered with the administration of the Selective Service System, a matter of legitimate concern to Congress.

The Supreme Court's decision, written by departing Chief Justice Earl Warren, began by reiterating the Cout's consistent unwillingness to recognize conduct as falling within the concept of "free speech" merely because its performance reveals a clear intention to convey an idea. As other courts speaking to this same issue have pointed out, using an example to which nerves are now only too sensitive, the political assassin surely cannot be permitted to argue that his act—expressive of deeply felt political views—is therefore immune from punishment.

But an equally intolerable extreme would be the view that nonverbal conduct, no matter how communicative, can be regulated or prohibited without regard for the First Amendment. The social importance of nonverbal protest has led one commentator to call it, quite aptly, the "poor man's printing press." And in any event, the Supreme Court is committed by precedent to a broader interpretation of "speech." Picketing and the display of a flag, for example, have been held to be protected forms of communication. Consequently, in the O'Brien case, the Court would have found it difficult to affirm the statute simply by labeling draft card burning "conduct" not "speech." Chief Justice Warren assumed for the purpose of the decision that under the circumstances O'Brien's act had enough of the elements of speech to compel consideration of the First Amendment.

The assumption that First Amendments interests were at stake by no means assured constitutional protection:

> This Court has held that when "speech" and "non-speech" elements are combined in the same course of conduct, a sufficiently important governmental interest in regulating the nonspeech element can justify incidental limitations on First Amendment freedoms.

A balance between the two interests, individual and governmental, must be struck. The balancing formula outlined in the O'Brien decision is comprised of three steps. Conduct which combines "speech" and "nonspeech" elements can be restricted or prohibited by Congress if: (1) the governmental interest supporting the regulation is "important or substantial"; (2) this same governmental interest is "unrelated to the suppression of free expression"; and (3) the restriction on expression is "incidental" and "no greater than is essential tò the furtherance of that interest." It is difficult to fault this as an abstract statement of the balance which must be struck if the umbrella of the First Amendment is to be extended (as it must be) beyond pure verbal communication. Where the O'Brien opinion falls down is in its perfunctory application of this formula. In each step, the Court ignored factors which common sense insists are relevant.

The first two steps are closely intertwined: is there a governmental interest, unrelated to the suppression of expression which lies behind the statue forbidding the destruction of draft cards, an interest which is substantial, compelling, or cogent? As the Court reaffirmed, Congress has authority to make all laws necessary and proper to the raising and supporting of armies, including laws providing for the registration and induction of individuals for training and service. From this base, the Court jumped to the following conclusion:

> The issuance of certificates indicating the registration and eligibility classification of individuals is a legitimate and substantial administrative aid in the functioning of this system. And legislation to insure the continuing availability of issued certificates serves a legitimate and substantial purpose in the system's administration.

More precisely, what is this substantial purpose? O'Brien's attorney had belittled the importance of the requirement, on which the Court here relies, that a registrant keep his draft cards (both registration certificate and classification notice) in his possession at all times. The Court found the purpose, or rather purposes, in some of the suggestions made by the government attorneys arguing the case. The requirement permits, it was urged, a suspected delinquent to prove compliance with the law in a manner convenient both to him and the Selective Service System: it operates as a safeguard against mix-ups in the registrant's file; in the event of national emergency, the cards permit a rapid, on-the-spot call-up no matter how far the registrant is from his local board: they facilitate communication between registrant and the Selective Service, cutting down on unnecessary reference to files, furnishing the registrant continual access to his Selective Service number and local board's address—and so on.

The Court's pliant acceptance of these speculative justifications for the law would perhaps be appropriate in the case of a regulation under attack solely for an alleged lack of reasonable legislative purpose; but it is much too superficial for a major confrontation between the First Amendment and Congressional power. There are few prohibitions for which a set of theoretically plausible purposes, unrelated to expression, cannot be spun. On past occasions, the Supreme Court has been more ready to see through such fabricated "governmental interests" when First Amendment freedoms were in jeopardy.

Like so many features of the Selective Service System, the regulation that a registrant keep his draft cards continually in his possession is a thoughtless carry-over of a policy which originated several wars ago. Under the Selective Service Act of 1917, regulations required the possession of either the registration certificate or final classification card. Registrants had the duty to show the card to Selective Service or police officials when called upon to do so.

During March of 1918, nine months after the initial registration of 10 million men, the Justice Department organized the first "slacker raids" in Pittsburgh. "Slackers," those unpatriotic enough not to register, were rooted

out. They were identified by their inability to produce a draft card. The greatest
and last "slacker raid" took place in New York City, the first week in September, 1918. *The Nation* reported (September 14, 1918):

> Men were torn from their wives' sides in the theatres, yanked out of street
> cars, pulled off milk-wagons and trucks of all kinds, which vehicles were left
> to stand where they were abandoned. Men from up-State and New Jersey—
> and there were thousands of them—who had no warning of the raid and had
> left their cards at home—were first taken to police stations and then to an
> armory, where everything was utter confusion and where many spent the
> entire night upon their feet. Numbers were held by the police who showed
> their registration cards, but were without their classification cards, which
> have never been issued by the draft boards of many up-State towns.

An estimated 75,000 were "arrested" in New York and nearby towns, fewer
than 3 per cent of them turning out to be men who had not registered. Spurred
by public outrage, President Wilson ordered an inquiry, and Congress con-
demned the raids.

Throughout World War II, the Justice Department was extremely careful to
prevent a recurrence. Even during the concentrated delinquency campaign in
early 1943, U.S. Attorneys were instructed that

> Mass raids, large-scale arrests, and indiscriminate challenging of men of
> selective service age are not warranted in view of the relatively small number
> of reported delinquencies and because of embarrassment and inconvenience
> to law-abiding citizens which such practices would entail.

But the possession requirement was not dropped.

Then, as now, willful nonpossession of a draft card, being the violation of a
regulation, was a crime. But during the war, of 15,758 convictions for draft law
violations, only 255 were for failure to possess draft cards. The 1946 annual
report of the director for the Federal Bureau of Prisons describes those guilty of
these technical violations as "mostly socially inadequate individuals of low
intelligence who were simply careless about their obligations under the act.
Many of these came to the attention of the authorities through arrests for
vagrancy or on other minor charges, and, because they did not possess draft
cards, were given Selective Service Act violation sentences."

In short, from the suspension of "slacker raids" in World War I until the
burning and returning of draft cards became a common form of protest against
the war in Vietnam, the duty to keep them on one's person amounted to an
atrophied regulation, and found its only vitality as a snare for a few unfortu-
nates. Under such circumstances, a strong presumption is cast against the claims
of those who find underlying it a "compelling" governmental interest.

Current treatment of the regulation by the government suggests that the
major effect of the requirement is to provide a means of punishing those who

violate the regulation as a form of dissent. If there were any significant concern with the sorts of problems enumerated by the Court, one would expect that violations by nondissenters would be taken more seriously. Yet neither the regulation nor supporting criminal provisions are systematically applied against the large numbers of American men who fail to carry their draft cards. In the first draft card burning case, U.S. District Judge Harold Tyler, Jr., conceded: "... almost certainly thousands of men in recent decades, *including the writer*, have unwittingly failed to carry their cards at all times without ever having been called to show or produce them." The government's true view of the regulation (until dissent clouds the picture) is that it is a mere technicality. If the registrant who has violated such a technical provision of the regulations is willing to cure his "delinquency" the Justice Department, as a general rule, does not prosecute. No doubt a principal reason for the lack of across-the-board enforcement is the severity of the penalty. The fact that there is no reluctance to apply the sanction when nonpossession is part of protest activity reveals the actual interest served by the provision, which is very clearly the punishment of protest and the suppression of dissent.

O'Brien's argument on this score relied on two other points, the circumstances under which the bill was enacted and statements made by the bill's supporters, which betrayed a desire to limit dissent. He cited Congressman Bray's diatribe on "Beatniks and so-called 'campus-cults' " who had "been publicly burning their draft cards to demonstrate their contempt for the United States and our resistance to Communist take overs," and the "filthy, sleazy beatnik gang led by a Yale University professor" which "just yesterday" demonstrated in Washington for the Vietcong.

The Supreme Court rejected this evidence of motive with a statement of its traditional, and justifiable, reluctance to strike down legislation on the basis of what some of the legislators may have said before voting. The Cout's detached search for a governmental interest seems just as unacceptable, however. To consider the circumstances of enactment as evidence of the governmental interest embodied in a statute is not subject to this same objection. And unless examined, symbolic protest activity is in jeopardy. A legislative body that chooses statutory language with care to avoid a prohibition which "on its face" is aimed at expression and to lay the foundation for a colorable claim of "substantial governmental interest" can vitiate First Amendment rights unless subject to deeper judicial scrutiny.

It is hard to imagine a case in which the events surrounding enactment could speak more clearly of the actual interest served by the legislation. Draft card burning emerged as a form of protest in the summer of 1965. When U.S. troops entered openly into the Vietnamese fighting in June and the force level rose, the draft and military recruitment became natural foci of anti-war sentiment. On July 29, 1965, about 400 people protesting the war picketed an army recruiting center in New York City. During the rally, several young men burned their draft cards. A week later, Rep. Mendel Rivers introduced a bill to make destruction of draft cards a crime.

There seems little doubt that the draft law already furnished a means of punishing this form of protest. After burning his draft card, the protestor had no way of complying with the regulation's command that he keep his card in his possession at all times. For willful violation of that regulation he faced criminal penalties. Nevertheless, Congress recognized a serious threat to the war effort and moved with unprecedented dispatch to pass the Rivers bill. Before a month had passed, it had been enacted into law.

The fact that certain conduct has gained widespread use as a symbol of protest before restrictive legislative action occurs cannot, of course, be permitted to tie the hands of Congress where there is truly "compelling" governmental interest in controlling the conduct. But it should lead a court to demand greater evidence of a substantial interest unrelated to the suppression of expression than could be offered for this statute.

The ultimate disappointment of the O'Brien decision is its failure to give any serious discussion to the final stage in the balancing formula initially set forth by the Court, i.e., whether "the incidental restriction on alleged First Amendment freedom is no greater than is essential to the furtherance" of the governmental interest underlying the regulation.

No doubt the Supreme Court considered this "an indirect and minimal abridgement of speech," to adopt a phrase used by the U.S. Court of Appeals (second circuit) in another draft card burning case. Yet for a number of reasons this mode of communication has great value, particularly to the American male under 21, so that its prohibition is no minor limitation on expression, notwith-standing the continuing unrestricted right "to criticize national policy as vigor-ously as [one desires] by the written or spoken word." O'Brien was denied direct participation in the democratic processes of change. He was too young to vote. The issue he addressed is one of the most momentous this nation has ever faced. Of course, he had the right to write and speak; but access to large-scale communication media in America comes at a high price. The failure of Congress to confront the issues of Vietnam made the need for a forceful appeal to the public all the more urgent.

Nor should it be forgotten that O'Brien, like most protesters against the war, sought to raise not just points of national policy (and morality) but also to challenge U.S. conduct on legal grounds. The courts, in which the Southern Negro found redress, have consistently closed their doors to arguments that the war is illegal in terms of our own constitutional processes and applicable international law. They have characterized these as "political questions" which are therefore nonjusticiable. Judge Ford refused to admit evidence or argument on the legality of the Vietnamese War in the Spock-Coffin conspiracy trial for precisely these reasons. Because of this doctrine of abstention, unrepresented young men are being required to serve in a war that they consider not only immoral but illegal, and are denied the opportunity to have their legal questions dealt with on the merits.

In this context, to characterize the restriction on expression which flows from the prohibition of draft card burning as "incidental" is unrealistic. Congressional reaction to a handful of burnings attests to the power of the symbol. The public burning of a draft card expresses with unique force the individual's stand on the Vietnamese War and the draft.

The misfortune of the O'Brien opinion is not to be found in its effect on David O'Brien. Nor does the misfortune lie in the decision's effect on future draft card burners. To the protester who makes the difficult decision to engage in dissent by returning his draft card or burning it, the moral issue is now only somewhat sharpened by the certainty that such conduct is not protected by the First Amendment and thus must be undertaken as a true act of civil disobedience. Instead, the misfortune, felt by the entire public, is that the country is now denied uninhibited expression of important views on a crucial issue in a singularly dramatic form.

CONCLUSION

When to a sense of frustration is added a belief that the frustrating conditions are morally wrong and that one's aspirations are just, the "success by hook or crook" approach leads not to selfish grabbing or to sly cheating, but to defiant disobedience. Sometimes people resort to this extreme (as they sometimes resort to grabbing and cheating), and on some of those occasions the world is indebted to them for calling attention to genuine injustice.

Resisters, in other words, are always social problems to those they resist; they irritate people who believe in the principles being resisted as well as those who would prefer not to be bothered. Unfortunately, as former Justice Abe Fortas observed, sometimes we need such irritants to call attention to the injustices being resisted. An alternative is to develop social arrangements that will call attention to injustices *before* resisters are pushed beyond "the limits which our organized, democratic society can endure." At the same time we must distinguish between baseless gripes and valid grievances.

Section D
RITUALISM

If people cannot achieve legitimately the goals their culture describes as proper to pursue, they need not resort to illegitimate means. One alternative is to give up, not the culturally prescribed means, but the *goals*. This is what Americans are often urged to do—to continue being industrious, patient, honest, and law-abiding *as ends in themselves* even if they do not anticipate that such conformity will make them healthy, wealthy, or wise. When the *means* to success are ends in themselves, people are encouraged to say, "I may not be successful, but I do my best. I hang in there. I can take it. And anyway, I'm honest."

The elevation of means into ends is the essence of ritualism. It is a mode of adjustment that may give the individual a sense of serenity, integrity, and self-acceptance in place of the frantic race for success in which he used to engage. In some cases, however, it is a mode of adjustment that produces social problems because the substitution of conformity to rules for realization of culturally approved goals is no easy road to self-respect. The individual is frequently haunted by feelings of inferiority, unconsciously if not consciously. Psychologists describe some neuroses in terms of outward conformity and inner turmoil. The individual is able to play the social roles to which he is assigned, but he suffers; he experiences a sense of failure and incompleteness.

Somewhat inconsistently, submission to rules is also a problem when the public feels there is not *enough* resistance. On the one hand, Americans lament the "success by hook or crook" adaptation; on the other hand they view with distaste those who submissively go through the motions of patterns that are supposed to lead to the good life. We shall examine some illustrations in Chapter 14.

290

chapter 14
Going through the motions

How many Americans are there who lead lives of quiet desperation? They contribute in little and not-so-little ways to the machinery of American society, but do so without hope for brightness in their lives. "Of happiness and of despair we have no measure."[1] Ritualistic persons sometimes are ignored; they are the expendable underdogs of American society. The selection that follows deals with two such underdogs, Katherine and Bernard Lavery. They would never have come to public attention had they not committed a crime, but otherwise they are indistinguishable from tens of thousands of young people who were caught up in the hardships of the Great Depression. Their story is included here *despite* their crime, which, after all, represented a departure from a generally submissive style of life.[2]

When Mrs. Bernard Lavery abandoned her twin girl babies one October morning, leaving one in a subway lavatory and the other in the vestibule of a church, she violated a law, or, as the legal phrase has it, she committed an act "against the peace of the People of the State of New York, and their dignity." She was arrested the same afternoon—detectives had merely to canvass the hospitals on Manhattan Island to find out what mother of newly born girl twins had been discharged that morning—and for about a year after that the People of

[1]Ralph Ross and Ernest Van den Haag, *The Fabric of Society*, New York: Harcourt, Brace and World, 1957, p. 191.
[2]From St. Clair McKelway, "A Case of Abandonment," *The New Yorker*, July 14, 1934. Reprinted by permission of Random House, Inc.

the State of New York, represented by sundry individuals and agencies, tried very hard to decide what to do about Mrs. Lavery.

Five or six newspaper reporters, including myself, were in the police station on West Sixty-eighth Street when Mrs. Lavery was brought in. The detectives told us they had also tracked down the woman's husband and that, at the moment, he was on his way to the station house. Then we learned that the husband hadn't had anything to do with the crime of which Mrs. Lavery was accused. She had written him from the hospital (she had been in a charity ward at the City Hospital on Welfare Island) and told him the babies were dead. His job as bellhop at a cheap hotel in the West Forties had prevented him from going to see her, because the visiting hours at the hospital came during his working hours at the hotel, and he couldn't afford to take any time off. So the telephone call from a detective had brought to the bellhop the first word that his wife was under arrest and the first word that his twins were alive. There were no secrets in this case, from the detectives' point of view, because the woman had confessed and the case was already cleared up. They left the door open, and we could see her sitting there. She was not unattractive. A slim woman, tired and pale, she was dressed rather smartly and looked very much like any one of the thousands of young working women you may see on the subway any day at the rush hour. On the police blotter her age was given as thirty. The reason she had abandoned her babies, she had told the detectives, was that her husband made only fifteen or twenty a week and that she knew he wouldn't be able to support twins. She had thought, when she was pregnant, that he might be able to support the one child they had expected.

The husband came into the station house after a while and was shown to the detectives' room. He sat down without touching his wife, and they talked earnestly, facing one another on two chairs the detectives had placed in a corner of the room. After two or three minutes, he turned half away from her and, looking at the ceiling, doubled up his fist and struck his own temple twice, sharply. Then his wife leaned forward awkwardly and put her head on his shoulder. He did not embrace her then; he let his arms hang down and kept his eyes on the ceiling. They sat like that, silently, until the detectives left them there together, coming out and closing the door. About a half hour later they took Mrs. Lavery to jail to await her arraignment before a magistrate the next morning. Lavery himself watched her get into the patrol wagon; then he walked off down the street. I walked after him and asked him whether he wanted to talk about it. "I could have supported them," he said immediately. "But *she* . . ." Somehow he put a large quantity of his own bewilderment and anger and hopelessness into the single pronoun. "She," he began again, and then, "*Listen*," he said in a different voice, "you can't do anything for me. Leave me alone, now, will you? Will you leave me alone?" He was a short, slight man with one of those ageless faces that bellhops seem to have more often than not. It was easy to picture him in his uniform, waiting for a call, bringing ginger ale or soda water, accepting a tip with a nod of thanks. At the hotel where he worked, they told me he was a faithful employee and that, while he was paid no salary, he averaged fifteen or twenty dollars a week in tips. Next day I learned that Lavery, having no money for a railroad or bus fare, had hitchhiked to Hartford and back the night before. There he had borrowed from a relative some money with which to bail out his wife. It had taken him all night long to make the trip, he was in the Magistrates' Court the next morning, and that afternoon, when I telephoned the hotel, they said he was back at work again—taking things to people in the rooms, standing around in his bellhop's uniform, holding out his hand for tips. A number of times in the weeks that followed, I found myself wondering what had happened to the Laverys and their twins, and so one day a few months later I spent an hour going over the records at the Criminal Courts Building. A good deal had happened, I found, and a great many facts about the Laverys had been gathered, but the case had not been disposed of. It wasn't until almost eleven months had passed that the courts decided what to do about Mrs. Lavery.

The history of the Lavery twins is brief. Both were discovered that October morning soon after their mother abandoned them, and they were taken to the New York Foundling Hospital, where they died, one after the other, within the month. Doctors said their death could not be blamed on anybody, that much more had been done for them at the hospital than the mother could have done for them in her home, and that they had been destined to die soon after birth because of a condition called marasmus—a wasting away, a withering, caused by prenatal malnutrition. The twins simply had no chance from the start, the doctors said.

Mrs. Lavery herself remained in jail only that one night. She appeared before a magistrate the next day, pleaded guilty to the charge of abandoning her babies, and was released on cash bail of fifty dollars, which was put up by her husband. The Laverys had lived in a furnished room on West Sixty-fifth Street before this, but now they moved to a furnished room in Long Island City. The bellhop kept his job and continued to earn fifteen or twenty dollars a week in tips. Mrs. Lavery's case proceeded automatically from the Magistrates' Court to the Court of General Sessions. There a Judge accepted her plea of guilty and paroled her in custody of the Probation Department of the Court. He would pronounce sentence three months later, he said, after the case had been thoroughly investigated.

One of the first things the probation officers found out was that Mrs. Lavery was not legally Mrs. Lavery. She had lived with Lavery for more than six years, but they had never been married. Her real name, it turned out, was Katherine Ryan. Dating from this revelation, the papers in the case refer to her as "Katherine Ryan, alias Mrs. Katherine Lavery." She was subjected to a mental and physical examination, when the investigation commenced, and it showed that she was "of average intelligence, but with a neurotic personality, emotionally unstable," and that she was "undernourished." The examining physician added that "from a purely and strictly psychiatric standpoint, without considering the social, environmental, and other factors in the case, it is respectfully suggested that the social rehabilitation possibilities are good, in view of the fact that the personality findings also indicate a number of favorable characteristics." Probation officers then investigated the social, environmental, and other aspects of the case. They found that Mrs. Lavery, as she preferred to be called, was one of four children. Her father, a bartender, had been unemployed for the past two years; her mother, who was described as "a quiet, well-spoken individual," had been taking in roomers. They owned a small house in Queens. Mrs. Lavery's elder brother, they found, was married and "maintaining his own home," as the report put it. One of her sisters had been totally blind since infancy; the other had been crippled since she was two years old, as a result of spinal meningitis. Until Katherine was eighteen, the probation officer found, she had been "an intelligent, normal child and most helpful to her mother, who was naturally preoccupied with the other two daughters." At that age, however, Katherine had become independent, had moved away from her home, had supported herself by working as a telephone operator in hotels in Manhattan, and had rarely visited her family.

Katherine had her first child about a year after she met Lavery. She quit her job at a small hotel on Columbus Avenue three months before it was born. When the baby—a girl—was about two months old, she brought it to her parents' home in Queens. The child's name, she told them, was Caroline Lavery. She left the baby there, saying she would be back, but she did not come back, and after some months the grandparents turned the child over to a foundling home. This baby lived. The probation officers found that the mother had visited her several times at the foundling home. During the six years Katherine was living with Lavery, she paid for her own clothes and contributed her share of the room rent and grocery bills, according to the probation officers' report. She worked as a telephone operator in various hotels in Manhattan, and in each case is remembered as a faithful employee. Her salary, at times, was as high as thirty-five dollars a week. It was in one of these hotels that she first met Lavery and, as the report says, "formed a strong attachment for him." The report is laconic about the Laverys. "They have always made their home in a furnished room," it says. Of the woman, "Her leisure is spent at home with her paramour, and save for an occasional visit to the motion pictures, she leads a rather colorless life."

Because Mrs. Lavery had pleaded guilty to the crime of which she was accused, it was entirely up to the General Sessions Judge to decide what to do about her. No trial was necessary, of course; no jury of twelve good men and true would sit in judgment and say, "We find the defendant guilty" or "We find the defendant not guilty." It was not necessary for one of the public prosecutors to build up a case against her, to denounce her as an enemy of society, to demand a heavy penalty. Mrs. Lavery was guilty, she admitted she was guilty, and when she appeared for sentence, the Judge had before him only the information gathered by the probation officers. He was evidently puzzled. "I do not know," he told her, "whether to put you in the House of the Good Shepherd or the Bedford Reformatory. It would probably be a good thing to put you in one or the other, because the way you are living I do not know but what you will abandon a couple more children. . . . But it goes against my grain to send a woman of your age to the House of the Good Shepherd or the Bedford Reformatory—one who is not a criminal, whose only offense is that she sins like a fool and then throws her progeny onto society." The Judge decided to defer the pronouncement of sentence for three months longer. "I want to be satisfied," he told her, "that you are going to make some kind of a genuine effort to live straight."

The fact that Lavery and Katherine had neglected to get married became from this time on the major issue of the case. A fairly nice legal technicality was involved. Under the old law pertaining to domestic relations in the state of New York, the Laverys' relationship might have been called a common-law marriage. They had lived "before the world," as the old law phrased it, as man and wife. But the status of such couples was made more explicit by the Legislature in a law which became effective in May, 1933. This law provided that no marriage should be valid unless solemnized by a clergyman, by an authorized official of a city or county, or by a written contract signed by both parties. People who lived together 'before the world' as man and wife no longer were to be regarded as legally married in this state, the new law provided. So the various individuals and agencies concerned with the case of the Laverys concentrated on this question of legal status and made a good deal of it. The Catholic Big Sisters were called in at the suggestion of the Judge, and a Miss Kelly was delegated to arrange a marriage between the telephone operator and the bellhop. Mrs. Lavery was given to understand that the Judge would have much more sympathy for her if the marriage were duly solemnized. But there were obstacles in the way of the denouement. Mrs. Lavery was a Catholic; Lavery was a Protestant. He refused to be married in her church, and she would not have the ceremony performed in his. The reports made by the probation officers on this phase of the case are voluminous. When it was evident that an impasse had been reached, Miss Kelly of the Catholic Big Sisters ceased her efforts to arrange the ceremony. No solution had been found when, on June 7th, ten months after the now dead babies had been abandoned, Mrs. Lavery appeared before the Judge to be sentenced. She looked extremely well; she had gained weight since her discharge from the maternity ward that October morning, and the fatigue had gone out of her face. She was, as before, smartly dressed—a white straw hat, long white gloves, a flowered dress clasped at her throat with a neat little stock. She was more than ever representative of the young women you see on the subway at the rush hour. Lavery did not come to court with her; he was working.

An attorney who had been acting for Mrs. Lavery without charge since her first arraignment spoke briefly in her behalf. He said that the religious difficulties had now been straightened out, and that he himself was to be a witness at the wedding, which was to be performed the next week at the Municipal Building.

"Well, I want to see the certificate," said the Judge. "I will defer sentence until two weeks this day."

"Couldn't Your Honor make it next week this day?" the attorney asked. "I'm not making anything out of this case, as you know, and I want to be rid of it as soon as possible."

"This day next week, then," said the Judge, and Mrs. Lavery departed, having spoken not a word.

Mrs. Lavery appeared before the Judge the next week, dressed in an attractive brown ensemble. The attorney began his speech a little hesitantly. He explained that Lavery worked until five P.M. every day. On the preceding Wednesday, he said, Lavery had got off a little early and had gone to the Municipal Building, with Mrs. Lavery and himself, but had arrived a few minutes too late; the Marriage License Bureau was closed, and nothing could be done. Lavery, the attorney said, had been afraid that he would be discharged by his employers if he asked for more time off that week, so now the marriage would have to take place the following week. The Judge was incensed. He talked for ten minutes or so, in angry tones. "I look more like a fool every day," he said. "I know you for what you are," he went on, turning to Mrs. Lavery. "You are a cruel, wicked woman who abandoned her children—you will come before this court one week hence, married, or this travesty on consideration will cease and you will go to the Bedford Reformatory. Just you think that over!" he told her, and Mrs. Lavery departed. Again, she had not spoken. Then the next week Mrs. Lavery's attorney handed the Judge a certificate of marriage, proving beyond all doubt that the telephone operator and the bellhop had been married the day before. The Judge chuckled with pleasure, looked at the attorney, at the court attendants, at Mrs. Lavery, still chuckling. The attorney grinned, the court attendants grinned, and Mrs. Lavery, standing at the bar awaiting sentence, smiled in a restrained way and looked around the courtroom self-consciously.

"All right," said the Judge, turning again to Mrs. Lavery, and letting out a final chuckle, "I suspend sentence. You are free. You need have no more worries about this case as long as you live straight. I have nothing further to say, as I do not wish to embarrass you further." Mrs. Lavery nodded and smiled and left the courtroom. The indictment that had charged her with committing an act "against the peace of the People of the State of New York, and their dignity" was handed to a clerk, who put it in an outgoing basket, to be taken to the file-room. I learned afterward from the attorney that Mrs. Lavery is working again now. She is a telephone operator in a hotel on the upper West Side and is making thirty dollars a week. She and the bellhop have moved away from Queens and are back in Manhattan again. They are living not far from their former address, in a furnished room.

Hold the dreary routine of Bernard Lavery and Katherine Ryan in mind while reading Sophocles' ode on man:

> Numberless are the world's wonders, but none
> More wonderful than man; the stormgrey sea
> Yields to his prows, the huge crests bear him high;
> Earth, holy and inexhaustible, is graven
> With shining furrows where his plows have gone
> Year after year, the timeless labour of stallions.
>
> The lightboned birds and beasts that cling to cover,
> The lithe fish lighting their reaches of dim water,
> All are taken, tamed in the net of his mind;
> The lion on the hill, the wild horse windy-maned,
> Resign to him; and his blunt yoke has broken
> The sultry shoulders of the mountain bull.
>
> Words also, and thought as rapid as air,
> He fashions to his good use; statecraft is his,
> And his the skill that deflects the arrows of snow,
> The spears of winter rain. . . .

The problem of lives wasting away in ritualistic submission is difficult to illustrate because humdum greyness does not often catch the eye of observers. More likely to catch the eye is the sudden breaking out of their routines by people who erupt in one way or another. We shall look at examples of this kind of behavior in a later chapter. In recent years, the breaking out of their submissiveness by American Negroes tends to be perceived by some as a social problem. In this chapter we want to call attention to the problems generated by the *failure* to break out. Consider the case of "Shorty," a Negro who today might be labeled an Uncle Tom.[3]

The most colorful of the Negro boys on the job was Shorty, the round, yellow, fat elevator operator. He had tiny, beady eyes that looked out between rolls of flesh with a hard but humorous stare. He had the complexion of a

---

[3]From Richard Wright, *Black Boy*, New York: Harper & Brothers, 1945, pp. 198-199. Copyright 1937, 1942, 1944, 1945, by Richard Wright. Reprinted by permission of Harper & Row, Publishers, Inc.

Chinese, a short forehead, and three chins. Psychologically he was the most amazing specimen of the southern Negro I had ever met. Hardheaded, sensible, a reader of magazines and books, he was proud of his race and indignant about its wrongs. But in the presence of whites he would play the role of a clown of the most debased and degraded type.

One day he needed twenty-five cents to buy his lunch.

"Just watch me get a quarter from the first white man I see," he told me as I stood in the elevator that morning.

A white man who worked in the building stepped into the elevator and waited to be lifted to his floor. Shorty sang in a low mumble, smiling, rolling his eyes, looking at the white man roguishly.

' I'm hungry, Mister White Man. I need a quarter for lunch."

The white man ignored him. Shorty, his hands on the controls of the elevator, sang again:

"I ain't gonna move this damned old elevator till I get a quarter, Mister White Man."

"The hell with you, Shorty," the white man said, ignoring him and chewing on his black cigar.

"I'm hungry, Mister White Man. I'm dying for a quarter," Shorty sang, drooling, drawling, humming his words.

"If you don't take me to my floor, you will die," the white man said, smiling a little for the first time.

"But this black sonofabitch sure needs a quarter," Shorty sang, grimacing, clowning, ignoring the white man's threat.

"Come on, you black bastard, I got to work," the white man said, intrigued by the element of sadism involved, enjoying it.

"It'll cost you twenty-five cents, Mister White Man; just a quarter, just two bits," Shorty moaned.

There was silence. Shorty threw the lever and the elevator went up and stopped about five feet shy of the floor upon which the white man worked.

"Can't go no more, Mister White Man, unless I get my quarter," he said in a tone that sounded like crying.

"What would you do for a quarter?" the white man asked, still gazing off.

"I'll do anything for a quarter," Shorty sang.

"What, for example?" the white man asked.

Shorty giggled, swung around, bent over, and poked out his broad, fleshy ass.

"You can kick me for a quarter," he said, looking impishly at the white man out of the corner of his eyes.

The white man laughed softly, jingled some coins in his pocket, took out one and thumped it to the floor. Shorty stooped to pick it up and the white man bared his teeth and swung his foot into Shorty's rump with all the strength of his body. Shorty let out a howling laugh that echoed up and down the elevator shaft.

"Now, open this door, you goddamn black sonofabitch," the white man said, smiling with tight lips.

"Yeeeess, siiiiir," Shorty sang; but first he picked up the quarter and put it into his mouth. "This monkey's got the peanuts," he chortled.

He opened the door and the white man stepped out and looked back at Shorty as he went toward his office.

"You're all right, Shorty, you sonofabitch," he said.

"I know it!" Shorty screamed, then let his voice trail off in a gale of wild laughter.

I witnessed this scene or its variant at least a score of times and I felt no anger or hatred, only disgust and loathing.

The degradation of Shorty was, in the eyes of Americans who believed in racial equality, a serious social problem; and the authors interpret the Negro Revolution as an effort to correct this problem (as well as others related to it). A similar problem is constituted by the lives led by the men and women in the following selection about unskilled workers.[4] The author, Michael Harrington, does not describe those lives in the detail with which McKelway described the Laverys or Wright painted Shorty; he is more concerned with the general forces that lead to ritualistic living, relieved only by occasional flashes of abandon.

On a cold evening in Chicago (winter is a most bitter enemy of the poor) I talked to a group of Negro workers. Until a short time before our meeting, they had worked in the meat-packing industry and were members of the Packing-house Workers Union. They had been making around $2.25 an hour, with fringe benefits and various guarantees for sick leave, vacation, and the like. More than that, they had found a certain dignity for themselves in that they belonged to one of the most integrated unions in the United States. (The industry had traditionally employed many Negroes; one factor was that much of the work was regarded as "dirty," that is, Negro, tasks.)

A number of these people had found jobs in a plant making artificial Christmas trees. They received $1 an hour and no fringe benefits. The shop was, of course, nonunion. Several workers were fired every day, and crowds gathered on Monday morning to compete for their places.

The $1 an hour was bad enough, but there was an even more important aspect to this impoverishment. When they worked at Armour, these employees knew a certain job security; they had rights in the shop because of the union. It was not only that their wages had been cut by more than half when the plant

[4]From Michael Harrington, *The Other America*, New York: The MacMillan Co., 1962, pp. 25-29, 133-135. © Michael Harrington, 1962. Reprinted by permission.

closed; it was also that they had been humiliated. This was particularly true of these Negroes. As members of a minority group, they had been fortunate to get such good jobs and to belong to a union that took civil rights seriously. Now that they had been thrust into the economic underworld, that racial gain was wiped out. The Christmas-tree shop hired Negroes only. That was because they were available cheap; that was because they could be "kept in their place."

One of the workers I talked to was a woman in her thirties. When she spoke, the bitterness was not so much directed against the low pay: what concerned her most was the "slavery" of her working conditions. She had to ask the supervisor permission to go to the bathroom. At any moment she could be fired for insubordination, and there was no grievance procedure or arbitration to protect her rights. She was vivacious and articulate, a born leader. So she tried to organize the shop. A majority of the workers had signed cards asking for a union election, but the National Labor Relations Board had postponed the date. The election will never take place. The Christmas-tree season is over, and these people are out on the streets again.

Yet the workers in the sweatshop considered themselves lucky. They were making $1 an hour, which was something. Two men I talked to were in a different classification: they had passed the line of human obsolescence in this industrial society. They were over forty years of age. They had been laid off at Armour in the summer of 1959. Eighteen months later, neither of them had found a steady job of any kind. "When I come to the hiring window," one of them said, "the man just looks at me; he doesn't even ask questions; he says, 'You're too old.' "

Other men talked of how racial discrimination worked against them when the plant closed. One technique is simplicity itself. A job is rated by a plant well over its actual skill level. Training and educational qualifications are specified in great detail. When the white worker applies, these criteria are waived. When the Negro worker shows up in the hiring line, the letter of the law is enforced. Technically, there has been no discrimination. The Negro was turned down for lack of skill, not because of race. But that, of course, is the most obvious and palpable evasion.

What happens to the man who goes eighteen months without a steady job? The men told me. First, the "luxuries" go: the car, the house, everything that has been purchased on installment but not yet paid for. Then comes doubling up with relatives (and one of the persistent problems in becoming poor is that marriages are often wrecked in the process). Finally—and this is particularly true of the "older" worker—there is relief, formal admission into the other America.

The Armour workers who became poor were, to a considerable extent, Negro. In attitudes toward poverty, there is a curious double standard. America more or less expects the Negro to be poor (and is convinced that things are getting better, a point to be dealt with in a later chapter). There is no emotional shock when people hear of the experience of these human beings in Chicago. The mind and the feelings, even of good-willed individuals, are so suffused with an unconscious racism that misery is overlooked.

But what happened at Armour is not primarily racial, even though the situation is compounded and intensified by the fact that Negroes are involved. The same basic process is at work in Pennsylvania and in Detroit.

In a brilliant report, Harvey Swados wrote of his first impression of Saint Michael, Pennsylvania: "It is a strange thing to come to a town and find it full of grown men. They stroll the narrow, shabby streets, chat at the corners, lean against the peeling pillars of the town saloon, the St. Michael Hotel & Restaurant, and they look more like movie actors than real human beings, because something is wrong."

That "something" happened on April 24, 1958, when Maryland Shaft Number 1 closed down. Since then some of the miners have been able to get jobs elsewhere. But for most of them, there are idleness and a profound change in the way of life. What, after all, do you do with a man who is a skilled coal miner? When the mine closes down, what industry do you put him into? He is physically strong; he has lived his life in a tight community of coal miners; and he has intense loyalties to his fellow workers and to his little town in the mountains. But he has a skill that is hardly transferable.

Some of the men from Maryland Shaft Number 1 got jobs in the steel industry, but they have already been hit by layoffs there. The automation process that destroyed the work in coal is spreading to steel: their problem is following after them. Others are working, for a fraction of their previous wage, as orderlies in hospitals and institutions, as janitors and stockmen in big stores.

But, again, the most humiliating part of this experience maims the spirit. As Swados puts it, "It is truly ironic that a substantial portion of these men, who pride themselves on their ability to live with danger, to work hard, fight hard, drink hard, love hard, are now learning housework and taking over the woman's role in the family."

For the miners have always been an almost legendary section of the work force. Their towns are as isolated as ships, and they have had the pride of métier, the élan of seamen. Their union battles were long and bloody, sometimes approaching the dimensions of civil war, as in the fabled Harlan County struggles. They had a tough life, but part of the compensation was the knowledge that they were equal to it. Now the job has been taken away, and the pride with it.

In many of these mining areas, there are small garment shops that are running away from union labor in New York and other established centers. Their pay is miserable, and they look for the wives of the unemployed. So the miners do the housework and hang around the saloon, and the wife has become the breadwinner.

In Detroit one can see still another part of this process: it is not minority poverty as with the Armour workers, nor is it depressed-area poverty as in the case of the coal miners. It is the slide backward, the becoming poor, that takes place in the midst of a huge American industrial city.

In 1956 Packard closed out a Detroit factory and destroyed some 4,000 jobs. What happened to the men and women involved has been carefully described in a special study of the Senate Committee on Unemployment Problems. The report is entitled, "Too Old to Work, Too Young to Retire."

When the Packard plant closed, the world fell in on some of the men. There were those who cried. They had worked in the shop for years, and they had developed a personal identification with the car they built. Some of them were particularly bitter because they felt the company had blundered by lowering standards and turning out an inferior product. They were laid off in 1956, but many of them had still not found regular work when the recession hit in 1958 and again in 1960.

The workers in the best position were those who were both young and skilled. Their unemployment averaged "only" a little better than five and a half months. The young and semiskilled were out on the street for an average of seven and a half months, the old, skilled workers for eight and a half months. Finally, the "old" semi-skilled workers (say, machine operators over forty-five) averaged better than a year of unemployment. The old and unskilled were out for fourteen months.

For almost every one of these human beings, there was a horrible sinking experience. Of those who were able to find jobs, almost 40 per cent took a position inferior to the one they had held. Skilled workers took semiskilled or even common-laborer jobs. Most of these did not become poor. They were humiliated and downgraded, but not dragged below the subsistence level. But some of the old, the unskilled, and the Negroes entered the other America in the late fifties. They came from a well-organized and relatively high-paying industry. They ended by becoming impoverished.

So it was in Detroit, Michigan, and the story is substantially the same as in Saint Michael, Pennsylvania or Chicago, Illinois. In the fifties and early sixties, a society with an enormous technology and the ability to provide a standard of living for every citizen saw millions of people move back. Some of them retrogressed all the way, and ended where they had been before the gains of the welfare state were made. Many of them slid back but did not become impoverished. . . .

This is how the Midtown researchers described the "low social economic status individual": they are "rigid, suspicious and have a fatalistic outlook on life. They do not plan ahead, a characteristic associated with their fatalism. They are prone to depression, have feelings of futility, lack of belongingness, friendliness, and a lack of trust in others." Translated into the statistics of the Midtown study, this means that the bottom of the society is three times more emotionally depressed than the top (36.2 per cent for the low, 11.1 per cent for the high).

A small point: America has a self-image of itself as a nation of joiners and doers. There are social clubs, charities, community drives, and the like. Churches have always played an important social role, often marking off the status of individuals. And yet this entire structure is a phenomenon of the middle class. Some time ago, a study in Franklin, Indiana, reported that the percentage of people in the bottom class who were without affiliations of any kind was eight times as great as the percentage in the high-income class.

Paradoxically, one of the factors that intensifies the social isolation of the poor is that America thinks of itself as a nation without social classes. As a result, there are few social or civic organizations that are separated on the basis of income and class. The "working-class culture" that sociologists have described in a country like England does not exist here, or at least it is much less of a reality. The poor person who might want to join an organization is afraid. Because he or she will have less education, less money, less competence to articulate ideas than anyone else in the group, they stay away.

Thus, studies of civilian-defense organizations during World War II showed that almost all the members were white-collar people. Indeed, though one might think that the poor would have more friends because they are packed densely together, there are studies that indicate that they are deprived in this regard, too. In one report, 47 per cent of the lower-class women said that they had no friend or no intimate friend.

Such a life is lonely; it is also insecure. In New Haven, Hollingshead and Redlich could find only 19 per cent of the people in the bottom class who thought that their jobs were safe. The Yale group described 45 per cent of the poor as "inured," and found that their motto was "We take what the tide brings in."

This fatalism is not, however, confined to personal experience alone, to expectations about job and family. It literally permeates every aspect of an individual's life; it is a way of seeing reality. In a poll the Gallup organization did for Look magazine in 1959 (a projection of what people anticipated in the sixties), the relationship between social class and political pessimism was striking. The bottom group was much more likely to think that World War III was coming, that a recession was around the corner, that they would not take a vacation in the coming year. As one went up the income scale, the opinion of the world tended to brighten.

This pessimism is involved in a basic attitude of the poor: the fact that they do not postpone satisfactions, that they do not save. When pleasure is available, they tend to take it immediately. The smug theorist of the middle class would probably deplore this as showing a lack of traditional American virtues. Actually, it is the logical and natural pattern of behavior for one living in a part of American life without a future. It is, sad to say, a piece of realism, not of vice.

Related to this pattern of immediate gratification is a tendency on the part of the poor to "act out," to be less inhibited, and sometimes violent. There are some superficial observers who give this aspect of slum life a Rousseauistic twist. They find it a proof of the vitality, of the naturalness of the poor who are not constrained by the conventions of polite society. It would be hard to imagine a more wrongheaded impression. In the first place, this violence is the creature of that most artificial environment the slum. It is a product of human density and misery. And far from being an aspect of personality that is symptomatic of health, it is one more way in which the poor are driven to hurt themselves.

Harrington's focus was on the poor, who live some distance from what Americans call the Good Life. As several of Harrington's remarks suggest, however, some of the poor break out of ritualistic submission in flashes of violence, lavish consumption, sexual adventuring, or bouts with the bottle. Significantly, popular speech often distinguishes between "the respectable poor" and the other poor. The "respectable" poor are presumably those who never break out.

But ritualism is not an adjustment confined to the poor. Some writers have suggested that, at least so far as the occupational world is concerned, mass industrial organization makes this a common experience.[5]

According to Marx, the modern factory hand is alienated from his work since he owns neither the means of production nor the product of his labor. Specialization has fragmented production so that each worker's labor has become repetitious, monotonous, and lacks opportunity for creativity and self-expression. The worker has little conception of the whole work process or of his contribution to it; his work is meaningless. He has little control over the time at which his work starts and stops or over the pace at which it is carried out. To this Marxian analysis, Weber added that this basic estrangement exists not only between the worker and the means of production, but also between the soldier and the means of warfare, the scientist and the means of inquiry, etc. This is not just a legal question of ownership (e.g., that the gun belongs to the army and not to the soldier) but rather that with ownership goes the right to control, and that those that provide the means also define their use; thus the worker, soldier, and researcher—and by implication all employees of all organizations—are frustrated, unhappy since they cannot determine what use their efforts will be put to since

[5]From Amitai Etzione, *Modern Organizations*, Englewood Cliffs, New Jersey: Prentice-Hall, Inc., Foundation of Modern Sociology Series, 1964, p. 42. Copyright 1964. Reprinted by permission.

they do not own the instrument necessary to carry out independently the work that needs to be done. When asked, "all said and done how satisfied are you with your work?" about 80 per cent of American blue collar workers answer "not satisfied." Alienation is a concept that stands for this sentiment and the analysis of its source in the Marxian-Weberian terms.

To be sure, the Human Relations approach has indicated some ways in which the resulting frustrations might be reduced, but, the Structuralists insist, there are sharp limits on the degree to which this can be achieved. The development of social groups on the job might make the worker's day more pleasant, but it does not make his task any the less repetitious or uncreative. Similarly, rotation eases the problem of monotony but does not change its basic nature since rotation is limited by the scope of the alternative jobs available, all similar in their dull, routine and meaningless nature. Workers, it is suggested, spend much of their working day in a semi-conscious delirium, dreaming about their major source of satisfaction, the post-work day.

This redirection of energy and interest toward off-the-job satisfaction is one source of indifference on the job.[6]

The indifferents are those who have come to terms with their *work environment* by withdrawal and by a redirection of their interests toward off-the-job satisfactions. They have also been alienated by the *work itself*, which has often been downgraded by machine processing and by assembly-line methods. This dual basis for alienation must be recognized. In industrial psychology the main effort has been to compensate for the deadening effect of the work itself by providing a happy work place. Less attention has been given to alienation from the job itself.

We are not speaking here of pathological kinds of alienation, but of modes of accommodation that often seem basically healthy. The typical indifferent has rejected majority values of success and power. While the upward-mobile strives for such values, obtainable today mainly through big organizations, the indifferent seeks that security which the organization can also provide for those who merely "go along." Such security seeking varies in accord with the demands of personality. One individual may have been taught to expect more than life can reasonably offer, and anxiety and frustration follow as his unrealistic claims are discounted. Another may have learned to expect less; he may refuse to accept success values or to compete for them. This role is encouraged by such bureaucratic conditions as hierarchy, oligarchy, and specialization.

The indifferent reaction, then, is the product of both social and organizational influences. But organizational factors seem to outweigh class-induced

[6]From Robert Presthus, *The Organizational Society*, New York: Vintage Books, 1965, pp. 208-209. Reprinted by permission.

mobility expectations. However strong such expectations, they rarely survive in an unsympathetic institutional environment. Today, many a potential entrepreneur languishes in some cul-de-sac because the organizational context no longer sustains his aspirations. The resulting accommodation may also reflect personal failures of nerve and energy, bad luck, and so on. But, essentially, indifference is manifested in a psychic withdrawal from the work arena and a transfer of interest to off-work activities. The employee "goes through the motions," paying lip-service to organizational values, but he no longer retains any real interest in the organization or in work for its own sake.

This accommodation may occur in two stages: alienation and indifference. The alienated are those who come into the organization with great expectations. They are determined to climb. But when bureaucratic and personal limitations blunt their hopes, they become alienated. Over a period of time, it seems, this reaction works itself into indifference. On another level, we are dealing with indifference as an *initial* orientation. Such individuals, usually of working or lower-middle-class origin, have been taught not to expect very much. Both socialization and work experience reinforce this perception of their life chances. And both alienation and indifference counter the organization's claims for loyalty, predictability, and hard work.

Although the preceding examples are drawn from adult life, a ritualistic accommodation can start earlier—in school, for example. Holt observed children in classrooms, and the "you" he refers to is the teacher whose class he was observing.[7]

In today's work period three or four people came up to you for help. All were stuck on that second math problem. None of them had made any effort to listen when you were explaining it at the board. I had been watching George, who had busied himself during the explanation by trying, with a pencil, to ream and countersink a hole in the side of his desk, all the while you were talking. He indignantly denied this. I showed him the hole, which silenced him. Gerald was in dreamland; so for the most part was Nancy, though she made a good recovery when asked a question. Unusual for her. Don listened about half the time, Laura about the same. Martha amused herself by turning her hand into an animal and having it crawl around her desk.

Watching older kids study, or try to study, I saw after a while that they were not sufficiently self-aware to know when their minds had wandered off the subject. When, by speaking his name, I called a daydreamer back to earth, he was always startled, not because he had thought I wouldn't notice that he had stopped studying, but because *he* hadn't noticed.

[7]From John Holt, *How Children Fail*, New York: Dell Publications, 1964, pp. 6-10. Copyright Pitman Publishing Corporation. Reprinted by permission.

Except by inflicting real pain on myself, I am never able to stay awake when a certain kind of sleepiness comes over me. The mind plays funny tricks at such times. I remember my own school experience of falling asleep in class while listening to the teacher's voice. I used to find that the "watchman" part of my mind that was saying, "Keep awake, you fool!" would wake me when the teacher's voice began to fade. But the part of my mind that wanted or needed sleep was not so easily beaten. It used to (and still does) counterfeit a voice, so that as I fell asleep an imaginary voice continued to sound in my head, long enough to fool me until the watchman no longer had the power to awaken me. The watchman learned, in turn, that this counterfeit voice was liable to be talking about something different, or pure nonsense, and thus learned to recognize it as counterfeit. Many times, I have dozed off with a voice sounding inside my head, only to have the watchman say, "Hey! Wake up! That voice is a phoney!"

Most of us have very imperfect control over our attention. Our minds slip away from duty before we realize that they are gone. Part of being a good student is learning to be aware of the state of one's own mind and the degree of one's own understanding. The good student may be one who often says that he does not understand, simply because he keeps a constant check on his understanding. The poor student, who does not, so to speak, watch himself trying to understand, does not know most of the time whether he understands or not. Thus the problem is not to get students to ask us what they don't know; the problem is to make them aware of the difference between what they know and what they don't.

All this makes me think of Herb. I saw the other day why his words so often run off the paper. When he is copying a word, he copies about two letters at a time. I doubt whether he looks beyond them, or that he could tell you, in the middle of a word, what the whole word was. He has no idea, when he begins to copy a word, how long the word is going to be, or how much room it may take up.

I watched Ruth during the period of the Math test. At least four-fifths of the time she was looking out the window; or else she played with her pencil, or chewed her fingernails, or looked at Nell to see what information she might pick up. She did not look in the least worried or confused. It looked as if she had decided that Math tests were to be done, not during the regular test period, when everyone else does them, but during conference period on Friday, with teacher close at hand, so that if she got into a jam she could get instant help.

She seems to find the situation of not knowing what to do so painful that she prefers to do nothing at all, waiting instead for a time when she can call for help the moment she gets stuck. Even in conference period today she did next to nothing. She was trying to sneak something out of her desk. She moves rather jerkily, so every time she raised the desk lid, I saw it out of the corner of my eye and looked at her. This was rather frustrating for her; however, she kept right on trying for most of the period, not a bit abashed by being caught at it all the time.

Remember when Emily, asked to spell "microscopic," wrote MINCOPERT? That must have been several weeks ago. Today I wrote MINCOPERT on the board. To my great surprise, she recognized it. Some of the kids, watching me write it, said in amazement, "What's that for?" I said, "What do you think?" Emily answered, "It's supposed to be 'microscopic.' " But she gave not the least sign of knowing that she was the person who had written MINCOPERT.

On the diagnostic spelling test, she spelled "tariff" as TEARERFIT. Today I thought I would try her again on it. This time she wrote TEARFIT. What does she do in such cases? Her reading aloud gives a clue. She closes her eyes and makes a dash for it, like someone running past a graveyard on a dark night. No looking back afterward, either.

Reminds me of a fragment of the Ancient Mariner—perhaps the world's best short ghost story:

> Like one, that on a lonesome road
> Doth walk in fear and dread,
> And having once turned round walks on,
> And turns no more his head;
> Because he knows, a frightful fiend
> Doth close behind him tread.

Is this the way some of these children make their way through life?

CONCLUSION

Not only "some of these children" but many adults "make their way through life" in dulled submission. Eighty percent of America's *workers* are "not satisfied" with their jobs, yet they do society's work. Eighty percent of America's workers are not social problems of the sort that make newspaper headlines. Are they, nonetheless, social problems? If American values say that people should lead lives of dignity, meaning, and vitality, then the answer is yes. And the authors of this book think American values say that.

Section E
EXPLOSION

The lives of quiet desperation glimpsed in the preceding chapter are one form of adjustment to disappointment, frustration, or deprivation. They are social problems from the point of view of those who think human lives should be lived more vibrantly. Furthermore, there is the chilling reminder of Edwin Markham, in his poem, "The Man with the Hoe," that desperation does not forever remain quiet:

> Oh, masters, lords, and rulers in all lands,
> How will the future reckon with this man?
> How answer his brute question in that hour
> When whirlwinds of rebellion shake all shores?
> How will it be with kingdoms and with kings—
> With those who shaped him to the thing he is—
> When this dumb terror shall rise to judge the world,
> After the silence of centuries?

Sometimes after centuries, sometimes after generations, and sometimes after only decades or moments, the casualties of certain modes of social organization explode. Their explosion generates counterexplosions, which fire off still further explosions in a chain reaction that can spiral into anarchy or repression. In the chapters comprising this section, we shall look at some examples from American society.

310

chapter 15
Vengefulness

The men with the hoes in the United States have included successive waves of laboring immigrants whose muscle power makes industrialization possible. But above all they have been the Negroes whose "immigration" was from the outset a coerced dehumanization. Certainly most Negroes have for generations borne their deprivation silently, and ritualistically "went through the motions." Then came the Detroit riots of 1967.[1]

At midnight, Hubert G. Locke, a Negro who is administrative assistant to the police commissioner, left his desk at headquarters and climbed to the roof for a look at Detroit. When he saw it, he wept. Beneath him, whole sections of the nation's fifth largest city lay in charred, smoking ruins. From Grand River Avenue to Gratiot Avenue six miles to the east, tongues of flame licked at the night sky, illuminating the angular skeletons of gutted homes, shops, supermarkets. Looters and arsonists danced in the eerie shadows, stripping a store clean, then setting it to the torch. Mourned Mayor Jerome Cavanagh: "It looks like Berlin in 1945."

In the violent summer of 1967, Detroit became the scene of the bloodiest uprising in half a century and the costliest in terms of property damage in U.S. history. At week's end, there were 41 known dead, 347 injured, 3,800 arrested. Some 5,000 people were homeless (the vast majority Negro), while 1,300 buildings had been reduced to mounds of ashes and bricks and 2,700 businesses sacked. . . .

[1]*Time*, August 4, 1967, pp. 13-15 (excerpt). Reprinted by permission from *Time*, The Weekly Newsmagazine. Copyright Time Inc. 1967.

Typically enough, Detroit's upheaval started with a routine police action. Seven weeks ago, in the Virginia Park section of the West Side, a "blind pig" (afterhours club) opened for business on Twelfth Street, styling itself the "United Community League for Civic Action." Along with the afterhours booze that it offered to minors, the "League" served up black-power harangues and curses against Whitey's exploitation. It was at the blind pig, on a sleazy strip of pawnshops and bars, rats and pimps, junkies and gamblers, that the agony began.

Through an informant, police were kept advised of the League's activities. At 1:45 a.m. Sunday, the informant, a wino and ex-convict, passed the word (and was paid 50¢ for it): "It's getting ready to blow." Two hours later, 10th Precinct Sergeant Arthur Howison led a raid on the League, arresting 73 Negro customers and the bartender. In the next hour, while squad cars and a paddy wagon ferried the arrested to the police station, a crowd gathered, taunting the fuzz and "jiving" with friends who had been picked up. "Just as we were pulling away," Howison said, "a bottle smashed a squad-car window." Then it began.

Rocks and bottles flew. Looting, at first dared by only a few, became a mob delirium as big crowds now gathered, ranging through the West Side, then spilling across Woodward Avenue into the East Side. Arsonists lobbed Molotov cocktails at newly pillaged stores. Fires started in the shops, spread swiftly to homes and apartments. Snipers took up posts in windows and on rooftops. For four days and into the fifth, mobs stole, burned and killed as a force of some 15,000 city and state police, National Guardsmen and federal troops fought to smother the fire. The city was almost completely paralyzed.

For the last couple of years, city officials had been saying proudly: "That sort of thing can't happen here." . . . When the trouble began outside Twelfth Street's blind pig, the 10th precinct at that early hour could muster only 45 men. Detroit police regard the dawn hours of Sunday, when the action is heaviest in many slums, as a "light period." The precinct captain rushed containing squads to seal off the neighborhood for 16 square blocks. Police Commissioner Ray Girardin decided, because of his previous success with the method, to instruct his men to avoid using their guns against the looters. That may have been a mistake.

As police gave ground, the number of looters grew. "They won't shoot," an eleven-year-old Negro boy said coolly, as a pack of looters fled at the approach of a busload of police. "The mayor said they aren't supposed to."

At 6:30 a.m., the first fire was in a shoe store. When fire engines screamed to the scene, rocks flew. One fireman, caught squarely in the jaw, was knocked from a truck to the gutter. More and more rioters were drawn to the streets by the sound of the sirens and a sense of summer excitement.

"The noise of destruction adds to its satisfaction," Elias Canetti notes in *Crowds and Power*. "The banging of windows and smashing of glass are the robust sounds of fresh life, the cries of something newborn." In Detroit, they proved to be—with the rattling of gunfire—the sounds of death. Throughout the Detroit riot there was—as in Newark—a spectacularly perverse mood of gaiety and light-hearted abandon in the mob—a "carnival spirit," as a shocked Mayor Cavanagh called it, echoing the words used by New Jersey's Governor Richard Hughes after he toured stricken Newark three weeks ago.

Looters skipped gingerly over broken glass to rake in wrist watches and clothing from shop windows. One group of hoods energetically dismantled a whole front porch and lobbed the bricks at police. Two small boys struggled down Twelfth Street with a load of milk cartons and a watermelon. Another staggered from a supermarket under the weight of a side of beef. One prosperous Negro used his Cadillac convertible to haul off a brand-new deep freeze.

Some of the looters were taking a methodical revenge upon the area's white merchants, whose comparatively high prices, often escalated to offset losses by theft and the cost of extra-high insurance premiums, irk the residents of slum neighborhoods. Most of the stores pillaged and destroyed were groceries, super-markets and furniture stores; of Detroit's 630 liquor stores, 250 were looted. Many drunks careened down Twelfth Street consuming their swag. Negro merchants scrawled "Soul Brother"—and in one case, "Sold Brother"—on their windows to warn the mobs off. But many of their stores were ravaged nonetheless.

The mobs cared nothing for "Negro leadership" either. When the riot was only a few hours old, John Conyers, one of Detroit's two Negro Congressmen, drove up Twelfth Street with Hubert Locke and Deputy School Superintendent Arthur Johnson. "Stay cool, we're with you!" Conyers shouted to the crowd. "Uncle Tom!" they shouted back. Someone heaved a bottle and the leaders beat a prompt retreat, not wanting to become "handkerchief heads" in the bandaged sense of the epithet. "You try to talk to these people," said Conyers unhappily, "and they'll knock you into the middle of next year."

Riots and looting spread through the afternoon over a 10.8-sq.-mi. area of the West Side almost as far north as the Northland Shopping Center. An entire mile of Twelfth Street was a corridor of flame; firemen answering the alarms were pelted with bricks, and at some point they abandoned their hoses in the streets and fled, only to be ordered back to the fire by Cavanagh.

Some 5,000 thieves and arsonists were ravaging the West Side. Williams Drug Store was a charred shell by dark. More than one grocery collapsed as though made of Lincoln Logs. A print shop erupted and took the next-door apartment house with it. In many skeletal structures the sole sign of life was a wailing burglar alarm. Lou's Men's Wear expired in a ball of flame. Meantime, a mob of 3,000 took up the torch on the East Side several miles away. The Weather Bureau's tornado watch offered brief hope of rain to damp the fires but it never came.

Readers of this book may associate such vengeful violence in America only with the recent expressions by black Americans of their fury. That would be a mistake. Reacting to the pain of enforced failure with explosive violence is a universal phenomenon. Consider the following account of white riots in New York City a hundred years before the Detroit riot. The prose of the writer of that time may be somewhat more purple than *Time* magazine's, but the event being described was similar.[2]

> The mobs that held fearful sway in our city during the memorable outbreak of violence in the month of July, 1863, were gathered in the overcrowded and neglected quarters of the city. As was stated by a leading journalist at that time: "The high brick blocks and closely packed houses where the mobs originated seemed to be literally hives of sickness and vice. It was wonderful to see, and difficult to believe [note] that so much misery, disease, and wretchedness can be so huddled together and hidden by high walls unvisited and unthought of, so near our own abodes. . . . To walk the streets as we walked them, in the hours of conflagration and riots, was like witnessing the day of judgment, with every wicked thing revealed, every sin and sorrow blazingly glared upon, every hidden abomination laid before Hell's expectant fire.

One might think that, after such an explosion, a mood of contrition overtakes the rioters. This is not so, however, when the desperation from which the outburst springs is so deep-rooted, as is shown in a journalistic account of the mood in the Detroit ghetto after the 1967 riot.[3]

> *He is a child of Detroit's ravaged ghetto, a lanky, spidery-legged kid whose hand-me-down pants stop a shin's length short of his narrow, pointy shoes. He sat with some of his pals on the railing outside an apartment house, gazing dully across Dexter Avenue at a block of charred ruins. It had been two weeks, but the acrid scent of smoke still hung in the air.*
>
> *"Those buildings goin' up was a pretty sight," the long-legged kid said. "I sat right here and watched them go. And there wasn't nothin' them honkies could do but sweat and strain to put it out."*
>
> *"Yeah, man," a pal chimed in, "it's about time those honkies started earnin' their money in this neighborhood."*
>
> *"You know," said Long Legs, "we made big news. They called this the country's worst race riot in history."*

[2]*Report of the Council of Hygiene and Public Health of the Citizens Association of New York*, 1866.

[3]*Newsweek.* "Report on Ghetto Mood in 1967," August 21, 1967, pp. 20-26. Copyright, Newsweek, Inc., August, 1967.

"Yeah," said another gangly kid, straddling the railing. "My kids goin' to study about that in school and they'll know their old man was part of it."

"We got the record, man," exulted another youth, the beefiest of the lot. "They can forget all about Watts and Newark and Harlem. This is where the riot to end all riots was held."

"That little girl that got shot, man," Long Legs said. "She shouldn't have been shot."

"That's the breaks, brother," Beefy replied, absently patting at the deep waves in his processed hair. "We in a war. Or hasn't anybody told you that?"

Everybody laughed.

They are another country, a land behind the looking-glass, a people as tragically distant from the ken of most white and many Negro Americans as the dark side of the moon. For decades, their world was invisible; now, in this fourth long, hot summer, it stands silhouetted in the light of a thousand fires—and as remote from understanding as ever. "First—let there be no mistake about it—the looting, arson, plunder and pillage which have occurred are not part of a civil-rights protest," Lyndon Johnson said in his post-Detroit television report to the nation. "That is crime—and crime must be dealt with forcefully, swiftly, certainly. . ." It was an accurate statement of the American law and the American will. But the hard-core ghetto—and particularly the ghetto young—speak quite another language.

And their tongue, in an hour of national peril, is well worth understanding. It is not the common tongue of Negro Americans. It tends at once to excite and chill those Negroes who have struggled somehow into a growing black middle class. It troubles many of the ghetto poor themselves—particularly the older poor whose lives are centered on the day-to-day issues of survival. It is instead the lingua franca of a minority within a minority: the angry young men consigned from broken homes through inadequate schools to a future of work at poverty wages—or, for more than one ghetto youth in four, the dole and the streets. It is the language of the people who make riots—and its use is spreading fast.

It is also the language of a garrison state. In the view from the street corners of Harlem or Watts or Detroit's West Side, the riots are rebellions, the rioters not criminals at all but the freedom fighters of an oppressed, beleaguered, powerless colony of the white world downtown. Words of bitterness suppressed for generations become the common currency. Stokely Carmichael and Rap Brown are the heroes because they say aloud, on national TV, what older Negroes had hardly dared think. "I hope you don't expect me to rap Rap," says a pert Harlem girl of 18 who wears her close-cropped "natural" coif almost like a flag of liberation. 'He's kinda crazy—but it's a feel-good crazy.''

There is now an air of desperation in the ghettos. Some say Whitey may listen; others actually believe he might even contemplate a Final Solution of concentration camps and gas chambers, but many of the ghetto young think the risk is worth all—even a man's life. Ed Bowen is a high-school dropout of 26; he fled from one failure to another, in the Army in Georgia, where he stole a jeep, wrecked it and was cashiered just thirteen days before his honorable discharge was due. Now he is back scuffling in Harlem, and he says: "People have been begging for years for a decent place to live, a job, some food, but they ain't got nothing, so they burn things down and maybe they'll get it." Bowen is, relatively speaking, an optimist. Others simply expect to die fighting—and are beyond caring. "I don't mind gettin' killed," says Donald, a jobless, 19-year-old corner boy in Chicago. "When I'm dead, they'll tell my kid, 'He died for a good cause'."

The cause, as the street corner sees it, is to seize the white man's attention by force, since a decade of nonviolent protest seems not to have altered the ghetto's life materially, and to make him look at what he has wrought. The riots are blind, deadly, destructive, criminal, yes—but to say they have nothing to do with "civil rights" is quite to miss the point. The rioters range, says Dr. Alvin Poussaint, a Negro psychiatrist at Tufts University, "from the plain damn angry to those with fantasies of taking over, to those who want a TV set, to those angry at their father and mother, to those caught up in hysteria, to those who will act only when they see the cops shoot someone." But he adds: "Rage is common to all of them." The rage is directed at the cheated hopes, the despond and finally the suffocating emptiness of the ghetto. "The chronic riot of their day-to-day lives," says Negro psychologist Kenneth Clark, "is, as far as they're concerned, no better than the acute riots . . . They don't have anything to lose, including their lives. It's not just desperation—it's what-the-hell."

Nor can the riots be written off as merely the holiday of the chronic criminal. In the benchmark insurrections of four summers—Watts, Newark, Detroit—roughly half the Negroes arrested on miscellaneous riot charges had no police records at all. "There is a growing body of myths emerging about the riots, ' said a UCLA task force reporting on a newly completed two-year study of Watts. "They center around the effort to distinguish between the 'good Negro' and the 'bad Negro' . . . This leads to the numbers game of guessing the percentage of 'bad Negroes' (2 to 5 per cent seems to be popular) and to a rationalization of better use of police power to deal with them." The task force's findings were quite to the contrary: its study indicated that 15 per cent of adult Watts Negroes actually joined the riot and 35 to 40 per cent more were "active"—and approving—spectators. And afterward, one Watts Negro in three approved of the riot; the majority who disapproved often expressed sympathy with the rioters or a sort of community pride that they had made the invisible man visible around the world.

Pride, indeed, is the first stunning fact discovered by the alien—and most whites today are alien—who crosses the line into that other country. "There's some sort of emancipation in it," says Poussaint. "It's like a festival, a sudden release of tensions, a feeling that they have freed themselves." Frederick J. Hacker, a white University of Southern California psychiatrist who crossed the line into postwar Watts, came back with similar findings. As Watts saw it, Hacker wrote, the riot "was the metamorphosis of the Negroes . . . from victims—historical objects—to masters . . . The people of Watts felt that for those four days they represented all Negroes, all the rebellions against all injustice. . . . What must be understood by the rest of America is that, for the lower-class Negro, riots are not criminal, but a legitimate weapon in a morally justified civil war.". . .

Efelka Brown, 29, is the assistant manager of a newly opened service station where Watts's equivalent of the Veterans of Foreign Wars, the "Sons of Watts," will train the idle young in a tradeable skill. "We rioted in Watts," says Brown. 'The Man put up the doctors' building down the street, they going to build us up a clinic and the way I heard, people don't have to pay but a dollar a year and that's for paper work. They have did this for us after the riot. What are these people riotin' about in other cities? They want recognition. . . and the only way they goin' get it is to riot. The only way . . . We don't want to overthrow the country—we just want what we ain't got."

And there is the equally real face of defeat. On the burnt-out block called Charcoal Alley No. 1, Henry Leonard Johnson Jr. lay flat in the grass, slugged at a 50-cent bottle of Applejack wine and delivered a soliloquy to a relentlessly sunny and utterly indifferent sky. He had, he announced, spent twelve of his 28 years in jail; as a consequence he could not find work; there is a car-wash job in Torrance, but Torrance is 20 miles away and Johnson has no car. So he lay in the grass and sipped his wine and told the sky, "F— Whitey. I don't believe in nothin'. I feel like they ought to burn down the whole world. Just let it burn down, baby.". . .

They roared on two wheels into "Burma Road"—Harlem's name for Lenox Avenue and braked for beers at the Royal Flush Bar. The car belongs to Joe-Joe, a chunky, dark 20-year-old who stuck through high school and now works at the Post Office. But the beerklatsch is on J.B., a young man of flash and dash in his crisp yellow sport shirt, his hip-hugging black gabardines and his rakish, stingy-brim straw hat. J.B., at 20, is a numbers runner; he has a hustle, and he has it made.

"The Man, he worried now," says J.B., "'cause he know we ain't takin' no more his s—. Anybody come rollin' into a city with tanks got to be afraid of somethin'. Anyplace you see a tank, you know there got to be a war goin' on, right? And that's what this is, baby—war!"

No one disagrees. Someone mentions Rap Brown.

"That's my man!" J.B. exclaims. "Ain't nobody in the world gonna get nothin' if he don't fight for it. The black man's been takin' low too long."

"That's right, that's right," says Skeeter. He is 19 and nowhere, a dropout

(at 14) living with a sister and an aunt, and whatever J.B. says, Skeeter echoes, "That s right."

But Joe-Joe half disagrees. "I used to watch ole Stokely up there on TV tellin' off the white people. I thought he was crazy, 'cause I thought he was gonna get hisself killed like Malcolm. But you know, when a man says what all the time you been thinkin', you wonder if maybe you ain't crazy. I mean like if you feel inside knotted all the time, maybe it's better if you make some noise." He sips at his beer. "Like when I broke my big toe cuttin' the fool [roughhous- ing] out at Coney Island. I went on limpin' around grinnin', not lettin' on to nobody I was hurt. But I had to tell 'em 'cause I couldn't stand it no more. And like, you know, these two cats crossed their arms and made like a seat and carried me to the beach clinic. Now supposin' I hadn't said nothin'?"

So Joe-Joe figures that, if there is another Harlem riot, he will join in. "Man," he says, "you know my sister wouldn't let me in the street that last time. But I bet you I'm gonna get me somethin' next time . . . I just might break me some windows, grab me some rags and throw me some bottles."

J.B. isn't sure. He "wouldn't mind knockin' me some cracker heads togeth- er," but, like any budding entrepreneur, he thinks rioting might be bad for business. Yet he too will be there if a new riot comes. "I mean," he says, "that's where it's at."

And so the riots are, at least in part, a declaration of dependence on white America; they are as well, in a curious way, an act not of utter despair but of flickering hope that white America may at last listen. . . .

And the clock is running.

Percy Wiggins went into the Army with a police record, served a year in Vietnam, came home to Chicago three months ago confident that his service record would help him land a job. It hasn't, and now Wiggins is bitter. "I couldn't even get a job driving a cab," he said. "The lowest paid job in the world and I couldn't even get that. You know, now I feel I made a great mistake goin' to Vietnam. Over there I fought with the white guys and I was considered a man. Now I'm nothin' but a lousy dog."

So now he runs with the old crowd, the hard ghetto kids he thought he had outgrown in the Army, and he is beginning to speak their language. "I'm not sayin' it's good to burn down another man's home," he says. "But if that's what it takes to do it, I say burn it down."

Is it surprising that such casualties of American society as black Americans can abandon a tradition of submissiveness? Charles Silberman helps to explain how apathy developed into explosive fury.[4]

[4]From Charles E. Silberman, *Crisis in Black and White*, New York: Random House, Inc., 1964, pp. 293-294, 296-301. Reprinted by permission.

Despair and apathy, of course, are basic ingredients of any lower-class community, and a good many problems attributed to Negroes because of their race in fact are due to their class. But there is a special quality to the despair of the Negro slum that distinguishes it from any other. For the youngster growing up in Harlem or any other Negro slum, the gates of life clang shut at a terrifyingly early age. For one thing, the children become aware almost from infancy of the opprobrium Americans attach to color. They feel it in their parents' voices as they are warned to behave when they stray beyond the ghetto's wall. They become aware of it as they begin to watch television, or go to the movies, or read the mass-circulation magazines; beauty, success, and status all wear a white skin. They learn to feel ashamed of their color as they learn to talk, and thereby to absorb the invidiousness our very language attaches to color. White represents purity and goodness, black represents evil. The white lie is the permissible misstatement, the black lie the inexcusable falsehood; the black sheep is the one who goes astray (and when he goes astray, he receives a black mark on his record), defeat is black (the stock market crashed on "Black Thursday"), victory white. Even James Weldon Johnson's "Negro National Anthem" speaks of Negroes "treading our path through the blood of the slaughtered/ . . . Till now we stand at last/*Where the white gleam of our bright star is cast*." [Emphasis added]

Language aside, Negro children learn soon enough—from their father's menial job, or lack of it, from his mixture of fear and deference and hate of "the man"—that the world is white and they are black. And the odds are small indeed that a Negro child can grow up without being abused or patronized, without being convinced by a hundred big and small humiliations, that he has no worth and no chance. "One did not have to be very bright," Baldwin has written of his childhood in Harlem, "to realize how little one could do to change one's situation; one did not have to be abnormally sensitive to be worn down to a cutting edge by the incessant and gratuitous humiliation and danger one encountered every working day, all day long."

Negroes are given humiliation, insult, and embarrassment as a daily diet, and without regard to individual merit. They are convinced, as a result, that most whites never see them as individuals, that all Negroes look alike to whites, the theme of "facelessness" and "invisibility" runs through Negro literature. "No more fiendish punishment could be devised, were such a thing physically possible," the philosopher William James once wrote, "than that one should be turned loose in society and remain unnoticed by all the members thereof." The Negro is noticed, of course, for in rejecting them, white society must thereby notice him. But the Negro, too often, is noticed only to be rejected. "The dehumanized image of the Negro which white Americans carry in their minds, the anti-Negro epithets continuously on their lips," Richard Wright has written, 'exclude the contemporary Negro as truly as though he were kept in a steel prison."

This sense of rejection by American society, a sense which dominates the lower-class Negro's life, tends to destroy his feeling of responsibility to law and authority; law and authority are always white and middle class and always seem designed to keep the lower-class Negro in his place. It also creates a good deal of class conflict and antagonism within the Negro community. Lower-class Negroes tend to resent Negroes who have achieved economic success, especially if the success is in the white world, for they are convinced that whites have so stacked the cards against Negroes that none can rise through ability or merit. Hence, if another Negro has "made it" in the white world it must be because of favoritism, because he pandered to white prejudice or white vanities, and thereby betrayed his own race. (Since ability counts for naught in the white world, why else has he advanced while I'm held back?) This kind of intra-group hostility is fairly typical of disadvantaged groups—witness the "shanty Irish" resentment of the "lace-curtain Irish" a generation or two ago. And lower-class Negroes' resentment of "dickety" Negroes frequently exists side-by-side with a vicarious delight that "one of our boys has made it."

Most important of all, however, the Negro reacts to exclusion with anger and hate. Nor is it just the sullen, apathetic tenement dweller who hates "the man." On the contrary, it is hard to imagine how any Negro American, no matter how well born or placed, can escape a deep sense of anger and a burning hatred of things white. Some are better able to repress it than others, but few escape its demonic force. "To be a Negro in this country and to be relatively conscious," James Baldwin has written, "is to be in a rage almost all the time." With those Negroes who deny their hatred, the essayist-novelist J. Saunders Redding has written, "I have no quarrel . . . it is simply that I do not believe them." Some Negroes, he concedes, may be able to order their lives so as to avoid the experience of prejudice and discrimination—but to do so, in his view, requires an effort so great as to bring them to a psychopathic brink. "One's heart is sickened," he writes, "at the realization of the primal energy that goes into the sheer business of living as a Negro in the United States—in any one of the United States." It is impossible, in Redding's view, for a Negro to avoid a dual personality; inevitably, one part of him reacts to people and events as an individual, the other part reacts as a Negro.

The inevitability and the horror of this fact—the unending consciousness of color—were driven home to Redding by a traumatic experience he describes in his moving essay, "On Being Negro In America." The incident occurred during the thirties, when Redding was teaching at a Negro college in Louisville. His office window overlooked a white slum beginning at the edge of the campus. Standing at the office window one quiet winter Saturday, he saw a young woman lurching and staggering in his back yard, until she fell face down in the snow. He couldn't tell whether she was sick or drunk. "Pity rose in me," he relates, "but at the same time something else also—a gloating satisfaction that she was white. Sharply and concurrently felt, the two emotions were of equal strength, in perfect balance, and the corporeal I, fixed in a trance at the window, oscillated between them." The gloating won out. Redding decided not to go to her aid, but salved his conscience by calling the police to report "a drunken woman lying in the back yard of a house on Eighth Street." An hour later, the police came—and the next morning, Redding read on a back page of a newspaper that the woman had died of exposure following an epileptic seizure. "One can wash his hands," Redding concludes, "but the smudges and scars on the psyche are different."

Redding was troubled by the conflict between his instincts as a Negro and his instincts as a human being, and scarred by his decision to follow the former. A good many Negroes would have felt no such qualms of conscience afterward, nor would they have felt beforehand the tug of war Redding describes, between his desire to help the woman and his glee that a white person was in trouble. On Sunday, June 3, 1962, when news was flashed around the United States that a chartered airplane bound from Paris to Atlanta had crashed, killing 130 of the 132 aboard, Malcolm X, then the number two man in the Black Muslim movement . . . was delivering a sermon to fifteen hundred Muslims in Los Angeles. He immediately shared the good news with his audience:

I would like to announce a very beautiful thing that has happened . . . Somebody came and told me that [God] had answered our prayers in France. He dropped an airplane out of the sky with over 120 white people in it because the Muslims believe in an eye for an eye and a tooth for a tooth. But thanks to God, or Jehovah or Allah, we will continue to pray and we hope that every day another plane falls out of the sky . . . We call on our God—He gets rid of 120 of them at one whop.

. . . To be sure, the Muslims have been able to enroll no more than 100,000, and perhaps as few as 50,000, Negroes as active members. But they have captured the sympathy of an enormous segment of Northern urban Negroes, who are unwilling to embrace the Muslim's strict discipline and religious tenets but who are delighted to hear the anger they feel being expressed so clearly. "I don't know how many followers he's got," a Harlem cabdriver told *Life* photographer Gordon Parks, who had just left Malcolm X, "but he has sure got a hell of a lot of well wishers." The cabbie was one of the latter. "Those Muslims or Moslems, 'ever what you call 'em, make more sense to me than the NAACP and Urban League and all the rest of them put together," he told Parks. "They're down on the good earth with the brother. They're for their own people and that Malcolm ain't afraid to tell Mr. Charlie, the FBI or the cops or nobody where to get off. You don't see him pussyfootin' 'round the whites like he's scared of them." Asked whether the Muslims hated all white men, the cabbie replied succinctly that "if they don't, they should, 'cause [the whites] sure don't waste no love on us. I used to live in Mobile and I lived in Memphis and I've lived in New York for fifteen years," the driver finished, "and I've come to one conclusion. No matter where the white man is, he's the same—the only thing he respects is force. And the only things gonna change him is some lead in the belly."

Nor are the relatively uneducated the only ones to respond to the Muslim's siren song of hate. On the contrary, the Muslims have struck a responsive chord in the most sophisticated Negro circles—among men and women in the forefront of the drive for integration, as well as in those who have held themselves aloof from any contact with "the problem." "Malcolm says things you or I would not say," a former president of the New York NAACP chapter confesses in admiration. "When he says those things, when he talks about the white man, even those of us who are repelled by his philosophy secretly cheer a little outside ourselves, because Malcolm X really does tell 'em, and we know he frightens the white man. We clap."

As noted in the introduction to this section, explosions lead to counter-explosions. At any given point in a sequence of hostile responses by some persons to threatening behavior by others, it is of course difficult to say which is explosion and which is counterexplosion.

In the context of race, black Americans are to be understood as attempting to improve their bargaining power, enhance and exercise their legal rights, and evoke sentiments of solidarity and empathy from their fellow Americans. For many Americans such efforts are threats. They are as frustrating to many white Americans as second-class citizenship is to black Americans. To many white Americans, the frustrations of competition in a marketing society are such that only by asserting a sense of racial superiority can they avoid the sense of failure. Given such a state of affairs, explosive vengefulness is not a monopoly of blacks. Consider what happened in Selma, Alabama, in the spring of 1965 when Negroes, supported by some whites from the North, attempted to hold a peaceful march to symbolize their grievances.[5]

Filling out a marching form at Brown's Chapel was 16-year-old Viola Jackson of Selma (no relation to the late Jimmy Lee Jackson.) *Have you ever*

[5]From Warren Hinckle and David Welsh, "Five Battles of Selma," *Ramparts*, June 1965. pp. 26-28. Reprinted by permission.

been arrested? NO. *Have you ever been beaten?* YES. *Do you have any ailments that should be checked before the march?* NO. She handed in the paper and went outside where the marchers were forming.

The detailed form was typical of the style of military organization that the SNCC people and Dr. King's lieutenants adopted for the Selma campaign. The march itself was planned in military style: participants were to line up two abreast, grouped into squads of 25 people, and then into companies of four squads each. The leaders of the march—John Lewis of SNCC and Hosea Williams of SCLC—had originally planned to organize the squads on paper. But the last minute influx of marchers made that impractical, so everyone was ordered outside to the playground behind Brown's Chapel and told to line up in pairs. Forty-five minutes later, six companies were ready to march.

The Union leadership had, in its own way, prepared for the expected confrontation with the Confederate forces: four ambulances were parked on Sylvan Street, ten doctors and nurses, mostly from New York, had flown to Montgomery and driven to Selma the night before. They were volunteers of the Medical Committee for Human Rights. When the march started, they followed in the file of ambulances at the end of the line.

Viola Jackson found herself in the second company, first squad. Standing in front of her was a young Negro wearing a sweatshirt. His marching companion was a tall white youth wearing a blue windbreaker jacket, blue cap and carrying a round knapsack on his back. They introduced themselves. The Negro was Charles Mauldin, an 18-year-old junior at the R. B. Hudson High School, Selma's Negro high, and President of the 1500-member Selma Youth Movement. Slight of build and articulate of expression, he was polite and friendly. The white was Jim Benston, an unsalaried member of the SCLC Selma staff. Benston is 20 and blond and has a scraggly yellow beard. He is from Arkansas and is hated by the cops because they consider him a double traitor: to the South and to his Caucasian race. He became a prime target for clubbing.

The march began without heraldry. Viola Jackson and Charles Mauldin and Jim Benston walked close together as the three-block-long line moved slowly down Sylvan Street and up Water Avenue, through the Negro business district, to the bridge. Groups of Selma citizens stood in sullen, compressed groups on street corners and watched. The marchers passed the Selma Radiator Shop. A white man taunted Viola: "Black bitch. Got a white boy to play with, huh?" As they reached Broad Street—the main street of Selma that leads onto the bridge—a white woman driving a green pick-up truck tried to run down Benston. He leaped out of the way. Police had refused to direct traffic for the marchers, except to halt cars as the long line turned onto the bridge at Broad Street. So the marchers had to be wary of white citizens with cars. The last thing Viola and the two boys saw as they walked onto the bridge was the troopers and possemen stationed by the Selma Times Journal building, waiting patiently. They knew the marchers would be coming back.

The view from the other side of the Pettus Bridge—looking toward Selma—was less than inspiring. The old brick buildings that line the bluffs above the slow-flowing river were gradually falling away. The sloping bluffs were spotted with bricks, discarded building materials and decaying underbrush. Viola Jackson and Charles Mauldin and Jim Benston could look back at the river bluffs and the long line of marchers behind them on the bridge, but they couldn't tell what was happening ahead of them on the highway. All they could see were police cars, State Trooper cars, sheriff's cars—a silent, stationary armada filling all four lanes of the Jefferson Davis Highway. Viola whispered that she had never seen so many police cars in one place in her life. A large, surly crowd of Selma white citizens—hooting, snorting, like spectators at a bull fight—stood on the trunks of parked cars or jammed the frontage area of roadside businesses, seeking ring-side seats. Newsmen were herded together in front of the Lehman Pontiac building some distance from the marchers and assigned several troopers for "protection."

State troopers, headed by Major John Cloud, lined the highway three deep. Colonel Lingo watched from his automobile parked near Lehman's Grocery. As the marchers approached, Major Cloud hailed them: "This is an unlawful assembly,' he said. "You have two minutes to turn around and go back to your church." The leaders of the march were now within several feet of the phalanx of troopers who held their clubs at the ready. Major Cloud took out his watch and started counting. The silence was total. Exactly one minute and five seconds later Major Cloud ordered, "Troopers forward." The blue-clad troopers leaped ahead, clubs swinging, moving with a sudden force that bowled over line after line of marchers. The first groups of Negroes went to the ground screaming, their knapsacks and bags spilling onto the highway. The white spectators cheered.

The marchers, pushed back by the billy club attack, grouped together on the grassy, gasoline-soiled dividing strip in the center of the highway. They knelt and began to pray. The troopers rushed in again, banging heads, and then retreated. Viola and the two boys knelt together. For two minutes, a tense silence was broken only by the sounds of the Confederate forces strapping on their gas masks and the buzz-buzz-buzz of the cattle prods. Sheriff Clark ordered his possemen to mount up. "Get those god damn niggers—and get those god damn white niggers,' he said.

As the troopers heaved the first tear gas bombs into the praying Negroes, the crowd of several hundred white onlookers broke into prolonged cheering. "Give it to the damnyankees. Give it to the niggers." The first were feeler bombs; the marchers coughed and gagged, but didn't move. Then the troopers let loose with a heavy barrage of gas shells. Several bombs landed near Viola and the two boys, and then they couldn't see each other anymore.

For Charles Mauldin, it was like a quick visit to hell. "The gas was so thick that you could almost reach up and grab it. It seemed to lift me up and fill my lungs and I went down." Some of the marchers panicked and ran. They couldn't see where they were going and they ran into cars and buildings. A young girl collapsed inside the treads of a tractor. Mauldin pulled her out. Marchers scrambled over a barbed wire fence, tearing their clothes and scratching their stomachs, and ran down blindly toward the muddy river. The troopers, protected by gas masks, moved through the gasping, fainting Negroes and beat them with clubs. When Mauldin finally staggered in retreat back onto the bridge, a posseman on horseback rode by and hit him across the neck with an eight-foot bull whip. "What do you want, nigger, jump off the bridge? Well, go on, jump." The troopers and the possemen herded the fleeing Negroes across the bridge with cattle prods, clubs and whips. Those who were too young or too old to move fast enough got hit the most. When they got to the Selma end of the bridge, the possemen and deputies who had been patiently waiting there attacked them anew with clubs and whips and chased them through the streets down toward the Negro quarter.

For Jim Benston, it was worse. After the first tear gas attack, he lay on the ground trying to breathe. He looked up and a trooper was standing in front of him, staring down through the big goggle-eyes of his gas mask. The trooper slowly lifted his tear gas gun and shot it off directly into Benston's face. "I was knocked out for maybe five minutes. When I woke up I was in a cloud. I couldn't breathe and I couldn't see. I was coughing and I was sick. It was like the world had gone away. I laid there on the grass for a few minutes and then I felt around me, trying to see if anybody else was still there. I couldn't feel anybody. They were all gone. I was the only one left." Benston staggered off to his right, through a used car lot, and collapsed in a small field. A dozen or so other marchers lay there, bleeding, coughing, trying to catch their breath. Then Benston heard horses, and shrill rebel battle yells. The possemen were charging the band of prone marchers. All the posse had clubs and some of them had whips and they struck out at anything they could see. "They tried to get the horses to run over us," Benston said. "They came charging through where we were laying on the grass and tried to hit us with the horses, but the horses had more sense. One posseman tried to get his horse to rear up and land on top of a man near me, but the horse wouldn't do it. Horses have more sense." The marchers got up and ran toward the bridge. The possemen rode in front of them and set off tear gas bombs in their path, forcing them through the new pockets of gas. On the bridge, Benston was clubbed at least 25 times. As he ran down the narrow pedestrian sidewalk, possemen would take turns, galloping by, clubbing him, laughing. He pulled his knapsack up to cover his head and neck. "That knapsack saved my life," he said. Some of the possemen, crazy with excitement, tried to force their horses up onto the narrow walkway to run down the fleeing marchers. As the possemen galloped up and down the concrete bridge, swinging clubs and whips, one sheriff's volunteer leaned forward and screamed in his horse's ear, "Bite them, bite them, bite the niggers." The possemen chased Benston's group for two blocks into Selma, until the streets became crowded. Possemen don't generally whip people in public.

For Viola Jackson, it didn't last long. She was knocked down on the dividing strip and dug her fingernails into the ground. The thick tear gas hung like heavy cigarette smoke between the blades of grass and curled around her fingers. She managed to get up and tried to run, but she couldn't go on. Her breath came shorter. Then she couldn't see, and she fell down onto the ground and didn't get up. More shells fell nearby, and the gas covered her fallen body like a blanket.

The police at first wouldn't let the waiting Union ambulances onto the bridge to pick up the wounded. When they did, finally, the volunteer drivers and doctors and nurses worked frantically, loading the injured and racing them to the Good Samaritan Hospital.

Sheriff Clark's possemen chased the Negroes down to the housing project, but were stopped by Selma Safety Director Baker. Baker said he had his city police surrounding the project area and saw no need for further force. The Selma Times-Journal quoted Clark as replying to Baker: "I've already waited a month too damn long about moving in."

In the ensuing thirty minutes before the possemen and the troopers cleared out of the housing project, the First Baptist Church on Sylvan Street was raided by Confederates. They fired tear gas into the church, then went inside and threw a Negro teenager through a devotional window. They also tear-gassed one of the Negro homes along Sylvan Street and chased children through the project with their horses. Some of the younger Negroes began to throw bricks at the troopers, and, in a few moments of extraordinary juvenile passion, the troopers picked up the bricks and threw them back. The angry, shattered marchers crowded into Brown's Chapel where John Lewis of SNCC told them (before he went to the hospital for treatment of a head injury), "I don't see how President Johnson can send troops to Vietnam. I don't see how he can send troops to the Congo. I don t see how he can send troops to Africa and can't send troops to Selma, Alabama."

At the Good Samaritan Hospital, a modernistic building dedicated in 1964 and operated for Selma's Negroes by the Edmundite Fathers, the emergency rooms looked like a scene out of *Birth of a Nation*. The wounded marchers were propped on carts and tables and on the floor—bleeding and sobbing. The sickening odor of tear gas filled the emergency rooms. Tables were removed from the employees' dining room and the injured were laid on the floor. The tear gas victims, coughing and gasping violently, overflowed into the hospital corridors. Several hours later, most of the 84 people taken to the hospital were deposited in a makeshift recovery area—the lounge of the hospital's nursing home—to await friends or relatives. Seventeen were injured seriously enough to be admitted for treatment—fractured ribs, fractured wrists, head wounds, broken teeth. Among those admitted was Viola Jackson, 16, "for extended treatment of tear gas effect and hysteria."

After the Negroes in the project were forced indoors, Sheriff Clark's posse rode uptown, looking for more Negroes. They yelled at Negroes walking on the streets and beat with their night-sticks on the hoods of cars with Negro drivers. "Get the hell out of town. Go on. We mean it. We want all the niggers off the street.'

By dusk, not one Negro could be found on the streets of Selma.

Physically violent expressions of vengefulness are the most spectacular kind, but they are not the only kind, and they may not be the most unpleasant. Many people explode quietly, or, more exactly, manifest vengeful hostility in nonviolent but still deadly ways as, for instance, in "the pseudo-conservative revolt" in American political life. Richard Hofstadter explains what he means by "pseudo-conservative" as distinct from genuine conservatism in an article written to explain the Joseph McCarthy anti-Communist hysteria of the 1950's; the reader will recognize the appropriateness of Hofstadter's analysis to the resurgence of the pseudo-conservative revolt in the late 1960's.[6]

Who is the pseudo-conservative, and what does he want? It is impossible to identify him by class, for the pseudo-conservative impulse can be found in practically all classes in society, although its power probably rests largely upon its appeal to the less educated members of the middle classes. The ideology of pseudo-conservatism can be characterized but not defined, because the pseudo-conservative tends to be more than ordinarily incoherent about politics. The lady who, when General Eisenhower's victory over Senator Taft had finally become official, stalked out of the Hilton Hotel declaiming, "This means eight more years of socialism" was probably a fairly good representative of the pseudo-conservative mentality. So also were the gentlemen who, at the Freedom Congress held at Omaha over a year ago by some "patriotic" organizations, objected to Earl Warren's appointment to the Supreme Court with the assertion: "Middle-of-the-road thinking can and will destroy us"; the general who spoke to the same group, demanding "an Air Force capable of wiping out the Russian Air Force and industry in one sweep," but also "a material reduction in military expenditures",[7] the people who a few years ago believed simultaneously that we

[6]From Richard Hofstadter, "The Pseudo-Conservative Revolt," in Daniel Bell (Ed.), *The Radical Right*, Garden City, New York: Doubleday Anchor, 1964, pp. 77-91. Reprinted by permission.

[7]On the Omaha Freedom Congress see Leonard Boasberg, "Radical Reactionaries," *The Progressive*, December, 1953.

had no business to be fighting communism in Korea, but that the war should immediately be extended to an Asia-wide crusade against communism. . . .

The restlessness, suspicion and fear manifested in various phases of the pseudo-conservative revolt give evidence of the real suffering which the pseudo-conservative experiences in his capacity as a citizen. He believes himself to be living in a world in which he is spied upon, plotted against, betrayed, and very likely destined for total ruin. He feels that his liberties have been arbitrarily and outrageously invaded. He is opposed to almost everything that has happened in American politics for the past twenty years. He hates the very thought of Franklin D. Roosevelt. He is disturbed deeply by American participation in the United Nations, which he can see only as a sinister organization. He sees his own country as being so weak that it is constantly about to fall victim to subversion; and yet he feels that it is so all-powerful that any failure it may experience in getting its way in the world—for instance, in the Orient—cannot possibly be due to its limitations but must be attributed to its having been betrayed.[8] He is the most bitter of all our citizens about our involvement in the wars of the past, but seems the least concerned about avoiding the next one. While he naturally does not like Soviet communism, what distinguishes him from the rest of us who also dislike it is that he shows little interest in, is often indeed bitterly hostile to such realistic measures as might actually strengthen the United States vis-à-vis Russia. He would much rather concern himself with the domestic scene, where communism is weak, than with those areas of the world where it is really strong and threatening. He wants to have nothing to do with the democratic nations of Western Europe, which seem to draw more of his ire than the Soviet Communists, and he is opposed to all "give-away programs" designed to aid and strengthen these nations. Indeed, he is likely to be antagonistic to most of the operations of our federal government except Congressional investigations, and to almost all of its expenditures. Not always, however, does he go so far as the speaker at the Freedom Congress who attributed the greater part of our national difficulties to "this nasty, stinking 16th [income tax] Amendment."

What I wish to suggest . . . is that pseudo-conservatism is in good part a product of the rootlessness and heterogeneity of American life, and above all, of its peculiar scramble for status and its peculiar search for secure identity. Normally there is a world of difference between one's sense of national identity or cultural belonging and one's social status. However, in American historical development, these two things, so easily distinguishable in analysis, have been jumbled together in reality, and it is precisely this that has given such a special poignancy and urgency to our status-strivings. In this country a person's status—that is, his relative place in the prestige hierarchy of his community—and his

---

[8]See the comments of D. W. Brogan in "The Illusion of American Omnipotence," *Harper's*, December, 1952.

rudimentary sense of belonging to the community—that is, what we call his "Americanism"—have been intimately joined. Because, as a people extremely democratic in our social institutions, we have had no clear, consistent and recognizable system of status, our personal status problems have an unusual intensity. Because we no longer have the relative ethnic homogeneity we had up to about eighty years ago, our sense of belonging has long had about it a high degree of uncertainty. We boast of "the melting pot," but we are not quite sure what it is that will remain when we have been melted down.

We have always been proud of the high degree of occupational mobility in our country—of the greater readiness, as compared with other countries, with which a person starting in a very humble plae in our social structure could rise to a position of moderate wealth and status, and with which a person starting with a middling position could rise to great eminence. We have looked upon this as laudable in principle, for it is democratic, and as pragmatically desirable, for it has served many a man as a stimulus to effort and has, no doubt, a great deal to do with the energetic and effectual tone of our economic life. The American pattern of occupational mobility, while often much exaggerated, as in the Horatio Alger stories and a great deal of the rest of our mythology, may properly be credited with many of the virtues and beneficial effects that are usually attributed to it. But this occupational and social mobility, compounded by our extraordinary mobility from place to place, has also had its less frequent-ly recognized drawbacks. Not the least of them is that this has become a country in which so many people do not know who they are or what they are or what they belong to or what belongs to them. It is a country of people whose status expectations are random and uncertain, and yet whose status aspirations have been whipped up to a high pitch by our democratic ethos and our rags-to-riches mythology.[9]

In a country where physical needs have been, by the scale of the world's living standards, on the whole well met, the luxury of questing after status has assumed an unusually prominent place in our civic consciousness. Political life is not simply an arena in which the conflicting interests of various social groups in concrete material gains are fought out; it is also an arena into which status aspirations and frustrations are, as the psychologists would say, projected. It is at this point that the issues of politics, or the pretended issues of politics, become

[9]Cf. in this respect the observation of Tocqueville: "It cannot be denied that democratic instittuions strongly tend to promote the feeling of envy in the human heart, not so much because they afford to everyone the means of rising to the same level with others as because these means perpetually disappoint the persons who employ them. Democratic institutions awaken and foster a passion for equality which they can never entirely satisfy." Alexis de Tocqueville, *Democracy in America*, ed. by Phillips Bradley (New York, 1945), Vol. I, p. 201.

interwoven with and dependent upon the personal problems of individuals. We have, at all times, two kinds of processes going on in inextricable connection with each other: *interest politics*, the clash of material aims and needs among various groups and blocs; and *status politics*, the clash of various projective rationalizations arising from status aspirations and other personal motives. In times of depression and economic discontent—and by and large in times of acute national emergency—politics is more clearly a matter of interests, although of course status considerations are still present. In times of prosperity and general well-being on the material plane, status considerations among the masses can become much more influential in our politics. The two periods in our recent history in which status politics has been particularly prominent, the present era and the 1920s, have both been periods of prosperity.

During depressions, the dominant motif in dissent takes expression in proposals for reform or in panaceas. Dissent then tends to be highly programmatic—that is, it gets itself embodied in many kinds of concrete legislative proposals. It is also future-oriented and forward-looking, in the sense that it looks to a time when the adoption of this or that program will materially alleviate or eliminate certain discontents. In prosperity, however, when status politics becomes relatively more important, there is a tendency to embody discontent not so much in legislative proposals as in grousing. For the basic aspirations that underlie status discontent are only partially conscious, and, even so far as they are conscious, it is difficult to give them a programmatic expression. It is more difficult for the old lady who belongs to the D.A.R. and who sees her ancestral home swamped by new working-class dwellings to express her animus in concrete proposals of any degree of reality than it is, say, for the jobless worker during a slump to rally to a relief program. Therefore, it is the tendency of status politics to be expressed more in vindictiveness, in sour memories, in the search for scapegoats, than in realistic proposals for positive action.[10]

Paradoxically the intense status concerns of present-day politics are shared by two types of persons who arrive at them, in a sense, from opposite directions.

[10]Cf. Samuel Lubell's characterization of isolationism as a vengeful memory. *The Future of American Politics* (New York, 1952), Chapter VII. See also the comments of Leo Lowenthal and Norbert Guterman on the right-wing agitator: "The agitator seems to steer clear of the area of material needs on which liberal and democratic movements concentrate; his main concern is a sphere of frustration that is usually ignored in traditional politics. The programs that concentrate on material needs seem to overlook that area of moral uncertainties and emotional frustrations that are the immediate manifestations of malaise. It may therefore be conjectured that his followers find the agitator's statements attractive not because he occasionally promises to 'maintain the American standards of living' or to provide a job for everyone, but because he intimates that he will give them the emotional satisfactions that are denied them in the contemporary social and economic set-up. He offers attitudes, not bread." *Prophets of Deceit* (New York, 1949), pp. 91-92.

The first are found among some types of old-family, Anglo-Saxon Protestants, and the second are found among many types of immigrant families, most notably among the Germans and Irish, who are very frequently Catholic.

The Anglo-Saxons are most disposed toward pseudo-conservatism when they are losing caste, the immigrants when they are gaining.

Consider first the old-family Americans. These people, whose stocks were once far more unequivocally dominant in America than they are today, feel that their ancestors made and settled and fought for this country. They have a certain inherited sense of proprietorship in it. Since America has always accorded a certain special deference to old families—so many of our families are *new*—these people have considerable claims to status by descent, which they celebrate by membership in such organizations as the D.A.R. and the S.A.R. But large numbers of them are actually losing their other claims to status. For there are among them a considerable number of the shabby genteel, of those who for one reason or another have lost their old objective positions in the life of business and politics and the professions, and who therefore cling with exceptional desperation to such remnants of their prestige as they can muster from their ancestors. These people, although very often quite-well-to-do, feel that they have been pushed out of their rightful place in American life, even out of their neighborhoods. Most of them have been traditional Republicans by family inheritance, and they have felt themselves edged aside by the immigrants, the trade unions, and the urban machines in the past thirty years. When the immigrants were weak, these native elements used to indulge themselves in ethnic and religious snobberies at their expense. Now the immigrant groups have developed ample means, political and economic, of self-defense, and the second and third generations have become considerably more capable of looking out for themselves. Some of the old-family Americans have turned to find new objects for their resentment among liberals, left-wingers, intellectuals and the like—for in true pseudo-conservative fashion they relish weak victims and shrink from asserting themselves against the strong.

New-family Americans have had their own peculiar status problem. From 1881 to 1900 over 8,800,000 immigrants came here, during the next twenty years another 14,500,000. These immigrants, together with their descendants, constitute such a large portion of the population that Margaret Mead, in a stimulating analysis of our national character, has persuasively urged that the characteristic American outlook is now a third-generation point of view.[11] In their search for new lives and new nationality, these immigrants have suffered much, and they have been rebuffed and made to feel inferior by the "native stock," commonly being excluded from the better occupations and even from what has bitterly been called "first-class citizenship." Insecurity over social

[11]Margaret Mead, *And Keep Your Powder Dry*, (New York, 1942), Chapter III.

status has thus been mixed with insecurity over one's very identity and sense of belonging. Achieving a better type of job or a better social status and becoming ' more American" have become practically syonymous, and the passions that ordinarily attach to social position have been vastly heightened by being associated with the need to belong.

The problems raised by the tasks of keeping the family together, disciplining children for the American race for success, trying to conform to unfamiliar standards, protecting economic and social status won at the cost of much sacrifice, holding the respect of children who grow American more rapidly than their parents, have thrown heavy burdens on the internal relationships of many new American families. Both new and old American families have been troubled by the changes of the past thirty years—the new because of their striving for middle-class respectability and American identity, the old because of their efforts to maintain an inherited social position and to realize under increasingly unfavorable social conditions imperatives of character and personal conduct deriving from nineteenth-century, Yankee-Protestant-rural backgrounds. The relations between generations, being cast in no stable mold, have been disordered, and the status anxieties of parents have been inflicted upon children. Often parents entertain status aspirations that they are unable to gratify, or that they can gratify only at exceptional psychic cost. Their children are expected to relieve their frustrations and redeem their lives. They become objects to be manipulated to that end. An extraordinarily high level of achievement is expected of them, and along with it a tremendous effort to conform and be respectable. From the standpoint of the children these expectations often appear in the form of an exorbitantly demanding authority that one dare not question or defy. Resistance and hostility, finding no moderate outlet in give-and-take, have to be suppressed, and reappear in the form of an internal destructive rage. An enormous hostility to authority, which cannot be admitted to consciousness, calls forth a massive overcompensation which is manifest in the form of extravagant submissiveness to strong power. Among those found by Adorno and his colleagues to have strong ethnic prejudices and pseudo-conservative tendencies, there is a high proportion of persons who have been unable to develop the capacity to criticize justly and in moderation the failings of parents and who are profoundly intolerant of the ambiguities of thought and feeling that one is so likely to find in real-life situations. For pseudo-conservatism is among other things a disorder in relation to authority, characterized by an inability to find other modes for human relationship than those of more or less complete domination or submission. The pseudo-conservative always imagines himself to be dominated and imposed upon because he feels that he is not dominant, and knows of no other way of interpreting his position. He imagines that his own government and his own leadership are engaged in a more or less continuous conspiracy against him because he has come to think of authority only as something that aims to manipulate and deprive him. It is for this reason, among others, that he enjoys seeing outstanding generals, distinguished secretaries of state, and prominent scholars browbeaten and humiliated.

Status problems take on a special importance in American life because a very large part of the population suffers from one of the most troublesome of all status questions: unable to enjoy the simple luxury of assuming their own nationality as a natural event, they are tormented by a nagging doubt as to whether they are really and truly and fully American. Since their forebears voluntarily left one country and embraced another, they cannot, as people do elsewhere, think of nationality as something that comes with birth; for them it is a matter of *choice*, and an object of striving. This is one reason why problems of "loyalty" arouse such an emotional response in many Americans and why it is so hard in the American climate of opinion to make any clear distinction between the problem of national security and the question of personal loyalty. Of course there is no real reason to doubt the loyalty to America of the immigrants and their descendants, or their willingness to serve the country as fully as if their ancestors had lived here for three centuries. None the less, they have been thrown on the defensive by those who have in the past cast doubts upon the fullness of their Americanism. Possibly they are also, consciously or unconsciously, troubled by the thought that since their forebears hae already abandoned one country, one allegiance, their own national allegiance might be considered fickle. For this I believe there is some evidence in our national practices. What other country finds it so necessary to create institutional rituals for the sole purpose of guaranteeing to its people the genuineness of their nationality? Does the Frehcnman or the Englishman or the Italian find it necessary to speak of himself as "one hundred per cent" English, French or Italina? Do they find it necessary to have their equivalents of "I Am an American Day?" When they disagree with one another over national policies, do they find it necessary to call one another un-English, un-French or un-Italian? No doubt they too are troubled by subversive activities and espionage, but are their countermeasures taken under the name of committees on un-English, un-French or un-Italian activities?

The primary value of patriotic societies and anti-subversive ideologies to their exponents can be found here. They provide additional and continued reassurance both to those who are of old American ancestry and have other status grievances and to those who are of recent American ancestry and therefore feel in need of reassurance about their nationality. Veterans' organizations offer the same satisfaction—what better evidence can there be of the genuineness of nationality and of *earned* citizenship than military service under the flag of one's country? Of course such organizations, once they exist, are liable to exploitation by vested interests that can use them as pressure groups on behalf of particular measures and interests. (Veterans' groups, since they lobby for the concrete interests of veterans, have a double role in this respect.) But the cement that holds them together is the status motivation and the desire for an identity.

CONCLUSION

Chapter 13 presented cases of resistance to laws and conditions perceived as morally unjust. The social problems illustrated in the present chapter resemble those described in Chapter 13 in their violence, but they are different in their expression of blind fury, in the lashing out of persons at the end of their tether. These passionate eruptions are not civil disobedience; they are *explosions.*

These actions and inactions stem from a need for vengeance. When blacks gloat over white deaths, when white troopers riot against peaceful demonstrators' heads, when superpatriots reassure themselves of their identities by hating dissidents, these are obviously social problems. But we must remember that lying behind such social problems are social arrangements that allow and foster what Kenneth Clark called the "chronic riots" of peoples' lives; sometimes chronic riots become acute riots.

Section 7

SEARCH FOR GREENER PASTURES

Some social problems are generated when people pursue the wants that their culture holds out as good by modes their culture concedes are legitimate but fail to stay in a *relationship* that people think they should maintain. Since they conform to goals and to modes and since Americans are ambivalent about how long and under what condition people ought to remain in a given relationship, no matter how frustrating, some ambiguity exists about the problematic nature of the search for greener pastures. This ambiguity is reinforced by the positive value placed on mobility and change.

Thus migration and job-changing are sometimes viewed as normal or desirable activities but sometimes as problems. Divorce is another example. Laws provide for it, and an individualistic ethic encourages people to escape from an unhappy marriage. But divorce is also regarded by many as a social problem, especially when there are children. In the chapters comprising this section, we examine some of the ways in which a quasi-legitimate search for greener pastures produces results that some feel are social problems.

chapter 16
Pulling up stakes

Since there is no biological law that says Americans must be consistent, Americans are capable of insisting both that people should seek to improve themselves by pulling up stakes and seeking their fortunes where conditions seem more promising and also that people who do so are "problems."

Why "problems"? Immigrants to a strange place are often not prepared for the new way of life, and it is not prepared for them. Change entails readjustment. Some of the most painful readjustments Americans are faced with today are those brought about by the search by black Americans for greener pastures.[1]

The immigrants still pour in—not from County Cork, or Bavaria, or Sicily, or Galicia, but from Jackson, Mississippi, and Memphis, Tennessee, and a host of towns and hamlets with names like Sunflower, Rolling Fork, and Dyersburg. No single European ethnic group ever increased as rapidly, or accounted for as large a proportion of the big cities' population as the current wave of newcomers. The new immigrants however, are distinguished from the older residents neither by religion nor by national origin; they are Protestant, for the most part, and can boast of an American ancestry much older than that of the established city dweller. Their sole distinguishing feature is color: the newcomers are black.

The new immigration is changing the character of the big cities as much as did the older immigration from Europe. It is also profoundly altering the nature of race relations in the United States. Only twenty years ago, Professor Myrdal

[1]From Charles E. Silberman, *Crisis in Black and White*, New York: Random House, Inc., 1964, pp. 19-20, 25-42. Reprinted by permission.

reported "a sense of hopelessness in the Negro cause," stemming from the fact that Negroes "can never expect to grow into a democratic majority in politics or in any other sphere of American life." No longer; Negroes are beginning to see themselves as riding the wave of the future. They can begin to see the day when they will be in the majority in most large cities; already, they hold the political balance of power, although they have not yet learned how to take full advantage of the fact. Thus, the Negro vote catapulted an unknown, Jerome Cavanagh, into the mayoralty of Detroit in 1961, defeating a candidate backed by both businessmen and the United Automobile Workers. Negroes supplied 118,000 of the 139,000-vote plurality by which Chicago's Mayor Richard Daley won re-election in 1963. . . .

There had been a steady trickle of Negroes from the eleven states of the Old Confederacy since the end of the Civil War; emancipation had cut many Negroes loose from the land and started them wandering from place to place. In the last decade of the century, however, the number of Negroes leaving the Old Confederacy jumped to more than two hundred thousand from fewer than sixty thousand in the 1880-1890 period, and the number of migrants increased somewhat in the first decade of the twentieth century. The migrants included a great many of the preachers and politicians who had sat in Southern legislatures during Reconstruction and its aftermath, as well as less distinguished Negroes who had occupied minor political posts. But the majority were half-educated or illiterate country folk too restless or too proud to accept life on Southern terms.

It was World War One that broke the social and economic fetters that had bound Negroes to the rural South almost as effectively as slavery itself, for the war created an enormous demand for previously untapped sources of labor. Business was booming as the United States supplied the Allies with weapons and matériel; but combat had cut off the flow of immigrants from Europe. With labor the scarce factor of production even before American entry into the war, Northern industries began sending labor agents into the rural South, recruiting Negroes just as they had recruited white workers in Ireland and Italy during the nineteenth century. The labor agents promised jobs and frequently offered free railroad tickets. Negroes began to move North in such numbers—emigration from the eleven states of the Old Confederacy jumped from 207,000 in 1900-1910 to 478,600 in 1910-1920—that white Southerners began to fear a shortage of labor in their own region and took measures to stop the Northern labor recruiters. In Macon, Georgia, an ordinance was passed requiring labor recruiters to pay a license fee of $25,000 and barring their admission unless recommended by ten local ministers, ten manufacturers, and twenty-five businessmen. In Montgomery, Alabama, fines and jail sentences were imposed on anyone found guilty of "enticing, persuading, or influencing labor" to leave the city, and throughout Mississippi, agents were arrested, ticket agents were intimidated to keep them from selling tickets to Negroes, and trains were actually stopped.

The Negroes kept leaving nevertheless. Besides the agents for Northern firms, Northern Negro newspapers also encouraged the migration editorially, as well as through advertisements offering employment. *The Chicago Defender*, in particular, exhorted Negroes to leave the oppression of the South for the freedom of the North. Copies of the *Defender* were passed from hand to hand, and from all over the South, Negroes wrote to its editor, Robert S. Abbott, asking for help and advice. "I would like Chicago or Philadelphia. But I don't Care where so long as I Go where a man is a man," wrote a would-be migrant from Houston, Texas. From the Black Belt of Mississippi came this letter, showing the hopes that moved the migrants:

Dear Sir: *Granville, Miss., May 16, 1917*

This letter is a letter of information of which you will find stamp envelop for reply. I want to come north some time soon but I do not want to leve here looking for a job where I would be in dorse all winter. Now the work I am doing here is running a guage edger in a saw mill. I know all about the grading of lumber. I have been working in lumber about 25 or 27 years. My wedges here is $3.00 a day, 11 hours a day. I want to come north where I can educate my 3 little children, also my wife. Now if you cannot fit me up at what I am doing down here I can learn anything any one els can. also there is a great deal of good women cooks here would leave any time all they want is to know where to go and some way to go. please write me at once just how I can get my people where they can get something for their work. There are women here cookeing for $1.50 and $2.00 a week. I would like to live in Chicago or Ohio or Philadelphia. Tell Mr. Abbott that our pepel are tole they can not get anything to do up there and they are being snatched off the trains here in Greenville and a rested but in spite of all this, they are leaving every day and every night 100 or more is expecting to leave this week. Let me here from you at once.

American's entry into World War One stimulated migration still more. As men were drafted, the labor shortage was intensified. And the draft brought thousands of Negro soldiers to Army bases in the North, opening a vision of a world beyond that of the small town in which, until then, their lives had been bound. The heavy traffic of Negroes moving North in turn persuaded others living along the main routes to join the trek. A migrant from Decatur, Alabama, reported that perhaps a third of the city's Negro population decided to leave after seeing all the migrants riding through. "And when the moving fever hit them," he said, "there was no changing their minds."

While Negroes were being pulled to the North by job opportunities, they were also being pushed off the land in the South. The full impact of the agrarian revolution was reaching the Southern cotton farmer, and the Negro was hit hardest of all. Farmers in the hot, dry climate of New Mexico and Arizona were producing a longer staple, better quality cotton than the farmers in the old Black Belt could produce, and so cotton production of Negro-operated farms east of the Mississippi began to decline. Mechanization of agriculture also hurt the Negro farmers, most of whom were sharecroppers and tenants. Finally, the ravages of the boll weevil, which plagued the Black Belt after 1910, intensified the Negro cotton farmer's already desperate plight. "The merchant got half the cotton, the boll weevil got the rest," went a Negro ballad. And as if the boll weevil weren't enough, a series of floods during the summer of 1915 added to the Negroes' woes.

The Negro was pushed off the land—but he could find no place in the cities of the South, for poor whites who were also being forced off the land pre-empted the jobs opening up in Southern industry. Indeed not only were Negroes barred from jobs in the new textile mills and other industries springing up in the South, but they found their traditional occupations as well—as barbers and waiters, as carpenters, masons, and painters, as saw-mill operators—taken over by the desperate whites. And so the North, for all its faults, looked more and more like the promised land.

Once the forces of ignorance and inertia were overcome and a new pattern of behavior opened up, the movement northward rapidly gained momentum. The pull of demand continued after the end of the First World War, when the Immigration Exclusion Acts of the early twenties ended once and for all the immigration from Southern and Eastern Europe. And the agrarian revolution continued to push Negroes off the land, while discrimination barred them from jobs in Southern industry. Nearly 800,000 Negroes left the eleven states of the Old Confederacy during the 1920s, and almost 400,000 moved away during the Depression of the 1930s. Thus, the 1940 Census revealed that the Negro population outside the Old Confederacy had more than doubled in the preceding thirty years, increasing from 1.9 to 4 million. Within the Old Confederacy, by contrast, the Negro population had increased only 12 per cent. Yet these eleven states still contained over two-thirds of all Negro Americans.

World War Two really opened the floodgates. With ten million men in uniform and industry operating in full blast, labor again was a scarce and precious commodity. Negroes flocked to the assembly lines in Detroit, now turning out tanks and jeeps instead of autos; to the shipyards in Oakland, New York, and Camden; to the steel mills in Pittsburgh, Gary, and Chicago; to the aircraft plants in Los Angeles. After the war had ended, industry continued to boom; in the late forties and early fifties the auto companies sent labor agents fanning through the South to recruit Negroes for the busy assembly lines. In New York, Philadelphia, Chicago, and most other big cities, employment agencies still do a brisk business directing a steady flow of Negro women and girls to work as domestic servants in a newly affluent society.

Within the South itself, moreover, mechanization of agriculture has been forcing millions of people, black and white, off the land, even when there are no jobs in the cities. Thus, the number of farms in the United States declined by one-third during the fifties. As always, the Negro farmers were hardest-hit: the number of Negro farm operators dropped 41 per cent in the five years from 1954 to 1959, the latest year for which figures are available. Sharecropping—

once the predominant method of Negro farming—has almost disappeared: the number of sharecroppers, black and white, dropped from 541,000 in 1940 (and 776,000 in 1930) to a mere 122,000 in 1959.

The result has been an enormous shift of population from rural to urban areas: no fewer than 78 per cent of the counties of the United States suffered a net out-migration of population during the decade of the fifties. In the South itself, nearly four and a half million whites and two million Negroes moved from rural to urban places in the 1950s. The rural whites, for the most part, moved to Southern cities and towns, (though some 1.4 million left the South). Negroes on the other hand, left the South altogether: only 150,000 Negroes moved to Southern cities during the 1950s, since competition from white migrants, when added to traditional Southern discrimination, made it impossible for Negroes to find jobs in the Southern cities. In all, some 2.75 million Negroes left the South between 1940 and 1960.[2] Thus, the Negro population outside the Deep South has increased fivefold since 1910; it has nearly tripled just since 1940. Part of this expansion, of course, has come from natural increase rather than migration; but it is the migration of Negroes of child-bearing age that enabled the natural increase to occur outside the South. Within the South itself, migration has caused a substantial decline in the Negro population in rural areas; as a result, the population living in cities has jumped from 21 per cent in 1940 (and only 7 per cent in 1910) to 41 per cent in 1960.

Most of the Negroes moving to the North have crowded into the slums of the twelve largest cities, which in 1960 held 60 per cent of the Negroes living outside the Deep South. Between 1940 and 1960 the Negro population of New York increased nearly two and a half times to 1.1 million, or 14 per cent of the city's population. The Negro population of Chicago increased more than two and a half times to 890,000, or 24 per cent. In Philadelphia, between 1940 and 1960, the number of Negroes doubled to 529,000, or 26 per cent. The Negro population of Detroit has more than tripled to nearly a half-million, or 29 per cent of the city's population; and the Negro population of Los Angeles County has increased a phenomenal 600 per cent between 1940 and 1960, from 75,000 to 464,000. In recent years, moreover, Negro migration has fanned out to a host of smaller cities—Buffalo and Rochester, Toledo and Akron, Newark, New Haven, Fort Wayne, Milwaukee, Kansas City, Wichita.

The migration continues; Newark, which was 34.4 per cent Negro at the time of the 1960 Census, is now over 50 per cent Negro. But even if Negro migration were to stop completely (and it's bound to slow down), the Negro population of the large cities would continue to grow at a rapid rate, and Negroes would account for a steadily increasing proportion of the cities' population. For the

[2]The statistics, of course, refer to *net* changes in population. A good many rural Southern Negroes moved to Southern cities, taking the place of Negroes who had moved to the North.

Negro population is considerably younger than the white population of these cities; in addition, the Negro birth rate is considerably higher than the white. (In New Haven and Buffalo, for example, Negroes represent one person in eight out of the total population, but account for one birth in four.) Thus, Professor C. Horace Hamilton of the University of North Carolina, has predicted that Negro population outside the South will have doubled again by 1980, and that by the year 2,000, nearly three Negroes in four will be living in the North and West.

Were it not for the increase in their Negro population, the large cities would be losing residents at a rapid clip. For the stream of Negroes moving into the big cities has been paralleled by a stream of whites moving out to the suburbs. In the twenty-four metropolitan areas with a half-million or more residents, for example, the "central cities" lost 2,399,000 white residents between 1950 and 1960, a drop of 7.3 per cent. They gained 2,641,000 new Negro residents in the same period, a rise of over 50 per cent; Negroes now account for over 20 per cent of the population of these cities. In the suburbs, by contrast, the white population grew by nearly 16 million, or 65 per cent; Negro population increased by 800,000, or better than 60 per cent, but remained a small proportion—under 5 per cent—of the total suburban population. . . .

Like all previous immigrant groups, the Negroes have settled in the traditional "port of entry"—the oldest, least desirable section of the city, generally in or around the central business district. That is where the cheapest housing usually is to be found; more important, that is the only place the newcomers can find a place to live, since prejudice as well as income keeps them out of the "better" neighborhoods. (Immigrants, Negroes included, have always paid more for their housing, comparatively, than the established city dwellers. No urban industry is quite as profitable as slum manufacturing.) In Detroit, for example, the number of Negroes within an eight-mile radius of the central business district has increased eightfold since 1930, while the number of white residents has been halved.

The fact that many of today's migrants are black need not necessarily make for a "social problem." Black immigrants become a problem when white residents define their arrival as threatening or undesirable. But there are other kinds of problems generated by large-scale population shifts, regardless of whether those who are pulling up stakes are white or black. Thus, rural migrants to the cities predominate over migrants from urban to rural areas and thereby lead to occupational and educational problems.[3]

Cities are recipients of a young labor force at the expense of rural areas. With more automation and technology reducing the amount of human energy input,

[3]From *Urban-Rural Problems* by Lee Taylor. © 1968 by Dickenson Publishing Co., Inc., Belmont, Cal. Reprinted by permission of the publisher.

however, cities often do not need the type labor force they reap from the rural areas. Furthermore, rural areas have shared disproportionately in the expense of educating youth who migrate to other areas for work.

More recently the social problem of the situation is clearly that whatever education was obtained in the rural areas is inadequate, incorrect, or otherwise not appropriate for the needs of the labor force in the urban area. Far from reaping the benefit of the rural area's education, the modern city reaps the social problems—the residue of the rural population pushed out of its native area and into second- or third-rate urban places.

The rural-urban mobility of young people is further illustrated by reports in the fifties revealing that some 3½ million youth annually, between the ages of 10 and 19, departed from rural areas for cities.[4] More recently this tidal wave of rural youth moving to cities has subsided slightly, but the major impact continues. For many of these migrants the difficulties of being integrated into the labor force of cities will increase. The day when vast numbers of new workers are needed to fill rank-and-file unskilled assembly-line jobs is nearly ended. Automation and technology at various levels are eliminating some of these positions and reducing the expansion of others. Urban slums are growing, partly due to their own generation, and partly due to continual in-migration of rural people who are unprepared to compete for top positions. Few special programs are provided to assist rural youth in adjusting to their new environment. To facilitate adjustment, programs of guided mobility are needed.[5]

One example of an attempt to facilitate the integration of migrants is the establishment of special ungraded classes in Milwaukee. The city has been the recipient of out-of-state migrants, particularly from the rural South for some time. When the Ford Foundation made sums of money available for its Great Cities Project, Milwaukee was selected to help both in-migrants and those of longer duration of residence to improve their capacities for work and life in the urban community. The Milwaukee program is serviced at the elementary, junior high, and high school levels. The special classes are limited to an enrollment of twenty persons per teacher. They also have special social work and psychological services. Following individualized teaching and guidance, the students are moved into the regular school programs as quickly as possible.

A special program is being provided in the New York City schools for the teaching of English to newcomers who are primarily Spanish-speaking. The state supplements the city funds for these English classes. The enrollment in the classes is limited to twenty-five, and students who do not speak English are

---

[4]*Young Workers: Their Special Training Needs*, (Washington, D.C.: U.S. Department of Labor Office of Manpower, Automation, and Training, Bulletin No. 3, 1963), p. 10.

[5]Herbert J. Gans, "Social and Physical Planning for the Elimination of Poverty," paper delivered at a conference of the American Institute of Planners (October 17, 1962).

expected to receive individual instruction in oral English. Auxiliary teachers who are fluent in both Spanish and English serve as liaison between the school and the Spanish-speaking parents. Experimental instruction is also being developed through the use of language laboratory equipment.

Guidance and preparation programs are offered for adolescents and young adults in cities, by migration or by birth, who have experienced difficulty in the transition from school to work. Some are slow learners, have poor work habits and attitudes, possess limited abilities, and have unrealistic ideas concerning vocational goals. In times of relatively high unemployment this type of person is more apparent. With low unemployment more of them enter various jobs regardless of their attitudes or level of training.[6]

In other situations it is known that there is a virtual "shuttling" between Southern Appalachia and areas like Chicago. In some Chicago schools there is a heavy enrollment of young people from eastern Kentucky and West Virginia. About three-quarters of these children transfer in and out of school multiple times during the year. When there is employment in the area their parents move in, and when there is unemployment they return to their southern area. To facilitate the adjustment of the children in the schools an effort is made to assign a "pal" of the in-migrant's own age. Efforts are directed at parents to discourage the shuttling effect in moving children into and out of school.

Another problem dimension of migration concerns the cost of educating migrants' children. A heavy trend of migration to suburban areas both from urban and rural points of origin has been experienced in the United States in the past twenty years. Connecticut is one of those states in which suburban-directed migration is particularly heavy. For many small rural and suburban towns the impact of in-migrants creates critical problems in the provision of schools and other community services. Many of these services are financed primarily by a general property tax. In the absence of heavy industry and commercial establishments, this tax burden is on homes and farm property.

The cost of education in suburbia is increased because the newcomers are often in the child-bearing ages. The need for more schoolrooms, facilities, and teachers is increased disproportionately. Specifically, in the Connecticut situation the greatest increase of school population occurred in "rings" around the state's standard metropolitan areas. In the suburban fringe schools, there were 40 per cent more children enrolled in the mid-fifties than at the end of the forties. In the predominantly rural towns, a little more remotely located from the standard metropolitan areas, there was an increase of 30 per cent in school enrollments. The central cities of the standard metropolitan areas had the lowest rates of school population expansion.

[6]*Help for Out-of-Work Youth, A Manual for a Job Preparation Program in Your Community* (National Committee on Employment of Youth, 1963).

This situation is creating a disproportionate burden on the taxpayers in the fringe and small-town areas for the education of children of employees of the central cities. Over 80 per cent of the schools' tax budget comes from local sources. The balance comes from the state. In Connecticut, ten towns were studied in terms of the proportion of migrants and residents and their respective number of children and tax assessments. It was clearly found that there was a deficit in the local communities' cost of education. The nonmigrants were paying a disproportionate share in the cost of the education of migrant children. Twenty-seven per cent of the children in the schools were from migrant families who in turn had paid only 21 per cent of the towns' property taxes. The proportion of preschool children among the migrant families was even greater than that of their school-age children. Accordingly, it should be anticipated that the resident families will experience an even greater burden in the education of the migrant children.

The situation reported in Connecticut is much in contrast to the historic condition in which rural people paid for the education of youth who migrated to cities to make their economic contribution. Now, this kind of finding suggests that once again small-town and rural people are paying for the education of an area's youth, often not their own, who will contribute their work-force years to an area other than the place in which they are educated.

The next major dimension of migration and education has to do with the children of farm migratory workers. The number of migratory workers has remained about 500,000 for some years. About half of these workers were indigenous and the remainder come from Mexico (until 1964 when Public Law 78 expired, which had authorized their entry), the British West Indies, and Puerto Rico.[7] In many cases, the farm migratory laborers travel with their families. The education of their children is minimal indeed. The social problem associated with this situation is less one of large numbers of people and more one of human consideration in an affluent society. In most cases, the farm migratory workers propagate themselves in a limited and uninspired life cycle which is characterized by poor and unsanitary housing, inadequate and improper food, minimum health and medical care, quick maturation for children—with marriage and reproduction following shortly after puberty. Accordingly, the cycle is insured for another generation.

Numerous reports have been made on the condition of migratory workers. The report here illustrates the situation with reference to education.[8] The study

---

[7]*Farm Labor Fact Book* (Washington, D.C.: U.S. Department of Labor, 1959).

[8]Elizabeth Sutton, *Knowing and Teaching the Migrant Child* (Washington, D.C.: National Education Association, Department of Rural Education, 1960); and Emmit F. Sharp and Olaf F. Larson, *Migratory Farm Workers in the Atlantic Coast Stream* (New York: Cornell Agricultural Experiment Station, Bulletin 949, 1960).

areas were Palm Beach County, Florida, and North Hampton County, Virginia. The Florida location is "home-base" for many migrants. They operate out of there and hence spend more of the year in that community. The North Hampton County community is characterized as "on-the-trek." It is one of the locational areas for migrant employment, where the duration of stay is limited. In both locations, the work is characterized by vegetable and truck-farming agriculture. In the Florida area, the number of migratory workers varies by month, but in the winter period of November and December the number peaks between 12,000 and 14,000. Enrollment in the local schools fluctuates accordingly with continual entrance and withdrawal of the transient students. At peak enrollment periods, additional teachers are employed.

In North Hampton County the peak production period is usually reached in May, June, and July. Some 6,000 migratory workers are normally recruited for vegetable harvest at this time. The number of school children increases sharply during this period, but the record is not clear. It is near the end of the school season, and frequently the children do not enroll at all.

The investigators of this migratory school situation outlined it as follows: (1) the student's life is not related to the community in the usual ways; (2) migratory students must make repeated adjustments to various school situations; (3) in most communities there is little awareness of the migrants' need and little classroom appreciation for the contribution he and his family make; (4) migratory families lack a general appreciation for education; (5) parents are typically nonvoters and are unaware of the resources and services which should be available in the community.

Given the preceding situation, one of the basic challenges for educating these children is to establish rapport. The teachers themselves must become acquainted with their situation in order to better understand how the children might be reached. In the two communities studied, a big-brother–big-sister system was used to help migrants gain identification with resident students. Special classroom responsibilities were given to the migrant children to enable them to feel a part of the school's program. School bulletin boards announced the enrollment of these newcomers. The school paper featured articles concerning the new students. Teachers sent letters welcoming their parents to the community and to the school, and friendly home visits were arranged with them. All of these special items of attention take more time than in the normal operation of a school. Special resources must be provided and additional teachers must be supplied to carry out such individualized programs.

Many migratory children are academically retarded. Special teaching situations must be provided if they are to be reached. Special lessons must be provided and special curriculum must be arranged. Individual instruction was offered in the experimental situation. Small group instructional situations were established. Some class periods were specifically designated for review. A "helping teaching program" was established. These instructors taught half a day to assist the regular homeroom teacher in her full day's responsibilities.

In addition to arranging special programs for migrant children, there was the prior difficulty of placing them at the appropriate grade level. Few if any records of achievement were brought from prior schools. Special tests were constructed to assist school administrators in placing the children at the proper grade level. Regardless of their age, many of them needed to be placed at a primary level.

Special health practice education needs to be given to migrant children. Personal hygiene and grooming are subjects that have to be taught in the school. Food and nutrition are related subjects that must be discussed in school or be completely absent in their environment. Discussions of communicable and noncommunicable diseases, safety and first aid, sanitation, mental health, and so forth are all special needs of the migratory children.

Research in Florida and Virginia demonstrates that an in-depth educational experience can be brought to migratory children by expanding an identification with them, modifying the curriculum, providing special teaching personnel, teaching health practices, and so forth. The social problem in this situation is largely a conflict of values. There is little value for the dominant society's education. The migrants' position is easily maintained in their social system of survival, due often to their lower academic abilities. There is also a conflict of values in the migrant situation, because the upgrading of their education will tend to move them out of this deprived labor force position. Employers in the local community may seek to have such a cheap and relatively uneducated labor force. Accordingly, the special efforts which might be made in the schools to improve their education, work against their labor-force needs in the short run. It has been long observed that in the United States in general and in rural America in particular school boards are controlled by a conservative middle class. The orientation is toward an academic education for the few and a vocational education for the many. The educational opportunity for migrant children, or the lack of opportunity, falls well within this confrontation between traditional values and the dominant societal values generated from an urbanized origin.

Whether the migrants are in cities, suburbs, or rural areas, the details of their situations constitute a social problem in the local environment.

The problems stemming from extensive changing of residence or jobs are usually associated with disadvantaged persons' pulling up stakes. But problems are also generated by the search for greener pastures by more privileged members of the population, such as college and university professors.[9]

---

[9]From Theodore Caplow and Reece McGee, *The Academic Marketplace*, New York: Basic Books, 1958, pp. 233-236. © 1958 by Basic Books, Inc. Reprinted by permission.

The borderline between appropriate turnover and excessive turnover is, of course, difficult to determine. Nevertheless, there is good reason to describe the present turnover in many institutions as excessive. Turnover is excessive when senior faculty members appointed to lifetime positions in connection with long-range programs leave after two or three years. With respect to junior staff, the expenditure of time and effort in recruitment is altogether out of proportion to the average duration of appointment for the people recruited. In qualitative terms, turnover may be reckoned as excessive when a university consistently loses members of its faculty whose services are needed and wanted and who cannot be satisfactorily replaced. The instability and loss of continuity in long-range projects, in graduate instruction, and the development of new curricula which result from excessive turnover can scarcely be exaggerated. A handful of very eminent institutions are protected by the fact that their tenure appointments are usually accepted as permanent. Minor universities are often protected against excessive turnover by the harsh fact that most of the members of their faculties have no other place to go. But for most major universities, the constant comings and goings of professors are a perpetual threat to planning and continuity.

There is a curious complication which haunts the sleep of administrators in these universities—namely, that the hazard of appointing incompetent or idle men to tenure positions increases as the general rate of turnover increases. Inevitably, a certain proportion of all appointments made are poor appointments. In the theoretical extreme case, in which all tenure appointees retained their positions for life, the proportion of "deadwood" on the faculty would be the same as the proportion originally appointed. However, when there is considerable faculty mobility, the ablest members of the faculty will tend to be the most mobile because of their attractiveness to other institutions, and the least competent members will tend to be immobile. For a weak major university, there is a real danger that almost all its superior appointees will eventually be lured away, leaving a permanent cadre which has been rigorously selected for incompetence.

ADMINISTRATIVE FAILURE

There are a number of ways in which the workings of the academic marketplace contribute to administrative failure within each university—for example, by the internal dissension and low morale which follow the appointment of outsiders on unduly favorable terms. As we have seen, candidates for academic positions must normally be attracted from other positions of rather similar characteristics, and some bonus of rank, salary, or perquisites is expected in order to create a difference between the two positions. It is usually thought to be necessary to offer an outsider somewhat better terms as an inducement to move than an insider of exactly the same qualifications could obtain. As we have seen, this practice provides a perpetual incentive for everyone on the academic ladder to circulate among institutions. The result is a vicious circle, whereby the appointment of outsiders on unduly favorable terms causes dissatisfaction among the staff members in place, so that some of them seek their fortunes elsewhere, which requires more new appointments to be made by means of extra inducements, which has a further unsettling effect upon the remaining members of the staff. Meanwhile, the emigrants from this faculty going to their new institutions contribute to the same cycles there. It is possible to find departments which have remained in turmoil for decades through the operation of this mechanism.

A related consequence is the uneven growth or decline of departments or colleges within the university according to the fortunes of the marketplace. It often happens that a department loses two or three men in the same short period by sheer chance—for example, by the simultaneous occurrence of several retirements. When the persons involved are of high standing in the discipline, the fall in the department's prestige is appreciable, and it may result in a scramble of the remaining staff for positions elsewhere. In this way, decades of growth and development can be wiped out in a few months.

Another kind of search for greener pastures occurs when people become convinced either that their present spouse is an obstacle to happiness or that some other wife or husband will make them happier.[10]

Whatever goals or interests a formerly married man or woman may have had before the ending of marriage, they usually become subordinated after separation to the master aim of finding a new love relationship. The searching and testing for this relationship begin rather soon: most FMs (as I shall call the formerly married) have at least one, and many have more than one, emotional involvement within the first year, and the majority experience several of them within two or three years. Although these alliances could be loosely called love affairs, FMs themselves are extremely reluctant to use that straightforward term or to refer to themselves as being in love. They rely instead on an assortment of cautious euphemisms; instead of having a love affair, they have a *relationship*, an *attachment* or an *involvement*. They are not in love, but are *involved with, all tied up with, going with* or *very much interested in* someone. A man and a woman are not lovers, but *a thing* or *a pair*, or are *going together, going steady* or *seeing each other regularly*. Even though they are involved with each other, they may or may not *be committed* or *have a commitment*. But when an

[10]From Morton M. Hunt, *The World of the Formerly Married*, New York: McGraw-Hill, 1966. The excerpt is from Chapter 6 as it appeared in McCall's, October 1966, under the title, "The Rocky Road to Remarriage," pp. 127, 197-199, 201-202. Reprinted by permission. Copyright © 1966 by Morton M. Hunt.

involvement—especially one with a commitment—goes sour, it becomes an *entanglement*, perhaps even a *hang-up*, until the FM manages to detach himself or herself from it.

These terms reveal a good deal about the guarded and qualified attitude of FMs to their major goal. They are so eager to love again that they act on their emotions impetuously and rapidly; yet they are so mistrustful of those emotions and so unsure of their own judgment that they hold back part of themselves. Sometimes their impulses are so unstable that love is born and dies in a matter of days or weeks.

When FM lovers *do* permit themselves deep and strong feelings, they often are able to maintain them over a long period only by carefully avoiding any statement or action that constitutes emotional commitment—any sort of avowal that one loves the other wholly and exclusively. The affair may go on for months without there being any clear understanding as to what the lovers mean to each other; the very ambiguity of the relationship is what makes its closeness tolerable. Those who make open declarations of love are often thrown into panic by their own act and then flee to avoid the desired—and feared—commitment.

Such must have been the case with the man who briefly came into this woman's life: "A couple of years ago," she said, "I made a blind date with a lawyer from out of town. I don't ordinarily make blind dates, but a cousin had urged him on me. He walked in, we took one look at each other, and sparks flew. There was something we both felt that was like nothing I had known in two years as a divorcée. We went to dinner but never noticed the food. We couldn't talk enough, we got misty-eyed again and again, and choked up. He told me we would be married, and I wasn't even surprised—it was just that natural and inevitable. He took me home at five a.m., and said he'd phone at nine, when my kids had left for school. I was exhausted, but I couldn't sleep a wink. It had really happened to me at last, and all I could do was paint scenes of the future.

"I got up with the kids at seven-thirty, and watched the clock—it never ran so slow. At eight-thirty I was excited. At ten of nine I was as fidgety as could be. Nine o'clock, and I was perspiring. Five after. Ten after. My heart was palpitating and I was feeling funny in the stomach. Well, I waited by that phone all morning and all afternoon, and it never rang. Not that night, either. Not ever. I never heard from him. I was shattered. It took months before I got over it, and I still feel a little sick telling about it even now. It was a nightmare. It was like being out of your head, when nothing makes any sense."

Ambivalence about loving seldom takes such an extreme and overt form, but even in milder and half-concealed forms it is exasperating and depressing to the one who feels it, as well as to the innocent victim. A civil engineer of 44 says that he has a "natural impulse" to be kind, good and warm toward women; but as soon as this begins to have its effects on them, he becomes uncontrollably difficult and provocative, until he has broken up the budding relationship.

"I can't understand it," says one young woman who has been separated for half a year. "I was looking forward to running around with different men after my marriage broke up, and here I am sticking to just one man—almost against my will. But I keep getting waves of feeling *caught*—the closer he and I become, the more strongly I feel I *ought* to run around a bit first."

A 40-year-old book editor says that she has fallen in love half a dozen times in the past four years, but that "each time, soon after it becomes serious, I begin to see his faults or limitations and get a scared feeling that I'm not as deeply in love as I want to be and that maybe it will be hard to get out of it. And I start getting out right then."

In the man or woman who has never married, the inability to resolve this kind of conflict may be a symptom of a chronic neurosis; in most FMs, it is a symptom of a temporary neurotic state produced by stress and trauma. When the stress is removed and the damage done by the trauma is slowly repaired, the inability to resolve the conflict usually disappears.

Besides the inevitable inner conflicts of this transient neurotic condition, there are also external forces pushing and pulling the FM both ways. Among those which powerfully and persistently thrust him toward a permanent relationship are his relatives, friends and acquaintances—all those persons whose world he has deserted and to which they hope he will return. Their interest and their good wishes thinly mask their all-too-frequent disapproval and poor opinion of his way of life; it is obvious to him that to regain their approval and good opinion he must fall in love, genuinely and openly. While remarriage is the only final solution they thoroughly approve of, they will consider him as good as saved if he confesses to loving and renounces the false idols of freedom and casual sex. Moreover, even if he does not feel that the collapse of the marriage was altogether, or even chiefly, his fault, he knows that the world around him feels he failed in some important way. To love again would prove there was nothing missing in him; and to have that love result in a successful marriage—*that* would show them what kind of human being he is.

"What's new?" ask the FM's friends. "Have you met anybody nice yet?" It is a kindly, a hopeful query; but underneath the surface it means (or at least seems to mean) something else: Are you a whole person yet, or are you still an emotional defective? At first, people are solicitous about their separated and divorced friends; later, though they continue to ask, there is a subliminal note of impatience and criticism. For no matter how the question is phrased or spoken, the FM squirms, feeling somehow at fault if his answer is no.

Virtually all the leisure activities of adult society are built around couples rather than individuals. Most of the places one would like to go are places for men and women in pairs, not one by one. It is an extraordinary man—and an even more extraordinary woman—who can go alone to the ballet, a play, a country club or a good restaurant and be surrounded by people in pairs without feeling acutely self-conscious and going away moody and diminished in self-esteem. At parties given by married people, the FM, if currently unattached and alone, may feel conspicuous and ill at ease. The social awkwardness of the FM's life thus impels him to try to love better, in order finally to live better.

The pressures brought on the FM by his children similarly are transformed into a desire to love and remarry. The formerly married woman has an almost continual sense of guilt about rearing her children in a manless home, a situation she could remedy by finding the right man to love. (The formerly married man—except for the rare one with custody of his children—may also feel guilty; but this has less impact on him, since his remarriage usually would not change his children's home life.) When the children meet one of their mother's male friends and begin to like him, the pressure is greatly intensified. Let some new man be friendly and competent with her children, wakening a response in them, and she feels something in herself going out toward him—and may even some-times resent the fact that she is learning to care for him not for her own sake but for her children's.

Children sometimes complicate the situation even further by deliberately trying to make their parents care for someone they have met and can envision as a stepparent. Transparently hopeful, they may ask their mother about each new man: "Do you like him? Do you like him very much? Do you think you might marry him? Aren't you *ever* going to get married again?" Listening to such queries and pleas, she wants to love him in order to make her children happy.

A radio announcer in Florida, whose ex-wife works and leaves their nine-year-old son with a maid, believes his ex-wife would let the boy live with him if he remarried; as a result, he tried to convince himself that he was in love with a woman to whom his son took a liking:

"I thought myself in love with Sally for a couple of weeks only because of my son. He spent a solid week with me during Christmas and saw a good bit of her. She was wonderful with him—not too sweet, not coy, just natural and adult. One evening at bedtime, he said to me, 'I know it's very complicated, Dad, but could you please tell me, how much do you like Sally?' I told him I liked her very much. 'Do you *love* her?' he asked. I said I wasn't sure; it was hard to tell when liking becomes loving, and I needed lots of time to be sure. I turned out his light, but he said, 'Please, Dad, wait a minute. Dad, is there any possibility you and she will get married?' I explained the difference between possibility and likelihood, but he cut me off. 'Okay, okay,' he said, 'but is there any possibility? Because—don't tell her this—but I more than like her. I think I love her. I'd really like her for a second mommy.'

"I can't begin to tell you all the feelings this aroused in me—first, a resistance, then a feeling of guilt, then the question 'Well, why not?,' then a great rush of hope and of love for her. I thought, Maybe this is really the answer; maybe this would be the best thing for me, and for him as well. For about two weeks, I really believed it might work out; then she and I had one of those crazy fallings-out that we were forever having, and the whole dream blew apart."

In contrast to all the pressures that push the FM toward loving are those that pull him away—or at least impede his way. One is the lack of a divorce. Some people allow negotiations or a legal separation to drag on indefinitely, as a safeguard against new involvement. But others, passionately desiring divorce, are unable to obtain it from a spouse who refuses to cooperate or who sets impossibly harsh terms for cooperating. . . .

But the divorce, even if completed, can pose formidable obstacles to new love. Alimony and child support take a considerable portion of the income of many a middle-class FM man—the more so if he was the one who wanted the divorce and his wife was reluctant or felt herself treated unfairly. Quite often, alimony and child-support payments take from a third to a half of a man's net income; a larger fraction is not uncommon.

The average homemaker and mother trying to get along on a third to a half of her ex-husband's income has a thin time of it and must reduce her standard of living, get help from her parents or go to work until she finds another husband. But the ex-husband, though he can manage to live alone on what remains to him, may well feel a chill coming over his responses to any other woman when he calculates the dimensions of her need for support.

A 36-year-old electronics engineer in Detroit is persuasive on the subject: "Money problems have killed off the two important relationships I've had since the divorce. I can live modestly on what I have left after paying alimony and child support, but I can't see how I could support another woman—especially not one who would want to have more children. The first girl I got in deep with was struggling to keep herself and her two kids; her husband is a gambler and a bum, who sends money for the children only when she takes him to court. That looked like a mess for me to get into. I felt guilty, but I didn't want any part of it. The second one had no financial problems—she got good alimony from a well-to-do ex-husband—but she doesn't work, and her alimony would be cut off if I married her. And then, if we didn't work out, she'd have to get alimony from me. I felt I couldn't take a chance."

It is not only men whose feelings are stifled by financial factors; women suffer the same effect. A highly intelligent and attractive divorcée with three children says, "Most of the desirable men I've met have financial problems due to former marriages and would probably shy away when they learned that the child support I get really doesn't cover the expenses. So I never let myself get involved enough with them to get hurt."

Sometimes it is the existence of money, rather than its lack, that obstructs or spoils a love affair. Almost always a woman who gets alimony stands to lose it instantly and forever the moment she remarries. If her ex-husband is wealthy and the alimony is substantial, she is free and independent; with a new love and marriage, she is neither. For some, this is not an easy choice, and a certain number of them in such circumstances go from affair to affair, breaking away from each one if it begins to raise the threat of remarriage. A few dare to live with the man they love, remaining unmarried in order to continue receiving the alimony. But this is a desperate measure. It is degrading, guilt-producing because of its exploitation of the ex-husband, socially awkward, hurtful to the children, if there are any—and, sometimes, risky, since in certain states it provides the ex-husband with grounds for cutting off the alimony. One may fairly wonder how love came to have the reputation of being a mighty and all-conquering emotion when so many coarse, material concerns seem able to overthrow it.

Children, though they often act as an impetus toward loving again, sometimes act in just the opposite way. Rather often, a child will take a new man in Mother's life until the affair becomes serious and the child perceives that the new friend is a competitor; then he may misbehave, act hateful or provocative toward the interloper and make him seem like an upsetting influence.

"When I was seeing a great deal of Bob," writes one woman, "my twelve-year-old daughter grew sassy, threw tantrums and was impossible to handle. Then I told her I didn't think I would ever marry him, and she relaxed and became herself almost overnight."

Again, a man may simply not be able to act like the ideal parent the children's mother had in mind. "He was gentle and kind to my boys," writes another woman, "in fact, far more so than the man I finally married, but he was so easygoing and so permissive that I could see he would never set standards or be able to exert discipline." "He really didn't like my children," says another, "and I faced the fact that if it was a question of him or my children, I was going to pick them."

On the other side, a man may have misgivings, because of her children, about getting too deeply involved with a woman. "I'm a pretty good father with my own kids," says one man, "but hers were so mixed-up and wild that I hesitated at the thought of living with them and trying to get along with them. It didn't look like a promising way of life." Some men are drawn to much younger women, but shy away when the latter talk of wanting children. "I thought she was really it," says one man, "until she began speaking about how much she wanted at least one or two more kids. At fifty, I've been through all that. I'm beyond it, I don't want to start it all over again. I felt it was a difference we'd never be able to resolve." . . .

Having been through the experience of a disintegrating marriage, the Formerly Married are already familiar with the process of breakup and the anguish to be endured when it is prolonged. They are therefore very likely to want to break cleanly and swiftly, although very often one of the pair will not perceive that the breakup is real and will try to hold on briefly, or will be afraid to let go and may try to continue the relationship in a less binding form. The one who wants the clean break is eager to get through the period of transition as fast as possible, knowing from experience that he has resources not only within himself, but all around him. The one who tries to hold on, despite the fact that the affair is doomed, is not so much trying to salvage it as clinging to it out of desperation. Some begin looking around and dating other people before finally letting go of the old relationship; some deliberately postpone the break until after a holiday season, or the summer; some make the break but reach out for the other time and again.

Joan, who had much less experience and sureness of herself than Douglas, reacted in the latter way. She says: "We had more and more arguments about stupid little things, but I think we both knew we were feeling the big differences. One night we really pulled it all out in the open and got to talking about the things that bothered us in each other. About one or two in the morning, Doug said maybe I'd rather not see him any more at all, maybe the whole thing was hopeless, and I said I thought he was right. We both became sad and tender, rather than angry, and he left. I cried for hours. A couple of nights later, I just couldn't stand it alone, after Tina was asleep, and I phoned him and bawled my eyes out, and he came rushing over, and we sat up very late, holding onto each other and talking it all over.

"For a week, things seemed all right, and then we had another argument and another break. This time, I didn't get in touch with him for a week. But I felt lost—I had come to depend on this relationship, after fighting it in the beginning, and I was feeling terrible. I sent him another poem, scented with sachet, telling him how miserable I was, and he came by the next night with flowers. That time, it lasted about three days. About the fourth or fifth time we broke off—I can't remember which—I forced myself not to do anything to start it up again. Doug never made a move. I think he began running around with other women as soon as we first broke up. It was a bad time for me, but I wouldn't let myself give in any more. I despised my own weakness for having done so."

CONCLUSION

American history portrays the pioneers who pulled up stakes and sought greener pastures in the westward trek as heroes, but they were social problems to the Indians and Mexicans. A parallel situation exists today when rural Americans who seek a better life in the cities become problems to longer-established city dwellers. Floods of immigrants overtax the resources of the cities and force unwanted, uncomfortable, and costly changes on their inhabitants. Migrants also disrupt the stability of the communities they leave, and of themselves as they abandon one way of life without yet mastering the new one. Those who leave jobs or mates are similar in the disruptions they cause and in the sociopsychic no-man's-land in which they sometimes find themselves.

Yet behind these social problems lie others: the institutional arrangements responsible for "pushes" out of a given community, the cultural idea that bliss lies just around the next corner, the absence of social organization for smooth absorption into the next place, or the failure of institutions to allocate manpower, jobs, or mates reasonably to begin with.

Section G
DISAFFILIATION

One way of adjusting to frustration or the threat of frustration is to break off the painful relationship. In the previous section we saw how disaffiliation can lead to problems even when the relationship is broken in a legitimate way. When the relationship is broken in ways proscribed by a culture, the problematic nature of the behavior is clearer.

In the chapter dealing with disaffiliation, we shall consider two kinds of disaffiliation: "extrusion" and "secession." Extrusion is behavior that breaks off a relationship by expelling someone from it. Person A defends himself against frustration by getting rid of his frustrator in some way. Secession, on the other hand, is behavior in which the frustrated person himself abandons the relationship. In some cases, it is not clear whether A is extruding B or B is seceding from the relationship. In any case, the result is disaffiliation: a relationship culturally "supposed to" be maintained is broken off in ways that are culturally proscribed.

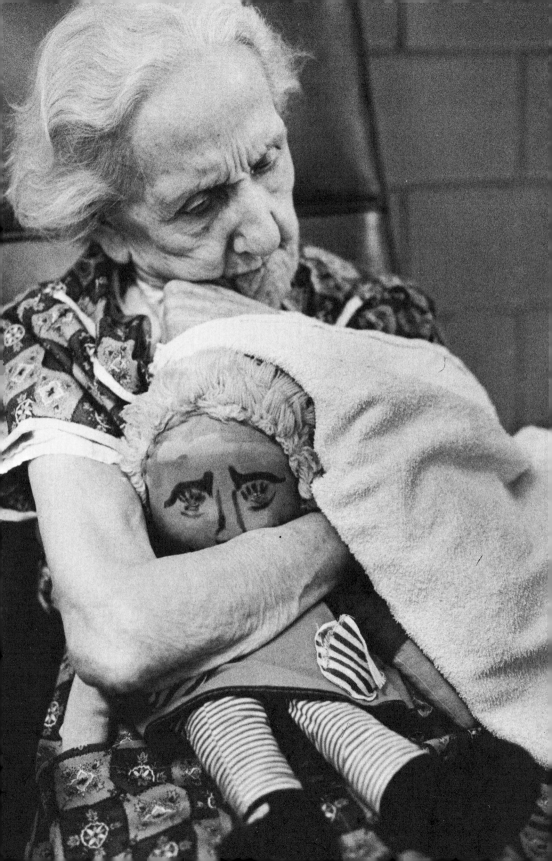

chapter 17
Extrusion and secession

In some contexts (for example, the public school), it is difficult to tell whether someone is being extruded from a relationship or is seceding from it. Are school dropouts "dropouts" or "pushouts"?[1]

In response to a series of questions about their attitudes toward school about half of our dropouts declared that they did not drop out of school but were asked or forced to leave. An example from an interview:[2]

I   Why did you drop out of school?

NDO I didn't drop out of school. They dropped me.

I   Why did they drop you?

NDO Well, when they dropped me there were a few other boys. . . .

I   How was it possible for you to remain in school?

NDO Oh, it was impossible for me to stay in school. I had to go down to Board of Education and see Dr_____, and he said that all my actions indicated

---

[1]From Seymour M. Miller and Ira Harrison, "Types of Dropouts," in Arthur Shostak and William Gomberg, eds., *Blue Collar World*, Englewood Cliffs, New Jersey: Prentice Hall, 1964, pp. 470-474. © 1964. Reprinted by permission of Prentice-Hall, Inc., Englewood Cliffs, N.J.

[2]"I" refers to the interviewer; "WDO" to a white dropout and "NDO" to a Negro dropout. Interviews averaged two hours. A limited number of the boys have so far been interviewed twice; the second time, some six months after they entered the program. Some parents have been interviewed. Italics and parenthetical materials in the interview excerpts are the authors'. The interview schedule and coding were primarily constructed by Dr. Arthur Pearl and the staff of the New York State Division for Youth.

that I didn't want to stay in school. So by going to night school and passing in my grades in March, maybe by next September I'd be allowed to get back into day school . . .

They would have stayed, most contend, if this pressure had not been exerted on them. They define themselves as "pushouts" rather than "dropouts." Obviously, such reporting cannot be taken at face value, and undoubtedly many acted so as to incite action to expel them from school, whether they intended that result or not. Most have been suspended from at least two schools.

The pattern is generally a great deal of residential mobility, so that many have attended eight different schools before leaving school in the tenth grade. In school they meet their friends and acquaintances; frequently, as they report it, these friends and others "wise around" and sometimes it is admitted that they themselves have done this as well. As one boy expressed it:

I   What did you like about school?
WDO The only thing I liked about school was recess and lunch.
I   Recess and lunch, huh?
WDO Yeah.
I   Okay. What didn't you like about school?
WDO Really to come right down to it, you know, I really didn't dislike school. I just didn't have time to do my work. I was always monkeying around. I think that was my biggest downfall. I think that if I hadda kept my mouth shut in class, you know, and never mind about my buddy next door, I wouldda got along okay. I don't know.

"Wise around" can include talking out loud, laughing, throwing paper, hitting students, drinking whisky. This action frequently ends in trouble— reprimands by the teacher, being grabbed or shoved by the teacher, having to stay after school, stand in a corner, or sent to the principal's or counselor's office. A boy explained his school departure in the following way:

I   Why did you come back up here?
WDO You see I was getting kind of old. You see they don't take anybody up to sixteen. That's all. When I went back to this (rural school) everything was going great. You see they got this new principal and this new principal wouldn't take it from the old principal about me, so he figured he'd try me out. So I was good. No trouble or nothing. Then all of a sudden one day this kid comes up and slugs me as hard as he could on the back. They'd been doing this because I'm from the city and they don't like city kids.
I   City? What city?
WDO Oh, this city (Syracuse) and New York. I told them I'd been down to New York and they don't like it. And so they kept on hitting me as hard as

they could. Then this one guy come up and hit me as hard as he could and then moved back. I turned around and swung and he moved and I hit the teacher and that was it.

I   What do you mean he moved? Where was the teacher?

WDO The teacher was standing in back of him. You see we were lined up and going down to the gymnasium and this kid was in back of me and he let me have it. You go by height and in the line I was near the end and the teacher was after you. So when this kid let me have it. . . .

I   Your back was turned?

WDO Yes. I was facing front. And he let me have it in the middle of the back. And so. . . .

I   The teacher didn't see him hit you?

WDO Yes. But the teacher didn't say nothing. Or he didn't have time. Once he hit me I let him have it.

I   What happened then?

WDO He dragged me down to the office and that was it.

I   Did you tell your side?

WDO I told my side.

I   What did the principal say?

WDO He says he didn't believe me but it would be better for me to get out.[3]

Sometimes, the principal suspends them from school and sometimes, it is two or three days before dropouts' parents discover that their child has been suspended. The dropout, however, usually returns to school or is able to re-enroll unless his sixteenth birthday is near. If this is the case, he is usually not returned to school, or, if he has past offenses, is not permitted to re-enroll.

This picture has been reported frequently in other communities. We want to make two comments which seem not to have been reported elsewhere:

(1) The boys are aggrieved by school: they frequently contend that they were not immediately involved in the event for which they have been kicked out and the teacher's misinterpretation of what was occurring led to their involvement in the event leading to their school dismissal.

They see the school personnel as "bugging" them, constantly keeping after them, until they finally have to defend themselves. The following excerpt relates this feeling:

I   I see. Now, do you feel any teachers were unfair to you?

WDO No. They were all fair to me.

I   Did you have any teacher that you didn't like?

---

[3] A number of our respondents claim to have been pressured by fellow students because they were new to a school and community. In contrast to the stereotype of the friendliness of the rural life, a number of urban boys reported, as in this interview, getting a rough reception when they moved to a rural school.

WDO No. Up to a certain point.

I   Well, tell me about it.

WDO I had an English teacher. He was a man too. Ah . . . I was doing my best to work, you know, and he always kept telling me I hadda do better and he *kept after me.* So one day I told him off and walked out of class and never went back.

. . .

(2) The boys, to our initial surprise, were not negative about school. School is a convenient place for meeting one's friends, and they miss it for this reason frequently. In reply to a question about the "fairness" of teachers, most indicated that they felt that teachers were fair. These excerpts from one interview indicate the general feeling of fairness:

I   What do you like about school?

NDO I like going to school. I enjoyed going to school, yeah. I don't know whether or not it was so much what I was learning, but I enjoyed going to school. One year I went to school every day and I still failed. . .

I   Was there anything about school that you didn't like?

NDO No. Not really. Only a few teachers. From time to time. . . . .

. . .

I   Could you tell me someting about the teachers that you mentioned before? What kind of people become teachers?

NDO More or less people who enjoy working with children or get some sort of a good feeling about helping young people and regardless of who they are.

. . .

I   Do you feel that any of your teachers you had in school were unfair to you?

NDO Oh, all my teachers were fair to me.

I   Weren't any unfair?

NDO No. Not really.

Further, many volunteered that some particular teacher had been particularly fair or interested in them. Yet, as one boy expressed it, "School and I just aren't friends."

What has struck us is that in a dropout population that has been particularly afflicted with school problems, there was not a pronounced rejection of school. Perhaps in retrospect after a difficult experience in the work-world, they romanticized school, but the important thing in terms of educational policy is to see the possibilities in their views. The youth are perplexed by school because it places great constraints on their behavior, is not intrinsically interesting, and does not have visible connection with the actual content of jobs on the outside. They recognize, however, that a high school diploma is a necessary *credential* for many jobs, although not an aid in these jobs.

The formal organization of schools may be an obstacle. One dropout was absorbed by drawing. When he could not continue his art classes because he was doing poorly in all his other classes, he left school. School personnel are perplexed by what they see as school-antagonism on the part of these youth, but the latter do not reject school out-of-hand. Teachers and administrators and difficult students have not learned how to become "friends," but there is more of a potential for this on the dropouts' side than has been realized. As one of the boys replied when asked, "How important is school?" "Well, I can't rightly say. I've never had a chance to know what school really is."

Now that they are out of school and have experienced the difficulties of the labor market, the majority of boys wished they had not left school, although many do not see on what basis they could have remained in that environment. It may be that, once boys in eighth grade or later have begun to move onto the school-leaving track, little will keep them in school. Perhaps it is after they have entered the labor market and tasted its possibilities and pitfalls that they then offer the greatest potential for satisfactory school performance. But in very few cities is there the flexibility which permits readmission any time during the year and provides special programs for the returnees.

Ninety per cent of our dropouts liked the following school subjects: math, science, physical education, art, and shop. English and social studies were courses our dropouts had the most difficulties with; they were dull and uninteresting. The potential of these generally disliked courses is revealed by a Negro dropout whose social studies teacher had the class "act out" historical events. He relates:

> You might think it was crazy, but you actually felt that you were there, at the Boston massacre. Now, why can't other teachers do that?

The great interest in science fields among our male dropouts and the "culturally deprived" generally has not been developed. Martin Mayer has pointed out that it is regrettable that the innovational programs in science teaching are mostly beamed at the elite schools, public and private, rather than at the slum schools, where they might capture the imagination of youth who find many school subjects uninteresting but not those in science. The constant reporting that many dropouts are too poor in mathematics to be able to benefit from advanced vocational and technical training underlines the inadequacy of science teaching.

Frustrated school teachers and administrators can make life so unpleasant for students that they are in effect pushed out (though the students get labeled 'dropouts '). But students can also behave so obnoxiously as to make expulsion a virtual certainty, which may be a covert way of dropping out. In either case, the status of "student" is abandoned and teachers are spared the job of teaching those difficult to teach.

Similar issues are present, although even more veiled by labels, in the case of welfare recipients, people lacking conventional relationships with economic or political institutions.[4]

Only 32 cities in the United States have total populations greater than the welfare population of New York City. Of 360,000 New Yorkers receiving public assistance, 200,000 are children. Another 20,000 children wander in and out of public-welfare institutions like New York sparrows looking for the spring. Who is responsible for these 220,000 children? How do they live? And who will dare face them 15 years from now?

The Department of Welfare of the City of New York is responsible for the care of all persons eligible for welfare aid within the five boroughs of the city. Nine thousand employees, including a social-service staff of 4,000, work for the department. Many of the social-service workers are in the process of resigning; the conflict between the utopian aims of New York State's Social Welfare Law and the realities they face daily in their territories has left them shattered and helpless.

In 1963, the Department of Welfare will spend $300 million. It will provide food, shelter, clothing, medical care and a potluck of sociological stew to an army of people who, through loss of money or inability to earn money, could not otherwise survive. The dollar cost is shared by local, state and Federal authorities. The moral cost is immeasurable.

The Social Welfare Law of New York State is a marvelously conceived document that spells out the American dream of total security. It charges the state with complete responsibility for all the needs of life, excepting Golden Books for children and contraceptive information for adults. New York City's Handbook for Case Units in Public Assistance specifically budgets money for more than 70 services, collectively designed to create for the have-nots the normal climate of 20th-century life.

For many of the aged, the disabled and the unemployed, public assistance is an immediate alternative to catastrophe. But what happens to the lives of tens of thousands of children, the aged and the disabled is so contrary to the law that the "dream of security" becomes a terrifying nightmare. And as long as inexhaustible funds are available to house children—if house is the word—to spoon-feed the aged into canvas mortuary sacks, to prop up the disabled and to file away the unemployed, 360,000 human beings will continue to be paraded as statistical icons by the Department of Welfare. Why? Because the Department of Welfare has not dared to admit, publicly and with candor, the enormity of the

[4]From Julius Horwitz, "The Grim State of Welfare," Look, March 26, 1963, pp. 72, 77-78, 80. Reprinted by permission of William Morris Agency, Inc. Copyright © by Cowles Communications, Inc.

social problems it faces, problems for which it has assumed a fatuous and dangerous responsibility. In self-defense, Welfare buries that responsibility in case records, in bureaucratic secrecy, in private guilt, in what John Dewey called "riotous glorification."

What really happens in the public-assistance world of New York City? No one can possibly know without taking the black notebook of a social investigator under his arm and walking into the rotting ghettos of New York: the great blocks of Harlem, East Harlem, the West Side, blocks so horrible that they would have awed the missionaries of the 19th century. The black notebook has become a symbol of living death to tens of thousands of New Yorkers. It lists the families for whom simple words like love, home, work, father are devoid of meaning. It lists families whom the rest of us have ruthlessly dumped into oblivion, to be hidden from our sight and banished from our thoughts.

These are the families who fall early prey to the drug pushers, the addicts, the muggers, the purse snatchers, the elevator thieves, the psychologically castrated men whose only proof of manhood is an out-of-wedlock baby, and the morally castrated welfare drifters who have brought panic to New York, a panic that pulses through thousands of brownstone blocks, where white, Negro and Puerto Rican families plot escapes with the same inner frenzy that infected Londoners during the bubonic plague.

For seven years, I carried the black notebook. There are many names in it. The names used in this article are not from my notebook. They are fictitious. The situations are not. They are composites of actual case histories. The black notebook is immediately recognized on the stoops of the sprawling slums of the East and West Side. That notebook brims with requests for beds, shoes, teeth, eye appointments, winter coats and the forbidden contraceptives. That notebook is a *"fenómeno"* to thousands of Puerto Rican families in New York. That notebook is more destructive to the American Negro than all the segregation laws of the South. That notebook has spawned the special "landlords" who swarm into the welfare offal like the worms that five-year-old Paula Rivera saw crawling into the mouth of a Mr. Clark during the three days he lay dead in the "single-room occupancy" brownstone owned by a Mr. Sheck. Paula's mother took her screaming out of the building; they slept on a friend's floor in East Harlem rather than return to Mr. Sheck's building.

You must walk through the West Side buildings to know what it's like to have Mr. Sheck for your landlord.

I've known Mr. Sheck as long as I've carried the black notebook. He owns five buildings on the West Side The five hold a total of over 200 families, if you count as a family any single, unattached person with one or more children. All the people in his houses are on welfare, except for an occasional tenant, unable or unwilling to move. Rents are $15 a week for a cube called a room, and $27.50 to $32.50 a week for a two-room furnished apartment, designed to house families with four or more children when no one else in New York City will house them. These two-room furnished apartments have been "decontrolled." This means that, for a start, the landlord can charge any kind of rent, and beyond that, anything goes.

Who would pay $30 a week for two rooms chopped out of a railroad flat, with broken walls, vermin, furniture that belongs in an incinerator, a front door through which rats enter as freely as the swarming children? Who would pay $30 a week, $65 semimonthly, $130 a month? The City of New York would and does. Why? The landlords know the answer. And the answer makes them inviolate. One of them said, "I run a pigsty for the City of New York. We're partners. See? The city pays me to keep these people off the street and out of everybody's sight, period. They aren't people. They're drunken, filthy, baby-producing pigs, and as soon as they die off, there are more to take their places. Nobody in City Hall would dare mention 'birth control.' They might lose votes, but they don't care about losing the whole city to these pigs. Nobody down there knows how these people live, because if they did, they would scream in their sleep. Me? I sleep, because I'm doing everybody a favor. I give the pigs four walls, and the city appreciates it, or, instead of paying me so well, they'd close me down tomorrow, just like they close down bookie joints and hustlers. But they won't, because there's no place else to put the 150 babies I've got urinating in my halls."

Slums are not a new story in New York. As soon as it took shape, the city became a massive slum. But the institutionalized slum, the publicly supported, high-rental slum, the slum that houses only welfare families, the slum that a child cannot forget, not in sleep, not in the ping of heroin, not in Rockland State Hospital, this is the new social-welfare slum.

Wilma Gilbort is one of Mr. Sheck's tenants. Open the door to Mrs. Gilbort's two rooms. You squeeze between the edge of the door and the edge of the stove and enter a dark hall that is a bedroom for five children, whose faces look at you with shattered innocence. Leonard, William, and Thomas sleep in the three-quarter bed. Deborah and Judy sleep in the single bed. Deborah has asthma. William is retarded. Thomas screams in his classroom. Leonard is in a PS 600 school, a kind of educational stopgap for children who are apt to fling themselves at our throats. The living room, where Roberta sleeps on a cot, hasn't seen sunlight since 1905.

Roberta is 14, and pregnant. Mrs. Gilbort is 41, and pregnant. This is Roberta's first pregnancy. It is Mrs. Gilbort's 16th. Her ten living children (one, Louis, is in prison) had seven different fathers—all with whereabouts unknown, except for George Williams in Pilgrim State Hospital and John Green in Manhattan State Hospital.

"I got caught this time, Mr. Horwitz," said Mrs. Gilbort. "I didn't mean to let it go this far.'

I could see her stomach pushing out the skirt held together by a diaper pin, a stomach that has heard 16 human monologues, five silenced by the probing of a clothespin.

"Generally I get rid of them, Mr. Horwitz, you know that from my old record. I don't see any reason for bringing more of them into the world."

"Where are you going to put this one? There's no room left for a second crib."

"In the dresser drawer. She'll grow up all right."

I opened my black notebook. "Who's the father?"

Mrs. Gilbort looked at me, trying to remember. Her mind strained for a name, a presence, a real man. She didn't remember, or she didn't know.

Roberta spoke up. Her slipper scraped on the floor. I thought it was the scratching of a rat. I did see a rat run under the crib. Charles saw the rat and smiled secretly at me. Charles is six.

"You know it was that super's helper on West 103rd Street," Roberta told her mother.

"Yes, I'm sure it was him," Mrs. Gilbort told me, relieved.

"Who's him? I need a name."

"He didn't have much of a name. They called him Pim. But that's not his real name. He's from Jersey. I don't know anything about him except that he was a super's helper."

"Did he actually work as a super's helper, or did he just sleep in the basement?"

"I think he just slept there more of the time."

"Did you tell him you were pregnant?"

"He wasn't around when I knew for sure."

"All right, we'll put the baby on the budget when it comes." The budget is now $172 semimonthly, or $344 a month, plus unlimited medical care, plus a clothing grant that can total $225 a year, plus household replacements as needed, plus the secure knowledge that each additional baby will be provided for out of the common treasury and buried in a common grave. (Mrs. Evins in Apartment 2B rushed into the buildings on West 104th Street begging for money to bury her six-year-old daughter Ellen when she died of a concussion, rather than see her dropped into a pauper's grave on Hart Island.)

I went upstairs, up the green hallway, newly painted for the housing inspectors, past the children rushing down into West 101st Street. Were they children? Every girl in Sheck's building over the age of 13 was pregnant, or had delivered a baby, or was imminently in the process of initiation. Like little girls playing with dolls everywhere, they believed their babies were real. The babies weren't real! The babies were hunks of flesh, laid down in dark rooms to age like meat, to be eaten when their taste appealed to rats, sodomites, drug pushers. And if they survived to the age of 18, they could expect to receive their own crisp IBM-processed public-assistance check, payable with the proper yellow identification card.

Mrs. Ringate lives on the first floor. Her door opens right into her toilet. The kitchen is a dark hole with a tiny refrigerator and a makeshift sink drained by leaking rubber hoses. Her two rooms hold five beds and two cribs, and cost $135 a month. The two cribs hold two babies born seven months ago on the 5th and 15th. Mrs. Ringate had her baby on the 5th. Her daughter Gloria had hers on the 15th. Gloria is 17. Mrs. Ringate is 37. Gloria "graduated" from a training school. Mrs. Ringate's oldest son Lawrence is in Dannemora prison. He threw a bottle of lye at his mother; it ate into her face and blinded her in one eye, almost blotting our her vision of him. I looked at Gloria and saw that she was pregnant again.

"Who this time?" I asked Gloria. The father of the first baby was Juan Martinez. He signed the form 384b admitting paternity, then vanished into the brownstones. Gloria told me that she wouldn't go looking for him, because she had heard he was pushing dope on West 88th Street. I could tell by Gloria's eyes that she heard only about every fifth word I uttered, and probably understood about as many as a well-trained cocker spaniel.

"I need a name for the record," I said to Gloria.

"Put down any name this time, Mr. Horwitz. I don't know his name for sure, and that's a fact. And it doesn't make any difference who's the father as long as you give me the checks." Gloria went into the toilet to comb her hair.

Mrs. Ringate showed me the letter from Dannemora advising her that her son would be discharged as soon as he was no longer capable of throwing lye in his mother's face.

"Will they let Lawrence out for real, Mr. Horwitz?"

"They might if they find the right pills."

"What do I do then?"

"Call the police and get an order restricting him from coming to your house."

"You know that won't keep him away. He'll come up the fire escape. He kicked the door in one time. One time, when I had the door blocked with the crib, he started to break in the wall. He'll do it again."

"Why?"

"You must know, Mr. Horwitz, you must know. I think if they let Lawrence out of that hospital, I'm going to take him South and show him his father's grave. Then at least he'll know he had a father once. He's a sick boy. I guessed that when I first saw him laying next to me. His eyes just looked like he shouldn't be looking out on this world. His eyes didn't have the surprise of a new baby. This is no place for him, not this world. He'll get shot in the head by the police or beaten to death in a street fight if they let him out. And if they keep him, then they've got to feed him all those years and watch him to see that he doesn't kill anyone in that hospital. Just send the checks, Mr. Horwitz, as

Gloria says. She hasn't the good sense of a three-year-old baby, but she knows about the checks, your checks. Do you know what she told me last night? I tried to talk to her about what she was going to do with her first baby and the coming baby, because she can't stay here—there's no room for us to breathe or for all of us to sit down and eat at the same time. Do you know what Gloria told me? 'Shut up, you pig. I'm getting my own check, ain't I?''

Mrs. Ringate spoke in a whisper, as though she believed her other children might survive if they didn't hear, but they lay on their beds, stiff, silent, straining, and they already knew.

I went into Anna Domingo's room on West 94th Street. Her mother, Rosa, lives in 2F. Anna lives in 4D. Her mother is a drug addict who has managed to fill two Department of Welfare case folders in eight years. Anna had to quit school. She had her first baby at 16 and now has a second baby. Her room is big enough to hold two cribs, a single bed, one chair, a table. The cooking is done in the community kitchen, and her babies' food is carried through trash-strewn corridors. Anna's brother lives with her mother in 2F. He sleeps with his mother. Incest would be the least of his mother's preoccupations.

"When are you going to get out of here?" I asked Anna.

"I look, Mr. Horwitz."

"I said, 'When are you going to get out of here?' You'll be having another baby in ten months."

"I won't have any more."

"How do you know?"

"I'll go to church and tell God that I won't have any more babies. I'll tell Him that I'm not His seed anymore."

"But you still have to get out of here."

"I will, Mr. Horwitz. If I get to be like my mother. I'm going to stick my head in an oven."

"Is she sleeping with your brother?"

"I don't know. I don't know what she does. She's high as soon as the check comes on the first and the 16th. I try to feed her after that. I don't know how she lives. I only know she's my mother because we used to be on the same welfare budget. I want to get off the budget, Mr. Horwitz, that's what I want to do more than anything else in the world. I hate being on welfare. I know I can't prove it to you now, but that's what I want to do, and that's what I *will* do. I'm looking for someone to take care of my babies. If I find someone, I can go out and work like the other people I see on the street."

"But, in the meantime, you're in this damn building."

"On check day, I'll move. I'll take my check before the landlord cashes it. He always takes his rent money first. He always says I owe him money for extra days. Why does he need *more* money from me, if the money I get is only enough to feed me and my babies for 15 days? I'll move on check day. I'll run."

I watched Anna "run" from Apt. 4D to Apt. 3C.

How do you stop the institutionalized welfare slums, the slums that turn New York's classrooms into bedlam, the slums that turn 220,000 children into potential criminals and their teachers into terrorized bureaucrats? How do you fight the institutionalized welfare slums, frequently disguised as Broadway hotels? What do you do with welfare slums hidden in blocks of crumbling, hacked-up, emasculated apartment houses, when they are protected by the guilt and fear of the Department of Welfare? Recently, a few sacrificial blocks and separate houses have been fed to the bulldozers. But what do you do when the shiny, vertical replacements are almost immediately befouled by the same forces that poisoned the tenements? What do you do when the cancer of welfare slums spreads to nursing homes, turning them into charnel houses? What do you do with the welfare slums that breed schizophrenia in children faster than the slums of the 19th century bred tuberculosis? And what of the welfare slums that are burgeoning all over the American urban landscape? For example, in 1961, Westchester County spent $11,806,990 on direct assistance, which was 27.5 percent of the total county expenditures, and Westchester is considered a prime refuge from the panic created by New York's welfare situation.

How do we stop the insensate drift toward impenetrable welfare slums? How do we smash an atom? Or place 12,000,000 men under arms? Or wipe out polio? Or send a chimpanzee to talk to the man in the moon? How?

The disaffiliating relationships in the welfare slum are horrifying enough. But the process is gradual—in comparison with the abrupt force with which the United States extruded Japanese Americans from their homes and from the entire West Coast in 1942.[5]

The outbreak of World War II found the Japanese community ill-prepared to meet the sudden stresses imposed upon it. Internal strains of group loyalties and identifications had eroded consensus and emphasized intergenerational conflicts. It is not certain—even though it is generally assumed—that the Manchurian invasion and the Sino-Japanese War resulted in an increase in either latent or manifest aggressions against the Japanese population on the West Coast. It is almost certain, however, that the Japanese had become highly sensitized to the ambiguity of their status, and the Alien Registration Act of 1940 underlined the defective status of the Issei.[6]

The growing crisis in the Pacific during the summer of 1941 precipitated a

[5]From Leonard Broom and John Kitsuse, *The Managed Casualty*, University of California Press, 1956, pp. 12-15. Published in *Culture and Society*, v. 6, pp. 1-26. Reprinted by permission.

[6]"Issei" refers to Japanese-Americans born in Japan, "Nisei" to Japanese-Americans born in the United States. "JACL" refers to the Japanese-American Community League.

series of "loyalty demonstrations" and formal renunciation of dual citizenship status by anxious Nisei under the leadership of the JACL. The loyalty issue raised before the war by the Nisei themselves was a recognition of their vulnerability. Despite the prolonged diplomatic crises, the Pearl Harbor attack found the Japanese on the West Coast psychologically and organizationally unprepared, and the most common reaction was one of utter disbelief followed by an acute sense of exposure. Movement was voluntarily restricted and, whenever possible, travel was avoided. Rumors that Japanese were being attacked and insulted heightened their feelings of fear and anxiety, but during the month of December the Japanese were comforted by the sympathy of their hakujin friends. In the first month of the war organized anti-Japanese sentiments were exceptional. However, the serious consequences of the war for the Japanese population were dramatized by FBI raids, which resulted in the internment of some 5,000 Japanese during the first few weeks. About one Japanese home in six had one member, usually the Issei father, interned. Issei were designated enemy aliens, their funds were impounded, the vernacular press was suspended, and travel was limited.

The major ethnic institutions collapsed, and community resources were dissipated. Language schools, Buddhist temples, *Nihonjinkai*, and other organizations were closed. The Japanese population indiscriminately destroyed possessions (art objects, letters, magazines, photographs, etc.) which they feared might be suspect. Even those Issei who were not involved in nationalistic organizations searched their homes for evidence that might incriminate them. The destruction of Japanese items symbolized the population's awareness of their extreme vulnerability.

The Japanese population had hardly begun to adjust to the initial impact of the war when anti-Oriental elements on the West Coast began their activity. Newspapers headlined the FBI raids for contraband, and reported and expressed increasing support for the evacuation of all Japanese aliens from the West Coast. Scattered acts of violence against Japanese, mostly by Filipinos, were magnified, distorted, and multiplied by rumors that swept through the Japanese community. Raids and arrests by the FBI in February, 1942, further demoralized the Japanese population. In almost every home Issei fathers were prepared to be picked up. The Japanese community was without leadership except for the Nisei-led JACL, which advocated full cooperation with the American authorities.

However, rumors were already being circulated that the JACL leaders were turning informers in order to secure special treatment by the authorities and to gain possession of Issei holdings. The focus of group hostility and resentment was sharpened by the JACL's declaration that it was the duty of the Japanese in America to prove their loyalty by aiding the authorities to apprehend suspicious persons. Arguments raged about whether Nisei could betray their Issei parents. From this it was a short step to open accusation of *inu* (dog, informer) against pro-American Nisei, and when the JACL urged the Japanese to cooperate in the evacuation, the majority of the population rejected its leadership and isolated its leaders. These preevacuation events laid the foundations for acts of violence against some JACL leaders in the relocation centers.

The foundations of the JACL leadership were weak and could not sustain the internal stresses that were aggravated by the threat of the evacuation. Nor was the dominant community any better organized to cope with the sudden crisis of civil liberties. Groups that ultimately worked vigorously to ameliorate the status of the evacuees were unorganized or silent.

By the end of January, 1942, two congressional committees, activated by West Coast pressure groups, were investigating means of evacuating the Japanese, including American citizens of Japanese ancestry. On February 13 a joint meeting of the Congressional Committees on Defense and on Alien Nationality and Sabotage passed a resolution recommending "... immediate evacuation of *all persons of Japanese lineage* and all others, aliens and citizens alike, whose presence shall be deemed dangerous or inimical to the safety of the defense of the United States from all strategic areas." General DeWitt of the Western Defense Command was already drafting a memorandum in favor of mass evacuation. He issued it on February 14, and five days later the President issued Executive Order No. 9066 authorizing the action.

The Tolan Committee hearings (February 21-March 12, 1942) were instituted at the behest of Carey McWilliams, Chief of the California Division of Immigration and Housing, with the intent of forestalling mass evacuation by giving a forum to moderate voices. The hearings boomeranged, and testimony chiefly supporting evacuation was reported by the press. But these unanticipated consequences were irrelevant, for the Executive Order had been given and the administrative acts were being instituted. The most effective opposition could have done no more than ameliorate the terms of the evacuation. It is just possible that the detention of United States citizens in relocation centers might have been prevented.

The events immediately following Executive Order No. 9066 comprised the most confusing of the many wartime experiences encountered by the Japanese. General DeWitt did not immediately use the power given him by the Order but awaited Congressional endorsement. On February 23 (four days after Executive Order No. 9066 was issued) the California coast near Santa Barbara was shelled by an unidentified vessel. This was the occasion for the publication of "eye-witness" accounts identifying the craft as a Japanese submarine and reports of signaling activities on shore. Two days later, on February 25, in the "Battle of Los Angeles" one to five unidentified planes were reported over the city which was blacked out. Antiaircraft guns were fired. Neither the vessel that reportedly attacked the Santa Barbara coastline nor the planes (if any) over Los Angeles have ever been identified as Japanese. However, the two incidents were dramatized and gave new support to demands for the immediate removal of all persons of Japanese descent from the West Coast. In response to these demands, General DeWitt issued the following statement:

> Military necessity is the sole yardstick by which the Army has selected the military areas from which the exclusion of certain groups will be required.
>
> Public clamor for evacuation from non-strategic areas and the insistence of local organizations and officials that evacuees not be moved into their communities cannot and will not be heeded, for considerations of national security must come first. . . .

On March 2, DeWitt issued Proclamation No. 1 designating the western halves of Washington, Oregon, and California, and the southern part of Arizona as Military Area No. 1, from which Japanese, German, or Italian aliens and *persons of Japanese ancestry* would be excluded. He announced that an evacuation program was being planned and advised the Japanese to evacuate the area voluntarily to "save themselves possible future trouble."

After hastily liquidating their businesses and properties, some Japanese moved into the interior agricultural regions of the three western states. Their reception by local residents was frequently hostile. Some evacuees attempting to cross state lines into the Rocky Mountain states were met and turned back by vigilantes. The resulting confusion was so great that on March 27, roughly three weeks after he had advised voluntary evacuation, DeWitt issued Public Proclamation No. 4 forbidding further migration of Japanese from Military Area No. 1.

Forbidden to move, and faced with the prospect of being moved into detention centers at a proximate but unknown date, the Japanese communities were disorganized. To continue work in such circumstances seemed futile, and many Japanese quit their jobs or closed their businesses. Many Nisei children withdrew from school. Military curfews imposed upon the Japanese curtailed ordinary travel and visiting, hindered those who continued to work, and handicapped those who attempted to make arrangements for the disposal of their property. Idleness increased the sense of self-consciousness, exposure, and vulnerability. Widespread and acute insecurity deterred the people from group activities which might have ameliorated the accumulating tensions or have enabled them to explore a new basis of community solidarity.

Another book gives further details of the evacuation and its results.[7]

The tale of injustices and manipulations to which the evacuees were exposed has been told and the arguments assessed often enough. For our purposes we

---

[7]From Leonard Broom and Ruth Riemer, *Removal and Return*, University of California Press, 1949, pp. 124-125, 128-130, 156-157. Copyright © 1949, The Regents of the University of California. Reprinted by permission.

need only to say that a segment of a population was precipitantly taken into custody. As a consequence they suffered damage to their status in the community, their security and self-esteem, their ability to earn, and their economic resources.

The timetable and plan of the Evacuation made large economic losses inevitable. For most of the population only one week elapsed between the notice of their Evacuation date and their actual removal. For some evacuees, particularly at the beginning of the program, as little as 48 hours were allowed for sale, rental, loan, storage, or even gift of real property and possessions. The following illustrates the confusion that hampered the efforts of Japanese Americans to salvage their property.

> On Tuesday, February 10, 1942, posters were put up on Terminal Island by Department of Justice order, warning all aliens that the deadline for their departure from the island was the following Monday, February 16. However, on February 11, without warning, a presidential order transferred Terminal Island to the jurisdiction of the Navy, and Secretary Knox instructed Rear Admiral R. S. Holmes, Commandant of the 11th Naval District in San Diego, to notify *all* residents [including citizens] of Terminal Island that their dwellings would be condemned and that they would be evicted within 30 days. This arrangement cancelled the order of the Department of Justice, and on the face of the matter it seemed to constitute a reprieve of eviction sentence. Before a week had passed, the residents of Terminal Island were ordered to be out within 48 hours of notification.

Nearly 2,000 persons had been evacuated from Terminal Island before Assistant Secretary of War McCloy sent Lieutenant General DeWitt a memorandum of recommendations about safeguarding the property of evacuees. The operation was an extemporized one and never provided for the minimal protective facilities. Mr. McCloy wrote, in his memorandum of February 20, 1942, in such generalities as the following:

> It will, of course, be necessary that your plans include provision for protection of the property, particularly the physical property, of evacuees. All reasonable measures should be taken through publicity and other means, to encourage evacuees to take steps to protect their own property. Where evacuees are unable to do this prior to the time when it is necessary for them to comply with the exclusion orders, *there is always danger* that unscrupulous persons will take *undue advantage* or that physical property unavoidably left behind will be pillaged by lawless elements. The protection of physical property from theft or other harm is primarily the responsibility of state and local law-enforcement agencies, and you will doubtless call upon them for the maximum assistance in this connection. Where they are unable to protect physical property left behind in military areas, the responsibility

will be yours, to provide reasonable protection, either through the use of troops or through other appropriate measures. The appointment by you of a property custodian and the creation by him of an organization to deal with such property in military areas *may become* necessary.

It was clear by February 19 that the Evacuation would be a mass movement involving all persons of Japanese ancestry, yet General DeWitt's *Final Report* states, "Prior to March 10, the General Staff of the Western Defense Command and Fourth Army had not engaged in any extensive planning or preparation for the program." . . .

No adequate storage facilities to protect the population from the exploitation of a buyer's market were provided. At the time of registration, which preceded actual removal by one or two days, evacuees were informed that they might take only such hand baggage as they could carry with them to the assembly centers, and were informed of the facilities of government warehouses. If he stored his property in the government warehouse, the evacuee signed a statement that read, ". . . no liability or responsibility shall be assumed by the Federal Reserve Bank of San Francisco for any act or omission in connection with its disposition. It is understood that no insurance will be provided on this property." The only suggestion of responsibility was the statement at the bottom of the personal property inventory list: "If the property herein claimed to have been delivered, and which actually was delivered, is lost, damaged, or destroyed *as the result of negligence* while it is in the possession or custody of the United States, or of any agency acting for it, the Congress of the United States will be *asked* to take appropriate action for the benefit of owners." In regard to motor vehicles, evacuees were informed, "Evacuees will not be permitted to take their motor vehicles to reception centers. No assurance whatever can be given that evacuees will be enabled at some future time to have the motor vehicles now owned by them returned for their individual use." If unable privately to dispose of the vehicle, the evacuee might ". . . deliver his motor vehicle to Federal Reserve Bank of San Francisco, as Fiscal Agent of the United States, for storage at owner's risk, without insurance; which storage will, in most instances be in open areas . . . and must of necessity be of a character which will subject motor vehicles to a more or less rapid deterioration."

The testimony of Mr. Dillon Myer, who was director of WRA, conveys the manner and consequences of the handling of evacuee property.

Mr. Myer. . . . The Federal Reserve Bank was designated to deal with the urban group and were given authority to provide assistance in the disposition, and assistance and storage and so on. *However, the people generally were urged to take care of their own goods and their own affairs because of the large problem involved.*

About ten per cent—as nearly as we can figure—of the folks did take advantage of the storage facilities for their personal property and the rest of them stored their goods in churches and schoolhouses or in individual homes or left them in storage. A small portion of it was properly guarded and a very great deal of it was vandalized.

Mr. Gwynne. Was what?

Mr. Myer. Vandalized. People broke in and opened trunks and tore them apart and stole washing machines and sewing machines and anything they could dispose of quickly.

Mr. Gwynne. Who did that?

Mr. Myer. We would like to know.

Mr. Gwynne. Was no attempt made by local authorities to maintain order?

Mr. Myer. I think there were some attempts made, but so far as I know no one was ever prosecuted for such actions. I have here three or four pictures which will give you an idea of the type of pattern. This [indicating] is one group where they broke in and this is another group. Here [indicating] they broke in where 800 families had their goods stored. I saw that with my own eyes a short time ago.

Mr. Gwynne. Was that vandalism the result of mob action?

Mr. Myer. No, generally speaking, it was not mob action. It was simply action on the part of individuals. In some cases they suspected the individuals who were custodians but were unable to prove it. In another case individuals broke in through skylights, and other ways, in the middle of the night. So far as I know there was no mob action in connection with this type of vandalism. However, there was vandalism of a mob type such as desecrating a cemetery but not any of this type that I know of.

These generalities may be made tangible by reference to our file of case histories. Experiences like that of Hideo Nakamura were not uncommon. Nakamura and his wife and two hired hands farmed 7.5 acres of leased land near Los Angeles. They had lived on this same tract for nine years, and had built a house and a barn. During the week between receiving notice and their actual removal, they sold their 1934 Chrysler sedan for $50 and their 1934 GMC one-and-a-half-ton truck for $40, a loss of $130 on 1942 wholesale Blue Book values. Unable to sell or to get a substitute operator, they abandoned the half-mature crops. They boarded up the buildings in which they stored household furniture, farm equipment, seeds, and fertilizer. The lease on the land expired, and when they returned after three and a half years in a relocation center, all their possessions, even the buildings, had been removed. They are unable to assign dollar values to these losses, and have no records to substantiate their claims. . . .

We found that about half of the property loss was through sales in which the evacuee was unable to realize the 1942 value of the property. Either he sold in the buyer's market during Evacuation, he was unable to protect his interests in a sale contracted after Evacuation, or the property had so deteriorated through mismanagement or vandalism during his absence that even at later inflated selling prices he could not recover the 1942 dollar value. Only when there was a business transaction have we an indication of the losses from deterioration and the less drastic forms of damage. Thus there is a category of hidden loss that is not assessed.

Abandonment of property was more important for farm families than for other occupational groups. Had the evacuees been willing to take a loss of 90 per cent or more, most of them might have been able to make a sale. Their failure to sell on such disadvantageous terms must be viewed in the context of the Evacuation. Upon being removed to the assembly center, they did not know whether they would be able to return to their homes in a matter of days, weeks, or years. The decision of a very few not to sell may have been due to their stubbornness and refusal to be a party to a business relationship that was regarded as exploitative. However, most such decisions may be viewed as a calculated risk in which the evacuee chose to risk a sure return of perhaps a tenth of his life savings in the hope that he would be able to salvage a more substantial part of it upon his return.

Although storage losses account for less than 10 per cent of the total dollar value lost, they make up about 20 per cent of the losses in personal and household property for each occupational group. Often these stored goods were the items of least dollar value but of great intrinsic meaning to the owners, articles of symbolic value that they could not bring themselves to sell.

"Other" reasons account for approximately 26 per cent of the total losses of all families. In this category were 40 per cent of the losses of business families. Reasons classified under "other" include such situations as inability to collect from debtors; confiscation by the government of cameras, "weapons" (e.g., Samurai swords), and radios; gifts to friends because fair sale or storage was found impossible; damage or deterioration during use by suboperators or renters; loss or damage in shipment from private or government storage to the relocation center; and fraud or disadvantages in negotiating and enforcing the terms of contracts.

The extrusion of Japanese-Americans was massive and spectacular because it was visited simultaneously on so many people. Over a period, however, more people may be the victims of a process of extrusion that operates on one person at a time. Such a process is illustrated by the extruding of the aged from many relationships by their friends and kin.[8]

As I passed through one of the wards I saw Mr. Yarmouth. He waved and motioned for me to come over. The first thing he asked was, "Do you live

[8]From Jules Henry, *Culture Against Man*, New York: Vintage Books, 1963, pp. 396-402. Reprinted by permission.

near my brother near King Street?" It seems that Mr. Yarmouth wanted me to find out if his brother was going to bring Mr. Yarmouth's other shoe. He pointed to his feet and I could see that he had a shoe on his right foot but none on his left. Mr. Yarmouth continued to tell me that he hoped his brother wouldn't let him down; his brother was supposed to bring his other shoe. I told him I lived on Maple and he said, "No, that isn't near my brother." He said if he only had his other shoe he could get up and around. He said that if his brother didn't get the shoe for him Reverend Burr would. The Reverend had promised that he would see about it. Mr. Yarmouth said, "Let's see, today's Friday isn't it?" and I said, "Yes." He said, "Well, there is still Saturday and Sunday maybe. I won't give up hope, I never give up hope." I said, "No, don't ever give up."

The record does not tell whether or not Mr. Yarmouth ever got his other shoe; but his dependence on relatives and children—who often do not come—for even a shoe, his anguish of hope, his sense of being trapped, are repeated themes.

The history of Mr. Yarmouth's eyeglasses is more complete than the brief tale of his missing shoe.

First day. Mr. Yarmouth waved at me and then motioned for me to come over to where he sat in a chair at the foot of his bed. I said, "Hi, how are you today?" He said "Fine," and then asked if I would make a phone call for him. I said I'd be glad to if I could. He then asked if I had a dime and I replied that I did not. It turned out that he wanted reading glasses that his brother had. He said that he had lost his and needed them badly. I told him that I would ask Miss Everson and left him to do so. I found her and told her that Mr. Yarmouth had asked me to call his brother about his glasses and she walked to the desk and wrote this down in a little green book. She was very friendly and said that sometimes the men didn't even have relatives and that then the hospital tried to take care of these things. I replied that I would tell him that I'd talked with her about it and she said, "No" and wrote something in the book. I thanked her and went back to the ward. Mr. Yarmouth asked me if I had any money and I said no, and I told him I talked with Miss Everson, and he said, "Who's that?" I explained that she was the charge nurse and was going to take care of his glasses. He seemed satisfied.

Who is Miss Everson anyway, and what is Mr. Yarmouth to her? "Sometimes," says Miss Everson, "the men [those identityless hundreds] don't even have relatives." As for this particular man, lacking particular eyeglasses, Miss Everson does not know whether or not he has a brother. Like a figure in a dream, writing in a phantom book where all that is written washes away, the charge nurse notes Mr. Yarmouth's request. But the act of writing is an act of magic and an act of pseudo-communication: by writing him down she has done away with Mr. Yarmouth, and the fact that Miss Everson is a make-believe listener writing a make-believe message makes the transmission of the observer's message and the writing in the book a pseudo-communication.

But to Mr. Yarmouth the communication was real:

> Third day. Mr. Yarmouth, who was sitting in a chair at the foot of his bed, beckoned me to come over, "Did you get my brother about my glasses?" I was absolutely amazed. I told him that I hadn't been able to make the call but that Miss Everson had written the request down. "Who's Miss Everson?" he asked. "When does the mail come?" I said I didn't know but that I would go and ask Miss Everson about the mail and the glasses. He kept urging me to find out even though I assured him I would as soon as I could find Miss Everson. (Later) Mr. Yarmouth beckoned to me wildly. "You forgot me," he said, "I knew you would." "No I didn't really forget you, Mr. Yarmouth, I just haven't found Miss Everson yet, but she's here somewhere." "Well, you be sure and tell me." I promised I would.

Mr. Yarmouth is sick—sick with false hope, a grave illness in the hospital. Symptoms of this disease are noisiness, demandingness, and the delusion that something one wants desperately is going to happen. The inner function of the delusion is to prevent the patient from thinking he is dead. Patients afflicted with false hope may become difficult to manage: for example, Mr. Yarmouth had the observer running back and forth stupidly between him and Miss Everson.

> When I found Miss Everson I told her that I had been amazed that Mr. Yarmouth had remembered me, and that he had asked me about his glasses. Miss Everson was very nice and seemed surprised too. She said, "Just tell him *you're* working on it."
> Then I went back to Mr. Yarmouth and told him "they're working on it—they're trying to get your glasses." He seemed satisfied and I left, waving at him as I went.

Miss Everson, who seems to understand the signs and symptoms well, handles the naive observer with sweet and consummate tact: "Just tell him *you're* working on it," she says. What else could she do? If the hospital were to call or write the patients' relatives for "every little thing" it would have to hire a special staff just to handle the phone calls and the correspondence.

The symptom that clinches the diagnosis of false hope is the anger of the staff at the patient.

> Fifth day. I noticed that Mr. Yarmouth had been moved to the left corner of the ward in Mr. Worth's place. He saw me, waved and asked me, "Have they come yet?" I called back, "Not yet."

> Sixth day. Mr. Yarmouth was still at his window. I went over to him and

asked what he was doing in his new spot and he told me that they had moved him around, he didn't know why, and that he had nothing to do but look at the wall. I replied, "Don't do that, look out the window." "I'm trying to," he answered. He was very subdued today.

Mr. Yarmouth had been moved for being argumentative and noisy: frustration over the glasses was more than he could bear.

Eighth day. Mr. Yarmouth sat in exactly the same position he has been in since he was moved into this section. He was sitting by the window facing the wall by his bed. He is so subdued it is striking. . . . When he saw me Mr. Yarmouth beckoned me to come over. He used to do this with a kind of devilishness but now he is almost lethargic, and when he asked me about his glasses and I told him I hadn't been able to find out about them he just accepted this, although in the past he has insisted that I let him know when I'll tell him. As I left he said, with a pathetic attempt to bolster his self-esteem, "Be sure to send the bill to me."

Mr. Yarmouth is "improving." He is giving up hope, yet his self-esteem still prods him into futile gestures of adequacy, as he clings to the idea and the memory of reading and of eyes that served him once:

Tenth day. Mr. Yarmouth with his back to the window. He asked me again about his glasses and I again told him that the order was written down. He knows he won't get them and so do I, so all of this is just a farce. I finally couldn't stand it any more and patting him on the shoulder told him I'd see him later.

Twelfth day. Mr. Yarmouth got out a Christian Science booklet to show me how he can read the larger headings but not the smaller print. "You know," he said, "I'm getting nervous, all I can do is sit here and read, and I have to have glasses." His request is only reasonable and I feel like a hell about it—how ineffectual can you be? Now he asks me about calling his nephew instead of his brother. We talked about Mr. Yarmouth's having been an oculist: "All the doctors used to call me and tell what they wanted and then I'd see that it was done and out on time. They depended on me."

Thus ends the saga of Mr. Yarmouth's glasses. Not once in his false hope did he make contact directly with one of the staff; his only channel of communication—or shall we say, pseudo-communication—was the observer. To him the hospital was a remote impersonal "They," inexorable and inscrutable like the prosecution in Kafka's The Trial. With not enough money for even a phone call, with nobody coming to see him, Mr. Yarmouth is marooned, and being marooned he is "nervous." When in his anxiety he argues with those around him, he is moved around and away from the patients he knows by the same "They" that promise to get his glasses but never do. He is punished for remaining human.

THE FEELING OF BEING DISCARDED

As one comes to know these patients one develops a feeling of unreality about their relatives: do they exist or don't they? Take the case of Mrs. Kohn.

> She was sitting in her wheelchair beside her bed, embroidering. She showed me the pillow cases and showed me how to make French knots. At first she talked slowly, but when she got on the subject of her neices she talked more rapidly. She took hold of my hand and held it. She said, "I have a niece living in town. Every year she goes to Wisconsin on vacation and sends me a card saying, 'I'll be seeing you soon,' and she never does come to see me."

The feeling of being discarded makes them cling to whoever shows a human interest. Holding on for dear life to their remnants of life and humanness is an idiosyncrasy of human obsolescence:

> I had only been in there for a few minutes when Mrs. Ramsey in her bed began calling out, "I'm cold, I'm cold. Cover me up." I walked over to her bed and she grabbed my hand and said, "Cover me, cover me up." I told her that her hands were cold and I pulled the covers up on them.

We have studied the process of becoming obsolete through the history of one man, Mr. Yarmouth; let us now observe a woman. Mrs. Prilmer was moved around, just like Mr. Yarmouth, because she was "noisy." Let us follow her for a few days:

> First day. As I entered the ward Mrs. Prilmer who was sitting on the edge of her bed motioned for me to come over, calling, "Here, here." I went over to her and she took my hand and held on to my arm trying to pull herself up, saying, "Take me to the office, call me a cab, I want to go home. Help me, I can't walk." I said, "I can't do that," but she said, "Yes you can." A patient walked up and said, "Are you her daughter?" and I said, "No." Then the patient said, "She has a daughter and three sons," and Mrs. Prilmer affirmed, "Yes, my daughter lives in Boston; my son comes to visit me every day." So I suggested that she talk to her son about going home, but she replied, "He isn't coming today." I asked, "But I thought you said he came to see you every day?" and Mrs. Prilmer answered, "But he isn't coming today." So I walked over to the aide Miss Jones who was making a bed on the other side of the ward and told her what had happened. She laughed and said, "She used to be so quiet. Tell her her son will be here this afternoon." But I mentioned what I had told her and what answer I had received. "Maybe it would be better if you told her." So Miss Jones went over. Meanwhile I started talking with Mrs. Kohn and she said, "I've been waiting for physiotherapy to come after me. Sometimes I sit here and wait all day and they don't come. I think I'd be just as well off sitting at home." I nodded and

Mrs. Kohn pointed to Mrs. Prilmer, saying, "She goes on like that all the time, even during the night. She stops anybody who'll talk to her; I think she's a little feeble-minded." Just then the aide walked away and Mrs. Prilmer called after her and said she wanted to go home. Jones answered, "I'll tell you what, I'll call the superintendent of the hospital; I'll send him over to see you, O.K.?" When Mrs. Prilmer said, "Yes," Jones and several of the patients laughed.

The record reads further: Finally I left just as an attendant was entering with a heavy cloth strap. Alice (another nurse-observer) asked if Mrs. Prilmer was going to be restrained with that. I said I thought so, but I didn't return to find out.

When people become obsolete, they are likely to be placed in caretaking institutions, and there they are often extruded still further from human relationships. Many people are obsolete before they grow old in the sense that no one wants what they have to offer. For them, the future is precarious, uncertain, and probably unpleasant. A poised readiness to break off relationships by seceding from them may be the only way to survive.[9]

One day, after Tally had gotten paid, he gave me four twenty-dollar bills and asked me to keep them for him. Three days later he asked me for the money. I returned it and asked why he did not put his money in a bank. He said that the banks close at two o'clock. I argued that there were four or more banks within a two-block radius of where he was working at the time and that he could easily get to any one of them on his lunch hour. "No, man," he said, "you don't understand. They close at two o'clock and they closed Saturday and Sunday. Suppose I get into trouble and I got to make it [leave]. Me get out of town, and everything I got in the world layin' up in that bank? No good! No good!"

In another instance, Leroy and his girl friend were discussing "trouble." Leroy was trying to decide how best to go about getting his hands on some "long green" (a lot of money), and his girl friend cautioned him about "trouble." Leroy sneered at this, saying he had had "trouble" all his life and wasn't afraid of a little more. "Anyway," he said, "I'm famous for leaving town."[10]

Thus, the constant awareness of a future loaded with "trouble" results in a constant readiness to leave, to "make it," to "get out of town," and discourages

[9]From Elliott Liebow, *Tally's Corner*, Boston: Little, Brown & Company, 1967, pp. 69-71. Copyright © 1967 by Little, Brown & Co. (Inc.) Reprinted by permission.

[10]And proceeded to do just that in the following year when "trouble"—in this case, a grand jury indictment, a pile of debts, and a violent separation from his wife and children—appeared again.

the man from sinking roots into the world he lives in.[11] Just as it discourages him from putting money in the bank, so it discourages him from committing himself to a job, especially one whose payoff lies in the promise of future rewards rather than in the present. In the same way, it discourages him from deep and lasting commitments to family and friends or to any other persons, places or things, since such commitments could hold him hostage, limiting his freedom of movement and thereby compromising his security which lies in that freedom.

Tally's individualistic flight is one way to deal with the problems a black American faces. Another way is through a *collective* secession from American culture and society: separatism. Separatism waxed and waned as a way out among Negro-Americans for almost a century, as an African commentator on the American scene points out.[12]

Until the early part of this century, most Negro leaders and many individuals among the first generation of educated Negroes proudly styled themselves "race men" who were above all concerned with reconstructing the economic, moral, and cultural life of their people. Today, however, such a reference is not only shunned but repudiated. The identification of middle-class Negro leaders with the masses of their race has grown increasingly tenuous and weak. They appear no longer to be seeking the dignity and the integrity of their race in America, but rather the political rights of Negroes as American citizens—a valuable goal in American life.[13] The bonds of race which bind them to the masses are increasingly loose and involuntary. They are no longer the leaders of their race, for they have arrived, i.e., gained entrance into white middle-class society. They cannot, however, take the millions of other Negroes along with them. They reject and despise the Negro masses, whom they deem responsible for what they know to be a continuing rejection by the whites, into whose society they are not really assimilated.[14]

[11] For a discussion of "trouble" as a focal concern of lower-class culture, see Walter Miller, "Lower Class Culture as a Generating Milieu of Gang Delinquency," pp. 7, 8.

[12] From E. U. Essien-Udom, *Black Nationalism*, Chicago: University of Chicago Press, 1962, pp. 2-16. Reprinted by permission.

[13] For a good discussion of "race values" and "race ends" among Negroes, see James Q. Wilson, *Negro Politics: The Search for Leadership* (Glencoe, Ill.: The Free Press, 1960), chap. XIII, "Goals of Negro Leaders." See also Gunnar Myrdal, *An American Dilemma* (New York: Harper, 1944) for the ambivalences in Negro behavior concerning "race ends"; Frazier, *op. cit.*, pp. 216 ff.; R. Kinzer and E. Sagarin, *The Negro in American Business: The Conflict Between Separation and Integration* (New York: Greenberg, 1952); St. Clair Drake and Horace Cayton, *Black Metropolis* (New York: Harper, 1945), pp. 716-54.

[14] We do not deny that there is greater social mobility among Negroes at the present time than in any other time in their history. In fact, it is for this reason that class distinction within the Negro group is acquiring new social significance. It makes the disparity obvious between the "fortunes" of the lower classes and those of the middle and upper classes.

White middle-class society, in reality, is not, and for a long time to come may not be, open to the millions of black Americans. But, in fact, neither is Negro middle-class society open to them. The inferior material and cultural standards of the Negro masses prevent them from entering either society. Their economic status, their moral habits, and the image they have been given of themselves, condemn them to live and die trapped in the Negro ghettos of the urban centers of America. In all probability, most will remain members of the lower class, despised by white and Negro middle-class society alike. The overwhelming objective limitations placed on their cultural, economic, and political aspirations make it impossible for them to escape from their community; they cannot wish away their racial identity. Whether they view it positively or negatively, they cannot be indifferent to it. It is the stuff of their lives and an omnipresent, harsh reality. For this reason the Negro masses are instinctively "race men." . . .

The nationalist leaders contend that the Negroes must become consciously aware of their identity as a group in America; they must realize their degradation and strive by individual and collective effort to redeem their communities and regain their human dignity. The Negro masses, unlike the middle and upper class, are seeking a way out of a sociocultural environment, a spiritual and psychological impasse, fostered by the stubbornly lingering mores of slavery and complicated during the present century by the urbanization of American society. The vast majority of black Americans, however, do not know how to liberate themselves. They look forward to that day when they will find themselves in the "promised land" without making any effort to bring it about. . . .

The concept of nationalism, which is germane to this study, may be thought of as the belief of a group that it possesses, or ought to possess, a country; that it shares, or ought to share, a common heritage of language, culture, and religion; and that its heritage, way of life, and ethnic identity are distinct from those of other groups. Nationalists believe that they ought to rule themselves and shape their own destinies, and that they should therefore be in control of their social, economic, and political institutions. Such beliefs among American Negroes, particularly among the followers of Muhammad, are here called black nationalism.

It must be admitted at the outset that neither the Nation of Islam nor any other black nationalist organization wholly conforms to this definition. Nonetheless, it may be helpful, in comprehending certain patterns of behavior among the black nationalists, to observe the degree to which they incorporate nationalist symbols, and in remarking deviations from the ideal type. Although black nationalism shares some characteristics of all nationalisms, it must be considered a unique type of separatist nationalism seeking an actual physical and political withdrawal from existing society. Apart from the unifying symbols of race and religion, it employs the heritage of abuse and indignity to which the

Negro people in the United States have been subjected and, perhaps more importantly, their common desire for self-improvement. Although most nationalisms involve the idea of race, they are able to develop historically within a definite geographical territory and can therefore easily evoke the common traditions and symbols of that region. The Nation of Islam, however, lacks both a territorial base and the symbolism drawn from either the Negro's past in the United States or from his African origins. This peculiar nationalism has placed its antecedents in what it believes to be "Arabian civilization," the highest development of which was reached in Egypt. It is also extraordinary that its belief in itself as a definite nation of people has produced absolutely no political program for the establishment of a national home. Rather, the final national homeland is guaranteed solely through eschatological beliefs taken from Old Testament prophecies.[15]

The ideas of an eventual return to a national homeland and of black redemption after the apocalypse (the latter a version of the Armageddon of the Book of Revelation) lend the movement two forceful ideological dynamics and inform it with an abstract world view. Both ideas have inspired religious zeal, loyalty to the movement and its leader, and personal sacrifices for the common good. The Muslims' sense of expectancy aids them in persevering and in sustaining their hopes. . . .

Elijah Muhammad makes his appeal primarily to the urban lower-class Negroes, who are for the most part migrants from southern rural sections where they had been accustomed to a way of life markedly different from that encountered in the city. In common with the white working class, they share the furstrations, anxieties, and disillusionments of contemporary urban life; but the Negroes' experience in adjusting to city life is additionally complicated and aggravated by their special status in American society. Black nationalism has its roots in these urban tensions and in the hopeless frustration which the Negroes experience in trying to identify themselves and their aspirations with white society. Compelled by segregation, discrimination, poverty, and ignorance to remain on the periphery of white society and to live and die within the subculture of the Negro ghettos, the Negro masses have had to disassociate themselves from white society. At the same time, however, they are compulsively attracted to it, since power, status, security, even beauty remain white priorities, white possessions. . . .

Black nationalists have in general attempted to deal with the problem of the

---

[15]For an excellent discussion of eschatology, see Norman Cohn, *The Pursuit of the Millenium* (London: Secker and Warburg, 1957), p. xiii. In Christian doctrine, the final struggle is to be between the hosts of Christ and the hosts of anti-Christ. In Muhammad's teaching, the struggle is to be between the Black Nation and the Caucasian race—the world of Islam and the world of Christianity.

Negro's ethnic identity by insisting that "what the Negro needs" is complete separation from the white majority and the establishment of a national home. Unlike the vast majority of American Negroes, the nationalists maintain that a positive identification with their "Negro-ness," or with their ancestral homeland, is a prerequisite to both personal dignity and effective social action. There is, however, no agreement among them as to what their ethnicity is. They are not even agreed upon a name for themselves. Some prefer "Afro-Americans," other "Aframericans," "Africans Abroad," "Persons of African Descent," "Asiatics," or simply "black people." . . .

Because it symbolizes the oppression of the Negro, the white culture's political and religious basis is rejected: the Muslims do not vote in local or national elections; they resist induction into the United States military services; and they categorically reject Christianity as the "graveyard" of the Negro people. The Negro subculture is as well rejected as "uncivilized," and as impeding their material, cultural, and moral advancement.

In order to create, to fashion a unified community, Muhammad first directs his attack against those forces which have so disastrously atomized and weakened Negro society. He seeks to provide the Negro with a spiritual and moral context within which shaken pride and confidence may be restored and unused or abused energies directed toward an all-encompassing goal; to heal the wound of the Negro's dual membership in American society. Specifically, Muhammad denounces the matriarchal character of Negro society; the relative lack of masculine parental authority which makes the enforcement of discipline within the family difficult; the traditional lack of savings- and capital-accumulation habits; and the folk belief that "white is right," which leads to a dependence upon the initiative of the white man. Personal indolence and laziness are sternly deprecated. Habits of hard work and thrift are extolled.

The Muslims disapprove of the expression of undisciplined, spontaneous impulses. The pursuit of a "righteous" life as prescribed by the "Laws of Islam" and by Muhammad's directives is seen as the major purpose of existence. These laws and directives prohibit the following: extra-marital sexual relations, the use of alcohol, tobacco, and narcotics, indulging in gambling, dancing, movie-going, dating, sports, long vacations from work, sleeping more than is necessary to health, quarreling between husband and wife, lying, stealing, discourtesy (especially toward women), and insubordination to civil authority, except on the ground of religious obligation. Maintaining personal habits of cleanliness and keeping fastidious homes are moral duties. The eating of pork, cornbread, collard greens, and other foods traditional among southern Negroes is strictly proscribed. No one is permitted to straighten his hair. Women may not dye their hair or conspicuously use cosmetics. Intemperate singing, shouting, laughing loudly are forbidden. Violation of any of these or other rules is punished immediately by suspension from the movement for periods ranging from thirty days to a maximum of seven years, depending on the gravity of the offense. The most important sanctions which appear to regulate the behavior of Muslims are loss of membership in the movement and the chastisement from Allah.

Muhammad's effort to inculcate a sense of self-esteem in the Muslims by encouraging them to practice and assimilate habits that we associate with the middle class is obvious in his teachings. The quest for respectability within and without the Negro community is a primary goal. Their enthusiastic desire to be independent of white control is demonstrated partly by their willingness to overstretch their resources in order to maintain private elementary and high schools in Chicago and Detroit. The effort to strengthen the Muslims' sense of pride is apparent in Muhammad's emphasis on the "glorious" past of the Black Nation: the special relationship between the Muslims and Allah and their connection with "Arabian-Egyptian" civilization.

It should be stressed, however, that Islam is not offered to Negroes merely as a divisive symbol. To the believers it is a living faith and a positive way of life, enabling them, in unacknowledged ways, to follow with devotion moral values reminiscent of the New England Puritans and to aspire to a style of life usually associated with the middle class. The Muslims, being the elect of God, are obligated to pursue a righteous life which would justify their special status in His sight. The pursuit of wealth is good only in so far as it enhances the common good—the elevation of the Nation of Islam and, in general, the masses of American Negroes. The Muslims are determined to rise on the social scale by their own efforts. Imbued with a common purpose, the Muslims appear to drown their fears, frustrations, anxieties, and doubts in the hope of attaining a national home and in the promise and assurance of redemption *now* in the "New World of Islam," purged of the suffering and corruption of the world about them. Such is the sense of "tragic optimism" which has characterized the organized effort of the Negro nationalists to assert their identity and to discover their human worth and dignity in American society.

CONCLUSION

The mix of extrusion and secession that makes up disaffiliation is difficult to disentangle. Probably a little extrusion lies behind every secession, and a little secession has invited every extrusion. Whatever the mix, the result is a sweeping under the rug of those for whom the society has no real place—including those it has maimed, used up, or failed to nurture properly, and those it simply doesn't know how to reclaim. At times the rug bulges in disquieting ways. Then people speak of a "welfare mess." At times, someone peeks under the rug and reveals the horror there.

Occasionally extrusion is spectacularly dominant, as in the detention of Japanese-Americans; at other times, as with many Negro-American movements, secession is dominant (albeit following years of exclusion if not extrusion). Occasionally, for Americans like Tally, there is no real place; they remain poised to secede, one jump ahead of extrusion.

Section H

SEARCH FOR NEW MEANINGS

Relationships may be severed in other ways besides pulling up stakes or disaffiliating, both of which involve a continuing pursuit of the goals most Americans cherish. Some people adjust to the strains of life by simultaneously disengaging themselves and by rejecting the cultural goals others value. They devote themselves to different goals; they search for different answers to the meaning of life. Such people are called "problems" by members of the society who feel their values threatened when others scorn them. They are not problems in the sense that anyone else is deprived of life, liberty, or property. They are problems in the sense that others may be deprived of the sense of security coming from supportive unanimity.

As has been observed many times in this book, human beings do not have instincts to tell them what is worthwhile to do; they depend on cultural definitions. But cultural definitions of the good and the beautiful *have no external or objective validation.* Security in the conviction that one is living his life "meaningfully" and that the things for which he makes sacrifices are *"really worthwhile"* is not easy to come by. It is strengthened when everyone else agrees and shaken when some people sneer.

When others claim that the truly worthwhile life is the opposite of what one stands for, what is one to do? One might change, and conversion experiences do occur. But to the degree that one was committed to his former values, conversion is difficult. It scarcely ever occurs except after painful disorganization and doubt. Disorganization and doubt *are* painful; people seek to avoid them. One way of doing so is to view those who reject one's morality and aesthetics as "social problems." They are not to be taken seriously; they are to be "corrected." This kind of behavior can lead into implacable divisions in society, with each side seeing the others as anti-Christ.

In Chapter 18 we look at some efforts to reinterpret life that run the risk of being regarded as social problems.

chapter 18
Reinterpreting life

Chapter 2 suggested that Americans tend to equate material possessions with the Good Life. Although Americans say they are religious, what they often mean is that it is a good idea to attend religious services. Their real religion, Will Herberg suggested, is The American Way of Life, a secular faith. The Judeo-Christian tradition exists within American culture, although it seems for most Americans more of a museum piece to be taken out and dusted off for ceremonial occasions than a directing influence on daily life. However, its existence, especially those aspects of it that denounce the "things of this world" in favor of eternal salvation, offers an alternative meaning of life for some people in place of dominant secular values. Consider, for example, Jehovah's Witnesses.[1]

One hundred and eighty thousand Jehovah's Witnesses, from every part of this country and about 130 other lands, recently gathered in New York for what they called a Divine Will International Assembly. It was the largest gathering of any kind ever held in the city, and it drew attention as never before to this group, which in recent years has been growing more rapidly than any other religious organization.

The Witnesses impressed New Yorkers not only with their numbers, but with their diversity (they include people from all walks of life), their racial unself-consciousness (many Witnesses are Negroes) and their quiet, orderly behavior (in contrast to the religious controversy, and hostility, they have often aroused). In

[1]From Wayne Phillips, "What Impels Jehovah's Witnesses?" New York *Times Magazine* August 10, 1958, pp. 15, 48-49. Reprinted by permission.

streets, subways, buses, everywhere New Yorkers looked they seemed to see the Witnesses wearing their yellow and purple badges with the legend: "God's Kingdom Rules—*Is the World's End Near?*"

The Witnesses' most striking belief is that since 1914 Satan has ruled the world, but that, in the rapidly approaching Battle of Armageddon, God—whom they call Jehovah—will destroy Satan and all other evil in the world. Thereafter, they believe, God will rule the world and those who have accepted his rule will live on in life everlasting. In one of his many talks at Yankee Stadium and the Polo Grounds, both of which the Witnesses took over for eight days, their leader, Nathan H. Knorr, told them that civilization stands now "at the threshold of a peaceable, happy and life-giving world."

"This is the grandest news," he declared, "although it means that we are living at the end of this worry-filled, problem-wracked, insane, loveless old world. We want the new. We are eager to leave the old."

Jehovah's Witnesses, who take this name from Isaiah xliii, 10 ("Ye are my witnesses, saith the Lord, and my servant whom I have chosen * * *."), grew from a small Bible class organized at Alleghany, Pa., near Pittsburgh, in 1872 by Charles Taze Russell. As the movement spread, a printed course of Bible instruction was evolved and sold from door to door. The Watchtower Bible and Tract Society, which printed these courses and is the organizational form of the movement, was first incorporated in 1884. The name Jehovah's Witnesses was not formally adopted until the first international meeting at Columbus, Ohio, in 1931.

It was a small movement and most people became aware of it only obliquely —by seeing one of its members standing on a street corner offering copies of its semi-monthly publications *The Watchtower* and *Awake!* for sale at 5 cents a copy; by having one of its members call at the door and endeavor to interest them in reading the Bible; by passing the obscure Kingdom Halls that were opened in cities throughout the country, and where Bible study classes are held five days a week.

All baptized Jehovah's Witnesses regard themselves as ministers ordained to devote their lives to preaching the Bible to all men. They work at what they call "temporal jobs" only to supply their essential material needs. All their other energies are devoted to studying the Bible and the techniques of their ministry.

Repeatedly the religious beliefs of the Witnesses have involved them in controversy. They do not believe in saluting the flag, interpreting this as a form of obeisance before temporal imagery that would conflict with their spiritual loyalties. They fought a long and bitter fight up to the Supreme Court before winning the right of their children to attend schools without taking part in flag saluting ceremonies.

For somewhat the same reasons, the Witnesses do not accept military service, and during World War II draft days they claimed exemption on the ground that they were all ordained ministers preaching to the public. Draft boards sent hundreds of young men associated with the Witnesses to Federal penitentiaries.

Another Witness belief forbids blood transfusions—a position they base on the Biblical injunction against eating blood. When, as occasionally happens, one of their children lay close to death and it seemed only a transfusion could save his life, parents have firmly forbidden it, despite extreme public pressure.

The Witnesses cite references to both the Old and New Testaments for all their beliefs, using all translations of the Bible, although their interpretations of these references differ greatly from those of other faiths. They believe the true meaning of the Bible is prophetic and is constantly being unfolded to men, and they deny any possible conflicts within it. They condemn other faiths for what they consider erroneous additions to and elaborations of the teachings of the Bible. Witnesses do not believe in the immortality of the soul, or a fiery hell, or that Christ died on the cross. They believe that only 144,000 persons will go to heaven and that all but about 15,000 of them are already there; that all others who die have no hope of life hereafter or resurrection. Such teachings have brought mob violence, imprisonment, torture and death to Witnesses in countries where other faiths are officially maintained.

In 1942 when Mr. Knorr was chosen as their president, the organization had 115,240 adherents in fifty-four countries. This year, the number of ordained Witnesses reached 780,000 scattered over 164 countries and territories.

The extent of their influence, however, may better be measured by their publishing activity. The basic book expounding their doctrine, "Let God Be True," first appeared in 1946, and so far 16,167,846 copies have been published. Their magazine, *The Watchtower*, published 3,550,000 copies of each issue in fifty languages, including such little-known African dialects as Cinyanja, Ibo and Xhosa.

The expansion of the Witnesses has been a matter of increasing concern to other faiths. Most of their adherents are apparently being attracted from those other churches.

Following are interviews with a number of Jehovah's Witnesses who attended the International Assembly. All talked willingly and openly about their reasons for embracing what they call "The Truth," and all were apparently deeply convinced of their beliefs. . . .

Mr. and Mrs. Wilfred Childs had come to the convention from their home in the summer resort town of York Harbor, Me. In their late twenties, they have been married three years and have no children. Mr. Childs, who has trouble with his hearing and sight, never learned to read too well, and works as a mechanic on automobiles and trailer trucks. His wife augments his $40-a-week take-home pay by caring for an invalid woman.

Florence Childs came from a French Canadian family that had moved south into Maine. She was brought up as a Roman Catholic, but had never been a very regular churchgoer. Her first contact with the Witnesses came two years ago when one of them—Mrs. Norma Vigneau of Portsmouth, N. H.—called at her door.

"She got me interested in reading the Bible," Mrs. Childs said, "and I found that if you knew where to look there were many answers to the questions the priests always told me were mysteries and had to be accepted on faith."

For more than a year Mrs. Childs continued her studies under Mrs. Vigneau's direction. "I didn't dare tell my husband about it; he was death on any kind of religion," she said. "But finally I had to tell him, because I wanted to go to one of the talks at the Kingdom Hall in Portsmouth, and I couldn't get there unless he drove me."

Mr. Childs had been raised in northern Vermont as a Methodist, but long before had rejected any church. "I was shocked when my wife first asked me," he said. "But I finally agreed to take her when she told me all they did was study the Bible. I've always had a lot of respect for the Bible, but never had any use for the way the churches used it."

About a year after his wife was baptized, Mr. Childs also accepted baptism— "because I was convinced the Witnesses preached just what was in the Bible and nothing else." Although they live twelve miles from Portsmouth, they get to meetings there three times a week, work together every day on their studies of the Bible, and, once a week, go out together door-to-door to try to interest others. . . .

Norma Vigneau, the 34-year-old Witness who first came to the door of Mr. and Mrs. Childs, had her first contact with the Witnesses in the same way—when a member of the Portsmouth group called on her. Mrs. Vigneau, brought up in a family of New England Unitarians and a graduate of Lasell Junior College in Auburndale, Mass., was shocked by what he preached.

"I felt sorry for him," she recalled. "I asked myself: 'How could anyone be so ignorant as to believe these things?' I felt it was my duty to invite him in, get out my college textbooks and show him why he was wrong."

To rebut his arguments, though, she found she had to delve deeper and deeper not only into her college texts but into the Bible, and over a period of months she found it was she, rather than he, who was being persuaded.

"I began to realize that in college I had been taught to think in circles," she said. "Nothing was black or white there; everything was the same neutral shade of gray. Finally I began to wonder what I was fighting against—here was something that was simple, straightforward, honest and beyond doubt."

The time came when she had to reveal her interest to her husband, Bob, who had been brought up in a Methodist family but had little use for any church. After the war, he and a partner had opened a gasoline station in Portsmouth, but he became fed up with that business, sold out to his partner, and was using the money to build an apartment house.

For quite a while he just went along, indifferently, with his wife's new ideas. But gradually he found the preachings striking a sympathetic chord.

"During the war my eyes were opened to a lot of things," he said. "I heard the politicians and preachers telling us we were fighting to create a better world. After the war I looked around and saw the United States grabbing everything she could get everywhere, and the people everywhere hating us and telling us to get out. I knew there was nothing better about the world. It became so I got sick every time I picked up a newspaper. I knew this couldn't be what God wanted in the world, and when the Witnesses got me started reading the Bible I found out it wasn't." . . .

Otto Smith, who is 33, came to the New York gathering from Anchorage, Alaska, where he has lived since the war. But he is originally from a strict Baptist family in Corpus Christi, Tex. His dissatisfaction with the faith of his parents broke into the open during the war, he recalls.

"I was a gunner on B-24's stationed in England and flying over Germany," he said. "Before every mission the Protestant, Catholic and Jewish chaplains would get us together and pray. And I kept thinking how over there on the other side the ministers and priests were doing the same thing. 'Now, how can God listen to all of them?' I kept asking myself. It wasn't until I came in contact with the Witnesses that I understood that He wasn't listening to any of them."

Otto was working as an automobile salesman in Anchorage when the first Witness he ever met came to his door and, after a talk, left a copy of "Let God Be True." Otto read it and other literature, and began studying the Bible.

"My wife was dead set against the Witnesses at first," he said. "She comes from East Texas, and they don't have much use for Witnesses down there because of the flag-saluting business before the war." But gradually, Otto said, he interested his wife also, and they were baptized together in 1952. . . .

Among the physicians who have accepted the beliefs of the Witnesses is Dr. F. D. Roylance of Haworth, N.J. Dr. Roylance, 48, is a graduate of the Columbia College of Physicians and Surgeons and is secretary of the medical executive committee of the Englewood, N.J., Hospital.

"I was baptized by my parents in the Disciples of Christ when I was 12 years old," Dr. Roylance said, "but after starting our own family my wife and I began attending the Congregational Church."

For about ten years, he said, he had been studying the Bible on his own, looking for answers to spiritual questions that puzzled him. Occasionally he listened to talks by Fundamentalist preachers on his car radio as he rode between calls on patients.

"But I first learned about the Witnesses," he said, "from a patient who started bringing me Watchtower literature. 'This makes sense,' I said after I read it, and I wrote to the Watchtower. They sent a brother to see me."

In November, 1956, Dr. Roylance was baptized and began to give all the time he could spare from his practice to study and preaching. For him it meant a severe family crisis.

"My wife is very much opposed to all this," he said. "She is Italian, but her father took the family out of the Roman Catholic Church before they came to this country. She still goes to the Congregational Church, and she resents very much the time that this takes from my work and our three children."

Professionally, he said, it had not caused the problems that others might expect. "I recognize that there are cases where a blood transfusion is the best thing that can be done to save a life," he says, "and if a patient is not a Witness and wants the transfusion I don't have any hesitation about prescribing it."

Among the Witnesses who came from foreign countries to the New York Assembly was Max Liebster, 43, born and raised in an Orthodox Jewish home at Reichenbach, near Frankfurt, Germany. Two days after the war began in 1939 he was arrested and sent to a prison at Pforzheim. "For four months I was on my knees every day all day praying for understanding," he recalls. " 'Why, why,' I asked, 'should God permit this persecution of his chosen people?' "

After four months, he was put on a prison train to be taken to the concentration camp at Oranienburg near Berlin. In the car with him was a Jehovah's Witness.

"This man was a farmer," Mr. Liebster said. "His wife had been killed, his five children taken away and sent to a Nazi training center. But he said he would go to prison rather than fight for Hitler. Never before had I seen a man who loved God's commandment more than himself or his family. For fourteen days on the train we were together and talked. He told me how Christ was proven in the Hebrew scriptures—and he quoted the scriptures to me from his head, for they had taken his Bible from him."

At Oranienburg Mr. Liebster saw this Witness tortured and finally killed rather than consent to serving in Hitler's army. "I saw it with my own eyes," he said, "and I made up my mind that I, too, would witness to the truth with my life if I were released."

Later he was moved to a succession of other camps until he reached Buchenwald. There the Germans had confined Leon Blum, the French Socialist leader, in a house set apart from the barracks, with a Witness assigned as his orderly. On May 15, 1945, just after the liberation, Mr. Liebster and two other former Jews were baptized as Witnesses in Leon Blum's bathtub.

"Altogether 10,000 Witnesses were sent to concentration camps," Mr. Liebster said. "Eight thousand came out, but 2,000 were too crippled to work. The 6,000 who were left started preaching all over Germany. Now there are a little over 60,000 of us in West Germany and another 25,000 in East Germany." . . .

What do the varied experiences of these Witnesses add up to?

It would be wrong to make any blanket conclusions about Jehovah's Witnesses and what motivates them on the basis of a handful of interviews. But through them run certain common threads: a deep yearning for religious experience, a conviction that the world is becoming increasingly worse, a desire to find some fundamental explanation of why, a wish to escape from worldly conflict and confusion, and a prayer that, somewhere in the undefined future, things will be better. In addition, and possibly more important, it seems clear that these people—who otherwise probably would have been both alienated from and outside any religious influence—have sought and found in the Jehovah's Witnesses a framework that provides them with both the purpose and strength for the kind of personal morality all religions seek to espouse.

Whether it is fair to term Jehovah's Witnesses a social problem is debatable. Certainly, though, their radical rejection of secular society causes difficulties with their neighbors. And their refusal to bear arms or to participate in the political process would greatly weaken the American political system—if they were more numerous. Furthermore, the Witnesses are not the only religious sect that feels that it must separate itself from American society and pursue other goals. The Amish provide another illustration.[2]

Behavior in the Amish community is oriented to absolute values, involving a conscious belief in religious and ethical ends, entirely for their own sake, and quite independent of any external rewards. This orientation to . . . absolute values, requires of the individual certain unconditional demands. Regardless of any possible cost to themselves, the members are required to put into practice what is required by duty, honor, personal loyalty, and religious calling. The fundamental values and common ends of the group, recognized by the people and accepted by them, have been designated as the charter. A charter need not be reduced to writing to be effective in the little community; it may be thought of as the common purpose of the community, corresponding to a desire or a set of motives embodied in tradition. . . .

To the Amish there is a divine spiritual reality, the Kingdom of God, and a Satanic Kingdom that dominates the present world. It is the duty of a Christian to keep himself "unspotted from the world" and separate from the desires, intent, and goals of the worldly person. Amish preaching and teaching draws upon passages from the Bible which emphasize the necessity of separation from the world. Two passages, perhaps the most often quoted, epitomize for the Amishman the message of the Bible. The first is: "Be not conformed to this world, but be ye transformed by the renewing of your mind that ye may prove what is that good and acceptable and perfect will of God." This to the

[2]From John Hostetler, *Amish Society*, Baltimore: Johns Hopkins Press, 1963, pp. 47-52, 58-62, 66-69, 132-135, 143-145. Reprinted by permission.

Amishman means among other things that one should not dress and behave like the world. The second is: "Be ye not unequally yoked together with unbelievers; for what fellowship hath righteousness with unrighteousness? and what communion hath light with darkness?" This doctrine forbids the Amishman from marrying a non-Amish person or from being in business partnership with an outsider. It is applied generally to all social contacts that would involve intimate connections with persons outside the ceremonial community. This emphasis upon literalness and separateness is compatible with the Amish view of themselves as a "chosen people" or "peculiar people."

The principle of separation conditions and controls the Amishman's contact with the outside world; it colors his entire view of reality and being. Bible teaching is conditioned by the totality of the traditional way of life. Compatible with the doctrine of separation is the doctrine of nonresistance. By the precepts of Christ, the Amish are forbidden to take part in violence and war. In time of war they are conscientious objectors, basing their stand on biblical texts, such as "My kingdom is not of this world: if my kingdom were of this world, then would my servant fight." The Amish have no rationale for self-defense or for defending their possessions. Like many early Anabaptists they are "defenseless Christians." Problems of hostility are met without retaliation. The Amish farmer, in difficulty with the hostile world around him, is admonished by his bishop to follow the example of Isaac: after the warring Philistines had stopped up all the wells of his father Abraham, Isaac moved to new lands and dug new wells. This advice is taken literally, so that in the face of hostility, the Amish move to new locations without defending their rights. . . .

Amish preaching and moral instruction emphasize self-denial and obedience to the teaching of the Word of God, which is equated with the rules of the church. All ministers constantly warn their members to beware of worldliness. Long passages from the Old Testament are retold, giving prominence to crucial events in the lives of Abraham, Isaac, Jacob, Joseph, and Moses. The escape of the Israelites from Egyptian bondage and Moses's giving of the law are sermon themes; punishments meted out to the lawbreakers are emphasized. The themes: "Offenders were executed for breaking the law," and "we are not better than they," are emphatically stressed. The choice put before the congregation is to obey or die. To disobey the church is to die. To obey the church and strive for "full fellowship," that is, complete harmony with the order of the church, is to have *lebendige Hoffnung,* a living hope of salvation. An Amish person simply puts faith in God, obeys the order of the church, and patiently hopes for the best.

Separation from the world is a basic tenet of the Amish charter; yet the Amish are not highly ethnocentric in their relationships with the outside world. They accept as a matter of course other people as they are, without attempting to convert them to the Amish way of life. But for those who are born into the

Amish society, the sanctions for belonging are deeply rooted in the belief in separatism.

The people of the little community have an "inside view" as well as a contrasting "outside view" of things. The doctrine of separation shapes the "outside view," and in discussing further aspects of the Amish charter we turn now to the "inside view." . . .

Once the individual has been baptized, he is committed to keep the *Ordnung* or the rules of the church. For a single person this means keeping one's behavior more in line with the rules than before. With marriage the individual assumes responsibility for keeping the rules as well as for "building the church," which means taking an active part in promoting the rules. The little Amish community is distinctive from other church groups in that the rules governing life are traditional ways not specified in writing. These rules can be known only by being a participant. The rules for living tend to form a body of sentiments that are essentially a list of taboos within the environment of the small Amish community.

All Amish members know the *Ordnung* of their church district and these generally remain oral and unwritten. Perhaps most rules are taken for granted and it is usually those questionable or borderline issues which are specified in the *Ordnung.* These rules are repeated at the *Ordnungsgemee* just preceding communion Sunday. They must have been unanimously endorsed by the ordained body. At the members' meeting following the regular service they are presented orally, after which members are asked to give assent. If there is any change from previous practice, allowing a new innovation or adaptation, this change is not announced. The former taboo is simply not mentioned. A unanimous expression of unity and "peace" with the *Ordnung* makes possible the communion. But without unity there can be no communion.

The following *Ordnung* of a contemporary group, published in English, appears to be representative of the Old Order Amish, except for those portions indicated by brackets. That it appears in print at all is evidence of change from the traditional practice of keeping it oral. This *Ordnung* allows a few practices not typically sanctioned by the Old Order: the giving of tithes, distribution of tracts, belief in assurance of salvation, and limited missionary activity.

ORDNUNG OF A CHRISTIAN CHURCH

Since it is the duty of the church, especially in this day and age, to decide what is fitting and proper and also what is not fitting and proper for a Christian to do, (in points that are not clearly stated in the Bible), we have considered it needful to publish this booklet listing some rules and ordinances of a Christian Church.

We hereby confess to be of one faith with the 18 articles of Faith adopted at Dortrecht, 1632, also with nearly all if not all articles in booklet entitled "Article und Ordnung der Christlichen Gemeinde."

No ornamental bright, showy form-fitting, immodest or silk-like clothing of any kind. Colors such as bright red, orange, yellow and pink not allowed. Amish form of clothing to be followed as a general rule. Costly Sunday clothing to be discouraged. Dresses not shorter than half-way between knees and floor, not over eight inches from floor. Longer advisable. Clothing in every way modest, serviceable and as simple as scripturally possible. Only outside pockets allowed are on work eberhem or vomas and pockets on large overcoats. Dress shoes, if any, to be plain and black only. No high heels and pomp slippers, dress socks, if any, to be black except white for foot hygiene for both sexes. A plain, unshowy suspender without buckles.

Hat to be black with no less than 3-inch rim and not extremely high in crown. No stylish impression in any hat. No pressed trousers. No sweaters.

Prayer covering to be simple, and made to fit head. Should cover all the hair as nearly as possible and is to be worn wherever possible. [Pleating of caps to be discouraged.] No silk ribbons. Young children to dress according to the Word as well as parents. No pink or fancy baby blankets or caps.

Women to wear shawls, bonnets, and capes in public. Aprons to be worn at all times. No adorning of hair among either sex such as parting of hair among men and curling or waving among women.

A full beard should be worn among men and boys after baptism if possible. No shingled hair. Length at least half-way below tops of ears.

No decorations of any kind in buildings inside or out. No fancy yard fences. Linoleum, oilcloth, shelf and wall paper to be plain and unshowy. Overstuffed furniture or any luxury items forbidden. No doilies or napkins. No large mirrors, (fancy glassware), statues or wall pictures for decorations.

[No embroidery work of any kind.] Curtains either dark green rollers or black cloth. No boughten dolls.

No bottle gas or high line electrical appliances.

Stoves should be black if bought new.

Weddings should be simple and without decorations. [Names not attached to gifts.]

No ornaments on buggies or harness.

Tractors to be used only for such things that can hardly be done with horses. Only either stationary engines or tractors with steel tires allowed. No airfilled rubber tires.

Farming and related occupations to be encouraged. Working in cities or factories not permissible. Boys and girls working out away from home for worldly people forbidden except in emergencies.

Worldly amusements as radios, card playing [party games], movies, fairs, etc., forbidden. [Reading, singing, tract distribution, Bible games, relief work, giving of tithes, etc., are encouraged.]

Musical instruments or different voice singing not permissible. No dirty, silly talking or sex teasing of children.

Usury forbidden in most instances. No government benefit payments or partnership in harmful associations. No insurance. No photographs.

No buying or selling of anything on Sunday. It should be kept according to the principles of the Sabbath. [Worship of some kind every Sunday.]

[Women should spend time doing good or reading God's Word instead of taking care of canaries, goldfish or house flowers.]

Church confession is to be made if practical where transgression was made. If not, a written request of forgiveness should be made to said church. All manifest sins to be openly confessed before church before being allowed to commune. I Tim. 5, 20. A period of time required before taking new members into full fellowship.

Because of great falling away from sound doctrine, we do not care to fellowship, that is hold communion, with any churches that allow or uphold any unfruitful works of darkness such as worldliness, fashionable attire, [bed-courtship, habitual smoking or drinking, old wives fables, non-assurance of salvation, anti-missionary zeal] or anything contrary to sound doctrine.

The rules of the Amish church cover the whole range of human experience. In a society where the goal is directed toward keeping the world out, there are many taboos, and customs become symbolic. There are variations in what is allowed from one community to another in the United States and Canada. Custom is regional and therefore not strictly uniform. The most universal of all Amish norms across the United States and Canada are the following: no electricity, telephones, central-heating systems, automobiles, or tractors with pneumatic tires; required are beards but not moustaches for all married men, long hair (which must be parted in the center, if allowed at all), hooks-and-eyes on dresscoats, and the use of horses for farming and travel. No formal education beyong the elementary grades is a rule of life.

The *Ordnung* is an essential part of the Amish charter. It is the way in which the moral postulates of society are expressed and carried out in life. The charter is constantly subjected to forces of change, a source of conflict to be discussed later.

The Amish have their own symbolism which provides a basis for common consciousness and a common course of action. We may hypothesize that in a simple society like the Amish the people themselves become symbolic, and not their achievements as in world civilization. The horse and buggy, the beard of the married man, and the styles of dress—all take on symbolic meaning. All Amish know that this is the accepted way of doing things, and symbolism becomes an effective means of social control as the nonconformist can quickly be detected from the conformist. Symbols which are universal in all Amish communities include the following: hooks-and-eyes on the Sunday coat and vest of all men, trouser styles that have no fly-closing but a flap that buttons along the waist, wide-brimmed black-felt hats for men, white organdy caps for women, plain rather than patterned or striped dresses for women, uncut hair for women, and long hair cut in bangs for men. All these symbols together constitute a world of social reality, a way of life that teaches how people should live and what they should imitate.

An illustration of convention which is symbolic is the way courtesy is expressed among the Amish. Acts rather than words perform this function. In a small society where convention is understood few words are needed between actor and alter to make meanings precise. Words of courtesy, as expressed by the English-speaking world, are conspicuously absent among members of the Amish family and community. The dialect contains few if any words of endearment between husband and wife, but young people of courting age frequently employ

English words of endearment. Amish parents who hear "English" couples exchange words like "honey" and "sweetheart" have remarked that such a relationship is probably anything but "sweet." There are no words in the Amish spoken language that correspond to "pardon me" or "excuse me." Children might use such English terms in their play but persistence in using them in family relationships would not be approved. They would be accused to trying to be "society" persons. "Oops" is sometimes used to indicate that a certain act was not intentional. "Please" and "thank you" are not a part of table manners nor a part of everyday conversation, but children are taught to say *Denki* (thank you) and *Willkomm* (you are welcome) when giving or receiving gifts on special occasions.

Acts of politeness are much more characteristic than words. The wife may brush the husband's hat on Sunday morning before he gets around to it. The act requires no "thank you." If the husband is thoughtful he will carry the toddler, help his wife into the carriage, and tuck the blankets around her. Belching is a normal occurrence around the dinner table and conceived as a sign of good appetite with no thought of discourtesy. A boy who was chewing his food vigorously at the breakfast table was greeted by his older brother with the words: "Fer was machst so weischt?" (Why do you make so ugly?) The boy did not reply but modified his behavior. However, in the presence of English people the Amish will adopt the polite language of the outsider. An Amish woman walking along a village sidewalk who approached a woman washing her sidewalk said "pardon me" as she stepped over the washed part of the sidewalk.

Symbolism in Amish life performs the functions of communication. When much of life is governed by symbols, fewer words are needed for communication. The conspicuous absence of words of courtesy in the Amish dialect would appear to be a function of the importance of symbols, making such words unnecessary. Like dress patterns, the speech habits have also been preserved in the New World. Polite language in Medieval Europe was characteristic of the nobility and not of the peasant groups. Actions among the Amish speak louder than words of courtesy. Acts and intentions are understood, while words of courtesy which might be adopted from the English language would not be understood. The large number of symbols which function within the Amish society aid the growing Amish child to find his place within the family, the community, and within the world of the Amish people.

Anything that can be perceived through the senses can be symbolized, and in Amish society styles of dressing become very important as symbols of group identity. The garb not only admits the individual to full fellowship but also clarifies his role and status within his society.

The hat, for example, distinguishes the Amishman from the outsider and also symbolizes his role within his social structure. When the two-year-old boy discards a dress and begins wearing trousers for the first time, he also receives a stiff jet-black hat with three or more inches of brim. Hat manufacturers produce at least twenty-eight different sizes and a dozen different styles of Amish hats. The bridegroom in Pennsylvania gets a telescopic hat that is worn during the early married years. The hat is distinguished by a permanent crease around the top of the crown. Grandfather's hat has a four-inch crown and a four-inch brim. The bishop's hat has a four- and one-half-inch crown, slightly rounded, and a wide seam around the brim. A hat which has a flatter crown is worn by the rank and file of Amish fathers. The outsider may never notice these differences, or if he does he may regard them as accidental. But to the Amish these symbols indicate whether people are fulfilling the expectations of the group. A young man who wears a hat with a brim that is too narrow is liable for sanction. The very strict Amish congregations can be distinguished from the more progressive ones by the width of the brim and the band around the crown. Thus when the writer's family moved from Pennsylvania to Iowa, one of the first adaptations to make was to take out the scissors and cut off some of the brim. This made my brothers and myself more acceptable to the new community of Amish. At the same time the act symbolized other adaptations that had to be made to adjust to a more "westernized' group of Old Order Amish.

Limiting education to the elementary grades prevents exposure to many areas of scientific knowledge and vocational training. It functions also as a form of boundary maintenance. New inventions and knowledge find their way into the little Amish community by many diffuse and delayed means. As soon as the law will allow, Amish children are taken out of school for work at home. The Amish viewpoint is that "Our people are engaged in some form of agriculture and we feel positive that as farmers we are better off with only a common school education. Education does not build muscle like tilling the soil in the open field and sunshine with lots of hard work. If a boy does little hard work before he is twenty-one, he probably never gets to like it afterward. In other words, he will not amount to much as a farmer."

Conflict over the school question arose in Pennsylvania, a few years later in Ohio, and continues in some areas. Pennsylvania law requires that children attend school until their seventeenth birthday but that children engaged in farm work may be excused through permits when they reach the age of fifteen. The conflict arose when it became clear that some Amish children completed grade eight more than once because their parents were opposed to sending them to high schools. When the parents were summoned to court and refused to pay their fines on grounds that this would admit to being guilty, they were sent to jail. Friends and businessmen paid the fines to release the parents. Some were arrested as many as ten times. The Amish took the position that compulsory attendance beyond the elementary grades interferes with the exercise of their religious liberty. Meanwhile a compromise plan has been worked out in Pennsylvania where pupils who have completed grade eight report to special "Saturday" schools conducted by the Amish themselves. Some of the more progressive Amish groups have allowed their children to enter the high school believing that it is not wrong to comply with the law. The Old Order Amish state that their children are needed for agricultural labor at home and that farming does not require higher education. The Amish leaders believe that exposure to the consolidated high school would constitute a real danger to their future community life. An Amishman who was called to court for challenging the school attendance law said: "We teach our children not to smoke or use profane language and do such things as that. I know most of the high school pupils smoke cigarettes and many girls I guess too. . . . It is better to have them at home. . . ."

The Amish strategy is merely one of withdrawal from the world. In some areas school boards have been able to keep the one-room school open in deference to the Amish, and in other areas where consolidation has occurred the Amish have built their own schools. The establishment of their own schools in recent times is an attempt to avoid participation in the centralized school and to bypass its whole socializing influence, rather than for the purpose of religious indoctrination. However, there seems to be a tendency after several years of experience for some schools to take over from the home the function of teaching religion.

The Old Order Amish are firm in their stand against formal education in the American high school. It is an effective means of maintenance, especially when linked to the doctrine of shunning. With set limits to the amount of knowledge a young person can acquire on one hand, and with the dread of censure (and of excommunication) on the other, one can scarcely find a more effective way of bounding the little community. A person who receives knowledge outside of the Amish bounds equips himself for capable living outside of the Amish community but makes himself liable to the severe sanctions of the ban and shunning. Limited knowledge preserves the existing order of things; it reinforces traditional values by keeping alternate courses of action to a minimum. Traditional values and stereotypes are thus maintained by unfamiliarity with alternate courses of action. Furthermore, questions about in-group practices are kept to a minimum.

Jehovah's Witnesses and the Amish reinterpret life by elevating into a central principle an aspect of the culture that most Americans regard casually or segregate in a corner of their lives: the religious aspect. Other Americans find new meanings by giving unusual emphasis on other American values, by embroidering on another theme. One such theme is sex. Americans cannot be accused of taking sex casually; on the contrary, ours is said to be a sex-obsessed society. But the dominant mores reserve sexual relations for a monogamous pair. Some Americans, however, seem to be moving toward preoccupation with sexual pleasure, with or without monogamy. This preoccupation underlies the phenomenon of spouse swapping.[3]

"Just about every Saturday evening my husband and I invite some of our friends over, or we go to their place," "Mrs. Clark" was quoted as saying, "and we have a very sociable visit and a few cocktails, and then we all start taking one another's clothes off and we have a sex party."

But she insisted to the Kronhausens that there was nothing remarkable about the "switchers": "People who share sex differ from other people only in that they have no false shame about undressing in front of their friends and engaging in sex freely with one another in the same room. Otherwise there's nothing special about us. We are all pretty conventional people, and anyone can join us at the beach, or at a ball game or a Sunday picnic and never notice anything unusual. Yet most of us could have been in a simply *heavenly* sex party the night before. It's something that no one would ever know or suspect."

She is absolutely right. "Swingers" are amused, when they are not annoyed, by the widespread misconception (among the "clydes") that wife-swappers must be boozers, bohemians, drooling lechers, atheists, and irresponsible, negligent parents, if indeed they acknowledge parenthood at all.

The facts, as every sociologist and psychologist who has investigated the "modern marrieds" attests, are quite to the contrary: The women are capable housekeepers, protective mothers, dutiful and loyal wives. The men are interested fathers, devoted husbands, and excellent providers, usually with high-paid and very respectable jobs. Very few run bars, work in show business, are artists, or have any connection with any other lines of work that might be considered "off-beat" by some. Instead they are, according to all accounts, professional men, engineers, photographers, writers, government employees, business executives, military officers, and the like, with a few notable exceptions, as we shall see later in this chapter. These are not the people who throw wild, drunken, noisy parties that awaken the neighbors and bring the police. (The last thing in the world that "swingers" want to do is attract the attention of anyone outside their own special world.) Their children—and most of them do seem to have children—don't run loose, uncared-for, and are not sexual delinquents. (The "switchers" take great pains to prevent their children, as well as the rest of the world, from learning about their unusual sex lives. Children are usually left with relatives, far from the scene of festivities, when a sex party is held.) These are stable, rational people whose lives, as nearly as a neighbor or casual acquaintance or business associate can tell, are well-ordered and sedate. (And so they are, except for sex.)

---

[3] John Warren, *The Age of the Wife Swappers* (New York: Lancer Books, 1966), pp. 57-60, 96-98. Reprinted by permission of Lancer Books, Inc.

They are, in short, the kind of people you'd want for your neighbors—if you didn't know about their sexual code (or, depending on your own attitudes, if you *did* know.)

Even among the "swingers" there are areas of approval and disapproval. Way out deviates—people with strong drives toward sadism, masochism, homosexuality, bestiality, fetishism, and so on—are unwelcome in the swap clubs; they have their own groups and call themselves, in the special cant of the sexual underworld, "bizarre."

Better known than spouse swappers is a group that has attempted to find new meaning in an expressive style of life. They are the "hippies," who differ from the spouse swappers also in rejecting the material values the latter presumably share with respectable middle-class people. The hippies made news a decade ago with their substitution of "spontaneity" for conventional planning for the future, of communal living for conventional privacy, of "love" and "flower power" for conventional marketing-bargaining-legalistic-bureaucratic relationships, and of "simple basic living" for the conventional infatuation with material gadgets and elaborate comforts. It is too soon to make assessment of the hippies' impact on American culture; that they were "a problem" to many there is little doubt. In the eyes of others, the pity is that they did not succeed more in affecting American values. We speak of the hippie movement in the past tense, because there is some reason to suppose that, in many respects, the movement is dead.[4]

A 19-year-old boy, tall and blond and very thin, with crooked teeth and a delicate, girl child's face, wipes his nose on his poncho, hitches up his rucksack and thumbs his way out, away from the Haight. He is leaving because, he says: "Leary is a fake. The underground newspapers are fake. Lot of the young kids are fake. Maybe the Diggers aren't fake—maybe.

"I've had six bad trips; the last time I was turning into the sidewalk. Pellets [LSD] don't scare me, though. I'll keep dropping them. It's the cops, wearing black gloves, four of them coming from each direction on both sides of the street, busting everybody. You've got to show ID to the cops and you have to leave your ID at the distributing office to get newspapers to sell. I might go to Colorado or West Virginia; I know somebody there with a cabin."

He doesn't know what day it is and he can't remember whether his parents live in India or Denver. He had pneumonia four times during his stay in the Haight-Ashbury district. He thinks he has been there for seven months, but he knows he left home two years ago and went directly to the Haight. It is more than he can cope with to reconcile the dates.

---

[4] From Earl Shorris, "Love is Dead," New York *Times Magazine*, October 29, 1967, pp. 27, 113-116. © 1967/65/68/58 by the New York Times Company. Reprinted by permission.

The hippie movement is over. In January, the Human Be-In drew a crowd estimated at 10,000 to San Francisco's Golden Gate Park. On Oct. 6, the funeral which was to mark a hippie death-and-rebirth ceremony, staged and publicized by many of the same people, drew fewer than a hundred of the lingering faithful.

The alternative to the "computerized society" has proved to be as unsatisfactory to its adherents as the society that gave birth to it. The hippie philosophy, in which Buddha reads Tarot cards, Confucius is an astrologer and Hesse peddles acid, was incapable of sustaining a mass movement. With the help of LSD it quickly turned inward, and the possibility of a hippie community was lost, for a community of solipsists, each "doing his own thing," is a contradiction without hope for synthesis. The notion of order grew out of observation of organized society; it was not imposed upon it. The political animal described by Aristotle, thrust into a disordered hippie community, must adopt a life style contrary to his nature, which over a protracted period is unendurable.

Without a viable, unifying philosophy, the hippies became prey to disease, commercialism, publicity, teeny-boppers, boredom, one another and the psychopathic criminals who found them the easy underbelly of the white middle class. The motorcycle gangs and the junkies prowl Haight Street in San Francisco. In the East Village of New York the "plastic" hippies come home from their uptown jobs to be mugged and robbed. The murder of Linda Fitzpatrick and James L. (Groovy) Hutchinson was shocking, but the East Village hipsters knew it, or something like it, was coming. The mixture of large quantities of middle-class whites, angry blacks and drugs had been seething for months; the explosion was, if anything, overdue.

Hostility is not now uncommon among the hippies themselves. Knives have appeared. The children in the streets no longer ask; they demand. Four newly arrived hippies were sitting on the sidewalk in the Haight. One was begging "small change" from tourists. Two others were busy with piercing the left ear of the fourth. They were too young to grow beards and too fresh from home to have long hair. Their blue jeans were dirty and their feet were bare. One of them called out to a passing tourist: "Want to see us pierce his ear?" The tourist smiled and continued walking. The young hippie snarled after him: "How would you like me to put a hole in *your* ear?"

Superspade, who sold drugs to hippies, was recently murdered, put in a cloth bag and thrown off a cliff north of San Francisco. The confessed hippie murderer of another drug peddler was arrested with his victim's arm in his possession. A San Francisco hippie filmmaker sent this message to his Los Angeles counterpart: "If you come into the Haight, we'll smash your cameras and bust your head." Those hippies who do not attach some mystical significance to these events have begun to wonder if the term "Love Generation" is a misnomer.

It is not easy for a hippie to be filled with love. Life in the movement has been disillusioning for most of them. Macrobiotic diets, instead of prolonging life, make one more susceptible to disease. The hippie life perverts middle-class values rather than exorcising them. The dream of nirvana dies quickly. Bad trips lead to suicide, murder or madness. Good trips lead to a mushy brain. Lucy is in the sky with zircons.

A worker in the Hip Job Corps explained: "I left the East Village two months ago because everything went sour for me. I was all up in the air and when I came down my feet were pointing toward California, so I came out here to a commune that's on a farm. That wasn't any good, so I came to the Haight. A lot of the people I was told to look up here had left. A different kind of people are here. The spirit has changed. The people here are running away, looking for someplace to hide. I think I might go to Big Sur."

Boredom, perhaps more than any other single factor, appears to have brought about the moribund state of the movement. Turning inward, many of the hippies apparently found there wasn't enough there to sustain them. They went to kicks instead, but marijuana experiences become repetitive, Methedrine is a drug with vicious side effects, there is no variety in total sexual promiscuity even for the few who are able to attain it, and the example of Timothy Leary, fear of the bad trip and publicity about the permanent damage that may be done by LSD limit the number of trips they dare to take.

A psychiatrist described the LSD pattern in a woman patient: "When she took LSD she had a very good experience. She believed she communicated with God. During the experience and immediately afterward, she felt a heightening of life. Within a short time, however, her life returned to the normal pattern, and she became depressed. The further she got from the period of ecstasy, the more depressed she became."

The moment of ecstasy has also passed for the hippies. The promises of the hippie life were illusory. Sex in the hippie world belongs to the seniors; the freshmen just arrived from Connecticut and Minnesota find there are five boys to every girl and the girls want the drug peddlers or musicians or any boy who has established himself as the hippie version of the letter man. The best the freshman can hope for is occasional group sex in a crash pad, a homosexual experience or a gang rape. While the parents are studying the Kama Sutra in a suburban bedroom in an effort to find the joys they imagine their children get spontaneously, the children are having sex, if at all, in the style their parents have forsaken as too square for the swinging sixties.

The hippies who left the suburbs in protest against the worship of money and material possessions found there is more talk about money on Haight Street than on Wall Street. Hippie bands fly first-class and buy extra seats for their instruments; Chester Helm of the Family Dog claims he earns a quarter of a million dollars a year; the owner of a hippie dance emporium has a corps of financial advisers; the poster makers are rich; the drug peddlers are rich; hippie bands are anxious to do singing commercials or play for the Opera Fol de Rol; Ken Kesey wanted desperately to sell the film made on his Intrepid Trips bus tour to General Electric for use in advertising.

Middle-class children, suddenly without money, become obsessed by it. There is resistance, but it is pitiful. "It's no good to have any money," a hippie boy said. "You get some money and you think of all the dope you could buy and sell and how much money you could get." The Diggers claim to despise money, but a leader of the group, which gives away food, clothing and furniture, finds it difficult to talk of anything else. "A cat comes up to me selling peace buttons. I say to him that he should give them away, be free, end the buyer-seller relationship; then we can be brothers." The cause of peace is insufficient; brotherhood must be established around the one theme that outshines drugs in the hippie world.

Having professed their disdain for middle-class values, the hippies indulge in them without guilt. It is the same talent for self-delusion they apply to other aspects of their lives: An obviously hostile young man is described by his girl friend in terms that would have astonished George Orwell's characters in "1984": "He's not hostile. He's got so much love in him that it comes out aggressively."

In the same vein, the leader of a hippie commune is called a "nonleader," and the "underground" newspapers sell hundreds of thousands, perhaps millions, of copies every month. The publisher of the first underground novel talks anxiously of the probability of having the unbound, mimeographed book reviewed in The San Francisco Chronicle. The people who blame the mass media for the failure of the movement continue to turn handsprings at the sight of a press card.

At the height of the hippie movement, they were deluged with social services: a free medical clinic, free legal service, free stores, help for runaways, Jewish Welfare Organization social workers. Long lists of addresses, names and phone numbers to call in case of trouble were posted in the windows of Haight Street stores. White, middle-class children needed help and the white, middle-class community responded generously.

As the hippie world loses its lily-white complexion and black faces and Spanish accents become commonplace in the streets, the social services, perhaps coincidentally, are being withdrawn. The free medical clinic is closed; the legal organization is curtailing its services; the Diggers can't pay their rent and other organizations are phasing out.

The hippies' supporters plainly don't like the Negroes: "They are coming into the neighborhood to get white girls." The hippies themselves see the Negroes as intruders: "We had some grass, a lid [$5 worth]. And this spade comes up and grabs it. Then he pulls a switchblade. There were a couple of spades, big ones, but there were a hundred hippies. We could have got 1,000, 15,000. We could've creamed him. So he gave back the lid." Negroes are blamed for the increasing use of Methedrine: "They get some nice white chick, the kind your mother would want you to go out with, and they shoot her full of speed. Then they gang her, 14, 15 of them, and she never knows what's happening." At the end of the Methedrine jag, when she crashes, she will know.

The preponderance of hippies come from the middle class, because it is there even among adults that the illusion of the hippies' joy, free love, purity and drug excitement is strongest. A man grown weary of singing company songs at I.B.M. picnics, feeling guilty about the profits he has made on defense stocks, who hasn't really loved his wife for 10 years, must admire, envy and wish for a life of love and contemplation, a simple life leading to a beatific peace. He soothes his despair with the possibility that hippies have found the answers to problems he does not dare to face. Unfamiliar with slum life, preferring illusions, he and his wife buy *art-nouveau* posters and smoke marijuana on Saturday night. The hippies, they say, have caused them to re-examine their own values, which they are more willing to suspect than those of the hippies.

Michael Stepanian, an attorney for HALO (Haight-Ashbury Legal Organization), says that when he calls the mother of a young girl from Connecticut who has been arrested for possession of marijuana, the mother invariably asks him: "Where did I go wrong?" In a time of race riots, the Vietnam war and the hydrogen bomb, it has not been difficult for the hippies to shake the confidence of the generation in power, the *malaise* generation. Of course, they raise valid questions; it is in their solutions that they fail.

Churchmen of several denominations have taken a deep interest in the hippies. A newly ordained priest, fresh from his first marijuana experience, said: "I want to work in the Haight-Ashbury; that's where it's at." The vice chancellor of the Archdiocese of San Francisco opened a conference of Catholic Charities by urging the delegates to visit the Haight-Ashbury to test their competency and their consciences. In an age of technology, during which organized religion has been losing its hold on the population, particularly youth, the hippies offer new hope for the churches. Already attuned to mysticism, with a large percentage of close personal friends of God among them, claiming to have renounced worldly goods in favor of spiritual values, they have a kinship to the church which makes them attractive prospects for conversion. The nuns who walk down Haight Street tell them they are like the early Christians. However, the hippies have neither a Jesus of Nazareth nor a New Testament to sustain them. While persecution strengthened the bond among the early Christians, forcing them into close, secret groups, the hippies are faced with publicity.

"Men give more credit to things they understand not," wrote Montaigne, coming close to the true religion of the hippies, for they will believe in almost anything that fails the test of reason. The necromantic Bishop Pike is a hippie hero. Lenore Kandel, author of "The Love Book," is the leading witch in the Haight-Ashbury, where witchcraft is accepted with a seriousness unequaled since the Salem witch trials. Events are canceled because of curses or bad omens; astrology is the science of the movement, and stores advertise: "All your metaphysical needs here." The few serious students of Eastern religions abandoned the hippie life long ago, leaving their unlettered teeny-bopper brothers to reationalize drug-taking with sidewalk Sanskrit. Among the leftovers of the Eastern-religion aspect of the movement is a sign over a rack of psychedelic books:

SHOPLIFTERS!
Remember Your
KARMA!

That sign and others like it in every store frequented by hippies are of little avail. Hippies steal—from stores, from tourists, from one another. The Diggers' Free Store has been looted at night of goods they would have given to the thieves during the day. A hippie who had been arrested on a narcotics charge complained that the police had left the door to his apartment unlocked when they took him to jail. A few hours later, released on bail, he returned to the apartment to find it looted bare.

Stephanian, the HALO attorney, says that a disproportionate number of all the arrests in San Francisco are made in the Haight-Ashbury district. He calls it police harassment and points out some of the ironies of the situation. Possession of narcotics, including that old rocking chair, marijuana, is a felony, but possession of Methedrine, by far the most destructive drug used by hippies, is only a misdemeanor. The majority of the arrests involve the very young, fresh from suburbia and making only a brief visit to the hippie life. They have no experience with city life or drug usage; consequently, they are often caught "holding," while the wily older hippies, peddlers and junkies rarely put themselves in danger.

The police harass the hippies and the hippies harass the police. The signs of the drug culture are everywhere in the movement. The underground papers, the art, even signs in the streets tell the police the hippies are using drugs. What choice do the police have? Two of the organizers of the Death of Hippie Funeral described the funeral this way, knowing they would be quoted:

"We stayed up all night before the funeral, drinking beer and smoking dope in the Psychedelic Shop. At about 2 in the morning, a taxi driver came in and he stayed up all night, too, smoking dope and laughing. It was a joyous night.

'The ceremony was at dawn. It was beautiful, first-class theater. Then a coffin appeared in the Panhandle [part of Golden Gate Park]. I don't know how. A guy from Kentucky played Blue Grass violin. He led the music while the funeral procession went around the police definition of the neighborhood. People put things in the casket, like clothes, beads, personal papers, marijuana.

Then we burned the casket in the park and danced around the fire. Then the firemen came. Some people sat in the fire while the firemen were hosing it down."

The funeral coincided with the closing of the Psychedelic Shop, which had come to the end of its lease, was $6,000 in debt, and was about to lose one of its co-owners to Napa State Hospital for 90 days of psychiatric observation at the request of the court. Its closing and the changing of the name to the Be Free Shop was announced with a poem:

Psychedelic Shop
Jan. 3, 1966-Oct. 6, 1967
Once upon a time
there was a Psychedelic Shop
that tried to save the world
and succeeded . . .

A manifesto was published, entitled "Death of Hippy End/Finished HIPPYEE Gone Good bye HEHPPEEEE DEATH DEATH HHIPPEE."

"Media created the hippie with your hungry consent," it began. "Be somebody. Careers are to be had for the enterprising hippie. The media cast nets, create bags for the identity-hungry to climb in. . . . NBC says you exist, ergo I am. Narcissism. Plebian vanity. . . . the FREE MAN vomits his images and laughs in the clouds because he is the great evader. . . . the boundaries are down. San Francisco is free now. The truth is out." It ended with the Declaration of Independence.

Following the announcement of the Death of Hippie, the patrons of the I and Thou Coffee House completed a discussion of the subject by making signs and posting them on the windows and walls of the coffee house:

"LIFE TO THE DEATH & DYING."
"Celebrate death/mourn the living."
"Thank you for telling us we can now be free."
"A meaningless death in a meaningless life."
"NOW THAT YOU'VE FOUND ANOTHER KEY/WHAT ARE YOU GO-ING TO PLAY?"

The effect of the state of the movement upon the pseudopsychedelic businesses in the neighborhood is documented by the history of one such store. "Before hippies got famous," said the owner, "we made $2 or $3 clear every day. It was enough for us to live on. That's all we wanted. This spring and summer we cleared $25 on weekdays and over $100 a day on weekends. Now it's down to $8 or $10 a day." The owner of a new store at the south limit of the Haight saw the Death of Hippie postings as "the handwriting on the wall" for his enterprise. Panicked, he put a sign in his window announcing an anti-Death of Hippie March to leave from his store on the closing day of the Death of Hippie Celebration, the day designated as "Silence Reigns." At the appointed time, five beardless boys appeared in front of the store.

The concept of the Free Man, which was to replace the media's hippie label is at best a murky one in the minds of its ex-hippie proponents. Philosophy is not a strong point with the high-school-dropout mentality of the movement; the unexamined life may be no life for man, but it appears to be satisfactory for love children. They express freedom with the fascist overtones of the true believer. To be free, according to the leaders of the Death of Hippie group, is to live the life of a hippie. Either one accepts the values of the Free Man movements and acts in accordance with them, or one is not free. But solipsism is not individualism. The Free Man is the complete follower, and nothing else will do, for the hippies are ruthless, utterly without empathy or compassion for anyone outside the movement.

Peter Berg, a nonleader of the Diggers, Death of Hippie, Free City, etc., defines freedom in part as "the end of the need to produce." And there the hippies are generally in agreement, for they are true consumers. In their utopian economy, the beggar takes the place of the owner of the means of production as the one who lives off the labor of the working class. After Eden, the choice is limited to being a producer or a parasite, and the hippies choose not to produce. Thus, the hippies become parasites on the flank of established society—albeit parasites with a certain sting—rather than an alternative to that society.

At one time the hippies hoped that their stores would all be cooperatives: "We thought we would export hippie arts and crafts to the straight world; that would sustain us." But their arts and crafts are controlled by a small group of young men on the make and there are no cooperative hippie stores.

"Prices in the Haight are very high," a hippie girl singer said. "In the Haight you pay double what you would pay anywhere else for incense." The stores are mostly boutiques catering to tourists and the hippies who get enough money from home to pause in their panhandling, as one girl did, and go into a boutique to buy a pair of $40 boots. An advertisement for flower children posters in The Oracle, a hippie newspaper dedicated to mysticism and incomprehensibility in an illegible format, contains a coupon urging the reader to "Fill out, cut out, chant an incantation, and send to: BEAUTIFUL POSTER THINGYS/CAPITOL RECORDS DIST. CORP."

The hippies generally blame the mass media for commercialization, overcrowding and the other problems that made life in their communities intolerable; they will, in fact, agree to no other cause. An estranged hippie, who makes 8-mm. movies, said: "The movement is dead. It's being dissected. In order to be dissected a thing must be dead—we don't believe in vivisection in America."

Certainly the hippies are the most publicized meditative religious group in history. The publicity brought the tourists and the tourists brought commercialization. Publicity also brought the record companies, dress manufacturers, social workers, researchers, teeny-boppers and a 70-year-old Hindu wise man who preaches from his storefront temple against the use of drugs. "I got too plastic," a retired hippie said. "The vibrations just aren't good any more. These new people are extremely selfish. They don't meditate." The manager of a rock 'n' roll band, who is of the mystic persuasion, said "The hippie scene has moved to the country to get away from the center of infection. In the city there is too much compromise." He commutes daily to his San Francisco office from Marin County, whose per capita income is among the highest in the world.

The love generation became the flower children, who have now taken up tribal relationships, in which the standard family unit is enlarged to a group of perhaps 10 or more. These tribes ordinarily live in one apartment, as in the case of a girl who supported herself and her tribe by baby-sitting. A month after the tribe moved in with her, she found that they had been using her telephone to make long-distance intertribal calls while she was out at her work. She threw them out. Now she has a new tribe living with her, but she has had her telephone disconnected. She is tenacious, but there is a limit to the tribal experiences she will put up with.

The shrinking of the movement began with the opening of school. The average age of the hippie, which dropped from 23 to 16 during the summer, is up again; social workers estimate that 90 per cent of the teen-age hippies have returned to school. The movement is seeking rejuvenation but its energy is gone, sapped by its own unreconcilable contradictions, by the vicious quality of hippie life, and by the commercial uses of its meager artistic production, which will be in evidence in Fifth Avenue and Union Square store windows and on Top-40 radio stations long after the movement that will replace the hippies has made a firm beginning in the underground.

Camus's statement, "I rebel, therefore, I am," is incapable of supporting life when the rebellion proves to be only a perversion of the values which set the world out of tune in the first place. The only clear thrust of the movement was its opposition to nuclear war, but hardly anyone is in favor of nuclear war; it is the circumstances of our lives that may drive us into the holocaust, and as the hippies come to realize that the movement has failed to redirect the inherent avarice and aggressiveness of its own members, let alone the entire world, they despair and abandon the movement.

The movement that was founded as an alternative to the "computerized, mechanized society" and chose electric musical instruments to play its leitmotiv has foundered in the very slough it created. Some hippies are moving to the country to live in garbage-heap communes, like the recently closed Morning Star in northern California, but the communes are only a prolonging of the death agonies of the movement. Most of the hippies are going back home or back to school; few of them ever intended to do anything else. "These were my wild years," said an ex-hippie college student. "I didn't want to spend them just sitting in a classroom. Now it's over. You have to get an education to get along in this world."

Although a formal census of the movement was never taken, there were reports that tens of thousands of young people had become hippies. It was an exciting vacation for at least that many American teen-agers, but the number of young people who intended permanently to drop out of society into a life of LSD, Methedrine and Eastern religion was never very large. Most of the hippies were "plastic," and they were the first to abandon the movement. Returning to "straight" society was easy for them. For the true believers a *rapprochement* with society is not easy. Transition is unacceptable to them, for faith mitigated is faith lost, and the movement had only faith and drugs to sustain it. There is nothing left now but the reluctance to admit failure, and that too is passing. All but a few have returned—or will return—to society, most of them with a better perspective for having been outlaws for a while. The others will remain somewhere outside, marked by veneral disease, life-shattering experiences, felony convictions, or with their minds jellied by LSD and Methedrine, the victims of a failed adventure in search of the perfect, ineffable groovy.

Despite the possible twilight of the hippies, cults which repudiate materialism are still quite common on the American scene. Consider the cult glorifying masculine strength and beauty; dozens of magazines recount the achievements of weight lifters and body builders; the values of the physique cult are not those of material success. Or consider the cults associated with particular movie stars. No doubt these are carefully nurtured by publicity men for materialistic reasons indeed, but an idolatrous devotion to Bob Dylan and other folk singers exists apart from the organization of fan clubs. And women have been placing flowers on the grave of Rudolph Valentino for 30 years.

Do these cults have anything in common aside from their implicit rejection of material success as the paramount goal? We suggest that most cultists— idolatrous "rock" fans, physical culturists, nudists, spiritualists, and vegetarians— share a romantic disregard of the limitations of the human situation. They believe that certain exercises or certain foods or certain incantations will guarantee health, wealth, or happiness. Such romanticism is a problem because, for people who remain in touch with reality, it guarantees disillusionment. A case in point is a romantic manifestation once so widespread in American society that the term "cult" seems inappropriate: romantic love as the basis for establishing enduring relationships between men and women. Romantic love is a less prominent form of romanticism today than it used to be, perhaps because it is so individualistic. Nowadays the collective form of romanticism embodied in cultish devotion to "participatory democracy" or communal living is more widespread.[5]

Angelina is a tall, striking blonde in her mid-forties, with a husky voice and a motherly, forthright air about her. She had been a successful interior decorator in a well-known college town in Oregon. Following her divorce, Angelina decided to rent some of the extra bedrooms in her house to students.

"I was shocked seeing people dirty and with unwashed hair—until I got to know them better and saw their soul reflected in their eyes. They wanted country life and animals. They wanted to be creative and to be themselves. At that time, I was attending a Unitarian church. I talked to the minister about starting a commune. He said it wouldn't work."

Angelina felt she needed new ideas and viewpoints, and she went to the Esalen Institute at Big Sur, California. She stayed three months. "I could see so much, feel so much, I thought I was really called."

Upon returning to her business, which she had left in competent hands, Angelina decided to sell out and was able to do so at a favorable price. "I made up my mind I wanted the family feeling. At this point, it was like Providence when I heard about the hundred and fifty acres. The price was so reasonable, I thought there was something wrong with the place. But when I saw it—with the half-dozen springs, three streams, and mixed timber—I knew this was the spot for a nature commune."

Angelina started the commune two-and-a-half years ago with a young couple she had met at Esalen. Today, there are thirty young people and eight children in the community. Twelve of this group are called "stable"; they have made a commitment to the commune. Median age within the commune is in the mid-twenties. Sixty-five per cent of the group are young men. There are many high school and college dropouts, but also a number of successful former businessmen and professionals, several teachers, and two engineers.

This commune, with Angelina as its prime mover and guiding spirit, is just one of many such living arrangements that have mushroomed around the country. Over the past few years, the commune movement has grown at an unprecedented and explosive rate, and there is every indication that this is only the initial phase of a trend that is bound to have far-reaching implications for the function and structure of our contemporary society. Some traditional institutions are already beginning to feel the impact of this explosive growth.

The commune movement has passed far beyond its contemporary origins in hippie tribalism and can no longer be described as a movement for youth exclusively. There are a rapidly growing number of communes composed of

[5]From Herbert A. Otto, "Communes: the Alternative Life Style," *Saturday Review*, April 24, 1971, pp. 16-21. Reprinted by permission.

persons in their mid-twenties to upper thirties. A source at the National Institute of Health has estimated that more than 3,000 urban communes are now in operation. This figure closely corresponds to a recent *New York Times* inquiry that uncovered 2,000 communes in thirty-four states.

Certain common viewpoints, almost a *Weltanschauung*, are shared by members of the contemporary commune movement. First, there is a deep respect and reverence for nature and the ecological system. There is a clear awareness that 70 per cent of the population lives on 1 per cent of the land and that this 1 per cent is severely polluted, depressingly ugly, and psychologically overcrowded. Commune members generally believe that a very small but politically influential minority with no respect for the ecological system of the beauty of nature exploits all of the land for its own gain. Surpassing the credo of conservationist organizations, most commune members stress the rehabilitation of *all* lands and the conservation of *all* natural resources for the benefit of *all* the people.

Anti-Establishment sentiment is widespread, as is the conviction that a change in social and institutional structures is needed to halt man's dehumanization and to give him an opportunity to develop his potential. Considerable divergence of opinion exists on how social change is to be brought about, but there is general agreement that the commune movement contributes to change by bringing man closer to himself and to his fellow man through love and understanding.

Communes widely accept the idea that life is meant to be fundamentally joyous and that this is of the essence in doing, and enjoying, what you want to do—"doing your thing." Work in this context becomes a form of joyous self-expression and self-realization. Many commune members believe that existence can be an almost continuous source of joyous affirmation. They usually trace the absence of authentic joy in contemporary society to the confining nature of many of our social institutions, the stifling of spontaneity, and the preponderance of game-playing and of devitalized artificial ways of relating socially.

A strong inner search for the meaning of one's own life, an openness and willingness to communicate and encounter, coupled with a compelling desire for personal growth and development, are hallmarks of the movement. A strong anti-materialistic emphasis prevails; it decries a consumption-oriented society. In many communes, what does not fit into a room becomes commune property. A considerable number of communes aim for the type of self-sufficiency through which they can exist independently of "the system."

There is a strong trend toward ownership of land and houses by communes. Leasing arrangements have not proved satisfactory; in too many instances, landlords have canceled leases when community pressures were exerted. The non-urban communes I have visited are strongly aware of ecological factors, and, because of this, members usually had consulted with local health authorities concerning the construction and placement of sanitary facilities. Among the urban communes, toilet and bath facilities were in most cases short of the demand.

Marked preferences for vegetarianism and for organically grown food are noticeable in the commune movement. Many individual members also experiment with different health diets. Roughly 40 per cent of the communes I visited were vegetarian; 20 per cent served both vegetarian and non-vegetarian meals. The remainder served meat when available—usually two to six times a week. This third group, although not vegetarian by choice, liked their vegetarian meals and expressed very little craving for meat. Whenever possible, communes concentrate on growing and raising their own food. An estimated 60 per cent of the urban communes are now purchasing some or most of their supplies from health-food stores or similar sources.

Not surprisingly, the commune has become the repository of repressed man's erotic fantasy. I was continuously told that visitors who come not to learn and understand but to peek and ogle invariably ask two questions: 'Who sleeps with whom?" And, "Do you have group sex?" There appears to be much fantasizing by outsiders about the sex life in communes.

Although there is considerable sexual permissiveness, I found a high degree of pairing with a strong tendency toward interpersonal commitment in a continuing relationship. Nudism is casual and accepted, as is the development of a healthy sensuality, and natural childbirth, preferably within the commune is encouraged. Group sex involving the whole commune occurs quite rarely, although there may be sexual experimentation involving two or more couples or combinations. . . .

Interest in spiritual development is a dominant theme in most communes. Study of and acquaintance with Eastern and Western mystics and religious philosophies is widespread. Religiosity and denominationalism were seldom encountered. On the other hand, I was struck by the deep commitment to spiritual search of so many members in all the communes I visited. Many members were trying different forms of meditation, and books on Eastern religions and mysticism were prominent on shelves.

I find that although there is some overlapping of functions and categories, a number of distinct types of communes can be recognized and are found in operation.

·   The Agricultural Subsistence Commune: The main thrust is to farm or till the soil (mostly organic farming) so that the land will provide most, if not all, needs and make the commune independent and self-supporting. Many of these communes cultivate such specialized crops as organically grown grain, vegetables, and other produce, which are then sold to health-food stores, health-food wholesalers, or supermarkets.

- The Nature Commune: Emphasis is on supporting the ecological system and on the enjoyment of nature. Buildings and gardening or farming plots are designed to fit into the landscape to preserve its natural beauty. Everyone "does his own thing," and economic support for subsistence usually comes from such varied sources as sale of produce and handicrafts, wages from part-time work, welfare support, etc.

- The Craft Commune: One or several crafts, such as weaving, pottery making, or carpentry (including construction or work on buildings outside the commune), occupy the interest of members. They often spend considerable blocks of time enjoying the exercise of their craft with the income contributed to the commune. Many of the craft communes sell directly to the consumers as a result of local, regional, or sometimes national advertisements and publicity. Profit margins vary since the vast majority of such communes do not subscribe to the amassing of profits as the primary aim of their enterprise. Included in this category are the multimedia communes that specialize in light shows, video tape, and filmmaking.

- The Spiritual/Mystic Commune: The ongoing spiritual development of members is recognized to be of primary importance. There may be adherence to a religious system, such as Buddhism, Sufism, or Zen, and a teacher or guru may be involved. Studies of various texts and mystical works, use of rituals, a number of forms of meditation (such as transcendental or Zen meditation), and spontaneous spiritual celebrations play key roles in the life of the commune. Several of these communes also describe themselves as Christian and have a strong spiritual, but not denominational, emphasis.

- The Denominational Commune: There is a religious emphasis with membership restricted to those of particular denomination. Examples are the Episcopalian Order of St. Michael, in Crown Point, Indiana, and the Catholic Worker Farm, in Tivoli, New York.

- The Church-sponsored Commune: Such a commune may be originated or sponsored by a church. There is usually a religious emphasis, but denominationalism is not stressed.

- The Political Commune: Members subscribe to or share a common ideology. They may identify themselves as anarchists, socialists, pacifists, etc. Emphasis is on the communal living experience with others sharing the same viewpoint. This is seen as fostering the individuals' political development. The commune is rarely engaged in direct social action in opposition to the Establishment.

- The Political Action Commune: Members are committed and practicing political activists (or activists-in-training) for the purpose of changing the social system. Classes are conducted, strategy formulated and carried out. The commune may be identified with a minority cause or be interested in organizing an industry, community, or ghetto neighborhood. It often identifies itself by the single word "revolutionary."

- The Service Commune: The main goal is social service. Emphasis is on organizing communities, helping people to plan and carry out community projects, offering professional or case-aide services, etc. Some of these communes include members from the helping professions. There are several such communes in the Philadelphia and New York ghettos; another example is the Federation of Communities, which services several locations in the Appalachians.
- The Art Commune: Artists from different fields or the same field come together to share in the stimulating climate of communal artistic creativity. As compared with the craft commune, members of the art commune are often painters, sculptors, or poets, who usually sell their art works independently rather than collectively. There are poetry and street theater communes in Berkeley and San Francisco.
- The Teaching Commune: Emphasis is on training and developing people who are able both to live and to teach others according to a particular system of techniques and methods. Communes whose purpose or mainstay is to conduct a school or schools also fall into this category.
- The Group Marriage Commune: Although members may be given the freedom to join in the group marriage or not, the practice of group marriage plays an important and often central role in the life of the commune. All adults are considered to be parents of the members' children.
- The Homosexual Commune: Currently found in large urban areas, with admission restricted to homophiles. The aim of these communes is to afford individuals who share a common way of life an opportunity to live and communicate together and to benefit from the economies of a communal living arrangement. Some of the communes subscribe to the principles of the homophile liberation movement. From a recent ad in *Kaliflower*, the biweekly information journal for communes in the San Francisco Bay Area: "OUR GAY COMMUNE HAS ROOM FOR TWO MORE. CALL AND RAP."
- The Growth-centered Commune: The main focus is on helping members to grow as persons, to actualize their potential. There are ongoing group sessions; sometimes professionals are asked to lead these. The commune continues to seek out new experiences and methods designed to develop the potentialities of its members.
- The Mobile, or Gypsy, Commune: This is a caravan, usually on the move. Cars, buses, and trucks provide both transportation and living quarters.

Members usually include artists, a rock group, or a light-show staff. The mobile commune often obtains contributions from "happenings" or performances given in communities or on college campuses.

· The Street, or Neighborhood, Commune: Several of these communes often are on the same street or in the same neighborhood. Ownership of property is in the hands of commune members or friendly and sympathetic neighbors. Basically the idea is of a free enclave or free community. For example, in a recent *New York Times* article, Albert Solnit, chief of advance planning for California's Marin County, was reported at work "on a city of 20,000 for those who wish to live communally." Several neighborhood or city communes are in the planning stage, but none to my knowledge has as yet been established.

Among the major problems faced by all communes are those involving authority and structure. Ideally, there is no one telling anyone else what to do; directions are given by those best qualified to do a job. In practice, strong personalities in the communes assume responsibility for what happens and there is a tendency toward the emergence of mother and father figures. There are, however, a clear awareness of this problem and continuing efforts toward resolution. At present, opposition to any form of structure, including organizational structure, is still so strong that communes have found it almost impossible to cooperate with each other in joint undertakings of a major nature. Interestingly enough, communes with transcendent or spiritual values are the most stable and have the highest survival quotient. It is my conclusion that the weekly or periodic meetings of all commune members, which are often run as encounter groups, have a limited effectiveness in the resolution of interpersonal problems and issues. Although trained encounter leaders may be present as facilitators, their effectiveness is often considerably curtailed due to their own deep involvement in the issues that are the subject of confrontation. One answer to this dilemma might be to bring in a trained facilitator or for communes to exchange facilitators.

It is difficult to determine to what extent narcotics represent a problem for communes precisely because their consumption is as casual, widespread, and accepted as is the downing of alcoholic beverages in the business community. Marijuana and hashish are widely enjoyed, while use of such hard drugs as heroin is seldom encountered, especially in the non-urban communes. In a number of communes where drug use was extensive, I noticed a general air of lassitude and a lack of vitality. I also had the distinct impression that "dropping acid" (LSD) was on the decline; among commune members there seemed to be a general awareness of the danger of "speed," or methedrine. A number of communes are totally opposed to the use of narcotics, especially those with members who were former drug addicts. In most communes the subject of drugs periodically comes up for discussion so that changes in the viewpoint of the commune flow from the experience of the members. Similarly, problems of sexual possessiveness and jealousy appear to be less critical and are also handled by open group discussion. I noticed a tendency toward the maintenance of traditional sex roles, with the women doing the cooking and sewing, the men cutting lumber, etc. Upon questioning this, I repeatedly received the same answer: "Everyone does what they enjoy doing."

Another major problem in most communes is overcrowding and the consequent lack of privacy and alone-time. Rarely does a member enjoy the opportunity of having a room to himself for any length of time. The common practice is to walk off into the woods or fields, but this is an inadequate substitute for real privacy.

Community relations remains a major and critical problem since many communes are "hassled" by authorities or are located amid unfriendly neighbors. As one member described it, the emotional climate in a hassled commune is "full of not so good vibes—you don't know what they will try next, and you keep looking over your shoulder. That takes energy." Today's commune members generally have a clear awareness of the importance of establishing good community relations.

Many of the communes that have got under way this past year or are now being organized are beginning on a sound financial basis. This trend appears to be related to the strong influx of people in their mid-twenties, early or mid-thirties, and beyond. These individuals have financial resources or savings and are, for the most part, successful professionals and businessmen with families.

One example is the Morehouse Commune, which now consists of thirteen houses in the San Francisco Bay Area, two in Hawaii, and another in Los Angeles; total assets are in excess of $2-million. Morehouse was founded a year and half ago by Victor Baranco, a former attorney who is now head of the Institute of Human Abilities, in Oakland, California. There are several categories of membership or involvement in this commune. Members who belong to "the family" give all their assets to the commune, which then "takes care of them," although family members are expected to continue to make a productive contribution within their chosen fields. All income from family members goes into a general fund, but if a family member wishes to withdraw, his assets are returned, including a standard rate of interest for their having been used. Each Morehouse commune in effect makes it own arrangements with members, who may be paid a salary or placed on an allowance system. All communes have a house manager, who assigns tasks or work on a rotating basis. In some Morehouse communes, certain categories of members pay in a fixed monthly sum (as much as $200) toward expenses.

About a third of the Morehouse couples are married and have children. According to one member, "There is no pressure to be married or unmarried. Nobody cares who lives with whom." Morehouse is a teaching commune built around a philosophy and way of life often described by group members as "responsible hedonism." The commune trains its own teachers and offers a considerable number of courses, such as Basic Sensuality, Advanced Sensuality, and Basic Communication.

The aim and credo of this group are taken from a description of the Institute of Human Abilities published in the commune journal *Aquarius*: "We offer the tools of deliberate living; we offer the techniques of successful communication on any level. We offer the knowledge of the human body and its sensual potential. And we offer love to a world that holds love to be suspect."

The rapid growth of the Morehouse communes is by no means an isolated example. A minister in Los Angeles founded a social-service and action-type commune that within a year grew to seven houses. Other instances can be cited. An unprecedented number of people want to join communes. In all but a few instances I was asked to conceal the name and location of the commune to make identification impossible. "We don't know what to do with all the people who come knocking on our door now," I was told repeatedly. In every commune, I heard of people who had recently left either to start a new commune or to join in the founding of one.

There is considerable mobility in communes, which is symptomatic of an endemic wanderlust and search. If people have to leave for any reason, once they have been exposed to communal living, they tend to return. They like the deep involvement with others in a climate of freedom, openness, and commitment. This feeling of belonging has been described as both "a new tribalism" and "a new sense of brotherhood." One young woman with whom I spoke had this to say about her commune experience: "When a white man walks into a room full of other whites, he doesn't feel he is among brothers like the black man does. In the communes, we are now beginning to feel that man has many brothers. . . . There is a new sense of honesty. You can say things to each other and share things like you never could in the family. I never had so much love in my whole life—not even in my own family." She also indicated, however, that commune living is highly intense and possibly not for everyone: "In the commune, there is nothing you can hide. Some people can't take it. They get sick or they leave."

CONCLUSION

Human beings have an insatiable appetite for meaning. The world must make sense. Our participation in it must seem meaningful to us. This is one reason why culture is so important.

When people have a web of meaning at odds with the rest of society, like the Amish, they jealously guard it against the larger world's contamination. When their confidence in the meaning of their subculture begins to fade or when their personal experiences show contradictions in the "symbolic universes"[6] they have accepted, they often convert to new meanings (such as those offered by Jehovah's Witnesses), evolve new philosophies like the hippies, or make sex a center of their lives, like the "spouse swappers."

Are these "problems"? As symptoms of a loss of meaning in the dominant secular culture, they are felt as problems by those whose faith in their own symbolic universes are threatened by them. But it might equally well be argued that those whose secular faith is so fragile constitute the real problem.

[6]See Peter L. Berger and Thomas Luckmann, *The Social Construction of Reality*, New York: Doubleday Co., 1966.

Section 9
SEARCH
FOR OBLIVION

Some people cannot enjoy what their culture defines as enjoyable, either because they have not been persuaded that those delights *are* the point of life or because they cannot obtain them, even if they do agree that they are desirable. Some of these persons, as we have seen (Chapter 14), may ritualistically continue to conform to their culture's prescriptions of how one should act toward others and continue also to maintain their relationship with others, in spite of their emptiness.

Still others among those who find the culture goals unrewarding, erupt in open or controlled rage against those who seem to frustrate them, as we saw in Chapter 15; and others react by breaking away from old relationships and by asserting new conceptions of "the Good Life." We examined instances of this reaction in Chapter 18.

There is a final category of persons who respond differently to the pain of malintegration with their societies. These are people who not only cannot derive enjoyment from their culture's conception of the Good Life, but in addition cannot either explode, *or* resign themselves to "going through the motions," *or* find "new meanings." They cannot because their personality systems or their biological capacities or their social situations are not such as to allow them to. Oblivion is the remaining possibility.

We shall look at some ways of searching for oblivion in Chapter 19.

428

chapter 19
Ways of numbing it

The inventive mind of man can be relied on to find relief from the psychic pain to which his sociocultural inventions expose him. One pain reliever is alcohol. Selden Bacon, Director of the Center for the Study of Alcohol at Rutgers University, describes the functions of alcohol—and some of the problems it generates—as well as providing a reminder of some features of complex societies that give rise to the psychic pains discussed in earlier sections of this book.[1]

As you are all aware, alcohol is a depressant. It allows, through its depressing function, a relaxation of tension, of inhibition, of anxiety, of guilt. There is no need to define narrowly the meanings incorporated in these words. I will consider, however, the areas of behavior and attitude which are most commonly colored with these emotional characteristics. The listing I shall present is quite arbitrary. Around what personal problems of adjustment do anxiety, tension, guilt, and the like arise?

I would suggest the following: (a) the individual's opinion of himself; (b) gaining and holding the respect and the affections of others; (c) conflicting with others, through self-assertion, through criticism, through out-and-out aggressions; (d) over-all security in ownership, prestige, and personal safety, as they are tied up with money; (e) responsibilities accepted in the achievement of specific goals; and (f) sexual matters.

[1] From Seldon D. Bacon, "Alcohol, Science, and Society," *Journal of Studies on Alcohol*, 1945, pp. 190-195. Reprinted by permission of the copyright owners. Copyright by Journal of Studies on Alcohol, Inc., 1945, 1954, New Brunswick, N.J.

This is a purely descriptive listing. It may seem to imply that these six are totally separate matters. They are not! The list is merely a convenient set of handles by which one can pick up and examine the package labeled "one human being." The handles alone are meaningless.

In a complex society these areas of behavior and attitude are more greatly challenged, are more difficult to live through or adjust to, than they are in a simpler society. For a very simple example, take the matter of self-assertion or the exhibition of aggression. In a world of extraordinary dependence on others, aggression is very dangerous. In a complex, specialized, stratified society we are continually in situations where we are dependent on others, and the others do not seem to care much about us. Elevator operators, waiters, salespeople, clients, partners—all of them have it in their power to frustrate us. By the very nature of the system they must frustrate us somewhat, since they serve fifty or five hundred other people in addition to us, and we must take our turn; that is ineradicable in association. So we get angry. But we cover it up. The complexity of society increases the incidence of aggression-provoking situations. The complexity of society renders the expression of aggression ever more dangerous.

Consider the matter of prestige, or recognition from others. In a society in which there is great homogeneity of activity, where most people do about the same things in the same way, the range of prestige is smaller. You are a good, a mediocre, or a bad workman. Furthermore, in a simple society the tangible marks of success, such as conspicuous consumption or ownership, are also limited in variety and quantity. In a complex society, however, the situation is dramatically different. There is an extraordinarily refined hierarchy of prestige. Much of the prestige goes with the position rather than with the individual's talent or exertion of effort or pleasing personality.

Furthermore, recognition and prestige depend more and more on obvious, often tangible, symbols. In the simple society, it is easy to tell who is an efficient, pleasant person. In the stratified, special society, it is not easy. People are more and more inclined to give recognition according to conspicuousness and wealth. There is not the time, there is not the knowledge, there is not the personal interaction on a variety of levels of experience, for people to judge. Yet, despite this weakness, the need to get good persons for specialized positions is pressing, and the goal of gaining prestige is enhanced. The result, of course, is increased apprehension, increased sensitivity, increased tension.

In a complex society where personal relationships are more and more specialized, impersonal, and competitive, and where various specialties are not understood by others, recognition, respect, and prestige are more intensely desired, are more difficult to attain, and are, perhaps, more suspect, than in simpler societies. This results in frustration, envy, aggression, and anxiety which do not appear in such marked form from this source in simpler societies.

The increased complexity of our social existence has increased social responsibilities. One of the outstanding characteristics of high position in any of our ways of life is increase in responsibilities. For many hierarchies we may say that the assumption of higher office is matched by an increase in the anxieties a person carries. One of the earmarks of the executive is his ability to assume anxiety with understanding and with poise. The person in the lowest rank carries very little anxiety about the function of the organization. At 5 P.M. he quits work and forgets about it, although he still carries personal anxieties. The high-ranking man carries his anxiety concerning the whole organization all the time. The one has little or no prestige and little or no anxiety on this account; the other has much prestige and much anxiety.

The general over-all security represented by money in a complex society has already been discussed. The increased anxiety from this source reflects through all of the significant emotional areas that were listed, in addition to possessing a ranking of its own. Although it weighs most obviously on the people in the lowest economic ranks or in marginal positions, it can be equally oppressive to people who, while not threatened with starvation, are threatened as to their social position and prestige.

Time forbids dealing with the other emotional areas. It is, or should be, sufficiently clear that interpersonal relationships and personal satisfactions are more difficult, are more anxiety provoking, are more exhausting, in a complex society.

The advantages of a complex society are manifest, but there is a price to pay. That price is intangible, difficult to measure or define. It can roughly be labeled as emotional insecurity for the individual. Since alcohol can reduce the impact, can allow escape from the tensions, fears, sensitivities, and feelings of frustration which constitute this insecurity, its role will be more highly valued. . . .

It has been pointed out that specialized and formal groups have become more powerful and have extended their functions while all-purpose and intimate groups have been weakened. If the drinking of alcohol and its effects were limited to the area of one of these specialized groups, sanctions could be efficient; or if the society were simpler, more homogeneous, more dominated by some all-purpose, personally intimate and significant association, sanctions could be significant. The drinking of alcohol and its effects, however, infiltrate all manner of acts, associations, and ideas. The attempt to exert sanctions over this wide, loosely organized area will be met with opposition, argument, and relatively unabashed violation. The sanctioning authority will not be recognized. The ideology behind the attempt will be challenged. Social classes, minority groups, religious groups, locality groups, and other categories will not have the identity of purpose, understanding, and experience which would allow such action to proceed smoothly. The complexity of society is of manifest significance with regard to this point. Furthermore, the question of control can itself create further disorganization in the society. This, of course, is quite irrelevant to the physical and psychological properties of alcohol.

In a society already impersonal, competitive, individualistc, and stratified, the effect of excessive drinking on the individual is dramatic. I would only draw attention to the fact that the complexity of the society, and the concomitants of that complexity as here described, exaggerate and speed the deterioration process in the maladjusted person.

Now let us recapitulate the particular sociological viewpoint on alcohol here presented: Social complexity, in the case of Western civilization dominated by economic specialization, has enormously increased the number and variety of goods and services, has improved quality beyond measurement, and can produce with unparalleled speed. This is as true of alcoholic goods and services as of others. Complexity has also resulted in horizontal and vertical stratification, in mutual ignorance and disinterest of societal subgroups, in extreme interdependence of subgroups and of individuals, in the emergence of money as a controlling factor in human life, and in an individualism marked by the increased power of each person and the decreased power of such all-purpose, intimate groups as the family and the small neighborhood.

In relation to alcohol, these concomitants of social complexity have had the following seven effects:

1. They have practically eliminated three functions of alcohol which were of minor importance in primitive society, namely, food value, medicinal value, and religious-ecstasy value.

2. They have enhanced the need for integrative mechanisms in the society which are personally significant. The pleasure group is important here, but other meetings are not excluded. The function of alcohol in depressing certain inhibitions, anxieties, aggressions, and tensions, thus allowing relaxation, has increasing significance, since it can help in this process.

3. These concomitants of complex society have increased, compared with simpler societies, the weight of the anxieties of most individuals, and have added new anxieties. The depressant function of alcohol thus becomes more significant, especially since these anxieties are directly related to the most basic human drives.

4. The very nature of the specialization process has created a network of relationships, activities, wealth, social position, and so on, which revolve around the business of alcohol, thus bringing into existence a set of factors not present in the simpler society, a set of factors unrelated to the physiological or psychological properties of alcohol.

5. The complexity of society increases the need, if the society is to exist, for

434   Social Problems

sharp discrimination, caution, accurate responses, timing, cooperation, and the acceptance of responsibilities. Alcohol, taken excessively, can deteriorate all of these.

6. The nature of the complex society makes social control over behavior that is not strictly compartmentalized into one or another institution an extremely difficult task. The drinking of alcohol and its effects are not present in only one institution or pattern of behavior but infiltrate throughout; the drinking itself is largely in the loosely organized area of individual recreation. Control of drinking behavior in the complex society is therefore a more difficult problem than in the simpler society.

7. The individual in the complex society has a far more formidable task in integrating himself to groups and ideas in a satisfying way, is equipped with more personal choice, and belongs to looser, more specialized, less personally satisfying associations. The excessive use of alcohol can more rapidly and thoroughly destroy such participation in complex societies than it can in the simpler, more general, more intimate groups of primitive societies. The power of alcohol to deteriorate personality is thus enhanced in complex society.

Bacon points to *general* sources of tension and anxiety in a complex society and to the tendency in such a society for social control of alcohol use to be ineffective. A concrete example of ineffective control is provided in the following case history of the evolution from a "tension reliever" into a full-fledged alcoholic.[2]

I was never a very heavy social drinker. But during a period of particular stress and strain about thirteen years ago, I resorted to alcohol in my home alone, as a means of temporary release, as a means of getting a little extra sleep.

I had problems. We all have them, and I thought a little brandy or a little wine now and then could certainly hurt no one. I don't believe, when I started, that I even had in mind the thought that I was drinking. I *had* to sleep, I *had* to clear my mind and free it from worry, and I *had* to relax. But from one or two drinks of an afternoon or evening, my intake mounted, and mounted fast. It wasn't long before I was drinking all day. I had to have that wine. The only incentive that I had, toward the end, for getting dressed in the morning was to get out and get supplies to help me get my day started. But the only thing that got started was my drinking.

I should have realized that alcohol was getting hold of me when I started to become secretive in my drinking. I began to have to have supplies on hand for the people who "might come in." And of course a half empty bottle wasn't

---

[2]Taken from *Alcoholics Anonymous*, Alcoholics Anonymous World Service, pp. 375-376. Reprinted by permission of the Director of A.A. World Services, Inc.

worth keeping, so I finished it up and naturally had to get more in right away for the people who "might come in unexpectedly." But I was always the unexpected person who had to finish the bottle. I couldn't go to one wine store and look the man honestly in the face and buy a bottle, as I used to do when I had parties and entertained and did normal drinking. I had to give him a story and ask him the same question over and over again, "Well, now, how many will that bottle serve?" I wanted him to be sure that I wasn't the one who was going to drink the whole bottle.

Many more Americans use alcohol to numb their fears and anxieties than become so fully addicted to it as to be labeled "alcoholics," although no sharp line can be drawn between an habitual user of alcohol and an alcoholic. Another numbing device, the use of heroin, is more clearly addicting. It progressively takes over the user and succeeds in freeing him psychologically from the burdens of responsibility.

Drug addiction as an escape from life is regarded with peculiar horror by the general public—as the phrase "dope fiend" indicates. Actually, heroin does not make addicts fiendish. An addict who has just taken "horse" is less likely to behave aggressively or boisterously than a student who has just visited the neighborhood tavern. It is true, however, that an addict who cannot get the drug his body demands becomes desperate; he will do almost anything for a "shot." (Some students of addiction have suggested that making heroin available to addicts under medical supervision would not only reduce the considerable crime associated with the traffic in illegal drugs but also the physical suffering of addicts.[3]) The following case history of a sixteen-year-old Negro addict, Charlie Reed, shows the underprivileged background from which most addicts come.[4] It is no accident that drug addiction is found disproportionately among Negroes and Puerto Ricans.

Mr. Hargraves turned at East 100th Street and headed toward the slum block lying between First and Second Avenues, where Charlie had his home. It is part of a wretched area in which the police records show an alarming incidence of narcotic addiction. Six-story cold-water tenements, their fronts fretted with moldering fire escapes, line both sides of the street, except at a point in the middle of the block where the city has torn down one of the most decrepit buildings, leaving a makeshift play lot that is strewn with debris. Seven grocery stores and five churches, including a synagogue and Mr. Hargraves' branch of the

---

[3]Methadone treatment is a modified application of this principle.

[4]From Eugene Kinkead, "Sixteen," *The New Yorker*, November 10, 1952, pp. 44-63; copyright 1951 by The New Yorker Magazine, Inc. Reprinted by permission of the Editorial Department of *The New Yorker*.

East Harlem Protestant Parish, occupy ground floors in the tenements, as do a barbershop, a social club, and a primitive steam laundry, whose tiny doors were open as we went by, giving us a glimpse of some incredibly antique wooden tubs teetering above a suds-sloshed floor that was overrun by a swarm of scrawny cats. The windows of the groceries were piled with grimy tins of Treet and Spam, and the facades of the churches bore crudely hand-lettered legends along the lines of "Jesus Calls" and "Sinners, Repent!" Even on that shining spring morning, the street looked drab and lifeless, as though it had not yet awakened from the activities of the night before. Mr. Hargraves had told me that in this section of the city three-year-olds can be seen playing happily on the street two or three hours after midnight. . . .

After locking the station wagon, Mr. Hargraves led me to what he called the parish house, a ground-floor flat at the rear of 311 East 100th Street, across the street from his church. Its clean, freshly painted three rooms contrasted sharply with the dark, strong-smelling hall outside. I had told Mr. Hargraves that before talking with Charlie about his experiences as a junkie—as a person who uses dope is generally called in the world of narcotics—I wanted to learn a little about the boy's background and the community in which he lived, and when we had settled ourselves in chairs, he started out by giving me a brief picture of the parish he works in. He said that most of his colleagues in the parish are, like himself, recent graduates of Union Theological Seminary. The parish, which was organized in 1948, extends from Ninety-ninth to 104th Street and from Lexington to First Avenue.

"When we first came here, we went around and knocked on doors to get acquainted," Mr. Hargraves said. "It was an eye-opening adventure. Across the hall from Charlie's apartment, for example, I found two Puerto Rican families who had been living together in three rooms for six months without knowing each other's last names. In another house, an old Negro lady of seventy-five was living all alone with six cats and six dogs, each with its own little filthy bowl in the center of the room. Poverty, love, and ignorance are all mixed up here. Last Christmas-time, one woman took in a family of five—utter strangers to her—to give them a bed and a warm place to stay over the holy season. Usually, in this neighborhood, apartments have a kitchen and just two or three other rooms. The gas range is the principle source of heat. In cold weather, it's kept burning most of the day."

Mr. Hargraves turned to the matter of family economics in the block. Family incomes, he said, vary widely, but individual earnings are for the most part low. Relief money is, of course, a big factor in the life of the community. "The Department of Welfare has a schedule of payments designed to take care of almost every conceivable domestic situation of the needy," Mr. Hargraves said. "Its checks—they're usually cashed around here in Jenny's Market, on Second

Avenue—arrive on the fifth and twentieth of the month. Those are red-letter days for the block. I'd say that five distinct economic groups live here, and—as far as the adults are concerned, at least—they keep quite separate. First, there are the aristocrats, amounting to about five per cent of the total—Jews, Italians, and West Indian Negroes who came here around 1910 as immigrants. They're familiar with the scene, regard it as their home, and keep on living here because they like it, despite the fact that there are apt to be high-salaried individuals in their families, such as pressers in the strictly unionized garment industry. Next—about ten per cent, I imagine—are Puerto Ricans who came to New York in the first wave of emigration from the island, around 1920. They've brought up their children as Americans and are better off financially than the third group—some thirty per cent—who are Southern Negroes who came here during the twenties. This third class is the one Charlie Reed's family is in. These people form a hard-working lower stratum of society, with obscure jobs that often require several hours' travel to get to and from each day. It's odd how far people around here seem to have to go to find work. Well, next there's the largest unit—about forty per cent—made up of newly arrived Southern Negroes and Puerto Ricans. Right now, they're in a state of ferment. Some of their customs tend to make them the laughing stock of the block, but, of course, they're only going through the same period of adjustment that the other groups went through before them. They seem to have a corner on menial kitchen and hospital work. The last, and in many ways the most difficult, group is the shady class. It runs to around fifteen per cent, and is composed of people who have broken off from the other groups. Its children rarely go to school. Their parents never look out for them. Both young and old are always either on the border line of crime or right in the midst of it—mixed up in the numbers racket, muggings, prostitution, and selling dope, to adults as well as to minors like Charlie Reed.

"From youngsters like Charlie who have come to us for help, we know that there are still more than twenty juvenile addicts in this block alone. We also know that in this district more than half the young people who have reached eighteen have taken dope in some form or other. Of these, a substantial percentage, ranging somewhere from a quarter to a third, have got hooked—become addicted, that is. The stronger boys seem to use drugs a few times and then stop. That's the end of it for them. But with the weaker ones the whole pattern of life is likely to be changed."

Mr. Hargraves said that the hub of a slum boy's social life in East Harlem is his gang. The neighborhood gangs are much more democratic than the adult groups; they tap all levels for membership. Organized to provide excitement in an otherwise dull society, the gangs have junior, intermediate, and senior divisions, and take in boys of anywhere from around twelve to twenty. The main juvenile gangs in Charlie Reed's area are the Latin Lords, the Viceroys, the

Turbens [sic], and the Redwings, none of which are to be confused with the 107th Street gang of adults that testimony at the Kefauver Committee hearings here linked with Charles Luciano in the dope-smuggling racket.

"Boys join their neighborhood gangs to improve their social status," Mr. Hargraves said. "It's a perfectly natural, boylike thing to do, I suppose. The bad part about it is that when trouble—or what's called a rumble—with another gang starts, they find that even if they're afraid to fight, they'd better not show it. It's a funny thing, though. Some boys don't like to go in for that sort of thing, and refuse to join gangs, and the other boys look up to them for it. And here's another funny thing. Although boys usually get their first experience with drugs through their older friends in the gang, the ones who get hooked drop out of the gang and drift off in little knots by themselves. That's what happened to Charlie and his two friends, Buff and Bugsy. They were prominent members of their gang until six months ago, when they started using heroin. For the last two months before they went to Bellevue, they'd been main-lining—you know, injecting the drug directly into a vein. Gradually, they drew away from the people and activities they'd formerly liked, and began wandering around the neighborhood like wraiths. Then their families got in touch with me, and two weeks ago I took them down to Bellevue to see if something could be done to cure them. They were in pretty bad condition by that time—thin and dirty, with their clothes unkempt and their eyes glazed. They had taken a shot somewhere just before getting in the car, and were on the nod—sitting there with their eyes open, but hardly able to talk and practically asleep, and their heads bobbing like mechanical dolls. Of course, they're all cleaned up now. Inside and outside, they're different boys. But in view of the case histories we've had on the block, all I can say is that we *hope* they'll stay this way."

I asked Mr. Hargraves about Charlie's family. "That's an important part of it, of course," he said. "Like so many other young users on the block, Charlie comes from a broken home. Up here, society tends to be matriarchal in the less prosperous families. That is, couples live together and have children, and sometimes they're married and sometimes they're not, but almost always the man is a transient or a weakling and the lease of the apartment is in the woman's name. She gets the relief check, too, and tries to hold the family together. Charlie's home is a good example of that. Some twenty-five years ago, as a teen-age girl, his mother came up here with *her* mother from South Carolina and settled in the block. She married and had Charlie and Sammy, his brother, who is a year older, before she and her husband separated. Then, by a second man, she had two girls, who are now ten and twelve, and a boy, who's nine. Finally, she married her present husband, and they have a son of two. Charlie's older brother Sammy is a settled boy and a good student, but the mother doesn't seem to care much for him. The eight members of the family live in a three-room-and-kitchen flat on the third floor rear that she gets rent free by acting as superintendent of the building—cleaning the halls, collecting the rents, and such. She also does part-time work in a laundry, and her husband is a dishwasher, and what they earn, together with relief, comes to about sixty dollars a week, and they manage fairly well financially. The mother is popular as the building superintendent because she does a good job and looks after her neighbors when they're sick. Charlie is crazy about her. He doesn't get along with his stepfather so well, but he just loves his mother. She's a big, handsome mulatto. Very much the queen of her household, I'd say."

I thanked Mr. Hargraves and set out down the street for Charlie's flat. He opened the door at my knock, and I stepped into the kitchen, as one usually does in tenements of ancient architectural vintage. Sammy was down on his knees mopping the floor. A little dog was tied to a leg of the sink. Beside the sink were some paper bags of refuse topped by soggy coffee grounds. The door of a closet hung open, revealing a toilet inside, and nearby was a tiny bathtub of the old-fashioned claw-foot kind. A string of wash hung drying in the hall leading from the kitchen to the other rooms. In the first room, although it was mid-morning, three of Charlie's brothers and sisters were still sleeping. This did not surprise me, for Mr. Hargraves had told me that children in that region often don't get up until afternoon, at least on weekends.

I had been in the kitchen only a few minutes when Charlie's mother came in from the landing with a mop and a pail with which she had been cleaning the stairs. She stood erect, with animated eyes and a face that was still attractive for all her many years of backbreaking existence. "This is a friend of Archie's, Mom," said Charlie.

She greeted me warmly. "Won't you sit down?" she said, indicating a sagging sofa against the kitchen wall.

"No, let's go up on the roof," said Charlie quickly. "We can talk better up there."

Charlie and I climbed the stairway to the roof, where we sat down on a wall in the bright sunshine, and Charlie began telling me about his difficulties and frustrations. He said he wanted to become a city fireman, but most of the time he doubted whether he would ever be able to pass the tests. When I said I couldn't see why he didn't have as good a chance as the next fellow, he looked grateful. "Firemen ain't like cops," he said. "They *save* people." I asked him if he had a girl, and he replied that he was fond of a Puerto Rican girl in the block but that he felt hopeless about his chances of marrying her. "For all the color the Puerto Ricans got in their race, they sure act strictly like white people about their women," he said bitterly. "They're Jim Crow just like down South that way. A Puerto Rican girl's family will whip her if she's going out with a colored boy, even if he's three shades lighter than her. If she don't stop going out with him, they'll throw her off the roof. And yet this girl I'm talking about, her brother and me is good friends in the gang." . . .

Charlie told me he had been led to taking dope by smoking marijuana early in the winter that he became fifteen. The first time he tried it was when he and some of the other members of his gang were coming back from Ward's Island after watching a soccer game. One of the boys handed him a butt and told him to inhale on it if he wanted to feel good. He took a few drags but felt nothing. In fact, he smoked marijuana off and on that whole winter without experiencing any kick. Then the warm weather came, and the drug hit him. "You feel peppy," he said. "You want to dance. When you walk, you really got that nine-foot glide. And it's good to listen to music when you been smoking reefers. It feels so nice just to hear it." Charlie did some of his smoking at stag parties in neighboring flats, but most of the time he smoked outside—in yards and parks and on rooftops—where the telltale sweetish herbal odor of the drug wouldn't be so likely to draw attention. Charlie said he learned that for the best results, marijuana smoke should be inhaled deeply and the smoke then blown out into cupped hands and inhaled again through the nose.

Tolerance to marijuana can be acquired fairly quickly, and shortly after Charlie became sixteen, he found he was no longer walking with that nine-foot glide. Then he started on heroin, or "horse." He and Bugsy first tried the white powder together, taking turns snuffing in the phone booth of a candy store. Buff had given it to them, saying that he'd tried it and that it was better than marijuana. Both Charlie and Bugsy knew what heroin was. They had even heard that some Harlem boys had died from taking it. I asked Charlie why, under the circumstances, he and Bugsy so much as accepted the stuff from Buff. He looked at me with surprise. "Buff was our pal, wasn't he?" he said stoutly. "Hell, I wasn't going to miss nothing." The snuffing stage lasted about a month. Then the trio turned to skin injections, using hypodermic syringes that they bought at a drugstore, and from that it was only a step to main-lining. Charlie said that when he realized he was hooked, he grew frightened. He tried to switch back to marijuana, but found he couldn't. "It made me sick at my stomach and left a terrible taste in my mouth," he told me. "It never works, the fellows say. You have to stay on the horse kick until you kick it."

Charlie said that heroin made him feel separated from the rest of the world. "It's a different feeling than when you're on marijuana," he went on. "You're relaxed. You ain't got a care from here to Brooklyn. A cop can come up to you and talk to you, and you won't get nervous or anything. When you're on marijuana and a cop comes up and talks to you, you're leery and you want to run. But not on horse. You talk right back to him." One of Charlie's favorite pastimes when he was taking heroin was to give himself a shot and then go to a movie, often at the Triboro Theatre, on 125th Street, which daily offers three features of the more lurid sort. He would buy a ticket, take a seat in the balcony, and stay there for hours, smoking regular cigarettes, one after another, and aimlessly watching the fantasies on the screen, which helped heighten and prolong his own fantasies. Often, during these reveries, his cigarette would burn his fingers. "I'd just sit there and goof," he said. Always in his fantasies he was big, important, powerful, "If somebody was to come up to me then and say, 'Let's have a swimming race or a home-run-hitting contest or something like that,' I wouldn't pay no attention to him," he told me. " 'What the hell,' I'd say to myself, 'I know I can lick him.' "

During the last two months before Charlie went to Bellevue, when he was main-lining, he injected himself with heroin three times a day—in the morning, at noon, and at night. When he couldn't manage it on time, he told me, he felt weak in the knees, headachy, and feverish, and cigarettes tasted like hay. He took the morning and evening shots in the toilet in his family's flat and the other in a washroom wherever he happened to find himself around noon. In those days, he would frequently start out for his high school—Samuel Gompers, in the Bronx—and never get there. He carried his hypodermic outfit around with him in a pocket of his jacket. It consisted of a syringe, some capsules of heroin, a soot-blackened spoon in which he diluted the drug with water and warmed it over a match, a thick rubber band to raise a vein in his arm, and a dab of cotton. Charlie said he never injected himself outdoors, because he had been told that if a person should be touched by a breeze while using a hypodermic needle, a bubble of air would enter the vein and later "freeze the heart."

As a main-liner, Charlie used three capsules of heavily cut heroin a day. He bought the drug, at a dollar a capsule, mostly from a twenty-three-year-old dope peddler—or pusher—named Pete, who lived on East Ninety-ninth Street and whom Charlie would meet in a lunchroom on Second Avenue. Once or twice, he bought his supply from a Puerto Rican who walked brazenly down the street calling *"Caballo! Caballito!"* ("Horse! Horsie!") Pete told Charlie he didn't really know where the stuff was coming from; he said he thought it might be from New Jersey. The biggest dealer in the neighborhood, whom Charlie said he was acquainted with but didn't patronize, ran his business right in his second-floor tenement apartment, and some of his customers, after making a purchase, would "take off"—as young addicts call injecting themselves—in the hallway just outside the door of the flat. During Charlie's two months of main-lining, he got hold of the three dollars a day he needed for the drug by working as a runner in the numbers racket and by some lucky breaks in a floating dice game. Buff had a job in a grocery store, and Bugsy became a petty thief. "We helped each other out with money," Charlie said. All three of the boys lost their interest in the gang, and were unconcerned when, toward the end, the other members wouldn't let them hang out on the gang's favorite street corner. "They told us, 'We don't want you junkies lousing us up,' " Charlie said. "I don't blame them. Hell, the gang has enough trouble with the cops as it is, without no junkies under-foot." . . .

. . . I went up to Charlie's flat. I arrived as the family was finishing supper, which had apparently consisted only of thick cold-meat sandwiches. Charlie and his stepfather, a slight, pimply Negro of about forty, were arguing over which one of them should take the day's garbage downstairs to the cans in front of the building. "Take it down, Charlie, you hear me?" said the stepfather.

"Like hell I will," said Charlie.

"It's your turn, God damn you!" the stepfather yelled.

"Don't you cuss at me, you skin-dirty louse!" Charlie yelled in return, whereupon the man rushed at him with upraised fist.

Charlie's mother stepped decisively between them, and sent each sprawling backward with a push. "Mind your manners!" she said. "Both of you! You hear me?"

"I'll take it down," said Sammy.

"Come on," Charlie said to me, picking himself up off the floor. "Let's get out of this stinking hole." On the way down the stairs, he denounced his stepfather profanely. "I don't see how Mom puts up with him, nohow," he said. "I'd as soon touch a rat. She's going to get rid of him one of these days, too. You mark my words." . . .

. . . Charlie and I went into a lunchroom down the block for a Coke and a piece of pie. We were joined by Bugsy, who proved to be congenial and talkative. Bugsy told me about a swell job he had had the year before. He had been a mortician's assistant, he said, at ninety-five dollars a week, and had had a luxurious apartment over the mortician's shop, with dim lights, flowered curtains at the windows, a tile floor, and a tile fountain with bubbling water. Bugsy also gave me a full description of his job—of going to people's homes to pick up bodies, of comforting grief-stricken families, and of preparing the remains. "But I gave up the work because it was too unfriendly," Bugsy said. "Nobody ever came to see me."

Charlie gave him a look. "You sure feeling comfortable," he observed.

Later that night, I dropped in to see Mr. Hargraves. He told me Bugsy was back on heroin again. I asked him about the boy's ninety-five-dollar-a-week job and the fancy apartment. "Rubbish," he said. "Just a junkie's fantasy."

Two weeks afterward, Mr. Hargraves called me to say that Charlie himself had gone back on heroin—less than two months after being discharged from Bellevue. He was slinking in and out of doorways again, and often stayed out all night. A few days later, Mr. Hargraves called me a second time. Charlie, he told me, had been arrested by a plainclothesman, who, as they say in Harlem, had lucked out on him; that is, the officer had picked him up merely on suspicion, searched him in a hallway, and found his dope outfit. So Charlie was held for possession and remanded to the Tombs to await trial.

A couple of days later, I went to see Charlie's mother. From time to time, as we sat and talked on the sofa in the kitchen, she plucked despairingly at a bright-colored scarf she wore around her head. Charlie, she said, had been in the hands of the police once before. "And that wasn't his fault," she added. "That was when a crazy Spanish man stabbed him." She explained that Charlie on that occasion had been down on the street, leaning through the window of a car talking to a friend, when a Puerto Rican he had never seen before came by and knifed him in the back. "Man *must* have been crazy," she said. "Drunk or crazy. But the cops took Charlie along, too. This here's different. Now he's in trouble with the law on his own. I don't know what to do," she went on. "It just worries me and worries me all the time." For a couple of weeks before Charlie's arrest, she told me, he had been sleeping either at Buff's or Bugsy's. "He had trouble with my husband," she said. "My husband miss his overcoat, a real beautiful California wrap. Them boys must of pawned it. And some of my rent money was gone, too. I don't know which one of them done it. They all stick together."

Charlie had grown crankier and crankier in the days just before his arrest, his mother told me. "I used to think I understood that boy," she said, in a low voice. "I had real trouble raising him up. He had asthma bad, you know. But now I don't know if I knows him at all. I could tell when he started taking that stuff again, though. I says to him, 'You promised me, Charlie, when you came out of the hospital, you ain't never going to do that no more.' I never knew how he take it, or nothing. I was awful stupid. Then, one day about three weeks ago, I pull out of his pocket this thing all wrop round with a rubber band, with a needle and a black spoon in it. I says, 'Glory God, this is it!' I shows it to him. 'Son,' I says, 'you deep in wrong.' He beg me so hard to give it back to him, and say he going to throw it away, that I give in and do. But he trick me. He hide it someplace, and I never did find it no more. Later, when I says to him, 'I see you taking that stuff again,' he lies. He says, 'You ain't see me take nothing.' I says, 'I may not *see* you take nothing, but I can tell when you done did it. I can tell the difference in you.' Then he yells at me, 'You see how you is? You talking like that *makes* somebody take something.' Oh, he was terrible cranky." The mother told me she suspected that her son, Buff, and Bugsy had been injecting themselves off and on in the bedroom that Charlie shared with Sammy in the flat. The door to it could be fastened on the inside with a hook. "The three of them would go in there and set the hook," she said. "After a while, I says to Charlie, "Why you fasten that door?' 'I just want to talk secrets with my friends,' he says. 'You don't have to hear everything we talking about.' "

I asked Charlie's mother how she could tell when her son had been taking heroin. "Right off, he seems happy," she replied. "Wants to dance. Comes around and kisses me. Says, 'Mom, I love you!' Then he gets a book. He tries to read and falls asleep. I'd sure like to know where he was getting it. I talked to Archie about this, and he say the police made a lot of arrests of pushers, but every time they do, new ones pop up in the same place. It seem just like some big business company." She asked me what I thought they would do with Charlie. I said I had no idea. "I sure hope they cures him this time," she said.

Drug addiction is a good example of clinging to a ruinous habit. For whatever reason the individual began taking opiate drugs, to relieve pain or fatigue, for thrills, because his friends were using them, he soon discovers disadvantageous aspects of the practice. (a) Heroin is extremely expensive because he must purchase it from illegal "peddlers." (b) Once he is physiologically habituated, he cannot stop using the drug without experiencing violent nausea and other unpleasant physical symptoms. (c) Being known as a "dope fiend" isolates him psychologically; his family and friends condemn him in words or action; employers have no desire to hire him; he is liable to arrest and imprisonment. Nevertheless, it is difficult to effect permanent cures. At the United States Public Health Service Hospital in Lexington, Kentucky, addicts from all over the country come for treatment. Not only is physiological dependence on the drug eliminated, but the patient also gets considerable psychological help. When he leaves the hospital, he is "cured" in a medical sense. Notwithstanding, he is likely to go back to the drug, sooner or later. Why? Because he knows that opiates provide relief from physical and psychic pain. When he encounters defeats and discouragement in his effort to readjust himself, there is a temptation to fall back upon them. True, drugs brought him trouble as well as relief, but at a low moment he is more likely to remember the relief than the trouble. He takes a small "shot." Having failed to resist temptation once, he will probably put up less objections to the drug the next time that troubles beset him. Soon he is "hooked" again.

Usually vicious circles are involved whenever individuals resort to the withdrawal mode of adaptation. The alcoholic *knows* that drinking broke up his marriage. Withdrawers expose themselves to social rejection, not because of ignorance but because of a vested interest. That is to say, they are loath to give up their mode of adjustment because, in the short run, there are only meager compensations for such a sacrifice. True, both foresight and hindsight point in the same direction: Give it up; it is ruining you. But at any one moment the choice is between a familiar escape and vague, uncertain hopes for the improvement of a bad situation. Furthermore, as the situation worsens—a consequence of the withdrawal—it looks to the individual less and less probable that giving up his solace will do any good.

The addict abdicates responsibility for his life—unlike other problematic adjustments to the strains of life in the United States: the ritualist, the con artist, or the seeker for greener pastures, who accept responsibility for their lives, albeit creating problems for others. Responsibility is incompatible with looking for oblivion.

Even the addict is more in control of himself than are people who adopt another mode of numbing the pain of adaptive failure, insanity. The following interpretation of schizophrenia regards it as a process by which the individual tries to avoid this pain.[5]

In the Eastern religion, Zen Buddhism, the goal is to achieve Enlightenment. The Zen Master attempts to bring about enlightenment in his pupil in various ways. One of the things he does is to hold a stick over the pupil's head and say fiercely, "If you say this stick is real, I will strike you with it. If you say this stick is not real, I will strike you with it. If you don't say anything, I will strike you with it." We feel that the schizophrenic finds himself continually in the same situation as the pupil, but he achieves something like disorientation rather than enlightenment. The Zen pupil might reach up and take the stick away from the Master—who might accept this response, but the schizophrenic has no such choice since with him there is no not caring about the relationship, and his mother's aims and awareness are not like the Master's.

We hypothesize that there will be a breakdown in any individual's ability to discriminate between Logical Types whenever a double bind situation occurs. The general characteristics of this situation are the following:

1. When the individual is involved in an intense relationship; that is, a relationship in which he feels it is vitally important that he discriminate accurately what sort of message is being communicated so that he may respond appropriately.

2. And, the individual is caught in a situation in which the other person in the relationship is expressing two orders of message and one of these denies the other.

3. And, the individual is unable to comment on the messages being expressed to correct his discrimination of what order of message to respond to, i.e., he cannot make a metacommunicative statement.

We have suggested that this is the sort of situation which occurs between the preschizophrenic and his mother, but it also occurs in normal relationships. When a person is caught in a double bind situation, he will respond defensively in a manner similar to the schizophrenic. An individual will take a metaphorical statement literally when he is in a situation where he must respond, where he is faced with contradictory messages, and when he is unable to comment on the contradictions. For example, one day an employee went home during office hours. A fellow employee called him at his home, and said lightly, "Well, how did you get *there*?" The employee replied, "By automobile." He responded

[5]From Gregory Bateson, Don D. Jackson, Jay Haley, and John Weakland, "Toward a Theory of Schizophrenia," *Behavioral Science*, Vol. 1, No. 4, October 1965, pp. 253-259. Copyright by James. G. Miller, M.D., Ph.D., Editor. Reprinted by permission.

literally because he was faced with a message which asked him what he was doing at home when he should have been at the office, but which denied that this question was being asked by the way it was phrased. (Since the speaker felt it wasn't really his business, he spoke metaphorically.) The relationship was intense enough so that the victim was in doubt how the information would be used, and he therefore responded literally. This is characteristic of anyone who feels "on the spot," as demonstrated by the careful literal replies of a witness on the stand in a court trial. The schizophrenic feels so terribly on the spot at all times that he habitually responds with a defensive insistence on the literal level when it is quite inappropriate, e.g., when someone is joking. . . .

The theoretical possibility of double bind situations stimulated us to look for such communication sequences in the schizophrenic patient and in his family situation. Toward this end we have studied the written and verbal reports of psychotherapists who have treated such patients intensively; we have studied tape recordings of psychotherapeutic interviews, both of our own patients and others; we have interviewed and taped parents of schizophrenics, we have had two mothers and one father participate in intensive psychotherapy; and we have interviewed and taped parents and patients seen conjointly.

On the basis of these data we have developed a hypothesis about the family situation which ultimately leads to an individual suffering from schizophrenia. This hypothesis has not been statistically tested; it selects and emphasizes a rather simple set of interactional phenomena and does not attempt to describe comprehensively the extraordinary complexity of a family relationship.

We hypothesize that the family situation of the schizophrenic has the following general characteristics:

1. A child whose mother becomes anxious and withdraws if the child responds to her as a loving mother. That is, the child's very existence has a special meaning to the mother which arouses her anxiety and hostility when she is in danger of intimate contact with the child.

2. A mother to whom feelings of anxiety and hostility toward the child are not acceptable, and whose way of denying them is to express overt loving behavior to persuade the child to respond to her as a loving mother and to withdraw from him if he does not. "Loving behavior" does not necessarily imply "affection"; it can, for example, be set in a framework of doing the proper thing, instilling "goodness," and the like.

3. The absence of anyone in the family, such as a strong and insightful father, who can intervene in the relationship between the mother and child and support the child in the face of the contradictions involved.

Since this is a formal description we are not specifically concerned with why the mother feels this way about the child, but we suggest that she could feel this way for various reasons. It may be that merely having a child arouses anxiety about herself and her relationships to her own family; or it may be important to her that the child is a boy or a girl, or that the child was born on the anniversary of one of her own siblings, or the child may be in the same sibling position in the family that she was, or the child may be special to her for other reasons related to her own emotional problems.

Given a situation with these characteristics, we hypothesize that the mother of a schizophrenic will be simultaneously expressing at least two orders of message. (For simplicity in this presentation we shall confine ourselves to two orders.) These orders of message can be roughly characterized as (a) hostile or withdrawing behavior which is aroused whenever the child approaches her, and (b) simulated loving or approaching behavior which is aroused when the child responds to her hostile and withdrawing behavior, as a way of denying that she is withdrawing. Her problem is to control her anxiety by controlling the closeness and distance between herself and her child. To put this another way, if the mother begins to feel affectionate and close to her child, she begins to feel endangered and must withdraw from him; but she cannot accept this hostile act and to deny it must simulate affection and closeness with her child. The important point is that her loving behavior is then a comment on (since it is compensatory for) her hostile behavior and consequently it is of a different *order* of message than the hostile behavior—it is a message about a sequence of messages. Yet by its nature it denies the existence of those messages which it is about, i.e., the hostile withdrawal.

The mother uses the child's responses to affirm that her behavior is loving, and since the loving behavior is simulated, the child is placed in a position where he must not accurately interpret her communication if he is to maintain his relationship with her. In other words, he must not discriminate accurately between orders of message, in this case the difference between the expression of simulated feelings (one Logical Type) and real feelings (another Logical Type). As a result the child must systematically distort his perception of metacommunicative signals. For example, if mother begins to feel hostile (or affectionate) toward her child and also feels compelled to withdraw from him, she might say, "Go to bed, you're very tired and I want you to get your sleep." This overtly loving statement is intended to deny a feeling which could be verbalized as "Get out of my sight because I'm sick of you." If the child correctly discriminates her metacommunicative signals, he would have to face the fact that she both doesn't want him and is deceiving him by her loving behavior. He would be "punished" for learning to discriminate orders of messages accurately. He therefore would tend to accept the idea that he is tired rather than recognize his mother's deception. This means that he must deceive himself about his own internal state in order to support mother in her deception. To survive with her he must falsely discriminate his own internal messages as well as falsely discriminate the messages of others.

The problem is compounded for the child because the mother is "benevolently" defining for him how he feels, she is expressing overt maternal concern over the fact that he is tired. To put it another way, the mother is controlling the child's definitions of his own messages, as well as the definition of his responses to her (e.g., by saying, "You don't really mean to say that," if he should criticize her) by insisting that she is not concerned about herself but only about him. Consequently, the easiest path for the child is to accept mother's simulated loving behavior as real, and his desires to interpret what is going on are undermined. Yet the result is that the mother is withdrawing from him and defining this withdrawal as the way a loving relationship should be.

However, accepting mother's simulated loving behavior as real also is no solution for the child. Should he make this false discrimination, he would approach her; this move toward closeness would provoke in her feelings of fear and helplessness, and she would be compelled to withdraw. But if he then withdrew from her, she would take his withdrawal as a statement that she was not a loving mother and would either punish him for withdrawing or approach him to bring him closer. If he then approached, she would respond by putting him at a distance. *The child is punished for discriminating accurately what she is expressing, and he is punished for discriminating inaccurately—he is caught in a double bind.*

Not only boys with mothers like the one Bateson and his associates describe are caught in "double binds." Many Americans feel damned if they do and damned if they don't by pressures of American society to come to terms with bargaining, competitive self-orientation and authority. One can deal with double binds not only by closing off all contact with the world through catatonic stupors, paranoid suspicions, or hebephrenic giggles but also by vengefulness, theft, and religious conversion. Ultimately, one can deal with them by self-destruction. "The best high of all is death," says the addict, only a step away from it. Some people take the final step when the point of their life is gone, as Ernest Hemingway apparently did.[6]

Ernest ... was getting depressed about his work, although I could never clearly determine whether it was because he did not like what he wrote or because of difficulty he was experiencing in writing. I would mention friends and try to tell him about them, but he really wasn't interested. I tried to discuss the general form of the Nick Adams screenplay I was about to start on, but he wasn't interested in that either.

On April 18th I went to a cocktail party in New York which Harvey Breit

[6]From A E Hotchner, *Papa Hemingway* New York: Random House, 1966, pp. 283-288, 297-303. Reprinted by permission.

had given to celebrate the publication of George Plimpton's book. It was a good party with good people and at one point Harvey suggested we call Ernest and all talk to him. I did not want to say that Ernest was in no condition to chat on the phone with the hubbub of a gay cocktail party in the background, so I tried to prevent the call by pretending I didn't have Ernest's unlisted phone number with me, unfortunately Harvey found it in his address book.

First Harvey spoke to him, then George, and they were merry and funny and George told him how well his book was going. When I came on, Ernest said, "Hotch, please try to hold off these calls." His voice was dead, the words coming at me like rocks falling down a well. "It's gotten pretty rough. I can't finish the bloody book. I've got it all and I know what I want it to be but I can't get it down." Harvey and George, looking happy, were watching me, so I curved my mouth up and tried to keep my eyes down on the phone.

I said some terrible inanity like, "Well, it's good that you're that far."

"Hotch, I can't finish the book. I *can't*. I've been at this goddamn worktable all day, standing here all day, all I've got to get is this one thing, maybe only a sentence, maybe more, I don't know, and I can't get it. Not any of it. You understand, I *can't*. I've written Scribner's to scratch the book. It was all set for the fall but I had to scratch it."

"Then they'll do it in the spring."

"No, no they won't. Because I can't finish it. Not this fall or next spring or ten years from now. *I can't*. This wonderful damn book and I can't finish it. You understand?"

When I hung up, Harvey said, "He sounds fine, doesn't he?" That was April 18th. At eleven o'clock Sunday morning, April 23rd, I received a call from Ketchum. Ernest was in the Sun Valley Hospital under heavy sedation, sodium amytal every three hours, nurses around the clock.

When Mary had come into the living room that morning, she had found Ernest standing in the vestibule, where the gun rack was; he was holding a shotgun in one hand, with the breech open; he had two shells in his other hand. There was a note propped up on top of the gun rack addressed to her. Mary knew that Vernon Lord was due to come by to take Ernest's blood pressure, so she just tried to hold Ernest's attention until he got there. She knew he had been terribly depressed about his inability to write, but she had had no inkling that his depression had driven him this far.

Ernest was calm and did not make a move to put the shells in the chamber, so Mary did not mention the gun at all but asked for the note. Ernest refused to give it to her but read her a few sentences here and there. There was a reference to his will and how he had provided for Mary and she wasn't to worry. Also, that he had transferred thirty thousand dollars to her checking account. Then he got off the letter and onto his latest worry, which concerned filing income taxes for the cleaning woman; talking on and on about how the Feds were sure to get him for the cleaning woman's taxes, and then Vernon arrived. When Vernon took hold of the gun Ernest let him have it without a protest.

Vernon had already put in a call to the Mayo Clinic and I was asked whether I would contact Dr. Renown and brief him on the situation.

Vernon phoned at four-thirty that afternoon. He reported that the Mayo doctors were insisting that Ernest go to Rochester voluntarily but that Ernest absolutely refused to go.

"I called Dr. Renown," I said, "and he was to call Mayo and then call you."

"He has. He made all the Mayo arrangements and discussed procedures, but I don't think he knows about this condition they've imposed, that Ernest go of his own free will. Hell, he doesn't have any *free* will! What are they talking about? I have my associate, Dr. Ausley, helping me with Ernest, but we're fighting the clock. We don't have proper facilities for this kind of thing and, Hotch, honest to God, if we don't get him to the proper place, and *fast*, he is going to kill himself for sure. It's only a question of time if he stays here, and every hour it grows more possible. He says he can't write any more—that's all he's talked to me about for weeks and weeks. Says there's nothing to live for. Hotch, he won't ever write again. He can't. He's given up. That's the motivation for doing away with himself. At least, on the surface. And that's what I have to accept because I'm not equipped to deal with anything beneath the surface. But that's strong enough motivation as far as I'm concerned, and I can tell you I'm worried sick. We've got him shot full of sodium amytal, but how long can we keep him in that state? I can tell you it's a terrible responsibility for a country doctor. It's not just that he's my friend, but he's *Ernest Hemingway*. We've *got* to get him to Mayo. '

For the rest of that day we phoned back and forth between New York, Ketchum, Hollywood and Rochester, but the Mayo doctors could not be induced to come to Ketchum or vary in any way from their adamant policy that patients must enter the clinic voluntarily. Dr. Renown suggested to Vernon Lord several procedures to be tried on Ernest to induce his co-operation. I wanted to go to Ketchum to help out, but Dr. Renown thought I should wait and go as a second echelon if Vernon failed.

The following day Mary phoned, terribly shaken. There had been a night-marish incident. Vernon had finally gotten Ernest to consent to re-entering Mayo, and the charter plane had been summoned from Hailey. Ernest said, however, that before he went there were some things he had to get from the house. Vernon said he would send Mary for them, but Ernest said they were things he had to get himself and he would not go to Mayo without them. So Vernon reluctantly consented, but first he called Don Anderson, who is six foot three and over two hundred pounds, to come along. Vernon took the nurse and Mary also.

They drove up to the house, the five of them, and Ernest started toward the door, followed by Don, then the nurse, then Mary and Vernon. Suddenly Ernest cut loose for the door, slammed it and bolted it before Don could get there. Don raced around to the other door, charged into the house and spotted Ernest at the gun rack, holding a gun and ramming a shell into the chamber. Don hurled himself at Ernest and knocked him down. There was a terrible struggle over the gun. Vernon had to help. Luckily, the safety had been on so it did not go off. Ernest was now back at the hospital, more heavily drugged. . . .

I felt I should get to it quickly now, and I did, but I said it very gently: "Papa, why do you want to kill yourself?"

He hesitated only a moment; then he spoke in his old, deliberate way. "What do you think happens to a man going on sixty-two when he realizes that he can never write the books and stories he promised himself? Or do any of the other things he promised himself in the good days?"

"But how can you say that? You have written a beautiful book about Paris, as beautiful as anyone can hope to write. How can you overlook that?"

"The best of that I wrote before. And now I can't finish it."

"But perhaps it is finished and it is just reluctance . . ."

"Hotch, if I can't exist on my own terms, then existence is impossible. Do you understand? That is how I've lived, and that is how I *must* live—or not live."

"But why can't you just put writing aside for now? You have always spent a long time between books. Ten years between *To Have and Have Not* and *For Whom the Bell Tolls* and then ten years more until *Across the River*. Take some time off. Don't force yourself. Why should you? You never have."

"I can't."

"But why is it different now? May I mention something? Back in 1938 you wrote a preface for your short stories. At the end of it you said you hoped you could live long enough to write three more novels and twenty-five more stories. That was your ambition. All right—*For Whom the Bell Tolls, Across the River and into the Trees* and *The Old Man and the Sea*, not to mention the unpublished ones. And there're more than twenty-five stories, plus the book of Paris sketches. You've fulfilled your covenant—the one you made with yourself—the only one that counts. So for God's sake why can't you rest on that?"

"Because—look, it doesn't matter that I don't write for a day or a year or ten years as long as the knowledge that I *can* write is solid inside me. But a day without that knowledge, or not being sure of it, is eternity."

"Then why not turn from writing altogether? Why not retire? God knows you have earned it."

"And do what?"

"Any of the things you love and enjoy. You once talked about getting a new boat big enough to take you around the world, fishing in good waters you've never tried. How about that? Or that plan about the game preserve in Kenya?

You've talked about the tiger shoot in India—Bhaiya's invitation—there's that. And at one time we talked about your going in with Antonio on the bull ranch. There's so damn many things . . ."

"Retire? How the hell can a writer retire? DiMaggio put his records in the book, and so did Ted Williams, and then on a particular good day, with good days getting rarer, they hung up their shoes. So did Marciano. That's the way a champ should go out. Like Antonio. A champion cannot retire like anyone else."

"You've got some books on the shelf . . ."

"Sure. I've got six books I declare to win with. I can stand on that. But unlike your baseball player and your prize fighter and your matador, how does a writer retire? No one accepts that his legs are shot or the whiplash gone from his reflexes. Everywhere he goes, he hears the same goddamn question—What are you working on?"

"But who cares about the questions? You never cared about those phony tape measures. Why don't you let us help you? Mary will go anywhere you want, do anything you like. Don't shut her out. It hurts her so."

"Mary is wonderful. Always and now. Wonderful. She's been so damn brave and good. She is all that is left to be glad for. I love her. I truly love her." A rise of tears made it impossible for me to talk any more. Ernest was not looking at me; he was watching a small bird foraging in the scrub. "You remember I told you once she did not know about other people's hurts. Well, I was wrong. She knows. She knows how I hurt and she suffers trying to help me—I wish to Christ I could spare her that. Listen, Hotch, whatever happens, whatever . . . she's good and strong, but remember sometimes the strongest of women need help." . . .

On the flight back to New York I thought about Mary's suggestion about a place that had access to the out of doors where Ernest could enjoy good air and scenery while receiving treatment. I knew now that he could be reached. On the hilltop he had been momentarily clear and lucid about his troubles. Sitting there in the plane, I could not help but try to reason out, from what he had said, what the forces had been that had crushed him. He was a man of prowess and he did not want to live without it: writing prowess, physical prowess, sexual prowess, drinking and eating prowess. Perhaps when these powers diminished, his mind became programed to set up distorted defenses for himself. But if he could only be made to adjust to a life where these prowesses were not so all-important . . .

I found myself thinking about his *dicho*: man can be defeated but not destroyed. Maybe it could work that way, even though Ernest favored its contrary brother. Ernest Walsh's words came back to me: "It will take time to wear him out. And before that he will be dead."

Mary was living in New York now, and we both consulted Dr. Renown about a new place that would be better suited to Ernest's needs. He suggested The Institute of Living in Hartford, Connecticut—small cottage residences, open grounds in a scenic setting, fine staff, long-term intensive care a specialty. Mary flew up to inspect it and consult with the director.

She thought that in all aspects the institute would be splendid for Ernest and brought back brochures and literature for me to look at, but again she faced the problem that transfer was not possible without Ernest's consent. Since this was a psychiatric institution and there was no way to disguise that fact, his resistance to it was foreordained. She wrote to the Mayo doctors, asking their assistance in influencing Ernest, but they replied that they would not aid in such a transfer since they did not feel it was to the patient's best interest. On the other hand, the institute was very deferential to Mayo's and insisted on playing a completely passive role. . . .

That was the situation when I left for Europe. Toward the end of June I received a note from Mary telling me that when she had arrived in Rochester the Mayo doctors had put pressure on her to let Ernest go along to Ketchum. In fact, they had already told Ernest that he could go, and he was counting on it. The doctors said that they felt Ernest was on the threshold of a new phase and needed to prove to himself what he could do in Ketchum. Mary said she had again brought up the institute, but the doctors very firmly said that such a transfer would definitely set Ernest back and couldn't be considered; that, in fact, it would destroy the new confidence which they had so painstakingly built up. They said that Ernest was between sixty to seventy percent of his normal self and that was plenty good to sustain him. Mary said she tried to protest but that with such little psychiatric knowledge it was futile. So she was resigned— fearful but resigned. She had rented a car and George Brown was flying out from New York to drive them through the northern states to Ketchum.

On July 2nd I flew from Málaga to Madrid, where I stayed overnight to catch the morning jet for Rome. As I was leaving the hotel elevator to go to the airport on the morning of the third, Bill David hurriedly entered the lobby. He had driven all through the night, virtually the length of Spain, to tell me that Ernest had shot himself and to be with me at this moment. I was glad he had. But what Ernest had done did not really hit me deeply at that time. It took months for that to happen.

On the flight to Rome I read the details of what had happened. As Dr. Renown had predicted, there were banner headlines on the front pages of newspapers everywhere I went. The Associated Press dispatch said that Ernest had been cheerful during the three-day drive through the northern states and appeared to enjoy himself. That on his first night home he had had a pleasant dinner and had even joined Mary's singing one of their favorite songs, "Tutti Mi Chiamano Bionda." Then, according to Mary, early the following morning a shotgun exploded in the house. Mary ran downstairs. Ernest had been cleaning one of the guns, she said, and it had accidentally discharged, killing him.

CONCLUSION

All of the problematic behavior discussed in this book are ways of dealing with the anticipated or actual pain of frustration in a materialistic, competitive, commercial society with authoritative do's and don'ts built into it. The ways of dealing with such pain that are considered in this final chapter are special ways. They amount to abandoning aspirations, relations, *and* efforts to improve the situation. They are not ways of coping with frustration; they are ways of *numbing the pain.* The ultimate of these is death.

This is a grim note on which to end this book. Yet we do not think that the existence of social problems, even very serious ones, justifies despair. As theologian Reinhold Niebuhr once said, "Nothing that is worth doing can ever be completed in the life of one generation." With good will and increased knowledge of societal functioning, it should be possible for modern societies to cope more successfully with "social problems."

Appendix

Postscript

Social problems are phenomena that are disapproved of by persons who call them "social problems." Two major kinds of these phenomena may be distinguished; and two categories of persons who disapprove of them also may be distinguished.

The two kinds of phenomena are:

1. Some persons "put out," that is, "produce" more of something than they "ought to."
2. Some persons do not put out or produce as much of something as they "ought to."

The two categories of persons who might disapprove of them are:

1. Those who are on the receiving end of the "too much" or the "too little."
2. Those who do the "too much" or the "too little" producing.

Four kinds of social problems emerge from a cross-tabulation of the two distinctions:[1]

---

[1] A further distinction might be made here between "disapprovers" who *actually* are either the receivers or the producers and those who observe them and *vicariously* disapprove. In the first case, the disapprovers are saying, in effect, "there is a social problem in that *we* are surfeited, deprived, strained, or slacked." In the second case, the disapprovers are bystanders who are saying, in effect, "there is a social problem in that *they* are more surfeited, deprived, strained, or slacked than 'such people' or 'human beings' ought to be—whether *they* think so or not." This distinction makes for interesting and significant refinements in the discussion of social problems (and for much argument about whether something is "really" a problem or not); but we shall not develop it here.

NATURE OF THE PHENOMENA

	Too Much Is Produced	Not Enough Is Produced
Those on the Receiving End	The disapprovers feel *surfeited* with, for example, pollution, noise, obscenity, ("over"-) population, propaganda, congestion, commands, red tape, violence, etc.	The disapprovers feel *deprived* of material goods, (food, clothing, housing, or other goods), or of respect, privacy, income, recognition, prestige, etc.
Those on the Producing End	The disapprovers feel *strained* at having to "spend" too much time, effort, attention, care, money (either in taxes, prices, rents, interest, wages), etc.	The disapprovers feel *slacked* at not having enough of their goods or services or ideas accepted, or at having "no place to put their energies." (The "social problems" of unemployment, underemployment, of being "put on the shelf" in retirement, of not being taken seriously as adolescents, etc.

THE PERSONS WHO DISAPPROVE

An implication of this classificatory scheme is that social problems are relative. How much is too much or too little depends on subjective standards derived from cultures. This is discussed in more detail in the text.

Textbooks attempting to analyze these various kinds of social problems choose among several alternative approaches. One approach is to make some assumption (often implicit) about the subjective or cultural standard to be adopted and then to describe the frequency and incidence of the phenomena. (How income is distributed, for example; or how many people are deprived of adequate housing or health care; or what the juvenile delinquency rate is; and so on.) Another approach is to focus on the *causes* of the problems; and still another is to focus on various *solutions* to them.

We make these points in order to distinguish the approach of this book from other approaches. It does not present statistics on the extent or seriousness of social problems; and it does not offer solutions. Statistics become outdated; and solutions can come only after diagnosis of the genesis of the problem. We focus on "causes." We locate causes in cultural standards and in the nature of the ways available to people for adapting to the frustrations (or threats of frustration) generated by their biological and social positions vis á vis the standards.

That is our *theoretical* approach. *Pedagogically*, our approach is to attempt to provide for the beginning student vivid imagery for some of the abstract concepts of the discipline. Hopefully, concrete illustrations will make students aware of the close-up human realities that get summarized in sociological principles. Sometimes that concrete reality is sordid; sometimes it is poignant, pathetic, or even tragic; sometimes it is comic; sometimes it is inspiring. Nearly always it is complex. Rarely, if ever, does a *concrete* human phenomenon illustrate one sociological concept neatly. (The utility of scientific abstraction is to enable us to abstract from the complexity of an event *general* principles so that we can analyze their operation one at a time or in carefully controlled interaction with another.)

But abstract theories are not one thing and the real world something else, as unsophisticated minds may think. To be useful, general principles must describe the real world, but the real world is such a densely packed, simultaneously interacting *collection* of elements and principles that their separate identities are often indistinguishable.

One risk of our attempt to illustrate principles concretely is that the student might direct his attention to the richness of the illustrative human cases and lose sight of the general point. Minimizing that risk will require conscious effort on the part of the student—on the encounter-group principle, "no gain without pain." New insights—learning—require effort. Another risk of the approach taken in this book of helping students to understand the real world by learning concepts in the light of concrete illustrations stems from the fact that the social problems we consider are generally concrete actions of concrete *people.* Readers may conclude that the "causes" of the problems lie in the people. "If only they acted differently, there would be no problems," some might conclude; and others might say, "These authors are implying *psychological* explanations of problems, not *sociological* ones."

Nothing could be further from our intention; the reader is hereby warned against that risk. A difference between "psychological" and "sociological" emphases has been aptly summarized in the aphorism that the sociologist is not so much interested in the behavior of the animal in the maze as he is in the architecture of the maze. We would put it slightly differently: we are interested in the behavior of people, but our main focus is on the structure of the society (the "architecture of the maze") that causes them to behave as they do. We would add, however, that all determinants of behavior are not in the external situation—the environment—of the individuals. That old debate is obsolete; nearly all scholars understand that behavior is the result of a complex *interaction* between what is in the actor and what is in his situation.

Nevertheless, in the human case, a large amount of "what is in the actor" is there because of what *was* in his situation *yesterday* or ten years ago. As we explained in Chapter 1, the culture into which a person is born (part of his situation at birth) *becomes* part of his personality as he internalizes it in the process of growing up. Our emphasis, then, is on two ways in which peoples' *social environment* contributes to their behaving in ways that get called "social problems." One way is by putting into *them* certain cultural definitions of themselves and their world; the other is by putting them *into* certain situations (the "maze") in which they must act out these definitions.

Thus our emphasis is on helping students to understand both cognitively and empathically *how the world seems* to the concrete persons whose behavior is regarded as "problematical." This is a microscopic approach to social problems as distinguished from an aggregative approach that would discuss social problems in terms of general conditions and processes of "societal maladaptation" or "malintegration."[2]

Chapter 1 explained the general principles involved. Chapters 2 to 5 described the special American definitions and "maze structures" that operate on people. Chapters 6 to 19 discussed fourteen kinds of *concrete behavior*, engaged in by Americans, that are called "social problems" and that result from phenomena discussed in the first five chapters. In these last fourteen chapters the student runs the greatest risk of forgetting the principles and getting lost in the richness of human drama. That is why we have added this postscript: to remind the reader of the forest whose trees he or she has just viewed.

[2]This latter approach is followed in a companion volume, Harry C. Bredemeier and Judith Getis, *Environment and People: Some Current Problems* (New York: John Wiley and Sons, forthcoming).

Author Index

The names of contributing authors are shown in CAPITALS

Subject Index